Produced by
Time Out Paris
100 rue du Fbg-St-Antoine, 75012 Paris
Tel: +33 (0)1.44.87.00.45 / Fax: +33 (0)1.44.73.90.60
E-mail: editors@timeout.fr

Published by
Time Out Guides Ltd
Universal House, 251 Tottenham Court Road,
London W1T 7AB
Tel: +44 (0)20 7813 3000 / Fax: +44 (0)20 7813 6001
E-mail: guides@timeout.com

Chairman Tony Elliott
Managing Director Paris Karen Albrecht

Editor Rosa Jackson
Sub Editor Maryanne Blacker
Production Editor Alison Culliford
Consulting Restaurant Editor Alexander Lobrano

Editorial Assistants Rob Orchard, Nick Petter
Research Frances Dougherty
Additional research by Dinah Nuttall, Linda Rosso

Consulting Editor Natasha Edwards

Editorial Director Peter Fiennes

Written and researched by: Maryanne Blacker, Julie Chang, Simon Cropper, Alison Culliford, Natasha Edwards, Duncan Fairgrieve, Hannah Feldman, Ethan Gilsdorf, Phoebe Greenwood, Neil Haidar, Laura Higgins, Joanna Hunter, Rosa Jackson, John Laurenson, Alexander Lobrano, Sophie Lyne, Nicola McDonald, Nicola Mitchell, Stephen Mudge, Rob Orchard, Lisa Pasold, Nick Petter, Clothilde Redfern, Vivian Rehberg, Emma Roberts, Louise Rowland, Ben Salzillo, Lucia Scazzoccio, Katherine Spenley, Sharon Sutcliffe, Kate van den Boogert

Additional contributions by: Karen Albrecht, Kathie Bergquist, Thomas Burgess, Geoffrey Finch, Chris Fremantle, Pamela Grant, Marlowe Hood, Kate Horne, François Murphy, Amy Parker, Toby Rose, Rosalind Sykes

Art Director Paris Richard Joy
Photography Tom Craig, Karl Blackwell
Cover Photography Tom Craig
Ad Design Paris Philippe Thareaut, Edna Wargon
Group Art Director Guides John Oakey

Sales & Administration Manager Paris Philippe Thareaut
Advertising Co-ordinator David Jordan
Advertising Executive Olivier Baenninger
Group Commercial Director Lesley Gill
Sales Director/Sponsorship Mark Phillips

Managing Director Mike Hardwick
Group Financial Director Keven Ellis
General Manager Nichola Coulthard
IT Director Simon Chappell
Circulation Director Jim Heinemann
Marketing Director Christine Cort
Marketing Manager Mandy Martinez
Production Manager Mark Lamond
Accountants Sarah Bostock, Abdus Sadique
Guides Co-ordinator Anna Norman

Marketing & Distribution Manager Paris Colin Shaw
Tel:+33 (0)1.44.87.04.19 / Fax:+33 (0)1.44.73.90.60
Distribution Executive London Sue Carter
Tel: +44 (0)20 7813 6060 / Fax: +44 (0)20 7813 6039

Special thanks to: Jean-Pierre Bordaz, Philippe Landry, Bruno Midavaine

Although every effort has been made to ensure the accuracy of the information contained in this publication, the publisher cannot accept responsibility for any errors.

All rights reserved throughout the world. Reproduction in whole or in part, by any means whatsoever, is forbidden save with the express permission in writing of the publishers.

Edité par Time Out Guides Ltd, Sté de Droit Britannique, 251 Tottenham Court Road, London W1P OAB, G.B.
Directeur de la Publication: AMM Elliott.
Responsable de la Rédaction: Peter Fiennes.
Principal Actionnaire: Time Out Group Ltd.

Imprimé à Imprimeries Quebecor Services, rue des Epinettes, ZI Sud de Torcy, 77200 Torcy. Dépôt Légal 2e trimestre 2002.

Copyright ©Time Out Group Limited 2000.
ISBN: 0903446642
Distribution by Seymour Ltd +44 (0)20 7396 8000
Service Diffusion France: +33 (0)1.44.87.04.19

Contents

About This Guide The content and how to use it	**6**
A La Carte Index Where to…	**8**
Special Offers for Readers	**15**

French Cuisine	**11**	**On the Town**	**103**
Bistros	13	Cafés	104
Haute Cuisine	40	Bars & Pubs	117
Brasseries	45	Tea Rooms & Ice Cream	127
Trendy	51	Wine Bars	129
Classics	55	Eating & Entertainment	133
Contemporary	58	Gay & Lesbian	134
Regional	60	Clubs	135
Fish & Seafood	65	Shops & Markets	137
Budget	67	Home Delivery	141
Vegetarian	74	Learning & Tasting	143

International	**77**		
Africa & Indian Ocean	79		
The Americas	81	**Lexicon**	**146**
Caribbean	84	**Alphabetical Index**	**148**
Eastern Mediterranean	85		
Far East	87	**Arrondissement Index**	**153**
Indian	91		
Italian	93		
Japanese	96	**Arrondissement Map**	**159**
Jewish	98		
North African	99	**Street Map**	**160**
Spanish	100		
Other International	101	**Métro Map**	**162**

The editors would like to thank the many readers who wrote in with suggestions for this guide. We encourage you to share your opinions with us, both on the places listed and places you think we should be covering.

For weekly Paris restaurant updates and a selection of key Paris events, see the *Time Out Paris* section inside *Pariscope*, every Wednesday at all Paris newsagents, €0.40.

And for more information on Paris sights, shopping, accommodation and arts, buy Penguin Books' annual *Time Out Paris Guide*.

See www.timeout.com for up-to-the-minute listings on Paris and 32 other cities worldwide.

Time Out Paris Eating & Drinking **3**

About this Guide

How to use the listings
Restaurants are divided into sections denoting the type of establishment and the style of food you can expect to find there. Within each section, restaurants are listed in order of *arrondissement*, or area, then alphabetically. We also provide two indexes (see p148): one by *arrondissement* and type of restaurant, the other alphabetical.

Critics' picks ★
A star after the restaurant's name indicates that it is a critics' favourite, one of the best in its category.

Telephones
Paris and Ile de France numbers begin with 01. If you are calling France from abroad leave off the 0 at the start of the ten-digit number: country code 33.

Transport
The Métro or RER stop listed is the one nearest the restaurant. Two stops are listed if they are both very near the restaurant and on different Métro lines.

Opening hours
Times stated for restaurants apply to service hours, when you can order food, rather than opening and closing times. Those given for bars and cafés are opening and closing hours, with food service hours if relevant.

Credit cards & currency
The following abbreviations are used: AmEx: American Express; DC: Diners' Club; MC: Mastercard; V: Visa. Visa is the most widely used. A ·15 minimum usually applies to credit card transactions. Most Paris restaurants will not accept travellers' cheques.

20th Arrondissement

PAP ★
3 rue Nexiste Pas, 20th (01.11.11.11.11). M° Bout-du-Monde. **Open** Mon-Fri noon-2pm, 7-10pm; Sat 7-10pm. **Average** ·45. **Prix fixe** ·30. **Lunch menu** ·25. **Credit** AmEx, DC, MC, V. **Wheelchair access**.

Supremely talented young chef Genesé Quoy has taken the new fashion for comfort food to the extreme at his achingly attractive vest-pocket dining room in the distant reaches of up-and-coming Ménilmontant (don't forget your visa, machete and malaria tablets). Star decorator Jack Garçon, best known for his tongue-in-cheek bordello decors complete with formidable madams, has outdone himself here by creating the over-the-top nursery that we all secretly pine for. We were seated promptly in tasselled Second Empire high chairs by rather fearsome, black-aproned matrons who gleefully chose fluffy, freshly laundered bibs to match our outfits (admirably treating us, in our Gap pastel flannels, with the same respect proffered to those in Bébé Dior gear). Then we were ready for the *amuse-bouches*: delectable little spoonfuls of quivery foie gras wrapped in baby spinach, so smooth it slipped right down our shirts. Instead of the usual *entrée-plat-dessert* triumvirate, the menu at PAP is shrewdly divided into two categories: purée and mash. Choose the purée and ingredients will be whizzed before your eyes in a state-of-the-art blender; mash, for the traditionalists, is chewed and spat out by the selfless waitresses, who for once are pleasantly curvy. Our neighbour, a well-known Lithuanian anthropologist, moaned with pleasure at every spoonful of his truffle, broccoli and sweet potato mash while his bored-looking trophy wife toyed listlessly with her celery, caviar and apple '*mash minceur*', but we couldn't resist the more innovative purée of *lisette* (baby mackerel), *encornets* (baby squid) and caramelised baby turnips: a palate-awakening meeting of earth and sea. Our only complaint: we were burped without so much as a by-your-leave before we had even finished our blissfully tepid vanilla milkshakes.

Service & tipping
Address waiters as *monsieur* and *madame* (or *mademoiselle*, considered a compliment if she's young-ish), or say '*s'il vous plaît*' to get their attention. Don't be too dismayed if waiters are abrupt – they are usually overworked – but if they seem outright rude, don't be afraid to show that you have a backbone. When you want your bill, ask for it – except in overly popular places, waiters don't like to give the impression they are rushing you out.

Prices and prix-fixe *menus*
Average means the average cost *à la carte* for a three-course meal without drinks. If no average price is listed, this means that the only option is the fixed-price *menu*. In our listings, Prix fixe indicates the price for the restaurant's set-price *menu*. If served only at lunch, the fixed-price *menu* is listed separately under Lunch menu. Within reviews, we use italics to indicate the French usage of the word *menu*, designating a fixed-price meal. Prices on restaurant menus (and listed in this guide) must by law include a 12-15 per cent service charge. A small tip of one to three euros (or small change in a café) is a nice, though entirely optional, gesture.

Services
Restaurants are busiest at lunch between 1pm and 2pm. In the evening, the French rarely venture into a restaurant before 8.30pm, much later in trendier places. Popular restaurants often have two sittings, around 8pm and 10pm. For a meal in the middle of the afternoon, try brasseries, cafés, wine bars and tea rooms.

Apéritifs, wine, water & digestifs In the more expensive restaurants, wine waiters might make it hard for you to refuse Champagne or other apéritifs, which can add significantly to your bill. Many French diners simply stick with a good bottle of wine. As well as the standard 75cl bottles, wine comes in half bottles (37.5cl) and in carafes or *pichets*, usually of 25cl (*un quart*), 46cl (*un pot*) and 50cl (*un demi-litre*, or *une fillette* if served in a tall carafe).

A matter of course French meals usually consist of three courses – *entrée* (starter), *plat* (main course) and *dessert* – although at more formal restaurants, there may be an additional *amuse-bouche* or *amuse-gueule* (appetiser or hors d'oeuvre), a fish course before the main course, cheese (before dessert), and petits fours served at the end with the coffee. This is invariably black (*un express*) – if you ask for a *café au lait* after dinner, expect to receive a strange look.

Loafing Bread is served free with any French café or restaurant meal and you're entitled to as much as you can eat – don't be afraid to ask for more, or to have it changed if it is stale.

Smoking/Non-Smoking Let's face it, France is a nation of smokers. Although by law every restaurant now has to have an *espace non-fumeurs* (non-smoking area), many simply seem to hang a 'no smoking' sign over the table nearest the loos, and no-one seems to protest when people light up in no-smoking zones. A few restaurants, especially Asian ones, now offer separate non-smoking rooms.

Dress You are what you wear in Paris. Restaurant goers on the whole opt for the 'smart-casual' look, so while you won't need a tie, leave the bermuda shorts and tracksuits behind. Haute cuisine restaurants normally expect a jacket and tie.

Reservations It's always a good idea to book at popular restaurants. Famous haute cuisine establishments take bookings months ahead (they will ask you to call back to confirm the day before your meal) and the most currently fashionable bistros require booking up to a few weeks ahead. However, it's also worth trying at the last minute to see if there's room. Some hard-to-book tables are much more accessible at lunch.

Bar & café customs Drink prices often vary in a café: they're cheapest at the bar, more at a table and even more sitting outside. There will often be a further increase (*majoration*), generally about 50 cents, after 10pm. If you want a table, sit down and wait for the waiter to arrive. You pay after you've finished your drink, even at the bar, except in Anglo-Irish-style pubs where you pay as you order.

The euro
The euro came into circulation in France on 1 January 2002 with the rate of exchange set at 6.55957 francs to one euro; the franc was withdrawn on 17 February. Prices in this guide are given in euros; all prices were checked after the introduction of the euro. Where necessary (some restaurants hadn't yet converted their prices) we translated into euros using the official rate. Paris restaurants have, on the whole, ruthlessly bumped up their *à la carte* and set *menu* prices, sometimes by several euros.

Wheelchair access
Where this is stated in the listing, the restaurant features full wheelchair access, including toilets. It's worth ringing ahead to check if an establishment can cater for you.

No payment of any kind has secured or influenced a review in this Guide. Time Out maintains a strict policy of editorial independence, and advertisers are never guaranteed special treatment of any kind: an advertiser may receive a bad review or no review at all.

Café - Restaurant

Open daily
Non-stop service
from 7.30-midnight

Terrace in summer
Private salon

... a brasserie remixed to a
modern tune - the place to be for
years to come ...

café de l'alma

5 avenue Rapp, 7th
Tel: 01.45.51.56.74

A la Carte

Where to turn to satisfy your appetite for cheese, celebrities, romance and rugby.

Where to go ....

...to eat After Midnight
Bon, Trendy
Chez Papa, Budget
A la Cloche d'Or, Bistros
Fogon St-Julien, Spanish
Georges, Trendy
Joe Allen, The Americas
Korova, Trendy
Les Philosophes, Bistros
Le Tambour, Bars & Pubs
La Tour de Montlhéry (Chez Denise), Bistros
See also p45, Brasseries

...to drink After 2am
Café Carmen, Cafés
Café des Phares, Cafés
Café le Bastille, Cafés
Le Crocodile, Bars & Pubs
La Distillerie, Bars & Pubs
Harry's Bar, Bars & Pubs
Mathis, Bars & Pubs
Les Mousquetaires, Bars & Pubs
Aux Troix Mailletz, Bars & Pubs
Viaduc Café, Cafés
Le Select, Cafés

...to eat Al Fresco
L'Absinthe, Bistros
L'Alivi, Regional
Bistrot Mazarin, Bistros
La Cagouille, Fish & Seafood
Café Marly, Cafés
Café Noir, Bistros
Closerie des Lilas, Bistros
Contre-Allée, Bistros
Châlet des Iles, Classics
La Fontaine de Mars, Bistros
Georges, Trendy
La Girondine, Bistros
Le Grizzli, Bistros
Laurent, Haute Cuisine
Le Parc aux Cerfs, Bistros

Pavillon Montsouris, Classics
Les Philosophes, Bistros
Pitchi Poï, Jewish
Le Pré Catelan, Haute Cuisine
Restaurant du Palais-Royal, Contemporary
Le Zéphyr, Bistros

...for Ancient Walls
L'Ami Louis, Classics
Anahi, The Americas
Auberge Nicolas Flamel, Bistros
Le Coupe-Chou, Classics
L'Ecurie, Budget
Le Grand Véfour, Haute Cuisine
Perraudin, Budget
Restaurant Pho, Far East

...for the Artworks
Baz'Art, Cafés
The Bottle Shop, Bars & Pubs
La Coupole, Brasseries
Guy Savoy, Haute Cuisine
Le Méditerranée, Fish & Seafood
Le Stresa, Italian
Pause Café, Cafés
Le Pictural Café, Cafés
Wadja, Bistros

...for a Business Lunch
L'Astor, Contemporary
Bath's, Regional
La Butte Chaillot, Bistros
Chez Georges, Bistros
Chez Michel, Bistros
Chez Savy, Bistros
Chiberta, Contemporary
La Closerie des Lilas, Classics
Les Elysées, Contemporary
Gallopin, Brasseries
Goumard, Fish & Seafood
Le Grand Colbert, Brasseries
Le Maxence, Contemporary
L'Oulette, Contemporary
Tante Jeanne, Bistros
Le Vaudeville, Brasseries

...for a Carnivorous Feast
Au Boeuf Couronné, Brasseries
Le Bouclard, Bistros
La Casque d'Or, Regional
Chez Jenny, Regional
Chez Omar, North African

L'Ecurie, Budget
Le Gavroche, Bistros
Georget, Bistros
La Maison de l'Aubrac, Brasseries
Le Nemrod, Bistros
Le Père Claude, Bistros
Le Petit Rétro, Bistros
Savy, Bistros
Sebillon, Bistros
La Tour de Montlhéry (Chez Denise), Bistros

...to Celebrity Spot
L'Ami Louis, Bistros
Anahi, The Americas
Brasserie Lipp, Brasseries
Café de Flore, Cafés
Le Fumoir, Bars & Pubs
Natacha, Bistros
Le Square Trousseau, Bistros
Le Stresa, Italian
404, North African
See also p51, Trendy

...for the Cheese Course
Astier, Bistros
Le Bistro de Gala, Bistros
Chez Michel, Bistros
Chez René, Bistros
Les Fernandises, Regional
Le Graindorge, Regional
Le Grand Véfour, Haute Cuisine
Montparnasse 25, Classics
Pierre Gagnaire, Haute Cuisine
Restaurant Au Pressoir, Classics

...with Children
Altitude 95, Bistros
Brasserie Flo, Brasseries
Café Cannibale, Bars & Pubs
Cap Vernet, Brasseries
Chicago Pizza Pie Factory, The Americas

La Coupole, Brasseries
Fogon St-Julien, Spanish
Hard Rock Café, The Americas
New Nioullaville, Far East
Pizza Milano, Italian
Quai Ouest, Contemporary
Thoumieux, Bistros
Le Troquet, Bistros

...for Cinema History
Café de Flore, Cafés
Café de la Mairie, Cafés
La Casque d'Or, Regional
Hôtel du Nord, Bistros
Pause Café, Cafés
Le Verre à Pied, Cafés

...for Cocktails
Café Mabillon, Bars & Pubs
Chez Richard, Bars & Pubs
China Club, Bars & Pubs
Le Crocodile, Bars & Pubs
Les Etages, Bars & Pubs
Favela Chic, The Americas
F.B.I Paris, Bars Pubs
Harry's Bar, Bars & Pubs
The Lizard Lounge, Bars & Pubs
Le Rosebud, Bars & Pubs
Tanjia, Trendy
Le Train Bleu, Brasserie
See also p119, Hotel Bars

...in Designer Style
Alcazar, Brasseries
L'Avenue, Brasseries
Barbara Bui Café, Cafés
Barrio Latino, Bars & Pubs
Boca Chica, Bars & Pubs
La Butte Chaillot, Bistros
Café Beaubourg, Cafés
Café Marly, Cafés
Colette, Cafés
Handmade, Cafés
Maison Blanche, Contemporary
Maison Prunier, Fish & Seafood
Renoma Café, Contemporary
Wax, Clubs
Web Bar Cafés
Wok, Far East
Yen, Japanese
59 Poincaré, Contemporary
See also p51, Trendy

...for unusual Desserts
Les Amognes, Bistros
Café des Délices, Cafés
Chiberta, Contemporary
Dame Jeanne, Bistros
L'Epi Dupin, Bistros
Ghislaine Arabian, Haute Cuisine
O'à la Bouche, Bistros
Petrossian, Contemporary
Pierre Gagnaire, Haute Cuisine

Le Régalade, Bistros
Restaurant du Palais-Royal, Classics
Le Violon d'Ingres, Classics

...on a Diet
Alcazar, Brasseries
L'Avenue, Trendy
Baan Boran, Far East
Bon, Trendy
Blue Elephant, Far East
Colette, Cafés
Hôtel Costes, Contemporary
Kifuné, Japanese
Tanjia, Trendy
See also p56, Japanese.

...with your Dog
Bistro Mazarin, Bistros
Café-Bar Le Nemours, Cafés
Café Beaubourg, Cafés
Le Clown Bar, Wine Bars
Khun Akorn, Far East
Le Suffren, Brasseries

...for Exotic Beers
La Fabrique, Bars & Pubs
Ghislaine Arabian, Haute Cuisine
La Gueuze, Bars & Pubs

...before/after a Film
Bar à Soupes, Budget
Bio.It, Budget
Le Comptoir du Relais, Wine Bars
La Coupole, Brasseries
Les Editeurs, Cafés
Fish, Wine Bars
Korean Barbecue, Far East
Nils, Budget
Le Reflet, Cafés
Le Rendez-vous des Quais, Cafés
Le Select, Bars & Pubs

...on a First Date
404, North African
Café Marly, Cafés
China Club, Bars & Pubs
Le Clown Bar, Wine Bars
Julien, Brasseries
Le Kiosque Flottant, Bars & Pubs
Le Reminet, Bistros
Les Zygomates, Bistros

...for Game
Auberge le Quincy, Bistros
La Biche au Bois, Bistros

Chez Casimir, Budget
Chez Michel, Bistros
Chez Toinette, Budget
Michel Rostang, Haute Cuisine
Au Petit Marguery, Classics
Le Repaire de Cartouche, Bistros
A Sousceyrac, Bistros

...with Grandma
Angelina's, Tea Rooms
Le Dôme, Fish & Seafood
Ladurée, Tea Rooms
Le Pavillon Puebla, Regional
Le Soufflé, Classic
Le Train Bleu, Brasseries
La Truffière, Classics

...with a Group of Friends
Alcazar, Brasseries
Bali Bar, Far East
Le Café du Commerce, Budget
La Catalogne, Spanish
Chez Gégène, Eating & Entertainment
L'Escapade, Budget
Fajitas, The Americas
Man Ray, Trendy
Sinostar, Far East
La Table d'Aude, Regional
Thiou, Trendy
La Tour de Montlhéry (Chez Denise), Bistros

...for the Kitsch
Atlas, North African
La Charlotte en Ile, Tea Rooms
La Chine Masséna, Far East
Le Dénicheur, Cafés
La Galoche d'Aurillac, Regional
Le Kitch, Cafés
Au Pied de Cochon, Brasseries
A Sousceyrac, Bistros

...for a Late Lunch
Le Bistro du Peintre, Cafés
L'As du Fallafel, Jewish
La Bocca, Italian
Café Marly, Cafés
Café du Commerce, Budget
Café Ruc, Brasseries
Camille, Bistros
La Chine Masséna, Far East

6 Time Out Paris Eating & Drinking

A La Carte

L'Entracte, Cafés
Georges, Trendy
La Grande Armée, Brasseries
Le Grizzli, Bistros
L'Interlude, Budget
Juvéniles, Wine Bars
Restaurant Pho, Far East
Soufflot Café, Cafés
Zimmer, Cafés

...for unusual Loos
Le Bar Dix, Bars & Pubs
Bon, Trendy
La Chaise au Plafond, Cafés
China Club, Bars & Pubs
L'Etoile Manquante, Cafés
La Folie en Tête, Bars & Pubs
Goumard, Fish & Seafood
Le Lèche-Vin, Bars & Pubs
The Lizard Lounge, Bars & Pubs
Le Pantalon, Bars & Pubs
Lou Pascalou, Bars & Pubs
La Tour d'Argent, Haute Cuisine
Viaduc Café, Cafés

...for Live Music
Batofar, Clubs
Chez Jean, Budget
Cithéa, Clubs
L'Entrepôt (14th), Cafés
La Flèche d'Or, Bars & Pubs
Hard Rock Café, The Americas
La Paillotte des Iles, Carribean
Au Petit Tam-Tam, Africa & Indian Ocean
Ti-Jos, Regional
Aux Trois Mailletz, Bars & Pubs
See also p133, Eating & Entertainment

...to Play Pool or Billiards
Blue Bayou, The Americas
Flann O'Brien's, Bars & Pubs
Lou Pascalou, Bars & Pubs

...for a Romantic Meal
L'Astrance, Contemporary
Café des Délices, Cafés

Châlet des Iles, Classics
Le Coupe-Chou, Classics
Ghislaine Arabian, Haute Cuisine
Julien, Brasseries
Lasserre, Classics
Laurent, Haute Cuisine
Le Pavillon Montsouris, Classics
Le Pré Catelan, Haute Cuisine
Restaurant du Palais-Royal, Contemporary
La Tour d'Argent, Haute Cuisine
Le Train Bleu, Brasseries

..to talk about the Rugby
La Maison de l'Aubrac, Brasseries
Barfly, Bars & Pubs
Brasserie de l'Isle St-Louis, Brasseries
The Frog & Rosbif, Bars & Pubs
Kitty O'Shea's, Bars & Pubs
Au Métro, Budget
La Régalade, Bistros

...for Interesting Salads
Apparement Café, Cafés
Baan-Boran, Far East
Bistro du Peintre, Bistros
Bon, Trendy
Café Beaubourg, Cafés
Chez Papa, Budget
L'Entracte, Cafés
Le Grizzli, Bistros
Joe Allen, The Americas
Le Relais Gascon, Budget
Spoon, Food and Wine, Trendy

...for rare Spirits
L'Alsaco, Regional
La Cagouille, Fish & Seafood
Dominique, Other International
Les Fernandises, Regional
Mazurka, Other International
Maison Prunier, Fish & Seafood
Pitchi Poï, Jewish
Au Trou Gascon, Classics
See also p40, Haute Cuisine.

...for a Timewarp
Anahi, The Americas
Au Babylone, Budget

Chardenoux, Bistros
Chartier, Budget
Chez Catherine, Bistros
Chez Georges, Bistros
Chez René, Bistros
Chez Savy, Bistros
Aux Crus de Bourgogne, Bistros
Julien, Brasseries
Perraudin, Bistros
Au Petit Marguery, Classics
Le Petit Rétro, Bistros
Le Train Bleu, Brasseries

...for Smoke-Free Air
Bofinger, Brasseries
Chez Germaine, Budget
Dong Huong, Far East
L'Ebauchoir, Budget
Lao Siam, Far East
Nobu, Trendy
A Priori Thé, Tea Rooms
Les Quatre et Une Saveurs, Vegetarian

...to be a Student
Le Bar Dix, Bars & Pubs
Les Caves de Bourgogne, Cafés
Chez Gladines, Budget
Chez Gudule, Cafés
L'Escapade, Budget
La Flèche d'Or, Bars & Pubs
The Hideout, Bars & Pubs
La Palette, Cafés
Au Petit Suisse, Cafés
Polidor, Budget
Le Reflet, Cafés
Tabac de la Sorbonne, Cafés

...for a meal on Sunday
Alexandre, Regional
Altitude 95, Bistros
L'Alivi, Regional
L'Amazonial, Gay & Lesbian
Ambassade d'Auverge, Regional
Les Ambassadeurs, Haute Cuisine
L'Ardoise, Bistros
L'Assiette, Bistros
Benoît, Bistros
Le Bistrot d'à Côté Flaubert, Bistros
Le Bistrot d'Hubert, Bistros
Le Bistrot des Vignes, Bistros
La Bistro du 19, Bistros
La Bocca, Italian
La Brasserie Italiana, Italian
Le Bristol, Haute Cuisine
La Butte Chaillot, Bistros
Café Noir, Bistros
Camille, Bistros
Caves Saint Gilles, Spanish
Le Chalet des Iles, Classics
Aux Charpentiers, Bistros

Chez Aida, Africa & Indian Ocean
Chez Janou, Bistros
Chez Jenny, Regional
Chez Paul (11th), Bistros
Chez Paul (13th), Bistros
Chez Toutoune, Bistros
Contre-Allée, Bistros
Doïna, Other International
L'Eclèche et Cie, Gay & Lesbian
L'Espadon, Haute Cuisine
La Fermette Marbeuf, Classics
Flam's, Regional
La Fontaine de Mars, Bistros
Le Dauphin, Bistros
Galerie 88, Vegetarian
Gli Angeli, Italian
Au Grain de Folie, Vegetarian
Grizzli Café, Bistros
Le Jules Verne, Haute Cuisine
Ma Bourgogne, Bistros
Le Meurice, Haute Cuisine
La Paillotte des Iles, Carribean
Le Pamphlet, Bistros
Le Parc aux Cerfs, Bistros
Le Père Claude, Bistros
La Petite Chaise, Bistros
Le Petit Marseillais, Bistros
Les Philosophes, Bistros
Piccolo Teatro, Vegetarian
Pizza Milano, Italian
Les Quatre et Une Saveurs, Vegetarian
Le Reminet, Bistros
La Rôtisserie de Beaujolais, Bistros
Sebillon, Bistros
Au Soleil de Minuit, Other International
Thoumieux, Bistros
Au Tibourg, Bistros
La Tour d'Argent, Haute Cuisine
La Truffière, Classics
Vasco de Gama, Other International
La Vieux Bistro, Bistros
Le Vieux Métiers de France, Classics
Au 35, Bistros
Le V, Haute Cuisine
See also p45, Brasseries, p98, Jewish, p87 Far East, p91 Indian, p81 The Americas, and p65, Fish & Seafood.

...for a Sunny Café Terrace
Café Beaubourg, Cafés
Café de Flore, Cafés
Café de la Musique, Cafés
Café du Marché, Cafés
Les Caves de Bourgogne, Cafés
La Chope Daguerre, Cafés
Les Deux Magots, Cafés

La Palette, Cafés
Pause Café, Cafés
Le Rendez-vous des Quais, Cafés
Le Rostand, Cafés
Le Soleil, Cafés
Tabac de la Sorbonne, Cafés
Vavin Café, Cafés

...with a Vegetarian Friend
Alexandre, Regional
L'Alivi, Regional
L'Arpège, Haute Cuisine
L'As du Fallafel, Budget
La Bastide Odéon, Regional
Bio.It, Budget
Bon, Trendy
Chez Marianne, Jewish
Au Coco de Mer, African
Favela Chic, The Americas
La Fresque, Budget
Macéo, Contemporary
Maison Blanche, Contemporary
Pause Café, Cafés
Le Safran, Bistros
Le Souk, North African
Spoon, Food and Wine, Trendy
La Voie Lactée, Eastern Mediterranean
Willi's Wine Bar, Wine Bars
See also p74, Vegetarian, and p95, Italian.

...for the View
Altitude 95, Bistros
L'Eté en Pente Douce, Cafés
Le Flore en l'Ile, Tea Rooms
Georges, Trendy
Le Jules Verne, Haute Cuisine
Le Kiosque Flottant, Bars & Pubs
Maison Blanche, Contemporary
Le Progrès, Cafés
La Table O & Co, Regional
Le Totem, Cafés
La Tour d'Argent, Classics
Ziryab, North African

...for Weekend Brunch
Amnesia, Gay & Lesbian
Barfly, Bars & Pubs
Blue Bayou, The Americas

Café Cannibale, Bars & Pubs
Café Charbon, Bars & Pubs
La Fabrique, Bars & Pubs
The Lizard Lounge, Bars & Pubs
M's Coffee Room, Cafés
Pitchi Poï, Jewish
A Priori Thé, Tea Rooms
Quai Ouest, Contemporary
Le Réservoir, Eating & Entertainment
Le Safran, Bistros
Zebra Square, Brasseries
404, North African

...For the Wine List
Astier, Bistros
L'Auberge Nicolas Flamel, Bistros
Chez Georges, Bistros
Ghislaine Arabian, Haute Cuisine
A la Grange Batelière, Bistros
Le Passage, Bistros
Les P'tits Bouchons de François Clerc, Bistros
Nobu, Trendy
Le Récamier, Classic
Spoon, Food and Wine, Trendy
Taillevent, Haute Cuisine
La Tour d'Argent, Haute Cuisine
La Truffière, Classics
Wadja, Bistros
Willi's Wine Bar, Bistros
See also p129, Wine Bars

...with a Writer
La Belle Hortense, Wine Bars
Café des Lettres, Cafés
Café de Flore, Cafés
Les Editeurs, Cafés
Le Fumoir, Bars & Pubs
La Maroquinerie, Eating & Entertainment
Le Perron, Italian

...on Your Own
Alcazar, Brasseries
L'As du Fallafel, Jewish
Le Bar à Huîtres, Fish & Seafood
Fish, Wine Bars
Garnier, Brasseries
Isse, Japanese
Maison Prunier, Fish & Seafood
Spoon, Food and Wine, Trendy

le chênevert

Open Mon-Sat from 11.30 am-6.30 pm
48 boulevard Haussmann, 9th
M° Chaussée d'Antin La Fayette
Tel : 01.48.74.94.71

Lafayette GOURMET
www.lafayettegourmet.com

Special Offers for Readers

The special vouchers on this page will get you free drinks all over town (subject to the Terms and Conditions below).

Terms and Conditions of Readers' Offers

All offers on this page are subject to the following conditions:

- Offers apply to a maximum of two people per voucher.
- Vouchers are good for one use only.
- To claim offers, readers must present the original of the related voucher, which will be kept by the venue.
- None of these offers can be used in conjunction with 'happy hour' promotions or with any other offer or discount.
- While these offers are designed to be valid any time, they may be subject to space and/or availability. Ring ahead if you want to be absolutely sure; phone numbers are printed on the vouchers.
- *Time Out* informs its readers that it can not take responsibility for other parties taking part in this promotion.
- All outlets mentioned have agreed to participate with offers as stated. Any enquiries relating the the promotion should be addressed to them. *Time Out* can not be liable for failure by any such establishment to honour their offer.
- For further details contact Time Out Paris, 01.44.87.04.19.

L'ABUS DE L'ALCOOL EST DANGEREUX POUR LA SANTÉ. CONSOMMEZ AVEC MODÉRATION.

Time Out Voucher / Bon
The Frog & British Library
114 av de France, 13th (01.45.84.34.26). M° Bibliothèque.
Free pint of microbrewed beer

Time Out Voucher / Bon
The Frog & Princess
9 rue Princesse, 6th (01.40.51.77.38). M° Mabillon.
Free pint of microbrewed beer

Time Out Voucher / Bon
The Frog & Rosbif
116 rue St-Denis, 2nd (01.42.36.34.73). M° Etienne Marcel.
Free pint of microbrewed beer

Time Out Voucher / Bon
The Frog at Bercy Village
25 Cour St-Emilion, 12th (01.43.40.70.71). M° Cour St-Emilion.
Free pint of microbrewed beer

Time Out Voucher / Bon
Le Bar des Ferailleurs
18 rue de Lappe, 11th (01.48.07.89.12). M° Bastille.
One free draught Heineken, 6-9pm

Time Out Voucher / Bon
La Pomme d'Eve
1 rue Laplace, 5th (01.43.25.86.18). M° Maubert-Mutualité.
Buy one drink, get one of the same type free

Time Out Voucher / Bon
The Moose
16 rue des Quatre Vents, 6th (01.46.33.77.00). M° Odéon.
Two Moosehead beers for the price of one (valid until 31 Dec 02)

Time Out Voucher / Bon
The Lizard Lounge
18 rue du Bourg Tibourg, 4th (01.42.72.81.34). M° Hôtel de Ville.
Buy one cocktail, get one free (outside of happy hour)

Time Out Voucher / Bon
The Bottle Shop
5 rue Trousseau, 11th (01.43.14.28.04). M° Ledru-Rollin.
Buy one cocktail, get one free (outside of happy hour)

Time Out Voucher / Bon
Stolly's
16 rue Cloche-Perce, 4th (01.42.76.06.76). M° Hôtel de Ville.
Buy one cocktail, get one free (outside of happy hour)

Time Out Voucher / Bon
Café Klein Holland
36 rue du Roi de Sicile, 4th (01.42.71.43.13). M° St-Paul.
Buy one pint of Grolsch get one free

Time Out Voucher / Bon
Fubar
5 rue St Sulpice, 6th (01.40.51.82.00). M° Odéon.
Buy one cocktail of your choice, get a second one free

Time Out Voucher / Bon
Mixer Bar
23 rue Ste Croix de la Bretonnerie, 4th (01.48.87.55.44). M° Hôtel de Ville.
Buy one cocktail get one free

Time Out Voucher / Bon
L'Envol Québécois
30 rue Lacépède, 5th (01.45.35.53.93). M° Place Monge.
Buy one draught beer get one free

Time Out Voucher / Bon
Café Oz
18 rue St-Denis, 1st (01.40.39.00.18). M° Châtelet-Les-Halles.
Two draught beers (middy, schooner or jug) for the price of one

Time Out Voucher / Bon
Café Oz
184 rue St-Jacques, 5th (01.43.54.30.48). RER Luxembourg.
Two draught beers (middy, schooner or jug) for the price of one

Time Out Voucher / Bon
Café Oz
1 rue de Bruxelles, 9th (01.40.16.11.16). M° Blanche.
Two draught beers (middy, schooner or jug) for the price of one

Time Out Voucher / Bon
McBride's Irish Pub
54 rue St-Denis, 1st (01.40.26.46.70). M° Châtelet-Les-Halles.
Happy hour prices at any time with this voucher

Time Out Voucher / Bon
Charli's Pub
24 rue Keller, 11th (01.48.07.80.99). M° Bastille.
Buy one draught or bottled beer, get one free

Time Out Voucher / Bon
Murphy's House
10 rue de la Chaussée d'Antin, 9th (01.40.22.08.10). M° Chaussée d'Antin.
Buy one drink, get one of the same type free

Enough to turn Marco Pierre white.

Time Out London
EVERY WEEK

FOOD

French Cuisine

Bistros	**13**
Haute Cuisine	**40**
Brasseries	**45**
Trendy	**51**
Classics	**55**
Contemporary	**58**
Regional	**60**
Fish & Seafood	**65**
Budget	**67**
Vegetarian	**74**

Restaurant La Rose de France

Ideally located on the "Île de la Cité", central Paris' historic island, La Rose de France will win you over with its relaxed service, fine wines and delicious food. The terrace (weather permitting) is one of the most beautiful in Paris.

24 place Dauphine, 1st. M° Pont-neuf or Cité
Tel: 01.43.54.10.12 - www.la-rose-de-france.com

Le Train Bleu
RESTAURANT
Traditional French Cuisine

Restaurant Le Train Bleu listed historical monument

Paris • Gare de Lyon • Place Louis Armand, 12th
Tel: 01.43.43.09.06 - Fax: 01.43.43.97.96 - www.le-train-bleu.com

Bistros

Some of the best chefs in Paris work their magic in modest bistro kitchens.

The perennial Parisian bistro continues to flourish in the face of epicurian fads. These congenial dining rooms are all about preserving simple French culinary traditions and sometimes, especially in the case of younger chefs, reworking them. Homestyle cooking is a key ingredient, so too are fresh seasonal produce and, best of all, affordable prices – set-price *menus* are generally great value and are guaranteed to satisfy any and all plate expectations. Wine, too, is well-priced. From modest neighbourhood bistros with weathered walls and oodles of old-world warmth to spacious contemporary rooms you'll find food in all its guises – sauced, seared, sautéed, stewed and served with aplomb. In Paris, when bistro food is good, it's excellent, often giving the hauty high cuisine places a run for their considerable money. Bistros such as **Chez Savy**, **Chez Georges**, **Chardenoux** and **Chez René** are renowned for their timeless, familiar dishes (the latter's *coq au vin* is worth a cross-country pilgrimage) while **Chez Michel**, **Le Pamphlet**, **La Régalade** and **L'Os à Moëlle** interpret the classics (roast farm chicken in basil sauce with polenta, for example). *Vive l'évolution*.

1st Arrondissement

L'Absinthe
24 pl du Marché-St-Honoré, 1st (01.49.26.90.04). M° Tuileries. **Open** Mon-Fri noon-2.30pm, 7.30-10.30pm; Sat 7-10.30pm. Closed one week in Aug. **Average** €35. **Prix fixe** €25, €31. **Credit** AmEx, MC, V. **Wheelchair access**.

This cheerful, inviting bistro, partly owned by Michel Rostang, stands in stark contrast to the stunning glass shopping mall that dominates the *place*. Initial impressions confirm that L'Absinthe has all the attributes of the perfect neighbourhood restaurant – an interesting menu, relatively keen prices and friendly staff. Add to this an excellent wine list and what more could you want? Well, unfortunately, the food was a real disappointment this time. From the €31 *menu*, we started with *ravioles de Royans aux langoustines* (€5 supplement). Boiled until they were completely soft, these mini raviolis were then bathed in a thick, dark, fishy sauce, in which a couple of woolly-textured prawn tails floated. A main course of whole roast sea bass (€3.05 supplement) was more successful – the fish sparklingly fresh and crisp-skinned – but the dish was marred by the strangely textured, pale green mousse that accompanied it. Pike-perch with oyster mushrooms and chicken *jus* (€4.57 supplement) proved duller than it sounded, and the mushrooms were greasy and far too salty. The speciality dessert, *cigare de Havane*, a rolled-up crunchy crêpe filled with prune and Armagnac cream, vied with the Saint Véran 99 Domaine Guy Saumaize (€23) as the most interesting part of the meal. A better bet for a quick and simple lunch.

L'Ardoise
28 rue du Mont-Thabor, 1st (01.42.96.28.18). M° Concorde or Tuileries. **Open** Wed-Sun noon-2.15pm, 6.30-11pm. Closed 25 Dec-3 Jan, first week in May, three weeks in Aug. **Average** €29. **Prix fixe** €29. **Credit** MC, V.

Some people get annoyed by the decor so minimal as to be non-existent, as if L'Ardoise should be shouting out that it's a restaurant not some unreconstructed café, but we actually rather liked its unassuming neutrality that tells you to focus on the food. For chef Pierre Jay, who trained at the Tour d'Argent, merits attention. From a blackboard menu that balances fish and meat, classic and creative, we had a starter of marinated anchovies served with a black olive *tapenade*, and an interesting *cassolette* of slow-cooked vegetables in a delicate green and orange coulis. Calf's liver cooked in sherry vinegar, topped by a crispy disc of potato slivers, could have been a touch more pink, but we loved the swordfish in an excellent orange-flavoured butter sauce set off by tiny peas and a fresh coriander leaf salad. The renowned *quenelles au chocolat* weren't on the *menu* that day, so we staved off chocolate cravings with a *pavé chocolat framboises* (three chewy chocolate macaroons with raspberries and vanilla ice cream) and got mildly sozzled on a brandy-glass of morello cherries in Beaujolais. Jay comes from Mâcon in southern Burgundy, reflected in vintage photos and the tilt of the mostly-under-€30 wine list.

Chez La Vieille ★
1 rue Bailleul/37 rue de l'Arbre Sec, 1st (01.42.60.15.78). M° Louvre-Rivoli. **Open** Mon-Wed, Fri noon-2pm; Thurs noon-2pm, 7.30-9.30pm. Closed one week in Aug. **Average** €34. **Prix fixe** €32. **Lunch menu** €23. **Credit** AmEx, DC, MC, V.

If you find yourself despairing over how Paris is changing, nothing will set you right like a meal in this splendid little bistro. Arriving here you breathe in a deep dose of Paris, which comes from the cobbled-together decor, the earnestness of the waitresses and the now-antique sound of a rotary phone ringing. The main-floor dining room only has six or seven tables, ditto upstairs, where we dined in the company of a wine importer and his son, a chain-smoking starlet and a silver-haired film type. With its long windows overlooking lovely 18th-century houses, and handsome black-and-white photos of the old Halles, the upper floor is a pleasant place to be. The assorted starters are brilliant – help-yourself terrines of duck and brawn, lentils, courgettes stuffed with veal, avocado and tomato salad with hard-boiled egg, marinated leeks and a sublime *céleri rémoulade*. We shared this spread, along with delicious bread and an order of Corsican *charcuterie*. Mains were homely and appealing, too – veal braised with green olives and cannelloni stuffed with ewe's milk cheese. We washed it all down with a bottle of Alzipratu, a lovely Corsican red, split an order of plump stewed prunes and left wishing that this place were open more often in the evening.

Le Cochon à l'Oreille
15 rue Montmartre, 1st (01.42.36.07.56). M° Les Halles. **Open** Mon noon-3.30pm, Tue-Fri noon-3.30pm, 7-10.30pm; Sat noon-3.30pm. Closed one week in Feb. **Average** €24. **No credit cards**.

Every table had an extra glass for the owner on the night we visited. Our arrival was apparently the occasion to break out the Champagne, because he plopped down three glasses and sat down with us, filling each to the brim with an excellent de Telmont. Unfortunately, with no waiter to take up the slack in this tiny bistro, our orders never got processed – too many tables and too many glasses got between the convivial owner and the kitchen. The friendly if strained chef eventually took our order himself. The food, when we got it, was excellent – classical bistro fare whose components were all of unusually good quality, from the baked camembert on a bed of salad with pecans to the *confit de canard* with its garlic-sautéed potatoes, to the sweet, fresh strawberries and crème fraîche for dessert. The setting is charming – tiles on the walls depict the old Halles market and seats are made from original wooden Métro benches. But although a dose of patience and good humour helped make the evening more memorable than anything else, four hours of amiable inebriation proved wearing. Despite our highest compliments to the chef, we understand the evening's particular style was in no way exceptional. If the meals were priced more reasonably we might be willing to risk it again, but as it is we recommend this place only for those with a sense of adventure.

Le Dauphin
167 rue St-Honoré, 1st (01.42.60.40.11). M° Tuileries. **Open** daily noon-2.30pm, 7.30-10.30pm. **Average** €34. **Prix fixe** €32. **Lunch menu** €23. **Credit** AmEx, DC, MC, V.

After a wobbly start a year ago, this very conveniently located bistro just steps from the Comédie Française and the Louvre has found its groove and is now serving excellent southwestern food under the direction of chefs Edgar Duhr and Didier Oudill of the Café de Paris in Biarritz. With its art deco wrought iron, stained glass windows and bare wood tables, this place pulls a diverse crowd of knowing locals and lucky or well-advised foreigners. The €32 three-course *menu* is a good buy, too, with starters such as a delicious terrine of foie gras, lentils and potatoes with a small salad, or *txangurro*, a Basque speciality of marinated raw scallops finely sliced and served on a bed of chopped tomato and dressed fiddler crab in abalone shells. Though *parrillas*, or grills, of fish and vegetables are another Hispano-Basque classic, we opted for the roast shoulder of lamb for two; this was a generous and flavourful dish of tender, crunchy-skinned shoulder of lamb and two cuts of lamb loin on a bed of sliced potatoes which had been cooked with broth in an open copper pan. Following such a hearty meal, the luscious poached peach made for a perfect conclusion. From an intelligent selection of reasonably priced wines, a red Gaillac was very pleasant. Although the bread was stale and service absent-minded, we'd happily return for a relaxed and hearty meal.

Le Safran
29 rue d'Argenteuil, 1st (01.42.61.25.30). M° Tuileries or Pyramides. **Open** Mon-Sat noon-2.15pm, 7-11pm; Sun 11am-6pm. **Average** €38. **Prix fixe** €24.39, €36.59. **Lunch menu** €13.57. **Credit** AmEx, DC, MC, V.

Longtime Paris restaurateur Caroll Sinclair, who now runs this sunny yellow bistro, shops at the organic market and is proud of her organic beef. Less inspired was the waiter, who told us unapologetically that no tuna was available though the day's lunch *menu*, limited to three choices for each course, included a tuna tartare and tuna steak. When we asked about the vegetarian *menu*, he looked at us blankly and said, 'it's vegetables'. But prepared how? 'Just steamed', he said, seeming puzzled that we should care. Beef it was, then. We started with *samosa*-like triangles of *brik* pastry filled with tasty pork and bean sprouts, and succulent eggplant layered with roasted red peppers and ricotta. Then came the tender (though slightly burnt) oxtail, served inventively with moist wheat cooked with cabbage, beans and chickpeas, and an artistic stack of minced beef with Middle Eastern spices, layered with potato purée. Saffron crème brûlée was disappointingly overcooked, with a chewy sugar crust, and a so-so chocolate fondant with hazelnuts confirmed that desserts are not Sinclair's forte. What impressed us were the rich flavours and her obvious passion for cooking. Her eyes lit up when we asked for more details on the vegetarian *menu*. 'I had such a creative menu planned for today. But I don't understand — no-one ordered it.'

Get your claws into lobster at Aux Crus de Bourgogne

La Tour de Montlhéry (Chez Denise)

5 rue des Prouvaires, 1st (01.42.36.21.82). RER Châtelet-Les Halles. **Open** 24 hours Mon 7am-Sat 7am. Closed 14 July-15 Aug. **Average** €35. **Credit** MC, V. **Wheelchair access.**

With its red-checked tablecloths, barrels of wine just inside the door, smoke-ambered walls and saucy waiters, this venerable night owl's roost is so quintessentially a Parisian bistro that it comes close to being a pastiche of itself. What saves it from tipping into Disney, however, is the hearty-eating French blowhards among the jolly crowd and the traditional, sturdy and generous food – a meal here is anything but self-conscious. Even during the grim days of mad-cow panic, our neighbours were defiantly and happily tucking into gigantic and delicious-looking rib steaks, stuffed cabbage and kidneys. For the more cautious or faint-hearted, start with the dense *terrine du chef* or the *frisée* salad loaded with freshly made garlicky croutons, and then go on to the roast lamb with unctuous white beans, lamb chops served with some of the best *frites* in town – they're handmade, a real rarity these days – or the salmon in herb sauce. Desserts run to slabs of sponge cake doused with rum, fruit tart and crème caramel, and you can be sure you'll end up chatting with your neighbours since this place is famously convivial, abetted by the good, cheap house Beaujolais.

Willi's Wine Bar

13 rue des Petits-Champs, 1st (01.42.61.05.09/www.williswinebar.com). M° Pyramides. **Open** Mon-Sat noon-2.30pm, 7-11pm. **Average** €32. **Prix-fixe** €32. **Lunch menu** €25. **Credit** MC, V.

There's an appealing atmosphere of low-key Anglo-French stylishness at this long-running and very popular *bistro à vins* near the Palais-Royal and, along with good food and some excellent wines, this attracts a diverse international crowd – expats, tourists, French media and fashion types. Although the staff could be friendlier, they will bail out anyone who appears to be floundering. The huge chestnut beam overhead creates most of the decor, along with posters that have been designed for the restaurant and small bunches of wild flowers on the white-linen-dressed tables. Our most recent meal here got off to a puzzling start, though, since the waiter decided to pour white Crozes Hermitage instead of the St-Joseph we had ordered, saying he'd change it if we didn't like it. Though we'd have preferred the St Joseph, this seemed more trouble than it was worth. So we tippled and nibbled the excellent bread until first courses of asparagus and fava beans in a heavenly, herb-brightened vinaigrette, and artichokes successfully served with avocado purée arrived. A juicy slice of lamb from the Corrèze and tuna steak with sun-dried tomatoes were both slightly overcooked but were full of flavour and a treat with a superb bottle of 1999 Domaine de l'Oratoire Saint Martin Cairanne, a heavenly Côtes du Rhône. One of us finished the wine with a plate well-chosen and nicely aged cheeses, while the other revelled in a *chaud-froid* of pears with a glass of delicious Rivesaltes dessert wine. A pleasant and relaxed meal, which is exactly what one expects of this well-run restaurant with an admirable undertone of connoisseurship.

The best Bargains

- **Le Hangar (3rd)** Understated excellence.
- **Baracane (4th)** A south-western feast.
- **L'Affriolé (7th)** A bistro worth cloning.
- **Le Rocher Gourmand (8th)** Small but seductive.
- **Chez Michel (10th)** A hidden treasure.
- **Astier (11th)** Great food, exceptional wines.
- **L'Avant-Goût (13th)** Crowd-pleasing.
- **La Régalade (14th)** A foodie's fantasy.
- **L'Os à Moëlle (15th)** Perfectly judged.
- **Le Troquet (15th)** Culinary sincerity.

2nd Arrondissement

Chez Georges

1 rue du Mail, 2nd, (01.42.60.07.11). M° Bourse. **Open** Mon-Sat noon-2pm, 7-9.30pm. Closed three weeks in Aug. **Average** €50. **Credit** AmEx, MC, V.

The good, solid food and conviviality at Chez Georges is confirmation that the Parisian bistro of old is alive and well. Every table in this classic long, mirrored room is taken – every night. And they come as much for the food and atmosphere as the motherly waitresses who glide about dishing out plates and advice. Starters are paragons of simplicity – a bowl of warm Puy lentils in a vinaigrette with grated onion; *frisée* tossed with warm bacon chunks and topped with a poached egg. Main courses are cooked with care; juicy, rose-coloured *steak de canard* with meaty ceps and text-book *sole meunière*, which was considerately suggested by the waitress when she sensed us hesitating over the sole baked with wine and sour cream on the menu. Desserts include tried-and-tested profiteroles filled with ice cream and inundated by a warm, dark chocolate sauce, and a slice of pear Charlotte with a meringue centre in a custard lake. A small selection of wine on the stencilled menu, all around €22-€24, appeals to all pockets, but if you've got money to spare and spend peruse the longer, printed list.

Aux Crus de Bourgogne

3 rue Bachaumont, 2nd (01.42.33.48.24). M° Sentier or Les Halles. **Open** Mon-Fri noon-2.30pm, 7.45-11pm. **Average** €34. **Prix fixe** €22.20 (dinner only). **Credit** AmEx, MC, V. **Wheelchair access.**

With its checked tablecloths, potted palms, old mirrors and wine-red curtains, this bistro is a Parisian refuge from the cold. Locals come for fresh foie gras and an informal evening out, while tourists arrive on the trail of its celebrated fresh lobster. The foie gras comes in various forms, from a hot *escalope* to a meltingly smooth terrine, served with a generous green salad and fried potatoes. Lobster addicts can indulge their habit with a whole lobster for a mere €14.50. The *charcuterie* platter consisted of intensely flavoured smoked ham balanced by tangy gherkins, while the rocket salad combined sharp Corsican ewe's cheese with peppery leaves. The roast salmon, dressed in nothing but a whisper of crusted sea salt, was perfectly complemented by buttered tagliatelle. Our favourite dessert is the frozen nougat: a pyramid of silky ice cream with a crackle of praline in a zesty strawberry coulis. We were tempted by the lemon-vodka and Poire Williams sorbets but unwisely chose the *millefeuille*, which, despite its gravity-defyingly light and flaky pastry, was disappointingly dry. But after-dinner Cognac, served in generous doses, more than made up for it.

Le Gavroche ★

19 rue St-Marc, 2nd (01.42.96.89.70). M° Bourse or Richelieu-Drouot. **Open** Mon-Sat 7am-2am. Closed Aug. **Average** €29. **Prix fixe** €13 (until 10pm). **Credit** MC, V.

This wine bistro near the Bourse continues to pack in the regulars and delight passers-by. Slabs of roast lamb, plates of black pudding, platters of thick beef, extra extra rare, are carried past in a whirl of activity, all destined to be washed down with one or more bottles of Beaujolais. The menu would be a cliché if it weren't so very good, from the fresh radishes served plain with salt and butter to the ham lunch special (check out the massive ham bone waiting to be carved beside the bar). If you have a hankering for the classic *steak-frites*, come with a friend and share the special beef plate for two. It's a lunch worthy of the two serious heavyweight businessmen who impressed us featherweights by working their way through three courses including this platter. Order a bottle of excellent Beaujolais (€12.96), or take a cue from the media types at the next table and drink Brouilly. The wine is superior and well-priced, specially bottled for the restaurant from reliable Burgundy contacts. Try to find room for the lovely crème caramel. We were smitten by the smiling waitress, who even while run off her feet managed to joke with lone diners. Booking is recommended for lunch, as the place fills up instantly, but you also can drop by La Gavroche after the theatre for a late dinner.

Le Tir Bouchon

22 rue Tiquetonne, 2nd (01.42.21.95.51). M° Etienne-Marcel. **Open** Mon-Fri noon-2.45pm, 8-11pm; Sat noon-2.45pm, 8-11.30pm; Sun 8-11pm. Closed 25 Dec and 1 Jan. **Average** €28. **Lunch menu** €12.20, €17.50. **Credit** MC, V.

This unpretentious bistro on a small, cobbled road near the lively rue Montorgueil feels inviting and warm thanks to its ochre colours, bare stone walls and candle-lit tables. Just as reassuring on a cold winter's day was the food. To start, try the *chèvre chaud* in a light filo pastry, the tasty salmon *quenelles*, or mini peppers stuffed with a fine *brandade de morue* (salt cod puréed with potatoes). We were impressed by the wide variety of main courses – quite a feat given the minuscule kitchen staffed by three contortionist chefs – half of which were fish, such as baked pike-perch in *sauce Nantua* (a creamy crayfish sauce). Red meat lovers are equally well catered for, the highlight being a tender venison steak topped with a melted slice of foie gras, served in a dark, meaty gravy with a well-matched accompaniment of glazed carrots. The reasonably-priced desserts were rather unadventurous – crème brûlée, lemon tart *et al* – but the *délice de praline* lived up to its name, consisting of a delicate butterscotch-flavoured mousse scattered with grated praline. Service was noticeably stressed.

3rd Arrondissement

L'Ami Louis

32 rue du Vertbois, 3rd (01.48.87.77.48). M° Arts et Métiers. **Open** Wed-Sun 12.15-2pm, 8-11pm. Closed Aug. **Average** €76. **Credit** AmEx, DC, MC, V.

If any given object is worth what someone will pay for it, then roast chicken and chips at L'Ami Louis must be worth the €60 price tag (for two). This famed bistro does have a magical quality, from its black facade with red-checked curtains to its carefully preserved pre-war interior, complete with stovepipe, bevelled mirrors and copper pots. The romantic setting, and very exclusive atmosphere – few, after all, can afford the luxury of a €100 bistro meal – seems to be enough for its faithfuls, who are willing to overlook serious flaws. Yes, the food is cooked over a wood fire which gives the house speciality, chicken, a delectable, smoky skin and rich *jus*, but the bird came apart so easily, and tasted so bland underneath that skin, that we wondered if it was even a farmer's chicken (the menu does not claim that it is). The accompanying skinny *frites* are beautifully presented in a perilous heap, but also proved rather tasteless. Our starter of twelve plump snails was fine, but we found wilted, brown leaves in our salad. The highlight was pecan ice cream on a plain white plate, for a cool €17. We might have been sceptical, but L'Ami Louis is so popular that dinner is booked up a full month ahead (it's easier to get in at lunch).

L'Auberge Nicolas Flamel

51 rue de Montmorency, 3rd (01.42.71.77.78/www.nicolasflamel.forez.com). M° Rambuteau. **Open** Mon-Fri noon-2.30pm, 8-11.30pm; Sat 8-11.30pm. **Average** €34. **Credit** AmEx, MC, V.

This bistro boasts that it's in 'the oldest house in Paris', and indeed it has an authentic old-world feel with broad exposed beams, heavy brass chandeliers and a dark wooden staircase. The service is flawless: both the waiter and the owner, Natan, were friendly and efficient, and the new chef Samuel Marciano emerged from the kitchen on several occasions to chat with diners about his latest creations. Despite this congenial backdrop, our last few visits have all been marred by the somewhat uneven cuisine, and the arrival of Marciano has not entirely resolved this. The fricassée of delicate oyster mushrooms came drowned in a very plain cream sauce, and the poached egg seemed an afterthought. A *beignet de foie gras* was an expensive flop consisting of an overly sweet caramelised doughnut filled with an undercooked morsel of foie gras. Main courses were more successful: steamed pike-perch was accompanied by light mashed potatoes and set off by a subtle mandarin sauce. Even better, the restaurant's flagship *gigot de sept heures* – a medieval recipe of slow-cooked lamb – was a tender, meaty delight. Pineapple *clafoutis* took a while to arrive, but was worth the wait: warm and meltingly soft in a luxuriant *crème anglaise*. The wine list is extensive thanks to Natan's frequent forays to wine auctions.

Camille

24 rue des Francs-Bourgeois, 3rd (01.42.72.20.50). M° St-Paul. **Open** daily noon-midnight. Closed 25 Dec. **Average** €28. **Lunch menu** €16 (Mon-Fri), €19 (Sat). **Credit** AmEx, DC, MC, V.

Camille is a sweet traditional bistro – slightly cramped and always packed – in the heart of the Marais. Groovy locals rub shoulders with grubby tourists and all manner of clients squeeze in for the standard bistro fare: good, sustaining stuff such as bundles of warm leek in a creamy vinaigrette, goat's cheese salad or, for a change, *accras* (salt cod fritters) with spicy sauce. Main courses run from *cassoulet* to kidneys with mustard, from veal with port sauce to salmon with tagliatelle and cream. We've tried them all on repeat visits and thumbs go up all round. For dessert simple is best, a *tarte Tartin* or the tart of the day. Wines are reasonably priced, staff are good humoured – it's an agreeable spot and a good address to know in this part of town.

Chez Janou

2, rue Roger-Verlomme, 3rd (01.42.72.28.41). M° Chemin Vert. **Open** daily noon-2am. **Average** €23. **No credit cards.**

There's something about Chez Janou. It's hard to put your finger on exactly what – the staff is friendly if somewhat frenetic, the decor is charming but unremarkable, and the food is reliable rather than great – but from where you're sitting, indoors or on the tiny terrace, the world somehow looks like a better place. Double-billed as a bistro and a *restaurant Provençal*, Chez Janou treads a rather varied line between the two. The grapefruit, avocado and prawn salad and the tuna tartare served with an onion marmalade are always excellent; for main courses the fish pie is disappointing and the lamb cutlets passable, while the duck is consistently delicious. Sweet tooths should not miss the chocolate mousse: where else in Paris – or anywhere – do get to help yourself to as much as you want? But the real draw is (to borrow from Arletty) the atmosphere. The workers may be rushing around, but for those lucky enough to be dining here, there's a prevailing feeling of convivial calm. It's real, too – on several occasions we have been allowed to move to a different table to continue drinking while they cleared up around us. We don't know who Janou is, but we know that we like him.

La Fontaine Gourmande

11 rue Charlot, 3rd (01.42.78.72.40). M° Filles du Calvaire. **Open** Tue-Fri noon-2.30pm, 7.30-10.30pm; Sat 7-10.30pm. Closed one week in Apr, three weeks in Aug. **Average** €28. **Credit** MC, V.

This tiny restaurant tucked away from the tourist crowds to the south feels like a bit of a secret, one you'd be loath to give away to even your best friends. Indeed, the stone walls, dark wood tables and impeccable cooking seem to come right out of a fantasised image of the Parisian restaurant: refined, yet informal. At lunch simple food is available, but this is one place where you shouldn't deprive yourself of the right to indulge. From a menu that changes every season, the homemade foie gras terrine with Calvados was smooth and creamy, ripe with apple perfume. Nor did the creamy crab

Bistros

Pop your corks at Le Tir Bouchon

soup disappoint. Further proof that the kitchen does the difficult job of preparing fish and meat with equal aplomb, a salmon *ballotine* with long-cooked chicory was melt-in-your-mouth tender, if a tad too salty. But the high point was the *pigeonneau confit*, the delicate small bird perfectly preserved without being greasy or heavy. Hard to eat to be sure, but worth every stolen morsel. After all this indulgence, we had to pass on dessert, but next time we'll definitely come prepared.

Georget
64 rue Vieille-du-Temple, 3rd (01.42.78.55.89). M° *St-Paul.* **Open** Mon-Fri noon-2pm, 7.30-10pm; Sat 7.30-10pm. Closed Aug. **Average** €31. **No credit cards**.
The first evidence of non-image-conscious, anachronistic dining: no sign of 'Georget' over the door. Look for 'Restaurant Robert et Louise', and enter the draughty, wood-smoke-filled chamber whose beamed interior is like a massive country kitchen, with heavy peasant tables, an open kitchen and blazing fire pit at the far end. Openness is, in fact, Georget's principal charm: you watch as a cleaver is taken first to a hunk of scrap wood to splinter kindling, then to a Renault-sized side of beef sitting at one end a long table (we sat at the other), where after much fussing your *côte de boeuf* or *contre-filet* is hand-selected, hacked and thrown sizzling onto the wood-fired griddle. As your meal sizzles away (be it lamb chops, black pudding or a mushroom-garnished *omelette forestière*), octogenarian matrons fry potatoes and slice *rillettes*, a boy arrives from the courtyard to deliver lilacs and *bisous*, a poodle whines for its bowl of water. We found the food rib-sticking in the most pleasing sense possible: buttery grilled prawns, earthy *escargots* served in the shell, crisp *confit de canard*. Although not quite as *à point* as we'd ordered, the juicy beef, served on a wooden board, still melted effortlessly down our throats. A bottle of decent Cahors (€13.72), and the fluffy *Charlotte au chocolat* are respectable sidekicks to the main show. Georget produces a timeless tableau – it could be 1910 or even 1620 were it not for the rotary dial phone and the location one block from one of the Marais' more popular café corners.

Le Hangar
12 impasse Berthaud, 3rd (01.42.74.55.44). M° *Rambuteau.* **Open** Mon 6.30pm-midnight; Tue-Sat noon-3pm, 6.30pm-midnight. Closed three weeks in Aug. **Average** €28. **No credit cards**.
Hidden down a tiny impasse, across from the hubbub of Beaubourg, Le Hangar treats its regulars (and if you've been once you're bound to go back) to imaginative classical cuisine with, for the price, remarkable attention to detail. The refurbished warehouse bears no sign of post-industrial pretension: staff are friendly and efficient. All that's missing is softer lighting – we beg the owners to consider investing in 40-watt bulbs. For starters we chose generous salmon tartare and an inspired chilled avocado soup, not too rich and topped with balls of tongue-teasing red pepper sorbet. Main courses included fabulous pan-fried foie gras accompanied by a long-time, in-house favourite, olive oil-potato purée, and a good, herb-filled rendition of steak tartare. Chocaholics will be hard-pressed to choose between the hot, oozing chocolate cake and the airy, but no less scrumptious, *soufflé au chocolat*; we had both. There are plenty of wines under €15 with some decent half bottles for around €8.

Le Pamphlet ★
38 rue Debellyme, 3rd (01.42.72.39.24). M° *Filles du Calvaire.* **Open** daily noon-2.30pm, 7.30-11pm. Closed 1-15 Jan, 5-21 Aug. **Average** €27. **Prix-fixe** €27. **Lunch menu** €20. **Credit** V. **Wheelchair access**.
When we first found this welcoming auberge on a tiny street on the northern fringes of the Marais two years ago, we often had the rustic, beamed dining room almost to ourselves. Word has since got out, and a mixed crowd of internationals and stylish locals packs the place out nightly, so book ahead to enjoy the friendly, relaxing atmosphere and great food. The menu changes regularly, but we loved recent starters of fresh baby pea 'gazpacho' (perhaps it was the dash of Espelette pepper that inspired the name?) poured over thin slices of foie gras and Bayonne ham, smoked salmon on a potato blini in a caviar-garnished cream sauce, and plump asparagus garnished with duck gizzards on rocket. Main courses were lovely, too, including a tuna steak on a *pipérade*-inspired bed of eggs scrambled with tomatoes, and juicy chicken breast with a crust of toasted hazelnuts. The cheese course is a tangy slice of *brebis* with green salad, while luscious desserts include strawberries roasted in salted butter and served with original and refreshing celery ice cream, a melting chocolate cake and a refreshing citrus fruit salad. Coffee is served with coconut macaroons and prunes marinated in *eau de vie*, and the brief wine list offers a variety of well-chosen and affordable bottles, from a Bourgogne Passetoutgrain for €15 to an Haut Médoc for €28.

Le Petit Marseillais
72 rue Vieille-du-Temple, 3rd (01.42.78.91.59). M° *Rambuteau.* **Open** daily noon-2.30pm, 8-11pm. **Average** €34. **Credit** AmEx, MC, V.
Ever since this cosy, happy, desperately trendy little place run by two childhood friends from Marseille – they're the muscular guys behind the bar – opened it's been packed with a hip, friendly, mixed crowd that chats easily between tables. Which is just as well, since you're packed in cheek-by-jowl in this small room with dark red walls, black wood tables and chairs, and vintage Murano glass chandeliers. The menu runs to appealing Marseillais home cooking, just the type of food you'd like to find if you were lucky enough to snag an invitation to a *cabanon* (privately owned sea shack) down in this increasingly fashionable port city on the Med. The blackboard changes regularly, but starters such as the oyster mushroom sautée with garlic and parsley or mixed salad with *pétoncles* (tiny scallops) are appealing, as are main courses such as sautéed squid, roast lamb, and tagliatelle with *pistou* sauce and hunks of parmesan. Most people don't bother with dessert, but tarts and cheese are available, and the Domaine d'Ott Côtes de Provence is excellent drinking at €20. Ideal for a night on the town with friends.

Le Réconfort
37 rue de Poitou, 3rd (01.49.96.09.60). M° *St-Sébastien Froissart.* **Open** Mon-Fri noon-2.30pm, 8-11pm. Closed one week in Aug. **Average** €28. **Credit** MC, V.
On our third attempt, at the end of the second dinner service, we only just managed to squeeze in here – booking is a must at this popular bistro. A good sign, we thought, and indeed it was. The decor is eclectic bordering on schizophrenic: rustic wooden beams, Chinese lanterns, red velvet upholstery and portraits of Indian film stars. It's strange, at first, to be eating in a gothic Bollywood country house, but ultimately we were charmed. The creative touches continue: the menus are printed into the first pages of old leather-bound romance novels (the menu was the better of the two reads). We started with fresh white mushrooms covered with warm goat's cheese and sprinkled with lemon – this alone would have made our visit worthwhile. So, with spirits high, we flew at our main course of Argentinean steak with *gratin dauphinois*. The meat, cooked rare for French tastes, was a good cut, while the garlicky *gratin* proved, once again, to be the stalwart of side dishes. Our chocolate fondant with *crème anglaise* didn't raise any eyebrows; but everything after the starter was inescapably *dénouement*. In keeping with the

Au Grain de folie

Montmartre's Vegetarian Restaurant

24 rue de La Vieuville, 18th
Mº Abbesses Tel: 01.42.58.15.57
Open daily noon-2.30pm,
evenings 7.30-11.30pm (Winter 7-10.30pm)
Complimentary tea/coffee with this ad

La Victoire Suprême du cœur

Vegetarian restaurant

HEALTHY, NATURAL FOOD THAT WILL FULFIL YOUR BODY AND SOUL'S DEEPEST CRAVINGS

41 rue des Bourdonnais, 1st
Mº Châtelet • Tel: 01.40.41.93.95
Monday to Saturday from noon to 10pm

La Brasserie de l'Isle-Saint-Louis

55 Quai de Bourbon, 4th.
Tel: 01.43.54.02.59

In the heart of Paris, a true French brasserie.

Open noon - midnight.
Closed Wednesdays
& lunchtime Thursdays

---

l'Auberge Nicolas Flamel

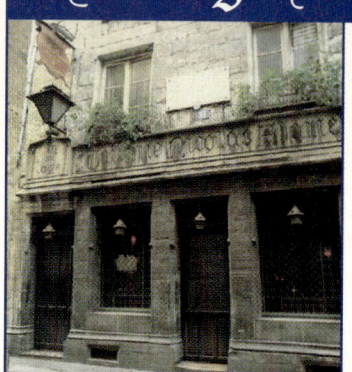

- Built in 1407, the oldest house in Paris
- High quality Bistro food
- Excellent selection of wines at vineyard prices
- Next door to "Les Bains"

51 rue de Montmorency, 3rd
Mº Rambuteau
Tel: 01.42.71.77.78
www.nicolasflamel.parisbistro.net

Chez Bibi

Specialities:

Duck confit
Stuffed cabbage
Aligot
Salers Beef
Duck magret with honey and cêpes

Set - menu for lunch choice of €14 or €20

Set - menu for dinner €20

Restaurant Aveyronnais
5 rue Mandar, 2nd

Tel: 01.40.26.70.55 Fax: 01.40.26.70.22
Open from Tuesday to Sunday
12pm-2.30pm and 7.30pm-11.30pm
Mº Sentier/Etienne Marcel

AU MOULIN A VENT

Meat specialities from the Salers region
BEAUJOLAIS SPECIALITIES

Open Tue-Fri noon-2pm, 7.30-11pm,
Sat 7.30-11pm

Alexandra Damas Spanu
20 RUE DES FOSSÉS SAINT BERNARD, 5TH.
TEL: 01.43.54.99.37 - FAX: 01.40.46.92.23

theme of the decor, a variety of spices – cumin and coriander most notably – made some unexpected appearances. Justly popular.

Taxi Jaune
13 rue Chapon, 3rd (01.42.76.00.40). M° Arts et Métiers. **Open** Mon-Fri noon-2.15pm, 7.30-10.30pm. **Average** €26. **Lunch menu** €11.89, €12.81. Closed three weeks in Aug. **Credit** MC, V.
This shrine to the yellow taxi is oddly decorated with dinky toys arranged around a revolving metal plate of painted food and a wacky yellow mirror surrounded by automobile parts. The cuisine, however, is more conventional and has no link with the yellow taxi's New York origins. Starters were fresh and well-prepared; we enjoyed the artichoke salad and the carpaccio of smoked salmon and tuna balanced precariously on a bulging bed of crisp green salad. The main courses showed real culinary flair: small portions of juicy, caramelised pork and a perfectly-cooked tuna steak in a light cream sauce. The highlight of the meal, though, was the vegetables: a delicate cauliflower purée dressed with mandarin segments, chicory baked with ham and gruyère, crunchy potato *rösti*, as well as spinach and mangetout. The desserts were pretty good as well – an above-average *tarte Tatin* which collapsed under the fork into buttery apple chunks, and a dark, rich and soft chocolate cake on a brittle praline base. A grinning chef emerged at one point to survey the scene and chat with the many regulars.

4th Arrondissement

Baracane
38 rue des Tournelles, 4th (01.42.71.43.33). M° Bastille or Chemin Vert. **Open** Mon-Fri noon-2.30pm, 7pm-midnight; Sat 7pm-midnight. **Average** €25. **Prix fixe** €24.50, €35. **Lunch menu** €9.50, €14. **Credit** MC, V.

This long, skinny bistro serves as a quiet respite from the madding Bastille and Place des Vosges crowds. Owner Marcel Baudis (now running the bistro L'Oulette in the Bercy *quartier*) hails from Montauban in south-west France, so the countrified flavours respect his roots while still surprising the most jaded of city diners. After scanning the list of regional *pâtés*, preserves, wines and *bonbons* available as take-home souvenirs, we began with a smoky Jerusalem artichoke soup with bacon, and a stuffed *cou* salad, a duck's neck terrine with mushroom accents and a watercress, walnut and lamb's lettuce topping. Mains kept the positive momentum going: a fresh trout pan-fried with hazelnuts, parsley and butter, and a hearty pastry-wrapped *croustade* of roasted feta, mushrooms and green vegetables. Generous desserts arrived as part of the €24.50 *menu*: a daringly cooked grapefruit in sabayon (a sweet egg yolk and wine sauce), and the house speciality, *tourtière aux pommes*, which also included prunes and Armagnac in its crispy pastry shell. Fine service and fabulous value make up for the rather plain decor.

Benoît
20 rue St Martin, 4th (01.42.72.25.76). M° Châtelet or Hôtel-de-Ville. **Open** daily noon-2pm, 8-10pm. Closed Aug. **Average** €90. **Lunch menu** €38. **Credit** AmEx, DC, MC, V.
What makes a €90 bistro meal worth the investment? Nothing much beyond snob appeal, judging from a recent experience at Benoît. Yes, the vintage dining room with its etched glass partition has the postcard look of an old Parisian bistro, and the white-aproned waiters play the part perfectly. But we've had better and just-as-atmospheric meals for €25 elsewhere. A starter of cold tongue layered with a foie gras mousse pleased the tongue-lover at our table, while the day's special of a hot morel terrine was not a terrine at all but simply hot morels with cream – pleasant enough. Ten minutes after ordering the classic *canard aux navets* for two, we decided to test the service by ordering a side-dish of potatoes. The waiter replied with a polite, *'oui, bien sûr'*. The roast duck arrived – overcooked – with a *jus* that had not been degreased, though the turnips were tasty. No sign of our potatoes until after we had finished the duck, then the boring potato cake arrived in a small gratin dish. The meal's only outstanding moment was a towering strawberry cake, quivering layers of fruit, pastry, custard and cream. Our budget restricted us to a fruity Chinon which nicely accompanied the food. Who goes to Benoît? Those with money to *flamber* who want an exclusive taste of the bistro experience.

Le Colimaçon
44 rue Vieille-du-Temple, 4th (01.48.87.12.01/www.lecolimacon.com). M° St-Paul or Hôtel-de-Ville. **Open** Mon, Wed-Sun 7.30pm-1am. Closed three weeks in Aug. **Average** €30. **Prix fixe** €14.50, €20.70. **Credit** AmEx, MC, V.
The centrepiece and namesake of this 18th-century, stone-walled, wood-beamed restaurant is the corkscrew staircase which must surely be the bane of the heavily laden waiters' lives. We were at first put off by the cramped seating, dim lighting and out-of-place Beach Boys tunes. But the waiters, expertly negotiatiating the stairs, came down from the kitchen with armloads of quality bistro food that helped us forget the incongruities. A liver, bacon and oyster mushroom fricassée astounded us with its deep, meaty sauce, while the mussels in cream sauce were better than average. Prawns sautéed in Cognac and a silky poached hen pan-fried salmon ruined our post-holiday diets. Meaty dishes such as duck *confit*, pork tenderloin and steak tartare fill out the sizeable *menu*. A la carte, the bill adds up more quickly than you'd expect; stick to the *formule* if you're on a budget. More than 12 euros for a half-bottle of Georges Duboeuf Beaujolais seemed outrageous, though the *tarte Tatin* with raspberry coulis sweetened the taste in our mouths. Le Colimaçon seemed a bit pricey considering the plain decor and offhand service: the food deserves a better stage and players.

Le Dôme du Marais ★
53bis rue des Francs-Bourgeois, 4th (01.42.74.54.17). M° Rambuteau. **Open** Tue-Sat noon-2.30pm, 7.30-11pm. Closed Aug. **Average** €38. **Prix fixe** €28-€38.50. **Lunch menu** €15, €23. **Credit** AmEx, MC, V.
In Paris, you never know what's behind the facade. Here, it's a striking octagonal-shaped restaurant with gilt walls and red flourishes crowned by a striking dome. There's even a slender gallery above the dining room with a few tables for two. The building pre-dates the Revolution, and from 1920 to 1930 it was the auction room for the French state-owned pawnbrokers. Now it's firmly in the hands of chef Pierre Lecroute and his food is as classy as the decor. An ample serving of scallops from Normandy roasted and splashed with a light curry sauce, and a spring vegetable soup with loads of delicately sliced veggies and fresh herbs, were super starters – light and full of flavour. Then came choice roasted guinea fowl with duck liver sauce and irresistibly green broad beans, and *daurade grise* (sea bream) teamed with curry and a mound of spring vegetables. Desserts were good, too, a simple vanilla *millefeuille* with tiny whole fresh strawberries plopped around it, and a wickedly rich trio of dark chocolate: *parfait*, mousse, and a warm, runny mini-gâteau. Small wonder smart-looking French folk and internationals fill the dining room. Beware, however, the non-smoking area – it's actually the covered courtyard at the entrance to the restaurant and is devoid of gilt and ceremony.

Grizzli Café
7 rue St-Martin, 4th (01.48.87.77.56). M° Hôtel-de-Ville or Châtelet. **Open** daily 9am-2am. **Average** €22. **Credit** AmEx, MC, V.
With a recent change in ownership, one of the most beloved bistros in Paris has been given a dramatic updating. If the endearing sepia quality has sadly gone missing, along with many of the classic bistro dishes Le Grizzli was known for, the new designer look is attractive, the food is still good and the non-stop serving hours make this a great address to bear in mind for a late lunch. The lighter, modern bistro cooking is appealing, and you can also get salads or pasta if you want something simpler. This place has one of the best terraces in town, since it's on a reasonably quiet pedestrian street, and a recent lunch began pleasantly with delicious *croustillant de chèvre* (goat's cheese inside fried pastry leaves) in basil oil and tomato sauce and an earthy terrine of aubergine and mozzarella. Main courses of sautéed scallops with tender chopped leeks and grilled tuna steak on a bed of sautéed courgettes were satisfying, though portions were small. The wines served by the glass are good, as was the strawberry tart, and the crowd here has become younger and more stylish. Note that the Grizzli also serves brunch in addition to lunch and dinner.

Ma Bourgogne
19 pl des Vosges, 4th (01.42.78.44.64). M° St-Paul or Bastille. **Open** daily noon-1am. Closed Feb. **Average** €33 **Prix fixe** €32. **No credit cards.**
No-one can deny that the setting – under the arcades of the picture perfect place des Vosges – is superb, and while there are temples to gastronomy on the square this isn't one of them. It belongs instead to the no-fuss, no-frills school of eating: grills, salads and an apparently famous steak tartare (which was stampeding out the door and onto French-speaking tables). Salads such as cucumber with tomatoes and green beans, and the *sarladaise* with smoked duck, *frisée*, duck liver pâté, walnuts and red onion, were fresh and nicely done but mains were less successful. The roast chicken and chips described by the waiter as *'exceptionnel'* was, in the flesh, rubbery fowl with greasy, soft chips, and the salmon with sorrel sauce, while better, was congealing. Orders are hurled electronically to the kitchen via the waiters' hand keypad. It's a tourist roost and that quintessential Paris view (and English-speaking staff) make the unexceptional food easily digestible.

Les Philosophes
28 rue Vieille-du-Temple, 4th (01.48.87.49.64/www.cafeine.com). M° Hôtel-de-Ville. **Open** daily 9am-2am (food served noon-1.15am). **Average** €26. **Prix fixe** €15.55-€25. Brunch daily 9am-5pm €16.77. **Credit** MC, V.
Reopened in 2001 after months of impatient waiting by loyal fans, Les Philosophes has been remodelled to fit in with its high-visibility Marais location. The interior is a classier version of its old self, with subtle lighting and high-end art on the walls. Prices have also been renovated in an upward direction (the menu hadn't changed but the chef promised refurbishment). Expect superb specialities such as their succulent and chubby duck thigh in honey and black pepper. With daily specials, the chef seems a little unsteady: mussels in a tasty chive broth were mushy and half unopened, and a well-cooked grilled pickerel fillet with fennel and morels was unharmoniously paired with melon chunks and blackcurrant sauce. Light and airy, the lovely-to-look-at mango fondant pie was up to the standard of Les Philosophes' amazing espresso cake, caramelised and crispy on the top, dense chocolate in the middle, with a crumble crust. The bustling staff was extremely courteous, finding time to translate the entire menu for a Dutch couple. Breakfast, brunch and snacks can be had inside or on the ample terrace when the kitchen isn't in full swing.

Au Tibourg
29 rue du Bourg-Tibourg, 4th (01.42.74.45.25/www.autibourg.com). M° Hôtel-de-Ville. **Open** Mon-Fri 7-11pm; Sat, Sun noon-11pm **Average** €23. **Prix fixe** €14.05-€24.05. **Credit** MC, V.
An exceptionally friendly welcome awaited us at Au Tibourg. Granted, we were the only customers at the time, but the pleasant service continued even as the bistro filled up. The owners abide by a remarkably civilized yet fatal policy: when customers order the house wine, the bottle is left on the table. At the end of the meal, the waiter checks how much is left, then simply charges for what has been drunk. The outcome is obvious enough. Starters such as *mousseline* of green asparagus with trout eggs sounded better than they tasted, which

Le Buisson Ardent, a flaming star

Macis & Muscade

The innovative cuisine here, which uses natural aromatic essences (thyme, osmanthus, turkish rose, neroli...), will test your tastebuds and delight your palate.

Set menu lunch & dinner: €23
Special lunch set menu: €12

Open Tue-Fri noon-2pm, Sunday brunch noon-2pm
Dinner Tue-Sun 8pm-10.30pm, Fri-Sat 8pm-11pm

110 rue Legendre, 17th M° La Fourche - Tel: 01.42.26.62.26

Le Berthoud
Since 1963

"The menu is a wonder of conservative, bourgeois *cuisine de ménage*" –Le Figaro

"Soup-lovers are well respected here" –Le Monde

"A Montagne-Sainte-Geneviève institution (...) delicious (...) tradition is a good thing here" –Zurban

"Getting back to basics with *Bouillon*, *Pot au feu* and home made butter" –Les Bonnes Adresses

Lunch: suggestions from €9 to €15
Evenings: menu at €28
or €35 à la carte

Open daily except Sat lunch and Sun

1 rue Valette, 5th. M° Maubert-Mutualité
Tel: 01.43.54.38.81 - Fax: 01.43.54.98.38
e-mail: axelmx@club-internet.fr
www.leberthoud.fr

Auberge "d'chez eux"

DON'T MISS ONE OF THE BEST CLASSIC FRENCH BISTROS IN PARIS!

Complete Lunch Menu... €28 / €33.50

Cuisine Bourgeoise • Foie Gras Cassoulet
Confits • Frogs' Legs

Great choice of desserts

(Just off Place des Invalides)

www.chezeux.com

2 avenue de Lowendal, 7th • M° Ecole Militaire • Tel: 01.47.05.52.55

was slightly bland. Our roast lamb chops *à la provençale* tasted as though they might have actually been cooked in Provence and posted to Paris some time later in specially designed dehydrating envelopes. Sadly, the *pommes boulangères aux oignons*, a pleasant distraction, were served in rather conservative portions. We decided to skip dessert but did stay long enough to enjoy the only loo we've encountered with its own waiting room – fully stocked with Marais-relevant reading.

Le Vieux Bistro

14 rue du Cloître-Notre-Dame, 4th (01.43.54.18.95). M° Cité or RER St-Michel.
Open daily noon-2pm, 7.30-11pm.
Average €38. **Credit** MC, V.
It couldn't have a more touristy location, but Le Vieux Bistro had long attracted an understated fashion crowd for its reliable classic fare and cheery service. Then it changed owners in December 1999, and though an initial meal since then proved reassuring, a recent visit convinced us that standards have seriously slipped. Our meal started with an unfortunate incident – the waiter knocked over a wine glass, sending shards flying into one of our bags. He took the bag away and picked the glass out within view of our table – well-meaning but embarrassing. On this summery day, we grabbed seats on the terrace and ordered gazpacho and retro avocado-and-prawn salads – the first tasted like nothing other than cold, packaged tomato soup with a few cucumber bits added, while the second reminded us of a school canteen. *Quenelles* in *sauce Nantua* were both doughy and greasy; fried sole tasted fine but came with flabby overboiled potatoes; pigeon with fresh foie gras and fried apples came closest to making us happy. With a bottle of inexpensive Bordeaux and no dessert – the kitchen had closed by the time we asked for one – this meal cost more than €122 for three. It's easy to do better, even in this area.

5th Arrondissement

Bistro Jef

9 rue Cujas, 5th (01.43.29.20.20). M° Cluny-La-Sorbonne/RER Luxembourg. **Open** Mon-Sat noon-2pm, 8-11pm. Closed 29 July-17Aug.
Average €25. **Prix fixe** €23.63 (dinner only). **Lunch menu** €12.50.
Credit AmEx,DC, MC, V.
Chez Pento is no more; long live Jef. The old Latin Quarter stalwart has come back under a new owner, rejuvenated and much more serious about its food. The art deco light fittings, high ceilings, banquettes and giant windows remain, and in have come today's deep terracotta walls, a dulcet jazz-funk backing and carefully prepared *cuisine du terroir* with a south-western edge. A lentil salad came with a well-judged dressing and a heap of warm, perfectly sautéed chicken livers, just crisp on the outside, soft and pink inside; the *verdure du jour* was a herby, mixed green salad. For mains we opted for slices of rosy roast beef with puréed potato and pike-perch in saffron sauce with rice, both served with sautéed courgettes. For dessert, two variants on the crème brûlée: its regional ancestor *crème catalane* and the original *crème Aubert au pain d'épices*, with well-caramelised crust and a delicious base of crumbled spice bread. The owner is from the Bordelais, so this is a place where the Bordeaux choices, such as our Château Pessac-Léognan at a reasonable €23.48, are worth trusting.

Le Buisson Ardent

25 rue Jussieu, 5th (01.43.54.93.02). M° Jussieu. **Open** Mon-Fri noon-2pm, 7.30-10.30pm. **Prix fixe** €26. **Lunch menu** €14.50. **Credit** AmEx, MC, V.
Le Buisson Ardent, which roughly translated means the 'the burning bush', is a fine example of a sophisticated 21st-century bistro. The cooking is traditional but with modern twists and presentation. On a busy midweek lunchtime the attractive, well-renovated trad decor was humming with a mixed crowd of tourists, business people and academics. A table of lady trade unionists had little positive to say about anything except their delicious starters such as a tomato *millefeuille* with feta or the more traditional salad topped with *gésiers confits* and a poached egg, while we tucked into the exceptional homemade bread. We opted for the *rognon de veau entier* for a small supplement to the price of the three-course *menu*. The veal kidney was perfectly cooked, served on a bed of braised vegetables, and deliciously accompanied by several *pots* of the very drinkable house red. Crème brûlée with chestnut cream proved that fiddling with a classic dish can work, the purée prominent enough to attenuate the eggy richness of the cream. The cheese was a fairly meagre selection but well-chosen and in perfect condition. Service was friendly, if stressed.

Chez René ★

14 bd St-Germain, 5th (01.43.54.30.23). M° Maubert-Mutualité. **Open** Tue-Sat 12.15-2.15pm, 7.45-11pm. Closed Aug.
Average €46. **Prix fixe** €39.50 (dinner only). **Lunch menu** €28. **Credit** MC, V.
Every ten years or so since René Cinquin opened this place in 1957, the staff have gathered for a photo that's framed and added to the other ones hanging by the door. And, as far as change is concerned, that is pretty much that. These days it's not René but his son Jean-Paul who chats with the diners but there's still the same heavy silver cutlery, thick starched linen, black-jacketed waiters and honest hard work in the kitchen; this is a place that exudes quiet confidence in its own traditions. Our starters – slices of tangy black radish in a cream and chive sauce and a sizzling plate of oyster mushrooms – were simple but in a winsome kind of way. But the *coq au vin*? This is the reason for coming here. The secret of the dark, succulent sauce is no stock, just a good twenty minutes constantly stirring flour and butter over the feeblest of flames before adding the wine – just as René's granny taught him to do. Similar skills go into the *boeuf bourguignon*, which is also served up in a cast-iron casserole in fine old style. After all that, we were expecting something a bit more grandmotherly from the rice pudding. Bit of a let-down. A portly fellow diner had the better idea of ordering the cheese, which impressively came in two courses: cow's milk and goat's milk. A fine way to finish off a bottle of perfectly adequate house Beaujolais.

Café Society

In her role as the quirky Amélie in Le Fabuleux Destin d'Amélie Poulain won the French nation's heart before working her magic abroad. She lives in Paris, in the 20th arrondissement.

'My favourite areas are Belleville and the Butte Chaumont. One of the restaurants that I love in that area is the **Le Bistro des Soupirs** (*see p39*). It's really good, and it's like being in a provincial restaurant – it doesn't feel like Paris at all. The decor is old fashioned and tacky, and the clientele isn't at all fashionable. I also like **La Flèche d'Or** (*see p117*, **Bars & Pubs**) – it's an old train station and the windows there are really beautiful. In the Marais I enjoy **Le Loir dans La Théière** (*see p127*, **Tea Rooms**). Inside it's like a Jeunet film set. There's something childlike about it – nothing is the same and none of the seats match. I love that. I really like **Anahi** (*see p81*, **The Americas**) – *the* banana with *dulce di leche* is fantastic - I would go there just for that. I don't often go clubbing, but I have been to **Le Queen** (*see p135*, **Clubs**) and the music was great. I don't really spend time in most of the Costes places, but I do like **Café Marly** (*see p104*, **Cafés**) – it has a very calming atmosphere.

Chez Toutoune

5 rue de Pointoise, 5th (01.43.26.56.81). M° Maubert-Mutualité. **Open** Tue-Sun noon-2pm, 7.30-10.45pm. **Average** €35.
Prix fixe €33.50. **Lunch menu** €22.
Credit AmEx, MC, V.
The menu proclaims it 'cuisine of the sun' and there's some truth in that. Starters such as a *millefeuille* of artichoke, tomato and finely sliced fried bread, and *caviar d'aubergine* topped with a poached egg were satisfying, but mains such as the undercooked cod with vapid orange butter, endives and cardamom were disappointing and limp. The faux-Provençal decor – a swirly mix of green and burnt red that wouldn't be out of place in a great auntie's parlour – and some sun-drenched murals aim to create Provence in Paris. Bah humbug! The service could be a lot sunnier: we had a 20-minute wait for menus, wine arrived after starters, and dessert ('truffles', or bland white ice-cream balls drenched in cocoa, and chilly crème brûlée) appeared too quickly. The €33.50 *menu* includes a tureen of soup plus picks from the *carte*, but watch the supplements.

Le Coupe-Chou

11 rue de Lanneau, 5th (01.46.33.68.69/ www.lecoupechou.com). M° Maubert-Mutualité. **Open** Mon-Sat noon-2pm, 7pm-1am. **Average** €46. **Prix fixe** €24, €32.
Credit AmEx, MC, V.
Cut the prices in half and we would give Le Coupe-Chou a rave review. It's true this restaurant has *je ne sais quoi*, in bags: an open fire in winter, lots of little rooms full of romantic nooks and crannies and – best of all – a kind of 18th century chill-out zone full of comfy old furniture where you can lounge *après*-dinner with brandy and cigars. The problem is you've got to shell out €24, even €32 for the sort of lunch a French lorry driver would pay €11 for, wine included. A propos the wine, at €15 a bottle, the Cuvée Coupe-Chou – a Nuits St-Georges, according to our waiter – tasted like a passable little Burgundy, nothing more. Worse still, you have to put up with a looped cassette of the sort of music they would have played in the supermarket had they had such things in Bach's day. *Frisée aux lardons*, duck *confit*, crême-brûlée plus 'Air on a G-String' equals Tourist Trap. Be warned.

Les Degrés de Notre-Dame

10 rue des Grands-Degrés, 5th (01.55.42.88.88). M° Maubert-Mutualité.
Open Mon-Sat noon-10.30pm.
Average €25. **Lunch menu** €9.60.
Prix fixe €21, €23. **Credit** MC, V.
It is not easy to have an inexpensive, OK lunch near Notre-Dame. And it still isn't exactly easy once you've found your way to this place. But follow these simple instructions and you should just about manage it. 1. Try to get a seat on the terrace overlooking a quiet and pretty corner of Paris 2. Ignore the American in the beret at the next table; he's probably harmless. 3. Order the quite-good-value €9.60 lunch *menu* rather than the quite-a-large-rip-off €21 meal. 4. Choose things that require minimal culinary care. Our French onion soup was almost rigid with what we suspected to be stock cube and the salmon tagliatelle was a watery, salty pile of disappointment. Go for the herring salad or the *boudin* (black pudding). 5. Avoid the house wine, bought in apparently inexhaustible quantity from the Polish airline LOT. 6. Don't ask if there's some link between this establishment and Poland; the service is rude enough as it is. Enjoy your meal!

L'Equitable

1 rue des Fossés-St-Marcel, 5th (01.43.31.69.20). M° Censier-Daubenton or St-Marcel. **Open** Tue-Fri noon-2.30pm, 7.30-11pm; Sat 7.30-11pm; Sun noon-2.30pm.
Average €34. **Prix fixe** €28.
Lunch menu €20.50, €25 (Tue-Fri).
Credit AmEx, V.
Although they've made an effort with some bright oil paintings, the almost soporific decor is at odds with the cuisine. We expected die-hard respect for tradition; instead we found in chef Yves Martin dishes that were light and inventive: lots of *timbales* and spices, a crispy wafer of something here, a tangy chutney there, lots of fish and plenty of vegetables in a register that goes from classic veal kidneys to exotic emperor fish cooked in a banana leaf. We began with a neat salad of fresh crabmeat in a *timbale* of julienned vegetables with a scoop of refreshing tomato sorbet, and a *marbré* of ham hock and foie gras on Puy lentils in a cream dressing. Guinea fowl two ways was fricasséed in a curry sauce, its leg in a *parmentier*, and an excellent slab of flaky fresh cod came with savoy cabbage and crispy *coppa* slices. We finished with lavender-honey ice cream doused in honey, its sweetness offset, a bit, by pink grapefruit segments, and crème brûlée over a base of *griotte* cherries. Quiet but accomplished.

Les Fontaines

9 rue Soufflot, 5th (01.43.26.42.80). RER Luxembourg. **Open** Mon-Sat noon-3pm, 7-11pm. **Average** €30. **Credit** MC, V.
Walk past Les Fontaines at breakfast time and it resembles any local Parisian café: plastic-topped tables, leatherette banquettes, neon lighting and diverse students and office workers stopping in for a coffee. Come mealtime, though, and there's not a place to spare, as the tables, transformed by white tablecloths, fill with local worthies from the *mairie*, neighbouring hairdressers and publishers, foodies and lucky tourists. We've sometimes found the food unspectacular but our latest visit laid doubts to rest as, after oysters and the prettily presented chicory, walnut and blue cheese salad (any health considerations waived by the huge dollop of mayonnaise), the regular steaks and calf's liver were supplemented by autumn specials that show they know their game. We dug into pheasant with muscat and raisin sauce and tender, roast *noisettes de biche* in a red wine and blood-based sauce, which came with all the trimmings: roast apple, red-wine-soaked pear, lozenges of carrot and celeriac purée. This left us with room only to share a sundae glass of *mousse aux deux chocolats* (creamy white on top, bitter dark below) and finish off our well-priced 1993 Givry at €28. Reserve, and come with time to spare – this is slow food territory.

L'Intermède

4 bd du Port-Royal, 5th (01.47.07.08.99). M° Gobelins. **Open** Tue-Sun noon-2.30pm; Tue-Sat 7.30-10.30pm. Closed three weeks in Aug. **Average** €23. **Prix fixe** €20.60, €27.50. **Lunch menu** €12.50, €17.
Credit AmEx, MC, V.
Into its third year of new managment, the state of the L'Intermède's awning still doesn't inspire confidence – faded yellow letters on a torn and stained green background – but once inside the aesthetics improve. A simple and classy layout consists of about 20 well-spaced tables, each with spotless (before we sat down) white cloths and gleaming cutlery. On the phone, on arrival, and *à table*, the service remains equally pristine. All our choices from the €27.50 dinner *menu* were described with care and pride. The *croustillant de chèvre aux asperges* was a complicated-looking but delicious starter while the salmon *'merrine'* – terrine from the *mer* – should not be eaten with a large main dish as it is comically big. The best mains are the fish and seafood plates but other dishes were pleasant: a tender *magret de canard* was served with a lovely broccoli purée, though the accompanying roasted potatoes seemed to have been rationed. The wine list is excellent but could benefit from the addition of

a few lower priced bottles. Another example of an above-average bistro almost empty while the McDonald's across the street was packed.

Le Moulin à Vent
20 rue des Fossés-St-Bernard, 5th (01.43.54.99.37). Mº Jussieu. **Open** Tue-Fri noon-2pm, 7.30-11pm; Sat 7.30-11pm. Closed Aug, Christmas. **Average** €49. **Credit** MC, V. **Wheelchair access**.
This bistro had long been one of our favourites, so it was with some anticipation that we came here after a change of owner. The first signs were good: the decor of polished copper, gleaming wood and portholes remains untouched. This is the kind of place where tables have to be pulled out to let diners slide onto the banquette and the babble can become rather deafening. Arriving early, we were inexplicably seated elbow-to-elbow with the only other couple in the dining room, but never mind — we were here for the juicy meat for which this restaurant is so famous. As a prelude, we had a salad of rather limp green beans topped with tasty morsels of foie gras, and quartered artichoke hearts on a salad of *frisée* that had seen better days. A steak with roquefort sauce was excellent, as always, but a side dish of sautéed potatoes seemed rather meagre and not particularly toothsome, while a succulent *coq au vin* came with just one small steamed potato. We felt somewhat heartened after a hearty serving of prunes and pure ice cream with Armagnac, and pear and chocolate sorbets, but the kitchen is clearly cutting corners. Our bottle of 1999 Moulin à Vent tasted fine but, perhaps coincidentally, we both had headaches the next day.

Le Reminet
3 rue des Grands-Degrés, 5th (01.44.07.04.24). Mº Maubert-Mutualité or St-Michel. **Open** Mon, Thur-Sun noon-2pm, 7.30-11pm. Closed two weeks in Aug, two weeks in Feb. **Average** €32. **Prix fixe** €17 (dinner only, Mon, Thur). **Lunch menu** €13 (Mon, Thur, Fri). **Credit** MC, V.
This is just the snug little bistro you were hoping to find in the Latin Quarter. Friendly young chef Hugues Gournay does some excellent cooking in his minuscule kitchen, the service is prompt and smiling, and there's an atmosphere of well-being. It can be a bit noisy when the narrow dining room – with its two crystal chandeliers, red velvet curtains and bouquet of flowers on the bar – is full, so come early or late for a quiet *tête-à-tête*. Specials change regularly, and recently included a superb starter of house-smoked salmon in dill cream on a crispy potato *galette*. The lentil salad with poached egg, thin slices of foie gras and smoked duck breast is a house favourite, and a fine way to begin a meal here, as is the dense, richly flavoured duck terrine. Main courses of sautéed scallops with young leeks and pan-fried steak with Cuban-style black beans were delicious, although we'd have happily eaten more than four scallops. Tiny, caramelised Caribbean bananas, and a rich chocolate *délice* were enticing desserts, and the interesting wine list includes the house Bordeaux Château La Tulière.

La Rôtisserie de Beaujolais ★
19 quai de la Tournelle, 5th (01.43.54.17.47). Mº Jussieu. **Open** Tue-Sun noon-2.15pm, 7.30-10.30pm. **Average** €29. **Credit** MC, V.
Lashings of trad dishes such as onion soup, snails in garlic, *coq au vin*, Lyonnais sausage, *confit de canard* and grills are the order of the day in this jolly bistro overlooking the Seine. Although owner Claude Terrail also has the nearby, and much loftier, Tour d'Argent, this little sister is more country comfort than cut crystal; that means warm leeks in a creamy vinaigrette, oyster mushrooms (*pleurottes*) with garlic and parsley as starters, and super mashed spuds partnering plump chicken legs hot from the rôtisserie for mains (the duckling and pigeon with garlic spuds looked great, too). Lamb *navarin en croûte* has baby carrots, beans and snow peas and comes with a pastry *béret* and a gravy that just has to be mopped up with chunky wholemeal bread (basket at hand). Desserts run from *tarte Tartin* to titanic floating islands – the wit at the table opposite quipped it was more a continent than an island. Decor is dead cheery – yellow-checked cloths, walls adorned with autographs and photos of celebs and staff – and the service is a perfect match. The Beaujolais goes down a treat, too.

La Table de Michel
13 quai de la Tournelle, 5th (01.44.07.17.57). Mº Maubert-Mutualité. **Open** Mon 7-11pm, Tue-Sat noon-2.30pm, 7-11pm. Closed Aug. **Average** €38. **Prix fixe** €27. **Lunch menu** €19. **Credit** AmEx, MC, V.
The Michel in question was previously the owner and chef of a popular trad French restaurant on the Butte aux Cailles. Now in a prime position a stone's throw from the famous Tour d'Argent restaurant, the chef has returned to his Italian origins and is doing his personal take on Franco-Italian fusion cuisine. Delicate *crostini* as an appetiser were followed by a tomato and mozzarella salad, in which the peeled tomatoes formed an artistic dome over the buffalo cheese, bathed in a rich basil and balsamic vinegar dressing. A luscious *feuilleté d'escargots* was equally successful. Our mains included a perfectly cooked, pungent *risotto aux cèpes* and a winning *tagliatelle au foie gras*, served in a filo pastry basket, the rich sauce enhanced by slices of foie gras. We were tempted by brie stuffed with roquefort and walnuts, a clever variant on the Italian mascarpone/gorgonzola version, but went for *panna cotta*, a classic preparation of the creamy vanilla dessert with a punchy bitter cherry coulis. With a bottle of exceptional Chianti and a bill of around €107 for two we will be back for more.

6th Arrondissement

Au 35
35 rue Jacob, 6th (01.42.60.23.24). Mº St-Germain-des-Prés. **Open** daily noon-2pm, 7-11pm. **Average** €31. **Lunch menu** €15, €19. **Credit** MC, V. **Wheelchair access**.
You might expect St-Germain to be full of bistros such as this and yet they've become a surprisingly rare breed. An endearingly cramped interior (the kitchen is up a flight of perilous stairs), murals on the walls and Yves Saint Laurent's Love prints made as New Year wishes set the scene for the tweedy publishers and local ladies who pile in for the lunchtime *menu* (apparently dinner is more international). If many customers are clearly regulars, the friendly *patronne* was genuinely welcoming to us first-timers, coming to check we were content. The food echoes the mood: simple, French home cooking with plenty of personalised touches. We began with a nicely crisp green bean salad with parmesan, then main courses of chicken in a tarragon cream sauce with basmati rice and a flaky, snowy-white steamed cod fillet with an interesting, if slightly dry, purée of potatoes and black olives. Desserts ran to a *moelleux au chocolat*, pink grapefruit salad with honey or brie de meaux and a green salad. The house *pot* of red cabernet sauvignon cost a satisfactory €9.

Allard
41 rue St-André-des-Arts, 6th (01.43.26.48.23). Mº Odéon or RER St-Michel. **Open** Mon-Sat 12.30-2.30pm, 7.30-11pm. Closed three weeks in Aug. **Average** €49. **Prix fixe** €30.49. **Lunch menu** €22.87. **Credit** AmEx, DC, MC, V. **Wheelchair access**.
If St-Germain seems to be turning into a suburb of Milan with the proliferation of Italian restaurants (happily, many of them very good), it's reassuring to come across a sadly endangered but truly excellent example of that increasingly rare species, the traditional bistro, in what many consider to be one of the most quintessentially Parisian neighbourhoods. With its vanilla-coloured walls, coat rack in the narrow hall connecting the two small dining rooms – the front one with the big zinc bar has more atmosphere – this restaurant has a delicious pre-war feel, and this first impression is very much confirmed by the kitchen itself, on view as you step in off the street. It sends out glorious Gallic grub that's exactly what everyone dreams of finding in Paris, which is to say wholesome, hearty traditional dishes prepared using excellent produce. Winter is the perfect time of the year for this place – start with sliced Lyonnais sausage studded with pistachios and served with potato salad in delicious vinaigrette or maybe a sautée of wild mushrooms, and then chose between one of the three classics: roast shoulder of lamb, roast Bresse chicken with sautéed ceps or roast duck with olives. All three are superb, but be forewarned that portions are enormous – our duck for two would easily have feed three. Finish up with the *tarte fine de pommes* and go with one of their good if slightly pricey Bordeaux, which are perfect with this food.

Au Bon Saint-Pourçain
10bis rue Servandoni, 6th (01.43.54.93.63). Mº St-Sulpice or Mabillon. **Open** Mon-Sat noon-2.30pm, 7.30-10.30pm. Closed Aug. **Average** €30. **No credit cards**.
Au Bon Saint-Pourçain draws lots of Anglos; the night of our first visit, we sighted only one French-speaking couple among the dozen or so parties enjoying generous portions of solid bistro food. The €13 house red from the Allier/Loire Valley region, which shares the same name as the bistro, proved a fine match for the heady flavours of the first courses: young rabbit in aspic with a tomato coulis, velvety vegetable soup and warm leek-vinaigrette salad. Our mains included a tuna steak, slightly overdone for our taste (we'd not been asked how we'd wanted it) and covered with a satisfying fennel/tomato sauce; roast chicken in a dark mushroom and tarragon gravy; and the *brandade de morue*, a warm purée of cod, cream and mashed potatoes, a tad salty but filling.

Grill seekers at La Rôtisserie de Beaujolais

Desserts also keep to the traditional: chocolate cake, *tarte Tatin* and a superior crème brûlée whose perfect burnt sugar crust was like breaking through a thin layer of ice. A second visit confirmed the host's unruly temper: he complained to other tables about our tardiness saying we ruined his evening despite there being no second sitting. The food here is much more palateable than the service.

Les Bookinistes

53 quai des Grands-Augustins, 6th (01.43.25.45.94). M° St-Michel.
Open Mon-Fri noon-2.30pm, 7-11pm; Sat 7-11pm. **Average** €53. **Lunch menu** €23, €26. **Credit** AmEx, DC, MC, V.
There are good and not-so-good things about this Guy Savoy offshoot. The food is smart and seasonally-driven. The sunny-yellow walls studded with mirrors and multicoloured 'frames' make a fitting partner. It's the uneven service that jars; the wad of young waiters could do with some buffing up because they're a poor match for the food. Dishes might include avocado and prawns in red chicory leaves with a curried herring sauce; tuna tartare with soy bean and sunflower sprouts; grilled saddle of rabbit with carrots and pearl-like steamed radish; and roasted John Dory with capers, olives, yellow pepper and olive-oil-mashed potato. The desserts are crowd-pleasers – lime macaroon filled with regal mango sorbet and served with coconut cream, or a blood-red 'cappuccino' of sour cherries and strawberries. Nice, too, is the offer of wine by the glass (starting at €4.60), or better still a bottle of chilled red Sancerre at €34. The word has long since spread: on our visit the bulk of the diners were English-speakers.

Brasserie Fernand

13 rue Guisarde, 6th (01.43.54.61.47). M° Mabillon. **Open** Mon-Sat noon-2.30pm, 7pm midnight. Closed Aug. **Average** €30.50. **Credit** MC, V. **Wheelchair access.**
In the throng of restaurants around the Marché St-Germain, there are those that cater to tourists, to style fiends, to expats – and the wilfully shabby bistro that has pandered to a set of hip St-Germain intellectuals for decades. Brasserie Fernand (more a bistro despite the name) cleverly manages to be a bit of each: a friendly, relaxed place unlike some of its more cliquey neighbours. They were quite happy to let us chat well into the afternoon, as the *patron* behind the bar that divides the two dining rooms burst out with occasional peals of song. The blackboard reads like a round-up of bistro and regional standards, but it proved just the sort of food we wanted to eat: simple dishes prepared with care and some imagination. A Provençal-inspired 'tarte' consisted of warm goat's cheese and *pistou* over gently melted courgettes, onions and tomatoes atop filo pastry. Oxtail *parmentier* was an elegant sandwich of succulent, shredded stewed meat between two layers of purée and its generously truffled gravy; the *entrecôte* came with a pile of bone marrow and excellent purée. Desserts focus on fruit and ice cream themes: vanilla ice and black cherries in kirsch, fromage frais and berry coulis. A welcome find.

Aux Charpentiers

10 rue Mabillon, 6th (01.43.26.30.05). M° Mabillon or St-Germain-des-Prés.
Open daily noon-2.30pm, 7-11.30pm. **Average** €32. **Prix fixe** €24.70. **Lunch menu** €19. **Credit** AmEx, DC, MC, V.
No matter how hard it tries to maintain the atmosphere of an old-world bistro, Aux Charpentiers becomes less and less distinguishable from new-world uniformity typified by the tourist-populated, Gap logo'd shopping mall that has taken the place of the old St-Germain market. The food, however, remains consistently pleasing and the price can't be beat for the neighbourhood. On our last visit, an overwhelming urge for fish led us away from the traditional meaty fare offered in the *prix fixe* and towards an impressively grilled, fresh-tasting sea bass. A lamb's lettuce and beetroot salad was the perfect precursor to so much tastiness. The fish soup less so, having arrived too tepid to melt the heaping mounds of gruyère that accompanied it. Desserts, like the decor, are traditional, simple and solid. Staff who have not forgotten that genuine French waiters are supposed to be condescending and snide will, all the same, recommend a wine to properly suit your meal. Ours picked a €18.29 Chinon to complement our fish.

Brasserie Fernand wipes the slate with bistro classics

Chez Marcel

7 rue Stanislas, 6th (01.45.48.29.94). M° Notre-Dame-des-Champs. **Open** Mon-Fri noon-2pm, 7.30-10pm. Closed three weeks in Aug. **Average** €27. **Lunch menu** €13. **Credit** MC, V.
The most eye-catching thing about Chez Marcel's unobtrusively welcoming interior, as we ambled in for a late lunch, was a vivid apricot tart, bulging with fruit. The next impression was that all the customers looked happy. We soon found out why. Chez Marcel offers a lunch *menu* of well-executed classics. But it pays to venture into the *carte*. The beautifully presented cold artichoke was a whopping specimen bathed in a tangy vinaigrette, the leaves neatly arranged around the heart, topped with chopped tomato for colour. The duck breast *à l'orange* came thickly sliced, just pink enough inside, in a textbook rendition of the classic sauce. From the specials we chose the *civet de cerf*. Served with tagliatelle, a robust venison stew masterfully complemented by a sprinkle of mild red peppercorns. Then a short breather to finish off our €13 Beaujolais nouveau and ponder the desserts. The apricot tart, light on pastry and heavy on fruit, proved as good as it looked. We even persuaded the host, Mr. Daumail, to tell us about the bistro (which started as a bar in 1915) and his travels in Africa. We forgot to inspect the bookcase in the corner, but it's a welcome excuse to go back.

Le Sabot Saint-Germain

6 rue du Sabot, 6th (01.42.22.21.56). M° St-Germain-des-Prés. **Open** Tue-Sun, noon-2:30pm, 7-11pm. **Average** €25. **Credit** MC, V.
This 'clog' is the latest incarnation of the former En Ville, and though the chef has stayed on, the traditional menu is still finding its legs. The meal started off strongly with a crisp spinach salad, served with warm duck *gésiers* (gizzards), and excellent snails in a garlic-strewn *cassolette*. While the main course duck was delicious in its traditional honey coating, the tuna steak was frankly disappointing, overcooked and depressing in a mysterious brown sauce. We were willing to forgive this rather typical French fish error because of the charming service, which made us feel like personal guests of the hostess. There's good attention to detail here: fresh flowers and wonderfully comfortable new banquettes make these wood-beamed rooms a calm retreat from inclement weather. Large groups can be tucked into cosy corners without interrupting the peaceful atmosphere. Our mood was only briefly shaken when the drinks fridge in the back leapt into gear, sounding like a holdover from the Soviet war machine. Fortunately it soon subsided and we relaxed, polishing off our excellent La Bastide wine (a good deal at €13.45 a bottle). The best dessert was a nicely tart lemon crème brûlée.

L'Epi Dupin

11 rue Dupin, 6th (01.42.22.64.56). M° Sèvres-Babylone. **Open** Mon 7-10.30pm; Tue-Fri noon-2.30pm, 7-10.30pm. Closed Aug. **Prix fixe** €28.20. **Lunch menu** €17.53. **Credit** AmEx, MC, V.
Though we've long admired the cooking of chef François Pasteau, a recent visit to this pocket-sized bistro proved disappointing. This place has now become so well-known that the clear imperative of both the kitchen and the off-handed and rather patronising staff is to turn tables. Forced to accept a 7pm reservation, we were squeezed into a stuffy corner table. We began with tempura of minuscule langoustines on a tasty pineapple-and-fennel chutney and oxtail with preserved tomatoes and unusual mustard ice cream. If both dishes were interesting, they tasted overly sweet and came in small portions. Main courses of cod on a bed of too-sweet shredded vegetables and over-salted salmon wrapped in soggy filo pastry and served with spinach purée arrived lukewarm. A tiny slice of brie went well with the rest of our white Menetou-Salon, the least expensive bottle at €18.29 from an over-priced, uninspiring list. We hadn't finished our desserts – excellent poached peaches in caramel sauce and drab rhubarb compote with apple purée – before our coffee arrived, and the bill seconds later. This place needs a serious rethink. The cooking and service should be more thoughtful, and a few tables should be removed.

Josephine 'Chez Dumonet' ★

117 rue du Cherche-Midi, 6th (01.45.48.52.40). M° Duroc. **Open** Mon-Fri 12.30-2.30pm, 7.30-11pm. **Closed** one week in Feb, throughout Aug. **Average** €61. **Credit** AmEx, MC,V.
This is the kind of bistro people dream of stumbling across on an icy day. Behind crisp white curtains lies an interior with cracked-tile floor, frosted tulip lamps, huge mirrors and acres of warm wood ministered by a handful of courteous waiters. This trad terrain with atmosphere and without attitude doesn't come cheaply, unfortunately, but the mix of English-speaking tourists and incessantly chatty locals don't mind because Jean-Christian Dumonet's cooking seems almost worth it. Black truffles from Quercy starred in his line-up of winter dishes and the creamy omelette generously studded with this earthy tuber is a great, if extravagant, starter. Less expensive are a chicory and roquefort salad or slices of warm artichoke hearts in lime butter. For mains try plump scallops *à la provençale*, an ample duck *confit* or crowd-pleasing *boeuf bourguignon*. The gamey hare or pigeon *millefeuille* are, in season, hard to resist. For a grand finale try the puffed-up Grand Marnier soufflé.

Le Mâchon d'Henri

8 rue Guisarde, 6th (01.43.29.08.70). M° Mabillon. **Open** daily noon-2.15pm, 7-11.15pm. **Average** €24. **No credit cards.**
A not unpleasant joint, albeit cramped, with red tiles, tiny tables and a haunting, oversized painting depicting previous diners sums up Le Mâchon d'Henri's straightforward approach. The food won't arouse rancour but doesn't wow you, either. A courgette terrine in tomato coulis revealed a pleasing nutmeg undertone, while roasted red pepper doused in quality olive oil was adequate; neither appetiser suggested the chef had added his own flair. A nicely braised *filet mignon* of pork was hampered by a sauce of nothing more than Dijon mustard and cream. Likewise, a freshwater pike *quenelle*, while possessing a certain intrigue, lacked complexity and was unfortunately served with monochrome, plain rice, accentuating the plate's overall blandness. Chocolate mousse and a puffy cherry *clafoutis* rounded out an under-achieving meal that demonstrated competence but little imagination. On the plus side, the elbow-to-elbow space almost guarantees you'll meet other diners; our chipper neighbours, two doctors from Arizona, grilled us for insiders' tips on the city. Rue Guisarde is a popular pedestrian street, which might explain why Mâchon d'Henri attracts a steady crowd, despite the middling fare.

Le Nemrod

51 rue du Cherche-Midi, 6th (01.45.48.17.05). M° Sèvres-Babylone. **Open** Mon-Sat 6am-11pm. Closed two weeks in Aug. **Average** €26. **Prix fixe** €20 (dinner only). **Credit** MC, V.
Not too many hybrids exist in Paris where you can choose between gulping down a two-second coffee, lingering over a full-on three course French meal, or snacking on an excellent plate of *charcuterie* and carefully chosen glass of wine at virtually any hour of the day. At Le Nemrod, you can do exactly that amidst a plentiful crowd of locals, tourists, and fashionistas refuelling after a spree at nearby Bon Marché. If such a prospect fills you with an urge to celebrate (which it just might if you' ve ever roamed the streets at 3:30pm, desperate for anything other than a crêpe or sandwich for a late lunch) why not start off with a plate of quivering Quiberon oysters? Follow with a special of the day, such as the weighty *cuisse de lapin confit* or a hearty *saucisse* served with a healthy dose of *aligot* (an Auvergnat classic of garlicky mashed potatoes and cheese). Only slightly less robust are the numerous *salades composées*. The *périgourdine*, or duck frenzy as we renamed it, was sublime. No matter what you choose, wash it down nicely with a glass or bottle from the well-selected wine list.

Le Parc Aux Cerfs

50 rue Vavin, 6th (01.43.54.87.83). M° Vavin or Notre-Dame-des-Champs.
Open Mon-Thur, Sun noon-2.30pm, 7.45-10.30pm; Fri, Sat noon-2.30pm, 7.45-11.15pm. Closed Aug. **Prix fixe** €24, €29 (dinner only). **Lunch menu** €19.50, €25. **Credit** MC, V. **Wheelchair access.**
As with the nearby Luxembourg gardens, the famous former romping grounds of Marie de Médicis, much of what happens at Le Parc Aux Cerfs is just for show. Our meal began well with a round of *mûrier*, a one-up on the traditional *kir*, in which robust red wine melds with rich blackberry liqueur to extraordinary results. The olives on our table were of the tinned and rather bland variety, but no matter – we had more substantial things in mind. For starters, we couldn't get enough of the wild mushroom-studded oxtail terrine, much more free form and stew-like than expected. Sautéed scallops were also tasty, though drenched in cream sauce. The meal's big disappointment was the *confit de canard*. Dry and salty instead of moist and savoury, the poor duck had seen happier days. And yet the veal kidneys were just right, their earthy taste tweaked by a mouth-tickling sauce made from sherry vinegar. Desserts were competent but challenged no expectations. We could have overlooked any flaws had it been warm enough to sit outside in the lovely little garden or, failing that, at one of the few tables perched on the whimsical iron mezzanine.

Wadja

10 rue de la Grande-Chaumière, 6th (01.46.33.02.02). M° Vavin. **Open** Mon-Fri noon-2.30pm, 7.30-11pm. Closed Aug. **Average** €28. **Prix fixe** €13.57. **Credit** MC, V.
Wadja has been around in some form or other ever since it was a cheap café for Montparnasse artists from the studios next door. Today it houses a pretty interior with changing art exhibitions. Service is friendly and the food a pleasant reminder of how exciting and varied bistro cooking can be when it draws on French regions and seasonal produce. Once we came here to discover that Wadja had gone Corsican for the month, but more regular *à la carte* dishes include calf's liver, red mullet, *gigot de sept heures* (lamb stewed for seven hours), *cassolette*

l'Écurie

Miny welcomes you to her charming Parisian restaurant in the heart of the Quartier Latin.

58 rue de la Montagne, Sainte-Geneviève, 5th. (on the corner of rue Laplace) • Tel: 01.46.33.68.49 • M° Maubert-Mutualité
Open Mon, Wed-Sat noon-3pm, 7pm-midnight.
Tue, Sun 7pm-midnight

Le Trumilou
RESTAURANT

Traditional French Cuisine

Just a few steps away from the Isle Saint Louis, with a lovely view of Notre Dame and the Panthéon

3 course menu: €16.50 - 2 course menu: €13.50

84 quai de l'Hôtel de Ville, 4th. M° Hôtel de Ville. Tel: 01.42.77.63.98

Open daily noon-3pm & 7-11pm (10.30pm on Sunday)

Le Christine
Restaurant

Come and try our traditional cuisine in a setting typical of St Germain des Prés.
Open Mon to Sat 6pm-midnight

Mr and Mrs Bazan
1 rue Christine, 6th. M° Odéon
Tel: 01.40.51.71.64 Fax: 01.42.18.04.39
lechristine@avantscene.com

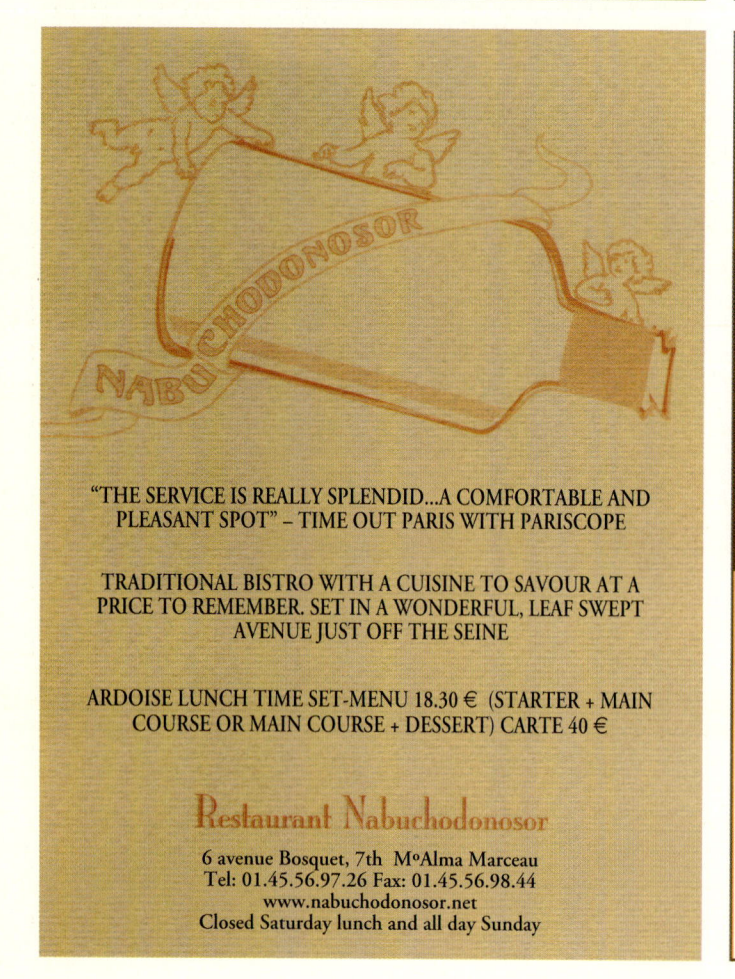

Restaurant Nabuchodonosor

"THE SERVICE IS REALLY SPLENDID...A COMFORTABLE AND PLEASANT SPOT" – TIME OUT PARIS WITH PARISCOPE

TRADITIONAL BISTRO WITH A CUISINE TO SAVOUR AT A PRICE TO REMEMBER. SET IN A WONDERFUL, LEAF SWEPT AVENUE JUST OFF THE SEINE

ARDOISE LUNCH TIME SET-MENU 18.30 € (STARTER + MAIN COURSE OR MAIN COURSE + DESSERT) CARTE 40 €

Restaurant Nabuchodonosor
6 avenue Bosquet, 7th M°Alma Marceau
Tel: 01.45.56.97.26 Fax: 01.45.56.98.44
www.nabuchodonosor.net
Closed Saturday lunch and all day Sunday

Eric Corailler's Bistrots

Le Bistrot de Paris

Authentic regional French cuisine
Wines from the vineyard
Open daily - English Spoken

Le Bistrot de Paris
33 rue de Lille, 7th. M° Rue du Bac
Tel: 01.42.61.16.83
www.le-bistrot-de-paris.fr

Le Bistrot des Vignes
1 rue Jean Bologne, 16th.
M° La Muette or Passy
Tel: 01.45.27.76.64

of snails, and an intriguing fig and anchovy starter. The €13.57 daily *menu* is truly remarkable: three courses of whatever chef Didier Panisset has decided on for that day. On our last visit, starters of pumpkin soup (a little thin), delicious marinated peppers and fresh sardine *tarte fine* were followed by hake in filo pastry with carrot mousse, and caramelised sautéed pork with courgette purée before a dessert of two *choux* puffs filled with vanilla and chocolate cream. The wine list is clearly a labour of love, combining wines from all over France, maps and quite useful descriptions of producers – our bottle was a sophisticated 1996 Régnie from the Beaujolais region.

7th Arrondissement

L'Affriolé ★
17 rue Malar, 7th (01.44.18.31.33). M° *La Tour-Maubourg or Invalides.* **Open** Tue-Sat noon-2.30pm, 7.30-11pm. **Average** €29. **Prix fixe** €29. **Lunch menu** €19. **Credit** AmEx, MC, V.
Chef Thierry Verola's bistro is a gem. The decor of terra-washed walls is odd, but it doesn't matter a whit since you'll be happy here from the moment you've spread your napkin. Verola's lovely wife and a well-drilled team of young staff make you feel instantly at home, going about their tasks with an admirable seriousness that doesn't preclude a natural warmth. Radishes and a pot of *rillettes* come as soon as you're seated, and the bread is excellent. The market *menu* changes regularly, but is consistently appealing. On a warm night, we loved the iced gazpacho with basil and a deliciously earthy cream of mushroom soup garnished with a *piquillo* pepper stuffed with diced vegetables. Main courses of braised beef cheeks with an imaginative *gratin* of smoked potatoes, and a *croustade de morue* – cod, cumin, raisins and sweet potatoes inside a fine, crunchy pastry leaf – were excellent. We finished up with a pear 'hamburger' – two crêpes enclosing poached pear, apple, raisins, pistachios and sesame seeds – which was good but a little heavy, and a cheese course of *caillé de chèvre* with shallots, leeks and Espelette pepper. Warm miniature *madeleines* were served with coffee and we dawdled over our Morgon, a nice pick from a good list.

Altitude 95
First level, Eiffel Tower, Champ de Mars, 7th (01.45.55.00.21). M° *Bir-Hakeim/RER Champ de Mars.* **Open** daily noon-3pm, 7-11pm. **Average** €60. **Prix fixe** €45. (dinner only). **Lunch menu** €17.50, €25.70. **Child's menu** €8.50. Lift ticket to first level €3.70. **Credit** AmEx, DC, MC, V. **Wheelchair access.**
Your obligatory reservation lets you cut to the front of the lift queue, so be prepared for the nasty glare of tourists who've been patiently waiting a half an hour to ride up the side of the Eiffel Tower. Altitude 95 prolongs the Jules Verne-like theme, with a *20,000 Leagues Under the Sea* steel and chrome interior which imparts a subterranean gloom, even on a sunny day. But no, you're aloft over the city, in a different sort of Disneyesque fantasy, and the food half lives up to the setting. There's the '*table du chef*' three-course lunch *formule* at €25.70, and two courses cost €17.50, but you're not given a lot of choice. A cured ham and artichoke salad was far from inspirational, but the smooth cauliflower soup, sprinkled with poppy seeds, took off the windswept chill. The tender chicken leg on top of ordinary noodles covered with a muddy sauce only partly satisfied while the salmon with potato purée in a tomato butter shined: fresh and vivid on the eye and tongue. We'd ordered the *gâteau au chocolat* but more of a hazelnut mousse pastry arrived, still delicious despite the false advertising. Altitude 95 is pleasant and family-friendly (kids get colouring books and puzzles), with multilingual menus and no attitude.

Au Bon Accueil
14 rue Monttessuy 7th (01.47.05.46.11). M° *Alma-Marceau.* **Open** Mon-Fri noon-2.15pm, 7-10.30pm. **Average** €40. **Prix fixe** €29. **Lunch menu** €25. **Credit** MC, V.
Located in one of the discreetly wealthy streets beneath the Eiffel Tower, this is a good place to lunch after inspecting the *chef d'oeuvre* of the great French engineer. It's a bit suity, but bearably so, and the staff try to make you believe you're welcome even if you're not wearing a tie. Even if you arrive with a baby. The food is refined French peasant: our excellent-value lunch *menu* offered, for example, a very good fricassée of *girolle* mushrooms and *petit gris* snails. This is the sort of thing that's usually served in chunky crockery with a lot of garlic. Here, a watercress sauce made it much lighter and fresher. Similarly, the braised beef with carrots was approached with subtlety and care. The meat was perfectly tender and even if the sauce tasted too salty and we could barely distinguish the green celery leaves that were supposed to accompany the carrots, we were left in no doubt: the chef has skill. Our decanter of Côtes de Thongues – an outstanding *vin de pays* from the Languedoc – went heartily well with the beef. And our puddings (walnut and quince crumble, roast figs, warm *moelleux* oozing with chocolate sauce) were pleasing to the eye and sumptuous in the mouth.

La Cigale
11bis rue Chomel, 7th (01.45.48.87.87). M° *Sèvres-Babylone.* **Open** Mon-Fri noon-2.30pm, 7.30-11.30pm; Sat 7.30-11.30pm. **Average** €25. **Credit** V. **Wheelchair access.**
We were welcomed into the Cigale by the French *patronne*, who exuded the sort of fashion-conscious style you would expect from this chic, pastel-shaded bistro just behind the Bon Marché store. The menu is dominated by seasonally changing soufflés, both sweet and savoury, which seem a big hit with ladies who lunch and the business regulars. The latter benefit from a superior welcome to that dished out to blow-in foreigners. Any rancour is quickly forgotten as we tucked into a moist chicken liver terrine accompanied by an almost fluorescent red *compote d'onions*. For our main courses we turned our back on good-looking fish and simple grills and plunged into the world of the soufflé. A *maroilles* and cumin version was a clear winner, the palate-liftingly strong cheese making a piquant contribution to a potentially bland dish. The curried *gambas* version was equally successful, served with a side salad which included a couple of seared prawns to concentrate the flavour. With a glass or two of our delicately coloured Sancerre rosé remaining, we couldn't resist sharing a chocolate soufflé with an intense chocolate sauce.

Le Clos des Gourmets
16 av Rapp, 7th (01.45.51.75.61). M° *Alma-Marceau.* **Open** Tue-Sat 12.15-2.30pm, 7.15-10.30pm. Closed Aug. **Prix fixe** €30 (three courses, dinner only). **Lunch menu** €22 (two courses), €27 (three courses). **Credit** MC, V.
The first sign that 'gourmets' are indeed the clientele that Arnaud and Christel Pitrois aspire to comes when callers are informed, in no uncertain terms, that dinner reservations can be made for 7.30pm or 9.30pm only. The earlier sitting is clearly aimed at foreigners: Parisians tummies rarely stir before 9pm. The meal kicked off brilliantly with an appetiser of delectable *tapenade*; the black olive paste had a delicate, nutty fragrance. From a choice of five starters, a market garden salad of mixed leaves was gossamer-light in taste as they were in weight; the walnut oil and fresh fennel gave it saving zip. As for the aubergine 'caviar', it was certainly reminiscent of the precious eggs if you took in the elfin serving, while the accompanying squid tasted sweet and tender. The main courses, though, were proof that Arnaud Pitrois has a master's touch. The fried sea bass fillet with a green asparagus fricassée came with roast potatoes that burst with flavour under their deliciously chewy skins. Succulent farm chicken thighs were roasted in basil sauce and served with an airy polenta. Fourme d'ambert, a cross between stilton and gorgonzola, was a satisying end to the meal, along with an exquisite chocolate mousse with caramelised banana. The Domaine de la Bernarde 1997 (€29.70), a gold-medal-winning red from the Var, was worth every centime. Conclusion? Take away the stop-watch so everyone can relax, add a touch of generosity (but stop overdosing on salt), and you have a real gem.

La Fontaine de Mars
129 rue St-Dominique, 7th (01.47.05.46.44). M° *Ecole-Militaire or RER Pont de l'Alma.* **Open** daily noon-3pm, 7.30-11pm. **Average** €38. **Lunch menu** €14 (Mon-Fri). **Credit** AmEx, MC, V.
This bistro has offered traditional *cuisine bourgeoise* by the Boudon family for the past ten years. Red-and-white checked cloths adorn the tables on the two floors. Adding to the atmosphere are friendly waiters, the clanging bell from the kitchen, and decor ranging from copper cake moulds to a gramophone, from a sewing machine to old-fashioned pepper grinders. A little on the pricey side, starters are mostly meat-based, such as a beef cheek and foie gras terrine with a lemony celeriac sauce, but we also tried a warm pâté of ceps and herbs, served with alfalfa and lamb's lettuce. Main dishes include duck specialities such as *magret*, served in a sweet sauce with braised chicory, or *cassoulet* and *confit*. We also enjoyed grilled cod served on white beans. From a tempting dessert list, we sampled *tourtière landaise*, layers of paper-thin pastry with warm apples and prunes, served with prune and Armagnac ice cream. This is a good place for simple, hearty standards, and for a bottle of the fruity Cahors wine. Book for an early dinner so you don't miss out on the specials.

Nabuchodonosor ★
6 av Bosquet, 7th (01.45.56.97.26). M° *Alma Marceau.* **Open** Mon-Fri noon-2.45pm, 7.30-11pm. Closed three weeks in Aug. **Average** €35. **Lunch menu** €18.30. **Credit** AmEx, MC, V. **Wheelchair access**.
The cigar-wielding Eric Rousseau makes his customers feel instantly at home in this elegant restaurant. Then again, anyone who names their place after a 15-litre bottle of Champagne has to be a natural *bon vivant*. Chef Thierry Garnier's *carte* is an inventive take on traditional French cuisine, with meticulously prepared dishes such as a rich, creamy chestnut soup with earthy-tasting snails, and a delicious mound of fresh goat's cheese served with peppers marinated in olive oil. Spotting *daube provençale* among the main courses, we were impressed: part of France's culinary heritage, this reich meat stew is an endangered dish, even in Provence. Preferring a lighter meal on the evening that we visited, we went sea-side. Roast langoustine tails were dawn-fresh, served with a delicate pepper sauce and perfectly cooked spinach. Roasted sea bream was less successful, being slightly overcooked and served on a bundle of rigid vegetable sticks. From a choice of five desserts, we chose a refreshing lemon-balm-flavoured fruit soup and masterful bittersweet candied orange in a crispy batter with vanilla ice cream. As for the fascinating wine board, if our celestial Quincy Lavault Rouze 2000 was anything to go by, Rousseau – who jokingly offered to finish our wine – must be left with decidedly empty bottles when the lights go out.

In a casa all of its own: Casa Olympe

L'Oeillade

10 rue St-Simon, 7th (01.42.22.01.60)
M° Rue du Bac. **Open** Mon-Sat 12.30-2pm, 7.30-10pm. **Average** €27. **Credit** MC, V.
The most noticeable result of a change of ownership at this long-running bistro in a stylish little street is that the good-value *prix fixe* menu has vanished; what was once a rare bargain in a pricey neighborhood has become much more expensive. This could explain the fact that the sparse clientele on a winter night consisted almost entirely of Americans from surrounding hotels, most of whom didn't speak French well enough to be aware of the patronising, impatient and almost nasty service they were receiving. The bored hostess who took our orders – we were a table of six, all French-speaking – rolled her eyes when asked to explain various dishes, shrugged when asked if it would be possible to have the wing as part of an order of guinea hen, and finally fled when we asked to divide the bill between two credit cards. The sour atmosphere notwithstanding, the food is still good French home cooking, if lacking the imagination and freshness it once had. Start with roasted goat's cheese on salad, or rabbit terrine, but avoid the mushy marinated peppers, and then try the guinea hen with sauerkraut – perfectly cooked and generously served – the impeccable *sole meunière* served with fresh spinach, or a steak. Desserts have a nursery slant, running to marinated prunes and *île flottante*, and the St-Nicolas-de-Bourgeuil is pleasant at €12.96.

Le Petit Troquet

28 rue de l'Exposition, 7th (01.47.05.80.39)
M° Ecole-Militaire. **Open** Mon, Sat 7-10.30pm; Tue-Fri noon-2pm, 7-10.30pm. Closed three weeks in Aug. **Average** €27. **Prix fixe** €26.50. **Credit** MC, V.
Owners Dominique and Patrick Vessière – hostess and cook respectively – have been serving their elegant clientele for eleven years. Patrick's cooking stands out for its use of fresh herbs, and the unmistakeable taste of quality olive oil. Every plate comes attractively decorated with a patterned splash of sauce. In the *croustillant de moules*, mussels are gently sautéed in a concentrated vegetable and meat stock, chives and parsley are added, and the whole is wrapped in *brik* pastry. Another delicious starter was *céleri rémoulade* with Granny Smith apple and marinated salmon: tasty and creamy, although the bite-sized salmon bits could seem frugal. We continued with a nicely cooked sea bream fillet in lemon and thyme sauce, served with a juicy, skinned tomato succulently stuffed with bacon and shredded cabbage. An excellent way to end a meal here is with the French classic, crème brûlée. We also tried the *gratin de clémentines*, made with eggy *sabayon* sauce; if only the clementines had been in season, it would have been divine. The wine list is limited and pricey, but includes a selection of vintages worth trying with this sophisticated fare.

La Petite Chaise

36 rue de Grenelle, 7th (01.42.22.13.35).
M° Rue du Bac or Sèvres-Babylone. **Open** daily noon-2pm, 7-11pm. **Prix fixe** €24, €29 (two courses). **Credit** AmEx, MC, V.
The staff-diner ratio at this ancient restaurant (dating from 1680) is reminiscent of haute-cuisine establishments; the decor is sedate with an incongruous Mediterranean touch (yellow fabric walls, sea-green ceiling mouldings); and, after a two-and-a-half month revamp, there's no hint of its celebrated age. With a €29 *prix fixe* menu, pricey wines, and a tasteless Touraine for penny-pinchers (€15 a bottle) we got the impression that La Petite Chaise was having an identity crisis. The food, though, was a pleasant surprise. Starters were carefully prepared and full of flavour: finely sliced salmon marinated in dill and mustard and an unctuous house foie gras were both spot on. Main courses incl-uded a saucy bowl of tender beef cheeks and a pleasingly pink *magret de canard* with a whole roasted pear. Desserts were less exciting; the passion fruit mousse cake was copious but undistinguished and the camembert chilled and under-ripe (its accompanying *salade aux pommes* was strangely devoid of apples). A good place for unadventurous visitors who will enjoy the formality and absence of noise.

Le Récamier

4 rue Recamier, 7th (01.45.48.86.58).
M° Sèvres-Babylone. **Open** Tue-Sat noon-2.30pm, 7.30-10.30pm. **Average** €55. **Credit** AmEx, DC, MC, V.
Tucked away on a leafy impasse, this long-running restaurant with a famous wine cellar and a tradition of Burgundian specialties has always been a place that puts on airs, possibly a reflection of its chic Left Bank clientele of editors and writers, local gentry and rich but worldly Americans. Though it's expensive, we've never minded much, since it has one of the loveliest terraces in town and the food has always been reliably good. A recent meal, however, put an end to our indulgent attitude. With a wet summer night keeping us off the terrace, we had a chance to notice that the grandmotherly brown decor is getting rather shop-worn. We saw a mouse in the loo, and the waiter cheerfully admitted that one of the house specialties – *jambon persillé*, shredded ham in parslied aspic – is not made on the premises. No nibbles were served with a pre-dinner drink, and first courses of *oeufs en meurette* (here, one egg in wine and bacon sauce) and eggy pike-perch mousse were disappointing. Two-and-a-half langoustines in basil were nicely cooked, but shockingly overpriced at €28.97. Happily the good if over-salted *boeuf bourguignon* was served generously enough to be shared. Desserts, including apple tart, sorbet and Charlotte Malakoff, didn't tempt so we finished up our pleasant Volnay instead, with the waiter hastily slapping the bill down on the table without being asked.

Thoumieux

79 rue St-Dominique, 7th (01.47.05.49.75).
M° Invalides or La Tour Maubourg. **Open** Mon-Sat noon-3.30pm, 6.45pm-midnight; Sun noon-midnight. **Average** €34. **Prix fixe** €28. **Lunch menu** €14 (Mon-Fri). **Credit** AmEx, MC, V.
If you're upset by the way things have been going in the world over the past 70 years or so, a couple of hours with an earthenware pot of Thoumieux's *cassoulet* should put you right for an evening at least. This big and popular bistro opened in 1923 and has stayed in the same family ever since. The red velvet banquettes, starched white tablecloths and sturdy cutlery are a testament to tradition, as are the polite, black-jacketed waiters. Likewise, there's not much on the menu you won't have eaten before but plenty you'll want to eat again. Choosing *à la carte*, we ordered some excellent goat's cheese and, thinking we had better eat it before they ban it, the oxtail terrine. In our experience, oxtail terrine is even better when it's served warm, but we enjoyed it nevertheless. Ask the waiter nicely and you might get away with sharing the enormous *cassoulet*. Otherwise there are strong bistro standards such as grilled sole or *côte de boeuf*. Feel like half a grapefruit to finish things off? Hey, you've come to the right place. It's right there on the menu for €2.29. Actually prices here have climbed €3 or so per person since our last visit but this remains the perfect address for a late and long Sunday lunch or winter supper.

Mad about cows

If ever vegetable cooking were to make inroads in France, 2001 should have been the year. A television programme on the mad cow scandal saw beef sales temporarily drop by 50 per cent – and, just as significantly, led the French to view other beloved foods with suspicion. Fish, at first considered a safe alternative to beef, began to flail when the national press revealed that farmed fish were being pumped up with polyphosphates and stuffed with additives to extend their shelf life. Even wild fish were found to contain worrying levels of pesticides and mercury. Lamb has been plagued by foot-and-mouth disease – illegal imports from Britain have been discovered in France – while chicken is recovering from a dioxin scandal and *charcuterie* is said to contain unsafe levels of carcinogenic nitrates.

Wander into **La Maison de l'Aubrac** (*see p45*, **Brasseries**) any night, though, and it's clear that the French are still mad about meat: they are simply turning into more knowledgeable and careful consumers. It's impossible to prevent every fraud – an inquiry recently found that the Limousin 'Blason Prestige' label had been illegally applied to more than 1,000 cattle at the end of the 1990s – but, increasingly, butchers and restaurateurs have been giving clear indications as to the origins of their meat. At the Maison de l'Aubrac the beef comes from the owner's farm in the Auvergne, while the fashion haunt **Anahi** (*see p81*, **Americas**) is famed for its Argentinean steaks. Star chef Alain Ducasse dropped beef from his menu just before opening **59 Poincaré** (*see p58*, **Contemporary**) at the height of the mad cow scare in France, but

Macéo takes its vegetables seriously

recently re-launched the restaurant as a New York-style steakhouse, with sides of beef fearlessly on display in the entrance. Some bistros, such as the popular St-Germain bistro **Chez Fernand**, continue to serve marrow bone to a carnivorous crowd.

A few chefs have reacted by giving vegetables pride of plate, most famously Alain Passard of the luxury Left Bank restaurant **L'Arpège** (*see p40*, **Haute Cuisine**). Asked why he dropped most meat dishes from his menu early in 2001, Passard replies, 'my hands were getting bored'. The fact remains that the decision – timed as it was during the mad cow panic – brought him a welcome publicity boost, especially among Americans and Japanese. Ducasse points out that his first vegetable menu dates from 1987, when he opened the Louis XV in Monaco. If €40 seems like a lot to pay for a plate of Passard spinach, some fashionable new restaurants such as **Korova** (*see p51*, **Trendy**) and **Maison Blanche** (*see p58*, **Contemporary**) are treating vegetables with respect. **Macéo** (*see p58*, **Contemporary**) and the bistro **Le Safran** also offer vegetarian menus that go well beyond the steamed-vegetables-with-olive-oil that pass for a vegetarian plate in many restaurants that bother to offer one.

Should you wish to indulge a passion for meat, the wisest approach is to seek out butchers and restaurateurs you trust – don't be afraid to ask questions. New regulations ensuring '*traçabilité*' mean that restaurant owners should always be able to identify the sources of their meats. And remember that 8,000 people die in road accidents each year in France, while only one meal in 100 million leads to any kind of illness.
Rosa Jackson

8th Arrondissement

Le Bistrot d'Anglas

29 rue Boissy d'Anglas, 8th (01.42.65.63.73). M° Madeleine.
Open Mon-Fri 9am-10pm, Sat noon-3pm. Closed Aug. **Average** €23. **Lunch menu** €15.70. **Credit** MC, V
In an area known for its designer boutiques and fashionable eateries, it would be easy to overlook this unprepossessing bistro. However, the place is popular with local shop workers grateful for the good-value *plat du jour*, and ladies-who-lunch, stopping to rest their swollen feet. So much so, in fact, that at 2pm on a Saturday, a single waitress was having great difficulty coping with the lunch rush. The perfunctory-bordering-on-rude 'welcome' we received sorely tempted us to walk out (this is exactly what another couple did), but our neighbour was so forthright in his praise for the food that we stuck it out. He had a point. The day's special, *tagliatelles aux écrevisses*, was well executed; *al dente* pasta with plenty of tender, juicy crayfish. Likewise, the *assiette du pêcheur*, chunks of salmon and various white fish with a *timbale* of risotto rice, laden with saffron and studded with pine nuts and sultanas. But not even a fine glass of Sancerre and a perfectly ripe, creamy st-marcellin cheese could compensate for the brusque and unsmiling service. As for dessert, despite accepting our booking for 2pm, by 2.45pm the kitchen staff had all left. Shame, because we fancied the sound of the roast apple with honey. The equally charmless host did, however, manage to rustle up a coffee.

La Maline

40 rue de Ponthieu, 8th (01.45.63.14.14).
M° Franklin D. Roosevelt. **Open** Mon-Fri noon-2pm, 7.45-10pm. **Average** €25. **Prix fixe** €29. **Lunch menu** €15. **Credit** MC, V.
This tiny, duplex bistro occupying a 1920s building is named after a poem by Rimbaud, and there's a nice framed photo of the restive poet, along with a very amusing series of 19th-century cartoons showing the type of person most likely to order a given dish. With terracotta-tiled floors and comfortable chairs, this is a pleasant and relaxed place, and the food maintains this friendly vibe. Duck foie gras on a bed of salad was delicious with the whole grain bread baked on the premises, and warm asparagus in a chive-spiked cream sauce with

Bistros

Try the southern comfort at Chez Catherine

country ham was appealing as well. Among the main courses, a lamb fillet on a bed of *lingot* beans in tomato sauce was satisfying, although the meat was rather lacking in flavour, and scallops on a bed of lentils with oven-dried tomatoes were quite good. The quince *tarte Tatin* was a pleasant dessert, while a thick slice of roquefort came on toast with a small salad. The brief wine list offers a variety of gently priced choices, from a Côtes du Rhône for €15 to a Menetou Salon for €22. With friendly service, easy prices and good music this is a good address to bear in mind in this part of town.

Le Rocher Gourmand
89 rue du Rocher, 8th (01.40.08.00.36). *M°* Villiers. **Open** Mon-Fri noon-2pm, 8-10pm; Sat 8-10pm. Closed Aug. **Average** €38. **Prix fixe** €30-€45. **Lunch menu** €25. **Credit** MC, V. **Wheelchair access**.
Chef Sébastien Gilles' compact but comfortable restaurant has become popular for his individual take on contemporary French cooking, which pulls off an appealing equilibrium between simplicity and sophistication. Gilles trained with Gérard Faucher of Restaurant Faucher, but brought none of the stuffiness of his teacher's pricey restaurant with him when he decided to go out on his own – this place is unpretentious and friendly. Typical of his style are starters such as a terrine of skate and courgettes and a *marbré* of foie gras with leeks and red-pepper *confit* and mains such as roast cod with poppy seeds on a bed of lemony spinach. Dishes are presented with real artistry, on carefully chosen plates. Try the 'soup' of fresh oranges with cumin and carrot sorbet for dessert if it's available. Service was polished, supervised from the corner by the very well-behaved baby of the house. A good bet if you want a memorable modern meal in Paris without spending a fortune.

Savy ★
23 rue Bayard, 8th (01.47.23.46.98). *M°* Franklin D. Roosevelt. **Open** Mon-Fri noon-2.30pm, 7.30-11pm (bar 7.30am-12.30pm, 3-8pm). Closed Aug. **Average** €30. **Prix fixe** €26.22. **Lunch menu** €18.29, €22.11. **Credit** AmEx, MC, V.
It's reassuring to find such a dead trad restaurant around exclusive avenue Montaigne, where almost everything now seems to have a theme or *dernier cri* designer decor. But don't be fooled, Savy has long been a favourite with the media barons from RTL radio just across the street, and the comfortable mirrored booths that run the length of the narrow dining room are perfect for discussing business strategy. Founded in 1901 as Bar Elie, when Madame Elie prepared one dish (roast pigeon), one day a week (Saturday), Savy gained its pretty, understated art deco identity in 1923. It changed hands in 2000, but owner Lionel Dégoulange has kept the Aveyronnais specialities and Cantal *charcuterie* and added superb Aubrac de Laguiole beef. If your image of the food of central France is of weighty volumes of sausage meat and cabbage, then be sure to start with the *farçou aveyronnais*, surprisingly light fried herb and chard patties, while other favourites include Puy lentils and *salade gourmande*. For main courses, go the meat route, such as the thick tender rump-steak *pavé* with Béarnaise sauce and crispy *frites*, although fish is brought in daily from the Breton port of Guilvinec. Desserts are mainly age-old favourites suited to business girths, but even a usually non-dessert-eating companion succumbed to the *tarte fine aux pommes*.

Sèbillon
66 rue Pierre-Charron, 8th (01.43.59.28.15). *M°* Franklin D. Roosevelt. **Open** daily noon-3pm, 7pm-midnight. **Average** €34. **Prix fixe** €28.97. **Credit** AmEx, DC, MC, V.
There's something reassuring about this slumbering, old-fashioned spot, the in-town branch of a venerable bistro in cushy Neuilly. A honeycomb tile floor, waiters in long aprons and a rather anonymous decor of dark wood and small brass chandeliers create an appealing backdrop for a solid feed on the house specialities: oysters and roast lamb. We enjoyed a glass of the house white over a tray of impeccably fresh oysters, then went for the fabled lamb. Tender and cooked pink, it was carved tableside and served with white beans by a very friendly waiter, who later stopped by to see if we wanted more. The accompanying *jus* was thin and a bit lacking in flavour, but the meat was excellent and the atmosphere festive. Tourists, many of them French in from the provinces, grandparents and grandchildren, and businessmen lingering over a brandy make up a heterogeneous mix. Having gone through our bottle of good Morgon-like lightning, we decided we wanted a last glass with coffee, something the French themselves wouldn't do, but the waiter happily suggested a half-bottle, in no way making us feel we were holding him up as the last in at lunch.

9th Arrondissement

Le Bistro de Gala
45 rue du Fbg-Montmartre, 9th (01.40.22.90.50) *M°* Le Peletier or Grands Boulevards. **Open** Mon-Fri noon-2.20pm, 7-11pm; Sat 7-11pm. **Average** €26. **Prix fixe** €29, €35. **Credit** AmEx, DC, MC, V. **Wheelchair access**.
With its framed photographs of actors and actresses, theatre posters alluding to the popularity of this place with a showbiz crowd, and brass lamps casting a soft light on every table, this bistro has an appealing cosiness, especially in a neighbourhood that's mostly given over to gyro stands and other cheap ethnic restaurants. Not far from a flock of inexpensive hotels, it's also clearly a front-desk recommendation, since on a rainy spring night we were flanked by studious Swedes on one side and vivacious Spaniards on the other. The kitchen is commendably serious, generously adding seasonal dishes like asparagus with a thick slice of grilled bacon, to a moderately-priced *menu*. Lentil soup garnished with foie gras was another very good starter, and we were delighted with main courses of scallops in their shells served on a bed of buttered leeks, and a delicious pastry filled with apples, preserved duck and potatoes and served with green beans. Unfortunately, the wonderful northern French cheeses once found here have vanished, to be replaced by a rather ordinary cheese plate, but desserts, including an apple *croustillant* and crème brûlée, are appealing. Eager service and a nice selection of inexpensive Loire Valley wines make this place a good bet in a central location.

Casa Olympe ★
48 rue St-Georges, 9th (01.42.85.26.01). *M°* St Georges. **Open** Mon-Fri noon-2pm, 8-11pm. **Prix fixe** €34. **Credit** AmEx, MC, V.
Once a star of the Paris night at her jet-setty restaurant Olympe in the 15th *arrondissement*, chef Olympe Versini has accomplished an admirable personal and professional transition at her superb bistro just off the Place St-Georges. The attractive mustard-coloured room with pretty Murano chandeliers and wall sconces pulls an interesting crowd – writers, designers, theatre people and other creative types – who come for the outstanding food on her regularly changing *prix fixe*. Well-paced, friendly service and a brief but very appealing wine list add to the pleasure of a meal here. Excellent bread and a fine 1998 Bernard Gripa St-Joseph got a recent meal off to a fine start, and the pleasure grew with the excellent starters – a poached egg with spinach and salted butter on a chestnut-flour *galette*, and a casserole of autumn fruits and vegetables, including pears, celeriac, pumpkin, kale and cardoons, braised in an iron casserole in luscious veal stock. Main courses of guinea hen with a single, large, wild-mushroom-stuffed ravioli, and pork fillet with homemade sauerkraut in a sublime sauce of vinegar, sugar, spices and veal stock, were rustic but deeply satisfying. Desserts were exceptional, too, including the Paris Brest – choux pastry filled with hazelnut cream – and a *croustillant de pomme* (apple baked in pastry) in salted caramel sauce. This is easily one of the best bistros in Paris.

Chez Catherine
65 rue de Provence, 9th (01.45.26.72.88). *M°* Chaussée d'Antin-La Fayette. **Open** Mon noon-3pm; Tue-Fri noon-3pm, 8-10.30pm. Closed Aug. **Average** €42. **Credit** MC, V.
Even if Catherine Guerraz weren't such a fine cook, one would be tempted by this place just for the pleasure of the dining room, from the polished copper bar to the cracked tile floor, bric-a-brac on the walls and lace curtains. Mercifully, the neon that outlines the ceiling is out of commission, but it still adds to an atmosphere that is gloriously postwar Parisian, as does the friendly service directed by Guerraz's charming husband, who also wields the very good wine list. Not surprisingly, such near perfection has not passed unnoticed – this place has found its way into the black books of concierges at many good hotels. The menu, which changes often, is an evolving and personal selection of dishes with a Provençal accent, plus a lot of sturdy and excellent bistro classics. Starters run from an elaborate mousse-like mushroom *timbale* garnished with crayfish tails – absolutely delicious – to roasted red peppers and a generous plate of Basque *charcuterie*, while main courses include a first-rate *steak au poivre* and a stylish rendition of *tagliata*, with strips of grilled steak served on a bed of rocket with parmesan shavings. Cheese is served as a plated course, but the quality is always good. Superb crème brûlée and cardamom-scented cheesecake are among the excellent desserts. An ideal place for a leisurely meal – but don't forget to book a week ahead.

Chez Jean
8 rue St-Lazare, 9th (01.48.78.62.73). *M°* Notre-Dame-de-Lorette. **Open** Mon-Fri noon-2pm, 7.30-10.30pm; Sat 7-10.30pm. Closed two weeks in Aug. **Average** €33. **Prix fixe** €32. **Credit** MC, V.
Despite the raucous party upstairs on the night we visited, Chez Jean downstairs offers sedate, discerning dining with staff who need no prompting to deliver the next carafe or basket of homemade bread. The deep red banquettes that line the high-ceilinged dining room suggest a star-worthy hang-out, but on our visit the only celebs were the attractively presented, superior dishes that delighted us right through to coffee. A mushroom and bacon soup possessed mysterious smoky undertones, while the outstandingly tender fresh skate fillet on a warm bed of *ratte* potatoes, tomatoes, olive oil and herbs was generous enough for a meal on its own. Main dishes kept up the momentum: the young guinea fowl roasted with peach slices and oversized shallots, and the slab of cod with a skirt of *beurre blanc* and tomato were both suffused like sponges with flavour. Just as fine were desserts: a light custard-like fresh raspberry gratin and the house special, a chocolate *cannelé* cake with a gooey centre, served with caramel sauce and coffee ice cream. The engaging Jean, who also runs La Maline in the 8th, has created a pleasant oasis whose menu, changing at least monthly, will bring us back.

A la Cloche d'Or
3 rue Mansart, 9th (01.48.74.48.88). *M°* Blanche. **Open** Mon-Thur noon-3pm, 7.30pm-3am; Fri noon-3pm, 7.30pm-5am; Sat 7.30pm-5am; Sun 7.30pm-3am. Closed Aug, Christmas. **Average** €34. **Prix fixe** €22, €25 (dinner only). **Lunch menu** €13.57, €18.29. **Credit** MC, V.
This late-night Pigalle institution has always been a hit with showbiz folk playing in the neighbourhood's many theatres or living in nearby Montmartre, and thus with groupies

Time Out Paris Eating & Drinking 25

Le Bouclard

Restaurant • Grandmother Cooking

1 rue Cavallotti, 18th • Tel/Fax: 01.45.22.60.01
E-mail: contact@bouclard.com /
contact@grand-mother-cooking.com

Le Soleil

At the Saint-Ouen flea market

The antique hunter's culinary find

Open daily noon-2.15pm & Thur-Sat dinner 8-10pm

109 avenue Michelet, 93400 Saint-Ouen
M°Porte de Clignancourt
Reservation required: 01.40.10.08.08
www.le-soleil.fr

LA POTÉE DES HALLES

RESTAURANT

Come and savour our traditional cuisine in an unspoilt 1900's bistro

3 rue Etienne Marcel, 1st
M° Étienne Marcel
Tel: 01.40.41.98.15
Open for lunch
Mon-Fri noon-2.30pm
dinner Tues-Sun 7pm-11.30pm

and wannabes hoping some of the glitter will rub off. Actress Jeanne Moreau's parents opened the restaurant in 1928 and the boozy, smoky smell of decades of late-night revelry still hangs among the kitschy, faux-rustic decor, held in by the heavy curtain draping the doorway. That it was disco diva Claude François' favourite hangout makes perfect sense. Dozens of vintage celebrity snaps hang between the crossed beams on the walls. The homemade French fare is all reliable if unimaginative, just the thing at 2am after a long evening strutting the stage – or waiting outside the stage door. Starters of *escargots*, lamb's lettuce with warm chicken livers and the house chicken liver pâté were all well executed, as was the soothing *confit de canard* on a bed of fried potatoes. The steak tartare stood out for its zesty seasoning and the plate of hefty golden chips. Prices are gentle, too, with a €25 three-course *menu* valid into the wee hours. Our €23.63 bottle of very drinkable Haut Canteloup Médoc bore a label reminiscent of Toulouse-Lautrec, perfect for the neighbourhood and the theatrical mood.

Les Comédiens

1 rue de la Trinité, 9th (01.40.82.95.95) M° Trinité. **Open** Mon-Fri noon-2pm, 8pm-midnight; Sat 8pm-midnight. **Average** €38. **Credit** AmEx, MC, V.

With a buzzy atmosphere and the type of decor of brick walls and bare wood floors that you might find in Soho or Times Square, this cosy, friendly bistro with an appealing bar and open kitchen is not only a good bet after the theatre, but a very pleasant place for a *tête-à-tête*. Stylish people – we were surrounded by a table of actors and actresses and two beautifully dressed buttoned-down banker types who would have been appropriate subjects for German erotic photographer Helmut Newton – come here to let their hair down and linger over drinks. The food is very good, too, including starters such as a meaty duck terrine served with salad or smoked salmon, followed by hearty main courses like a generous serving of mackerel poached in *court bouillon* or sautéed scallops with nicely made potato purée. Though the wine list is a tad pricey, there are several good bottles from the Loire, including a Chinon that teams well with this food. Exceptionally friendly and professional service.

A la Grange Batelière

16 rue de la Grange-Batelière, 9th (01.47.70.85.15). M° Richelieu-Drouot. **Open** Mon-Sat 12.15-2.30pm, 7.15-10.15pm. Closed Aug. **Prix fixe** €25.75, €26.65. **Lunch menu** €30.34. **Credit** AmEx, MC, V.

Well-spaced tables, attentive service, generous *formules* complete with *amuse-gueules* and *petits-fours*, and a long, lovingly inscribed wine ledger make this bistro near Drouot a useful choice for a business lunch. The pretty, vintage interior has been brightened up with fresh paint and, in the kitchen, chef Ludovic Cingla has similarly tried to refresh tradition. A quail and lentil salad was a surprisingly elaborate concoction of cold legs, a fan of smoked breast, a dainty Puy lentil salad and a small *mesclun*. An asparagus *velouté* turned out to be unexpectedly rich, with crème fraîche rather more evident than asparagus and an equally creamy smoked salmon *quenelle* in the middle. Two generous roasted sea bass fillets, with sautéed leeks and a langoustine cream sauce, proved more exciting than the pork tenderloin with rather slimy diced carrots, peppers and salsify. Desserts took in variants of all the current faves: a trio of mini crèmes brûlées included a very good orange version with candied peel, while the *moelleux au chocolat* was filled – lord knows how – with a lugubrious pistachio sauce, which conjured up visions of the creature from the green lagoon. Order with care, for this is ambitious classic cooking that would benefit from gutsier seasoning and a lighter hand with the cream.

La Table de la Fontaine

5 rue Henri-Monnier, 9th (01.45.26.26.30). M° St-Georges. **Open** Mon-Fri noon-2.30pm, 7.30-11.30pm. Closed two weeks in Aug. **Average** €27. **Prix fixe** €27. **Lunch menu** €22. **Credit** MC, V.

The British, you may or may not be proud to know, are responsible for the sprinkler that gives this place its name. It is one of 50 fountains called Wallace bestowed on the city by the 19th-century British Francophile of the same name. The leafy little square around it is full of Parisian charm and the bistro isn't bad either. The decor is perhaps more tasteful than interesting (ditto for the suity, handbaggy clientele) but this is a good address for a business lunch or supper with a genteel relative. We started with prawns and celeriac in a *rémoulade* sauce (like a prawn cocktail only posher) and the *ravioles de Royan*, tiny ravioli stuffed with morsels of cheese. Both were utterly delicious. Then came a superbly fresh and juicy slab of red tuna, splendid amid bright-coloured vegetables from Provence and paprika sprinkled across the rim of the plate. Our other main, a lamb *navarin*, was also a good-looker, arriving in its black, lidded casserole where (it was soon revealed) there were also carrots, spring onions and crunchy mangetout. Apple tart and ice cream posed no particular problems and coffee at the café terrace on the other side of the square completed an agreeable lunch.

Velly ★

52 rue Lamartine, 9th (01.48.78.60.05). M° Notre-Dame-de-Lorette. **Open** Mon-Fri noon-2.30pm, 7.45-10.30pm. Closed two weeks in Aug. **Average** €35. **Prix fixe** €20.60, €27.40. **Lunch menu** €20.60. **Credit** MC,V.

Odds are you'll agree that the only problem with this cosy little bistro behind pretty old-fashioned glass windows is that it's not just downstairs from your flat. Friendly service and an interesting crowd create a nice buzz – just as long as you don't get sent upstairs to the new dining room, which is a bit cold – as you peruse the regularly changing €27.40 *menu*. On a recent evening most of the stylish types who came in were greeted by name, always a good sign. The kitchen does homely, appealing food, too, including starters such as pumpkin soup or a poached egg on crunchy polenta in *jus*-spiked cream sauce with Sichuan pepper and mains such as stuffed cabbage, veal steak with small potatoes, red mullet on a bed of red cabbage and *supions* (small squid) on creamy, slightly overcooked rice with mushrooms. The food is generously and attractively presented, including a whole, perfectly ripened st-marcellin cheese, and desserts such as cocoa, pear and apricot sorbets. There's a nice wine list, too, with the Château du Puy Bordeaux a very good buy at €19.82.

10th Arrondissement

Chez Arthur

25 rue du Fbg St-Martin, 10th (01.42.08.34.33). M° Strasbourg St-Denis. **Open** Mon 7-11.30pm; Tue-Sat noon-2.30pm, 7-11.30pm. Closed Aug. **Average** €25. **Prix fixe** €20. **Credit** AmEx, MC, V.

For nearly 50 years, this late-night eatery has provided sustenance for hungry actors and audiences from the neighbourhood's many theatres seeking a post-performance treat. Jacky (Arthur's son) is there to welcome all of his clients as though they were stars. With nicely pressed linen, slightly cramped seating (all the better for mingling with rising celebrities) and intimate lighting, this romantic rendezvous aims to satisfy both hearty appetites and thrifty budgets with panache. From the two-course, €20 *menu*, we opted for the salmon tartare marinated in vodka with pepper-corns followed by pan-fried beef which was slightly tough but redeemed by an excellent creamy foie gras stuffing. The less carnivorous among us chose fresh cod with a rainbow assortment of *al dente* vegetables and basil and ricotta ravioli. Good dessert choices were an artfully caramelised crème brûlée and a *sabayon* which was tasty though a little short on the promised fruit. The wine list, slightly pricier than average for the basic house red or white, offers some bargains for connoisseurs.

Chez Casimir

6 rue de Belzunce, 10th (01.48.78.28.80). M° Gare du Nord or Poissonnière. **Open** Mon-Fri noon-2pm, 7pm-midnight. Closed three weeks in Aug. **Average** €24.39. **Credit** MC, V. **Wheelchair access.**

Celebrated bistros (think Thierry Breton's Chez Michel) don't have bargain basements, but occasionally they do spawn affordable offspring. Chez Casimir, a few doors down from Michel, is resolutely down-to-earth (stripped-down decor, plain wooden tables, blackboard menu) but its small selection of market-inspired daily specials betrays its parentage. Starters are simple but hearty, like the pots of homemade pheasant *rillettes* and gargantuan slices of *foie gras confit*. Main courses are similarly rustic, but with more than a hint of culinary fashion. The hands-down favourite *gigot d'agneau rôti*, for instance, was paired with a *gratin dauphinois* not of potato but of the modish *topinambour* (Jerusalem artichokes, once synonymous with war-time deprivation). Desserts, too, had that trendy-traditional edge: a rich, moist *fondant au chocolat* was topped with delicate balls of thyme ice cream and the humble *pain perdu* was layered with slices of roasted pear. Casimir's wines range from €11 to €24 a bottle; the clientele is eclectic and relaxed; and the staff remarkably accommodating.

Café Society

From New York to Senegal to the Great Wall of China – but most often in Paris, and especially in the heights of Ménilmontant – Jerôme Mesnager has painted spectral white figures on walls, fences and tree trunks. 'It's a symbol of the free human being', says this Paris artist, who is now based in the newly cool suburb of Montreuil.

A true Parisian, Mesnager remains attached to the 20th *arrondissement*, where he lived for several years. 'In the 20th there is a restaurant that you don't see from the street. It's called **Le Mistral** (401 rue des Pyrénées, 20th/01.46.36.98.20), named after the wind in the south of France. There is a little door that opens into a garden, where you can eat good regional cuisine such as duck *confit*. The dining room is also very pretty, with an atrium. Another restaurant that I like very much in Paris, a timeless place that reminds me of Inspector Maigret, is **Le Bourgogne (Chez Maurice)** (26 rue des Vinaigriers, 10th/ 01.46.07.07.91). You must go, it's really worthwhile. It's a family-run place where Parisian atmosphere is guaranteed. **Chez Gladines** (*see p67*, **Budget**) is a favourite of mine in the Butte-aux-Cailles area. You can eat big salads and on evenings when there's a rugby match you feel as if you're in the Pays Basque. One of the most fun bars that I know is **La Flèche d'Or** (*see p117*, **Bars**), over an abandoned railway track. I like **Les 3 Arts** (21, rue des Rigoles, 20th/01.43.49.63.95), which has live music. I'm suspicious of bars and restaurants that have a faux-old decor. Of course, I enjoy eating couscous in little neighbourhood restaurants and it's fun to have Greek food on the rue Mouffetard among the souvenir shops.'

Chez Michel ★

10 rue de Belzunce, 10th (01.44.53.06.20). M° Gare du Nord. **Open** Tue-Sat noon-2pm, 7pm-midnight. Closed Aug. **Prix fixe** €30. **Credit** MC, V. **Wheelchair access.**

Well-known among tourists and Parisians despite its out-of-the-way location in a pretty neighbourhood near Gare du Nord, Chez Michel is invariably full. Game season is an ideal time to eat here – our October meal started with a velvety, well-seasoned pumpkin soup, ladled out of a pumpkin shell. The surprises were a garnish of salted herring roe and tiny, crunchy croutons, which turn up in a lot of Thierry Breton's dishes. The chef's Breton roots (as in Brittany) come through in mains such as *kig ha farz*, a substantial *pot-au-feu* for two made with pork. We opted for game, though: boar chops, which turned out to be remarkably like pork, served with a cast-iron pot of small roasted potatoes and whole garlic cloves; and much gamier-tasting venison, cooked rare and accompanied by a creamy pumpkin gratin. Sensitive souls, be reassured that fish is also beautifully prepared here – one of our group ordered red mullet fillets with smooth olive-and-basil mashed potatoes. Desserts are equally rich: you can order two *petits pots de crème*, creamy vanilla custards served with madeleines; the intensely buttery Breton cake *kouing aman*; or perhaps stewed fruits with vanilla ice cream. The cheese board features a few carefully selected and perfectly ripened specimens presented on a black slate. Breton also runs Chez Casimir (*see above*).

Aux Deux Canards

8 rue du Fbg-Poissonnière, 10th (01.47.70.03.23). M° Bonne Nouvelle. **Open** Mon, Sat 7-10.30pm, Tue-Fri noon-2.30pm, 7-10.30pm. Closed 22 July-22 Aug. **Average** €38. **Credit** AmEx, DC, MC, V.

At first, you seem to be getting special treatment, hearing Gérard Faesch's cheery explanation of Aux Deux Canards' colourful history (a former clandestine HQ for a Résistance newspaper during the Nazi occupation) and the kitchen's ancient recipe for citrus rind sauces (you are implored to sniff the contents of jars which, bringing to mind specimens in a pathology lab, are in various states of decay). But after the about the sixth recital of his schtick ('For your initiation, you must taste spider legs and worms!'), fortunately, food comes to the rescue: a trustworthy menu of inventive takes on bistro cuisine, with lots of fruity touches. A pan-fried foie gras with blueberry compote proved surprisingly complementary. Tender *couteaux* (razor clams) in garlic butter and parsley brought to mind skinny, earthy escargots. Two thin tuna fillets, served with *beurre blanc*, puréed carrots, and courgette and potato gratins, were grilled to perfection. Though we didn't order the duck *à l'orange*, the plate is magnificently adorned with a candle lighting up a hollowed-out orange. An archetypal crème brûlée arrives with branding-iron ('Look at the two ducks!' our waiter declared, pointing at the dessert's crispy emblem before backing away into a cloud smoke). It's all quite enjoyable while being a bit over-the-top. You're allowed one cigarette with your aperitif and one with coffee: the previous no-smoking policy proved too ambitious.

L'Hermitage

5 bd de Denain, 10th (01.48.78.77.09). M° Gare du Nord. **Open** Mon-Fri 11.30am-2.30pm, 6.30-10.30pm; Sat 6.30-11pm. Closed one week in Aug. **Average** €32. **Prix fixe** €20, €30. **Credit** AmEx, DC, MC, V.

If you're looking for an alternative to the chains that dominate the environs of Gare du Nord, then this inconspicuous bistro slotted in amid the brasseries is a useful option, frequented by a local business set at lunch, as well as travellers from the Eurostar and Thalys. The long dining room, with tapestry chairs and brocaded walls that reek of the provinces, looks distinctly sad, but it's obvious that the Bergerons in the *salle* and chef François Déage take their food seriously. Cooking centres on traditional regional fare with some modern flourishes, daily dishes inspired by the morning's purchases at Rungis and a good-value three-course *menu*. We started with green asparagus and a well-textured duck terrine served with fig chutney, before a succulent line-caught sea bass fillet, from a daily catch of '*poissons sauvages de pleine mer*', served with a creamy polenta purée – closer to French-style purée (apparently inspired by Michel Rostang) than the coarser Italian version. Desserts are all homemade, including a *nougat glacé* with red fruit coulis and an inventive *millefeuille* filled with lemon-and-basil-flavoured cream.

Le Parmentier

12 rue Arthur Groussier, 10th. (01.42.40.74.75). M° Goncourt. **Open** Mon-Fri noon-2.30pm, 7.45-10.30pm. Sat 7.45-10.30. Closed Aug. **Average** €23. **Prix fixe** €19.51, €22.87 (dinner only). **Lunch menu** €12.20. **Credit** MC, V.

Le Parmentier is one of those hidden, little-known bistros that offers outstanding value in an intimate, feel-right-at-home setting. On a deadly quiet side street not far from the North African neighbourhood of Faubourg-du-Temple, this brightly lit gem feeds you quite well for €23. Choose your *menu* or *à la carte* selections from the same (frequently changing) list of a half-dozen starters and desserts, and a dozen meat, poultry and fish dishes that borrow from French, Italian and Eastern traditions. We enjoyed a decent carafe of red as the *tapenade* arrived, followed by a delicate corn polenta dripping with ash-striped morbier cheese, and a raw mushroom, chervil and crème fraîche salad that adequately revved our tastebuds. The curried *rascasse*, mild-tasting scorpion fish in a sauce of toasted mustard seed, and the fettuccini with prawns and cream both quietly satisfied, as did a slightly mushy apple crumble and smooth *fondant au chocolat*. Nothing knocked our socks off, everything was solidly acceptable, especially the price, and the service encouraged us to seek out Le Parmentier again.

11th Arrondissement

Les Amognes

243 rue du Fbg-St-Antoine 11th (01.43.72.73.05). M° Faidherbe-Chaligny. **Prix fixe** €28.20. **Open** Mon, Sat 8-11pm; Tue-Fri noon-2pm, 8-11pm. Closed three weeks in Aug. **Prix fixe** €20 (two courses), €30 (three courses). **Credit** MC, V.

If you just happened to be walking past this place the first thought to run through your mind probably wouldn't be 'I must eat here now'. But the nondescript exterior belies a cosy interior with beams holding up a low ceiling, and bare stone walls hung with contemporary paintings which, if pretty useless, are at least of warmish hue. What matters here is the food, which, even on the Monday night of our latest visit, drew a good crowd of locals with its bold Mediterranean tastes and colours. The marinated sardine tart, for example – who would have thought all that silvery, fishy tanginess could go so well with pastry base? Well, it does. And that, as they say, was just for starters. As a main course, salt cod fritters with tomato sauce were a bit burnt but still pretty good while our pudding will remain in our memory for years. Crêpes stuffed with cardamom-spiced aubergines: dazzlingly unusual and, with a rich, citrus *crêpe Suzette* sauce, absolutely delicious.

Astier ★

44 rue Jean-Pierre-Timbaud, 11th (01.43.57.16.35). M° Parmentier. **Open** Mon-Fri noon-2pm, 8-11pm. Closed Easter, Aug, Christmas. **Prix fixe** €23.50. **Lunch menu** €19.50. **Credit** MC, V. **Wheelchair access** (ring in advance).

Astier has a gained a reputation as one of those bargains from another age: four courses for an incredible €23.50. But don't be fooled, for it draws not skinflints but an eclectic, rather upmarket food-loving crowd, and the casual appearance (old corner bistro, tightly packed tables, pine panelling, photocopied menu) belies a surprising finesse in the kitchen. There's meat and cream, as one might expect, but also plenty of fish and seasonal ideas: on one hand, a tangy anchovy 'gâteau' starter (marinated anchovies on a base of potato and herbs) on the other, baked egg in a cream and morel sauce. Classic rabbit in mustard sauce with tagliatelle was succulent and lavish with the cream, while *perche croustillante*, perch and nutmeggy fresh spinach in filo pastry in a lemony *beurre blanc*, showed they can do light and modern too. Then on to one of the best cheese trays in the business – a generous basket that gets left on the table for you to help yourself. We restrained ourselves enough for summery desserts, baked apricots served warm with vanilla ice cream and a hot roast peach in a red fruit sauce. The wine list is famous and voluminous, but our bottle of Château Greysac, a Médoc cru bourgeois, from the less-exalted end of the spectrum, was good-value at €26.50.

C'Amelot

50 rue Amelot, 11th (01.43.55.54.04). M° Chemin Vert. **Open** Tue-Fri noon-2.30pm, 7pm-midnight; Sat 7pm-midnight. Closed Aug. **Prix fixe** €30. **Lunch menu** €20. **Credit** MC, V.

On a Saturday evening the cosy, narrow room was packed with a lively local crowd, enjoying the limited choice three-course *menu* at €30. Despite the charming staff we found the service slow, especially as all conversation was being shared with the elbow-to-elbow neighbours. The cuisine itself offers a rare degree of sophistication for the price, and one of our starters of a cream-dominated, chilled bean soup was heightened by little shavings of foie gras nestling among the croutons. Rabbit terrine was excellent but had taken on the temperature of the rather torrid evening. By comparison the main courses were slightly disappointing – a perfectly-cooked *entrecôte* came with soggy *grosses frites*; only the shallot cooked in goose fat lived up to its unctuous description. *Cuisse de canard parmentier* was a superior cottage pie which lacked any real gastronomic distinction. Things got back on course with the desserts, which featured a meltingly addictive *biscuit au chocolat* and an imaginative cold cherry soup, both served with a dollop of vanilla ice cream. A worthy bistro, with some excellent regional wines such as our rugged Côtes d'Auvergne, but one which is probably best visited on a quiet weekday.

Chardenoux

1 rue Jules-Vallès, 11th (01.43.71.49.52). M° Charonne. **Open** Mon-Fri noon-2.30pm, 8-10.30pm; Sat 8-10.30pm. Closed Aug. **Average** €30. **Credit** AmEx, MC, V. **Wheelchair access.**

Chardenoux's etched glass, moulded ceiling, marble bar and *belle époque* painted ladies keep it up there among Paris' most romantic restaurants, but it's the food that makes it a favourite of many Parisians as well as numerous Anglophones, ruled over with good-humoured equanimity by the all-female serving staff. We began with the *salade folle* of crisp green beans, sliced apple, slivers of excellent foie gras and a well-dressed mesclun, and a smooth cream of lentil soup. We remembered from a previous visit how good chef Bernard Passavant is at potent, flavour-packed sauces and the *daube* of beef cheeks *à la provençale* was no exception, in an almost black wine sauce with plenty of carrots and red peppers. All the same it was overshadowed by the dish of the day, very tender *biche* (doe) in a wonderful red wine and blackcurrant concoction, accompanied by potato purée equally dyed purple with blackcurrants, and sautéed black *trompette de la mort* mushrooms. We indulged in a chocolate and chestnut *fondant* and a rather crispy, frozen almond nougat with raspberry coulis while finishing off our fruity red Graves. The menu rarely changes, but the cooking remains good enough to make this a worthy choice for a celebration.

Le Chateaubriand

129 av Parmentier, 11th (01.43.57.45.95). M° Goncourt or Parmentier. **Open** Tue-Sat noon-2pm, 8-11pm (bar open till 2am). Closed three weeks in Aug, one week at Christmas. **Average** €23. **Lunch menu** €11. **Credit** MC, V. **Wheelchair access.**

With its sparse decor, frosted glass panels and a potted palm by the door there is something vaguely '40s about this airy bistro north of Oberkampf. Even the English owner and her waiter look the part – she in polkadots, he in a waistcoat and rolled sleeves – as they buzz between small, decently spaced tables. The food, however, is more reminiscent of Hoxton than occupied France, being an amalgam of New English cooking, French bistro staples and some Mediterranean influences (the chef is half-French, half-Portuguese). Arriving famished, we waited too long to order, but were pleased with the excellent starters of a *tarte* of fresh marinated sardines and *rillettes de lapin*, followed by a succulent beef cheek and perfectly pink, though ever so slightly stringy, shoulder of lamb. Both mains were served on a tagliatelle of lightly cooked spring vegetables – fennel, carrot and courgettes. Susan Hunt is importing Neal's Yard cheddar and stilton and reports French customers to be surprised and delighted by them. We couldn't manage the substantial-sounding desserts of crumble or chocolate fondant. The wines chalked on the blackboard were chosen by Olivier Camus, formerly of the Baratin bar, and range from €13 to €30. If you're fed up with snide comments about the English and food, take your French pals here for a revised opinion.

Chez Paul

13 rue de Charonne, 11th (01.47.00.34.57). M° Bastille. **Open** daily noon-2.30pm, 7pm-12.30am. **Average** €26. **Credit** AmEx, MC, V.

You'll notice Chez Paul because it's the one that always seems to have a queue out the door – all year round. This is a fantasy French restaurant; both floors have a hue that looks like it might owe more to tobacco pollution than paint, the walls are covered in Métro signs and indecipherable documents, and a maximum number of tables is packed into a minimum of space. The waiters and waitresses are frenetic and (mostly) friendly, although service is idiosyncratic rather than uniformly efficient; the menu groans with hearty traditional recipes and meat cuts to make the squeamish shudder. The old favourites are done well here. Chez Paul's steak is excellent, as is the foie gras with lentils. The servings are satisfying and reliably tasty. However, if you're thinking of something other than steak, choose with care – our perch with mushrooms was pretty drab, the taste of the fish all but drowned-out by a gloopy sauce, and the puddings are average. Make sure you book, and even then be prepared to wait.

Chez Ramulaud ★

269 rue du Fbg-St-Antoine, 11th (01.43.72.23.29). M° Faidherbe-Chaligny. **Open** Mon-Fri, Sun noon-3pm, 8-11pm; Sat 8-11.30pm. **Average** €35. **Credit** MC, V.

This hugely popular place with a cosy, found-at-the-fleamarket decor – funky old china and furniture, and one-offs like a vintage fridge – is another reason why the corridor of the 11th and 12th between Ledru-Rollin and place de la Nation is rapidly becoming the best part of town in which to find a real modern bistro. It packs out nightly with a crowd of happy, pennywise and rather arty punters, so be sure to book. The blackboard menu changes often, but typical well-made, homely dishes include a potato *galette* topped with smoked duck breast or pumpkin soup to start, followed by a steak with polenta sprinkled with bleu d'auvergne, or grilled John Dory. Desserts are appealingly grandmotherly, running to *blanc-manger* in almond sauce or roast quince with nougat cream. The great wine list includes some superb small-batch Côtes du Rhônes, and an aura of well-being hangs as heavily over the crowd here as the swirling fug of tobacco smoke.

Dame Jeanne

60 rue de Charonne, 11th (01.47.00.37.40/ www.damejeanne.fr). M° Ledru-Rollin. **Open** Tue-Thur noon-2.15pm, 8-11pm; Fri, Sat noon-2.15pm, 8-11.15pm. Closed three weeks in Aug. **Average** €30. **Prix fixe** €20. **Credit** MC, V

It's difficult to tell whether Dame Jeanne provides fine modern bistro dining that sometimes misses a beat, or a mostly out-of-tune experience that now and then strikes a pleasing chord. Quality ranges from sublime to middling, from a creamy risotto dotted with juicy bits of nicely seasoned chicken, to an utterly forgettable *parmentier* of stringy, flavourless duck meat topped with gummy mashed potatoes. Other dishes show great promise but are held back by imprecise cooking or inattentive seasoning. A starter of thinly sliced sea bream in creamy lentils, for instance, featured perfectly cooked fish but bland veggies, while scallops arrived over-salted but with a light though intense parsley sauce. Desserts were uniformly fine, however, including the classic *gâteau au chocolat* with a bitter chocolate sorbet, and warming fruit crumble with excellent vanilla ice cream. The red and ochre walls, wrought iron and soft lighting set a cosy scene, and service is friendly and light-hearted if a bit slow and unresponsive as the night wears on.

Les Jumeaux

73 rue Amelot, 11th (01.43.14.27.00). M° Chemin Vert. **Open** Tue-Sat noon-2.30pm, 7.30-10.30pm. Closed Aug. **Prix fixe** €30. (dinner only). **Lunch menu** €24. **Credit** MC, V.

Identical twins are always intriguing and this pair had the bright idea of opening a restaurant, one *jumeau* ducking and diving in the kitchen while his matching brother meets and greets the sophisticated local crowd of the increasingly fashionable rue Amelot. The room is airy, with well-spaced tables and changing contemporary art exhibitions, while the three-course *menu* for €30 featured precise and imaginative cooking. We began with a slice of good foie gras, an earthy *fricassée d'escargots* and an unusual and wholly successful camembert *brik*, a crisp pastry parcel filled with melting cheese enhanced by a scattering of cumin seeds. Main courses included a pink veal kidney served on a bed of stewed beetroot, moist and tasty rabbit, and a chunky piece of cod astride olive oil-perfumed mash. Two of us plumped for the cheese plate of the day with the last glasses of our powerful Madiran red, chosen from a list that includes a good choice of reasonably priced bottles. The two finely aged cheeses had been selected with the same care that typified the rest of the cuisine. An almond *financier*, accompanied by greengage plum compote and a dollop of chocolate mousse, was a well-balanced combination which finished off a highly recommendable meal.

Le Passage

18 passage de la Bonne-Graine, 11th (01.47.00.73.30). M° Ledru-Rollin. **Open** Mon-Fri noon-2.30pm, 7.30-11.30pm. Closed Aug, one week in spring. **Average** €25. **Credit** AmEx, MC, V. **Wheelchair access.**

Try to turn up at the Passage before your dining companion to have a chance to peruse the menu in peaceful solitude. It's a treat. And also very impressively long. There's an entire page for different types of Côte Rôtie, an outstanding Rhône Valley wine – and another for intestine as the aptly-named Passage boasts a dozen *andouillettes* (tripe sausages) created by numerous artisans of the stomach. The welcoming, woody decor is warm and pleasant and the place has a scrupulously salubrious feel. Perfect for lunch with mother. We chose to share a starter of deliciously creamy polenta and grilled vegetables before entering the wonderful world of digestive tracts: we went for a spicy Beaujolais *andouillette* made by a certain Monsieur Gast and didn't regret it for a minute. Did you know that one generally prefers white wine with *andouillette*? Neither did we but a bright, young Mâcon was a very convincing accompaniment. A perfect *café liégeois* and a cup of very good espresso confirmed our general impression of great care taken to get things right. An address to return to with pleasure.

Le Repaire de Cartouche

8 bd des Filles-du-Calvaire/99 rue Amelot, 11th (01.47.00.25.86). M° St-Sébastien-Froissart. **Open** Tue-Sat noon-2pm, 7.30-11pm. Closed Aug. **Average** €30. **Credit** MC, V. **Wheelchair access.**

The aura of conviviality and contentedness that prevails at this very popular bistro is easily explained: Rodolphe Paquin is an excellent cook, and his devoted regulars know it. Swift, friendly service completes the picture, so it's well worth booking a week ahead for dinner. Since setting up shop here four years ago Paquin has achieved real excellence, as expressed by a blackboard menu that follows the daily market and the seasons. If Paquin's style is generally down-to-earth, he can also send out

A touch of French polish at Chardenoux

splendidly sophisticated dishes such as an *emincé* of scallops with chicory and truffles. Reasonably priced game figures on his autumn menu, which also offers deliciously sturdy dishes such as a thick slice of farmhouse bacon, grilled and served on a bed of cabbage, or a generous, creamy veal stew. Desserts such as plum crumble or chocolate-filled roasted figs, and an imaginative and well-priced wine list round out the happy experience.

A Sousceyrac
35 rue Faidherbe, 11th (01.43.71.65.30). Mº Faidherbe-Chaligny or Charonne. **Open** Mon-Fri noon-2pm, 7.30-10pm; Sat 7.30-10pm. Closed Aug. **Average** €45. **Prix fixe** €30. **Credit** DC, MC, V. **Wheelchair access**.
Food-lovers and Francophiles speak reverently of this bistro, dedicated since 1923 to the riches of south-western cooking from the village of Sousceyrac in the Lot. Despite such good intentions, A Sousceyrac is a bit devoid of the legendary warmth associated with provincial France. Amidst respectably spaced tables set between soft-hued walls, voices are hushed, and the bourgeois diners demonstrate less exuberance than you might expect given food of such rich culinary lineage. Maybe it's because not all the food is actually that great. A salad of *langoustines en beignets* seemed the stuff of budget restaurants, bland and greasy. A duck terrine dotted with Agen prunes was also surprisingly insipid. The *soupe de fraises* was almost inedible: slices of underripe strawberries floating in a puddle of nearly soured red wine. But, in between, a deboned, foie gras-stuffed pigeon, a quail cooked to perfection with green grapes (never mind that both dishes had the same sauce), and the stunningly complex 1996 Crozes Hermitage that Mr Asfaux chose for us, made us forget all other offences.

12th Arrondissement

L'Auberge le Quincy
28 av Ledru-Rollin, 12th (01.46.28.46.76). Mº Gare de Lyon. **Open** Tue-Fri noon-2.30pm, 7-10pm. Closed one week in Feb, 15 Aug-15 Sept. **Average** €70. **No credit cards**.
For 30-plus years diners have been offered a homely welcome at this country-quaint bistro, looking more like your grandparents' kitchen or a vintage train carriage with its dim lamps, off-colour cartoons and cured meats. Robert Bosshard and his genial staff are more than attentive; they treat you as one of the family. Be prepared to be told not only what to eat but how to eat it: we were instructed to close our eyes and eat the airy leek tart with our hands. A trip to the loo takes you through the cramped kitchen to the courtyard where a tank of crustaceans await their stewed fates: a strong, generously sauced chicken and crayfish dish. We also savoured the beef-stuffed courgette, tomato and cabbage, reminding us of a Polish preparation, though the fare here is strictly the off-the-beaten path cuisine of the Berry and Ardèche. Can't finish a whole bottle of wine? No problem: you drink what you can and are charged accordingly. Awaiting you at the finish line are an above-par *mousse au chocolat*, rice pudding (with alcoholic raisins) and cookies, in giant bowls: you decide how much you can knock back. From the starting glasses of sparkling wine to the showy warming of the prune digestif, L'Auberge le Quincy lodged itself into our list of most memorable meals.

A La Biche au Bois ★
45 av Ledru Rollin, 12th (01.43.43.34.38). Mº Gare de Lyon. **Open** Mon-Fri noon-2.30pm, 7-10.30pm. Closed end July to third

La Cuisine Montorgueil

www.lacuisinemontorgueil.com

Tasting Menu: €43
Lunch Menu: €14.48
A la carte: €30

Southern cuisine in the heart of Paris

35 rue Mauconseil, 1st
Tel: 01.42.21.35.15 - Fax: 01.40.28.43.32
Mº Etienne Marcel or Les Halles

AMBASSADE D'AUVERGNE

In the heart of Paris, near the Pompidou Centre, discover our regional specialities in a typical décor and convivial atmosphere.

*Private dining rooms from 10 to 35 persons.
Open daily. Menu from €26.*

Time Out readers will be welcomed with a free "Le Pelou".

22 rue du Grenier Saint-Lazare, 3rd. Mº Rambuteau
Tel: 01.42.72.31.22

www.ambassade-auvergne.com

Le Bistrot de Cancale

30-32 boulevard de Vaugirard, 15th
Mº Montparnasse-Bienvenue
Tel: 01.43.22.30.25 – Fax: 01.43.22.45.13

week in Aug. **Average** €23. **Prix fixe** €20.60. **Credit** AmEx, DC, MC,V.
One look at the centrally placed antlers inside and you can guess the speciality. It's a game kind of place. The decor is woodsy and warm and the service dished out by Céline and Bertrand Marchesseau is so cheery, you can't help but wonder if you've crossed back into another decade. The food, too, recalls days past. Kick off with homemade terrines – rabbit, fish, duck and venison – a simple tomato salad or eggs poached in red wine, but leave lots of room for the robust mains. We ladled seconds, and thirds, of the bubbling *coq au vin* from its weathered pot and polished off a tender venison steak without a second thought to Bambi. Then it was on to the tray of well-chosen ripe cheeses and a pillowy apple tart with custard. And the wine list, with lots of bottles under €16, ensures further contentment. It's good, solid, filling food with pocket-friendly prices – and that means it's always in demand, so don't forget to book.

Les Bombis Bistrot

22 rue de Chaligny, 12th (01.43.45.36.32)
M° Reuilly-Diderot. **Open** Mon 8-11pm; Tue-Thur noon-2pm, 8-11pm. Closed two weeks in Dec. **Average** €36.
Lunch menu €13. **Credit** MC, V.
It's easy to understand the popularity of this little neigbourhood bistro – it has a lot of atmosphere, a mixed crowd, great food and friendly service. What surprises is that chef Hassan Nithsain can turn out such good food from the small stainless steel kitchen at the back of the room. Judging by our most recent dinner here, he runs a tight ship, since his food is impeccably cooked and beautifully presented (lunch is a simpler, neighbourhood affair). The blackboard menu changes regularly, but we were delighted by the generous rocket, artichoke and parmesan salad, a first-rate rabbit terrine and a soothing lentil soup to start, followed by grilled prawns with a delicious vegetable ragout, breaded halibut in a lemony sauce, and a good steak with *frites*. If this line-up was slightly less creative than others we've encountered here, the quality is unfailing. In fact, our only complaint is that main course portions were slightly small, but we were only too happy to console ourselves with the lovely chocolate cake. With a great wine list and comfortable seating, this is a perfect spot for dinner in a group, but be sure to book.

L'Ebauchoir

45 rue de Cîteaux, 12th (01.43.42.49.31).
M° Faidherbe-Chaligny. **Open** Tue-Sat noon-2:30pm, 8-11pm. Closed 15 Aug, Christmas and New Year. **Average** €25. **Lunch menu** €11.43, €16.80. **Credit** MC, V.
We still enjoy this place, although prices have moved steadily up out of the budget range. The airy main dining room, with its yellow paint, murals and ancient floor tiles, makes for a delightful dining ambiance with a worker's canteen feel, and service is friendly and efficient, easily handling the warm, relaxed crowd. A main of calf's liver in a honey and coriander sauce maintained the standards set by the excellent starter – *chèvre* terrine on a bed of greens and herb sauce – but lamb was disappointing, its flavours drowned rather than enhanced by the Provençal-style rosemary and tomato sauce. Sides of limp vegetables and dry, chewy sliced potatoes didn't seem to justify the increase in prices, but the widely-praised rice pudding was everything we could hope for – and served all-you-can-eat. Still, although the pistachio ice cream in the profiteroles was a happy thought, no overdose of chocolate sauce could disguise the burnt puffs. Despite the inconsistencies, the place is clearly a favourite in the neighborhood – reserve ahead on Friday and Saturday nights.

Le Saint Amarante

4 rue Biscornet, 12th (01.43.43.00.08).
M° Bastille. **Open** Mon-Fri noon-3pm, 8-10.30pm. Closed mid-Jul to mid-Aug.
Average €37. **Prix fixe** €29.
Lunch menu €22.20. **Credit** MC, V.
An unattractive facade not far from Bastille reveals a non-descript interior, deadpan service and a fairly inventive menu which, if not entirely successful, at least has the guts to unite usual bistro ingredients in uncommon ways. The night of our visit, the waiter quipped, 'If you share your food it's not our fault if you go hungry,' and, in response to a request for the non-smoking section, 'We are supposed to have one but, being French, we disobey the law'. OK, *monsieur* – just show us the menu, which turns out to be a small blackboard with half-a-dozen choices for each course. Melon with smoked ham, artfully tuna-stuffed tomatoes and a smooth courgette soup were anything but drab starters, and got our taste-buds humming. Mains were more uneven. The duck breast, dense as steak, was seasoned only by its own unadorned juices, and crunchy bits marred the tasty pea and potato purée. A leg of lamb with white beans got the flavour part right, but the cut of meat was tough. However, a fillet of pollack, with squid, calamari and spinach, was just right. If you don't like fruit or a decent chocolate *moelleux* for dessert, you're out of luck. Saint Amarante's main drawback is the limited selection, so choose wisely, perhaps seeking the advice of the straight-shooting waiter.

Le Square Trousseau

1 rue Antoine-Vollon, 12th (01.43.43.06.00).
M° Ledru-Rollin. **Open** Tue-Sat noon-2.30pm, 8-11.30pm. **Average** €38.
Lunch menu €20, €25. **Credit** MC, V.
This restaurant would be worth visiting for its superb 1900s interior alone, but what makes the place a must is its *joie de vivre*. It's a favourite with a media and film crowd; the diners are uniformly elegant in urban nomad gear. Even the friendly waiters, relentlessly handsome in their long white aprons, appear celluloid-wrapped. The food, though, is for real. We started with a silky-textured smoked salmon and candied lemon *timbale*; a tomato, cucumber and avocado *millefeuille* with mozzarella, refreshing red, green and white layers of natural goodness showered with chives; and poached eggs in a fine, nutmeg-scented cheese sauce with Japanese herbs. The main courses were just as satisfying, almost: plump farm chicken served with a mini, creamy risotto, tender strips of duck in a delicious cherry sauce, and chicken in Moroccan-style pastry, which was a little dry. For dessert, the serving of chocolate *quenelles* in a saffron custard was on the frugal side, but a delight nonetheless. The relatively steep wine prices may come as a surprise, given the good-value food, but the selection shows expertise in unearthing the best from Touraine, Burgundy, Auvergne and the Vaucluse. Our Les Roches Chinon 1996 (€21.34) was proof of this.

La Table du Marquis

3 rue Beccaria, 12th (01.43.41.56.77).
M° Gare de Lyon. **Open** Tue-Sat noon-2pm, 7.30-10pm. Closed two weeks in Aug.
Prix fixe €21.04 (dinner only). **Lunch menu** €12.20, €15.24. **Credit** MC, V.
Wheelchair access.
The handsome facade of this old café charbon (a turn-of-the-century café which once sold coal) presages an excellent meal in a simple but immaculate dining room painted white and yellow and decorated with contemporary art. In the democratic spirit of Beccaria himself, an Italian noble who penned a work that first set forth what were to become the rights of man, you get a fine, affordable feed here. In the evening, a meal starts with soup – perhaps puréed carrot or puréed lentil – brought to the table in a generously filled tureen, so that you can serve yourself. It's invariably delicious, but don't get carried away, since portions here are consistently ample. Start with the chicken-liver terrine with pistachios or sautéed oyster mushrooms and field mushrooms, and then try the *plat du jour*, often fish, or solid main courses such as tender roast pork with a bacon cream sauce and a big serving of lentils or stuffed rabbit with a cake of rosemary-scented aubergine caviar. Desserts by a skilled pastry chef include a coconut *blanc-manger* with raspberry sauce and a chocolate fondant. Excellent bread and a short, well-selected and inexpensive wine list round out the pleasure of a meal here. Less elaborate food is offered at lunch.

Illuminating conversation at Natacha

Les Zygomates

7 rue de Capri, 12th (01.40.19.93.04).
M° Daumesnil. **Open** Mon, Sat 7.30-10.30pm, Tue-Fri noon-2.30pm, 7.30-10.30pm. Closed Aug. **Average** €27. **Prix fixe** €23.
Lunch menu €13. **Credit** MC, V.
Nostalgia buffs will find the trek to this out-of-the-way restaurant more than worthwhile. With its marble counters, mirrored and etched glass walls and gorgeous ceiling tiles, this former 1930s butcher shop oozes charm – and the food is pretty good, too. Blackboard specials included a salad of foie gras with pine kernels and exceptionally plump ravioli of langoustine, aubergine and mushroom in a wonder-fully rich langoustine sauce. Next up, a nicely pink fillet of roast ducking dusted with nuts, and *rascasse* (scorpion fish) with herb-brightened tomato *concassé* – both garnished with dollops of mashed carrot, ratatouille and cauliflower gratin. Unfortunately, our chocolate tart was overly dry and we lamented not choosing the towering raspberry melba instead (ice cream desserts are always a good bet here). On a Monday night the place was packed, and service was friendly but slow.

13th Arrondissement

L'Aimant du Sud

40 bd Arago, 13th (01.47.07.33.57).
M° Les Gobelins or Denfert-Rochereau.
Open Tue-Sat noon-2.30pm, 7.30-10.30pm; 1 Apr-31 Aug Mon-Sat noon-2.30pm, 7.30-10.30pm. Closed one week at Christmas.
Average €24. **Lunch menu** €12, €15.
Credit AmEx, MC, V. **Wheelchair access**.
This contemporary bistro has become a hit with the locals who appreciate its relaxed atmosphere and good cooking at moderate prices. On sunny days, come for a meal on the broad and relatively quiet pavement terrace. Start off with a *fondant de légumes* with a tomato coulis or a melon *rosace*, sliced melon with smoked salmon, before feasting on generous mains such as tuna steak with toasted almonds, steamed cod with coriander or pork fillet in a Port and mushroom sauce. Roasted figs, fresh pineapple or an apricot gratin make for a homely offer of desserts and, in addition to the short but fairly priced wine list, there is an appealing selection of wines by the glass.

Anacréon

53 bd St-Marcel, 13th (01.43.31.71.18).
M° Les Gobelins or Saint Marcel. **Open** Tue, Thur-Sat noon-2.30pm, 7.30-11pm; Wed 7.30-11pm. Closed Aug. **Prix fixe** €30.
Lunch menu €19. **Credit** AmEx, DC, MC, V. **Wheelchair access**.
No place asserts the truth of the old adage, 'don't judge a book by its cover', as vehemently as this small and really rather ugly restaurant. We walked by it four times before accepting that we had indeed arrived at the right address. The atmosphere inside did little to improve the impression given by the bare facade. The head waitress comes off more military commando than hostess and the room, crowded with suit-clad locals dining early, fostered less conviviality than some barracks might. But, we forgot all that when we tasted André Le Letty's provocative cooking. An *amuse-bouche* of thick and creamy puréed peas smoothed our ruffled feathers. Our starters, a rich and livery rabbit terrine and a shellfish salad – more like a cold, creamed soup than a salad – were so tempting that we had to refrain from licking our plates dry. For mains, thin slices of rich duck breast were perfectly mated to a refreshing sauce of fresh grapefruit while an ample fillet of an unusual Mediterranean fish was cleverly nuanced by the herbal zing of juniper berries. We were not sure the licorice-infused crème brûlée was completely successful, but if you can squeeze it in, don't shy away from the plentiful mounds of goodness that call themselves *quenelles de chocolat*.

L'Avant-Goût ★

26 rue Bobillot, 13th (01.53.80.24.00).
M° Place d'Italie. **Open** Tue-Sat noon-2pm, 8-11pm. Closed three weeks in Aug. Average €32. **Prix fixe** €26. **Lunch menu** €10.60.
Credit MC, V.
Chef Christophe Beaufront bowled us over with his take on *terroir* at his buttercup-yellow bistro in the Butte-aux-Cailles. The blackboard

menu is designed to reflect the best seasonal produce. We loved the refreshing, chilled cucumber soup laced with tiny clams and a hot, asparagus gratin with an egg on top, both proof of how Beaufront can marry different textures and flavours. A lamb knuckle with spring vegetables showed a light touch to potentially rich food, well-seared calf's liver came with a hint of spice in the *jus* and a luscious *gratin dauphinois*, while the meringue and chocolate fondant concoction with orange sorbet that followed was a mouthwatering indulgence which left us satisfied, not stuffed. Add a pleasant Côtes du Rhône du Printemps wine of the month, friendly service that made everyone welcome despite the Saturday lunchtime crush and volunteered an extra plate, small cutlery and a toy for a small child, and this bistro merits all its plaudits. You need to book at least a week ahead in the evening, but we can't wait to go back.

Chez Paul
22 rue de la Butte-aux-Cailles, 13th (01.45.89.22.11). Mº Place d'Italie or Corvisart. **Open** daily noon-2.30pm, 7.30pm-midnight. Closed Christmas. **Average** €34. **Credit** MC, V. **Wheelchair access**.
Chez Paul is a beacon to professional types who lurk in the quirky 13th *arrondissement*, its white cloth and wood approach offering a quietly chic, but buzzy alternative to other offbeat spots along the strip. Tradition takes pride of plate (*pot-au-feu*, beef knuckle, bone marrow – in fact, bones galore) and you can eat your way from one end of a beast to the other, from beef tongue to tail or pig's ear to rear. Seafood makes an appearance on the blackboard menu with oysters, whelks and fish such as an excellent starter of pan-fried mullet fillets with olive *tapenade* and a main of monkfish nuggets in a creamy garlic sauce with gleaming green spinach. A classic saddle of lamb, with the house's famed mashed potatoes, was another good choice. Desserts such as *réglisse* (liquorice) ice cream and *marquise au chocolat* along with good-natured service and a *pot* of chilled Brouilly also went down well. On a Monday night the joint was jumping, so if you want a bone to pick, book.

La Girondine
48 bd Arago, 13th (01.43.31.64.17). Mº Glacière. **Open** Mon-Thur noon-2.30pm, 7.30-10.30pm; Fri noon-2.30pm, 7.30-11pm; Sat 7.30-11pm. **Average** €38. **Prix fixe** €19.50 (dinner only). **Lunch menu** €15. **Credit** AmEx, DC, MC, V.
If you happen to be visiting a friend or relative or, better still, leaving the nearby prison of La Santé, here's the perfect place to come and enjoy your freedom. On a warm day, make sure you reserve a table on the superb terrace under the shade of the conker trees where you'll be presented with an extraordinarily wide choice of dishes. From the blackboard specials we went for one of four scallop dishes, a scallop carpaccio with foie gras, as our starter. A less magnanimous critic might quibble with the over-generous dose of balsamic vinegar, but this was a successful meeting of unlikely ingredients, presented rather fetchingly with a dusting of cumin and grated carrot. The grilled turbot, though the most expensive dish of the day, proved worthy but a bit dull. Our best main, recommended by the good-natured waitress after due consultation with the relevant authorities, was the beef with sherry: crispy outside, good and bloody within. The gravy was a credit to the unequalled sauce-making skills of the French. Our pudding, a crème brûlée full of deliciously juicy baked strawberries, was, like much of the cooking at the Girondine, a little original and very pleasant.

Au Petit Marguery
9 bd du Port-Royal, 13th (01.43.31.58.59). Mº Gobelins. **Open** Mon-Fri noon-2.30pm, 7.30-10.15pm. Closed Aug, 24 Dec-5 Jan. **Prix fixe** €32.77-€50.30. **Lunch menu** €25.15. **Credit** AmEx, MC, V.
Come October and you can barely enter a patch of woodland or moorland in France without coming across shotgun-bearing gunmen and their dogs *à la chasse*. In Paris one of the best bets for trying their bag is the ruby-coloured Petit Marguery. True, the restaurant serves up guinea fowl and steaks all year round, but in autumn it comes into its own and a crowd of all ages comes here to join the game. Our kindly waiter knowledgeably launched into the different preparations on the three-course *menu-carte*. Mild pheasant and gamier hare terrine, each studded with foie gras, were followed by wonderful main courses: *noisettes de biche*, tender venison in wine sauce with raisins and pine kernels (€7.62 supplement), and a house speciality, *lièvre à la royale*, a dome of rich, shredded hare's meat in a magnificent sauce of wine, offal and blood that showed what French culinary tradition is all about. Desserts go from the mildly to the wildly alcoholic – expertly risen Grand Marnier soufflé, lime sorbet with Marc de Gewurztraminer, cherries in *eau de vie*.

Le Terroir
11 bd Arago, 13th (01.47.07.36.99). Mº Gobelins. **Open** Mon-Fri noon-2.30pm, 7.45-10.15pm. Closed Easter, three weeks in Aug, Christmas. **Average** €38. **Credit** MC, V.
The Terroir is your classic bustling bistro: tightly packed tables, a corny mural of exotic lands, jokey *patron* and a zinc bar where many people start their dinner munching radishes over an *apéro*. The menu is firmly attached to tradition and the glories of French *terroir* – the emphasis here is on fresh, quality ingredients, simply prepared. But be warned, helpings are gigantic so come with an appetite. We started with wonderful *girolles* – a mushroom that can become lamentably soggy, but here, simply sautéed with shallots, were plump and succulent – and a plate of fresh, grilled sardines. Other favourites are the help-yourself terrines or a chopping board laden with *charcuterie*. Then a juicy, rumpsteak *pavé* with a mound of green beans and a length of spicy *boudin noir aux deux pommes* (black pudding with sautéed potatoes and apples). The wine list is short and uninformative, so if in doubt ask; the *patron* whisked out a wonderful, complex half-bottle of Larivet Haut-Brion (€22.87) for us that we've spotted at twice the price elsewhere.

14th Arrondissement

L'Assiette
181 rue du Château, 14th (01.43.22.64.86). Mº Mouton-Duvernet. **Open** Wed-Sun noon-2.30pm, 8-10.30pm. Closed Aug. **Average** €63. **Lunch menu** €35. **Credit** AmEx, MC, V.
Perhaps it's the price you pay for precise cooking with top-quality products, but we find it hard not to look sideways at a bistro dinner for two that can top €135 without breaking a sweat. Then again, L'Assiette's clientele don't seem to care a bit. They come for the fine food and the casual charm – photocopied menus, peeling paint, bare wood floors and all. We can't quite bring ourselves to call the €35 lunch *menu* a bargain, but it's a more affordable way to approach chef Lulu's deft, south-western hand with superbly chosen ingredients. Starters include great-looking mesclun greens with a nutty, herb-infused vinaigrette, and fluffy pan-fried salmon blinis, whose undersalting was redeemed by an accompanying *quenelle* of tangy taramasalata. Main courses featured whole pan-fried sardines cooked until their skin crisped slightly while their flesh remained silken and juicy. Veal kidneys arrived perfectly pink and topped with sliced scallions, whose acidity provided an excellent balance to the meat's richness. Desserts are plain, but the well-executed *oeufs à la neige* and crème caramel offered a soothing end to the meal. The south-western-focused wine list also stretched our budget.

Contre-Allée
83 av Denfert-Rochereau, 14th (01.43.54.99.86). Mº Denfert-Rochereau. **Open** Mon-Fri, Sun noon-2pm, 7.30-10.30pm; Sat 8-10.30pm. Closed Christmas. **Average** €35. **Prix fixe** €25-€35. **Credit** AmEx, MC, V. **Wheelchair access**.
This popular modern bistro takes its name from the parallel streets that run alongside the wide avenues of this elegant district, allowing for pleasant summer dining under the stars. The welcome is friendly and the decor is as discreetly chic as the locals who frequent the place. We particularly like the way the garden has been lit up to give a rush of green from the back windows. The menu is full of imaginative Mediterranean fare and caters as much for those who want to eat healthily, lightly, even meatlessly as for the hearties. We began with a *millefeuille* of aubergine, *confit* tomatoes, deliciously grainy polenta and plenty of good olive oil. Our best main, eaten with a couple of glasses of crisp, fruity Chardonnay, was fried perch with tiny white beans, a few more of those tomatoes and a tangle of deep-green seaweed to give that gung-ho taste of life on the ocean wave. Pudding was slices of pear soaked in red wine with an exquisite apricot coulis, and wild cherry ice cream with what looked like a small garden gate made out of chocolate positioned rather fetchingly on the top. This is a good place to come for a fine lunch that won't leave you comatose for the rest of the afternoon.

Natacha
17bis rue Campagne-Première, 14th (01.43.20.79.27). Mº Raspail. **Open** Mon-Sat 8.30pm-1am. Closed Aug. **Average** €38. **Credit** MC, V.
Natacha is one of those restaurants that divides opinion. There are those who maintain that it is, in a fantastically low-key way, very, very cool: previous diners have found themselves surrounded by the international glitterati and any-colour-so-long-as-it's-black-pack; others, denied the chance to jostle for elbow room with Mick Jagger (allegedly) point out it's a pricey restaurant in an out-of-the-way location. Clearly this depends on who's in town, but for those of you who are more interested in what's going on at your own table than somebody else's, Natacha manages to successfully combine good

Sniff out some truffles at Le Troquet

looks with friendly, even efficient, service. The food, unlike the company, is reliable: we recommend the generous salmon tartare and the particularly succulent *gambas à la provençale*. Our lentil salad, steak and tiramisu, however, were not outstanding – although the generous serving of chocolate coffee beans that came with the tiamisu was. Book well in advance and get a table upstairs – on quiet nights the main room can lack atmosphere.

L'O à la Bouche

124 bd du Montparanasse, 14th (01.56.54.01.55). M° Vavin. **Open** Tues-Sat noon-3pm, 7pm-midnight. Closed three weeks in Aug. **Average** €38. **Prix fixe** €24.90, €29.90 (dinner only). **Lunch menu** €15, €19. **Credit** AmEx, MC, V.

We were always rather put off by the tacky word play of this restaurant's name, but putting mouthwatering prejudice aside, it was a pleasant surprise to find a sophisticated restaurant with excellent service and well placed tables, despite the rather unfortunate red and yellow wannabe Tuscan colour scheme. Frank Paquier's *menu* at €29.90 for three courses and €24.90 for two courses has a tendency to work too hard for its effects. A starter of mussel and lentil soup was excellent but gained nothing from the blob of cream cheese and crispy bacon garnish; on the other hand, the galette of *pied de veau* was an original creation, crispy and unctuous at the same time. A main of moist rabbit astride an over-sophisticated polenta revealed that this Italian classic is not the chef's strong point. The *boeuf bourguignon*, prettily presented in a casserole, was a good version of this classic red wine stew, although the chunks of beef were rather insignificant. We resisted the puddings, including the tempting yet ubiquitous *fondant au chocolat* on the *menu* and a more spectacular hazelnut soufflé *à la carte*. A little fine-tuning of the cuisine seems to be needed to bring the hint of pretension into sharper focus.

Les Petites Sorcières

12 rue Liancourt, 14th (01.43.21.95.68). M° Denfert-Rochereau. **Open** Mon-Fri noon-2pm, 8-10pm; Sat 8-10pm. **Average** €29. **Lunch menu** €18.50. **Credit** MC, V.

Forget the hokey decor (red velvet entry curtains, Hallowe'en theme lamps and a vast assembly of airborne witches), the real sorcery is in the kitchen. Christian Teule conjures up sophisticated French classics with a contemporary twist, spot-on every time. The rich lentil soup, cushioning a delicately earthy *foie gras poêlé*, was crowned with a drizzle of balsamic vinegar, while the splendid *boudin noir* tart, rings of grilled black pudding, caramelised onion 'jam' and a dense square of crisp pastry, was defiantly light. Main courses included a lemony *blanquette de veau*, a thick Aubrac steak, and a juicy hunk of pink *canard rouennais* with crisp, honey-pepper skin. Seamless service (once Mme Teule had dispensed her rather brusque welcome) ensured that desserts, most cooked to order, arrived just as we were wanting them. And the magic continued. The pear *clafoutis* was moist and almondy, and the warm chocolate tart – *sablé* pastry encasing an intense bittersweet soup – a chocoholic's fantasy. In contrast to the food, wines tend to be pricey, although the low-end options are more than drinkable; our 1996 Côtes du Rhône at €22.10 was a smooth match for the meal. For a lucky few this is a neighbourhood bistro, but for those outside the enchanted circle, it's well worth the trip.

La Régalade ★

49 av Jean-Moulin, 14th (01.45.45.68.58). M° Alésia. **Open** Tue-Fri noon-2pm, 7pm-midnight; Sat 7pm-midnight. Closed Aug. **Prix fixe** €30. **Credit** MC, V.

We returned to La Régalade after a long absence and were relieved to find that the tireless Yves Camdeborde is still meeting his own demanding standards. The provincial-style dining room was as lively as ever and reservations remain notoriously hard to obtain – we waited two weeks for a weeknight table. We started with a typically south-western dish: chilled raw oysters with hot, slightly spicy chipolata sausages. These oysters were particularly fleshy, which made the contrast even more intense. Another starter, the langoustine carpaccio, was a delicate dish in a tangy marinade. Continuing with the fishy theme, the spider crab with fennel and tomato was a surprising concoction of crab meat in a smooth, aromatic sauce, gorgeously presented in its shell atop a bed of coarse salt. More wintery was a main of juicy roasted capon, served with chestnuts. Don't expect big portions or generous accompaniments here – flavour is the thing. One of us couldn't resist the towering Grand Marnier soufflé, Camdeborde's signature dessert, but regretted not having ordered the more original grapefruit in Campari jelly, which combines a childishly delightful wobbly texture with very adult bitterness. Washed down with fruity red wine from the Béarn for about €18 a bottle, this meal was just the 'fashion food' antidote we had been craving.

Le Vin des Rues

21 rue Boulard, 14th (01.43.22.19.78). M° Denfert-Rochereau. **Open** Tue-Sat 10am-1am. Closed one week in Feb, early Aug-early Sept. **Average** €23. **No credit cards.**

The spirit of former owner and local legend Jean Chanrion still looms large at this rustic restaurant, after his succession by Didier Gaillard and wife Niky. If blustery Jean's presence was somewhat formidable, gentle giant Didier is congeniality and calm incarnate, and his abundant moustache and ample form hint at the heartiness of the food to come. A starter of *cervelas* (pork sausage) with pistachios delivered the first exquisite dose of indulgence; sardines marinated in basil on a bed of fresh lettuce provided a more restrained option. A main course of roast quail cooked with grapes and wild mushrooms was terrifically tender and perfectly seasoned. It appeared to be the choice at most tables, where an air of reverence reigned. The *andouillette* (tripe sausage), which we ordered in a foolhardy fit of bravura despite the most diplomatic warnings from Didier, is not for the uninitiated. Half of it, obviously of the utmost freshness, was shamefacedly consumed, and the trauma melted away as Didier enjoined us to contemplate the dessert menu – a choice of apple sorbet with Calvados, prunes in wine, strawberry soup or *clafoutis* with mirabelle plums.

15th Arrondissement

Le Bistrot d'Hubert

41 bd Pasteur, 15th (01.47.34.15.50). M° Pasteur. **Open** Mon-Fri, Sun 12.30-2.30pm, 7.30-10.30pm; Sat 7.30-10.30pm. **Average** €37. **Lunch menu** €18.50, €27.50. **Credit** AmEx, MC, V. **Wheelchair access.**

Lime-washed grey walls, pretty blue tiles and a huge, creamy marble dresser hosting bottled preserves and soup tureens set the scene – upmarket country. But there's a twist, and it's not just the decorative skeins of garlic. The *menus* come in two guises: 'tradition' and 'discovery'. 'Tradition' ranges from black pudding sautéed in duck fat to very delicious free-range chicken with tarragon, honey and caramelised chicory. And, for starters, a pretty terrine of fresh leeks, spinach, smoked and fresh salmon with nut oil. 'Discovery' offers choice pan-fried swordfish doused with soy sauce, lemon, diced courgette and red pepper on a bed of mashed potato, and a life-enhancing butterscotch and apple mousse flavoured with Calvados and served with slivers of caramelised orange rind in gentian liqueur. It's attractive food in an attractive setting that seems to be appreciated by everyone from stylish suits to grannies in pearls. Staff are competent and friendly, and if you're flying solo you can perch at the counter overlooking the open kitchen.

Chez Les Frères Gaudet ★

19 rue Duranton, 15th (01.45.58.43.17). M° Boucicaut. **Open** Mon-Fri noon-2pm, 7.45-10pm; Sat 7.45-10pm. **Prix fixe** €26.68. **Credit** AmEx, MC, V.

If this new restaurant were anywhere but on a quiet street in an outlying part of the 15th *arrondissement*, it would surely have become a popular word-of-mouth address by now, since the food is excellent and a very good buy. For the time being, however, it remains an insider's address with an assiduous local following of professional couples in the evening and a television and UNESCO crowd at noon. The calm of this salmon-coloured dining room, formerly L'Ammonite, is part of its charm, since tables are well-spaced and service well-paced and friendly. The Gaudet brothers in the kitchen – Jean-Yves, the chef, who trained at Lucas Carton and L'Ambroisie, among other restaurants, and Hugues, the pastry chef – serve truly delicious traditional French dishes with a stylish gloss of modernity. Start with the salad of skate, cabbage and walnuts, the marinated oysters or the homemade foie gras, and then try main courses such as the delicate *dariole de homard*, a sort of flan with a few discreet morsels of lobster, served with a baked apple, or the delicious *bourride*, a creamy, garlicky soup with monkfish. Desserts are first-rate, including orange-sauced crêpes, runny chocolate cake and a pear poached in Muscat wine with a slice of sugared brioche toast. This quiet spot is well worth a trip across town.

La Dînée

85 rue Leblanc, 15th (01.45.54.20.49). M° Balard. **Open** Mon-Fri noon-2.15pm, 7.30-11pm. Closed three weeks in Aug. **Prix fixe** €25.90 (two courses), €29.20 (three courses). **Credit** AmEx, MC, V.

Largely because of the remote location of his restaurant and the fact that he had previously blazed his own path by doing a pricey *à la carte* menu as opposed to the good-value *prix fixe* offers that other young chefs use to build their reputations, Christophe Chabanel has been the dark horse among the new generation of up-and-coming Paris talent. Now he has introduced a *menu* that makes his talent more accessible, and it's very much worth finding your way to this quiet corner to sample his sophisticated and inventive cooking. The new *formule* changes according to the market, but runs to dishes such as smoked salmon with cucumbers in horseradish cream and a *croustillant* of pig's trotter with goat's cheese and salad as starters, and main courses such as honey-glazed pork spare ribs with Madras rice and delicious veal rib roast with spring onions and caramelised carrots. Fine desserts include a grapefruit terrine with honey and a luscious chocolate mousse. The wine list is still a bit pricey, and service can be stilted, but overall this mannered little place is well worth the trip.

La Folletterie

34 rue Letellier, 15th (01.45.75.55.95). M° La Motte-Picquet-Grenelle. **Open** Tue-Sat noon-2pm, 7.30-10pm. Closed two weeks in Aug. **Average** €22. **Prix fixe** €21, €23. **Lunch menu** €17, €21. **Credit** MC, V.

Chef Frédéric Breton produces a bargain €21 three-course *menu*, whose sophistication and accomplishment belie the price and position of the restaurant. A quiet lunch found the vaguely

The food police

Even if you're not privy to the backroom theatrics of your favourite neighbourhood bistro, anyone who has worked in a kitchen can imagine dozens of horrifying food preparation practices. Fortunately, even in this country of ancient plumbing, frequent *bisous* and baguettes handed over, well, hand-to-hand, France does have stringent hygiene regulations.

Thirty-eight Préfecture de Police health inspectors, working with the Direction des Services Vétérinaires and the Direction de la Protection du Public, are charged with checking not only 13,000 Paris eateries but also 8,500 food distribution centres, 1,500 butchers, 2,600 hospitals and schools – more than 25,000 establishments where meat, fish and vegetables are packaged, processed, prepared or served. Meanwhile, the Direction Générale de la Concurrence, de la Consommation et de la Répression des Fraudes, aka the Fraud Squad, ensures that fish advertised as sea bass is not farm-raised, or that the chef's *tarte maison* doesn't come from Picard.

Usually a half-day, on-site visual inspection is enough, but sometimes samples are taken back to the lab for analysis, where inspectors can look for nasty bacteria and fraudulent food. If the *contrôleurs* find incongruous mould on a camembert tray or cockroaches skittering about the *plat du jour*, they'll levy a €1,524 fine. Bigger bucks – as much as €5,336 – must be paid if restaurants are caught serving expired meat or fish. Each year about 30 shut-downs are ordered in Paris.

A typical inspection report might list the following minor infractions: meat stored and transported without containers, dirty ceilings, cheese displayed on soapy plates, and old-style tile in the kitchen, where bacteria can fester in the cracks. One in ten restaurants are accused of dishing up expired food and 95 per cent are considered to lack adequate freezers. During a particularly fruitful raid in September 2000, after a coordinated Goutte-d'Or operation involving inspections of more than 100 establishments, police seized rotten crocodile, porcupine, and monkey meat, as well as 'spoiled caterpillars'. Illegal boa and iguana have also been found.

The fact that even a venerable institution like the Jewish food emporium Jo Goldenberg was nabbed in 2001 suggests inspectors are neither complacent nor prone to favouritism. Goldenberg's troubles began back in 1999 with seizures of poorly frozen carp and spoiled meat; his establishment was charged again in March 2001, with 'repugnant uncleanliness'. But Goldenberg, who said the food was destined for his pets, not the dining room, persuaded the police to keep him in business, citing 'decades without complaint from my customers'. Inspectors can be lenient with older Parisian establishments, admits Marie-Noëlle Boyer, a police brigadier and inspector. 'One can't completely renovate a restaurant because it lacks a door or because there's not enough room for three separate freezers', she says.

Naturally, some restaurants entirely escape the gaze of inspectors who, collectively, can only visit 6,500 establishments a year. Proprietors are asked to regulate themselves, using booklets which translate verbose regulations into digestible language. The detailed French and EU hygiene statutes require, for example, that beef and poultry not be stored side-by-side, and that hot water be available for employees to wash their hands.

Meanwhile, with mountains of unrefrigerated meat in full view of diners, a certain ancient bistro beloved for its no-frills steak grilled before your eyes probably violates at least one rule. But the food is scrumptious. The lesson seems to be, don't allow hyper-vigilance to spoil each and every meal. And, if your veal cutlet tastes suspiciously like turkey breast, report the fowl play to the food police. *Ethan Gilsdorf*

Direction des Services Vétérinaires (DSV), 107 bis rue du Faubourg Saint-Denis, 10th (01.44.79.51.51).

Café Les Parisiennes

10 rue Brise-Miche, 4th
Tel: 01.42.78.44.11
M° Rambuteau

restaurant - cocktails
open daily 8am-2am

heated terrace
in front of the
Centre Pompidou

cocktail happy hour
daily 5-8pm

'Deep-jazz' DJ evenings
4-8pm Fri-Sat

Café Le Petit Pont

1 rue du Petit-Pont, 5th
Tel: 01.43.54.23.81
M° St Michel

open daily
5am-3am

world food, cocktails
heated terrace with a
splendid view of Notre-Dame

'House-garage' DJ nights Thur-Sat

www.panamcafe.com

Le Petit Rétro is big on fine food and decor

Mediterranean-style room pretty deserted, but the staff were welcoming and attentive. From the blackboard *menu*, we began with a *millefeuille* of filo pastry, layered with a flavoursome seafood mousse, and some crisp roquefort croquettes. Our main courses kept up the high level of presentation; delicate morsels of duck's legs were topped with a savoury mixture of vegetables and couscous in a sea of blackcurrants. The combination of textures and flavours showed a genuine talent, and while a veal dish was a simpler creation, it featured meltingly tender meat and an onion-rich sauce. Pausing to appreciate our red Chinon, chosen from the short but interestingly personal wine list, we contemplated the eternal pudding or cheese question. We plumped for one of each: the cheese was a generous selection, while the *moelleux au chocolat* was an unusually good version of what is becoming a wearisome restaurant cliché. Here it was a moussy, tart-shaped slice, which provided a pungent chocolate fix to end our meal.

L'Os à Moëlle ★
3 rue Vasco-de-Gama, 15th (01.45.57.27.27). Mº Lourmel. **Open** Tue-Sat 12.15-2pm, 7.30-11.30pm. Closed Aug. **Prix fixe** €32 (dinner only). **Lunch menu** €27. **Credit** MC, V. **Wheelchair access**.
The lace curtains and the sleepy location of this place do attract lunching *dames d'un certain âge*, but the evening we visited it was also populated by a crowd of young locals, attracted by the fine cuisine of chef Thierry Faucher and his team. On offer is a six-course *menu dégustation* which might sound dangerously close to gluttony, but we consumed the modest-sized portions of delicately prepared food without remorse. We started with a flavoursome pheasant broth sprinkled liberally with fresh coriander which set the tone for the ensuing delicacies. The first fish course was a colourful creation of oven-cooked red mullet offset by slow-cooked sweet red peppers and lightly caramelised onions, all served with a beetroot coulis. This was followed by another great fish course of marked contrasts, with a choice between sea bream, roasted in rosemary and thyme and accompanied by leeks cooked in a buttery sauce, or perfectly cooked sea bass on a bed of *trompette de la mort* mushrooms married unusually with a pronounced lobster sauce. The meat course consisted of either gamey wild duck in a cep mushroom sauce studded with peppercorns, or succulent lamb delicately roasted with a head of garlic. This feast was rounded off by a slice of ewe's milk tomme, and a good selection of desserts including the chef's winning *quenelle de chocolat* in an unctuous saffron cream. Just opposite is the sister restaurant, La Cave de l'Os à Moëlle, which serves earthy dishes in an informal *table d'hôte* atmosphere.

Le Père Claude
51 av de la Motte-Picquet, 15th (01.47.34.03.05). Mº La-Motte-Picquet-Grenelle. **Open** daily noon-2pm; 7.30-10.30pm. **Average** €53. **Prix fixe** €22, €24. **Lunch menu** €27 (Mon-Fri). **Credit** AmEx, MC, V.
The house speciality here is clear from the outset with Asterix-style hunks of meat sizzling on a flaming spit behind the bar: this is an ideal place for carnivores with hefty appetites. The starters cover traditional, solid fare, such as farmhouse terrine, homemade foie gras (though the latter in rather disappointingly parsimonious portions), or an excellent salad of tasty crayfish in a light vinaigrette. The main courses focus on the rôtisserie, with the odd fish dish as a concession to lighter appetites. The mixed grill is a meaty feast of thinly sliced steak, black pudding, chunks of lamb and chicken, all with the trademark spit-roast taste. Under this mound of meat was a surprisingly fine *gratin dauphinois*, delightfully creamy with wafer-thin slices of potato and – of course – a golden crust. The crème brûlée was good, and again very much a beltline-expander. This restaurant is frequented by affluent and stocky locals, Japanese tourists and – given the photos adorning its walls – the odd ravenous celeb.

Les P'tits Bouchons de François Clerc
32 bd du Montparnasse, 15th (01.45.48.52.03/www.lesbouchonsdefrancoisclerc.com). Mº Duroc or Montparnasse. **Open** Mon-Fri noon-2.30pm, 7-10.30pm ; Sat 7-10.30pm. **Prix fixe** €31.25 (dinner only). **Lunch menu** €21.19. **Credit** AmEx, MC, V.
Les Bouchons is a place where Bacchus and Dionysus might have liked to meet even though the wines are no longer sold 'at cost' as they were before. The restaurant now makes the totally unverifiable claim that it has 'the cheapest wine list in France'. A glass of velvety Château Fonrazade Saint Emilion Grand Cru 1996 proved good value at €5.18, given the estate's prestigious location just next to Angélus, and the Pernand Vegelesses 1998 at €3.04 was just an average buy as was the Pouilly Fumé '99 at €4.42. The *menu* is decent enough and the cooking seems to have improved since our last visit as attested by our starters of a piquant, ultra-fresh crayfish gazpacho with creamy *pistou* (for a €1.52 supplement) and refreshing tuna carpaccio, although the accompanying vinaigrette was rather too tart. We enjoyed our roasted veal garnished with beans and garden peas sprinkled with diced ham, but although the pike-perch *goujonettes* were tangy with their onion and olive compote, the fish itself lacked flavour. Desserts were delicious, particularly the aniseed-spiked rhubarb crème brûlée, and service was friendly and efficient.

Le Sept/Quinze
29 av de Lowendal, 15th (01.43.06.23.06). Mº Ségur or Cambronne. **Open** Mon-Sat noon-2.30pm, 8-11pm. Closed three weeks in Aug. **Average** €26. **Prix fixe** €23.30 (dinner only). **Lunch menu** €15, €21. **Credit** MC, V.
On the premises of a 1950s vintage café not far from UNESCO, a young team has created an attractive dining room whose ochre walls and wood tables lend it a miscellaneously Mediterranean allure. This backdrop sets off a stylish young crowd in the evening, who linger over well-cooked and inventive dishes that are variously Provençal, Italian and Spanish. The brief menu is complemented by daily specials, which may include a delicious homemade vegetable soup with a dab of saffron *aïoli*, or linguine with fresh goat's cheese and roasted pine kernels. Grilled polenta with roasted red peppers and parmesan shavings was pleasantly seasoned with thyme, while very good main courses of chicken breast stuffed with goat's cheese, and veal scallops sautéed with sage were accompanied by a bowl of potato purée. Good desserts included *panna cotta* and an excellent take on a *millefeuille* with layers of crunchy caramelised pastry alternating with lemony cream. The Château Haute Fontaine Corbières from the brief wine list was very drinkable at €15. In addition to its talented chef, this place has affable service and an agreeable soundtrack, giving it the young, edgy atmosphere of a restaurant in New York's Tribeca or London's Soho.

Le Troquet
21 rue François-Bonvin, 15th (01.45.66.89.00). Mº Cambronne or Sèvres-Lecourbe. **Open** Tue-Sat noon-2.30pm, 7.30-11pm. Closed three weeks in Aug, one week at Christmas. **Prix fixe** €28, €30 (dinner only). **Lunch menu** €22, €24. **Credit** MC, V.
After polishing his technique in Christian Constant's famed kitchens, the burly Christian Etchebest took the reins of this bistro from his uncle a few years ago. Decorated with 1930s light fixtures and bawdy drawings alongside a proudly displayed Crillon certificate, the restaurant feels deceptively old-fashioned. If Etchebest's Basque-inspired cooking has occasional country touches, his style is far more modern than the surroundings suggest. Choosing from a limited but tempting lunch *menu* , we started with fresh goat cheese on crisp pastry, sprinkled with Espelette pepper and served with just-cooked red cabbage. Vegetable soup sounded virtuous but, to our delight, turned out to be a creamy, cardamom-scented blend, which we ladled ourselves on to foie gras and a spoonful of *crème fraîche*. Both mains were stunning: a thick tuna steak wrapped in cured ham was served with a rich squash purée, while a plump farmer's chicken breast stuffed with *tapenade* was accompanied by deeply flavoured cabbage cooked with juniper, pork and olive oil. Desserts of soft meringue with roasted figs, and a *crème renversée* (upside-down custard) with raspberries, were less remarkable. But we could hardly complain, especially given the excellent service, with Etchebest bidding farewell to each diner.

16th Arrondissement

Le Bistrot des Vignes
1 rue Jean-Bologne, 16th (01.45.27.76.64). Mº Passy or La Muette. **Open** Mon-Thur, Sun noon-2.30pm, 7-10.30pm; Fri, Sat 7-11pm. **Average** €26. **Credit** AmEx, MC, V. **Wheelchair access**.
Although much of the stylish-by-day 16th turns sleepy at night, that could easily change if more people hear about this place. On a quiet street across from Notre-Dame de Passy, Le Bistrot des Vignes is making a subdued noise of its own. There is no *prix fixe*, but the menu is simple enough: all starters are €6.10, main courses €13.60, and desserts or cheese plates €6.10. Among the starters, the artichoke-heart salad garnished with thick ribbons of smoked salmon and poached egg is not to be missed. Duck *confit* was flavourful without being greasy, though the real prize goes to the heavenly garlic potatoes that come with it: brown and crisp on the outside, piping hot inside. An ample *souris d'agneau* (knuckle of lamb) arrived in a small casserole, resting on a bed of beautiful white beans. After this a dark chocolate fondant seemed excessive, so we took the

plunge – and weren't disappointed. Considering the quality of the food, the discreet, café-like atmosphere and the hospitality of English-speaking Eric Corailler and crew, we imagine that this secret will soon get out.

La Butte Chaillot
110bis av Kléber, 16th (01.47.27.88.88). M° Trocadéro. **Open** Mon-Fri, Sun noon-3pm, 7.30-11pm; Sat 7.30-11pm. **Average** €37. **Prix fixe** €30. **Credit** AmEx, DC, MC, V. **Wheelchair access**.
Before this place was *relooké* it was starting to feel a bit like a business-class airport lounge. The large number of American customers probably felt right at home – and a little bit cheated as a consequence. But the architects and designers have done a good job, adding caramel-coloured walls, chocolate chairs and a sort of cigar 'terrace' to the mezzanine and sexy white plastic walkway that were already here. The reason that it attracts so many Americans isn't the decor, it's because the owner is super-chef Guy Savoy. So we were all eager expectation when our seared tuna steak starter with poppyseed, apple and celery *'rémoulade'* winged into view. First impressions, however, were of small mingled with dull – we were shaking the salt-cellar in disbelief. The caramelised sea bream fillet with a risotto of ratatouille vegetables and parmesan came closer to tasting as good as it sounded but it still didn't quite make it. And, sorry to say, those of Guy's boys who weren't just taking it easy that night were simply taking the mickey. We finished with a *coulant* of (as it was to turn out, aptly-named) bitter chocolate before having to point out to the waiter come bill-time that he'd charged us for an extra, totally imaginary pudding. Time, perhaps, for Guy Savoy to make sure this place doesn't forget the basics.

Les Ormes ★
8 rue Chapu, 16th (01.46.47.83.98). M° Exelmans. **Open** Tue-Sat 12.15-2pm, 7.30-10pm. Closed Aug, first week in Jan. **Average** €37. **Prix fixe** €32 (dinner only). **Lunch menu** €21.50, €26. **Credit** AmEx, MC, V.
Although he's tucked away in a tiny, dressy dining room – yellow fabric walls and formally set tables – in a fairly remote part of town, it's worth the trip to discover the cooking of talented young chef Stéphane Molé. Molé trained with Joël Robuchon, and his pedigree shows in delicious cooking that's at once lusty and refined. The brief, good-value *prix-fixe* – three courses plus cheese from the excellent *fromagerie* Alléosse – changes almost daily according to what Molé finds in the market, but typical dishes include *quenelles de brochet* (pike-perch dumplings) with *sauce américaine*, snails and wild mushrooms with a sorrel *timbale*, pumpkin soup garnished with morsels of sautéed lamb sweetbreads, John Dory with wild mushrooms and artichoke hearts in a verjus sauce, and boneless veal knuckle with *gnocchi*. Desserts are excellent, too, from a runny *moelleux au chocolat* to an individual *tarte Tatin*, and the wine list offers many good buys, including a superb Cornas at €43. A favourite of sedate locals, the dining room draws its liveliness from a growing number of word-of-mouth diners from other parts of town.

Le Petit Rétro
5 rue Mesnil, 16th (01.44.05.06.05). M° Victor-Hugo. **Open** Mon-Fri noon-2.30pm, 8-10.30pm; Sat 8-10.30pm. Closed Aug. **Average** €30. **Lunch menu** €17, €21. **Credit** AmEx, MC, V.
One reason to go to Le Petit Rétro, with its art nouveau floral tiles, zinc bar and tall mirrors dating from 1910, is that it's a listed monument. Another good reason is the generous portions of traditional French food, prepared with flair. The dark wood and closely packed tables lend an intimate feel that encourages conversation with strangers. We sat next to two distinguished old ladies from the neighbourhood, dressed in Chanel. On the other side, we talked with an expat couple who urged us to write a negative review as this is their favourite restaurant in the area. They ordered the top-notch foie gras, and the *escargots* served in a pastry shell with a luscious cream sauce. We opted for the starter of the day, the prawn and asparagus salad served on a bed of chicory dressed in lemon and olive oil. The presentation was a delight and the prawns were sweet and abundant. The tangy goat's cheese pasta was homemade and showered in a sweet tomato coulis that created a pungent pairing. Mains were also reliably good: four whole, perfectly fresh red mullets came served on a bed of just-wilted spinach. A crisp white Sancerre from the judicious wine list made a pleasant match. For dessert, our neighbours insisted that we try the *moelleux au chocolat*, a warm and rich ending to a fine meal. Bookings are essential.

Le Scheffer
22 rue Scheffer, 16th (01.47.27.81.11). M° Trocadéro. **Open** Mon-Sat noon-2.30pm, 7.30-10.30pm. Closed Sat in July and Aug, 25 Dec-2 Jan. **Average** €24. **Credit** AmEx, MC, V. **Wheelchair access**.
A stone's throw from the busy Trocadéro, Le Scheffer is a tourist-free haven for French family-style dining. OK, so the BCBG couples (French Sloanes), some with immaculate *enfants*, aren't your average family, but their palates are reassuringly classical. Start with *os à moelle*, unctuous marrow bone which you slather on bread and top with coarse salt, or a hearty slice of duck terrine paired with onion jam: both guaranteed to take the edge off your appetite. Main courses include *confit de canard maison*, a crispy rendition of that bistro standard, and salmon grilled *à l'unilatéral* (a one-sided cooking method that ensures moistness is retained) and topped with fresh herbs. We washed it all down with a tasty *pichet* of Chinon (well-priced at €8) and braced ourselves for dessert. A mound of profiteroles, drenched in rich, dark chocolate, vied with the fluffy *île flottante* for top sweet and we were glad of both. There's no *avant-garde* gastro-nomy here, no unbeatable ambiance, and your dinner will probably have lows as well as highs. But there's something inescapably 'authentic' about a night at Le Scheffer – checkered tablecloths, vintage posters and a stern *patronne* not withstanding. Be sure to book ahead; even on Monday, it's a packed house.

17th Arrondissement

Le Bistrot d'à Côté Flaubert
10 rue Gustave-Flaubert, 17th (01.42.67.05.81/www.michelrostang.com). **Open** daily 12.15-2.30pm, 7.30-11pm. Closed one week in mid-Aug. **Average** €46. **Lunch menu** €27. **Credit** AmEx, MC, V.
Michel Rostang pioneered the star chef's bistro when he took over the old *épicerie* next door in 1987, kept the pretty period interior and began serving up what he felt genuine bistro food should be. Today, the marble racks carry wine bottles (go for the excellent-value house Bordeaux red) and the shelves are lined with vintage Michelin guides, toby jugs and 19th-century novelty pitchers. Of course, the great thing about this chef's bistro is that you get things you wouldn't normally expect in a bistro at all. While we've eaten at other members of the Bistrot d'à Côté before we can't help feeling that the original, nestling under the watchful eye of mother next door, is best. Starters, especially, have a degree of sophistication that surely reflect *haute cuisine* roots. We started with a wonderfully complex *pressé* of asparagus, sundried tomatoes and *coppa* ham accompanied by a raw artichoke and parmesan salad to create a fantastic array of textures, and marinated *lisette* (baby mackerel fillets) with mushrooms, carrots and mesclun. Main courses are simpler but well prepared, with the emphasis on fine-quality meat (there's always a beef offering of the day) and in a democratic move you have a choice of accompaniments. We opted for lamb from the Pyrenees in a crumble crust with garlic shortbread biscuit and a bowl of smooth purée and *dos de lieu* (pollack) with spicebread crust and *jus*, with *légumes niçois*, which, while reflecting the season, were not as good as the perfect julienned vegetables we had adored in the autumn. Then on to fruit salad with sprig of thyme and lemon and thyme ice cream, and the tiny pots of chocolate that have become a Rostang classic. Just what a bistro should be like – only better.

Le Clou
132 rue Cardinet, 17th (01.42.27.36.78). M° Malesherbes. **Open** Mon-Fri noon-2.30pm, 7.30-10.30pm. Closed two weeks in Aug. **Average** €30. **Lunch menu** €18. **Credit** AmEx, MC, V. **Wheelchair access**.
This red-fronted former brasserie is somewhat off the beaten track, but its combination of honest cooking, smiling service and terrific value makes it well worth seeking out. Though keeping costs down means that tables are crammed together, the decor is classier than you'd expect, with white tablecloths, decent glassware and an abundance of dried flowers. Chef and owner Christian Leclou eschews gimmickry in favour of careful sourcing of ingredients, producing rustic dishes like a chunky *terrine de volaille*, or a more refined *croustillant d'escargots*, made with *petits-gris* and filo pastry. Fish features strongly on the daily-changing menu, with, for example, a warm salad of *coquilles St Jacques* and cod cheeks, or a huge fillet of pan-fried sea bass, resting on chopped, roasted tomatoes. But the star (and one of the few permanent menu fixtures) must be the rosemary-scented, five-hour simmered, *confit d'épaule d'agneau*, meltingly tender and served with a smoky aubergine purée. Desserts maintain the high standard, with a homemade *nougat glacé*, studded with walnuts and candied angelica, and an excellent *moelleux au chocolat*. Wines are sourced just as carefully as the food – Leclou tasting and buying directly from the *vignerons* in many instances – making for some truly remarkable prices.

Macis & Muscade
110 rue Legendre, 17th (01.42.26.62.26). M° La Fourche. **Open** Tue-Fri noon-2pm, 8-10.15pm, Sat 8-10.15pm, Sun noon-2pm. **Prix fixe** €23 (dinner only). **Lunch menu** €16. **Credit** AmEx, DC, MC, V.
Tucked away in the gallopingly trendy Batignolles district, this popular bistro is not only

Le Bouclard has carved itself a choice reputation

great value for good, unusual food but an interesting close-up on how a Paris neighbourhood gentrifies. Retired shopkeepers and SNCF employees walking their dogs pass by the front windows and peer in curiously at the cross-section of moneyed couples – from young and hip with media jobs to mid-40s bohos who are currently buying up nearby flats. What makes this place more interesting than usual is the imaginative but judicious use of floral essences to enhance and elongate the natural tastes of their good produce. A few drops of strawberry vinegar brightened a lentil salad with sliced Morteau sausage, and ditto the use of neroli, or orange-flower essence, in a salad of sautéed monkfish on a bed of lamb's lettuce. Rather than a gimmick, this is actually a subtle, fascinating and usually successful experiment. Rabbit roasted with prunes and gently dosed with davana, an Indian herb that smells like figs, was excellent, while the Osmanthus flower used with duck breast and peaches sort of went missing. Finally, a chocolate *marquise* was lit up by cardamom. Pleasant service and good wines complete the experience.

Le Morosophe

83 rue Legendre, 17th (01.53.06.82.82). M° La Fourche. **Open** Mon-Fri noon-2.30pm, 8-10.45pm; Sat 8-10.45pm. **Average** €23. **Prix fixe** €22.87. **Lunch menu** €11.43, €16.77. **Credit** AmEx, MC, V.

This café transformed into a warm bistro with bare wood tables and strips of African fabric on the walls is extremely popular with the young trendies who are colonising the Batignolles neighbourhood. The friendly, cigar-smoking owner knows most of the regulars but is a genial host to all comers, and his interesting menu mixes trad bistro fare with various foreign dishes. You can start with roasted marrow bones, tabouleh, a delicious courgette flan, pasta salad with pesto sauce and ham or ravioli with three different fillings, and then choose from a daily special – a *coquelet* with sautéed mushrooms on a recent night – or interesting main courses such as *andouillette* with snails, an appetising *boudin blanc* or a vegetarian plate, among other options. Go with the chocolate fondant cake or the fruit gratin for dessert. The owner is rightfully proud of his good-value wines from the Languedoc-Roussillon.

La Table de Lucullus

129 rue Legendre, 17th (01.40.25.02.68). M° La Fourche. **Open** Tue-Fri 12.30-2pm, 7.30-11pm; Sat 7.30-11pm. Closed Aug, one week in Feb/Mar. **Average** €43. **Lunch menu** €21.34. **Credit** MC, V. **Wheelchair access.**

Though the decor may seem inauspicious, this pocket bistro is the workplace of one of Paris' most interesting young chefs. Self-taught Nicholas Vagnon has a keen palate, demonstrated by a market menu that is inventive without ever missing a beat. The chef himself came to take the order at the table next to us and not only cheerfully translated his menu into excellent English but stuck up for himself when someone said he didn't like French fish sauces. 'You haven't tried mine yet,' he said amiably. 'I don't use cream and butter.' Excellent bread got the meal off to a fine start, and Vagnon and his waiter recommended two first-rate wines, a white Montlouis from the Loire and a fruity Morgon. Starters of langoustine carpaccio and brilliantly garnished foie gras were as delicious as they were impressive, and main courses were excellent, too. Haddock with artichoke hearts in a lemon juice and olive oil emulsion was perfectly cooked, while a casserole of shredded lamb, cracked wheat, fresh mint and dried fruit was hearty but delicate. We finished with a wonderful cheese course and fresh figs with raspberries. It's essential to reserve.

Tante Jeanne

116, bd Péreire, 17th (01.43.80.88.68/ www.bearnard-loiseau.com). M° Péreire. **Open** Mon-Fri noon-2.30pm, 7-10.30pm. Closed Aug. **Average** €53. **Prix fixe** €37. **Lunch menu** €30. **Credit** AmEx, MC, V. **Wheelchair access.**

Like many high-profile chefs, Burgundian star Bernard Loiseau has opened up a number of cheaper outlets. In Paris these form a gaggle of 'Aunts'. Poor old Auntie Jeanne suffers initially from her decoration, which borrows from all decades of the last century and ends up looking like the dining room of a pretentious, three-star provincial hotel. The staff are welcoming and plentiful, but we were somewhat surprised to be brought a plate of thin, pre-sliced *saucisson* and a bowl of potato crisps in a city where amuse-bouches have been raised to an art form. Rather than the €37 *menu*, we opted for two courses from the more interesting-looking *carte*. The starters were disappointing: a dish of crab meat on Tarbais beans was a good concept spoilt by an overwhelming dill dressing, while a very cold rabbit and olive terrine was timidly flavoured albeit generous. Things perked up with our main courses – a *palombe* (wood pigeon) with a *grand-mère* garnish of potatoes, bacon and mushrooms was carved at the table with some ceremony. Slightly too rare and tepid, it was tasty enough, but the legs, which were removed for flash grilling and served on a salad, were rendered acridly unpleasant. The winning dish was a good piece of hot foie gras served on an excellent sweet corn pancake. The wine has a gentle mark-up and our Brouilly for €19.82 was light and delicious. Good *mignardises* with the coffee almost made us regret not having ordered dessert from the traditional selection.

Branches: Tante Marguerite, 5 rue de Bourgogne, 7th (01.45.51.79.42); Tante Louise 41 rue Boissy-d'Anglas, 8th (01.42.65.06.85).

Tête de Goinfre/ Cave du Cochon

16/18, rue Jacquemont, 17th (01.42.29.89.80). M° La Fourche. **Open** Mon-Sat noon-2pm, 8-10.30pm. **Average** €22. **Credit** MC, V.

The Tête de Goinfre started 12 years ago and its neighbouring overspill the Cave du Cochon has been going for five: two restaurants rolled into one with a common kitchen and, judging by the numbers they were turning away, they're on to something. We ate in the latter; a jolly yellow bistro with red gingham tablecloths and lots of porky paraphernalia in the form of paintings, pho tos and ornaments. A hearty menu (go hungry) featured an old-school fixed *plat du jour*, and it being Thursday this meant *tête de veau* – alas no takers! Instead we started with the *bricoles de Goinfre – andouille*, garlic sausage, an aromatic pork and hazelnut terrine and crudités, which could have served two and was great value at €6.40 – and a salad of smoked *magret*. Next up, top notch black pudding with apple and mash and a rather less successful salmon steak, curiously served with a prawn cocktail sauce and more mash. It's probably wise to stick to the meat dishes: *bavette* with shallots, duck *confit*, and pan-fried veal escalope. A fruity house red was fairly priced at €7.93 the carafe. Desserts are simple: chocolate mousse, crème caramel or tart of the day. The hard-pushed service (the staff ran back and forth to the kitchen next door) was amicable but it lacked the twinkly charm of the moustached owner, Jean-Pierre Starck, who presides in the Tête de Goinfre.

Le Troyon

4 rue Troyon, 17th (01.40.68.99.40). M° Charles de Gaulle-Etoile. **Open** Mon-Fri noon-2.30pm, 8-11pm. **Average** €30. **Prix fixe** €30.45. **Credit** AmEx, MC, V

The tastefully understated interior of Le Troyon, all ochre walls and brown and cream chess-patterned banquettes, promises a sophisticated, modern dining experience. That is, to some extent, what follows – although the quality of the fare remains disappointingly patchy. Still, chef Jean-Marc Notelet's way with herbs and spices gives dishes an original twist which attracts a varied crowd of Parisian regulars and clued-in tourists. We opted for the *prix fixe menu*, choosing from a mix of light seasonal dishes and robust classics. The mussels in a cream and herb sauce with mushrooms, green beans and peas, although beautifully presented, were rather insipid, while tangy morel mushrooms with garlic and shallots couldn't have been better. The grilled saddle of lamb (for two) didn't live up to its billing: the topping of mixed Oriental herbs failed to disguise the flavourless meat. A touch lazy, too, to team the meat with identikit vegetables to the ones used in the mussels starter. Things were redeemed somewhat by excellent desserts: warm raspberries with yoghurt ice-cream and a superbly crunchy yet melt-in-the-mouth *moelleux au chocolat*. Service was polite but slow.

18th Arrondissement

Le Bouclard

1 rue Cavalotti, 18th (01.45.22.60.01). M° Place de Clichy. **Open** Tue-Fri noon-2.30pm, 8-11.30pm; Mon, Sat 8-11.30pm **Average** €46. **Lunch menu** €16, €21. **Credit** AmEx, MC, V.

The eclectic menu in this compact, traditional-style bistro a short walk from the Moulin Rouge highlights French rural cooking, with dishes such as *cassoulet* and prized regional meats including T-bone veal steak from Corrèze and saddle of lamb from Limousin. Owner Michel Bonnemort also makes tourists feel at home by offering European culinary landmarks: along with rabbit terrine and foie gras *maison* there are starters such as Spanish serrano ham (which we found too dry) and swordfish carpaccio. Dover sole is also on offer, as well as vegetarian dishes and the ever-so-British apple crumble. French gourmets of the old school are likely to pounce on the leeks with *gribiche* sauce – mayonnaise with chopped eggs and capers. The bistro makes a particularly potent, mustardy variety. In contrast, our haddock *parmentier*, a fish pie with mashed potatoes, lacked flavour, while the accompanying green salad, although huge, had a vinaigrette that tasted dangerously close to the bottled kind. The roasted farm pigeon, however, was tender and fragrant, served with a mini casserole of fresh garden peas. The apple crumble, although too sticky, had a redeeming, pleasant cinnamony flavour. The wine list is limited, given the pricey *carte*, but the Saumur Champigny turned out to be an excellent choice at €21.34.

L'Entracte

44 rue d'Orsel, 18th (01.46.06.93.41). M° Abbesses or Anvers. **Open** Wed-Sat noon-2pm, 7-10pm; Sun noon-2pm. Closed Aug. **Average** €30. **Credit** MC, V.

Tucked away in a side street near Sacré Coeur, this little bistro pulls a crowd of locals, which includes the winsomely flamboyant, always-dressed-in-blue female impersonator Michou and his band, for delicious home-style cooking. Not easy in a neighbourhood under siege from tour buses. There is something confidential about this address, which adds to the fun of a night out here. Be sure to book as it's always packed. Run by Carlos and Sonia, he in the dining room and she in the kitchen, it's a relaxing, friendly place. Start with the onion soup or herring marinated in white wine, and then try the rack of lamb or *steak au poivre* before finishing up with a slice of luscious fruit tart.

L'Etrier Bistrot

154 rue Lamarck, 18th (01.42.29.14.01). M° Guy-Moquet. **Open** Tue-Sat noon-2pm, 7.30-10.30pm. Closed three weeks in Aug. **Average** €38. **Prix fixe** €19.82 (dinner only). **Lunch menu** €12.50, €18.29. **Credit** MC, V.

Scarlet curtains, candles and Verdi on the CD player make l'Etrier that teensy-weensiest bit camp. But in a district that generally prefers to take a walk on the dull side, that's not a bad thing. We came in from the shivering cold to a warm welcome, a complimentary glass of dry white and a saucer of hazelnuts. Not a bad start. First courses, though, were a bit of a let-down. Avoid the *endive Tatin* unless sugary chicory is your thing, and beware the *estouffade* of snails cooked in veal stock with carrots marinated in red wine: it tasted like a musty cellar. The tables are well-spaced at l'Etrier, conducive to conversation which, at ours, had turned negative by the time the mains – sea bass, and a slab of warm foie gras melting over a fillet of beef – showed up. But these were good. Very good. We were, only then, glad that we had come in.

La Galère des Rois

8 rue Cavallotti 18th (01.42.93.34.58). M° Place de Clichy. **Open** Mon-Fri noon-2.30pm, 7.30-11pm; Sat 7.30-11pm. Closed three weeks in Aug, one week in Feb. **Average** €34. **Lunch menu** €14.50. **Credit** MC, V. **Wheelchair access.**

A skip and a jump from the splendours of Cézanne's studio is this curious and charming street which, at nightfall, turns into a picture gallery as the shopkeepers lower their shop fronts' metal gates which have been painted by the students from the local art school. Come at lunch when they serve a cracking *menu* to a mix of local workers. Georges Bataille fans will enjoy the *oeufs mollets*, all the sexier for being ever-so-slightly undercooked and ravishingly accompanied by succulent slices of hot duck's liver. Warming to our duck theme, we chose a pretty good *confit de canard* as our main. Fatty? For sure. But you might as well quibble about olive oil being oily. For pudding, there being nothing duck-based, we went for recommendable praline chocolate *croquant* with *crème anglaise*. Drop in after a morning stroll around the nearby Montmartre Cemetery.

Le Moulin à Vins

6 rue Burq, 18th (01.42.52.81.27). M° Abbesses. **Open** Tue-Sat 6pm-2am. Closed last three weeks in Aug, one week at Christmas. **Average** €31. **Credit** MC, V.

The spirit of Montmartre – a little rustic, a little wild and very *bon vivant* – is alive in this bistro-on-the-hill. This is largely thanks to the *patronne* Danielle Bertin-Denis, who did the world a big favour by giving up a career in banking to open up this place. Her deeply impressive wine list is the result of regular travels through France in search of the tremendously good for surprisingly little. – and, if you don't know your stuff, she'll take pleasure in choosing for you. All the *charcuterie* is specially delivered from the Béarn, home region of Dumas' Three Musketeers, Dani herself and the best *boudin* in France. We kept to south-western specialities for the mains, with a duck *à l'orange* that was tender, unfatty and utterly delicious, before lingering over our bottle of Vacqueyras with a shared selection of cheese from the platter. It gets noisy in here, it's very smoky and the tables are crammed in pretty tight. But it's a treat – and if you're very, very lucky, Dani might even sing.

Aux Négociants

27 rue Lambert, 18th (01.46.06.15.11). M° Château-Rouge. **Open** Mon noon-12.30pm, Tue-Fri noon-2.30pm, 8-10.30pm. Closed Aug. **Average** €23. **Credit** MC, V.

Don't be put off by the cramped tables or the prime view of the public toilets outside; this place belongs to a dying breed of rustic bistros. Locals stand at the bar debating furiously and there are photos on the wall to prove it. The best choice of apéritif is surely the Coteaux de Layon, a fortified white wine from the Loire Valley. The attitude to the food here is generous: our traditional rabbit pâté starter was simply left on our table in its Pyrex dish with a large earthenware pot of *cornichons* for us to help ourselves. There's little choice and no frills but the hearty portions and comforting homemade food make for a real treat. The approach to wine is equally down-to-earth – you order a bottle and return what you haven't drunk, paying according to how many markers have been revealed. The *boeuf bourguignon* was better than any we'd had in Burgundy and the strawberry tartlets and chocolate mousse were as good as *grand-mère*'s. Not an ideal place for a first date but a brilliant choice for when you crave genuine French home cooking.

Le Petit Caboulot ★

6 pl Jacques-Froment, 18th (01.46.27.19.00). M° Guy-Moquet. **Open** Mon-Fri noon-2pm, 8-11pm, Sat noon-2:30pm, 8-11pm. Closed two weeks in Aug. **Average** €25. **Lunch menu** €10. **Credit** MC, V. **Wheelchair access.**

When the *confit de canard* arrived crisped to perfection, we knew we would come back. With all the trappings of a friendly neighbourhood bistro, and then some, you'll wish this were your local; and judging from the crowd on a Monday night that's no secret. *Brique de chevre aux pommes*, a crisp pastry of apple and melting goat's cheese on a bed of salad, is the place to start. Tasty, very tasty, and not too filling. *Foie gras maison* is also well worth a try. The *confit* (ask for it *bien grillé*) – dark, succulent, and with a skin that crunched like heaven – was one of the best we've had in a restaurant and the haddock *brandade*, flakes of smoked fish blended with moist potato purée and oven-browned, was 100 per cent comfort food. We weren't sure it could get better – until the *tarte Tatin* arrived. Ubiquitous in bistros but so rarely right, this one, caramelised to the core, had us booking our return. Mosaic pillars, a huge curved bar and a vast collection of old

Restaurant - Wine Bar
LE CHAUDRON DES SORCIÈRES
and MOUSTIQUE
IN CONCERT EVERY SATURDAY EVENING

IN THE BASTILLE AREA

WELCOMES YOU
MONDAY TO SATURDAY
FROM 6PM TO 2AM
RESERVATIONS:
01.40.09.04.47

7 RUE DE LA FORGE ROYALE, 11TH. M° LEDRU ROLLIN

---

foodunlimited

open non-stop daily
from 12 to 11 pm
except mondays and
tuesdays from 12 to 6 pm
great sunday brunch !

restaurant coffee-shop
168, rue saint martin 75003 paris - tel: 01 42 77 06 06
a few steps from the Pompidou Center

Le Polidor

In the heart of the Quartier Latin, a historic surrounding dating back to 1845… Enjoy fine French cuisine.
Prix fixe: €18, à la carte: avg. €20, Lunch menu: €9

Big choice of French regional wines and a unique selection of spirits on offer.

41 rue Monsieur-le-Prince, 6th, M° Odéon.
Tel: 01.43.26.95.34. Open daily for lunch and dinner.

Bojangles
American Restaurant

SOULFOOD ★ JAZZ ★ BON TEMPS

47 rue Rodier, 9th. M°Anvers
Tel: 01.42.81.98.20 - e-mail: bojangles@paris.com

enamel adverts (look for the Arabic Kodak) evoke a bygone era. There's an extensive wine list to match all budgets; our Alsatian white at €14.50, cool, fruity and a match for the foie gras, tasted like something more pricey.

Le Petit Robert

10 rue Cauchois, 18th (01.46.06.04.46). M° Blanche. **Open** Tue-Sat 8.15-11.30pm. Closed 20 Jul-25 Aug. **Prix fixe** €24. **Credit** MC, V.
Just around the corner from the red lights of Pigalle, this cosy restaurant is an unexpected find. It's made up of three small connecting rooms with wood-panelled walls where art and newspaper clippings hang in sturdy gold frames. Leopard-print bar stools and soft eclectic jazz music add to the homely feel of the place. The menu is handwritten and the prices democratic: €24 for three courses. Starters include Russian cucumber soup, oyster mushrooms with lemon, fresh anchovies, spicy pâté and a jellied *museau de boeuf* but we opted for the fresh artichoke – the tastiest we'd ever had, with gorgeous, tender purple and green leaves to dip in a fine vinaigrette. The chicken with preserved lemons and farmer's black pudding were both pleasantly rustic and served with hearty baked potato slices and soft green runner beans. The dessert list is short but original. A minute pot of tart ginger-flavoured cream rounded off our meal.

19th Arrondissement

Le Bistro du 19

45 rue des Alouettes, 19th (01.42.00.84.85). M° Buttes Chaumont or Botzaris. **Open** Sun, Tue-Fri noon-2.30pm, 7.30-11pm; Sat, Mon 7.30-11pm. Closed Aug. **Average** €29. **Prix fixe** €12.05, €28.80. **Credit** MC, V.
Amid the mindless '80s French pop music, cooking diplomas, froofy curtains, ribbons, hearts and plug-in angel, serious attention is paid to each dining detail: goose *rillettes* to begin, the palate-blasting sorbet in Cognac between courses, and the throwback 'ladies' menu' *sans* prices. Dishes can be had *à la carte*, but you're far better off signing up for the *prix fixe*, which gives you a full choice of three courses, plus Champagne (in a chilled flute), wine and coffee. We started with a salmon, artichoke, walnut and radish salad and the grilled *escargots* with garlic nut oil, both inventive and fresh. The duck with roast peaches was equally pleasing, and a monkfish and fennel stew, chock-full of veggies, served as further evidence of the chef's skill. Desserts such as made-to-order profiteroles and *tarte maison* lived up to expectations set by earlier courses. The exceptional food and value will entice us back.

La Cave Gourmande ★

10 rue du Général Brunet, 19th (01.40.40.03.30). M° Botzaris. **Open** Mon-Fri 12.15pm-2.30pm, 7.30-10.30pm. **Prix fixe** 28.97 (dinner only). **Lunch menu** 24.39. **Credit** MC, V.
A meal at this excellent and very relaxed bistro will make you wonder how it can be that American-born Mark Singer is so much the quiet man of the Paris resaturant scene, especially since he has a long and impressive CV (a succession of distinguished French kitchens since he began his career at the age of 14). Singer's latest setting is the restaurant where chef Eric Frechon, now at Le Bristol, forged his reputation, and Singer's menu offers a comfortable continuity in terms of both price and quality. The dining room itself doesn't amount to much – think renovated café – and service could be friendlier considering the setting, but overall there's a mood of bonhommie in the room as a contented, mostly local crowd and a few well-advised and pennywise gourmets from other parts of town feast on perfectly cooked rustic-chic dishes such as a cream of white bean soup with mussels and cockles, strips of duck breast with savoy cabbage and hazelnuts, and grilled scallops with tiny potatoes in a pleasantly seasoned cream sauce.

Restaurant L'Hermès

23 rue Mélingue, 19th (01.42.39.94.70). M° Pyrénées. **Open** Tues-Sat noon-2.30pm, 7.30-10pm. Closed Aug. **Average** €30. **Prix fixe** €22.10. **Lunch menu** €12.20. **Credit** MC, V.
L'Hermès returned from summer 2001 holidays with an interior facelift, now all vivid yellows and floral, country-print tablecloths. The cheeriness extends beyond the decor: we were thoroughly welcomed and there is now a non-smoking room. We witnessed a genuine love of invention and playfulness, from the poetically phrased, weekly-changing *menu* to the south-western-inspired food. A langoustine, foie gras and veggie medley, stuffed into a crispy crêpe, kept pace with the other starter, a slice of silky-smooth eggplant custard with tomato. *Confit de canard* can be dry and tough, but our watchful waiter brought over an incredibly moist and tender thigh, served with a tart pickle relish, blinis, potato gratin and roasted tomatoes. A cod fillet in richly-flavoured saffron sauce also made a splash. Try expertly crafted desserts such as prune, Armagnac and orange flower water cake. Wines are on the pricey side.

20th Arrondissement

Le Bistro des Soupirs (Chez Raymonde)

49 rue de la Chine, 20th (01.44.62.93.31). M° Gambetta. **Open** Tue-Sat noon-2.30pm, 7.30-9.45pm. Closed 12-28 Aug. **Average** €34. **Prix fixe** €13.50 (two courses), €15 (three courses). **Credit** MC, V. **Wheelchair access.**
Le Bistro des Soupirs, aka 'chez Raymonde', is an oddly thriving old world bistro. We were seated in a twee room in the back with net curtains, bird-patterned tablecloths and baskets of dusty silk flowers. The unseasonal menu, heavy on classics, offered starters between €6-€11 and main courses up to €23 which were all served with *'pommes au couteau-specialité maison'*, (aka chips). *Oeufs cocottes crème de morilles* and *crottin de chèvre aux amandes* were both unremarkable: the mushrooms, bland; the goat's cheese, dry. The main courses arrived after a painfully long wait, animated by the *patronne* complaining to a neighbouring table about a recent debilitating hygiene inspection and her unsuccessful attempts to sell the restaurant. Veal kidneys, nicely pink in a mustard sauce, were served with the obligatory chips. The duck breast and green bean salad from the blackboard included four tiny shavings of duck, cold cooked carrots and the kind of white dressing more commonly found on a green salad with a *croque monsieur* in a tabac. Dessert, a rather solid crème caramel, was pronounced *'maison'* with a proud grunt. The bill for all this, washed down with a half jug of Provence rosé, came to a hefty €59.46 – sigh.

Le Bistrot des Capucins

27 av Gambetta, 20th (01.46.36.74.75/ www.le-bistrot-des-capucins.com). M° Père Lachaise or Gambetta. **Open** Tue-Sat noon-2pm, 7.30-10pm; Sat 7.30-10.30. Closed three weeks in Aug; one week Christmas/New Year. **Average** €30. **Prix fixe** €17 (Tue-Fri), €19 (Sat), €23. **Credit** AmEx, MC, V.
Caught between tradition and the trendiness of nearby Oberkampf, the streets around Père Lachaise offer slim pickings for gourmets. Gérard Fouché aims to change that with his cheerful bistro, which is popular with food-loving locals. They come here not for the spruced-up-café decor – pink paper over orange tablecloths, cheap white chairs, horrid floral curtains – but for the good-value, if slightly inconsistent, *prix fixe*. A *pressé* of leeks and fine foie gras, held together with tasty jelly, came with a superfluous creamy white sauce. Another starter, the *duo de ravioles*, proved to be unexciting green and red ravioli in a fresh-tasting but too buttery wild-mushroom sauce. More inspired was a fillet of grey mullet – an often-neglected fish – in red wine sauce with sweet onion jam and smooth, lemony celeriac purée. *Entrecôte d'Aubrac* sounded tempting, but the steak had too much fat and the thick-cut *frites* were just a little too dry. Fouché makes a real effort with desserts: we tried his *cannellé*, a moist Bordeaux cake served here with melon sorbet and dried apricot purée, and an ill-judged *parfait glacé* with lavender flowers and honey, rather too much like eating the sachet from your underwear drawer. Service by a rugby player is efficient, though it slows down as the dining room fills up. He thoughtfully recommended the cheapest wine, a pleasantly fruity €10 Côtes du Frontonnais.

Arty eaters congregate at Le Zéphyr

Café Noir ★

15 rue St-Blaise, 20th (01.40.09.75.80). M° Porte de Bagnolet. **Open** daily 7pm-midnight. Closed 1 May, Christmas and New Year. **Average** €28. **Credit** MC, V.
One of several restaurants along this cobbled, pedestrian street, Café Noir has a compact but blissfully quiet terrace in summer. It would be a shame, though, to miss the quirky interior with its collections of hats and coffee pots – an Italian mocha machine done up as a puppet hangs over the bar. Packed on a Saturday night despite highish prices for the area, Café Noir has the feel of a restaurant that has hit its stride. Our meal started with refreshing pinwheels of smoked salmon and avocado, served with a nicely dressed salad. Tasty plaice with pesto, accompanied by lightly cooked bean sprouts and salicorne seaweed, was a conservative choice compared to 'tandoori' *gambas* and chicken livers with rice pilaf. Mildly spiced in the French fashion, the surprisingly compatible seafood and meat were pink and succulent. The big portions left us with room only to share a prune, pear and chocolate *tourtière*, whose paper-thin crust had turned sadly chewy from over-vigorous reheating. Blue-and-white check tablecloths and neon strip lights take you back in time, but the fairly expensive wine list is intriguingly modern with selections such as our complex Irancy Bienvenue (50cl for €19.81).

Le Zéphyr

1 rue du Jourdain, 20th (01.46.36.65.81). M° Jourdain. **Open** Mon-Fri noon-2pm, 8-11pm; Sat 8-11pm. Closed Aug. **Average** €30. **Prix fixe** €26. **Lunch menu** €11.05. **Credit** AmEx, DC, MC, V. **Wheelchair access.**
Le Zéphyr might seem out-of-the-way, but it doesn't take long to see that an arty young population inhabits this old-fashioned part of Belleville. The gorgeous art deco dining room always buzzes with conversation, and in summer the terrace tables are equally popular. What we love most about this bistro, though, is the food. Ignoring the €26 *menu*, which seems a little sad compared to the *carte*, we started with a pumpkin flan topped with quivery pan-fried foie gras and a citrusy vinaigrette, and an unlikely-sounding but exquisite soup of chicory and maroilles (a potent northern cheese) with curry, elegantly served in a big white bowl. Warm oysters in a truffled sabayon (a whipped, wine-based custard) were as wonderful as they sound. Just as impressive was roast wild duck with lavender honey, spiced polenta and quince. The only flaw was slightly overcooked *sandre* (pike-perch), served with an apple and sweet pepper chutney, rich potato purée and lightly cooked bean sprouts. Of the desserts, our favourite was the day's special: banana mousse sandwiched between layers of coconut and chocolate, with passion fruit ice cream. Affordable wines included the full-bodied and smooth Visan Cuvée St-Vincent 1991.

Beyond the Périphérique

Le Soleil ★

109 av Michelet, 93400 St-Ouen (01.40.10.08.08). M° Porte de Clignancourt. **Open** Mon-Wed, Sun noon-3.30pm; Thur-Sat noon-3.30pm, 8-10.30pm. **Average** €35. **Credit** MC, V.
Behind the windows of this former café near the flea market, the atmosphere feels light-years from the gritty, busy world outside, and at the center of this little planet of bonhommie is a deep devotion to good eating. So good is the food here, in fact, that this place is becoming something of a cult word-of-mouth address in Paris food circles, with the jovial waiter at a recent dinner confirming that both Alain Ducasse and Pierre Gagnaire had recently been customers. Once the food comes, you'll see why, since this place could give a real lesson to many other restaurants. Quite simply, everything is outstanding – from the mound of yellow butter from the Cotentin region of Normandy that comes with the sourdough bread from a secret bakery in Neuilly, to a salad of *haricots vert* with shavings of foie gras, to partridge with savoy cabbage, and a huge *entrecôte* in a deep, ruddy, delicious wine sauce. The wine list is excellent, too, as are desserts, including what must surely be the best *baba au rhum* in Paris. Reservations are essential.

Haute Cuisine

The luxury experience isn't only about food – every detail conspires to make you feel giddy.

After a brief revival caused by the migration of many of the capital's most exalted chefs to hotel dining rooms, the future of the most elaborate – and most expensive – cooking in the French food chain looks wobbly again.

The main problem is that modern tastes privilege simplicity, and even if the menus at restaurants such as **Alain Ducasse**, **Le Bristol** and **Le Pré Catelan** implicitly seek to justify terrifying tariffs by showing off the pedigree of their produce under sub-headings such as *Le boeuf*, *Les langoustines* and so on, a fish is still a fish. This particular quandary has perhaps been most clearly highlighted at **L'Arpège**, following Alain Passard's nervy decision to serve mostly vegetarian food – he now grows his own vegetables. Even if it's delicious, how can sautéed spinach with an orange-zest-brightened carrot purée possibly be worth €40?

In fact, it's been a long time since haute cuisine seemed so irrelevant to the future of French cooking. With the exception of exceptionally brave and imaginative chefs such as **Pierre Gagnaire**, haute cuisine is no longer a cutting-edge laboratory of where taste might go, but rather an exquisite and often rather over-stuffed museum to enjoy on a special occasion. If you want this experience served up with classical grandeur in all respects, **L'Espadon** at the Hôtel Ritz has been once again offering a sublime *la-vie-en-rose* experience since chef Michel Roth returned to the kitchens where he'd worked for many years. For something more modern, try **Guy Savoy**, who has an instinctive talent for preparing dishes that are light, luxurious and exceptionally festive – in other words, he knows how to deliver a contemporary haute cuisine experience.

Le Carré des Feuillants
14 rue de Castiglione, 1st (01.42.86.82.82). M° Tuileries. **Open** Mon-Fri noon-2pm, 7.30-10.30pm; Sat 7.30pm-10pm. Closed Aug. **Average** €100. **Prix fixe** €138 (dinner only). **Lunch menu** €58. **Credit** AmEx, DC, MC, V. **Wheelchair access**.
This restaurant is just a wisp away from being one of the very best in town. Chef Alain Dutournier's cooking remains altogether excellent – simple, elegant, light, inventive and deeply flavoured. Our seven-course tasting menu was a tour de force of refined and luxurious fare. A bright, briny oyster served in its shell with seawater jelly felt like a summer swim. Delicate, juicy turbot was coated with a brilliant lemon sabayon, the citrus at once foiling and elevating the soft richness of the fish. Then came a small package wrapped with impossibly thin potato ribbons. Cutting into it revealed pink foie gras and steely grey caviar, a decadent combination of luxuries from both land and sea. And, if the test of great kitchen is its ease with classic preparations, this one excels beautifully with juicy little herb and parmesan-encrusted lamb chops and a savoury *jus*. Our cheese course was a slab of silken goat's cheese dotted with plump yellow raisins and drizzled with fruity olive oil. Dessert featured a towering *millefeuille* of wild strawberries, puff pastry, and an intense vanilla Chantilly. The only downsides are a criminally high-priced wine list (very little under €70), rather drab decor, and occasionally amateurish service. Without these imperfections, Le Carré des Feuillants would be a truly extraordinary place to dine. With them, it is merely excellent.

L'Espadon ★
Hôtel Ritz, 15 pl Vendôme, 1st (01.43.16.30.80/www.ritzparis.com). M° Madeleine or Concorde. **Open** daily noon-3pm, 7.30-11pm. **Average** €183. **Prix fixe** €141.80 (dinner only). **Lunch menu** €63. **Credit** AmEx, DC, MC, V. **Wheelchair access**.
With lavish silk swaggers on gilded windows, a painted ceiling of fluffy little clouds and Murano wall sconces, this place purrs luxury. And now, with the return of chef Michel Roth, who had left to work at Lasserre, one of the most sumptuous dining rooms in the world is yet again one of the best restaurants in Paris. Service is a sort of cross between a classical ballet and a Prussian artillery troop drill, but perfect in any event. Everything about our meal here was gracious and pure pleasure, from the welcome to the live harp and violin music in the dining room and the astonished pleasure of the Japanese couple next to us when their waiter addressed them in their own language (staff speak five languages beyond French). Most importantly, the food is outstanding. Promptly served an appetiser of soy-marinated tuna and excellent bread, we received a second nibble after ordering, a delicious pinwheel of smoked salmon filled with a minute dice of vegetables and tiny cockles. Breton lobster and mesclun salad dressed with raspberry vinegar, hazelnut oil, lobster coral and salmon eggs impressed us, while a crayfish tail *brochette* with powdered pistachios and an accompanying creamy shellfish soup was luscious and very creative. Further evidence of well-reasoned inventiveness came with main courses of a perfectly cooked veal chop in a polenta crust and a superb if slightly overcooked whole sea bass with a lemongrass-spiked cream sauce and a wonderful side dish of coco beans, *girolle* mushrooms, runner beans and tomatoes. Though the cheese trolley looked lovely, we went for desserts instead, including a sublime poached peach with lemon sorbet and what might be the best *millefeuille* in Paris. The wine list has been revised, too; they offer a credible selection of foreign wines, plus fairly priced choices such as our 1996 Côtes de Beaune Cent Vignes for €88.

Le Grand Véfour
17 rue de Beaujolais, 1st (01.42.96.56.27). M° Palais-Royal. **Open** Mon-Thur 12.30-2pm, 8-10pm; Fri 12.30-2pm. Closed Aug. **Average** €244. **Lunch menu** €70.13. **Credit** AmEx, DC, MC, V.
Our lunch at the Grand Véfour fell into the trap of starting with the best: starters of *chipirons* (small squid) with tangy, minced squid stuffing and a delicate salad of tomato, broad beans and fennel, and jellied tuna terrine (looking much like a *traiteur* offering), before the uninspiring main course choice of salmon, cod, pork or *tête de veau*. This is clearly a place where, despite the numerous gastronomic accolades for chef Guy Martin, the already pretty-expensive lunch *menu* is decidedly second-best – we're not asking for truffles or caviar, but even so. Pork presented like a little cottage loaf with a garam masala topping was pink, succulent and moist. However, cod fried in butter with a scant scattering of capers, accompanied by a curious pasta tube filled with a *brandade*-style purée of fish, potato and diced vegetables, was distinctly dull; we've had more interesting fish in many a bistro. A *palet* of hazelnut ice cream and glossy milk chocolate was decorative and rich, but the sort of thing you'd find in a sophisticated pâtisserie, while its ice-cream component had made the biscuit base spongy. The '*biscuit à la rhubarbe*' turned out to be a small, warm sponge cake filled with what seemed to be rhubarb and apple compote, sweetened so as to have lost any interesting tartness. The promised olives were presumably the dark lumps in the sugar-flake wafer. Owned by the Champagne house Taittinger, Le Grand Véfour has a well-oiled big business feel. Come by all means for a well-behaved, dignified meal in a beautiful setting, but not to widen your gastronomic frontiers. Even the historic aura reveals a certain degree of myth: the Grand Véfour began as the Café de Chartres in the 1780s and received its present decoration in the later 19th century, so could we be really sure we were sitting at Napoléon's table? Note that the confirmation policy is exercised with excessive zeal – the first time we tried to eat here, our table had been given away after just one attempt to reach us, on the very same morning. If you want to receive suitable fawning, it clearly helps to arrive with an armful of Hermès carrier bags.

Le Meurice
Hôtel Meurice, 228 rue de Rivoli, 1st (01.44.58.10.10). M° Tuileries. **Open** daily noon-2pm, 7-10.30pm. Closed Aug. **Average** €95. **Prix fixe** €95, €145 (dinner only). **Credit** AmEx, DC, MC, V. **Wheelchair access**.
It's a delight to bask in the magnificence of this room overlooking the Tuileries. Excellent service and the comfortable intimacy created by generously spaced tables with hand-carved armchairs create an atmosphere that's the very definition of a Parisian palace hotel. The menu seeks to stun as well, with food that is calculated to be simultaneously luxurious, traditional and innovative. Following an *amuse-gueule* of tuna tartare with *cornichons* and capers, starters were excellent: lobster salad with summer vegetables, and more inventive poached eggs in a breadcrumb crust on a bed of *girolle* mushrooms with young salad leaves. Next, we sampled the langoustines with a caramelised garlic sauce and rack of lamb with small hazelnuts, watercress, and its own *jus* with fresh almonds. Both were excellent, though a guacamole-like salad with the langoustines gilded the lily. If the food here is generally beyond reproach, it tends to be overelaborate. This baroque touch worked brilliantly with desserts, however, including a sublime nougat soufflé with a side dish of apricot marmalade, and roast figs with a raspberry and fig pastry, raspberry sauce and sorbet. Add flawless service and an exquisite wine list, and you find a dining room that's been restored to the front row of Parisian restaurants.

L'Ambroisie
9 pl des Vosges, 4th (01.42.78.51.45). M° Bastille or St-Paul. **Open** Tue-Sat noon-1.30pm, 8-9.30pm. Closed Aug. **Average** €215. **Credit** AmEx, MC, V. **Wheelchair access**.
There's perhaps no better address in Paris to dine with a virgin – an haute-cuisine virgin, that is – than this exquisite restaurant off the elegant place des Vosges. However, the fact that a meal here can easily head beyond €450 a couple must be addressed before any trilling over the beauty of the dining rooms or the magnificent food. Is it even decent to spend so much money on a transitory experience? Well, in this instance, aside from the egregiously overpriced desserts, the money could well prove worth it. Choose between the front room, with its Renaissance look, the 19th-century salon with more natural light, or a very intimate back dining room, all impeccably decorated. We declined an apéritif, but happily nibbled on cheesy *fougères* (choux puffs), until a sublime hors d'oeuvre arrived – early-season scallops, cooked with stop-watch precision and served on a bed of laser-fine ceps in a perfectly balanced lemon cream sauce. This was so good that it completely derailed our conversation, but when sublime first courses of feather-light langoustines with spinach between two nearly transparent sesame wafers in a perfect curry cream sauce, and foie gras with plump raisins and quince arrived, we abandoned ourselves to the intriguingly restrained experience of heightened public sensuality that haute cuisine at its best provokes. Main courses were magnificent, too – a turban of perfectly cooked sea bass on a bed of *duxelles* (finely chopped mushrooms) and petals of cep, and turbot with preserved citrus rind, mustard seeds and braised chicory. Unlike past meals here, this one was graciously and gently propelled by attentive, almost friendly service – when we started to exchange plates so as to sample each other's first courses, the waiter arrived instantly with fresh silverware and more toast for the foie gras. Things slackened slightly at the end, when our Meursault had been left to overchill, but overall this was a spectacular meal, which we'd repeat often if we could.

Hiramatsu
7 quai de Bourbon, 4th (01.56.81.08.80). M° Pont Marie. **Open** Tues-Sat noon-2pm, 8-10pm. **Average** €120. **Prix fixe** €95. **Credit** AmEx, DC, MC, V.
Japanese chef Hiroyuki Hiramatsu has created a bona fide culinary event with his spectacular new restaurant seating only 18 on the Ile St-Louis. First off, the food is absolutely brilliant as a sort of Zen tribute to the great traditions of French haute cuisine. If the Japanese and the French share a cult of produce and presentation, the alluring lightness of the former is infinitely more modern than the usual richness of the latter, and by creating a cuisine that seems to be almost entirely fat-free and using rich produce in homeopathic doses, Hiramatsu has created something entirely new. Then there is the stunningly handsome and understated dining room, with traditional stone floors but sleek leather armchairs, frosted glass partitions and tiny spotlights between all of the beams overhead creating a warm light. Like the cuisine, the decor speaks of a certain humility, which is echoed by the five waiters. Easily the most important new restaurant to open in Paris in the new century, this place serves sublime Nippo-French dishes such as a salad of raw pigeon breast, savoy cabbage and foie gras, which is poached at the table in hot bouillon, scallops with oysters and mushrooms, and a stunning coffee-cream-brown sugar riff on cappuccino for dessert. The wine list is a masterpiece, too; rely on the vast knowledge of friendly young sommelier Hideyoshi Ishizuka to make an original choice.

La Tour d'Argent
15-17 quai de la Tournelle, 5th (01.43.54.23.31/www.tourdargent.com). M° Pont Marie or Cardinal Lemoine. **Open** Tue-Sun noon-1.30pm, 7.30-9.30pm. **Average** €120. **Lunch menu** €59.46. **Credit** AmEx, DC, MC, V. **Wheelchair access**.
La Tour d'Argent has always been blessed with position and personalities. Walls of signed cards downstairs attest to its pedigree: Dali, Chanel, JFK, Roosevelt, Henry IV, Liz and Phil (minus the corgis), Bogey and Bacall, Orson Welles, Sinatra, Cocteau, Pagnol and all manner of majesties have graced its tables. Suavely suited owner Claude Terrail, with his trademark carnation, even creeps past each table of his gastro-museum wishing all '*bonjour et bienvenue*' and grasps the ring-encrusted hands of regulars. Naturally, partaking of this doesn't come cheap, but if you forgo the night lights and opt for lunch and the daytime view of Notre-Dame, the Seine and Paris rooftops, then a bank loan won't be necessary. The lunch *prix fixe* offers some Tour d'Argent classics plus contemporary dishes and a few suggested wines, though you can do just as well if you're willing to wrestle with the wrist-punishing wine list. We enlisted the sommelier's help to find a half-bottle of 1988 Clos des St-Ursules for €51.07, a wonderfully complex Burgundy that complemented both fowl and fish: moist duck *à l'orange*, a breast and leg with candied orange rind and a rich, meaty sauce, and red mullet fillets with vegetable-stuffed courgette flowers. Starters of a 'mosaic' of foie gras and rabbit flavoured with Sauternes wine, and langoustine tails in a tangy curry sauce with salad, also didn't disappoint. Duck is the restaurant's signature dish and almost one million Daffys have given their all since 1919; the sauce is made with much silver ceremony in the dining room. We also polished off a *millefeuille* of fresh raspberries and strawberries and a *délicieux chocolat* and stuffed in a few mini-tarts and macaroons as we lingered over coffee and the cathedral view.

Haute Cuisine

On top of the world at La Tour d'Argent

L'Arpège
84 rue de Varenne, 7th (01.45.51.47.33/ www.alain-passard.com). M° Varenne. **Open** Mon-Fri 12.30-2pm, 8-10pm. **Average** €205. **Prix fixe** €304.90. **Credit** AmEx, DC, MC, V. **Wheelchair access**.

With much fanfare, chef Alain Passard announced in early 2001 that he was moving away from meat in favour of a new haute cuisine based mainly on vegetables and seafood. It was a bold move – even if meat continues to appear regularly on his menu – and Passard is spearheading a movement that will surely be very influential. His restaurant has also been partially redecorated, with Baccarat inserts in the chair backs that match those sunken into pear-wood panelling on the walls. A wall has been removed, giving the main room a spacious feel. Predictably, perhaps, businessmen at several tables muttered that they liked the old menu better, while Japanese and American diners seemed generally enchanted by excellent new dishes such as sea urchins with nasturtium flowers and leaves, a very delicate vegetable couscous and a brilliant dish of lobster sautéed in mustard with a garnish of tiny red onions from Roscoff. After appetisers of small fava beans, herbs and parmesan and the house classic, avocado mousse with caviar, starters of *girolle* mushrooms and sautéed spinach with an orange-brightened carrot purée were rich with butter and appealing, though the vegetable stock-based sauce on the mushrooms didn't quite succeed in bringing out their earthy taste the way a veal stock might have, and both dishes were shudderingly expensive given the raw materials. A main course of scallops wrapped in bay leaves and served on a bed of young leeks was superb. A featherweight *millefeuille* with praline butter cream was outstanding, while first-of-the-season Plougastel strawberries in a light hibiscus syrup seemed rather too simple in this setting. Not surprisingly, the pricey wine list offers an expanded selection of whites. Overall, if you don't mind the conspicuous consumption of sautéed spinach for €40, Passard is doing some really brilliant cooking.

Le Jules Verne
Second Level, Eiffel Tower, Champ de Mars, 7th (01.45.55.61.44). M° Bir-Hakeim or RER Champ de Mars. **Open** daily 12.15-1.45pm, 7.15-9.45pm. **Average** €100. **Lunch menu** €49 (Mon-Fri). **Credit** AmEx, DC, MC, V.

Do you dream of dining on the second floor of the Eiffel Tower, 123 metres above the Paris streets? You'd better book now – despite its seven-day opening, in summer you'll need to reserve as much as three months in advance (it is, however, always worth trying on the day). If you are one of the lucky few, prepare for a sensory treat. In addition to the vertigo-inducing trip in the private lift and the soaring views over the city, Alain Reix's food offers an exciting array of contrasting tastes and textures, intelligent and unusual combinations and lots of luxury ingredients. Our summer *menu dégustation* (€109.76) kicked off with smooth duck foie gras with citrus chutney, a chewy, lemony biscuit and a sprinkling of *fleur de sel* and Sichuan peppercorns. This was followed by a well-seasoned tuna tartare, balanced on a disc of minestrone aspic and crowned with a *quenelle* of Aquitaine caviar (from sturgeon caught near Bordeaux). Following this was a *petit pain soufflé* – a perfect, golden sphere of light dough, stuffed with delicate crab meat and bathed in a creamy shrimp sauce, and a steamed fillet of red mullet with green asparagus and a foamy lettuce emulsion. Next, a refreshing muscat and thyme sorbet before a superb veal *entrecôte* with tiny broad beans, girolles and summer truffle, and finally two desserts: summer berries with passion fruit jelly, and a rich, dark, chocolate mousse, with salty caramel and the thinnest of shortbread biscuits. Service is multilingual, polite and unobtrusive, and, certainly at lunch, families are made very welcome. The decor – a mix of the 1880s (cast-iron chairs echoing the tower's construction) and the 1980s (black-stemmed wine glasses and octagonal plates, a throwback to nouvelle cuisine) is totally in keeping with this national monument. The fine wines are likely to give your wallet a hammering (we chose a Crozes Hermitage 97 from Graillot at €50.31), but we were too giddy to care.

Alain Ducasse au Plaza Athénée
Hôtel Plaza Athénée, 25 av Montaigne, 8th (01.53.67.65.00/www.alain-ducasse.com). M° Alma-Marceau. **Open** Mon-Wed 8-10.30pm; Thur, Fri 1-2.30pm, 8-10.30pm. Closed 21 Dec-31 Dec, 14 Jul-20 Aug. **Average** €220. **Prix fixe** €190, €250. **Credit** AmEx, DC, MC, V. **Wheelchair access**.

After working for execu-chef Alain Ducasse for nine years, Jean-François Piège, the real cook in the kitchen here, has not only learned but perfected his master's lessons, making this one of the finest restaurants in Europe. Though Piège's name doesn't appear on the menu, the jet-setting Ducasse no longer pretends that he'll be the one making your white-truffle-and-duck-foie-gras ravioli or any of the other superb dishes recently found on his autumn menu. All it takes is a meal in the fish bowl, as the dining room that overlooks the kitchen here is nicknamed, to understand that the impeccable culinary choreography of this kitchen produces the maestro's results whether he's around or not. The dining room by Patrick Jouin, done in sort of a post-modern pastiche on all things Louis, offers a spectacularly beautiful setting for a meal, with gun-metal grey arm chairs, crystal chandeliers inside huge moiré drums and splashes of apricot carpeting. Service is superb and so is the food, which is all about luxury and beauty, making it occasionally just a whisker soulless. Try classics such as the langoustines in a creamy *nage* topped with Oscietra caviar, or seasonal offers such as an earthy tart of ceps with crayfish or an elegant duckling in fig leaves with a sauce of aged vinegar and pan drippings. Ducasse also offers vegetarian main courses and an innovative *menu* that allows you to sample three half-portions of any dish of you choose, plus cheese and dessert for €190. A sumptuous wine list, cheeses by Bernard Antony, the celebrated Alsatian *maître fromager*, and excellent desserts round out the glamour here.

Les Ambassadeurs ★
Hôtel de Crillon, 10 pl de la Concorde, 8th (01.44.71.16.16/www.crillon.com). M° Concorde. **Open** daily noon-2.30pm, 7-10.30pm. **Average** €145. **Prix fixe** €135. **Lunch menu** €62 (Mon-Fri). **Credit** AmEx, DC, MC, V. **Wheelchair access**.

Les Ambassadeurs is the exclusive residence of visiting dignitaries, celebrities and travellers of substantial means. In such exalted company, it's perhaps not surprising that gentlemen are required to wear a tie, even for lunch. The dining room is spacious and incredibly opulent; acres of marble, polished mirrors, gilt decoration and crystal chandeliers conjure up a mini-Versailles. Service is quite formal, although not without charm. Dominique Bouchet's cooking oozes classical technique. *Marbré de foie gras de canard et artichaut en gelée de boeuf* was astounding – thick layers of smooth, rich foie gras, juxtaposed with firm, earthy, olive-hued artichoke heart, held together by a translucent beef jelly. A main course of *supions farcis à la basquaise* produced the most tender baby squid you could imagine, plump with a stuffing of finely shredded peppers and served with a not-bad risotto. A crab-and-apple *Charlotte* and *brandade de morue* with a *sauce vierge* were flawless, if rather less interesting. The lunch *menu*, while not a bargain, does include *petits fours* and generous desserts – sophisticated pecan brownies, a cocoa bean nougatine with a raspberry coulis and a *vacherin glacé comme en Alsace* – an imposing snow-white meringue and ice cream gâteau, dispensed from a silver trolley. The wine list has some very grand bottles at even grander prices, but what else would you expect? We drank a delicious half-bottle of Chablis 1er Cru Montmains 1995 from Droin, for €38.

Le Bristol
Hôtel Bristol, 112 rue du Fbg-St-Honoré, 8th (01.53.43.43.00/www.hotel-bristol.com). M° Miromesnil. **Open** daily noon-2.30pm, 7-10.30pm. **Average** €130. **Prix fixe** €57, €110. **Credit** AmEx, DC, MC, V. **Wheelchair access**.

Our meal at Le Bristol got off to an unpromising start when one of us nearly swallowed an industrial-size staple that had been lurking in the langoustine tempura *amuse-bouche*. When we showed the waiter the offending object, he turned the same starched tint as our tablecloth, placed it gingerly on a plate and rushed it into the kitchen, returning with contrite apologies. The rest of our meal was coloured by this isolated (we can only believe) but alarming incident – trying to put it out of our minds, we forged on with our €57 *menu*, an unusual evening bargain for a luxury restaurant. A starter of warm coco beans with clams and tender squid could have used more assertive seasoning, as could flakes of snowy white cod in a frothy truffle cream sauce, topped with a rather superfluous egg yolk. Then came a surprise dish – the chef's apology for our mishap – of two outsized macaroni stuffed with artichoke and more truffle and generously topped with melted parmesan. Delicious, but salty and rich. Mains reminded us of superior bistro fare: a thick sea bass fillet cooked in hazelnut oil with small, sautéed artichokes, and a rosy veal kidney with crushed ratte potatoes. The waiters made a gesture with a free cheese course from a nicely ripened selection. A generous serving of golden mirabelle plums caramelised in brown sugar, and watery poached figs again showed a certain inconsistency. Our bottle of subtle Faugères Château de la Liquère 1998 (€39.64) went down easily, but the overly conscientious waiters kept pouring more water, even charging us €7.32 for a second bottle we hadn't ordered. Along with a shocking €36.59 for two glasses of Port, this brought our bill to €204.28 – no extra charge for the staple.

Time Out Paris Eating & Drinking 41

Le Cinq

Hôtel Four Seasons George V, 31 av George V, 8th (01.49.52.70.00/www.fourseasons.com). Mº George V. **Open** daily noon-2pm, 6.30-10.30pm. **Average** €150. **Prix fixe** €200. **Lunch menu** €60. **Credit** AmEx, DC, MC, V. **Wheelchair access.**

The George V hotel has lost its glamorous, star-strewn patina in its new Four Seasons guise. The dining room, with its incongruous potted palms, is a formal place (compulsory jackets) leading into a courtyard for summer dining. Service fawns and scrapes just a little too much, but it is totally professional. At lunch the comparatively reasonable *menu* makes it a luxury dining experience worth considering. We found it difficult to turn down an offer of a glass of Champagne from a trolley of fizz, but be careful not to choose the vintage bottles if money is an issue. With our *menus* we were given tasty spoonfuls of foie gras mousse and crab lasagne, which raised our hopes for the excellence of the meal. Our starters of scallops with a vegetable garnish and a crab with a Thermidor (cream, mustard and cheese) sauce were bland, however, the crab meat even featuring some unwelcome shards of shell. Main courses were somewhat better: delicately cooked Scottish salmon with tiny squid in a timid red wine emulsion, and a scallop and mushroom risotto. This was a poorly named dish as it consisted of a perfectly seared ring of seafood, accompanied by a meagre spoonful of mushroom risotto. Things picked up with a good cheese board, unusually featuring a hunk of well-selected parmesan, but the highlight of the meal was undoubtedly the vanilla *millefeuille* with caramel coulis, a perfect Proustian version of the multilayered dessert. Sipping the last drops of our full-bodied white '99 Condrieu at €72 a bottle, served by a helpful sommelier, we felt that bolder flavours were needed.

Laurent

41 av Gabriel, 8th (01.42.25.00.39/ www.le-laurent.com). Mº Champs-Elysées-Clemenceau. **Open** Mon-Fri 12.30-2pm, 7.30-10.30pm; Sat 7.30-10.30pm. **Average** €120. **Prix fixe** €65, €130 **Credit** AmEx, DC, MC, V. **Wheelchair access.**

This pastel-pink 19th-century pavilion (in the time of Louis XIV, the site was occupied by a hunting lodge) serves as a luxurious lunch canteen for France's political and business elite. The pace is more relaxed in the summer, when meals are served on the pretty terrace, or in the evening, when gastronomes take time to savour Joël Robuchon's menu, prepared by Philippe Braun (Braun perhaps deserves a bit more credit – he has been in charge of the stoves at Laurent for ten years now, and Robuchon seems to spend most of his time on television). Dishes may appear simple, but in terms of quality of ingredients, precise timing and depth of flavour, the food is some of the best in the world. For those not on expenses, the €65 *menu du pavillon* (available at lunch and dinner) offers a selection from the *carte*, albeit in somewhat reduced portions. We sampled veal ravioli with crisp artichokes and a deconstructed gazpacho with the puzzling title *fondant de légumes 'Jérusalem 3000'*, followed by seared, marinated tuna with bitter-leaf salad and spit-roasted Bresse chicken with *girolle*-stuffed macaroni and an intense *jus*. For dessert, we couldn't resist two totally different but equally glorious strawberry concoctions – warm *fraises compotées* with a lemony fromage blanc sorbet and *tarte sablée* with wild strawberries and freshly churned vanilla ice cream. The wine list features lots of very grand bottles, but there is satisfaction to be had at around €50 (we followed the sommelier's recommendation with the excellent Bandol Château de Pibarnon '98, at €48.78). Oh, and service doesn't come any smoother than this.

Ledoyen

1 av Dutuit, 8th (01.53.05.10.01). Mº Champs Elysées-Clémenceau. **Open** Mon-Fri 12.30-2pm, 8-10pm. Closed Aug. **Average** €138. **Prix fixe** €119 (dinner only). **Lunch menu** €58. **Credit** AmEx, DC, MC, V.

The taxi driver told us that he would never have the opportunity to go to Ledoyen. Then the car door swung open into this world of ultimate Parisian privilege, and all egalitarian thoughts got lost in a haze of well-being. The Second Empire first-floor salon was hushed and wonderfully luxurious, with a romantic view over the trees of the Champs and the place de la Concorde. The good news is that at lunch this experience is available for the relatively reasonable price of €58 for a three-course *menu* prepared by chef Christian Le Squer. The appetisers featured caviar and foie gras, while a pre-starter of melon jelly topped with a bacon mousse was a comforting baby-food version of melon and Parma ham. Our first course was the *feuillantine de cèpes* with foie gras, the thinnest, crispiest layer of pastry hiding firm mushrooms and a tasty chunk of goose liver. We followed with one of the best pieces of *foie de veau* imaginable, a mighty pink slab coated with a tart fruit sauce; our other choice of eels in a slightly sweet sauce convinced us that we didn't really like the slippery creature, but the preparation was above reproach. Cleverly we chose the magnificent selection of cheese, knowing that with coffee we would be served a tempting selection of *mignardises*, which provided a dessert in their own right. The wine was served with great ceremony and we were guided to a fine half-bottle of Chablis '94 and a more expensive white Condrieu '91, a quality quaff. The cigar-smoking business crowd and studious Japanese ladies quietly appreciated the solemn beauty of the event.

Lucas Carton

9 pl de la Madeleine, 8th (01.42.65.22.90/ www.lucascarton.com). Mº Madeleine. **Open** Mon, Sat 8-10.30pm; Tue-Fri noon-2.30pm, 8-10.30pm. Closed Aug. **Average** €190. **Lunch menu** €64. **Credit** AmEx, DC, MC, V.

We wondered if there was a *manifestation* going on in place de la Madeleine on the day of our lunch at Lucas Carton – until we realised that the muffled yells which punctuated our meal were coming from the kitchen. This might not have been the voice of the great Alain Senderens himself – Frédéric Robert handles the day-to-day running of the kitchen – but there is no doubt that his perfectionism continues to pay off. We ordered the €64 *menu d'affaires*, whose businesslike name doesn't suggest culinary extravagance. A dish of tender little spiced squid perked up our palates before surprisingly adventurous starters: a carpaccio of tuna from St-Jean-de-Luz in the Basque country, refreshingly flavoured with shallot, pink ginger, aromatic oil and a crunchy spiced *tuile*; and melt-in-the mouth ravioli each filled with a small scallop and a slice of courgette, served in a buttery sauce with a pile of toothsome slivered courgette. As Senderens' signature duck *à l'Apicius* is available only *à la carte*, we chose another dish of roast duck with a sweet and spicy skin, served with an odd though quite enjoyable combination of sautéed leek and diced mango. Just as successful was a rabbit and foie gras *pastilla* wrapped in crisp filo pastry and showered, Moroccan-style, with a great deal of cinnamon. The vanilla *millefeuille*, a speciality, was nothing short of an ode to this towering queen of pastries: the caramelised *feuilleté* shattered under the fork, mingling with headily scented vanilla cream. We snubbed the too-familiar *coulant au chocolat* to try a soul-lifting dessert of puff pastry filled with orange mousse and served with a melting cocoa sorbet. Combined with one of the most sumptuous dining rooms in Paris – plum-coloured banquettes make it comfortable, while art nouveau carved-wood partitions with glass-encased butterflies give it splendour – and unsnobbish service (the sommelier served us refillable glasses of luscious Côtes de Beaune for €15.24 each), Lucas Carton delivers a hard-to-equal luxury experience.

Pierre Gagnaire

6 rue Balzac, 8th (0158.36.12.50/ www.pierre-gagnaire.com). Mº George V. **Open** Mon-Fri noon-2pm, 7.30-10pm; Sun 7.30-10pm (Oct-Apr only). Closed mid July-mid Aug. **Average** €190. **Prix fixe** €183. **Lunch menu** €80. **Credit** AmEx, DC, MC, V.

The only problem with a meal at Pierre Gagnaire is that it doesn't last long enough: to fully savour the fruits of his exuberant creativity, we would like to linger all day. Instead, we had to settle for a dizzying couple of hours in a dining room whose grey carpet, gleaming wood and minimalist modern art remind you that the food is all-important. Champagne cost €21.34 a glass, which blew our wine budget before the meal had started. The *amuse-bouches* could

Alain Ducasse au Plaza Athénée: the swishest of the swish

have been mistaken for Zen art — two cubes of monkfish on toothpicks rested in a bowl of chick-pea flour. After a few such nibbles, including a chilled velvet swimming crab soup, our waiter arrived bearing a multitude of plates. A Spanish-inspired starter from the autumn menu featured a succulent cod cake; different types of small squid with *lisette* (small mackerel), lightly cooked beetroot leaves and black truffle; and melt-in-the-mouth Bellota-Bellota Spanish ham with stuffed squid and divine fresh sardine. Just as complex was our other starter of cold, raw *gambas* in deeply flavoured olive sauce; bok choy with foie gras and a rooster's *sot-l'y-laisse* (a tantalising morsel also known as the 'oyster'); and risotto (cool by the time we got to it) with frogs' legs. The most intriguing of our main courses was the pink suckling lamb rubbed with ewe's milk curd and *nicchia* capers, served with toasted rice, Shanghai cabbage with *petit gris* snails and fennel shoots. Less inspiring was the more conventional thick slice of turbot in a turmeric cream sauce, served with an iced cucumber *jus*, a soft biscuit made with ewe's milk cheese, and slivers of dried pear. Sadly, we couldn't face *le grand dessert*, Gagnaire's seven-plate extravaganza, so settled for lovely *mignardises* with his own herbal tea. Gagnaire is often accused of over-experimentation, and his food does demand concentration, but France definitely needs at least one chef like him.

Taillevent

15 rue Lamennais, 8th (01.44.95.15.01/ www.taillevent.com). M° Charles de Gaulle Etoile or George V. **Open** Mon-Fri noon-2pm, 7.30-10pm. Closed Aug. **Average** €120. **Prix fixe** €130. **Credit** AmEx,DC, MC, V. **Wheelchair access.**

Taillevent is housed in a mansion rich in polished wood and precious paintings. Warmly welcomed, we were whisked up the gracious staircase and, nibbling on cheese puffs, we surveyed the stripped wood walls and chandeliers of our multicultural alcove – we clocked Japanese, Russian, Canadian and Spanish, the only French delegates being the waiters. Service is good-natured and top-notch, and an appetiser of chilled creamed courgette with a touch of red pepper signalled that a treat was in store. The signature lobster *boudin*, more soufflé than sausage, was packed with lobster meat and drizzled with a creamy shellfish sauce, while *galette de courgette*, a disc of puréed courgette, was studded with pretty spring vegetables and ringed with an earthy truffle tapenade. Chef Michel Del Burgo, we decided, has a heady grasp of technique and imagination. Then came the mains: *boeuf aux jus de truffes* – tough and almost past medium-rare – and sole fillets, cooked on the bone and doused with a creamy sauce of gritty cockles and one chewy razor clam. The fish was fine and a watercress purée a nice shot of colour and taste, but oh that sand. A *millefeuille à la vanille bourbon*, and a *sablé* topped with finely sliced strawberries and a caramelised candied ginger sauce, were sweet successes. The wine list has all the usual heavies but surprisingly there are bottles priced as low as €34; our Château de France 1997, a velvety Bordeaux, cost just €44.

Ghislaine Arabian

16 av Bugeaud, 16th (01.56.28.16.16). M° Victor Hugo. **Open** Mon-Fri noon-2.30pm, 7.30-11pm. **Average** €90. **Lunch menu** €45. **Credit** AmEx, DC, MC, V. **Wheelchair access.**

Several years after leaving Ledoyen, Ghislaine Arabian has opened a superb new restaurant on a quiet street in a laced-up part of town. Designed by decorator Laure Welfing, her new dining room is lavish but intimate, with gold leaf walls, white porcelain bearing her initials., and a frieze of moulded Italian glass tiles, but what really impresses here is the sheer talent and technique you find in every dish – Arabian is clearly happy to be back at work in the spectacular new kitchen that she's designed in the basement. It's interesting to encounter her northern French cooking after a pause, too, since it seems directional at a time when Parisians appear to be tiring of Provençal food. Following an appetiser of potato with a smoked spratt in a light cream sauce, we loved her grey shrimp croquettes with fried parsely – a true Belgian classic – and a spectacular *mille-feuille* of fresh vegetables. Sea bass cooked in a salt crust served with small white asparagus was light, flavourful, and beautifully served. Cheeses are supplied by Marie-Anne Cantin, but we couldn't resist desserts: a rhubarb *speculoos* biscuit with a strawberry compote and whole-milk ice cream and a parfait of chicory and spice breadcrumbs in a white beer sabayon; both were excellent. Prices are relatively reasonable for this level of cooking.

Jamin

32 rue de Longchamp, 16th (01.45.53.00.07). M° Trocadéro. **Open** Mon-Fri 12.30-2pm, 7.45-10pm. Closed Aug. **Average** €106. **Prix fixe** €76. **Lunch menu** €47. **Credit** AmEx, DC, MC, V. **Wheelchair access.**

Jamin wouldn't win any awards for design: the pink, frilly curtains and pale blue-green panelling make it feel like a slice of provincial France. It has neither the Tour d'Argent's view nor the gilt and cherubs of Les Ambassadeurs at the Crillon, and the waiters are a little uptight. But the food! For a mere €47 at lunch (evening meals are more expensive), chef Benoît Guichard offers a flawless haute cuisine meal, following in the tradition of the now-retired Joël Robuchon. Ours began with a tuna tart — tender, thinly-sliced fish on a bed of tomato, courgette and piquillo pepper, all atop paper-thin pastry – and a frothy, delicate-tasting asparagus soup with clams and langoustines. *Morue fraîche* – the trendy name for *cabillaud* (cod) these days – was a thick chunk of snow-white fish on a vivid green courgette purée, surrounded by red pepper sauce, while a tender rabbit fricassée came with tiny, succulent spring vegetables. From the mouthwatering dessert trolley we chose an intriguing grapefruit tart and pineapple *clafoutis*, and were offered generous servings of fresh sorbets and ice creams – just in case we were still hungry. Bargains are even available on the wine list: our fruity white Château Clément Termes Gaillac '99 cost just €18. Popular with a business crowd and chic locals, Jamin remains a pilgrimage – the ideal choice for a splurge, big or small, when food is what matters to you most.

Le Pré Catelan ★

route de Suresnes, Bois de Boulogne, 16th (01.44.14.41.14/www.lenotre.fr). M° Porte-Maillot, then taxi. **Open** Tue-Sat noon-2.30pm, 8-10.30pm; Sun noon-2pm. Closed 27 Oct-5 Nov, 9 Feb-5 Mar. **Average** €110. **Prix fixe** €87, €115. **Lunch menu** €55. **Credit** AmEx, DC, MC, V. **Wheelchair access.**

A liveried doorman rushes to open the taxi door and ushers you into the cool, elegant dining room, all crisp linen, cupids and rustling leaves outside the long windows. We had worried unneccessarily about going tie-less and fellow diners were having animated conversations fuelled by Champagne and, a little later, cigars. In contrast, the *amuse-bouche* was straight out of *Barbarella*, a sort of warm chlorophyll shot concocted from lettuce juice and froth of spring onion sap. The *prix fixe* lunch is an economical way to sample Frédéric Anton's cuisine, whose emphasis is on simplicity and produce. The ruse of calling each dish by an ingredient – '*La carotte*', '*Le cabillaud*' – quickly loses its glamour when you translate it into English. However, we were delighted by our starters. The duck foie gras was the best we had ever tasted, meaty and with a symphony of flavours hidden in the marbly pink and peachy slab, encrusted with Chinese spices. 'The carrot' consisted of rows of the young vegetables with a sweet caramel *pain d'épices* glaze. 'The cod' treated this noble but workaday fish with respect: pan-fried with a perfectly crispy crust, it came surrounded by a demure green herb sauce with olive oil and, surprisingly, curry, and was topped with crunchy, delicious fennel. 'The pigeon' was like a sweetmeat to set before a pasha: resting on a bed of couscous were exquisitely soft pink breasts poached in a spice bouillon. The sommelier selected our light '98 Château Pierrail red, good value at €22.87. Still with an appetite, we savoured a wonderful ashy goat's cheese that was virtually walking off the plate. *Mignardises* arrived to tempt us before the desserts: homely 'Banana' baked in a sugar sauce, and 'Chocolate', a triangular slice of *tarte fondante* with a plume of chocolate. If you prefer your food complicated, your decor minimalist and your service haughty, the Pré Catelan is not for you – we found it relaxed and congenial.

Guy Savoy

18 rue Troyon, 17th (01.43.80.40.61/ www.guysavoy.com). M° Charles de Gaulle-Etoile. **Open** Mon-Fri noon-2pm, 7.30-10.30pm; Sat 7.30-10.30pm. Closed Aug. **Average** €230. **Prix fixe** €175.50, €228.70. **Credit** AmEx, DC, MC, V.

The door slides open electronically at Guy Savoy – like the entrance to the exclusive lair of one of Bond's adversaries. Smiling staff lead you through a succession of rooms, all buzzing with conversation. The setting is luxurious yet thoroughly contemporary, with chocolate and tobacco hues and glass display cases housing a collection of African artefacts. The relative informality makes this like no other prestige restaurant in Paris. And so to the food. Almost as we sat down, the first *amuse-bouche* arrived. This was quickly followed by another, and yet another, this time a plate of three. The foie gras with *sel de Guérande* was memorable, others less so. We opted for the *menu prestige* – an eight-course selection of seasonal dishes, designed to show off the range of the kitchen. The main action started with a slice of *suprême de volaille de Bresse*, stuffed with foie gras and artichoke heart and studded with truffle: a beautiful, delicate yet earthy dish. *Langoustine éclatée*, with coconut and broccoli, was an exotic mouthful, while John Dory, roast on the bone and served with salsify and shallot confit, was simply excellent. Savoy's signature dish of artichoke soup with black truffle was a big disappointment this time. Strangely bland, it was only lifted by the warm brioche served alongside. *Noisettes* and *côtes* of venison came with a heavily reduced and downright salty *jus*, overcooked carrots and a thin potato and pistachio *galette* which tasted of cooking oil. The cheese trolley was followed by a dazzling *chaud-froid* of blood orange – warm compote and crystalline sorbet, with dried orange crisps; a chocolat fondant with chicory sauce; a tea sorbet and a mini slice of apple tart. You certainly get a lot for your €175.50. Watch out for the high cost of the apéritifs – our excellent late-harvest Riesling cost €18.29 a glass. (We also drank a '97 Côtes du Roussillon from Cazenove for a more reasonable €39.63).

Michel Rostang ★

20 rue Rennequin, 17th (01.47.63.40.77/ www.michelrostang.com). M° Ternes or Péreire. **Open** Mon, Sat 7.30-10.30pm; Tue-Fri 12.30-2.30pm, 7.30-10.30pm. Closed Aug. **Average** €145. **Prix fixe** €150. **Lunch menu** €59. **Credit** AmEx, DC, MC, V. **Wheelchair access.**

Grand options, including a luxurious six- or seven-course lobster and seafood *menu*, are available at Michel Rostang, but this is a place where even the lunch *menu* is well-thought-out and incredibly generous. An appetiser of clams, a delicate herb salad and a morsel of warm foie gras sitting in the half-shell was delicious preparation for the day's starter of *potimarron* (squash) soup topped with warm oysters and a lightly poached egg, and more rustic, oniony hot foie gras with a buckwheat galette, onions and tiny chanterelle mushrooms. *Omble chevalier* (lake char), with crisp roasted skin and firm, deep pink flesh was served with whole, long, cumin-scented carrots and a smooth green sauce of finely minced spinach and herbs laced with what looked like transparent caviar but were actually, the waiter confided, ingeniously prepared tapioca 'eggs'. Wonderful lamb was served with chanterelles and fresh peas on a fine purée. An unctuous nectarine sorbet as a refresher cleared our palates for pastry 'cigars' enclosing a light mousseline cream – and a rather richer kebab of figs skewered on an aromatic cinnamon stick, sitting on a moist *pain perdu*, accompanied by white chocolate ice cream. Early on all the chefs could be seen, through a glass window, white toques bobbing up and in an incredible hive of activity in the kitchen; later, Rostang came out to survey the scene. He is a collector, too – evident in the cheerful array of china figurines (De Gaulle, Napoléon, a bagpiper) on the shelves behind us, and the vintage bottles of Château Latour that sit regally behind glass in the cellar. This restaurant has a family feel: Madame Rostang runs the reception, and the waiters exude pride and loyalty. Lunch naturally draws a mainly business clientele, but these customers were clearly also appreciative foodies.

Wait and see

All good things to those who wait? Breaking into the ranks of a luxury restaurant is the first step on a potentially lucrative career path. So why are these restaurants, once deluged with applications from hopeful *commis*, now having trouble filling their lower orders?

'I made an investment in my future by working very hard when I was young', reflects Jean-Marie Ancher, *premier maître d'hôtel* at the lofty restaurant Taillevent. Starting his career at 16, Ancher climbed from the bottom to the top of the military style hierarchy – *apprenti, commis, demi-chef de rang, chef de rang, maître d'hôtel, premier maître d'hôtel* – in 26 years of 50-plus hour weeks, one of the quickest ascents in the business. But the long, winding road to *les grandes tables* is being ironed straight. *Maître d'hôtels* are becoming much younger as the business adopts the French technocrat's credo – qualifications over experience – and transforms from trade into profession.

The new standard route is to study at a prestigious Ecole Hôtelière for two to three years, and then, with a Bac professionnel, CAP (*certificat d'aptitude professionnelle*) or BEP (*brevet d'études professionnelles*) in hand, begin an internship at a *grande maison*. Those who don't obtain a *stage* of sufficient prestige in Paris may choose to train at celebrated tables in Provence, or travel abroad to improve their English. But, when apprenticeships come to an end, many up-and-comers are not keen to stick around for what they regard as ten years of thraldom before enjoying the rewards of haute cuisine. So, just as many young chefs are choosing to run their own bistros, exchanging crystal and porcelain for freedom, many young workers *en salle* are choosing to work as bigger fish in smaller ponds. With better hours.

The new 35-hour week introduced by Jospin's Socialist government is problematic in an industry that naturally lends itself to long days. 'Students are indoctrinated with the 35-hour system in school', laments Ancher. 'It is difficult to find young people who are motivated to work as we worked'. The haute cuisine circuit has always been fluid – all the *maîtres d'hôtels* are on a first name basis (a young waiter who goofs is a marked man). But, as restaurants are forced to hire more staff at the bottom rung, there are fewer opportunities for internal advancement. Consequently, there is more movement between restaurants than ever before as frustrated staff look elsewhere.

'Sixty per cent of people in the business have a real love for the profession', observes Ancher. But it is the other 40, the mercenary workforce, that worries many of the old guard. They predict that the subtle art of haute service will be lost to a new generation of callow agents and, at worst, replaced with perfunctory McService. *Nick Petter*

RESTAURANTS DE HAUTE MER

le bar à huîtres®

New, interior design by Jacques Garcia

TEMPTING, "Lobster" set-menu € 38

ALWAYS, our oysters cultivated at L'Ile d'Oléron

MONTPARNASSE : 112 Bd du Montparnasse, 14th. Metro Vavin • 01 43 20 71 01
St. GERMAIN : 33 Rue S' Jacques, 5th. Metro S'Michel • 01 44 07 27 37
BASTILLE : 33 Bd Beaumarchais, 3rd. Metro Bastille • 01 48 87 98 92

http://www.lebarahuitres.com

Brasseries

Big, brassy and always buzzing, brasseries sate seafood and steak cravings at all hours.

You'll see 'brasseries' on nearly every corner in Paris – today, the word often refers to cafés that serve food – but those featured in this chapter are more ambitious. Originally modest places where beer brewed on the premises was served with Alsatian food, the first Paris brasseries opened in the 16th century. With the influx of Alsatians in the 1870s, they took on their present form – extravagant dining rooms, often near train stations, known as much for the buzz as for *choucroute* and gargantuan seafood platters.

Though groups such as Flo and Frères Blanc have saved many a historic brasserie from ruin, the downside has been a standardisation of brasserie food that is becoming increasingly hard to ignore. Flo brasseries maintain a fairly high standard, while the quality at Frères Blanc restaurants varies from one to the next. A few independent brasseries continue to forge their own identities, while a new breed – led by Conran's **Alcazar** – dares to reinvent the decor and food.

Brasseries continue to be some of the most entertaining restaurants in Paris, often attracting a fascinating, mixed clientele. Keep your culinary expectations in check and enjoy the show.

Au Pied de Cochon

6 rue Coquillière, 1st (01.40.13.77.00/ www.pieddecochon.com). M° Les Halles.
Open daily 24 hours. **Average** €45.
Credit AmEx, DC, MC, V.
Wheelchair access.
You enter this temple to the trotter through doors with handles cast in piggy-extremity-shaped bronze and eat off crockery decorated with the picture of a pig clutching a knife and fork and sitting on a four-leaf clover (not so lucky for you, Buster). If you're having doubts about ordering a foot, take a look at the menu. They've got something called St Anthony's Temptation, an assortment of pig bits that makes *pied* seem positively banal. Once your crispy trotter arrives, accompanied by fries, watercress, *sauce béarnaise* and, in our case, a bottle of Chinon, it may not be immediately obvious what to do next; a pig's foot is a complicated anatomical construction containing 32 bones, so don't hesitate to ask for a bit of advice on how to go about eating one. Le Pied de Cochon has all the usual brasserie food for those who refuse to partake in the foot-fest and the onion soup and the oysters are rightly renowned. But that's all a bit like ordering an omelette in a curry house: this is a place to extend your gastronomic foothold.

Gallopin

40 rue Notre-Dame-des-Victoires, 2nd (01.42.36.45.38.). M° Bourse. **Open** Mon-Sat noon-12.30am. Closed mid-Jul-end Aug.
Average €34. **Prix fixe** €20.50-€30.50.
Credit AmEx, DC, MC, V.
Wheelchair access.
The welcome at Gallopin is sincere and solicitous, the service is polished and professional, and the gorgeous 1876 decor is maintained with care and pride. There's a certain clubby feel in the air, to be sure (the Bourse is just across the road, after all), but it's inviting rather than exclusionary: everybody is welcome to bask under the light of the stunning stained glass ceiling and enjoy the reliable, if mostly unexceptional, food. We opted for two of the *menus* and enjoyed fine oysters with dense rye bread and an admirably executed salmon and cabbage terrine. Alsatian *choucroute* featured deeply seasoned sauerkraut and juicy cuts of pork and sausage, but pan-cooked sea bream was rather cold, under-seasoned, and chock full of bones that should have been removed in the kitchen. Desserts include a 'floating island' of fluffy meringue with caramelised almonds in a pool of *crème anglaise* plus luscious ice creams and sorbets.

Le Grand Colbert

2-4 rue Vivienne, 2nd (01.42.86.87.88). M° Bourse. **Open** daily noon-1am.
Average €38. **Prix fixe** €24.39. **Credit** AmEx, DC, MC, V. **Wheelchair access.**
Tucked just behind the Palais-Royal, this vintage spot remains popular with an eclectic, mostly Parisian crowd. On a recent visit we found ourselves flanked by three young professionals swilling Heineken and chain-smoking Lucky Strikes and two earnest parents prodding their young daughters to sit up straight and eat their spinach. The main draw here is the atmosphere: intimate with soft lighting and cosy banquettes, impressive with huge potted palms and plenty of polished brass and burnished wood. The food plays second fiddle, but it's all good enough to justify an occasional visit. Our onion soup was nicely rich and savoury for a few bites, but quickly proved far too heavy to finish. A simple lentil salad revealed the kitchen's penchant for under-seasoning – evident throughout the meal. *Sole meunière*, however, was sweet and delicate and its accompanying mushrooms and spinach were cooked so they retained their warming natural flavours. A chicken *fricassée* was noteworthy for its plump, fresh morel mushrooms but not much else. Desserts were a notch above: a *Charlotte au chocolat* with an agreeably bitter coffee *crème anglaise* and undoubtedly the best green apple sorbet we'd ever had.

Le Vaudeville ★

29 rue Vivienne, 2nd (01.40.20.04.62). M° Bourse. **Open** daily 7-11am, noon-3pm, 7pm-1am. **Average** €32. **Prix fixe** €30.50 (dinner only). **Lunch menu** €21.50.
Credit AmEx, DC, MC, V.
Located just opposite the Bourse, this delightful standby fills up at lunch, dinner and weekends – not just because it is convenient to the Opéra, Grands Boulevards and *grands magasins* but simply because it's so much fun. Crowded and intimate, Le Vaudeville, like other members of the Flo chain, radiates its own personality and boasts a fanciful art deco interior. Manned by efficient and inordinately friendly staff, it maintains a pleasant buzz while offering dependable fare that will satisfy whether you've got three hours or 30 minutes to spare. We were in the latter category: a dozen *spéciales N° 3* oysters were meaty enough to make a dinner in themselves – as they should do at €27. An equally quick meal, grilled fresh cod, confirmed its status as our eternal favourite, salty and satisfying with its creamy potato purée and truffle sauce. Sophisticated comfort food that still tickles the palate.

Bofinger

5-7 rue de la Bastille, 4th (01.42.72.87.82). M° Bastille. **Open** Mon-Fri noon-3pm, 6.30pm-1am; Sat, Sun noon-1am. **Average** €42. **Prix fixe** €30. **Lunch menu** €20 (Mon-Fri). **Credit** AmEx, DC, MC, V.
Brasseries owned by the Flo group rarely offer any big surprises – good or bad – and Bofinger is no exception. Happily (for non-smokers, at least) the pretty downstairs dining room, with its domed glass ceiling dating from 1919, is fume-free – seating along the banquettes is fairly close but not irritatingly so. Founded in 1862, Bofinger was the first restaurant in Paris to serve beer on tap; today it's better known for its art nouveau decor, boisterous atmosphere and fairly good-value brasserie fare. The €30 *menu*, which included a half-bottle of very drinkable Provençal wine, is the obvious choice unless you want to splurge on a seafood platter. Our meal began with a generous portion of sunny yellow mussel soup, enlivened with shallots, parsley and croutons, and a slice of foie gras served simply with toasted *pain de mie*. Tender pork fillet with crushed potatoes was marred only by a slightly gloopy sauce, while crisp-skinned sea bream with nicely cooked courgette rounds was a success. We were pleased with our vanilla-blackcurrant *vacherin* and hearty pear *clafoutis*, but less impressed by a costly mistake on our bill which our waiter quickly rectified once we'd pointed it out (he had not been so quick during the meal itself – we were among the last to leave).

Brasserie de l'Isle St-Louis

55 quai de Bourbon, 4th (01.43.54.02.59). M° Pont Marie. **Open** Mon, Tue, Fri-Sun noon-1am; Thur 5pm-1am. Closed Aug.
Average €30. **Credit** MC, V.
Once beyond this brasserie's idyllic terrace, which offers a view on to the elegant back of Notre Dame, a rustic world of dark wood and mounted animal heads transports you far from the city. Families, smooching couples of all ages and a few guidebook-bearing foreigners filled the long room for Sunday lunch, seated elbow-to-elbow at wooden tables. Food, like the setting, is earthy and satisfying rather than refined. The day's special, roasted *poule faisanne* (hen pheasant) served Normandy-style with roast potatoes and apples, even contained authentic shot. *Coq au riesling*, although a bit messy-looking, had a richly flavoured sauce made with wine, bacon and mushrooms and came with classic boiled potatoes. Equally hearty was a tender pork knuckle served with apple sauce and cream. A bottle of fruity Côtes de Ventoux was good value at €13.70 (you pay for what you drink), but two scoops of Berthillon ice cream seemed steep at €7.50. Instead, stroll down the street for a cone.

Le Balzar

49 rue des Ecoles, 5th (01.43.54.13.67). M° Cluny-La Sorbonne. **Open** daily noon-midnight. **Average** €35. **Credit** AmEx, MC, V.
Our most recent meal at this long-running Latin Quarter brasserie next to the Sorbonne was reminiscent of bad sex with someone you love, except that in this case money was involved. The 1930s decor of this intimate dining room and the plain but reliable Gallic menu, plus a stylish crowd and cheerful professional waiters, have always epitomised a certain blowsy idea of the Left Bank. Unfortunately, we recognised none of the waiters, who seemed self-consciously aware of the fact that they were supposed to be playing a part, the crowd ran to self-conscious tourists and boisterous groups, and the food was drab, beginning with the stale bread. A pricey first course of asparagus was served water-logged and cold with a miserable hollandaise sauce – it had the consistency of scrambled eggs – while foie gras had a musty taste. Roast chicken was fine, if slightly overcooked; the *frites* were delicious but a side-order of spinach appeared to have been reheated several times, as did the *choucroute* accompanying a bland assortment of *charcuterie*. And, the lemon tart was soggy.

Restaurant E Marty

20 av des Gobelins, 5th (01.43.31.39.51/ www.marty-restaurant.com). M° Gobelins.
Open daily noon-midnight. **Average** €34.
Prix fixe €33. **Credit** AmEx, DC, MC, V.
With a handsome 20s and 30s decor, this is one of the too-rare Parisian brasseries that makes an honest effort in the kitchen. Unfortunately, our last meal here was decidedly uneven. The attractive dining room and interesting crowd make a good first impression, as do the delicious sourdough bread rolls. First courses of house-smoked salmon, neatly sliced, generously served, gently smoky and accompanied by hot rye toast, and a medley of spring vegetables dressed with a coriander-brightened vinaigrette and served in a filo pastry cup, were excellent. Then, following a long wait, main courses arrived: pleasantly seasoned steak tartare served with excellent *frites* and a small over-vinegared green salad, and the daily special, a disappointing *emincé de boeuf*, tough, flavourless, too-thick slices with a tasteless garnish of wild mushrooms and terribly overcooked wild asparagus. We missed some potatoes with this dish, and rather regretted the over-zealous pouring by the wine waiter, since he'd seen to it that our very good Gaillac was empty by the time the main courses arrived. Another endless wait followed before we got our good desserts – profiteroles in chocolate sauce and a lovely pistachio *dacquoise* with raspberries. When coffee was served without sugar, and it took five minutes to track some down, tempers started to fray, and it was obvious that other tables were similarly unhappy with the badly wanting service. Still, since it's a beautiful place and the produce is good, we'll give it another chance.

Alcazar

62 rue Mazarine, 6th (01.53.10.19.99/ www.conran.com). M° Odéon. **Open** daily noon-3pm, 7pm-1am. **Average** €45.
Prix fixe €21.34 (dinner only, at the bar).
Lunch menu €15-€25. **Credit** AmEx, DC, MC, V. **Wheelchair access.**
Alcazar opened with a fanfare in 1999 as a self-proclaimed 'brasserie for the 21st century'. The design is there all right, from the enviable collection of photos of writers in the hallway and the sleek, galleried restaurant with its banquettes, cleverly angled mirrors and open kitchen, to the upstairs bar with its long, slinky zinc, low chairs and Peter Beard photos (*see p117*, **Bars & Pubs**). Only the food somehow seems to have missed the mark and our lunchtime company numbered Brits with Eurostar vouchers rather than Parisian sophisticates. Alcazar describes its menu as a mix of French and English, the former presumably being the *confit de canard* and the steak tartare, the latter (apart from fish and chips) being that ever-so-English international fusion spin – bits of Thai here, tinges of Italy there – which would be a fine thing if only they got it right. Mussels stewed in coconut milk and ginger were fiery indeed but lacking in nuances; free-range chicken came with sadly slimy *julienne* of vegetables and a bowl of 'curry sauce' that appeared to consist of cream mixed with curry powder; while a starter of mozzarella, sun-dried tomatoes and guacamole in moulded gâteau form showed when you should leave a classic well alone. The steak tartare was decently prepared, although the soggy chips were just a bit too authentically British. Desserts were better. Nice space, shame about the food.

Brasserie Lipp

151 bd St-Germain, 6th (01.45.48.53.91/ www.brasserie-lipp.fr). M° St-Germain-des-Prés. **Open** daily 12.15pm-1am. Closed 24-25 Dec. **Average** €37. **Credit** AmEx, DC, MC, V.
It says a lot about Lipp that François Mitterrand, an epicurian extremist who liked nothing better than to eat endangered species, used to be a regular here. For the '*président-roi*' to have put up with such a banal bill of fare there must have been something special about the place itself. Perhaps it's the chunky-but-elegant art deco crockery or the exquisite ceramics with scenes from a colonial jungle climbing up to the ceiling but, let's face it, it's more likely to be that people of fame and influence have always come here – we spotted a very well-known French actor and France's top film producer the night we visited. But, just in case you think you're going to get an evening elbow-to-elbow with Juliette Binoche for the price of a steak tartare, here's the catch: if you're Mr and Mrs Nobody, you'll likely as not be seated upstairs, well removed from the action. So you might as well pay attention to the food. The starters are rather dull; sharing a plate of 12 Burgundy snails is an altogether better idea. As for the mains, you're best off going for one of three cuts of beef or choosing from the three *plats du jour*. Desserts include a rice pudding '*maison*' and, in season, wild strawberries. We were unimpressed by the house Bordeaux. Next time, we trust, the same appalling underestimation of our social worth will not be repeated and we'll be seated downstairs.

Vagenende

142 bd St-Germain, 6th (01.43.26.68.18). M° Odéon. **Open** daily 10am-2am. **Average** €35. **Prix fixe** €23. **Credit** AmEx, DC, MC, V. **Wheelchair access.**

Vagenende will always be popular for its ravishing *belle époque* interior and perfect position on the boulevard St-Germain. Fairly competitive pricing and the undeniable glamour of the interior mean that few visitors will be aggressively disappointed, but on our last visit the food never rose above the ordinary. A starter of prion-defying marrowbones served with coarse salt was excellent, but a plate of hot mussels and small scallops was lamely scattered rather than presented. Our main courses included a good piece of foie gras on an *aligot* base, a solid cheese and potato mound that wouldn't have passed muster in the Auvergne, a rather tepid *chateaubriand* with indifferent *frites*, and a timidly spiced suckling pig, on the desert side of dry. Puddings included a reasonably classic rum baba and a cheesecake, advertised as 'old fashioned', but only the first word of this description seemed apt, despite an uplifting berry coulis. The *vin du mois*, a country red from the Cévennes, was very rough for its €17.98 price tag, and we felt foolish for having fallen for such a simple marketing ploy.

L'Avenue

41 av Montaigne, 8th (01.40.70.14.91). M° Franklin D. Roosevelt. **Open** daily 8am-1am. **Average** €57. **Credit** AmEx, DC, MC, V.

Next to Nina Ricci on the swishest shopping street in Paris, this Costes brasserie is the place to rest weary Prada-clad feet when those Dior and Chanel bags start to weigh you down. Filled with dark suits and blonde tresses on our lunchtime visit, L'Avenue felt crowded and clamorous downstairs, but the spacious upstairs rooms were surprisingly peaceful – something about the padded setting makes diners speak in hushed tones. Seated comfortably in purple-velvet chairs, with a view of the Eiffel Tower from the round, cream-painted room, we sipped a festive glass of Champagne (€11) while perusing the stylish menu. A salad of whole lettuce was a popular choice but, craving more substantial fare, we ordered the lasagne with *coppa* (Italian sausage), spinach and gorgonzola – flavourful but overbaked with a dry crust – and monkfish in Thai curry sauce – cooked to tender perfection in a yellow sauce fragrant with turmeric, kaffir lime, lemongrass and coconut. Feeling hopeful, we ordered dessert, but it was a flop: a mushy mango crumble and a praline *millefeuille* whose pastry should have crackled but instead was flabby. Stick to unambitious fare and soak up the view – inside and beyond.

Le Boeuf sur le Toit

34 rue du Colisée, 8th (01.53.93.65.55). M° St-Philippe du Roule. **Open** daily noon-3pm, 7pm-1am. **Average** €38. **Prix fixe** €33.54 (dinner only). **Lunch menu** €21.57, €28.35. **Credit** AmEx, DC, MC, V.

Le Boeuf sur le Toit started out as a lively cabaret in the 1920s, taking its name from the comic ballet of the same era by Milhaud and Cocteau. Taken over by Groupe Flo in the mid-1980s, the brasserie was restored and enlarged, but echoes of *les années folles* remain in the grandiose art deco surroundings complete with gilt mirrors, wood panelling and gigantic geometrical lights. On a weekday night it was bubbling, benefiting from the Champs-Elysées revival and a temptingly priced *prix fixe*. The huge bank of oysters is one of the highlights here, but there are also some satisfying Mediterranean-style dishes *à la carte* – a satisfying '*millefeuille*' of feta cheese and grilled aubergine, and ravioli with ricotta and basil – alongside brasserie classics. Mains include a chunky venison steak with chestnuts or specialities such as the *andouillette de Troyes*. The wine list offers a good choice and a range of prices, including *pichets*.

Brasserie Lorraine

2-4 place des Ternes, 8th (01.56.21.22.00). M° Ternes. **Open** daily 8am-12.30am. **Average** €46. **Credit** AmEx, DC, MC, V.

For years, this venerable restaurant had an almost Cocteau-like elegance that set it apart from other Parisian brasseries, and the food was a cut above that served elsewhere – good quality salmon or lamb chops served with delicious *frites* and side orders of spinach or green beans. All this has disappeared without a trace since being taken over by the Frères Blanc. In fact, all that remains of the former atmosphere is generously spaced tables. Calling for a 9pm booking, we were told to come instead at 8.15pm to avoid a long wait at the bar. So how come the empty tables around us all night long? The only possible explanation for the nudge seems to have been a desire to keep the kitchen busy at an earlier hour. It took forever to get a half-bottle of Sancerre for apéritifs; finally we learned that they were out of half-bottles, and langoustines. Well, then we'd have oysters. Stiffly priced, they had been so carelessly opened that nary a one didn't have a shard of shell or two. A salad of chicory and green beans with delicious slices of smoked duck proved the better choice. *Sole meunière* was perfectly cooked, though, and accompanied by two nice waxy potatoes. Less successful was a 'creative' dish of cod with pine nuts and *piquillo* peppers stuffed with salt cod; the fish flaked as though it had been frozen, and the accompaniment seemed pre-made, too. Profiteroles were soggy under a tasteless chocolate sauce. Presented with a large bill for such a mediocre meal, we left this place for the last time.

La Fermette Marbeuf 1900

5 rue Marbeuf, 8th (01.53.23.08.00/ www.blanc.net). M° Alma-Marceau. **Open** daily noon-3pm, 7-11.30pm. **Average** €45. **Prix fixe** €27.90. **Credit** AmEx, DC, MC, V. **Wheelchair access.**

Jean Laurent struck gold when he bought this restaurant in 1978 and discovered that the '50s panelling hid a stunning art nouveau conservatory created in 1898 for the Langham Hotel. Beautifully restored since, the Fermette now belongs to the Frères Blanc group. The vintage decor is superb but, alas, the food is no match. A main of duck breast with peaches materialised as an over-done lump of meat showered in coriander leaves, accompanied by two lukewarm apricot halves and a bizarre cold, custardy peach flan; the chef was on safer ground with the relatively simple salmon tournedos. Ditto for the starter of Scottish smoked salmon, though the burnt toast was an oversight. The cold melon soup was nothing more than, well, mushy melon topped with coriander (again). Despite a long wait, the apricot *tarte Tatin* wasn't caramelised in the least and had a metallic tang. Decor aside, it's all a bit bland and formulaic (service included). Art lovers, ask for a table in the conservatory.

Le Fouquet's

99 av des des Champs-Elysées, 8th (01.47.23.70.60/www.lucienbarriere.com). M° George V. **Open** daily 8am-2am (last order 11.30pm). **Average** €76. **Prix fixe** €50. **Credit** AmEx, DC, MC, V. **Wheelchair access.**

On one of the first warm days of summer, a stroll down the Champs-Elysées seemed a more tempting prospect than usual. Despite regeneration in the surrounding area the number of dining possibilities on the avenue itself remains limited. Leading the field is Fouquet's; the 't' is sounded in French as a tribute to bygone times when English tea salons were all the rage. As the day was glorious we resisted the velvety interior of this Parisian institution and grabbed a table on the terrace, where a simpler menu is served. Although the entrance is paved with a celebration of the César film awards, we were surrounded by tourists rather than local glitterati. The staff was charming and encouraging to this polyglot crowd and our meal began with foie gras, which was tasty but held telltale veins which should have been removed during the preparation. The *plat du jour*, roasted tuna, came with a nice buttery sauce which made up for the overcooked fish, accompanied by well-prepared pasta interlaced with shredded vegetables. A fillet steak was a good-sized piece of meltingly tender meat with *pommes allumettes*, which were high on crunch. Prices reflect the location and the popularity of the place, but the wine list shocks with mind-boggling mark-ups and little available under €30 a bottle.

Garnier ★

111 rue St-Lazare, 8th (01.43.87.50.40). M° St-Lazare. **Open** daily noon-3pm, 7-11.30pm. Closed Aug. **Average** €50. **Prix fixe** €27-€38. **Credit** AmEx, DC, MC, V.

Since it reopened after a very smart renovation last summer, this venerable restaurant in front of the Gare St-Lazare has become one of the two or three best brasseries in Paris. The decor is an attractive mix of past and present, including dark wood floors, glass partitions, pear-wood chairs, feather-shaped 1950s vintage glass lamps and a few art deco touches. A relaxed and very mixed crowd of locals, tourists, theatre-goers, actors and business types makes for an unselfconscious but stylish atmosphere. If you're accustomed to the clamour and indifferent service of the chain brasseries, this place comes as a delightful surprise: tables are generously spaced and the waiters are friendly professionals. Tuna *rillettes* and croutons arrive as soon as you're seated, and whatever you choose, the quality of the produce and cooking are excellent. Garnier has some of the best oysters in Paris – you could make a feast of these alone – or try the sautéed baby squid and delicious, if expensive, tempura of langoustine tails served in a folded white napkin. Outstanding main courses include tuna steak *a la plancha*, served with tangy carrots and a decorative reduction of balsamic vinegar and pine nuts. Desserts are remarkably good, too, including *baba au rhum* – spongy cake doused with Martinique rum at the table, or a delicate vanilla *millefeuille*. The wine list, however, is rather expensive. For loners, the charming circular oyster bar is an ideal spot.

La Maison de l'Aubrac

37 rue Marbeuf, 8th (01.43.59.05.14). M° Franklin D. Roosevelt. **Open** daily 24 hours. Closed Aug. **Average** €38. **Credit** AmEx, MC, V.

On a Thursday night, just off the chic Champs-Elysées, we found ourselves hemmed in by scrums of big, beefy men tucking into plates of *saucisse aligot* (pork sausages with a mix of mashed potatoes, garlic and cheese), giant ribs of beef and juicy steaks. This rustic little Auvergnat corner, complete with wooden booths, paper placemats and glossy photos of man and beast (bulls in particular), is a beacon for rugby lovers and displaced country folk. We started off simply with a *millefeuille* of vegetables (consisting mainly of mozzarella) with slices of Bayonne ham, and a slab of fine foie gras before the meaty main events. We decided against the 'three meats platter' (tartare, sirloin steak and *boeuf pressé*) and went for slices of leg of lamb from the Lozère region, roasted and served with green beans and crisply fried potato slices – tender if a tad overcooked – and a perfectly grilled *entrecôte*. The accompanying green salad was fresh but gritty. The excellent wine list is a little pricey with good choices from the south-west, Rhône and Languedoc Roussillon. Service is friendly and efficient and the place, like a rugby line-out, is always jumping.

Restaurant Cap Vernet

82 av Marceau, 8th (01.47.20.20.40). M° Charles de Gaulle-Etoile. **Open** Mon-Fri noon-2.30pm, 7-11pm; Sat 7-11pm. Closed 1 July-31 Aug. **Average** €43. **Credit** AmEx, DC, MC, V.

Just off the Champs-Elysées, this very good brasserie with a predominantly seafood menu occupies an awkward if reasonably comfortable split-level space decorated in a twee nautical theme of blue walls and parquet floors. In spite of such a strategic location, it pulls an affluent, mostly Parisian crowd, who appreciate the quality produce and reliable cooking of a kitchen under the aegis of chef Guy Savoy. Settling in on the sunny terrace for lunch, we thoroughly enjoyed the smoked salmon tartare, a tidy mound of pleasantly smoky fish spread with avocado purée under a garnish of small spinach leaves, and a sauté of seasonal vegetables – asparagus, courgettes, mangetout, baby carrots – garnished with grilled bacon. A main

Alcazar: all things Brit and beautiful

course of steamed *demi-sel* cod with a shellfish sauce and mashed potatoes was excellent; however, a tuna steak, cut too thin to be cooked rare as ordered, arrived over-done. Better was a thick slab of salmon in a pleasant, herby green sauce, also garnished with mashed potatoes. A perfectly ripened st-marcellin went down a treat with the rest of a celebratory bottle of white Châteauneuf-du-Pape, and rhubarb tart was pleasant. The only drawbacks to this place are the relatively stiff prices and consistently inefficient and indifferent service – we waited forever for our order to be taken, were not shown the daily specials, were served the wrong wine and were generally ignored by thoroughly bored staff. Still, in season, they offer some of the best oysters in Paris (no shellfish is served on weekends), and if you're casting about for a Sunday meal, bear this place in mind since it's vastly better than most of the increasingly soulless and mediocre brasseries elsewhere in town.

Charlot, Roi des Coquillages ★
81 bd de Clichy, 9th (01.53.20.48.00). *M° Place de Clichy*. **Open** Mon-Wed, Sun noon-3pm, 7pm-midnight; Thur, Fri, Sat 7pm-1am. **Average** €53. **Lunch menu** €23.17, €27.90. **Credit** AmEx, DC, MC, V.
Aside from its endearing, campy glamour – you half expect to see Freddie Mercury, Donna Summer or Abba in this time-warp 1970s dining room decorated with apricot velvet banquettes and peculiar laminated lithographs of shellfish – the main reason that this long-running fish-house is so popular is its flawless catch-of-the-day menu. A curious but buzzy mix of tourists, night people, arty locals, he-and-she executive couples and good-humoured folks in from the provinces patronise this place and given such an eclectic clientele, staff are to be commended for their outstanding professional service. Depending on the season, the various seafood platters are what the regulars opt for, and even in the middle of the summer – off-season for many shellfish – the prawns, sea urchins and lobster are impeccable. Otherwise, start with the excellent fish soup, followed by a classic such as grilled sea bass with wild fennel stalks, tuna steak with ratatouille or superb *aïoli* (boiled salt cod and various vegetables served with lashings of garlic mayonnaise). Finish with *crêpes Suzette*, or the delicious *tarte Tatin* with cinnamon.

Au Petit Riche
25 rue Le Peletier, 9th (01.47.70.68.68/ www.aupetitriche.com) *M° Le Peletier*. **Open** Mon-Sat noon-2.15pm, 7pm-12.15am. **Average** €38. **Prix fixe** €22.10, €28.20 (dinner only). **Lunch menu** €22.10, €25.15. **Credit** AmEx, DC, MC, V.
At the turn of the century *le tout Paris* dined at the long-since-disappeared Café Riche, while lesser mortals, including actors, stage hands and chauffeurs, came to Au Petit Riche. An echo of the grandiose Café Riche survives since this place has beautiful etched glass windows, soaring ceilings, handsome wood panelling and a copper bar; turn-of-the-century framed cartoons and drawings add to the picture. Unfortunately, however, service was bored and awkward, and the food uneven. If first courses of coddled eggs and smoked salmon were decent enough, oysters were served warm and had been carelessly shucked so that they were showered with shell shrapnel. The cheese-capped veal chop, a speciality, was fatty and overcooked, and perch in a drab sauce, ditto. A seeming policy of segregating tourists from locals further dampened our spirits; a table of Americans whose halting but sincere attempts to speak French provoked nasty hilarity among the waiters. The selection of Loire Valley wines is excellent and our 1999 Chinon Losse Loup was delicious, as was a *savarin* topped with whipped cream. We might come back if in the neighbourhood but only for a light supper of starters and a nice Loire wine.

La Taverne
24 bd des Italiens, 9th (01.55.33.10.00/ www.taverne.fr). *M° Richelieu-Drouot*. **Open** daily noon-1am. **Average** €35. **Prix fixe** €24. **Credit** AmEx, DC, MC, V. **Wheelchair access**.
This non-threatening Grands Boulevards restaurant draws a tourist crowd looking for a reasonably priced shellfish extravaganza, as well as locals treating themselves to a night out. We found our fellow diners more interesting than our food, especially when the house *brochettes géantes*, gigantic grilled fish, meat and vegetable kebabs, arrived at the neighbouring table. We watched as the daring family tried to coax chunks of salmon onto their plates from the dangling spikes that hung from a central, circular rack like Damocles swords. A blackened Provençal tart with red mullet prompted the assumption that it was crispy and piping hot, when it was in fact ice cold and undercooked in the middle. An unremarkable *choucroute* and fillet steak with chips and *sauce béarnaise* followed. Insipid cabbage came studded with a small black pudding, a Montbéliard sausage, a pig's trotter and a slice of smoked pork. The steak was properly cooked but the portion of chips was stingy. With no hint of tarragon in the Béarnaise, they might as well have brought mayonnaise. We left the hard, over-refrigerated chocolate fondant untouched, and gobbled up the ice cream and chocolate sauce of our profiteroles. Pastry is not one of La Taverne's strong suits either.

Brasserie Flo
7 cour des Petites-Ecuries, 10th (01.47.70.13.59). *M° Château d'Eau*. **Open** daily noon-3pm, 7pm-1.30am. **Average** €39. **Prix fixe** €30.50 (dinner only). **Lunch menu** €21.50. **Credit** AmEx, DC, MC, V. **Wheelchair access**.
Dating from the late 19th century, Brasserie Flo is the foundation of Jean-Paul Bucher's Flo empire – and one of his least glitzy brasseries. That might have something to do with its location down a fairly remote and seedy alleyway, where it thrives on a post-theatre crowd. One Sunday lunch we found the dining room surprisingly calm and the waiters in good spirits, dodging catapulting children with the grace of tap dancers. Part Alsatian tavern with its wood panelling, part classic brasserie with its black banquettes, crisp white tablecloths, frosted glass and ceiling mouldings, the room felt so comfortable that we lingered for most of the afternoon, while the waiters indulged the catapults by playing an ancient nickelodeon. Food, too, was better than average for Flo. A generous salmon tartare was flavoured with whole peppercorns, onion, bay leaf, chives and thyme, and served on warm boiled potatoes. Both mains were beyond reproach: tender Scottish salmon with chunks of bacon, baked whole garlic cloves and bright-green spinach, and juicy roast veal with morels, served with a crisp and creamy rice *galette*. Our final indulgence was the decadent *coupe Flo*, cherry ice cream drowned in cherry liqueur, and a potent prune and Armagnac *vacherin*.

Julien
16 rue du Fbg-St-Denis, 10th (01.47.70.12.06). *M° Strasbourg-St-Denis*. **Open** daily noon-3pm, 7pm-1.30am. **Average** €38. **Prix fixe** €21.50 (lunch and after 10pm), €30.50. **Credit** AmEx, DC, C, V.
Thanks in part to Eurostar, Alain Ducasse and Sir Terence Conran, not to mention McDonald's and Pizza Express, eating out in the British and French capitals is becoming increasingly similar. However, seated in Julien's beautifully slinky art nouveau decor, with its painted glass panels, white globe lamps and zinc-topped mahogany bar by the artist Majorelle, there is no doubting that you are in Paris. Julien, created in 1902 and revamped in 1975 by the Flo group, is much more intriguing and less hectic than its sister brasseries, partly due to its out-of-the-way location on the border of the red light district of the rue St-Denis and the merchants of the Faubourg itself. Although its status as a listed monument is sufficient reason to pay a visit, the food is also very good, combining trusted brasserie staples with more innovative dishes. From the *carte*, we started with creamy and ripe st-marcellin, wrapped in bacon and roasted, served with wild rocket and walnut oil, and excellent fish soup, complete with croutons, gruyère and spicy *rouille* sauce. Toothsome and perfectly timed partridge came with a delicious cep and potato cake, while saddle of rabbit with fresh tagliatelle was boned, stuffed with pistachios and rolled. With due respect for the spirit of a bygone and more glamorous era, we tucked into vanilla-ice-cream-filled profiteroles, smothered in steaming chocolate sauce.

Terminus Nord
23 rue de Dunkerque, 10th (01.42.85.05.15). *M° Gare du Nord*. **Open** daily 11am-1am. **Average** €25. **Prix fixe** €30.50 (dinner only). **Lunch menu** €21.50. **Credit** AmEx, DC, MC, V.
There may be nothing particular to love about this brasserie besides its location if you're catching a train north (it's across the street from the Gare du Nord), but there certainly is plenty to like. The room is bright and well-appointed with sparkling chandelier, mosaic floors and comfortable leather banquettes; the welcome is warm, and the service is friendly and efficient. The towering shellfish platters – oysters, prawns, mussels, crabs *et al* – are probably the menu's safest bets, but the kitchen handles traditional brasserie fare well enough, too. Our plate of salmon with creamed lentils was fresh and well-seasoned, and the smoked fish platter was generous with at least a half-dozen offerings. The *jarret de porc* (pork knuckle), on the other hand, was thoroughly

Past perfect: the art nouveau Julien

Le Coupe-Chou

Fall under the charm of this Louis XIII style residence, with its little corners, hushed lights and candlelit dinners...

Lunch and dinner set menus: €24 or €32, or à la carte

Open daily, noon–2.30pm and 7pm–1am. Closed Sunday Lunch

11 rue de Lanneau, 5th. Mº Maubert-Mutualité - Tel: 01.46.33.68.69

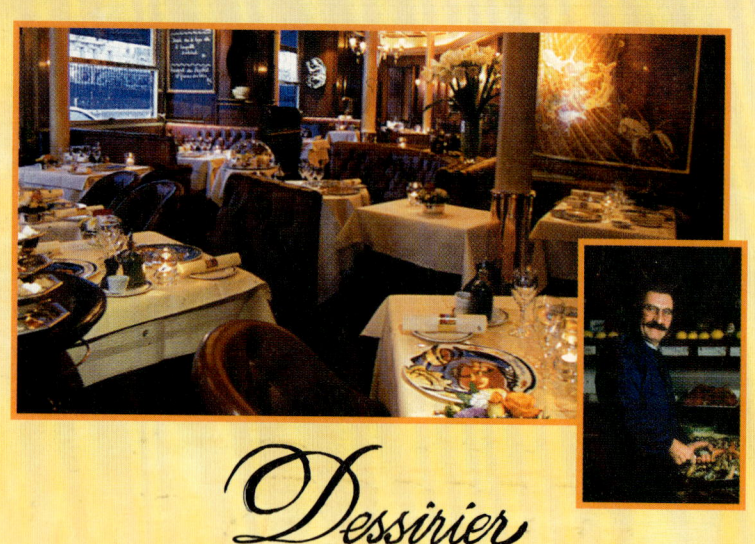

Dessirier

MICHEL ROSTANG

The great fish restaurant in Paris

Michel Rostang took over this seafood institution in 1996

Come and enjoy some of the sea's best:
Wild Sea-Bass in a salt crust
Whole John Dorry roasted (two people)
An extraordinary selection of oysters

Open daily • valet parking

9 place du Maréchal Juin, 17th. MºPereire • Tel: 01.42.27.82.14 • www.michelrostang.com

pedestrian – without the crackling skin that makes it worth the inevitable indigestion that follows – and its accompanying *choucroute* was limp and bland. Traditional desserts such as *tarte Tartin* and profiteroles are agreeable if not exceptional, and the wines are well-priced.

Les Grandes Marches

6 pl de la Bastille, 12th (01.43.42.90.32/ www.lesgrandesmarches.com). M° Bastille. **Open** daily noon-1am. Closed 16 July-1 Sept. **Average** €45. **Prix fixe** €30.50. **Lunch menu** €20.50. **Credit** AmEx, DC, MC, V. **Wheelchair access.**

The Flo group, responsible for restoring La Coupole, Brasserie Flo and Julien in period style, employed Elisabeth and Christian de Portzamparc to redecorate this modern brasserie near the Bastille Opera. It feels like an advertising agency lobby complete with colour-coordinated orange and grey chairs, menus and 'high concept' spiral staircase, while waiters in dark suits dash about like junior executives on deadline. We chose the attractive-sounding 'Opus' menu at €30.50 but, unfortunately, the performance was riddled with wrong notes. The starter, served fresh from the fridge with a basket of stale bread, was *pot-au-feu* of foie gras Jurançon style, a rich pâté with apricot, prune and raisin topped with a mild gelatine. Then came the bland duck steak with too-salty, soggy beans and the salmon steak with linguine and pesto sauce. We had barely finished our last bite of undercooked pasta when our items were cleared a beat too fast. The chocolate tart with pear sorbet and raspberry mascarpone with honey sauce did hit the spot, but as bored children swung off the banister we began to wonder, why come here? Neither the decor nor the food would bring us back.

Le Train Bleu ★

Gare de Lyon, place Louis-Armand, 12th (01.43.43.09.06). M° Gare de Lyon. **Open** daily 11.30am-3pm, 7-11pm. **Average** €45. **Prix fixe** €40. **Credit** AmEx, DC, MC, V. **Wheelchair access.**

This listed dining room has long been one of the most romantic restaurants in Paris, with magnificent 1900 vintage frescoes of the alluring destinations once served by the Paris-Lyon-Marseilles railroad, big oak benches with shiny brass coat racks, and a pleasant air of wistfulness and expectation derived from arrivals and departures. For years the food was so drab that it was only worth coming for a drink in the front bar with its big, cushy leather Chesterfields. But chef André Signoret is to be applauded for the sincere and successful effort that the kitchen is now making. Don't come expecting cutting-edge cooking, but rather fine renderings of French classics and first-rate produce. Lobster served on a bed of walnut-oil-dressed salad leaves was a generous, beautifully prepared starter – easily a luxurious supper on its own – while pistachio-studded *saucisson de Lyon* with a warm salad of small *ratte* potatoes was perfectly cooked and copious. Mains of veal chop topped with a cap of cheese and *sandre* (pike-perch) with a 'risotto' of *crozettes* (tiny squares of pasta from Savoie) were also pleasant, although given the size of the starters and the superb cheese tray, you could easily have a satisfying three-course meal here without a main. A large *baba au rhum* was split at the table, doused with good Martinique rum, and slathered with cream. Charming and efficient service adds to the pleasure of a meal here, and the only obvious improvement would be the addition of a few reasonably priced wines.

La Coupole

102 bd du Montparnasse, 14th (01.43.20.14.20). M° Vavin. **Open** Mon-Thur 8.30am-1am; Fri, Sat 8.30am-1.30am. **Average** €46. **Prix fixe** €30.50 (dinner only). **Lunch menu** €16.50-€29. **Credit** AmEx, DC, MC, V.

Given the sheer size of this restaurant it's amazing that it should ever fill up completely. But fill up it does, with a seething eclectic crowd of Parisians, suburbanites and tourists who come to live the Coupole experience. You can book at lunch, but evenings after 8.30pm (8pm on Fridays and Saturdays) are more complicated. After being issued with a ticket at the entrance, we joined the throng of some 30 or so wannabe diners at the bar and dutifully waited. Finally our number came up and we wedged into our table along with the dozens of others seated along the endless rows of banquettes. Service was good-natured with plenty of corny jokes from the wise-cracking waiters. It all adds to the atmosphere. We couldn't resist the truffled scrambled eggs for a starter and, although they looked fluffy and appetising enough, they were, predictably, almost a truffle-free zone. La Coupole has plenty of seafood on offer: one of us spent a good hour tackling a plate-sized crab while another managed a beautifully cooked *sole meunière* at a whopping €27.14. Fun, rather than a gastronomic experience, a meal at La Coupole makes for great people-watching at a timeless venue.

Le Suffren

84 av de Suffren, 15th (01.45.66.97.86). M° La Motte Picquet-Grenelle. **Open** daily noon-midnight. Closed Aug. **Average** €24. **Prix fixe** €18.90, €29.27. **Credit** AmEx, MC, V.

Near the Eiffel Tower it's a surprise to find a brasserie that feels so local – on our Sunday lunch the average age was well into the 70s, not counting the dogs. One of the few remaining independently-owned brasseries in Paris, the Suffren has a kitsch nautical theme with SS Suffren lifebuoys, model ships, lanterns and dark wood. Tables are informally set with red paper and many people opt for one of the good-value *menus* (not available on the terrace). *A la carte*, we liked the sound of one of the winter specials, the *omelette au truffes*: this unfortunately turned out to be dry, greasy and totally devoid of the heady truffle scent we had been craving. A generous salad of lamb's lettuce and beetroot was a safer bet. *Canard des bocages de l'ouest rôti aux pêches* sounded more elaborate than it tasted – peaches were not exactly in season, after all – but the duck itself was nicely roasted and tender, and a glass of Alsatian pinot noir made a decent match. Of the tempting ice-cream *coupes*, we finally settled on the *coupe papoue*, with meringue, and the extravagant *coupe ardéchoise*, with whipped cream and chestnut purée. Stick to straightforward fare at Le Suffren and enjoy the scenery.

Brasserie de la Poste

54 rue de Longchamp, 16th (01.47.55.01.31/www.brasserie-de-la-poste.com). M° Trocadéro. **Open** daily 11.30am-11.30pm. **Average** €23. **Prix fixe** €20 (lunch only). **Credit** AmEx, DC, MC, V.

The setting of subdued yellow paint, dark wood, and mirrors sporting old black-and-white photographs is pleasant enough but lacks a certain spark, and the same goes for the food. A starter of aubergine and goat's cheese in a pepper sauce would have been helped by a stronger cheese, and while the comté-stuffed ravioli were good, their plain cream sauce made for a monotonous flavour. For mains, we tried an excellent *andouillette* and a *sauté de veau* – a cosy, creamy stew laced with golden raisins. Dessert, a slice of dense, creamy chocolate in *crème anglaise*, looked promising but left an artificial aftertaste. Service was impeccable, friendly and efficient but, overall, nothing seemed worth the increase in prices since our last visit.

La Gare

19 chaussée de la Muette, 16th (01.42.15.15.31). M° La Muette. **Open** daily 12.30-3pm, 7.30-11.30pm. **Average** €33. **Prix fixe** €19, €24. **Credit** AmEx, DC, MC, V. **Wheelchair access.**

This was once a train station of the Petite Centure, the railway circling Paris built by Napoléon III. The ticket office is now the bar and the platforms downstairs have become a colossal dining area. After pushing the train theme hard,however, it seems the restaurant is now taking itself more seriously. Granted there are still giant poultry cut-outs on the walls but the menu, while still dominated by the rotisserie specialities, has been refined. Exploring the new starters, we were seduced by the *pince de tourteau* (crab) with an avocado mousseline, and the black truffle risotto. Stuck awkwardly into the middle of the rice was a grilled wafer of comté: unexpected and delicious. The no-nonsense main courses were excellent: the *gigot d'agneau*, accompanied with a *jus* so concentrated that it is served in a shot glass, was very tender and cooked exactly as we had requested. The portions seemed undersized until the giant bucket of accompanying purée was dropped off. A bit salty this time round but still divine, this traditional side dish is guaranteed to fill any gaps in your stomach. La Gare is in the heart of the posh 16th – if you ask for water, they will assume you want it from a bottle – but prices are varied and reasonable. Evenings are generally calm, but it is often packed for lunch with locals with coiffed pooches in tow and an international crowd from the OECD, just around the corner.

La Grande Armée

3 av de la Grande-Armée, 16th (01.45.00.24.77). M° Charles de Gaulle-Etoile. **Open** daily 7am-2am. **Average** €45. **Credit** AmEx, DC, MC, V.

Admirers of Napoléon Bonaparte might appreciate a more robust tribute to the Corsican upstart than the too-cool-to-be-serious decor for the Grande Armée, jointly owned by the Costes brothers and Jacques Garcia. Perhaps a brace of canon, or a *tricolore* brought back from Austerlitz shot through with gunfire. What you actually get is a couple of cut-out hussars and a bit of synthetic leopard skin (a reference to the Egyptian campaign perhaps?). The word *triomphe* is not the first to spring to mind. Still, with its red and blue walls, there is a cosy gloom about La Grande Armée that makes for intimate conversation. You'd say it was almost like a pub, if that weren't sacrilegious in a place dedicated to history's greatest anglophobe. The menu is strong on prawns, oysters and langoustines, as you'd expect in a Parisian brasserie, but as a starter the parmesan soufflé is an excellent re-working of the old French peasant dish. On to the mains – we wrote off the offer of a cheeseburger as a sort of joke and went for the duck *parmentier*, a delicious combination of duck *confit* and fluffy mashed potato topped with two sublimely-tender slices of piping-hot duck's liver. For pudding: a combination of tiny apple crumble, tiny apple pie and scoop of fresh apple ice cream called a *pom pom pomme*... like the sound of a distant artillery barrage. Or maybe a Costes brother choosing curtains.

Zebra Square

3 pl Clément-Ader, 16th (01.44.14.91.91/ www.zebra-square.com). M° Passy/RER Kennedy-Radio France. **Open** daily noon-3pm, 7.30-midnight. **Average** €36. **Lunch menu** €23. **Credit** AmEx, DC, MC, V. **Wheelchair access.**

Zebra Square is a concept restaurant; at least it tries to be. Part of the sleek Hotel Square complex (and bang opposite the massive and very '60s Maison de Radio France), it screams urban chic. Ebony floors, muted green banquettes and sand-tone walls recall the savannah, but then there's the zebra: minimalism meets safari kitsch. The floor mosaic, painted canvas, funky lamp – all sporting the zebra-skin motif – are OK, but when it comes to tablecloths, napkins and plates it's hard not to think of Elvis (remember Graceland's Jungle Room?). On the night we visited, the clientele was resolutely upmarket: monied locals, hip and not-so-hip, and Anglo-American businessmen. The only wildlife was a savage pigeon that raided patio nut bowls and sent a cocktail flying through a bank of potted trees. The safari theme does not extend to the menu; the house speciality is tartare. A copious plate of salmon, zapped with ginger and lime, was tangy enough, but beef laced with lemon, olive oil and fresh parmesan left us craving more citrus. Starters, such as the rocket with parmesan or the tomato and goat's cheese *tarte croustillante*, were pleasant if unexciting. For dessert we opted for the homely, red-berry crumble topped with *goût bulgare* ice cream. Like everything else it left us – hunting for that distinctive yoghurt taste – a tad disappointed. There's no doubt about it, Zebra Square is a trendy hot spot, but we couldn't figure out why. For all the effort, we left longing for a walk on the wild side.

Le Wepler

14 pl de Clichy, 18th (01.45.22.53.24/ www.wepler.com). M° Place de Clichy. **Open** daily noon-1am. **Average** €38. **Prix fixe** €14.70, €24.10. **Credit** AmEx, DC, MC, V.

There are lots of reasons to like this big brasserie overlooking the busy Place de Clichy, but unfortunately the food isn't one of them. Still, given its convenient location, great people watching, interesting crowd – lots of media and movie types, mixed with tourists and locals – and wonderfully ugly late '50s-early '60s decor, you can manage a decent meal here as long as you order very simply. In other words, avoid anything that requires real cooking, and especially dishes with sauces, since the kitchen here really isn't up to anything even remotely ambitious. We don't speak Polish, but we knew that the table of four next to us was very let down by the elaborate dishes they'd ordered, while a furtive-looking French trio discussing a revision to a screenplay seemed perfectly happy with their steaks. So, start with the oysters or maybe a salad, and then have a grill or the decent *choucroute garnie*, and finish up with ice cream or sorbet if you want dessert. Otherwise, the sandwiches served on the terrace at noon are perfectly fine, and this is one of the rare places in Paris where an interesting crowd of regulars perches to while away an afternoon reading or ruminating.

Au Boeuf Couronné ★

188 av Jean-Jaurès, 19th (01.42.39.54.54/ www.au-boeuf-couronne.com). M° Porte de Pantin. **Open** Mon-Sat noon-3pm, 7.30pm-midnight. Closed 1 May. **Average** €53. **Prix fixe** €25.92, €33.54, €10.67 (children's menu). **Credit** AmEx, DC, MC, V. **Wheelchair access.**

The mad cow scare certainly hasn't dampened Parisians' devotion to this old-fashioned brasserie near the site of the original La Villette abattoirs, which has been serving up massive portions of quality, chargrilled meat since 1930. Its solid, unruffled atmosphere and out-of-the-way location make you feel as though you're dining somewhere *en province*. The large, cavernous room, fitted out with the typical banquettes, wood panelling, mirrors and white linen cloths, has a charming faded elegance – the high-tech till appeared to be the only thing to have changed since circa 1962. The food is traditional French fare done impeccably, delivered by a team of unflappable waitresses in matching frilly white aprons. This year we decided to bypass the beef in order to explore less familiar portions of the menu. The enormous tournedos of salmon accompanied by steamed potatoes and *mirepoix* was of excellent quality and perfectly cooked. As was the juicy lamb chop with *herbes de provence*, served with watercress, grilled tomato and the famous *pommes soufflées*. The speciality here, though, is steak, and most of our fellow diners were enthusiastically tucking into some startling hunks of meat. Desserts were monumental: *crêpes Suzette* cooked dramatically at the table, profiteroles filled with ice cream and doused with chocolate sauce, etc. Dining at the Boeuf Couronné is a thoroughly enjoyable, nostalgic experience.

The best For Seafood

Garnier (8th)
Possibly the best oysters in Paris.

Restaurant Cap Vernet (8th)
Superb seafood, but only on weekdays.

Charlot, Roi des Coquillages (9th)
King-sized platters.

BERMUDA ONION

B.O

16 RUE LINOIS • 15TH • 01 45 75 11 11
OPEN DAILY 8 PM-MIDNIGHT & SUNDAY BRUNCH
"STAR" TERRACE • BAR • EVENING LOUNGE
UNDERGROUND PARKING
www.bermuda-onion.com

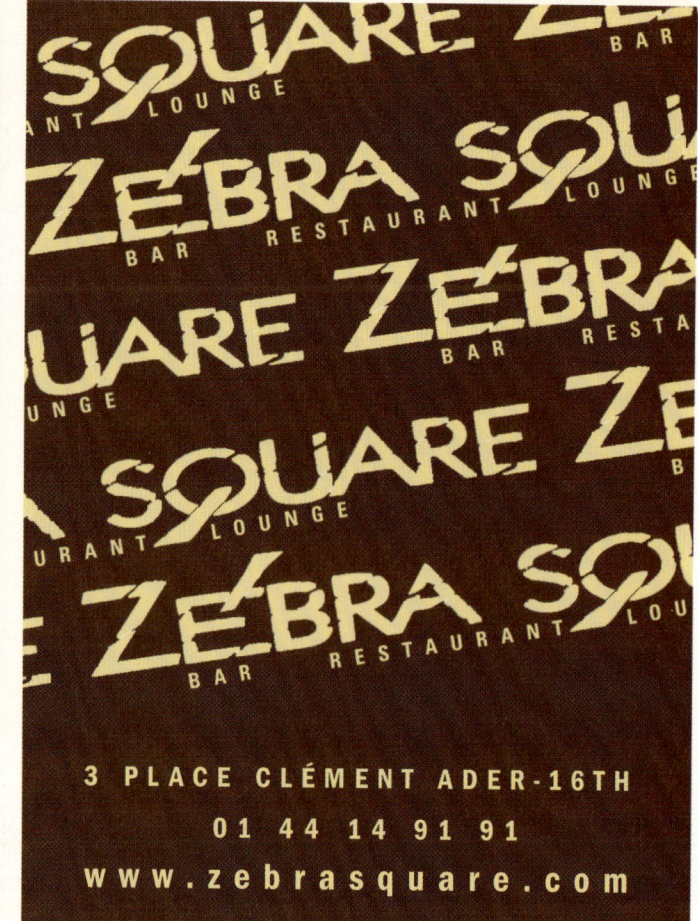

ZEBRA SQUARE
BAR RESTAURANT LOUNGE

3 PLACE CLÉMENT ADER - 16TH
01 44 14 91 91
www.zebrasquare.com

LE SOFA
BAR ———— RESTAURANT

A Bistro unlike any other...

Come for French cuisine with an exotic touch or enjoy a drink at our convivial bar...

21 rue Saint-Sabin, 11th • M° Bastille • Tel: 01 43 14 07 46 • www.lesofa.com
Happy Hour 6pm-8pm

Trendy

Eat with spoons, chopsticks and your fingers as you check out the global fashion set.

The past year has proved that fashion restaurants aren't just a fad in Paris. Probably the most talked-about new drop-dead designer dining room has been **Korova**, which serves lobster hot dogs to its calorie-counting crowd – though the recently opened **Cabaret** is causing a stir. **Nobu** was also a much-anticipated event, and shortly after its opening was pulling in punters who were as well-turned-out as its fusion food. **Spoon, Food & Wine** continues to wow the fashion pack with its puzzle-like menu and international wines.

Alongside these polished spots, a few long-established havens such as **Natacha** (see p13, **Bistros**), **Chez Omar** and **404** (see p99, **North African**), **Anahi** (see p81, **American**) and **Le Stresa** (see p93, **Italian**) attract a slightly less flamboyant fashion set.

Cabaret
2 pl du Palais-Royal, 1st (01.58.62.56.25). Mº Palais Royal. **Open** Mon-Fri noon-6pm, 8-11.30pm; Sat 8-11.30pm. **Average** €46. **Credit** AmEx, DC, MC, V. **Wheelchair access**.
Unashamedly designer maybe, but no red faces for service or cuisine. With a prime location near the Palais-Royal, Cabaret offers quality food overlooking either exhibition rollerblading on the *place* or exhibition posing in the cavernous white Jacques Garcia-decorated basement. The sizeable booths, which seat up to ten comfortably, have quickly become some of the top tables in town. The other option is the African-themed zone with crocodile skins on the walls and mock elephant-foot stools on the floor. Behind the African bar is a chill-out zone of wall-to-wall mattressing where the music is mercifully at conversational level. The menu is Costes-like at first glance, but house specials such as grilled duck and cod with spices are well-executed. Come midnight the venue turns itself over to a cool club which draws a sophisticated crowd that had given up on finding an uptown-fun party. In its short life Cabaret has played host to Kevin Spacey, Rupert Everett, Donatella Versace and Naomi Campbell. Another devotee is the deeply cool Momo.

Hôtel Costes
239 rue St-Honoré, 1st (01.42.44.50.25). Mº Concorde or Tuileries. **Open** daily 7.30am-1am. **Average** €75. **Credit** AmEx, DC, MC, V. **Wheelchair access**.
Costes positively bubbles with the young chattering classes, scanning the scene and braying in plummy French, English and Italian accents. In contrast to the Costes brothers' early postmodern ventures, designer to the stars Jacques Garcia has gone for pseudo-Napoléon III with an excess that is well into kitsch. Funky pop music makes hearing the conversation at the other end of your table impossible – after all, it's being seen rather than heard that is important. The food is far from Napoléon III in scale but augmented by precious little touches on the menu – *'le tigre qui pleure'* ('the tiger that cries', a Thai-inspired dish of minced beef with a piquant sauce), 'club sandwich & chips' and the *'toute petite'* chocolate and banana tart that proved not so much extremely small as extremely sweet. Four succulent but literally bite-sized *noisettes d'agneau* were arranged around a lone sprig of *mâche* (who ever said that nouvelle cuisine was dead?). Service is off-puttingly snooty, but the quality is decent and the action all around theatrically abundant.

Georges ★
Centre Pompidou, 6th floor, rue Rambuteau, 4th. (01.44.78.47.99). Mº Rambuteau. **Open** Mon, Wed-Sun noon-2am. **Average** €54. **Credit** AmEx, DC, MC, V. **Wheelchair access**.
What else would you expect in a modern art museum but an arty, modern restaurant? So here's Georges (named after Mr. Pompidou), with its brushed aluminium pods, translucent tables that glow at night, Philippe Starck-designed cutlery, strenuously hip soundtrack and staff to match. It's another of the Costes brothers' successful scene centrals. Daytime sees exhibition escapees and casual diners while night-time is more a Gucci groove. The food is fine without being fabulous (hard to compete with that view) and prices are on the high side. A cup-full of gazpacho was chilled and spicy, and the artichoke hearts with salmon slices were perfect for a hot summer's day. Also good was a roasted, well-seasoned ostrich steak; however, the tuna steak, although butter-tender, was nowhere near as pink as requested. We found the staff on the terrace breezier than those inside, who were incapable of rising above icy civility.

L'Esplanade
52 rue Fabert, 7th (01.47.05.38.80). Mº La Tour-Maubourg. **Open** daily noon-1am. Café 8am-2am. **Average** €46. **Credit** AmEx, DC, MC, V.
The view is stunning (directly opposite Les Invalides, beautifully floodlit at night), the interior sumptuous and slightly decadent (Jacques Garcia, naturally), the food modish (raw tuna with soy and *wasabi*, steamed vegetables), and the waitresses uniformly stunning, stylish and skinny. L'Esplanade is vintage Costes. The only thing that varies is the clientele – it might be the *arrondissement* or the carefully arranged cannonballs, but L'Esplanade attracts a slightly more mature customer; the profusion of gold buttons gives off a glare almost as distracting as Napoleon's dome. Our *belle sole meunière* was cooked (and filleted) to perfection, and the steak was also well cooked. For pudding we had no idea if *moelleux à la mode* was truly fashionable (certainly we couldn't imagine any of the waitresses eating it) but it was delicious. The fruit salad was thinly cut and decidedly ordinary – although thankfully not drenched in syrup.

Thiou ★
49 quai d'Orsay, 7th (01.45.51.58.58). Mº Invalides. **Open** Mon-Fri noon-2pm, 8-11pm; Sat 8-11pm. Closed Aug. **Average** €60. **Lunch menu** €26. **Credit** AmEx, DC, MC, V.
Let's just start by saying that Thiou serves what has to be the best Thai food in Paris. Hers is a simple mantra: super-fresh, high quality ingredients prepared with care and flair. And it's proved a big hit. Previously, Thiou was at the restaurant of Les Bains Douches so it's no surprise that fashion puppies, and hounds, decorate her new place, along with stylish young and old money, i.e. the locals. Start with juicy chicken satays and peanut sauce, a prawn soup heavy with lemongrass or cold, grilled aubergine topped with prawns and drizzled with a fish sauce vinaigrette (sounds awful, tastes great). Follow with impressive main courses such as *kae phad prik wan*, tender cubes of lamb sautéed with red and green pepper and served with fried rice, or grilled John Dory fillets with spinach, bean sprouts and soy sauce. Desserts are mainly fruit based; mini bananas with syrup and vanilla ice cream makes a good finisher. The wine list is reasonably priced – from €22.10 – the service is attentive and polite, and the setting is elegant and cosy. A nearby annexe specialises in fish.
Branch: Marine de Thiou, 3 rue Surcouf (01.40.62.96.70).

Le Buddha Bar
8 rue Boissy d'Anglas, 8th (01.53.05.90.00). Mº Concorde. **Open** Mon-Fri noon-3pm, 6pm-2am; Sat, Sun 6pm-midnight. **Average** €69. **Prix fixe** €60, €75. **Lunch menu** €32. **Credit** AmEx, MC, V. **Wheelchair access**.
Forget even B-list celebrities. These days Buddha Bar is divided between an international hotel crowd and suburbanites on an office night out – even if a famous face did turn up they would run from the constant and intrusive flash photography. The setting, of course, is as impressive as ever and booking a table at least gives an illusion of exclusivity when you see how the staff descend like Valkyries on anyone who tries to break free from the bar throng to get a peek at the enormous seated Buddha. For a place with such attitude, the food is surprisingly good, though pricey. We ordered a mixed plate of sushi from the separate sushi menu as a starter – large, well-presented and very fresh. From the main courses the steamed monkfish in banana leaf was rather tasteless but the curried prawns lipsmackingly good. Desserts featured the ubiquitous chocolate *moelleux* (listed as *fondant chocolat*), which lived up to expectations. In the hope that Johnny Depp might still turn up, the wine list soars to Château Pétrus at around €1,350, but in the lower price range there are some fine offerings.

Korova
33 rue Marbeuf, 8th (01.53.89.93.93). Mº Franklin D. Roosevelt. **Open** Mon-Fri, Sun noon-3pm, 7.30pm-2am; Sat 7.30pm-2am.

Thiou good to be true

CD days

Long gone are the days of faint tinkling ivories, a little lite-jazz or background muzak – these days what's coming out of the speakers is as important as what's coming out of the kitchen. The 'lounge' phenomenon and the reign of celebrity resto-DJs began way back in 1996 when Claude Challe put together the **Buddha Bar**'s first compilation CD. This temple to exoticism has never looked back; last year saw the launch of its third CD mixed by DJ Ravin. Matching the trans-pan 'fusion' food and oriental/colonial decor, the disk is a blend of what they call 'ethno-mystical' tracks, aka ambient Goa trance.

Requiring no joss sticks but equally exotic due to its A-list clientele is **Hôtel Costes**. Popular for its opulent decor and Costes-quality food, the place also owes its enormous success to the resident DJ and lounge supremo, Stéphane Pompougnac. His first Costes CD placed 80s diva Grace Jones alongside current electro faves K & D and De-Phazz – mixing up styles and taking underground sounds to a whole new audience. When not remixing Madonna or jetting off to Miami for a Gucci party, Pompougnac found time to work on Costes' recently released fourth CD.

Momo, urbane host of the **404** (see p99, **North African**), was one of the first to bottle his restaurant's atmosphere in home-friendly CD form, and the second CD, *Zoudge*, offers more *riad*-chic soundtracks from the likes of Natacha Atlas.

Man Ray and Conran's **Alcazar** (see p46, **Brasseries**) have been sure not to miss out on the fun. Man Ray gives its glam customers a chance to relax *chez soi* to its ambient lounge. Mezzanine's (Fridays at Alcazar) resident DJs Fabrice Lamy and Shade keep their foodies happy with seductive lounge and their weekenders lively with up-for-it house. The Brazilian cantina **Favela Chic** (see p81, **The Americas**) owes its inimitable party atmosphere as much to its trend-setting DJ as its potent cocktails. It seems the only trendy eatery/move your feetery without a CD is **Korova**, ironic considering it is the 'in' spot. *Phoebe Greenwood*

Café Society

Raghunath Manet has made the ancient south Indian dance form bharata natyam *his own, using ancient texts to resurrect the male tradition which had been all but lost. He also plays the veena, the oldest and most venerated south Indian instrument, and has recorded a fusion album,* Omkara *(Dreyfus Jazz), with famed jazz violinist Didier Lockwood and soprano Caroline Casadesus.*

'Food has always been very important to me. It's another art form, the expression of a culture. I've always gone back and forth between Pondichery and Paris, so I live in both countries. When I'm in Pondichery, I like to eat typical south Indian food such as *dosai*. But, wherever I am, I want to eat the food of that culture so I don't seek out Indian food in Paris, though I love to cook it at home for friends. Wherever I perform, people always reserve an Indian restaurant for me after the show. I have to tell them that I prefer to taste the local food! Indian food in other countries is necessarily adapted to local tastes. One Indian place I like in Paris is **Yogi's**. It's modern with a bit of a trendy feel and, though the cooking is inventive, the spicing reminds me of India. A typically French restaurant that's one of my favourites is **Le Gamin de Paris** (49 rue Vieille du Temple, 3rd/01.42.78.97.24), which is near where I live in the Marais. It's always fun. For vegetarian food I enjoy **L'Aquarius** (54 rue Ste-Croix de la Bretonnerie/01.48.87.48.71), which is also close to home. A place I love is the **Barramundi** (*see p 117*, **Bars & Pubs**), for its new French cuisine and wonderful, relaxing decor. When I go to a café I don't necessarily want to see other artists – I see them all day! – and that's why I like **La Tartine** (24 rue de Rivoli, 4th/ 01.42.72.76.85). It's a down-to-earth place that serves wine by the glass. Another café I go to often is **Le Louis-Philippe Café** (*see p104*, **Cafés**), which has a historic interior and good food, and is near the Cité des Arts where I rehearse.'

Average €50. **Lunch menu** €30.50 (Mon-Fri). **Credit** AmEx, DC, MC, V. **Wheelchair access.**
Owned by TV presenter Jean-Luc Delarue, this slick new restaurant is pulling in trendy punters like clockwork – Orange, that is, since it's named after the bar in the Anthony Burgess novel. The decor by architect-designer Christian Biecher recalls *The Avengers* and '60s-vintage airport lounges with white plastic pod chairs and dramatic lighting, and the Gucci and Prada clad crowd is earnestly see-and-be-seen. Service is rather friendlier than at most fashion restaurants, and the food is actually pretty good, though the most talked-about dish, the chicken roasted with Coca-Cola, is definitely best avoided, as is the pear and Parmesan pizza. Start with *ceviche* or the salad of quinoa with a *bouillabaisse* sauce and langoustines, and then try the salmon with cucumber ribbons and new potatoes, or fish and chips. Desserts, created by star *pâtissier* Pierre Hermé, are original and delicious, especially *pom, pomme, pomme* – an apple meringue tart served with an apple parfait made with apple compote, apple ice, chunks of Granny Smith and dried apple wafers. This is not a place where we'd aspire to becoming a regular, but it's amusing for a one-off meal.

Man Ray

34 rue Marbeuf, 8th (01.56.88.36.36/ www.manray.fr). M° Franklin D. Roosevelt. **Open** Mon-Fri noon-2.30pm, 7.30pm-12.30am. Bar daily 6pm-2am. Closed at lunch in Aug. **Average** €57. **Lunch menu** €20. **Credit** AmEx, MC, V. **Wheelchair access.**
Though the service is not in the same league of rudeness as the Buddha Bar (but then, what could be?), the diners have a degree more sophistication and the faux-Asian decor has a certain James Bondish appeal, Man Ray still leaves you feeling curiously empty. It's not just the effect of spending time in the company of the vacuous 'jet set', it is quite literally the food, which might as well have been constructed out of jelly for a film set. After a miserable previous experience, we were willing to give the place a second chance – but nothing has changed. From an extensive menu covering anything from Italian to Thai dishes we chose starters of an utterly flavourless chilled cucumber soup, and a 'cappuccino of langoustines' which reminded us of the sweet artificial cream used by downmarket British bakeries. The fish of the day, turbot fried in basil olive oil, was not bad, and a second fish dish of *sandre* (pike-perch) in a *girolle* sauce was edible, though the sauce swamped the fish completely. In terms of mediocrity desserts took the biscuit: *velouté de pêches* surrounding an industrial-tasting sorbet tasted and looked suspiciously like the syrupy nectar drinks you can buy in corner shops. The éclairs appeared to have been frozen and defrosted. Stick to cocktails at the bar or return for the Friday night soirées when DJs spin French Touch. But dinner? Forget it.

Nobu ★

15 rue Marbeuf, 8th (01.56.89.53.53). M° Franklin D. Roosevelt. **Open** Mon-Fri noon-3pm, 6.30pm-12.30am; Sat, Sun 6.30pm-12.30am. Bar daily 6.30pm-2am. Closed 25 Dec. **Average** €76. **Prix fixe** €98 (dinner only). **Lunch menu** €38, €76. **Credit** AmEx, DC, MC, V. **Wheelchair access.**
On the eve of the couture fashion shows, this slick new Japanese fusion restaurant with bare wood floors and tables had clearly struck a chord with the itinerant fashion and media crowd, since it was absolutely packed with Gucci and Prada devotees who didn't seem to blanch at the idea of running up a bill of €76 or more per person. This is the third Nobu, following the original in New York and one in London, and in Paris, the vibrant flavours and textures of chef Matsuhisa Nobuyuki's stylish hybrid South American-Japanese cooking are extremely welcome. Nobuyuki does intriguing dishes such as tempura of Florida rock shrimp (rather like a langoustine but from the Gulf of Mexico), a tomato '*ceviche*' (red, yellow and green tomatoes dressed with red onions and loads of fresh coriander), sublime sushi and sashimi, miso-marinated black cod cooked until it's more or less lacquered, and wonderful *à la carte* tempura. Start with an order of *endamame* beans sprinkled with salt, a popular Japanese snack, and then order the outstanding *ceviche* before hitting the sushi and sashimi. The wine list is very pricey, but includes some wonderful bottles such as the South African Neethlingshof sauvignon blanc (€36.59), and service is patient and efficient. Nobu is that rarest of things in Paris – a non-smoking restaurant – though you can smoke in the lounge downstairs, which is furnished with comfy leather armchairs.

Rue Balzac

3-5 rue Balzac, 8th (01.53.89.90.91). M° Franklin D. Roosevelt or George V. **Open** Mon-Thur 12.15-2.15pm, 7.15-11pm; Fri 12.15-2.15pm, 7.15-11.30pm; Sat, Sun 7.15-11.30pm. Closed three weeks in Aug. **Average** €46. **Credit** AmEx, DC, MC, V. **Wheelchair access.**
Rue Balzac, Johnny Hallyday's pad, is a cut above your average celebrity-owned restaurant. For a start, its consultant chef is Michel Rostang, who runs an eponymous haute cuisine restaurant and several bistros. The deco-inspired chairs and banquettes were looking a bit grubby despite the low lighting, but we liked the delicate gold chandeliers and tiny blue glass spotlights. The welcome was friendly enough, although it was a slack night for celebrity clients – only a young French radio comedian. The menu offers four options in each category of eggs, starters, pasta and rice, fish and meat, with specials written on a piece of glass. We started with rice-paper-thin slices of aubergine layered with a crab and aubergine filling, enhanced by dribbled lines of soy and peanut vinaigrettes. The *terrine de foie gras* with wild mushrooms was disappointing, however – served too cold with a cold piece of toast, the foie gras lacked salt or indeed any flavour at all and the dry *girolles* and radish with a smidgen of cherries did little to help. The sea bass fillet *a la plancha* with an artichoke and fresh coriander confit was better, the fish virtually perfect, soft and juicy with a herby crust. The other fish dish, light and grease-free squid and langoustines with sesame spring vegetables, came elegantly served on a napkin in a metal basket. A *soufflé fondant chaud au cacao amer* was richly satisfying and the *petits pots de chocolat crème*, served in two identical tiny pots with a puff pastry finger, were also good, though definitely the less indulgent choice. Wines are steeply marked-up but we enjoyed our crisp '99 Sancerre for €29.73.

Spoon, Food & Wine

14 rue de Marignan, 8th (01.40.76.34.44). M° Franklin D. Roosevelt. **Open** Mon-Fri noon-2pm, 7-11pm. Closed last week in July and first three weeks in Aug. **Average** €74. **Credit** AmEx, DC, MC, V.
When Alain Ducasse's world-food bistro opened several years ago, it had the effect of a fire alarm going off in a wax museum. Since then, Paris has changed – and, impressively, so has Spoon. Ducasse plays a sensuous game for assiduous gourmets, but most of the clientele here seem more interested in the brand name than in the food. We began our meal with a sublime *mousse d'étrilles* (velvet swimming crab) and a brilliant and original casserole of cod, aubergine and tomatoes with sesame cream, then sampled wonderful sea bass *ceviche* and rather mediocre lobster ravioli with anchovy cream sauce. Thai soup with cockles, prawns and squid was splendid, as was tuna fillet with a sautée of mixed vegetables wondrously garnished with garlic flowers. Our *grande bouffe* continued with spare ribs with *sauce diable* and potato chips, and a sublime grilled loin of rabbit with its liver and kidneys. We finished up with the best cheesecake in town and chocolate-dipped ice cream, and came away in admiration of the way this place keeps surfing the very best of fusion cuisine. Remarkable wine list, too – if only the help would lighten up a bit and stop being so arch.

Tanjia

23 rue de Ponthieu, 8th (01.42.25.95.00). M° Franklin D. Roosevelt. **Open** Mon-Fri noon-3pm, 8pm-1am; Sat, Sun 8pm-1 am. Closed Aug. **Average** €45. **Prix fixe** €53.36. **Lunch menu** €19.06. **Credit** AmEx, DC, MC, V.
We were expecting high voltage air kisses and a side of couscous at Tanjia, Les Bains Douches team's (Cathy and David Guetta and Hubert Boukobza) Moroccan restaurant. After all, Bobby (de Niro) and Jack (Nicholson) and all manner of Hollywouldbes, models and moguls pop in when in Paris. Once past the phalanx of black cling-wrap clad, wired-for-sound staff at the door (we had a reservation), we downed an overpriced, overly small cocktail in the bar downstairs and then settled in to the super-sheik restaurant upstairs. The food is better than you'd expect and the staff seem, believe it or not, attitude-free. The assorted starters for two – pricey at €13.72 a head but sufficient to feed a small army – included *briouates* (turnovers) of *gambas*, chicken and *chèvre*, aubergine caviar, and salads (give the sickly sweet carrot salad with orange flower water a miss). Then it's on to pigeon *pastilla* (crispy pastry with ground pigeon and almonds, dusted with icing sugar) and generous servings of mild lamb tagine (cooked ten hours with 25 spices) or couscous with organic veggies. Try the fig ice cream and order mint tea – just to see the waiters pour it deftly from a great height. Alas, our cool factor had melted and we couldn't adjourn to the bar afterwards – private party, they insisted.

Yogi's

13 rue du Commandant-Mouchotte, 14th (01.45.38.92.93). M° Montparnasse-Bienvenüe. **Open** Mon-Wed 8am-2am; Thurs-Sat 8am-5am (kitchen open until closing). **Average** €31. **Lunch menu** €13.95. **Credit** MC, V.
A rickshaw marks the entrance of this Indian bar-restaurant, strangely located at the entrance of a shopping mall. There's formal restaurant seating towards the back, but the over-the-top lounge area near the door is much more fun: there aren't many places in Paris where you can recline on satin sofas and drink cocktails under the wary eye of dragons and

Bon for your health

Korova: this tribute to Anthony Burgess runs like clockwork

Hindu gods, while Bollywood posters add an authentic note. The food ranges from the sublime to the ridiculous. Our tandoori grill plate included mysterious sausage meats and one scampi with no body, just the inedible head. But the south Indian dishes are spiced just as they should be. Alternatively, order nan bread (the coriander and almond flavours are particularly nice), with some dahl and yoghurt-based raita, and stick to drinks. Don't be put off by the price of beer; there are some peculiar misprints on the menu, so check with the waiter about what things are likely to cost.

Bon ★
25 rue de la Pompe, 16th (01.40.72.70.00). Mº La Muette. **Open** daily noon-2.30pm, 8pm-2am. **Average** €60. **Credit** AmEx, MC, V. **Wheelchair access**.
Philippe Starck's first venture as restaurateur has a rather fantastic setting: a sort of cross between *Alice Through the Looking Glass* (all sorts of coloured, distorted mirrors will do wonders – or not – for your waistline), Nero's Rome, with draped sofas, decadent candelabras and *coupes* of bright green apples, and a Heidi-esque wooden chalet. There's a courtyard with curious metal planters and glass clocks and a boutique section that stocks anything from organic olive oil to nappy-pin jewellery. What was missing, until recently, was food to live up to the surroundings. After a debut that was anything but *bon* (good), this trendy spot is not only back on track but is on its way to becoming a seriously good restaurant under the auspices of very talented chef Jean-Louis Amat. Amat formerly ran the Saint-James and two other excellent restaurants outside of Bordeaux in Bouliac, and after having been foolishly shown the door by a new owner, he's brought his vast experience and appetising south-western touch to Paris. Start with that delicious Bordelais combo of fresh oysters accompanied by tiny grilled sausages, and then venture on to other signature dishes such as skewered eel with artichokes or scallops steamed with seaweed. If this serious, regional cooking seems vaguely incongruous in the campy, kitschy dining room, one might hope that this evolution will prove the point that no matter how trend-conscious they may currently be, the French ardently insist on a certain standard of cooking.

Café de la Jatte
60 bd Vital Bouhot, Ile de la Jatte, 92200 Neuilly-sur-Seine (01.47.45.04.20). Mº Pont de Levallois. **Open** daily noon-2.30pm, 7.30-11.30pm. **Average** €46. **Credit** AmEx, DC, MC, V. **Wheelchair access**.
Enter this island from the Pont de Levallois on a lovely summer's day to breathe in the delicious scent of honey from the beehives hidden in the middle of the parkland – you'll be glad to have made the expedition. The Café is housed in a vast red brick building that was once Napoleon's riding school; today, a spectacular dinosaur skeleton strung from the ceiling decorates the main dining room. The menu is determinedly international with dishes such as spiced lamb curry with chutney and salmon sushi maki. We stuck to the more Gallic propositions of sea bream grilled with capers and wild asparagus, and farmer's duck *magret*. The result was generous portions of fresh, tender fish and vegetables and very tasty slices of duck. Less agreeable was the closeness of the tables on the vast terrace: cigar smoke billowed over our shoulders, while the amorous couple on our left let slip a little more information than we could digest. As for the waiters, they were so robotic in their efficiency that the customers could have been frogmen for all they cared. The desserts, such as fresh peach *suprême* with cinnamon syrup, were just as fresh and plentiful as the previous courses, yet it was a relief to flip-flop back to the tree-lined river bank.

Quai Ouest
1200 quai Marcel Dassault, 92210 St-Cloud (01.46.02.35.54). Mº Porte de St-Cloud. **Open** Mon-Sat noon-3pm, 8pm-midnight; Sun noon-4pm. **Average** €34. **Lunch menu** €17.50 (Mon-Fri). **Credit** AmEx, DC, MC, V. **Wheelchair access**.
Looking across the sparkling river to the tree-lined banks of the Bois de Boulogne, we felt far from the stresses of Paris. The world-weary floorboards had obviously seen a lot of use before this airy warehouse was ever a restaurant. The rust has been left on the frames of the many windows, but the atmosphere is prevented from becoming too rustic by the enthusiastic gas heaters that can keep 400 diners warm and cosy. So cosy, in fact, that you can feel your hair curling if you are unfortunate enough to be placed right under one. Despite its privileged location (and customers: we had to squeeze between a Lotus and a Jaguar E-type to get to the door) the prices are reasonable. We stopped by for the Sunday brunch, complete with clown and face-painting for the kids. Sitting in the adult-only annexe, we took advantage of the bottomless cups of coffee and all-you-can-eat pancakes – cunningly served as dessert, after the generous main brunch *plats* of salmon, chicken, chips, bacon and fresh fruit.

La Table du Marquis

Traditional French cuisine

Open Tuesday to Saturday
noon-2pm and 7.30pm-10pm

3 rue Beccaria, 12th • Tel: 01.43.41.56.77 • M° Gare de Lyon or Reuilly Diderot

---

CHEZ PAUL
— RESTAURANT DE TRADITION —

BUTTE AUX CAILLES • PARIS XIII • 01 45 89 22 11

Traditional French Cuisine

Open daily - even on Sundays!!
Lunch noon-2.30pm & dinner 7.30pm-midnight

22 rue de la Butte aux Cailles, 13th. M° Place d'Italie
Reservations recommended. Tel: 01.45.89.22.11

Classic

Familiarity breeds contentment; the defenders of French traditions tastefully deliver.

While food fads may come and go, in Paris there is a clutch of sentinels that retain a reverence for archetypal French cooking – a rewriting of the classics (be it decor or food) is rarely on the menu in these establishments. From lavish addresses such as **Lasserre**, with its thoroughly civilised clientele and retractable ceiling, to the freshly renovated **Violon d'Ingres**, kept perfectly tuned by former Crillon chef Christian Constant, these restaurants boldly fly the French flag in the face of fashion and fusion follies.

Le Poquelin
17 rue Molière, 1st (01.42.96.22.19).
M° *Palais Royal.* **Open** Mon, Sat 7-10pm; Tue-Fri noon-2pm, 7-10pm. Closed three weeks in Aug. **Average** €46.
Prix fixe €31.25. **Lunch menu** €24.35.
Credit AmEx, DC, MC, V.
Given the name of the street and the close proximity to the Comédie Française, it's no surprise that Molière looms large in this diminutive restaurant. It's named after him (his real name rather than his *nom de plume*) and his face, *trompe l'oeil* bookshelves and theatre masks decorate the walls. If you like chocolate-box pretty, you'll like this. The kitchen serves up agreeably traditional food with a nod to today: roast rabbit with mustard and green peppercorns and new potatoes, *rascasse* (scorpion fish) with Provençal vegetables, or starters such as smoked duck slices atop a crispy green salad, and spinach and coriander ravioli dipped in a light curry cream. *Oeufs à la neige* topped with cracked sugared almonds, and a vanilla ice-cream ball dusted with cocoa and served with raspberry coulis are fine finishers. *A la carte* prices are on the high side so stick with the *menu* as many of the best dishes make an appearance. Lunch is the domain of locals while internationals rule at night.

Le Soufflé
36 rue du Mont-Thabor, 1st (01.42.60.27.19). M° *Concorde.* **Open** Mon-Sat noon-2.30pm, 7.30-10.30pm. Closed public holidays. **Average** €38.11. **Prix fixe** €28.50-€35. **Credit** AmEx, DC, MC,V. **Wheelchair access.**
This matronly restaurant located in a chic hotel district attracts a fair amount of tourists and families with its sweet and salty versions of the 18th-century invention, the soufflé. Choices include savoury standards, such as cheese, ham, leek, mushroom and salmon, or sweet dessert ones such as lime, pear, chestnut and Grand Marnier. The waiters in crisp white jackets and blue ties are efficient, patient and ready to offer advice as well as take orders in fluent English. We started with a crowd-pleasing spinach soufflé and ended with rich chocolate and raspberry versions, puffed high with custardy centres. Sizeable portions came at an upbeat pace, served piping hot on quaint flowered dishes. We also enjoyed non-soufflé choices of fresh tomato stuffed with crab and chives, a buttery-soft rack of lamb and breaded sea bass with mashed sweet potatoes.

La Truffière
4 rue Blainville, 5th (01.46.33.29.82). M° *Place Monge.* **Open** Tue-Sun noon-2pm, 7-10.30pm. **Average** €49. **Prix fixe** €32, €65. **Lunch menu** €15, €21 (Tue-Fri).
Credit AmEx, DC, MC, V. **Wheelchair access.**
The long, intimate room is heavy on beams and lace and hung with tacky 'Paris' artwork of the worst kind. Lots of swirling and fiddling with crockery apes grand restaurants, but the welcome is warm and we were quickly enjoying an apéritif and studying the menu. We rejected the good-value set *menu* – too low on sexy truffles – and plumped for a meal laden with the musky black jewels. First up, scrambled eggs, in which truffle shavings produced groans of pleasure, and a salad with nuts and slivers of fresh truffle. The main courses of quail and rabbit with rich foie gras and truffle sauces were delicious but lacked the last degree of culinary refinement. Finally, a generous selection of cheeses and desserts which included a superb caramelised sweet potato concoction and the well-named *puits d'amour*, a 'well' from which sprung berries and *crème pâtissière*. It was probably not as deep as the pit left on our credit card, but we were led astray by the encyclopaedic wine list, and the admirable sommelier, whose advice led us to a peppery 1998 Gigondas and a half-bottle of powerful white Hermitage. The poor man had a difficult evening coping with some American businessmen who, *mon dieu*, claimed they preferred Chilean red to anything French!

Lapérouse
51 quai des Grands-Augustins, 6th (01.43.26.68.04). M° *St-Michel.*
Open Mon-Fri noon-2.30pm, 7.30-10.30pm; Sat 7.30-10.30pm. Closed mid July-mid Aug.
Average €77. **Prix fixe** €106. **Lunch menu** €30. **Credit** AmEx, DC, MC, V.
It's hard to imagine a more delicious historical setting for a meal than this ancient townhouse on the banks of the Seine. During the 19th century, its private *salons* were the setting for many an illicit romance, since a loophole in the law made adultery legal if it took place in a public setting. Our room was delightfully intimate, with timeworn wallpaper, a small red sofa and a big mirror covered in scratches – apparently the work of cheeky mistresses who used them to test the authenticity of their diamonds. If you ask for a *salon*, there is a catch — you must order chef Alain Hacquard's €106 *prix fixe menu*. Since some of the same dishes are available on the excellent-value lunch *menu*, served in the beamed dining room overlooking the Seine, you are clearly paying for the privacy – so you might as well make the most of it. We splurged on Champagne (€11 a glass) before starters of a sea urchin *brouillade* (scrambled eggs) with green asparagus, and barely-cooked langoustines with a *cristalline* of paper-thin beet slices and raspberry cream, and mildly spiced avocado '*saté*'. A scallop main course was perhaps a bit same-ish – a circle of just-seared seafood with garlic cream sauce and parsley *jus*. Heartier were two rounds of *biche* (doe) with pepper sauce, tender salsify and mango chutney with maniguette, a subtle pepper. Dessert also featured the spicing for which Hacquard is becoming known — *pain perdu* (French toast) came with a sweet chilli jam and herb sorbets. We couldn't resist the dramatic praline soufflé, doused in buttery rum sauce. After a few inconsistent years, Lapérouse seems to have found its footing – the waiters were friendly and efficient and the experience thoroughly memorable.

Violon d'Ingres ★
135 rue St-Dominique, 7th (01.45.55.15.05). M° *Ecole-Militaire or RER Pont de l'Alma.*
Open Mon-Sat 7-11pm. Closed Aug.
Average €76.22. **Prix fixe** €89.94. **Credit** AmEx, MC, V.
The long room is an essay in tasteful 21st-century classicism, with elegant porcelain urns and sepia prints. We arrived late, but were greeted with surprising warmth by the exemplary staff. Details such as the bread, canapés and amazing *petits fours* all indicate that chef Christian Constant's violin is perfectly tuned. Our meal began with a soup of coco beans, which had been transformed into a few spoonfuls of tantalisingly creamy goodness. Starters included a tomato and seafood *millefeuille*, prepared with such culinary dexterity that it seemed a shame to bring a knife to bear on it, but the winner was a plate of soft poached eggs, in a magically crisp coating topped with truffles. We chose the chicken tagine; the resulting dish was more like a gentle Thai curry, but nonetheless delicately flavoured. Only the miserable side portion of over-seasoned couscous disappointed. Perhaps more successful was a dish of long-cooked *joues de boeuf*, spoonably tender meat cooked to perfection with rich slivers of foie gras. We decided to share a dessert, which turned out to be spectacular. Souffléed potatoes had been lightly caramelised and filled with a coffee *crème pâtissière*, served beside a fluffy liquorice mousse, and the whole dish topped with piping hot chocolate sauce. Perhaps not something one should try at home. A few more reasonably priced bottles on the comprehensive wine list would lighten the bill considerably, but even paying more than €152 for two we left the restaurant happy.

Le Bistrot du Sommelier
97 bd Haussmann, 8th (01.42.65.24.85). M° *St-Augustin.* **Open** Mon-Fri noon-2.30pm, 7.30-11pm. Closed Aug, 24 Dec-2 Jan.
Average €55. **Prix fixe** €60-€100 (dinner only). **Lunch menu** €39, €54.
Credit AmEx, V.
'Bistrot' is perhaps a misnomer for this small but luxurious restaurant, run by Philippe Faure-Brac, who was named France's best sommelier in 1988 and the world's best in 1992. Chef Jean-Michel Descloux's *menu découverte*, served only to the whole table, is indeed a voyage of discovery. Each of the six courses is designed to complement the accompanying wine, tasted blind, with diners invited to guess the origin. A slightly salty green asparagus *velouté*, with tiny chicken dumplings, became an excellent foil for Guigal's white Côtes du Rhône '98. Delicious Graves de Vayres, Château Pichon-Bellevue '99, cut through the richness of thick slices of salt-cured salmon, served with chicory and a goat's cheese mousse. Braised *carrelet* (plaice) with coriander-spiced cauliflower was the backdrop to steely, concentrated Pouilly-Fumé from Jean-Claude Dagueneau. And as for the reds? Well, a silky '94 Volnay from Crotet partnered *mignon de porc* with pearl barley, followed by the mind-blowing Pomerol Château la Conseillante '89 alongside comté, st-marcellin and charolais goat's cheese (to be eaten in that order!). Finally, a notoriously difficult match, a bitter chocolate fondant with pistachio *crème anglaise*, was served with Carthagène, a sweet wine from the Languedoc, made from grenache and fortified with grape spirit. The sheer quality and variety of the 900 wines available, many by the glass, coupled with knowledgeable yet unstuffy service, make this a unique place for wine lovers.

Lasserre
17 av Franklin-Roosevelt, 8th (01.43.59.53.43). M° *Franklin D. Roosevelt.*
Open Tue-Sat 12.30-2pm, 7.30-10pm. Closed Aug. **Average** €137.20. **Prix fixe** €130 (dinner only). **Lunch menu** €55.
Credit AmEx, DC, MC, V.
The sky was a brilliant blue for the first time in weeks on the Saturday we went for lunch at Lasserre – which meant that we were treated to the open ceiling for which this restaurant is famous. The decor of pillars, potted plants, Saxe porcelain and a giant candelabra, none of which can have changed much since Lasserre's opening in the 1940s, otherwise errs on the side of stuffiness – as do the customers (we heard one asking for the *soustraction* rather than the *addition*, har har). The waiters, too, looked a bit stiff – this is not a place where it's easy to laugh out loud. The good news is that the food is excellent, even if you order the relatively cheap €55 *menu*. Jean-Louis Nomicos, formerly of La Grande Cascade, recently replaced Michel Roth and his cooking proved refreshingly modern, though classic dishes are still available *à la carte*. A foie gras flan with a frothy mushroom cream whetted our appetites for the starters: slightly oily courgette flowers filled with creamy aubergine and surrounded by slices of

Le Poquelin, a class act with Molière on the menu

Michel Rostang

www.michelrostang.com
bistrotrostang@wanadoo.fr

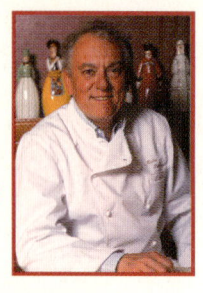

Le Bistrot d'à Côté — "La Boularde"
4 rue Boutard
92200 Neuilly sur Seine
Tel: 01.47.45.34.55

Closed Sat lunch and Sun all day
Valet parking

In the heart of the village of Neuilly sur Seine, and right near to La Défense, this authentic bistrot offers generous cuisine. You'll love to try the famous steaks (for two people) and the "Crêpes flambées" with Grand Marnier.

L'ABSINTHE
24 place du Marché
Saint Honoré, 1st
Tel: 01.49.26.90.04

Closed Sat lunch and Sun all day

Between the Place de l'Opéra and the Louvre, this modern welcoming bistrot guarantees a tasty and pleasant time.

Bistrot...côté mer
10 boulevard Saint-Germain, 5th
Tel: 01.43.54.59.10

Open daily, valet parking

Behind Notre-Dame Cathedral, Michel Rostang's daughter welcomes you to this charming little "maritime" bistrot. Discover inventive seafood cuisine, and sample dishes like the whole grilled sea-bass (for two).

Le Bistrot d'à Côté — "Flaubert"
10 rue Gustave Flaubert, 17th
Tel: 01.42.67.05.81

Open daily, valet parking

Right next door to his world-famous haute-cuisine restaurant, this is Michel Rostang's first bistrot. You'll want to come back when you've tried the delicious, traditional cuisine served here.

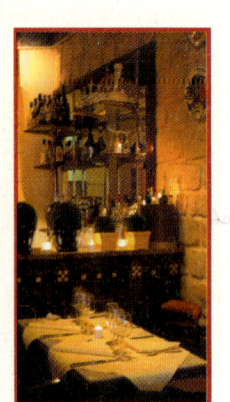

RUE BALZAC
3-5 rue Balzac, 8th
Tel: 01.53.89.90.91

Closed Sat-Sun Lunch, valet parking

Co-owned by French singer Johnny Hallyday and two steps away from the Champs-Elysées, a perfect place to enjoy modern French cuisine in a contemporary setting.

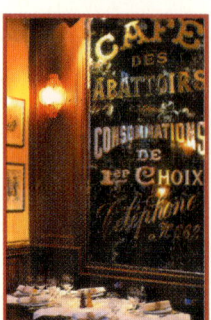

Le Bistrot d'à Côté — "Villiers"
16 avenue de Villiers, 17th
Tel: 01.47.63.25.61

Closed Sat lunch and Sun all day

Just next to the beautiful Parc Monceau, this real Parisian bistrot gives you the key to great wines at small prices, all accompanied by delicious nibbles. After-show dinners available until midnight (reservation only).

mini-courgette, strips of piquillo pepper and pine nuts; and langoustines, clams and rather dumplingish wontons in a rich langoustine cream. A main dish of John Dory served with stripes of carrots, olives, a parsley emulsion and lightly cooked spinach tasted as colourful as it looked; a saddle of rabbit elegantly served with the ribs, leg, kidney and liver had a Provençal-style accompaniment of slow-cooked young fennel and roasted tomatoes. Desserts were sensational – chocolate and pear cake with pecan ice cream and candied pecans, and Victoria pineapple caramelised in passion fruit with coconut sorbet and dried pineapple – and the Club de la Casserole Champagne made a festive accompaniment to the whole meal.

Maxim's

3 rue Royale, 8th (01.42.65.27.94/ www.maxims-de-paris.com). M° Concorde. **Open** Mon-Sat 12.30-2pm, 7.30-10pm. Closed 1 May, 1 Jan, 25 Dec. **Average** €91.46 (lunch), €152.43 (dinner). **Credit** AmEx, DC, MC, V. **Wheelchair access.**

Maxim's makes you want to suspend your cynicism. But walking into the glorious art nouveau dining room on an August night, it was hard to know what to think: tinny FM-radio music made us feel we had arrived too early, though other diners were tucking into their food. Tables are arranged around a dance floor with a view of the stage, but the real theatre is provided by fellow customers, all tourists on our visit – we watched as a waiter broke the ice between two self-consciously solo diners. Once the room began to fill up and the wild-haired pianist launched into his repertoire of smoochy classics, the atmosphere grew friskier. Does this make dinner at Maxim's worth the €325 we paid, and this while avoiding apéritifs, coffee and the priciest dishes? By no means. We were uninspired by the menu, divided into 'classics' and more contemporary dishes, and the cheapest wine cost €58 (we splurged on a bottle of Marsannay rosé for a ridiculous €74.70). Our meal started with a salad of tender but bland langoustines with overcooked coral lentils and mesclun salad, and two nicely pan-fried chunks of foie gras with caramelised mango and a refreshing linden blossom syrup. Then came a generous, juicy veal chop with a tasty but grey artichoke and foie gras purée, and two gleaming red mullet fillets with *tapenade* and a dry, undercooked basil risotto. Dessert costs an astronomical €22.11, but we splashed out on *crêpes Suzette* – not prepared at the table, and undistinguishable from the crêpe stand variety – and a tower of fresh raspberries with a gelatinous white chocolate mousse and raspberry sorbet. Despite the skilled and diplomatic service, Maxim's would be a blatant rip-off at half the price.

L'Oulette

15 pl Lachambeaudie, 12th (01.40.02.02.12). M° Cour St-Emilion. **Open** Mon-Fri noon-2.15pm, 8-10.15pm; Sat 8-10.15pm. **Average** €68.50. **Prix fixe** €27, €44. **Credit** AmEx, DC, MC, V.

Widely spaced tables guarantee confidential conversation in this delightful restaurant. After a warm but unobtrusive welcome from the manager we perused the apéritif list featuring quality sherries, served with informed comments from the waiter along with some dinky *amuse-bouches* of baby figs with country ham and *brandade* toasts. We opted for the four-course €44 evening *menu* which included a half-bottle of zippy white Sancerre from Mellot and a full bottle of deeply fruity oaked red Gaillac Château Adelaide. Our duck terrine arrived girdled in Jurançon jelly and studded with large nuggets of foie gras; the colourful *millefeuille* of sardines and tomato served with a parmesan and herb salad was a harmonious combination of textures and palate-teasing flavours. Our double order of duck *confit* proved a superb choice, its meat cooked to falling-off-the-bone perfection and accompanied by crispy golden potatoes and a tangy onion confit. A slice of beautifully ripened brebis was followed by a frothy prune sabayon and an impressive apple *tourtière* laden with almonds and hazelnuts and crowned with featherlight filo. To end our gastronomic experience we chose a mellow, fragrant Mexican Maragogype from the extensive selection of coffees.

Au Pressoir ★

257 av Daumesnil, 12th (01.43.44.38.21). M° Michel Bizot. **Open** Mon-Fri noon-2.30pm, 7.30-10.30pm. Closed Aug, 25-31 Dec. **Average** €100. **Prix fixe** €66. **Credit** AmEx, MC, V.

Once in the wood-lined, clubby interior of Henri Séguin's temple to serious eating we were quickly led to a table by the smiling *patronne*. Lunchtime saw an exclusively male clientele, popping out of their business suits in all directions, sporting complexions which keep cardiologists in work. We knew we were in for some serious food; even the appetiser of cold lobster soup was sublime. The starters included a special of the day, foie gras terrine with the contrasting texture of artichokes; we also tried a salad of warm roseval potatoes topped with foie gras. Both portions were generous and the preparation of the liver exceptionally fine. The sommelier suggested an excellent Bordeaux from the cheaper end of the list. The *tournedos aux cèpes* surpassed all expectations; not only was the meat spoon-tender but it seemed to be permeated by the rich mushroom sauce. An *escalope de foie gras chaud* was a perfect version accompanied by some nicely tart quartered apples. We had greedily watched the cheese trolley from the beginning of the meal and found ourselves with groaning platefuls. A dessert of wild strawberries magically held in thrall by spun sugar, accompanied by homemade vanilla ice cream, was unmissable. Our eye had also been caught by a silver chalice of *soupe au chocolat*, which turned out to be possibly the richest pudding we have ever tasted; later the dish and its accompanying sponge cakes had to be pulled away from us.

Au Trou Gascon

40 rue Taine, 12th (01.43.44.34.26). M° Daumesnil. **Open** Mon-Fri noon-2pm, 7.30-10pm; Sat 7.30-10pm. Closed 25 Dec-5 Jan. **Average** €56. **Lunch menu** €36. **Credit** AmEx, MC, V. **Wheelchair access.**

Excellent service, interesting and delicious food, wonderful wines – this place has it all. And it's completely democratic: the grannie in the floral-print from Clermont-Ferrand will be greeted and treated as warmly as any supermodel, politician or big-wig exec. Though the slick decor of bleached wood and halogen lighting installed during the summer of 2001 took some getting used to, the subtle updating of the south-western menu was shrewd and welcome. Piquillos rolled with grilled aubergine and tuna carpaccio, served with a Moroccan salad of chickpeas and avocado cubes with a nice gust of coriander, were delicious, while a thick steak of marinated salmon rolled in Provençal herbs and served with a small salad was pleasant, though the fish was a bit flabby and the herbs rather overwhelming. Come the main courses, red mullet with herbs was perfectly cooked, while the *confit de canard* was sublime, bursting with flavour under perfectly crisped skin, and garnished with sautéed ceps, fresh herbs, and a corn *galette*. *Tourte landaise*, apple-filled pastry served with prune ice cream and prunes, and a luscious melting chocolate cake served as finales to a splendid meal.

Les Vieux Métiers de France

13 bd Auguste-Blanqui, 13th (01.45.88.90.03). M° Place d'Italie. **Open** daily 11.30am-3pm, 7pm-midnight. **Average** €50. **Prix fixe** €23, €29. **Credit** AmEx, DC, MC, V. **Wheelchair access.**

The name refers to the antique looms of the nearby Gobelins factory and other ancient trades, rather than the modern apartment towers dominating this area. Behind the carved wooden and tinted glass exterior lurks a twee mini-château complete with stone walls, tapestries and a corner adorned with a lavish fabric tent. Run by Jean Bernard for the past two years, the restaurant continues to serve up good food at reasonable prices, a custom appreciated by a stream of French regulars. Starter standouts included the fricassée of wild mushrooms with poached eggs, and slices of smoked salmon with a buttery, salty crêpe. From the *carte* the shoulder of lamb was cooked to rosy perfection For dessert try the *vacherin* with rum and raisin ice cream or the house speciality, a thin, caramelised apple tart.

Le Pavillon Montsouris

20 rue Gazan, 14th (01.45.88.38.52/ www.pavillon-montsouris.fr). RER Cité Universitaire. **Open** daily noon-2.30pm, 7.30-10.30pm. Closed Sun Sept-Apr. **Average** €60.97. **Prix fixe** €41.77. **Credit** MC, V.

Le Pavillon Montsouris, with its *belle époque* pavilion and large shady terrace, is particularly pleasant for a leisurely meal. If only chef Jérôme Mazur's food consistently lived up to the setting in one of Paris' most beautiful parks. Nibbles of tiny black *niçoise* olives, pastry straws and roasted tomatoes, and a €8.38 glass of bubbly got us off to a grand start but our enthusiasm waned with the first spoonful of room-temperature (on a hot day) gazpacho garnished with two tiny, badly peeled crayfish tails. A *tarte fine* of preserved tomatoes and warm goat's cheese was better. The best main course was free-range chicken, roasted with garlic and thyme and served with wild mushrooms; the *veau fondant* – a chewy, stewy piece of meat with white asparagus – was best forgotten. Desserts of *savarin* with berries, and sorbet with fresh fruit were passable. Service is so-so and the wine list expensive, but the setting is such a winner that booking is essential.

Le Chalet des Iles ★

av Henri Martin/rue de la Pompe, lac du Bois de Boulogne, 16th (01.42.88.04.69). M° La Muette. **Open** daily noon-2.30pm, 7.30-10.30pm. **Average** €38.11. **Prix fixe** €22.87 (Mon-Fri); €32.01, €15.24 for children (Sun). **Credit** AmEx, DC, MC, V.

If Venus and St. Valentine had to pick a restaurant for their silver wedding anniversary, Le Chalet des Iles might well be it. Quite possibly the most romantic restaurant in the entire world and certainly in Paris, it represents the ultimate in loved-up dining. It's on an island in the middle of a lake and you have to take a cute little boat to get there. Ducks paddle lazily through the rushes as you cross and a smiling maître d' waits on the other side. Inside there's a roaring log fire, intimate little tables and unusually friendly service. The food is unfussy and excellent. We started with slivers of tuna carpaccio in a rich plum sauce and a simple but tasty *tomate-mozzarella* with sun-dried tomatoes. A main-course *carré d'agneau* was beautifully tender and accompanied by layers of roasted tomato and aubergine. Fish *pot-au-feu* came with crisp mangetout and baby corn and chunks of fresh salmon, cod and swordfish. A gorgeously-presented *croustillant de fruits rouges* was piled high with strawberries and redcurrants. On the way back over the lake, the moonlight glints off the water as little waves lap around the boat and the smiling maître d' waves a cheery goodbye. Impossibly romantic.

La Grande Cascade

Pavillon de la Grande Cascade, Bois de Boulogne, 16th (01.45.27.33.51). M° Porte Maillot, then taxi. **Open** daily 12.30-2.30pm, 7.30-10.30pm. **Average** €130. **Prix fixe** €54.12-€129.58. **Credit** AmEx, DC, MC, V.

With its dramatic fan-like glass porte-cochère over the terrace, where meals are served in good weather, this intimate pavillion tucked away in the Bois de Boulogne was built in 1856 as a hunting lodge for Napoleon III. Just across the street from the hippodrome, it makes a wonderful escape when you want to get out of town without going far, and even though star chef Jean-Louis Nomicos has moved on to Lasserre, Richard Mebkhout is proving to be a talented and able successor with a style that clearly shows the influence of Alain Ducasse. Start with the open tart of raw and cooked ceps with snails or the superb macaroni stuffed with black truffle, foie gras and celery root, and then go with the luscious hare *à la royale* or maybe the sole with capers and croutons for two. The young sommelier ably manages an interesting list, and has a particularly original selection of Provençal and Languedoc-Roussillon bottles, so ask for a suggestion. Finish your meal with the citrus tart and heavenly mango-chocolate ice cream, or delightfully retro *crêpes soufflées*.

The sky's the limit at Lasserre

Contemporary

Fusion food doesn't lead to confusion in the hands of these innovative chefs.

This has been a soul-searching time for French chefs (*Gault Millau* magazine went so far as to ask, 'Has French cuisine become naff?'). While many bistros continue to turn out food worthy of more pompous restaurants, other chefs are pointing their whisks to the future. The restaurant name on every critic's lips has been **L'Astrance**, run by chef Pascal Barbot. Barbot, and other chefs featured in this chapter, prove that when technique meets imagination, French cuisine is more than equal to any other.

L'Atelier Berger

49 rue Berger, 1st (01.40.28.00.00/ www.atelierberger.com). M° Louvre-Rivoli. **Open** Mon-Sat noon-2.30pm, 7-11pm. Closed 23-25 Dec. **Average** €38. **Prix fixe** €32. **Lunch menu** €23. **Credit** AmEx, MC, V.

Giant pine cones and rustic carved-wood baskets hint at chef Jean Christiansen's Norwegian origins, as do his pairings of meat and fruit and a marinated herring starter. His imaginative seasonal cooking is as surprising to look at as it is to eat. A deep-fried oyster (sadly, only one) came with a delicate, pale green asparagus *panna cotta*, just-cooked asparagus and crunchy celery in a vividly flavoured vinaigrette. A small portion of rich artichoke soup topped with seared fresh foie gras was artistically presented in a deep white bowl placed on a square black plate. Mains were served on yellow and blue floor tiles (not recycled, we trust): strips of succulent pink duck *magret* on a bed of couscous with shredded duck meat, orange and mustard; and tender monkfish on asparagus and purple potato. After the preceding dainty portions, desserts were a shock: a molten chocolate cake baked in a big white bowl, served with frothy cappuccino sauce, and a whole caramelised pear with spice bread ice cream.

Macéo

15 rue des Petits-Champs, 1st (01.42.97.53.85). M° Bourse or Palais Royal. **Open** Mon-Fri 12.30-2.30pm, 7-11pm; Sat 7-11pm; Sun 12-30-11pm. **Average** €48. **Prix fixe** €35, €38 (dinner only). **Lunch menu** €25, €34. **Credit** MC, V.

The room is gorgeous, with wedding-cake mouldings, a refreshingly spare decor and nicely spaced tables, and the kitchen has some excellent ideas, too, not the least of which is a serious approach to vegetarian dining – follow the asterisks to put together a meat-free meal. A cosmopolitan crowd out for a good time creates a good atmosphere, and the modern market menu is often excellent, to say nothing of the remarkable wine list, one of the best in Paris. The snag? The service. Having decided to splash out on a bottle of Priorat, a splendid and pricey Spanish wine, we got off to a festive start, but then the waiter slapped down *amuse-bouches* of *brandade de morue* with nary a word, or bread, before we had even tasted our wine. It finally came, as did a salad of perfectly cooked green beans with mushrooms, a poached egg, and mixed peppercorns, and a nicely made if slightly too-cold tuna tartare seasoned with lemongrass. A too-long wait ensued, and then redemption with the arrival of a sublime *tian* of veal, braised veal shank from the bone mixed with chickpeas and cinnamon and encased in aubergine skin topped with a slivered cucumber salad, and cold hake with mayonnaise on a bed of mixed vegetables. A lovely meal, but then a 15-minute wait for farmhouse cheddar with salad and fruit. Another eternal wait, and we bolted without coffee. Our waiter was too busy babying a table of high-spending regulars next to us.

Restaurant du Palais-Royal

110 galerie Valois, 1st (01.40.20.00.27). M° Palais Royal. **Open** May-Sept Mon-Sat 12.15-2.15pm, 7.15-9.30pm (tea 3.30-6pm); Oct-Apr Mon-Fri 12.15-2.15pm, 7.15-11.30pm; Sat 7.15-11.30pm. Closed late Dec-late Jan. **Average** €46. **Credit** AmEx, DC, MC, V.

Stroll through the Palais-Royal gardens in the summer, and it's hard not to feel envious of those privileged enough to dine on the terrace here. We visited when the restaurant had just reopened after renovations, and were pleasantly surprised by the modernised dining room – the walls are a warm brick red, the panelling has been cleverly painted silver and gold, and the chairs are upholstered in jewel tones. Best of all, there is a real non-smoking room, from which we admired the view on to the gardens. Having been pleasantly greeted by several staff, we chose from the small, seasonal menu. Duck foie gras 'maison' turned out to be a thick, round slab, served with mango chutney and toasted brioche, while thinly sliced raw scallops came with a bright green salad of small fava beans, snow peas and green beans. Tagliatelle with clams, tomato and leek was deeply flavoured, if a little sticky; the juicy tenderloin steak, served with symmetrically-stacked *frites*, remains a house classic. When we ordered a chestnut *millefeuille* for two, the waiters presented it on two plates, a mark of the thoughtful service. A few affordable wines, including pink Champagne, are available by the 50cl carafe.

Le Café des Délices ★

87 rue d'Assas, 6th (01.43.54.70.00). M° Vavin or RER Port Royal. **Open** Mon-Fri noon-2.30pm, 7.30-11.30pm. Closed Aug. **Average** €32. **Credit** AmEx, MC, V.

Gilles Choukroun made his name at the formal La Truite qui File in Chartres, but he's now forging his own identity with this casual restaurant near Montparnasse, where no-one will look at you askance if you order only a main course or just a starter. Behind the pretty art nouveau facade is a pared-down dining room with wooden tables and chairs, dark panelling and pink-tinged walls. We launched in with mains: roast *pièce de boeuf* – slightly too chewy, but flavourful – with a risotto-like mix of wheat and mimolette cheese, and crisp-skinned sea bream accompanied by white coco beans cooked with anchovies, coriander and lemon, and a fresh-tasting herb-filled *nem*. Strawberries in coconut milk with tiny lamb's lettuce leaves, sugary cereal and crushed lollipop showed the chef's sense of humour, while his signature dessert of sliced dates with fresh orange, crunchy pistachios, mint leaves and lemon sorbet was wonderfully refreshing.

Restaurant Hélène Darroze

4 rue d'Assas, 6th (01.42.22.00.11). M° Sèvres-Babylone. **Open** Mon-Sat 12.30-2.15pm, 7.30-10.15pm. **Average** €95. **Prix fixe** €89, €110. **Lunch menu** €60. **Credit** AmEx, MC, V.

Upstairs at Hélène Darroze is a quite different affair from the downstairs Salon: same plum velvet, soft orange and rust chairs and burgundy-stained parquet, but far more service and the well-spaced tables of a formal restaurant. In contrast to the dainty tapas downstairs, portions are ample but more classic, as Hélène Darroze – widely regarded as one of the most talented young female chefs in France – shows off her gastronomic credentials. Basque and south-western flavours are combined with far-flung influences. Introductory *amuse-gueules* (a glass of pumpkin *velouté*, two slivers of courgette tempura and a piquant spoon of anchovy), followed by caramelised turkey on lentils in balsamic dressing show how Darroze can mix influences and textures. The comparison of goose and duck foie gras came in almost too lavish helpings, the former *au naturel*, the latter *confit* and gently spiced, served with an exotic fruit chutney and mesclun. *Poulet fermier des Landes* was unspectacular though high-quality with wild mushrooms and a courgette and pasta garnish. Fresh, flaky cod in a clever hazelnut crust came with a wonderful combination of Noirmoutier potatoes and swathes of meaty cep. A *moelleux au chocolat* with a bitter chocolate ice cream and rum baba flambéed in Armagnac with berries followed by a trolley laden with caramels, marshmallow, macaroons and *pet-de-nonne* completed the generosity. Overall it's a more conventional eat than the experimentation of downstairs.

Le Salon d'Hélène

4 rue d'Assas, 6th (01.42.22.00.11). M° Sèvres-Babylone. **Open** Mon-Sat 12.30-2.15pm, 7.30-10.15pm. **Average** €46. **Credit** AmEx, MC, V. **Wheelchair access.**

At her casual downstairs salon, Hélène Darroze has abandoned the *entrée-plat-dessert* format for an array of inventive tapas-sized dishes, warm and cold, savoury and sweet. You can also order the *plat du jour* from upstairs but it's more interesting to choose the tapas, where Darroze updates south-western classics with Japanese and Mediterranean influences. We sampled smoked haddock *brandade*, raw marinated tuna with a Basque-style *pipérade*, a tangy salmon *ceviche*, subtle foie gras ice cream with Puy lentils, and melt-in-the-mouth slivers of foie gras prepared three ways (*au naturel*, with citrus and with Armagnac). Mini desserts – *moelleux au chocolat*, bitter chocolate tart, a glass of berry compote and a doll-sized slice of *gâteau basque* – allowed indulgence *sans* gluttony. Although fabulous, it did feel like a succession of cocktail party nibbles, so be prepared to order lots or settle for a very light lunch.

Le Maxence

9bis bd du Montparnasse, 6th (01.45.67.24.88). M° Duroc. **Open** daily noon-2.30pm, 7.30-10.30pm. Closed three weeks in Aug. **Average** €66. **Prix fixe** €60 (dinner only). **Lunch menu** €24, €31. **Credit** AmEx, MC, V.

Our recent meal at David Van Laer's vaunted restaurant was a shocking disappointment. Nothing from either the tasting *menu* or the *carte* lived up to expectations. The meal began with a listless *brandade de morue* on a triangle of spongey toast. Next came a 40-minute wait for cold, undercooked foie gras with dry, crumbly spice bread. We saw a flash of finesse in poached scallops with a delicate, foamy cream sauce, and tempura scallops served with an agreeably bitter onion relish. But the roasted quail with chopped truffle and truffle *jus* was a failure: the skin was soggy, the meat dry, and the tuber tough and tasteless, despite it being the height of truffle season. A *tarte* of wild duck, meanwhile, was large and hearty but underseasoned and rather pedestrian. Desserts escaped the kitchen in better form – a buttery crêpe filled with caramelised apples and an extremely rich, dense chocolate cake. Given the fine meals we've enjoyed here in the past, we can only hope this one was a fluke.

Ze Kitchen Galerie ★

4 rue des Grands-Augustins, 6th (01.44.32.00.32). M° St-Michel. **Open** Mon-Fri noon-2pm, 8-10.30pm; Sat. 8-10.30pm. **Average** €35. **Lunch menu** €20-€26. **Credit** AmEx, DC, MC, V.

Aside from ze awful name, this new place next door to Les Bookinistes is excellent. It's an attractive, comfortable modern bistro with a pleasant menu organised around four themes: soup, raw (as in fish), pasta and or grilled. This astute read on the way stylish Parisians want to eat these days is the work of William Ledeuil, who's been the head cook at Les Bookinistes ever since it opened. In many respects it's like a less expensive and rather more local version of Jean-Georges Vongerichten's expensive hit Market on the Right Bank. Ledeuil works in a kitchen visible through a window, modern art hangs on the walls, and the tables are set with Philippe Starck cutlery. Appropriately, you don't have to follow any particular order as you make your way through the menu either – start with the red tuna tartare with lemongrass and then have pasta shells stuffed with diced mushrooms, or begin with pasta and follow with duckling *a la plancha* in red onion *jus* and coriander. Finish up with the caramel macaroon or the baked apple, and go with the white Jarasse Côtes du Rhône or the red New Zealand Pinot Noir.

Restaurant Petrossian ★

18 bd de La Tour-Maubourg, 7th (01.44.11.32.32) M° Invalides or La Tour-Maubourg. **Open** Tue-Sat noon-2pm, 7.30-10.30pm. Closed Aug. **Average** €90. **Prix fixe** €53 (dinner only), €107, €136. **Lunch menu** €44. **Credit** AmEx, DC, MC, V.

Occupying an elegant dove-gray dining room upstairs from the boutique of this famous supplier of caviar and smoked fish, this is an intriguing restaurant for anyone after delicious and creative cooking. Yes, you can feast on the famed luxury products, but it would be a shame to forsake the cooking of chef Philippe Conticini, formerly of La Table d'Anvers. Best known for his sublime new-age desserts and pastries, Conticini is a remarkable cook all round. Start with wonderful *beignets* of taramasalata and move on to smoked salmon with white salmon sorbet, risotto with foie gras and carrots, or smoked swordfish with a corn compote and turnip *ragoût*, all beautifully presented and offering brilliant contrasts of taste, texture and temperature. The friendly *maître d'hôtel* arrived with a trolley of herbs and mixed up vividly coloured infusions to prepare the palate for desserts, the most amazing of which was the 'Teaser, five explosions of taste' – a colourful mixture of fruit coulis, jellies, and creams garnished with sugared pistachios in a glass bowl. This is a great choice for a special night out.

L'Angle du Faubourg

195 rue du Fbg St-Honoré, 8th (01.40.74.20.20). M° Ternes or George V. **Open** Mon-Fri noon-2.30pm, 7-11pm. Closed 27 July-21 Aug. **Average** €48. **Prix fixe** €35. **Credit** AmEx, DC, MC, V.

The estimable Taillevent has given birth to this relaxed contemporary spot, and it's an instant success with a curious crowd of trendies and older affluent couples who probably find the minimalist decor – Tuscan-red walls, tan floors, black wood tables with white linen runners – daring. The space is too spare and the dining room is awkwardly divided between an over-lit bar area and more comfortable seating behind a thick white pillar. Still, it's not unpleasant and the menu by young chef Stéphane Cosnier, former second to Taillevent's Michel Del Burgo, is excellent. Start with the salad of crunchy laser-thin vegetables in a well-made vinaigrette served on fine slices of tomme cheese, or the superb *lomo* of tuna – a roasted tuna steak with Espelette pepper, sesame seeds and a salad of slivered spring onions – to see how shrewdly and deliciously Cosnier has updated traditional bistro dishes. Mains are wonderful, too, including a snowy slab of roasted cod with a small salad and a 'condiment' of *brandade de morue* with fresh herbs, and roast lamb shoulder with black olives and garlic. Desserts are fresh and appealing: pineapple ravioli filled with mascarpone cheese, a passion fruit milkshake and raspberry *clafoutis*. Happily, the wine list reflects the younger crowd being targeted; there are several fine reds from the Languedoc-Roussillon at €16.

L'Astor

Sofitel Demeure Hôtel Astor, 11 rue d'Astorg, 8th (01.53.05.05.20/www.hotel-astor.net). M° St-Augustin. **Open** Mon-Fri noon-2pm, 7.30-10pm. Closed Aug. **Average** €100. **Prix fixe** €99.90. **Lunch menu** €50. **Credit** AmEx, DC, MC, V.

Having long admired the cooking of Robuchon-trained Eric Lecerf and appreciated the good value of the lunch *menu*, we decided to splurge on the evening *à la carte* selection. We were in fine spirits until a drab *amuse-gueule* of cucumber soup arrived before we had finished our pricey Champagne. The table had barely been cleared when our first courses arrived, but terrine of *poularde de Bresse* (fattened hen) with truffles and a perfectly seasoned herb salad, and interesting if overpriced grilled aubergine with fresh tuna were impressive. Potato salad with truffles, though, was terribly disappointing. The very expensive Condrieu was served lukewarm, we had to ask for bread several times, and waiters kept reaching in front of us –

quibbles perhaps, but not at these prices. More serious were three disappointing main courses – a sole fillet so full of little sharp bones that it was like eating a pin cushion, drab lamb sweetbreads and a boring chicken 'cannelloni', wrapped around morsels of truffle and foie gras. When we complained about the lethal sole, they offered us a bottle of Champagne. Desserts were spectacular, including a 'zephyr' of roses, a layered fruit parfait in a martini glass with delicious rose aspic, and a lovely, summery *nage de fruits*, mixed berries served with a first-rate basil-and-lemon sorbet, but overall this was a seriously disappointing and expensive meal. We'd try lunch again, though.

Chiberta
3 rue Arsène-Houssaye, 8th (01.53.53.42.00). M° Charles de Gaulle-Étoile. **Open** Mon-Fri noon-2pm, 7.30-10pm; Sat 7.30-10pm. **Prix fixe** €89. **Lunch menu** €44. **Credit** AmEx, DC, MC, V. **Wheelchair access.**
Chiberta has maintained a deserved reputation for innovative and enjoyable cooking through a succession of chefs (Eric Coisel is the current incumbent). With well-spaced tables, sophisticated black decor and friendly service, it draws a mix of executive types and splurging tourists. Start with the tartare of scallops, celery and Granny Smith apple, or frogs' legs with garlic; then sample delicious dishes such as lobster cooked with mint or a luscious pigeon smoked over beech wood, roasted and served with an excellent chicory and orange-zest garnish. The wine list is well-balanced and desserts are excellent: the delicious 'variation on cocoa' offers chocolate in five incarnations.

Les Élysées
Hôtel Vernet, 25 rue Vernet, 8th (01.44.31.98.98/www.hotelvernet.com). M° George V. **Open** Mon-Fri 12.30-2.15pm, 7.30-9.15pm. Closed Aug, two weeks in Dec. **Average** €130. **Prix fixe** €150 (dinner only). **Lunch menu** €52, €64. **Credit** AmEx, DC, MC, V. **Wheelchair access.**
An atmosphere of civilised pleasure prevails under this glass-domed ceiling designed by Gustave Eiffel. Among chandeliers and opulent flower arrangements, young waiters in dinner jackets perform a flawless ballet. Dreamy dating couples, foreign gourmets and canny Parisians know that Alain Soliverès is among the city's best chefs. His seasonally changing menu spans the south of France, and his style is earthy and precise. A starter of perfectly sautéed scallops was garnished with cubes of spicy Spanish *lomo* (dry-cured pork), parmesan and a dandelion and rocket salad, while a creamy risotto of *épeautre* (spelt) was redolent of black truffle and long-simmered meat stock. Sautéed fresh duck foie gras was surrounded with a reduction of sweet Banyuls wine, while a lamb shank with winter vegetables and a juicy pigeon with polenta were pure pleasure. After an excellent cheese tray, a *millefeuille* of dried pineapple, and chocolate fondant tart showed the kitchen's class.

Maison Blanche
15 av Montaigne, 8th (01.47.23.55.99) M° Alma-Marceau. **Open** daily noon-2.30pm, 8pm-midnight. Closed Aug. **Average** €91. **Lunch menu** €53.50. **Credit** AmEx, MC, V.
The Pourcel twins, the talented duo behind the Jardin des Sens in Montepellier, have done a brilliant job of reviving this perenially trendy mezzanine restaurant. The slick white decor with black accents is bracingly modern, and then there are the friendly young waiters dressed in black and the superb menu. It's the starters that star, with dishes as visually interesting as they are appetising: sea urchins stuffed with dressed crab and garnished with caviar; raw and cooked vegetables with beetroot caramel; *tarte Tatin* of shallots with grilled red mullet; and foamy chestnut soup. The best of the mains are sea bass baked with preserved lemons; pasta with tiny clams, fava beans, parmesan and pesto sauce; and roast duck fillet with a 'pastilla' of carrots and apricots in a spiced sauce. Desserts are brilliant, too, including a raspberry-filled *dacquoise* with wild peach sorbet, and preserved pink grapefruit with almonds accompanied by lemongrass sorbet, vanilla sauce, and grilled-almond toffee. And, they have the best selection of Languedoc-Roussillon wines in town.

Market ★
15 av Matignon, 8th (01.56.43.40.90). M° Champs-Elysées-Clemenceau. **Open** Mon-Thur, Sun noon-3pm, 6.30-10.30pm; Fri, Sat noon-3pm, 6.30-11.30pm. **Average** €100. **Prix fixe** €60 (dinner only). **Lunch menu** €24, €31. **Credit** AmEx, DC, MC, V.
Bankrolled by movie mogul Luc Besson and sporting a terribly glam if rather OTT 90s decor of African wood and dark stone by Christian Liaigre, this is one of the most fashionable restaurants in town. What's more, widely-travelled chef Jean-Georges Vongerichten – a man with a genius for producing irresistible new culinary hybrids – turns out some wonderful food. A meal opens with dazzling starters such as scallops marinated in citrus juice and garnished with roast peppers; potato and *chèvre* terrine with rocket *jus;* or cep, onion, walnut and garlic oil pizza. Then comes mains such as lobster with Thai herbs, duck breast with sesame *jus* and a crispy *confit* with tamarind sauce, or Bresse chicken with olives, ginger and coriander. Finish up with the runny chocolate tart or *panna cotta* with an exotic fruit salad. Choose a reasonably priced Côtes du Rhône wine from the excellent (but expensive) list.

Renoma Café Gallery
32 av George V/45 rue Pierre-Charron, 8th (01.56.89.05.89). M° George V. **Open** daily noon-2am. **Average** €50. **Credit** AmEx, DC, MC, V.
This polished new bar/restaurant could seem like one big ego trip for designer Maurice Renoma, whose photos adorn the walls, but it's run in association with chef-entrepreneur Thierry Burlot (also the brains behind the Armani Caffè and Joe's Café) and the food is more than simply design-conscious. A menu divided into 'vegetables and organic eggs', 'fish from lake and ocean', 'pastures of France', 'pasta, rice and cheese' and 'follies', allows you to eat a full meal or lunch on a luxurious plate of fried eggs with fresh ceps. A leek *pressé* came with fresh hazelnuts; grilled vegetables were generously served, drizzled in basil and olive oil. Tuna with radicchio and quail eggs was more cooked than the promised 'rosé', but the *poêlon d'encornets*, tiny squid sautéed with cherry tomatoes and basil, was spot-on. The L-shaped room offers two faces: one overlooking rue Pierre-Charron, the other, a doormen-warded gallery on avenue George V, with a long table, magazines, photos and a collection of modern design classic chairs and prototypes from Van der Rohe, Eames, Jacobsen, Bertoia et al. Add continuous service and a not-too-obtrusive soundtrack and you can see why it's already popular.

Shozan
11 rue de la Trémoïlle, 8th (01.47.23.37.32). M° Franklin D. Roosevelt or Alma-Marceau. **Open** Mon-Fri noon-2.30pm, 7-10.30pm. **Average** €65. **Prix fixe** €60.50-€91.50 (dinner only). **Lunch menu** €25.50, €30. **Credit** AmEx, DC, MC, V.
Owned by the Isawa family, which has been producing sake in Japan for 12 generations, Shozan shows how good 'fusion' cuisine can be when it's approached with intelligence. They even have a consultant dietician, while young German-born chef, Frithof Wimmer, orchestrates this East-meets-West style. A meal here begins with an elegant hors d'oeuvre: shot glasses containing a sublime sake, and maybe salmon tartare and a mousse of fresh cheese and avocado. Not to be missed are the sushi of grilled foie gras on seaweed-wrapped rounds of rice filled with rhubarb and apple chutney, and the langoustine tempura with a white asparagus mousse. Refined mains include a perfectly cooked tuna steak with a buckwheat crust, and loin of lamb wrapped in seaweed with miso paste. Desserts run from sesame-caramel wafers layered with pink grapefruit, served with a verbena infusion on a grapefruit jelly, to rhubarb compote dotted with tiny meringues in thyme-flavoured caramel sauce.

Stella Maris
4 rue Arsène-Houssaye, 8th (01.42.89.16.22). M° Charles de Gaulle-Étoile. **Open** Tue-Fri noon-2.15pm, 7.45-10.30pm; Mon, Sat 7.30-10.30pm. Closed two weeks in Aug, Christmas. **Average** €61. **Prix fixe** €70.50, €104. **Lunch menu** €42.80. **Credit** AmEx, DC, MC, V.
Japanese chef Tateru Yoshino worked with Joël Robuchon before setting up shop on his own. His guiding philosophy is the refined yet simple Japanese cooking style called *kaiseki* and, while most of the dishes in his seasonally changing (and 100 per cent organic) menu are clearly French, there is plenty to remind you of the chef's origins. The lunch *menu* began with tiny *crème de foie gras* and *accras* and an oyster *en gelée*, before a soul-gladdening, superbly flavourful chestnut *velouté* and a *millefeuille* of raw tuna and cooked aubergine, topped with caviar. We followed with a meltingly soft eel *blanquette* with chunks of grilled cucumber, and generous roast cod served in vegetable stock with leaves of Chinese cabbage. For dessert we chose a tangy sorbet selection and a clever fruit *yakitori*, delicious pieces of grilled pineapple, strawberry, banana and apricot skewered on a vanilla pod.

59 Poincaré
Hôtel Le Parc, 59 av Raymond-Poincaré, 16th (01.47.27.59.59). M° Victor Hugo. **Open** Tue-Fri noon-2.30pm, 7-11pm; Sat 7-11pm. Closed 24 Dec, 14-15 July. **Average** €90. **Lunch menu** €31, €39. **Credit** AmEx, DC, MC, V.
The wood-panelled, captain-of-industry style former premises of Alain Ducasse's namesake restaurant (since moved to the Plaza Athénée) is now the location of one of the oddest and most unreasonably expensive restaurants in Paris. First off, there's the strange decor – chrome-framed white leather high chairs at marble topped tables. Then, the concept: the ostensible idea here is to celebrate lobster (Canadian, not Breton) and beef, along with vegetables, in a sort of Gallic update of the American steakhouse concept. The place goes off the rails not because the food is bad – it's generally fine – but because it feels more like a marketing idea than a restaurant. Service is robotic and portions are tiny for really nervy prices – €13.50 for a casserole of winter vegetables; €14.50 for artichokes *à la grecque*, €11.53 for a baked apple with vanilla ice cream. Clearly, this place is aimed an expense-account clientele. If you're interested in Ducasse's take on casual dining, you're far better off going to Spoon, which has a similarly superb wine list, interesting food, and a more interesting crowd.

L'Astrance ★
4 rue Beethoven, 16th (01.40.50.84.40). M° Passy. **Open** Mon, Tue 8-10.30pm; Wed-Sun noon-2pm, 8-10.30pm. Closed one week in Feb. **Average** €61. **Prix fixe** €58, €76. **Lunch menu** €29. **Credit** AmEx, DC, MC, V.
Tucked away in a surprisingly hip space – slate-colored walls, a metallic ceiling, discreet lighting – this is quite simply one of the best restaurants to open in Paris for a long time. We first came across extremely talented young chef Pascal Barbot during his brief stint at Lapérouse, and his cooking has got even better. Barbot worked in Sydney, and this antipodean experience shows up in shrewd, chic, minimalist and absolutely delicious dishes such as his 'ravioli' of avocado and crab (crab in dressing between two thin slices of avocado), superb baked mussels with a Moroccan-style salad of grated carrots, a soup of milk and toast crumbs, and luscious scallops in peanut cream sauce – and these are just the starters. The stellar performance continues through main courses – red mullet cooked in a banana leaf and served with a superb tamarind sauce and a banana gratin, sautéed guinea hen with autumn vegetables and a cup of *bouillon* spiked at the table with a splash of Champagne, and cod with chestnuts and lime. Desserts are excellent, too. This is clearly cooking that Paris has been waiting for – clean, creative, and very modern.

Cruise past the caviar, Petrossian is a dessert island

Regional

Delve into the riches of the French countryside without taking the TGV.

While there's nothing quite like slurping *bouillabaisse* on a terrace in sunny Provence or sticking your snout into a steaming plate of *choucroute* in chilly Alsace, there's lots of country comfort to be found in Paris. Treasured islands of regional cuisine dot the capital, so it's possible to cross the country without ever leaving the city. In fact, these specialised restaurants offer some of the best food in town: you can have a Breton seafood experience at **Ty-Coz**, sample superb northern French cheeses at **Le Graindorge** and try the earthy Corsican specialities served by a number of proud island ambassadors. The south-west is particularly well represented both in this chapter and by bistro chefs such as Yves Camdeborde at **La Régalade** and Christian Etchebest at **Le Troquet** (*see p13*, **Bistros**). Lovers of Alsatian food should also visit classic Parisian brasseries (*see p45*).

Alsace

Alsace's schizo-identity (it was alternately French and German four times between 1870 and 1945) is abundantly apparent in its cuisine: a German hardiness coupled with a French elegance. Local ingredients star alongside introduced items – courtesy of Jewish immigrants – such as spices, foie gras and chocolate. Alsace's signature dish is *choucroute* (sauerkraut), spiced, salt-pickled cabbage traditionally topped with sausage, ham and pork, although fish or goose has been known to make an appearance, too. Both beer and local wine are poured into the culinary equation in dishes such as beer-braised ham hock, wine-soaked *truite à la riesling* and the meaty (and potatoey) *bäckaofa*. The region is also renowned for its *charcuterie*, freshwater fish, munster cheese, and, of course, fragrant white wines such as riesling, silvaner and gewurztraminer. Brasseries (*see p45*) originated in Alsace so you can be sure of finding (Alsatian) things that make you go 'woof' there, too.

Flam's

62 rue des Lombards, 1st (01.42.21.10.30/ www.flams.fr). M° Châtelet. **Open** Mon-Fri noon-2pm, 6pm-midnight; Sat, Sun noon-midnight. **Average** €11.50. **Prix fixe** €11.90, €16.90. **Lunch menu** €7.90. **Credit** AmEx, MC, V.

Flam's is part of a chain of restaurants offering *flammenküche*, Alsace's answer to the pizza. Thin slices of dough are covered with a variety of toppings, flame-cooked and served up on big wooden platters. You can order individual *küche* or do as we did and take one of the all-you-can-eat *formules*. The starters are not up to much – a rather sad chicken and pineapple dish came with painfully hot curry sauce and a cheese salad was hardly any better. Things started to look up, however, when we started on the *flammenküche* themselves. Order by the half or whole platterful, and, since they're fairly light, try a range of different flavours. We found the *tartiflette*, an oniony, bacony, potatoey extravaganza dotted with huge chunks of melting reblochon cheese, the best. Service was amazingly friendly and the place had something of a family atmosphere, with off-duty staff eating dinner together at a nearby table. Desserts were sweet versions of the mains; we managed a half-platter of delicious berry *küche* flambéed with kirsch.

Branches: 16 rue du Colisée, 8th (01.45.62.84.82); 4 rue de Tilsitt, 8th (01.42.56.84.40); 101 rue St-Lazare, 9th (01.48.74.74.90); 32 av du Maine, 15th (01.45.44.63.53); 25-27 av Corentin Cariou, 19th (01.40.36.13.00).

Café Runtz

16 rue Favart, 2nd (01.42.96.69.86). M° Richelieu-Drouot. **Open** Mon-Fri 11.45am-2.30pm, 6.30-11pm; Sat 6.30-11pm. Closed Aug, one week in May. **Average** €29. **Prix fixe** €17.54, €21.96. **Credit** AmEx, DC, MC, V.

Just the sort of cosy, spirit-lifting place we like to come to on a frosty winter's night, this wood-panelled brasserie-cum-restaurant felt a little stifling on a warm spring evening. A man-sized chunk of warm and unctuous onion tart got us off to a pungent start but the *poêlon* of six snails was just lukewarm and we didn't even bother to mop up the blandish garlic butter. Main courses were also a mixed affair. The firm haddock fillets in *beurre blanc* proved pleasingly tangy but the accompanying steamed potatoes were cold and almost as hard as when they were dug up. The other main course of *jambonneau* (ham knuckle) with an undistinguished *choucroute* failed to save the evening as the knuckle had been grilled to a crisp and the meat was positively teeth-wedging. The Black Forest gâteau was in a class of its own, bulging with plump black morellos steeped in kirsch, all nestled in an airy chocolate and Chantilly concoction, but the sorbets tasted and looked as though they could have emerged from any ordinary supermarket.

Chez Jenny

39 bd du Temple, 3rd (01.44.54.39.00/ www.chez-jenny.com). M° République. **Open** Mon-Thur, Sun noon-midnight; Fri, Sat noon-1am. **Average** €33. **Prix fixe** €16, €22.50. **Credit** AmEx, DC, MC, V.

Be prepared to queue, particularly at weekends, at this hugely popular brasserie, which thankfully seems to have changed little since being taken over by the Frères Blanc a few years ago. By the time we were seated, we had taken in the magnificent marquetry by Alsatian Charles Spindler, the festive atmosphere and the gargantuan platters of seafood and *choucroute* ferried deftly around the dining room by waitresses in regional dress. Our *tourteau* – a formidable beast with pincers to be reckoned with – was ordered as a starter but could easily have made a main course. Then came what has to be one of the best *choucroutes* this side of Alsace – a steaming mound dotted with crunchy juniper berries and topped with pork knuckle. Skip dessert – the iced *kougelhopf* tasted rather bland and the profiteroles were oddly reminiscent of cardboard – and splash out on an excellent bottle of Alsatian wine such as the 1995 riesling Les Murailles from Dopff et Irion or the Grand Cru Altenberg from Lorentz.

Le Bec Rouge

33 rue de Constantinople, 8th (01.45.22.15.02). M° Villiers. **Open** Mon-Fri noon-2pm, 7.30-10.30pm. Closed two weeks in Aug, 25 Dec-2 Jan. **Average** €23. **Prix fixe** €19, €23. **Credit** MC, V. **Wheelchair access.**

The owner of this Alsatian restaurant has done a shrewd job of updating the *gemütlich* image of the province for Parisian tastes – to wit, the place is still cosy, but the design has been streamlined. This extends to the campy disco soundtrack (one wonders what Donna Summer would make of *flammenküche*). Portions here are huge, so you can get away with a starter and a shared dessert. Otherwise, the three-course €23 *menu* is an excellent buy. Start with the copious and well-seasoned *salade du Bec* (smoked duck breast, spinach, walnuts and parmesan); the delicious *fleischnacka* (sautéed rounds of crêpe stuffed with ground meat and herbs on salad), or the *flammenküche*, here offered in three versions (traditional – onions and bacon – or topped with gruyère or munster cheese). Then go for the excellent *choucroute garnie*, *bibelkasse* (roasted brine-soaked pork with salad, sautéed potatoes and crème fraîche) or the pork spare ribs roasted in pine-tree honey. First-rate *charcuterie* comes directly from Colmar. Though it's unlikely you'll want anything more, the munster cheese is runny, odiferous and full-flavoured, or try the rhubarb strudel. Alsatian and other wines are served by the glass, carafe and bottle, which might leave you with a *bec rouge* (a red beak, like the Alsatian emblem the stork, or, in local slang, someone who's been at the bottle).

Branch: Le Bec Rouge Rôtisserie, 46bis bd du Montparnasse, 15th (01.42.22.45.54).

L'Alsaco ★

10 rue Condorcet, 9th (01.45.26.44.31/ www.alsaco.net). M° Poissonnière. **Open** Mon, Sat 7-11pm; Tue-Fri noon-2.30pm, 7-11pm. Closed last two weeks in July, month of Aug. **Average** €26. **Prix fixe** €20, €30. **Credit** MC, V. **Wheelchair access.**

We can vouch that L'Alsaco is a wonderful cure for the blues. From the minute you enter the cosy *winstub* you feel cossetted thanks to the rustic decor and motherly service. After Port apéritifs on stools at the bar we were settled in a wood-panelled back room painted with hunting scenes from where we could see the chef rolling *flammenküche* in his kitchen. All the Alsatian favourites are here, plus a few more unusual dishes such as *marmite marcaire*, a slow-cooked rustic stew that has to be ordered in advance (call at noon for dinner). But there is little point in ordering *à la carte* – the *menus* incorporate most dishes and are much better value. The jolly proprietor, Klaus Steger, has made a point of not providing a wine list – instead he will suggest one according to your budget and choice of food. Inspired by his expansive gestures we chose a 1997 riesling *vielles vignes* for €28.97 which was indeed the perfect accompaniment to *choucroute*. A starter of *pipalakass* – soft cheese mixed with onions and chives and served with waxy boiled potatoes – was substantial and the six snails were just garlicky enough. For mains we enjoyed *bäckaofa*, a hearty beef and potato stew not dissimilar to the Irish version, and the *choucroute maison*, which featured *jarret de porc*, thick streaky bacon and gammon plus *saucisse Vénitienne* on mounds of *choucroute*. But thank goodness we didn't finish everything on our plates or we would have missed out on the gargantuan slice of homemade *tarte aux mirabelles* with its pitted fruit set in a moist custard – quite simply delicious.

Auvergne

France's mountainous central region is famous not only for its folklore but also its foodlore: hale and hearty cooking that's perfect when winter winds are howling. Cured hams and sausages, sturdy soups and stews feature along with prime Salers and Limousin beef and *aligot* (a creamy mix of mashed potatoes, garlic and tomme cheese served in long strands straight from the pan). Auvergnat chefs also have stacks of 'insider knowledge' – skilfully stuffing cabbage with pork, veal with sausage meat, and ravioli with local cantal cheese. Cheese looms large in the region: the rich selection includes bleu d'auvergne, fourme d'ambert and st-nectaire. Team it with St-Pourçain, a fruity red wine. As Auvergnats own many Paris cafés, regional produce often features on café menus as well as in bistros such as **Chez Savy** and **Au Bon-St-Pourçain** (*see p29*, **Bistros**).

Ambassade d'Auvergne

22 rue du Grenier Saint-Lazare, 3rd (01.42.72.31.22/www.ambassade-auvergne.com). M° Rambuteau. **Open** daily noon-2pm, 7.30-10.30pm. **Average** €30. **Prix fixe** €25.90. **Credit** AmEx, MC, V.

Magnum bottles and rather maudlin oil paintings decorate this rustic two-storey house. Portions are suitably ample: a bowl of warm, garlicky green lentil salad could have served four people as a starter. We also tried the two summery soups, melon chunks marinated in honey and lemon, and a lovely chilled cream of corn. Mains are equally hearty and successful: a thick veal steak topped with tiny mushrooms; chicken roasted with garlic, potatoes and courgette; and a juicy grilled pickerel fillet with cabbage. *Aligot*, a classic Auvergnat potato-cheese dish, is whipped before your eyes, then pulled like toffee until it reaches the desired consistency. Less entertaining, the unfinishably huge pork and cabbage stew was also blander. Atypical desserts include hot strawberry gratin and verbena-scented frozen mousse. The professional, encouraging waiter made our decision to order a bottle of raspberry-like Chanturge seem informed rather than random. The menu also describes the many regional wines, which can be bought in the tiny boutique near the door. With mostly tourists in the less-picturesque upstairs room and a predominantly French crowd downstairs, we suspect that seating was segregated, so state your preference when reserving.

Bath's

9 rue de la Trémoille, 8th (01.40.70.01.09/ www.baths.fr). M° Alma-Marceau. **Open** Mon-Fri noon-2.30pm, 7-10.30pm. Closed Aug. **Average** €50. **Prix fixe** €70. **Lunch menu** €30. **Credit** AmEx, MC, V.

With its slick international clientele, this buttercup-yellow dining room in a quiet corner of the 8th *arrondissement* is a long way from chef Jean-Yves Bath's original restaurant in Clermont-Ferrand, the largest city in the Auvergne. Though his son runs the dining room with charm and the food is delicious, there's an odd mismatch between the cushy dining room with an odd painting of Clermont on black velvet and the chef's earthy cooking style. But Bath's food is a hit with moneyed businessmen, who appreciate such hearty, solid cooking. He brings a real sophistication to traditional Auvergnat fare, with elegant dishes such as ravioli stuffed with cantal cheese and green onions, or one of the most refined versions of stuffed cabbage to be found anywhere in France. It is the outstanding quality of the meat, including Salers beef and milk-fed veal, that appeals to many customers. Starters include foie gras and chopped artichoke, or cream of lentils. Given the superb cheeses of this region, it's slightly disappointing that they don't offer a proper cheese tray. Desserts aren't terribly interesting, but overall this restaurant well warrants its plaudits. It's pricey, though.

Au Casque d'Or

51 rue des Cascades, 20th (01.43.58.44.55/ www.aucasquedor.com). M° Jourdain. **Open** Mon-Fri noon-2.30pm, 7-11pm; Sat 7-11pm. **Average** €26. **Lunch menu** €11. **Credit** MC, V.

For a taste of Piaf's Paris, head to this winding Ménilmontant street, named after the streams that once tumbled through this part of town. The building has housed a restaurant for the past century, but Marc Cédat, its owner since 1998, has made it a shrine to the 1952 film *Casque d'Or*, starring Simone Signoret (whose strawberry blonde locks gave the film its name). Posters, drawings and photographs of *Casque d'Or*, much of which was filmed in this street, adorn the walls, and the jovial, down-to-earth atmosphere takes you back in time. In such a room, with its dark beams and wooden chairs, you might expect rustic fare, but this is Auvergnat cooking with a modern touch, matched with well-selected regional wines. It's hard to do better than the *entrecôte-truffade*, melting meat cooked perfectly to order (a little flag indicates its level of doneness) and served with a golden cake of potatoes with fresh tomme cheese, but the adventurous can order a tin of vintage sardines with salad and fennel sorbet. The chef is proud of his long-cooked and deeply caramelised suckling pig roasted

Ham it up at Le Bec Rouge

with *fleur de miel*, but refuses to tell even the waiters exactly what *fleur de miel* is. To start, we've never got beyond the *salade de gésiers*, fresh leaves mixed with succulent gizzards, though the *charcuterie* also looks tempting. A few traditional desserts are available but everyone orders the homemade ice creams: from rhubarb and verbena to more conventional chocolate and vanilla, they're a must.

La Galoche d'Aurillac
41 rue de Lappe, 11th (01.47.00.77.15). Mº Bastille. **Open** Tue-Sat noon-2.30pm, 7.30-11.30pm. **Average** €35. **Prix fixe** €24, €35. **Credit** MC, V.
Since 1949, Jean and Nicole Bonnet have run this proud family establishment as a tribute to their village Aurillac and its cuisine. The *galoche* or clog is represented by countless pairs pegged to the wooden beams and actually for sale at €77. The decor is a blast from the past and, as further proof of its authenticity, no decaf was available. Auvergne is no place for dieters: for starters we had generous portions of cold Puy lentil salad, and melon with cured Auvergnat ham. Then came our Saturday night specials, green cabbage stuffed with pork and a plate of steamed pork ribs, green cabbage, carrot and sausage, washed down with wine from Cahors. When we asked what was in the *saucisse auvergnate*, Mme Bonnet quipped, 'It's pig! Auvergne is all pig, of course!' For dessert we enjoyed a plate of ripe red raspberries, wild strawberries and blackberries and a creamy homemade chestnut ice cream with chestnut liqueur, another Auvergnat speciality.

La Maison du Cantal
1 pl Falguière, 15th (01.47.34.12.24). Mº Volontaires or Pasteur. **Open** Tue-Sat noon-2.30pm, 7-10.30pm. **Average** €38. **Prix fixe** €26. **Credit** MC, V.
The cheesy decor and tacky plastic terrace furniture belie one of the city's best regional French dining experiences. An extensive menu includes lighter fare such as a refreshing three-melon salad or a *cassolette* of snails and wild mushrooms in an earthy brown sauce. The moist sea bream, grilled whole with lemon, was one of three fish options for diners unaccustomed to the brawny culinary heritage of the Auvergne: *saucisse*, *boudin* (black pudding), and grilled calves' sweetbreads. The *confit de canard* – perfect rich meat beneath crisp skin – came accompanied by buttery garlic potatoes. An apricot tart with puff pastry had obviously been freshly baked, while the seemingly endless ice cream combinations persuaded us finally to settle on the cantalienne, hazelnut-flavoured with chestnut paste and whipped cream. The choice of house white, rosé or red with the three-course *menu* was a welcome touch.

Brittany

Brittany's best-known staple is probably the ubiquitious crêpe and its buckwheat cousin, the *galette* (see p67, **Budget**, for more crêperies). It serves as both main course and dessert and is usually washed down with cider. Not surprisingly, coastal Brittany also produces an abundance of France's top fish and shellfish. Look for *cotriade* (a mixed fish stew), *anguille* (conger eel), Cancale oysters, mussels and Breton lobster. Also highly regarded are the potatoes from Noirmoutier, sea salt crystals from the Guérande peninsula, pork products, such as *andouille* (tripe sausage), and lamb from Belle-Ile.

Ty-Coz ★
35 rue St-Georges, 9th (01.48.78.42.95). Mº St-Georges. **Open** Tue-Sat noon-2pm, 7-10pm. Closed two weeks in Aug. **Average** €46. **Prix fixe** €26 (dinner only). **Credit** AmEx, MC, V.
Ty-Coz earns top marks from us for its no less than perfect cooking and service. A warm welcome from the staff even though there had been a mix-up about bookings (our fault) made a positive beginning to what turned out to be one of our best meals this year. The only clichéd part about Ty-Coz (meaning little house) is perhaps the seadog cottage decor with its wooden beams, crockery dressers and sensational model ship. The restaurant does have absolutely superlative seafood: a whole fresh crab arrived glistening on a bed of iodine-packed seaweed looking as though it had just been caught. We spent an hour relishing the beast, savouring every last fleshy bit. The pleasure rating was just as high with the main of a generous fillet of golden smoked haddock with a side dish of beautifully cooked mushrooms and courgettes with colourful strips of carrot, beans and a sprinkling of parsley. The fish lay on a bed of savoury saffron rice surrounded by the best butter sauce we have ever tasted. Perhaps it was a hint of lime zest and a touch of curry powder that made it special. We picked a delicately fragrant Muscadet sur lie Cuvée Donatien, served chilled to exactly the right temperature. Our dessert – a crêpe that oozed melted chocolate – could not be faulted.

Ti-Jos
30 rue Delambre, 14th (01.43.22.57.69). Mº Edgar Quinet or Vavin. **Open** Mon, Wed-Fri 11.30-2.30pm, 7pm-12.30am; Tue noon-2.30pm. Closed three weeks in Aug, Christmas/New Year. **Average** €14. **Prix fixe** €11 (Mon-Fri). **Credit** AmEx, MC, V.
Terracotta floor tiles, white tablecloths and carved dark wood chairs create a simple, uncluttered Breton atmosphere. Behind the basket of fresh eggs on the counter, the cook turns out golden-brown, frilly-edged pancakes with a variety of fillings, from *saucisse* to *andouillette* to roquefort cheese. We tucked into the 'farmer's version' – onions, fatty bacon and a hearty dollop of crème fraîche. Fortifying stuff for a cold winter's day, especially when washed down with Ti-Jos' excellent cider at €4.88 for 50cl. Dessert fillings include maple syrup, chocolate and chestnut cream. Our favourite was the apple *crêpe flambée* with its pleasant hint of caramelised sugar and a generous belt of Calvados. For those who balk at the idea of crêpes for main and dessert, the evening *menu* has non-crêpe options such as *moules marinières*. The evening gets livelier as the pub downstairs fills up, and Ti-Jos often has live Breton music on Friday nights.

Burgundy

Burgundy's long history, wealth and world-famous wines have given rise to one of France's most refined and renowned regional cuisines. Even if many of the foods traditionally associated with the region, including snails (dubbed the oysters of Burgundy), frogs' legs and mustard, are now imported and locally prepared, there is some produce, such as tangy, pungent époisses cheese, that remains distinctly local. Much of the cooking originated as farm food: *jambon persillé*, chunks of ham in a parsleyed aspic jelly, and *oeufs en meurette*, poached eggs in a red wine sauce with onions, mushrooms and bacon, as well as classics such as *coq au vin* or *boeuf bourguignon*. Dijon is also famous for its *pain d'épices*, a spice bread first baked during the Middle Ages, and *kir*, the apéritif of blackcurrant liqueur and dry aligoté wine.

Le Relais Chablisien
4, rue Bertin Poirée,1st. (01.45.08.53.73). Mº Châtelet or Pont Neuf. **Open** Mon-Fri noon-2.30pm, 7-9.30pm. Closed three weeks in Aug. **Average** €35. **Credit** MC, V.
This rustic *relais* is more *vieille France* than you would imagine in the heart of Paris. A husband-and-wife team bustle through the beamed dining room, serving local businessmen and the odd intrepid tourist. The *plats du jour* carefully written out on the menu began stunningly well with a meaty homemade terrine accompanied by pungent onion chutney and a more original salad of warm potatoes topped with tasty morsels of pork cheek. The main courses were spoilt by poor presentation and vegetable overkill. The piquant *poulet fermier au vinaigre* would have been better served with just the mound of good rice, rather than the addition of tough broad beans and mushy courgettes. The excellent steak suffered from the same indifferent broad beans and under-seasoned potato wedges strewn with raw garlic; only the tasty wild mushrooms added to the dish. The service, however, was charming and the wine list outstanding, especially our Burgundy pinot noir. We resisted the puddings and finished off our meal with a potent *marc*.

Au Bourguignon du Marais
52 rue François-Miron, 4th (01.48.87.15.40). Mº St-Paul. **Open** Mon-Fri noon-3pm, 7.30-11pm; Sat noon-3pm. Closed mid-July-mid-Aug. **Average** €23. **Credit** AmEx, DC, MC, V.
This stylish, ten-year-old dining room with a dozen tables projects a paradoxical, refined yet casual, vibe. The genial English-speaking staff handles a steady stream of Anglophones who launch right into their native tongue without so much as a *bonsoir*. The owner doesn't mind, filling the place most nights despite no publicity and a brave ban on mobile phones. The food is equally pleasing. On a hopping Friday night, we settled on a starter of tender sautéed *girolles* with cured ham and parmesan shavings on a bed of rocket. Other starters included snails, and *oeufs en meurette*. *Gougères* (cheese puffs) stuffed with pâté and a selection of breads kept our mouths busy until the main event arrived: a luscious seared tuna steak, only slightly overcooked, in a herb vinaigrette with steamed spinach on the side. Other dishes included steak tartare, pan-fried beef with *frites* or mashed potatoes, and roast duck. A '97 aligoté nicely tied together our meal; fans of Burgundy will relish the wine list. We could just see the tiny kitchen: plates warming in the oven, mushrooms frying, a slice of *marquise au chocolat* being set into a swirl of raspberry and white chocolate coulis. It's best to reserve, though lunch is quieter.

Corsica

As distinctive as the Corsicans themselves, the robust food of this rocky Mediterranean island features aromatic herbs, soft white brocciu cheese (the Corsican version of ricotta, made with goat's milk in summer and ewe's milk in winter), cured meats, chestnuts, kid, lamb and wild boar (in season). The cooking reflects the island's two habitats, wild mountain and rugged coast, with a limited number of fish and shellfish dishes. As a result of the Genoese rule, there are Italian-inspired preparations, such as aubergine gratin or brocciu and tomato salad. Chestnut flour (courtesy of the chestnut forests) is used as a substitute for wheat flour in an earthy-looking polenta. Wine growing dates back to Phoenician times, producing zesty reds, whites and rosés.

L'Alivi

27 rue du Roi-de-Sicile, 4th (01.48.87.90.20). M° St-Paul. **Open** Mon-Thur, Sun noon-2pm, 7-11pm; Fri, Sat noon-2pm, 7-11.30pm. **Average** €35. **Prix fixe** €20 (dinner only). **Credit** MC, V.

This discreet corner of 'the beautiful isle' is worth seeking out if only for the cultural experience: the wooden tables, beams, stone walls, polyphonic music and old Corsican ferry posters perfectly reproduce the atmosphere of one of the island's excellent *ferme-auberges*. You can get into the feel of things by leafing through the Corsican dailies while sipping an apéritif such as a fruity Cap Corse, a sweet muscat, or the flagship beer, Pietra, made with chestnut flour. A filling but slightly watery country soup made with the ham bone, beans and other elements and originally designed to warm the bones of Corsican shepherds, together with a thick wedge of rustic *tarte aux herbes*, began our meal. We opted for roasted kid, which turned out to be a little high on the bone-to-meat scale. To accompany it we drank an excellent 1997 Oriu from Domaine Torracia from a selection of the best vineyard names such as Clos Capitoro, Orenga, Fumicicoli and Peraldi. Questions on the specific origins of Corsican cheeses were met with as much caricatural suspicion as if we were enquiring as to the whereabouts of Yvan Colonna. Only the owner could authorise our waiter to dispense the precious information. Sadly, he never arrived.

Vivario

6 rue Cochin, 5th (01.43.25.08.19). M° Maubert-Mutualité. **Open** Mon, Sat 7.30-11pm; Tue-Fri noon-2pm, 7.30-11pm. Closed one week in Aug, 25 Dec-2 Jan. **Average** €22. **Credit** AmEx, MC, V.

There is something of a clubby feel to Vivario, which might have to do with its dark wood interior and the fact that regulars know the menu by heart and order without even looking (or mispronouncing). Brocciu, the soft white Corsican cheese, features in several starters including the spinach and herb *tourte*, tomato salad and an excellent fluffy omelette oozing with the stuff. For main courses, the roast *cabri* (kid) was good enough to have every morsel stripped from its bones and the plate of salt cod doused with garlic disappeared almost as fast. We downed our last drops of rosé with some Corsican cheeses including an earthy *brebis* (sheep's milk cheese).

Casa Corsa ★

25 rue Mazarine, 6th (01.44.07.38.98). M° Odéon. **Open** Mon 7.30-11.30pm, Tue-Sat noon-2.30pm, 7.30-11.30pm. **Average** €30. **Lunch menu** €20. **Credit** AmEx, MC, V. **Wheelchair access.**

It was a brave move to open a regional restaurant in a heavily touristy, high-rent part of St-Germain but the locals have taken to the terracotta floors, ochre walls and old photographs of Corsica, and it's rightly thriving. The delicious food is generously served and fairly priced, and the blackboard menu is regularly revised. A starter of excellent Corsican *charcuterie* is nearly a meal in itself, while a savoury flan of leeks and *coppa* (cured Corsican pork loin) is delicate and full of flavour, as is a pastry filled with chard and served in a sauce of preserved onions. Main courses run from boar *civet* (a stew made with wine and enriched with blood) and a casserole of braised veal with olives, to sautéed baby squid with a tomato, garlic and basil garnish – as made in Bonifacio. Split the first-rate cheese plate.

Le Maquis

3 rue du Commandant Rivière, 8th (01.42.56.68.03). M° St-Philippe du Roule. **Open** Mon-Fri noon-2.30pm, 7.30-10.30pm; Sat 7.30-10.30pm. Closed three weeks in Aug. **Average** €35. **Credit** AmEx, MC, V.

This restaurant dispenses with the usual folkloric paraphernalia in favour of a more sober expression of Corsican culture in line with its swish location. From an *à la carte* menu that included a selection of the island's *charcuterie*, an intriguing tartare of red mullet and crab in pesto sauce and the delicious veal-olive *stuffatu* (stew), we chose a delicious *flan au brocciu*, made with ricotta-like Corsican cheese, whose texture was perfectly balanced: firm but creamy. To follow, the *aubergines bonifacio* was a flavourful combination of sweet oven-roasted tomatoes smothered in herbs and garlic with succulent, spicy strips of aubergine. This super-value dish at just €10 was enjoyed by the whole table. The roast kid was another resounding success, featuring man-sized chunks of meat, oven-cooked with a combination of fresh herbs from the Corsican *maquis* (scrub) and enough garlic to head off a host of vampires. The restaurant's posh location and representative regional cuisine, however, deserve a much wider selection of Corsican wines than currently on offer.

Paris Main d'Or

133 rue du Fbg-St-Antoine, 11th (01.44.68.04.68). M° Ledru-Rollin. **Open** Mon-Sat noon-3pm, 8pm-midnight. Closed Mon in Aug. **Average** €22. **Lunch menu** €11. **Credit** MC, V.

You'd better like your neighbours at this Corsican restaurant – chances are you'll either be sharing a bottle of wine with them or planning a vendetta by the end of the evening – but it seems to attract a likeable crowd of *bon vivants* of all ages. The menu, titled *'dossier Corse, confidentiel'*, makes tongue-in-cheek reference to the islanders' reputation for skullduggery and the specials of the day are found on a folded note tucked inside. The air of mystery is compounded by the fact that many of the dishes use uniquely Corsican ingredients, but our waiter was happy to enlighten us. The special of veal in Vico honey (Vico is a region) was unavailable by the time we ordered, but the two squiffy ladies to our right declared the *pignata marina* (a kind of bouillabaisse) *'délicieuse'*. We were perhaps unwise not to follow their lead – the tomato and brocciu salad was sparing, but the luscious baked aubergine was juicy and big enough to share. A lamb stew with olives was again nothing special, but when the roast kid arrived it caused gasps from the surrounding tables. The enormous plate contained what must have been a quarter of a goat, covered in sprigs of herbs and roasted, unpeeled garlic to smear on the meat. Among the desserts, many of which contain Corsican liqueurs, the honey ice cream is especially good. Corsican food is only served in the evenings.

Lyon

Lyon, the traditional gateway dividing north and south, earned its reputation as a gastronomic capital during the second half of the 19th century with the development of the *bouchon*, a small bistro that served simple home cooking at any time of day. While few genuine *bouchons* remain, Lyon's culinary emissaries in Paris continue to serve up the kind of hearty, homely fare common in Lyonnais homes. Go armed with an insatiable appetite: typical dishes include warm potato salad with sausage slices, tripe in various forms (*andouillettes à la Lyonnaise* or *tablier de sapeur*), *gratin dauphinois*, potatoes cooked with cream and sometimes cheese, and *poulet de Bresse*, the only chicken to be awarded the AOC (*appellation d'origine controlée*) status in France.

Moissonnier

28 rue des Fossés St-Bernard, 5th (01.43.29.87.65). M° Cardinal Lemoine or Jussieu. **Open** Tue-Sat noon-2pm, 7.30-10pm. Closed Aug. **Average** €34. **Lunch menu** €22.90 (Tue-Fri). **Credit** MC, V.

This classy-yet-casual restaurant, with its white linen, weighty silver and lamps fashioned from gnarled branches, serves up bulky, country-sized portions of food from Lyon and Franche-Comté. During a recent lunch two women made a meal from a forbidding cart wheeled in from the kitchen. If you order this, the *saladier*, you sample freely from a dozen or so bowls – cabbage and potato salad, lentils, red beans, *saucissons*, tripe – and the trolley moves on to the next victim. Or, try a simple salad of slightly bitter *escarole* and comté cheese, or the snails. Fish dishes such as the pike *quenelles* in Nantua (crayfish) sauce seemed expensive (€16 and up) compared to meats, such as roast rack of lamb with parsley or the *breuzi*, air-dried and salted beef from the Jura. While we expected the rooster to be less tender than chicken, it was overcooked to the point of being dry, its sauce revealing scant trace of the promised raspberry essence. Dessert made up for it: three *poires Bourguignonnes*, soaked in an outstanding cinnamon-wine brew, and apple-raisin crème brûlée.

Normandy

Dairy produce and apples are the hallmarks of Normandy fare. While the famed creamy sauces of the region are frequently flavoured with refreshing local cider or Calvados, a potent apple brandy, the cheeses, comprising some of France's finest cows' milk cheeses including camembert, livarot, neufchâtel and pont l'évêque, stand firmly alone. Despite the fields of cows – the dairy godmothers – pork is the favoured meat, and fruits, particularly apples and pears, act as a pleasantly sharp foil to the richness of much of the food. Try *porc à la normande*, cooked in cider with apples and onions. Seafood also features in *moules marinières*, *marmite dieppoise*, fish stew, and *sole normande*.

Les Fernandises

19 rue de la Fontaine-au-Roi, 11th (01.48.06.16.96). M° République. **Open** Tue-Sat noon-2.30pm, 7.30-10.30pm. Closed one week in May, Aug. **Average** €27. **Prix fixe** €21. **Lunch menu** €17. **Credit** MC, V.

Perfect camemberts are rare, but at Fernand Asseline's convivial bistro the selection of Normandy's finest – oozing, unctuous and ripened in-house – is virtually unbeatable. A large wooden platter, heaving with pungent cheese, was generously left at our table and no one grumbled when we carved a healthy slice of each of the eight varieties. The ones doused in Calvados and *lie de vin* (wine sediment) were superb, the walnut satisfyingly earthy, and the *nature* a must for the purist, but the best surprise was *foin* (delicately coated in, yes, hay!). Pre-cheese treats included poultry-laden starters – a salad laced with strips of tender duck and chicken livers on warm lentils – a nicely crisped duck breast paired with *gratin dauphinois*, and a tasty roast pigeon. If you've still got room for dessert, there are scrumptious cider crêpes and a *tarte aux pommes flambée* that's well worth ordering for the spectacle of the two-minute flame dance. The wine list is reasonably priced and there is a good selection of Calvados. Book ahead.

North

The hardy cooking of Picardy and Flanders is closely linked to that of neighbouring Belgium. Wine makes way for beer both at the table and in dishes such as *carbonnade*, a stew usually made with beef. The classic Belgian dish *moules-frites* (mussels with chips) pops up in northern French cities such as Lille while another import, *waterzoï*, a stew of chicken or fish and vegetables, also puts in an appearance. A favourite side dish is braised chicory, known as *chicon*. Also on offer are the particularly pungent northern cheeses such as maroilles, deep-orange mimolette (known as 'hollande' in the north) and, for the truly brave, sharp and salty vieux lille. Sweets include spice breads and *speculoos*, crunchy spice biscuits served with coffee. **Ghislaine Arabian** (*see p40*, **Haute Cuisine**) offers a sophisticated take on northern food.

Le Graindorge ★

15 rue de l'Arc de Triomphe, 17th (01.47.54.00.28). M° Charles de Gaulle-Etoile. **Open** Mon-Fri noon-2.30pm, 7.30-11pm; Sat 7.30-11pm. Closed two weeks in Aug. **Average** €38. **Prix fixe** €32 (dinner only). **Lunch menu** €24, €28. **Credit** AmEx, MC, V. **Wheelchair access.**

A meal in this relaxed art deco-style dining room on a quiet street near the Arc de Triomphe is a real treat, which is why it's almost always full of knowing regulars and well-informed tourists. Everything about this place pleases, from the rollmops and cucumber canapés served with apéritifs to the reasonable prices and welcoming chef Bernard Broux, who takes your order before scooting into the kitchen. Another pleasure: the service from a polite and well-drilled team of waiters. The regional card isn't overplayed, since you could easily have a meal here without heading north, but it would be a shame to miss such beautifully done Franco-Belgian specialties as *potjevleesch*, a jellied terrine of rabbit, pork and veal, or a delicate and generously served *waterzooï*. We loved our starters of perfectly cooked asparagus with a fresh herb salad and *potjevleesch*, and mains were excellent, too – grilled Scottish salmon in a delicate *beurre blanc* sauce and *waterzooï*, flavourful free-range chicken pieces poached in a creamy sauce and garnished with spring carrots, cauliflower, potatoes and courgette. The cheese course was a fine opportunity to finish our Château de Mille Côtes du Luberon, since the perfectly-aged selection of northern cheeses comes from Philippe Olivier in Boulogne-sur-Mer, one of the best cheese merchants in the north. Finish with an outstanding crème brûlée with rhubarb preserves.

Provence & South

Mediterranean cuisine's rapid rise to fame has contributed to a variety of misconceptions about southern French cooking. While it's true that olive oil is almost always used in preference to butter, and that garlic, tomatoes, courgettes and aubergines figure in many recipes, the cuisine is considerably varied and often much more delicate than is popularly thought. Fish, vegetables and pasta figure in the cooking of the Riviera and Provence. Signature dishes include *bouillabaisse* (a once humble fishermen's soup made from the lowliest part of the catch, which has become emblematic of Marseille), *les petits farcis*, baby vegetables with a veal, breadcrumb and vegetable stuffing, and *aïoli*, a garlic mayonnaise served with boiled cod, vegetables and potatoes. From Montpellier to the Spanish border the Italian influence yields to Catalan dishes, reflecting the fact that the area from Perpignan to the Pyrenees was once part of this Spanish province.

La Bastide Odéon

7 rue Corneille, 6th (01.43.26.03.65/www-bastide-odeon.com). M° Odéon. **Open** Tue-Sat 12.30-2pm, 7.30-10.30pm. Closed three weeks in Aug, 25 Dec-2 Jan **Prix fixe** €26, €32. **Credit** AmEx, MC, V. **Wheelchair access.**

Just like Provence itself, La Bastide Odéon is under constant siege from tourists and French alike. We made three attempts before we finally secured a booking; by 8pm on a Tuesday it was heaving with English speakers and by 10pm a new set of French faces had arrived. Chef Gilles Azuelos, who trained with Michel Rostang and Jacques Maximin, does traditional Provençal cooking with a contemporary twist. Starters of roasted aubergine layered with *tapenade* and

Berried treasure from Le Graindorge

topped with a sun-dried tomato, and a round courgette stuffed with creamy *chèvre* with spring asparagus, were smart and likeable. Mains included a fillet of remarkably tender *canette* (duckling) with aubergine caviar, and fresh cod garnished with capers and croutons, served with artichokes and onions. Also on offer, *pieds et paquets*, tripe and sheep's feet cooked with white wine and tomatoes – a Marseillaise speciality. While the food won approval, the service didn't. It was frenzied and fraught; our waiter was put out when we delayed ordering dessert and was that a curled lip when we went for tap rather than bottled water? The cooking is good but the speed of service and sittings create a feeling of mass catering, albeit upmarket.

Le Bistrot d'Alex
2 rue Clément, 6th (01.43.54.09.53).
Mº Mabillon or Odéon. **Open** Mon-Fri noon-3pm, 7-11pm; Sat 7-11pm. Closed 1-13 Nov.
Average €38. **Prix fixe** €26.
Lunch menu €16. **Credit** AmEx, MC, V.
With so many bistros offering bargain set *menus*, it takes some gumption to be frankly expensive. Le Bistrot d'Alex, formerly an uninspired Lyonnais, seems to be gambling on a clientele of wealthy Left Bankers and tourists in its rebirth as a Provençal bistro with prices reminiscent of St-Tropez. Whether this will work remains to be seen. The menu is brief – not necessarily a bad thing – but some of the most tempting dishes, such as squid *a la plancha* and fresh cod with olive mash, were unavailable. Very fresh fish and seafood are the specialities here, so all but confirmed carnivores should ignore the three meat dishes. The *assiette tropézienne* was a big plate of shelled prawns with roasted red peppers and aubergines and a bowl of *tapenade*, while meaty anchovy fillets came with *tapenade* toasts, warm potato wedges in oil and a beautifully dressed *escarole* and parsley salad. Feeling stuffed already, we tackled an *assiette du pêcheur* – tender red mullet, grouper, scallops and prawns with whole mushrooms stewed with tomato – and a dry, overcooked swordfish steak with floppy courgette rounds and mushrooms. Dessert of the day, a homely chocolate cake with a dollop of chocolate filling and plenty of crème anglaise, rounded out a satisfying meal. But with a half-bottle of white Provençal wine and two apéritifs, the €102.13 price tag seemed overly steep.

Pataquès
42 bd de Bercy, 12th (01.43.07.37.75).
Mº Bercy. **Open** Mon-Sat noon-3pm, 6.30pm-midnight. **Average** €26. **Prix fixe** €19.10-€26. **Credit** AmEx, DC, MC, V.
Pataquès is a Provençal word for 'brothel', and the menu cover features rosy-cheeked yokels grinning cheerily. Despite the risqué name, it's a classy, upmarket place, a soft-lit, linen-napkin sort of restaurant and a real find in this quiet area. Recently taken over by a new team from Italy, it still specialises in Provençal cuisine but with an Italian twist. A cheerful waiter led us to a candlelit table on the elegant terrace, enclosed by a wall of potted plants and sweet-smelling lavender. We started with ice-cold gin and tonics, accompanied by fried cheese appetisers and juicy green olives with a bite of garlic. A starter of plump langoustines came drizzled in pesto with a fresh rocket salad and slivers of crumbly parmesan, and an aubergine *parmeggiana* was cooked to melt-in-the-mouth perfection. *Lasagne de morue* was very good: tender slices of cod with rich tomato and herb sauce, layers of lasagne and still-melting mozzarella. The *sauté de veau* with gnocchi, however, was disappointing – undercooked and fatty, with a bland, unseasoned olive and artichoke sauce. An excellent *salade d'oranges* – thick chunks infused with a ginger and brown sugar dressing and topped with sweet crystallised violets – perked us up. We finished the bottle of €14.48 Saint Julien des Vignes and rounded off the meal with Italian coffees, marzipan sweets and complimentary sour lemon liqueurs.

La Table O & Co.
Oliviers & Co, 8 rue de Levis, 17th (01.53.42.18.04/www.oliviers-co.com).
Mº Villiers. **Open** Mon-Sat noon-2.30pm.
Average €20. **Prix fixe** €13.72, €19.82.
Credit AmEx, MC, V. **Wheelchair access**.
Once they get the painfully slow and disorganised service worked out, this latest branch of the boutique chain devoted to olive oil and olive-oil-derived products will be a pleasant place for a light, reasonably priced lunch. The setting is attractive and the food simple but good. The menu changes daily and features dishes prepared with the various oils on sale here. Select two or three dishes from the five on offer, which are served in little terracotta dishes fitted into a wooden tray. We liked the *brandade de morue* with Greek olive oil, the stuffed aubergines with Croatian oil, the stuffed peppers with Tunisian oil and the cheese-filled ravioli sprinkled with lemon-spiked oil, all accompanied by *socca*, slices of Niçoise-style chickpea flour crêpes. Desserts – a blancmange with watermelon preserves, strawberry *clafoutis*, baked apple with olive jam and chocolate mousse – were inventive and tasty.

Le Pavillon Puebla ★
corner of av Simon-Bolivar and rue Botzaris, parc des Buttes-Chaumont, 19th (01.42.08.92.62). Mº Buttes-Chaumont.
Open Tue-Sat noon-2.30pm, 8-10pm.
Average €55. **Prix fixe** €30, €40.
Credit AmEx, MC, V.
On a summer's night on the terrace of this romantic, time-worn French-Catalan restaurant in the Buttes-Chaumont park, you'll breathe the scent of the flowers and forest by candlelight and hear the chronic mating squawk of a lonely male peacock. We selected a chilled red Sancerre from the lengthy wine menu and settled back for a leisurely meal. To start we had zesty tomatoes with garlic on toast and serrano ham over fresh salad, and anchovies with sweet red peppers. Roast duck was sweetened perfectly with stewed ripe figs, and the lamb roasted with thyme and mushrooms practically dissolved in our mouths. We finished with fresh strawberries in a chilled strawberry sauce topped with scoops of vanilla and heavenly honey-almond ice cream. Overseeing the impeccable service was the owner and lively hostess for the evening. When asked if the restaurant was an old hunting lodge, she replied, 'Hah! Look at that wall. It's concrete. My husband built it the other day.' When we inquired about the strange bird noises, she said, 'Try listening to that 200 times a day!'

Savoie & Franche-Comté

If Savoie is best known for its superb cheeses, including beaufort, reblochon, tomme and the rare bleu de gex (a fine, sweet blue-veined cow's milk cheese that is only made at five dairies), there is much more to the region's menu than the raclette (cheese melted and served over boiled potatoes) and fondue that have become its claim to culinary fame. Baked vacherin is a particular delight; this runny, seasonal cheese is also often found on Paris cheeseboards. Fishermen on the shores of Lake Geneva land crayfish and *omble chevalier* (char lakefish), a delicate, much-prized freshwater fish. The influence of nearby Italy is evident in *crozettes*, tiny squares of pasta eaten buttered with – what else but? – grated cheese. Fine quality *charcuterie* includes *viande des Grisons* (air-dried beef), and smoked sausage. *Gratin dauphinois* and *ravioles de Royan*, tiny cheese-stuffed ravioli from the Vercors region, denote the adjacent Dauphiné, while Mondeuse, a hearty red, is the best-known Savoyard wine. On the Swiss border, the Franche-Comté's rich pastures yield a variety of excellent cheeses, most made with cow's milk. Smoked Morteau and Montbéliard sausages are served with warm potato salad as a first course or a hearty lunch. Excellent wines are produced around Arbois, including vin jaune, a sherry-like wine often used to season the cream sauces that partner poultry dishes.

Alexandre
24 rue de la Parcheminerie, 5th (01.43.26.49.66). Mº St-Michel or Cluny-La-Sorbonne. **Open** daily 6-11.30pm.
Average €15. **Credit** MC, V.
There are only three items on the menu and no desserts. Each selection is accompanied by lumberjack portions of salad, bread, potatoes

and a trio of squirt bottles containing ketchup, mayonnaise, and Béarnaise sauces. If you think of cheese fondue as a winter dish, try the popular *pierrade*, which allows you to grill beef strips, onions, mushrooms, peppers and tomatoes on a sizzling stone rubbed with oil, salt and pepper, in summer. The *fondue bourguignonne* is the third hearty selection consisting of similar beef and vegetable ingredients cooked in boiling oil. As one of us was a vegetarian, and each table is obliged to order the same dish, we opted for the cheese fondue. The board outside promises 'all you can eat', yet we could not imagine anyone possibly asking for more of these giants. We stuffed ourselves endlessly with comforting gooey mouthfuls and even then we had hardly made a dent in the pile of slightly dry dipping bread. As we left the last bits of cheesy bread to solidify on our plates, we couldn't help imagining the same event occurring in our arteries.

Chez Maître Paul
12 rue Monsieur-le-Prince, 6th (01.43.54.74.59/www.paris-avenue.fr/maitrepaul). M° Odéon. **Open** daily 12.15-2.15pm, 7.15-10.15pm. Closed Mon, Sun in July and Aug, 25 Dec-2 Jan. **Average** €40. **Prix fixe** €27, €32. **Credit** AmEx, DC, MC, V.
One of the most venerable regional tables in Paris, this grey-painted dining room specialises in the hearty cooking of the Jura and Franche-Comté regions. Many worried that the kitchen quality wouldn't survive the retirement of the founding couple several years ago, but the new owner remains committed to the job at hand. The €32 *menu* with a half-bottle of Bourgueil is an innovation that offers a hearty feed for a very fair price, although the quality of the wine is indifferent at best. Start with a plump Montbéliard sausage served with fresh potato salad, smoked salmon or a *salade comtoise* (ham, walnuts and cheese), or, *à la carte*, asparagus vinaigrette or *mousseline*. Then try the delicious chicken gratinéed in mushroom cream sauce with comté cheese, chicken with morel mushrooms in a cream sauce spiked with vin jaune, or calf's liver in a sauce of sweet vin de paille. Unfortunately there's no cheese tray, but a cheese plate is available and desserts such as walnut cake and *fondant au chocolat* in a sauce boosted by *liqueur de sapin* are good.

South-west

Combining Périgord (Dordogne), Bordeaux, Gascony and the Basque country, this part of France is known for its filling yet refined fare. Foie gras, the liver of fattened duck or goose, is a speciality of Gascony and the Dordogne. It is eaten in various guises; often very lightly cooked (*mi-cuit*) and served cold as a terrine (a 'pâté' is lower-quality, mixed with pork), or lightly pan-fried so that the inside still quivers. Duck also features heavily: *magret* is the breast of a fattened duck, and *confit de canard* is duck preserved in its own fat. Another famed dish is *cassoulet*, a rib-sticking stew of white beans, duck or goose *confit*, lamb and sausage. Look out, too, for tasty lamb from the Pyrenees. Bordeaux's contributions, unsurprisingly, often contain wine: *à la bordelaise* implies a red wine sauce, be it for steak or in a snail *cassolette*. Ceps and pricey truffles from the Périgord are also prized. Basque cuisine is often quite spicy thanks to the addition of Espelette peppers. Try *pipérade* (scrambled eggs with peppers, onions and ham), stuffed squid, tuna, delicate, raw-cured *jambon de Bayonne*, and the sheep's-milk iraty cheese of the Pyrenees.

La Fermette du Sud-Ouest
31 rue Coquillière, 1st (01.42.36.73.55). M° Les Halles. **Open** Mon-Sat noon-2.30pm, 7.30-10pm. **Average** €30. **Prix fixe** €22.20. **Lunch menu** €14.50.
Credit MC, V.
Near the former wholesale market of Les Halles, this slightly claustrophobic restaurant seems caught in a gastronomic timewarp. On a hot summer's day the owners, who seem to have a good regular clientele, made us feel particularly welcome. The *carte* and *menus* feature all the classic regional dishes, including a serious-looking *cassoulet* and *confits* galore. This being the hottest day of the year we chose with circumspection from the €22.20 *menu* – a starter of prawn cocktail, even with the addition of grapefruit segments, was the sort of dish which is the same from Pau to Prague, but the *salade landaise* was the works, loaded with warm *gésiers confits*, walnuts, ham and bacon. Main courses were equally wholesome, including a well-seasoned steak tartare and a *brochette* of perfectly pink veal kidneys, both served with a side plate of potatoes sautéed in duck fat. Ordering another *pot* of the excellent house red, we enjoyed a creamy dish of fromage blanc and an *île flottante*, a feather-light meringue streaked with crisp caramel bobbing on an ocean of *crème anglaise*.

Le Souletin
6 rue La Vrillière, 1st (01.42.61.43.78). M° Bourse or Palais Royal. **Open** Mon-Fri noon-2.30pm, 7.30-10.30pm; Sat 7.30-10.30pm. **Average** €27. **Credit** MC, V.
Old-fashioned on the outside, with its facade of polished wood, Le Souletin is just as warm and welcoming inside. Suit-clad men hang around the bar, joking with the *patronne*, who is cheerful and efficient even with unfamiliar foreigners. From a short menu featuring robust Basque food, we chose a frothy puréed white bean soup with lovely foie gras nibbles, and a substantial salad of nicely firm lentils with bacon, in a tangy vinaigrette. Mains were just as rustic and generous, in the true Basque tradition. *Axoa*, strips of veal in a sweet tomato and pepper sauce, was a fine choice. We ordered saddle of lamb with thyme, mostly for the crunchy fried potatoes that came with it. These turned out to be unevenly cooked but tasty nonetheless, while the meat was pink and succulent. Dessert was hardly necessary, but out of curiosity (and greediness), we tried a waffle with pan-fried pears (more Belgian than Basque) and a *coupe* of surprisingly good blackcurrant, lime and pear sorbets.

La Maison de la Lozere ★
4 rue Hautefeuille, 6th (01.43.54.26.64). M° St-Michel. **Open** Tue-Sat noon-2pm, 7.30-10pm. **Closed** first week in Jan, mid-Jul to mid Aug. **Average** €19. **Prix fixe** €20.50, €25. **Lunch menu** €15. **Credit** MC, V.
Just behind the Fontaine St-Michel, this restaurant provides delicious cuisine in an area where it is increasingly difficult to find decent regional cooking. A lunch visit found the tiny, beamed room buzzing with a crowd of regulars. All the tables are laid with a welcoming quarter-loaf of country bread, ready for you to hack off a chunk to accompany your starters. These included a plate of good-quality regional *charcuterie* and tasty *pâté caussenard* flavoured with juniper berries; the homemade soup, from one of the set *menus*, also looked tempting. Our table's tripe man, something of an endangered species these days, was more than happy with two authentic *tripoux* parcels accompanied by oniony sautéed potatoes, while veal fillet with prunes was tender and homely. A chestnut Charlotte was the most interesting of the puddings on offer, and with a bottle of excellent Domaine Hortus from the Languedoc at €19.90 and a house apéritif, the bill was a bargain. Added to which, the staff were attentive and welcoming. We'll be back on a chilly Thursday for their *aligot* (creamy potatoes, cheese and garlic) evening.

La Table d'Aude
8 rue de Vaugirard, 6th (01.43.26.36.36/ www.latabledaude.com). M° Odéon or RER Luxembourg. **Open** Mon noon-2pm; Tue-Fri noon-2pm, 7-9.30pm; Sat 7-9.30pm. **Average** €25. **Prix fixe** €25-€35 (dinner only). **Lunch menu** €12-€19.
Credit MC, V.
The senators and book editors in this Left Bank neighbourhood, joined by students, professors and other locals in the evening, are on to a good thing at this simple and convivial restaurant. Owner Bernard Patou and his wife Véronique take a contagious pleasure in serving up the best of their home turf, the Aude, a narrow department in the Languedoc-Roussillon that includes Carcassonne, Castelnaudry – famed for its *cassoulet* – and some of the most rapidly ascending vineyards in France, including Minervois and Corbières. Almost everyone orders the *cassoulet* as the main course, which comes piping hot in a small, high-sided ceramic dish filled to the brim with white beans, sausage and preserved duck. Start with a goat's cheese salad, or the improbably delicious *saladette du Cabardes*, mixed leaves with raw artichoke and slices of dried pork liver. The *poule de l'Aric façon grand-mère* is another soothing and satisfying main dish – chicken cooked with white wine, olives and mushrooms.

D'Chez Eux
2 av de Lowendal, 7th (01.47.05.52.55). M° Ecole-Militaire. **Open** Mon-Sat noon-2.30pm, 7.30-10.30pm. Closed three weeks in Aug. **Average** €50. **Lunch menu** €28, €33.50. **Credit** AmEx, DC, MC, V.
Wheelchair access.
A warm welcome from the *patron* and long-serving staff are a prelude to a complimentary *kir* and a hunk of excellent *saucisson*. The cosseting, interlinked rooms feel comfortingly provincial and the menu is an essay in a certain type of traditional French cuisine. Begin with either the salad trolley, which includes plump fresh anchovies, delicious long-cooked pearl onions plus other delicacies, or the equally tempting range of *charcuterie*. Our mains included a guinea fowl *grand-mère*, served in a copper pan and carved at the table on its comfortable bed of potatoes, bacon and mushrooms. If the bird itself was slightly dry, the intensely flavoured *jus* compensated for this. An enormous slab of calf's liver was coated in a melting mixture of shallots and sharp vinegar. The meat itself was slightly less pink than ordered, the sort of imprecision which is the downside to this rustic, country approach to big eating, but warming to the experience we tucked into the dessert trolley with gusto: a winning chocolate mousse, creamy vanilla ice cream, the first strawberries of the season and an impressive collection of stewed fruits.

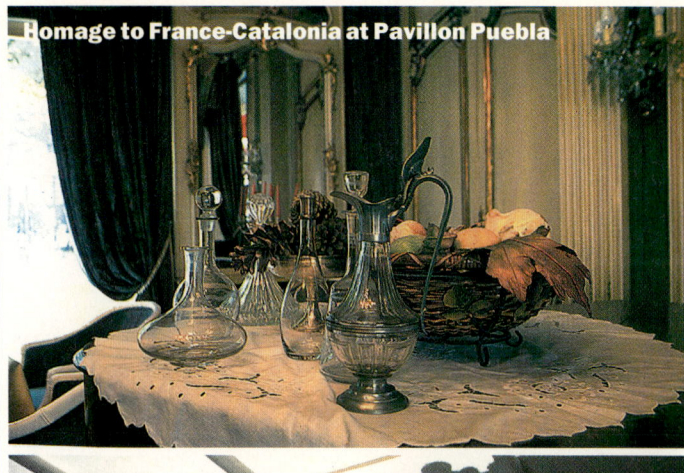

Homage to France-Catalonia at Pavillon Puebla

Fish & Seafood

Longing for a whiff of salty air? These restaurants land the sea at your table.

Though the nearest beach is hours away, chefs at the best fish restaurants in Paris take pride in offering squeaky fresh specimens such as you might find in Brittany, Normandy or the Mediterranean. Some specialise in one dish – oysters at **Le Bar à Huîtres** or *bouillabaisse* at **Le Keryado** – while others, such as the legendary **Le Dôme** and **Le Duc**, rely on the day's catch. Minimalist is still the preferred technique – fish is often served raw or barely cooked, with little seasoning – and the famous **Maison Prunier** has re-opened after renovations as a New-York style caviar house. If you're craving a giant seafood platter, head to one of the city's famous brasseries (*see p45*).

Goumard

7-9 rue Duphot, 1st (01.42.60.36.07/ www.goumard.fr). M° Madeleine. **Open** daily noon-2.30pm, 7.30-10.30pm. Closed two weeks in Aug. **Average** €68. **Lunch menu** €40. **Credit** AmEx, DC, MC, V.

Goumard's lovely tiled exterior seems to hint at things to come – and then you are led upstairs to a dining room totally bereft of art nouveau extravagance. The room has a new fish motif carpet and freshly upholstered chairs but you can't help but feel nostalgic for the restaurant's long-lost glory days, especially after a visit to the beautifully preserved loos. Feeling slightly out of place among the many dark suits, we put our minds to the pricey menu. The €40 lunch for skinflints – the term is relative here – offers no choice, so we splashed out on one *à la carte* meal. After a nice appetiser of mackerel with *tapenade*, we waited more than half an hour for our starters of *soupe d'étrilles* (velvet swimming crabs) from the *menu*, and crab salad. Both featured the same refreshing pile of crabmeat with diced courgette and carrot, one surrounded by a richly flavoured but lukewarm broth and the other by thick cream sauce in a starfish-shaped glass dish. The friendly service picked up at this point and our mains arrived promptly: the *menu's* sea bream fillet with small artichokes and roasted tomatoes, and three red mullet fillets with a side dish of fennel overkill (roasted, and puréed with fennel seeds and fresh leaves). Indisputably fresh, the fish helped us understand why Goumard remains popular. But, after a so-so dessert of caramelised quetsch plums with puff pastry and vanilla ice cream, we felt that our €129 (with two glasses of Chablis and coffee) might have been spent more pleasurably than in this business haunt. The new Champagne and oyster bar downstairs should bring back some of the former glamour.

Iode ★

48 rue d'Argout, 2nd (01.42.36.46.45). M° Sentier. **Open** Mon-Fri 12.30-3pm, 8.30-11.30pm; Sat 8.30-11.30pm. **Average** €34. **Credit** MC, V.

Something fishy has been going on in the rue d'Argout since Steve Arcelin opened the doors to his new-wave Breton bistro, Iode; and it's looking like just the kind of groovy gourmet set-up that the young fashionistas of this trendy pedestrian street (off-off Montorgueil) have been crying out for. Although most of the action takes place in the first-floor dining room – marble tables with plants (aquatic of course) and funky metal sculptures from artist Emmanuelle Chapelin – there is also a small bar downstairs with a back-lit shark-pool ceiling, and a terrace opposite. In the kitchen, more young Bretons: Arnaud (ex-Michel Rostang) and wife Sandrine Cren produce a menu with an accent on freshness, and there are daily deliveries, some direct from suppliers in Brittany. We chose a creamy, carefully seasoned tartare of *grenadier* and a pile of crisp deep-fried baby squid from the blackboard which also offered a salad of langoustines and goat's cheese and *mijoté de palourdes* (stewed clams). A generous John Dory fillet with *chorizo* 'scales' was served with artichoke heart, caramelised onions and mash; the swordfish steak simply grilled and drizzled with basil oil tasted delicious. There is duck breast with mango for die-hard carnivores. We shared a berry and citrus salad in a light mint syrup as we were stuffed to the gills, but heartier appetites could try *crêpes Suzette* with a glass of cloudy draught cider. Service was friendly and laid-back and the €79.58 bill for two, including a bottle of crisp white Côtes de Gascogne, seemed fair.

Le Bistrot du Dôme Bastille

2 rue de la Bastille, 4th (01.48.04.88.44). M° Bastille. **Open** daily 12.15-2.30pm, 7.15-11.30pm. **Average** €37. **Credit** AmEx, MC, V.

Le Bistrot du Dôme, an offshoot of the celebrated Dôme at Montparnasse, at first feels rather formal with its heavy white tablecloths, pretty vineyard canopy and lack of set *menu* at lunch. The waiter didn't flinch when we arrived with a two-month-old baby, though, and found a comfortable space for us in the quiet downstairs dining room (most people head for the livelier room upstairs). Written in chalk, the menu changes according to the day's catch. We settled on a refreshingly tangy sea bream and avocado *ceviche*, and an unusual smoked haddock and grapefruit salad that proved a little short on the grapefruit. A juicy John Dory fillet was nicely flavoured with warm spices, as were the accompanying carrots, but a tuna steak had been cooked to death, topped with a mustard sauce whose lurid colour and flavour reminded us of hot dogs. Berry gratin with fluffy sabayon, and a generous serving of soothing rhubarb compote finished off a lunch that had its share of flaws, but the relaxed atmosphere, pleasant surroundings and tempting selection of wines – all priced at €17.60 – would bring us back to fish for the best of the dishes.

Branch: Le Bistrot du Dôme Montparnasse, 1 rue Delambre, 14th (01.43.35.32.00).

Net returns from Le Dôme

Bistrot Côté Mer

16 bd St-Germain, 5th (01.43.54.59.10/ www.michelrostang.com). M° Maubert-Mutualité. **Open** daily noon-2.30pm, 7.30-11pm. **Average** €38. **Credit** AmEx, MC, V

Chef Michel Rostang's daughter Caroline has created a trendy Breton atmosphere, and her warm welcome and constant presence pleasantly animate a meal here. The menu, too, is well-conceived, priced and executed. Start with a choice of three different kinds of oysters, *céleri rémoulade* with fresh crabmeat, or roasted mussels with mushroom salad and tartare sauce or opt for a daily special such as a delicious terrine of marinated salmon layered with mashed new potatoes. Mains include excellent sautéed prawns on a bed of *orecchiette* pasta in a prawn and tomato sauce, grilled sea bass with black-olive polenta, and scallops cooked in their shells with small vegetables. Meat-eaters are catered for with a hefty *côte de boeuf* or lamb *pastilla* with Moroccan spices. Excellent desserts include a first-rate cocoa soufflé. The wine list, assembled by the sommelier at Rostang's main restaurant, has three subheadings that help you select the style you're after.

L'Huître et Demie

80 rue Mouffetard, 5th (01.43.37.98.21). M° Place Monge. **Open** daily noon-2.30pm, 7-11pm. **Average** €46. **Prix fixe** €17, €28. **Lunch menu** €11. **Credit** AmEx, MC, V.

Huître et Demie initially appears to be a typical Left Bank tourist haunt, complete with stone walls, beams and nasty piped music. The €28 *menu*, however, is excellent value, and is prepared with heart-warming, old-fashioned competence. We began with a *flan de pétoncles*, a light scallop mousse surrounded by a highly flavoured seafood sauce. Salad with slices of perfectly cooked *rognons de veau* (veal kidneys) was substantial and comforting. Neither of us could resist the half-lobster with rosemary butter accompanied by creamy tagliatelle, perhaps not the greatest lobster in the world but a bargain which raised the spirits. We ignored the *dame-blanche* (vanilla ice cream with whipped cream and chocolate sauce) and plumped for the *omelette norvégienne*, a French take on baked Alaska, which arrived ablaze with Grand Marnier. The far from ruinous bill showed that fish restaurants in Paris don't have to break the bank.

La Méditerranée

2 pl de l'Odéon, 6th (01.43.26.02.30/ www.la-mediterranee.com). M° Odéon. **Open** daily noon-2.30pm, 7.30-11pm. Closed Christmas. **Average** €46. **Prix fixe** €24.50, €29. **Credit** AmEx, MC, V.

Burgundy velvet seats and wall paintings of maidens, romantic goatherds, doves and fishergirls, painted by Manuel Vertès and Christian Bérard in the 1930s, conjure up the era when the Côte d'Azur was colonised by artists and literati, as do menus and plates adorned with virtuoso squiggles by Jean Cocteau in 1960. The focus is on fish with a Mediterranean touch; however, there are some meat options (steak, *magret*). From the *carte*, *bouillabaisse*, accompanied by a mound of croutons and a boat of *rouille*, consisted of a sturdy russet-red soup and saffronned potatoes. Although there were only three pieces of fish rather than the cacophony of species and the shellfish found in Marseille, it was enjoyable – but less of a good deal than the well-thought-out €29 *menu*. From this we chose, as a starter, a lightly blanched, round courgette stuffed with a nicely fishy *brandade*, dotted with fresh herbs, then a roast perch just crisp on the outside, flaky in the centre, on a bed of hot aubergine caviar. We finished off with *crème renversée* topped with caramelised egg white, accompanied by apple compote, and a warm *moelleux au chocolat*.

Le Divellec ★

107 rue de l'Universite, 7th (01.45.51.91.96). M° Invalides. **Open** Mon-Fri noon-2pm, 7.30-9.30pm. Closed one month in Jul/Aug. **Average** €107. **Lunch menus** €50, €65. **Credit** AmEx, DC, MC, V.

It may be the preserve of government ministers and high-flying corporate types, who don't bat an eyelid when told that the live lobster they have selected will set them back €150, but this well-mannered dining room is an exceptionally pleasant place for a splurge even if your means limit you to the €50 *menu*. Often in restaurants of this calibre, you get the proverbial fish eye when you opt for the cheapest *menu*, but never once during our superb meal were we made to feel like poor relations. Delicious appetisers of tiny grey North Sea shrimp, a fresh marinated sardine and *accras* (salt cod fritters) arrived immediately, and our very good, €33.54 Muscadet, one of the cheapest options, was expertly served. We were extremely impressed by the fish soup, served tableside and garnished with grated gruyère, garlicky croutons and a first-rate *rouille*, and a plate of Cancale oysters. Sautéed salmon on a bed of spinach in a lemony cream sauce spiked with herring roe was impeccably cooked, as was a thick cod steak in an excellent sauce of meat stock and red wine. Though decidedly traditional, they were very satisfying. Le Divellec offers a superb dessert trolley, brimming with chocolate mousse, fresh raspberries and straw-berries, fruit tarts, *oeufs à la neige*, poached blood oranges and other delicious choices; we chose timidly but, egged on by the waiter, ended up with plates of raspberries in cream, mousse, and fruit tart, a lavish finale to an excellent meal.

Les Glénan

54 rue de Bourgogne, 7th (01.45.51.61.09). M° Varenne. **Open** Mon-Fri 12.30-2.30pm, 7.30-10.30pm. **Average** €55. **Prix fixe** €22-€60. **Credit** AmEx, MC, V.

Chef Emmanuel Jerz doesn't shuck shellfish by the seashore; he does it in the landlocked 7th, steps from the Rodin Museum, where he's been turning out sedately sophisticated seafood dishes since early 2001. A shot glass appetiser of watercress coulis, topped with tomato *fondue*, wisps of deep-fried carrot and Lilliputian shrimp, revealed an attention to produce and presentation finely honed by stints at Lasserre, Guy Savoy and The Ritz. Starters of lentils studded with shrimp on a bed of lamb's lettuce gently drizzled with vinaigrette, and melting tuna carpaccio with squid ink, showed Jerz's grasp of technique and imagination. A main of cockerel on a disc of fluffy couscous was butter-tender, while a crisp, fresh fillet of *daurade* (sea bream) deserved a better prop than the almost-soggy mound of broccoli, beans and spinach. A trio of pan-fried fish with tagliatelle, however, worked a treat. *L'assiette Glénan* – seven sweet treats including a runny chocolate gâteau, coffee crème brûlée and a swirl of rich coffee cream – is 'the' dessert. The service dished up by partner Thierry Blenner was unfailingly polite and professional.

Le Guilvinec
34 Cour St-Emilion, 12th (01.44.68.01.35). Mº Cour St-Emilion. **Open** Mon-Fri noon-2.30pm, 7-10.30pm; Sat 7-10.30pm; Sun noon-2.30pm. **Average** €46. **Prix fixe** €26.68 (Mon-Fri, Sun lunch). **Credit** AmEx, DC, MC, V. **Wheelchair access**.
Located in an old stone warehouse, this very good new fish house offers an opportunity to discover an emerging neighbourhood. Inside, the stone walls remain bare, lighting is subtle, and old apothecary cabinets line one wall. The service is excellent without being stilted. Run by a Breton family – mum in the dining room with one brother, and another brother in the kitchen – this place has a relaxed atmosphere, and an appealing menu. The *menu* is market-driven and might run to pumpkin soup with langoustines, a mixed grill of fish, and crème brûlée, while *à la carte* the young chef shows off his solid training. Among the original dishes are a *roulade de homard*, rolls of country ham filled with shredded lobster and diced vegetables in a shellfish sauce, or the terrine of skate, *andouille* (tripe sausage) and *chèvre*, plus sea bass with delicious potato purée or John Dory with artichokes and horseradish croutons. The *croustillant à l'orange* with chocolate mousse and citrus caramel could well be the best of the desserts.

Le Keryado
32 rue Regnault, 13th (01.45.83.87.58). Mº Porte d'Ivry or RER Boulevard Masséna. **Open** Mon noon-2.30pm; Tue-Sat noon-2.30pm, 7.30-10.30pm. Closed Aug. **Average** €23. **Prix fixe** €17, €23. **Lunch menu** €9 (Mon-Fri). **Credit** MC, V.
Small and unpretentious, this blue-and-white bistro offers a fine daily fish *menu* but it's the *bouillabaisse* that shines. As soon as you walk in, the heady smell of garlic and lobster tempt you. Enjoy your complimentary *kir*, peruse the menu, but order the *bouillabaisse*: a heaped plate of fish, prawns and lobster, with a separate tureen of soup for just €21.50 per person. Take some rounds of toast, dot them with excellent homemade *aïoli*, select your fish, and pour a good ladle-full of soup on top. If you ask, they will bone and shell the fish and seafood before bringing them to your table, but it's more fun to do it yourself. No one stands on ceremony, and if the waiter catches you inelegantly tearing a fabulous fresh lobster limb from limb, he'll merely smile and nod. There are good traditional desserts and the wine list, while small, is well-chosen and well-priced.

Le Bar à Huîtres ★
112 bd du Montparnasse, 14th (01.43.20.71.01/www.lebarahuitres.fr). Mº Vavin. **Open** daily noon-2pm, 7-11pm **Average** €42. **Prix fixe** €18-€34. **Credit** AmEx, DC, MC, V.
Anyone after an oyster feast or the metropolitan bustle once associated with Parisian brasseries would be well-advised to head for a branch of this little chain instead, since both the quality of the seafood and the atmosphere easily better them. All three of these restaurants have been redesigned with a shell-themed scheme by decorator Jacques Garcia, and this stylish Baroque look is attracting bobo locals along with tourists and business travellers, as well as gangs of friends out for a night on the town. During a recent meal in Montparnasse, we were seated next to a pair of young Japanese women who, to our surprise, were given a menu translated into Japanese, and a bunch of junior blowhards from the Quai d'Orsay railing about *les anglo-saxons*; free entertainment as we made our way through a dozen superbly fresh and perfectly opened oysters and continued a first-rate meal with a tender, cooked-exactly-as-ordered tuna steak with *haricots verts* and roasted tomato garnish and a similarly generous sauté of sliced *encornets* (squid) with garlic and olive oil, plus rice. Even dessert – a nicely made fruit crumble and good quality lemon sorbet – proved satisfying.
Branches: 33 bd Beaumarchais, 3rd (01.48.87.98.92); 33 rue St-Jacques, 5th (01.44.07.27.37).

La Cagouille
10-12 pl Constantin-Brancusi, 14th (01.43.22.09.01/www.la-cagouille.fr). Mº Gaîté. **Open** daily 12.30-2.30pm, 7.30-10.30pm. **Average** €50. **Prix fixe** €23, €38. **Credit** AmEx, DC, MC, V.
Marble-topped tables, stubbly walls and a few ropes and pulleys suggest a rather basic seaside café but the cooking here is taken much more seriously than that. Owner-chef Gérard Allemandou believes in quality fish, simply prepared. Fish generally come grilled, fried or steamed with few garnishes except perhaps chopped parsley, sea salt or a drizzle of olive oil. After a delicious appetiser of hot cockles, we started with *fines de claire* oysters and a plate of thinly sliced, sautéed octopus, before half a dozen small whole fried red mullet and a perfect *daurade royale* (sea bream) in a buttery cockle stock, each accompanied by a side plate of new potatoes. Meanwhile, our two-year-old worked her way through a starter of monkfish tails – two, floured and fried on the bone, served with a 'tartare' of capers, salted anchovies and a boat of hollandaise sauce. Add good country bread, a wickedly bitter combination of chocolate fondant, dark chocolate ice cream and chocolate sauce, and a satisfactory white Graves wine of the month, and Montparnasse takes on the allure of the coast.

Le Dôme
108 bd du Montparnasse, 14th (01.43.35.25.81). Mº Vavin. **Open** daily noon-3pm, 7pm-12.30am. Café 8am-1am Closed Mon and Sun in Aug. **Average** €72. **Credit** AmEx, DC, MC, V.
While past orgies have concentrated on oyster platters, our last visit focused on more elaborate offerings. The potato *maxime* with salmon and *boutargue* – two slices of smoked salmon draped over a slim potato pancake plus a dollop of whipped cream vaguely dotted with orange roe – tasted not that different from what one might get at a decent PR banquet. The pillbox of raw salmon fillet filled with sea bream tartare and nicely seasoned with dill and peppercorns was more worthwhile. Fried brill with *girolles*, three sprigs of asparagus and a buttery sauce was delicate but very salty, while the four langoustine tails with fresh tagliatelle were redolent of premium olive oil but all a bit mushy. Our neighbours made out better with their oyster platter, massive hunks of grilled turbot in hollandaise sauce, and decadent follow-up of fried *céteaux* (small sole) with Béarnaise.

Le Duc
243 bd Raspail, 14th (01.43.20.96.30/ 01.43.22.59.59). Mº Raspail. **Open** Tue-Fri noon-2pm, 8-10pm; Sat 8-10pm. Closed Christmas, New Year, one week in Feb, three weeks in Aug. **Average** €83. **Lunch menu** €44. **Credit** AmEx, DC, MC, V.
The 30-year-old Le Duc continues to sail along smoothly, attracting wealthy fish lovers both foreign and French. Service is discreet but also friendly; from a wine list that gives room to reds despite the exclusively fishy menu, the cheerful sommelier navigated us towards a white St-Joseph from the Côtes du Rhône. Brothers Jean and Paul Minchelli, who founded this restaurant (named after the Duke of Buckingham, who once owned land on the Ile de Ré), were among the first in Paris to take a minimalist approach to fish cooking. Paul went on to open his own fish restaurant, Paul Minchelli, but the late Jean's wife Valérie maintains a lofty standard. Fish is often served raw, dressed at the last minute. We loved the salad of fresh crab, dressed at the table with olive oil and lemon, and barely cooked monkfish drizzled with olive oil and lime. More powerfully flavoured were six whole red mullet in a fiery chilli sauce. Portions are generous and the waiters insistent that plates are licked clean.

Maison Prunier
16 av Victor Hugo, 16th (01.44.17.35.85/ www.maisonprunier.com). Mº Charles de Gaulle-Etoile **Open** Mon-Sat 11am-1am. Closed two weeks in Aug. **Average** €69. **Credit** AmEx, DC, MC, V.

Fish for compliments at Le Guilvinec

Created in 1870, Maison Prunier is the Rolls-Royce of fish and seafood restaurants and its recent overhaul reinforces its claim to marine culinary fame. Upstairs is all luminous blonde wood (Scandinavian-style), while downstairs are gleaming black and bronze tiles and thick glass etched with fish and sturgeon motifs. This is the caviar bar and it's so art deco and chi-chi that wall-to-wall fedora and fur wearers would not be out of place. If you can't stretch to Beluga or French caviar at €645 and €300 respectively for three spoonfuls plus French vodka (Prunier's own), there are less pocket-punishing options. Try six briny Breton oysters, and wild Scottish smoked salmon – heaven on a fish fork – crab and crayfish salad, Joe's stone crab claws or the non-fishy Spanish *Bellota-Bellota* ham from acorn-only-eating pigs. Staff are fantastically accommodating and expert. Pierre Bergé – he of the house of Yves Saint Laurent fame – is the new owner so no doubt *la maison* will become a 'now sea this' place for fashion folk.

Vin et Marée
183, bd Murat, 16th (01.46.47.91.39). Mº Porte de Saint-Cloud. **Open** daily noon-2.30pm, 7.30-10.30pm. **Average** €40. **Credit** AmEx, MC, V. **Wheelchair access**.
Fish is their business at this mini-chain,, and they do a good job of it. The decor is insipid, the dishes unexperimental, and the only possible accompanying vegetable – potatoes creamed with olive oil – easy to ignore, leaving the focus strictly on consistently good, fresh seafood, deftly cooked. The purple tentacles twining through the *amuse-bouche* could be unsettling to some diners, but the clams browned in garlic with a chive and parsley sauce melted in the mouth, and the shrimp-stuffed spring rolls were a fun upgrade of the classic *traiteur* food. There were no surprises with either the young and tender pan-fried sole or the sea bream. Diners can also indulge in choices not scrawled on the giant blackboard, but should count on drastically higher prices – a whole lobster was going for €53. For dessert, the dark chocolate *chaud-froid* is a mouth-watering pleasure. As our spoons broke through the crust, the chocolate, rich and not too bitter, melted out over its raspberry sauce. Service was impeccable, super-efficient, friendly and personal. A fish-lover's refuge, with no unpleasant surprises.
Branches: 71 av de Suffren, 7th (01.47.83.27.12); 108 av du Maine, 14th (01.43.20.29.50); 276 bd Voltaire, 11th (01.43.72.31.23).

L'Huîtrier
16 rue Saussier-Leroy, 17th (01.40.54.83.44). Mº Ternes. **Open** Tue-Sun noon-2.30pm, 7-11pm. Closed Aug. **Average** €38.11. **Credit** AmEx, DC, MC, V.
Though the overlit modern decor has all the charm of a car-hire branch, this place serves some of the best oysters in Paris. L'Huîtrier pulls a festive crowd with its permanent 'three dozen for the price of two' bargain offer. The oysters come from Marennes-Oléron and are briny and delicious, as well as generously calibrated: their 'medium-sized' oysters are of a size which passes for large in many brasseries. They also offer a variety of decently priced white wines to accompany the shellfish. Sea snails, crab, pink prawns, clams, mussels and other crustaceans are also available on the festive *plateau de fruits de mer*. A brief selection of fish and other cooked shellfish is on offer, too: the small squid sautéed with garlic and parsley or the similarly prepared scallops are both pleasant. The soothing apple crumble is the dessert highlight.

Budget

Being a pauper in Paris is no problem if you bargain on no-fuss, filling food.

When it comes to eating well, Paris is surprisingly democratic. Yes, you can blow €150 and up on an haute cuisine dinner, but a mere €15 can buy you to a fine three-course meal with wine, especially at lunch.

Restaurants that proudly cater to a budget-conscious crowd most often focus on no-frills traditional fare such as *steak-frites*, *boeuf bourguignon*, *andouillette*, chicken and occasionally fish. Don't expect many vegetarian options, although more places have been making an effort lately, particularly such health-conscious self-serve spots as **Bio.It** and **La Ferme Opéra**.

In this chapter we have concentrated on restaurants where you can have an evening meal for €20 or less, but remember that many pricier bistros become accessible at lunch – when reservations are easier to come by at popular places such as **L'Epi Dupin** and **La Régalade** (*see p13*, **Bistros**). Many cafés also serve decent grub prepared with fresh ingredients (*see p104*, **Cafés**).

Ethnic food can be a bargain alternative. For affordable Chinese, Vietnamese and Thai food, head to Belleville or the 13th *arrondissement* (*see p87*, **Far East**). North African couscous restaurants (*see p99*) are another option, and there is a cluster of cheap Italian pizza and pasta joints around the Marché St-Germain (*see p93*).

1st Arrondissement

La Fresque
100 rue Rambuteau, 1st (01.42.33.17.56). M° Les Halles. **Open** Mon-Sat noon-3pm, 7pm-midnight; Sun 7pm-midnight. Closed ten days in Aug. **Average** €20. **Lunch menu** €11. **Credit** MC, V.
Hidden among Les Halles' collection of trendy and dodgy shops, La Fresque could easily pass unnoticed, but the sight of the lunch crowd as you walk through the door makes you wonder how you ever missed the place. Essentially a collection of corridors, the venue is nondescript apart from the frescoes in the main room (hence the name). Narrow tables are squeezed together and on our latest visit we had to wait a very long time before grabbing the waiter's attention. We opted for *à la carte* rather than the limited *menu*. Our generous starters of *tapenade* and *chèvre chaud sur toast* were as appetising as they were filling. The *tourte aux légumes*, which our waiter warned us was 'very vegetarian', lived up to its reputation: a wholesome mixture of densely packed veg in crisp pastry with a smooth carrot purée on the side. In the wake of the 'mad cow' scare La Fresque was serving ostrich: the red meat was tender and juicily pink, but the two big hunks defeated us. Servings are plentiful but a little more breathing room for everyone might result in more consistent food and service.

Le Petit Flore
6 rue Croix des Petits Champs, 1st (01.42.60.25.53). M° Palais Royal or Musée du Louvre. **Open** Mon-Sat 6am-8pm. Food served Mon-Sat noon-2.30pm. Closed Aug. **Prix fixe** €12. **Credit** DC, MC, V. **Wheelchair access**.
Guy and Annie Dellac, owners of the former L'Oustal Dellac, have moved to a chic location just off rue St-Honoré. Fortunately, the exceptionally warm service and very reasonably priced south-west influenced dishes that their popular bistro was known for have moved with them. The terrace is bordered by a sea of blossoming flowers in hanging baskets. Inside, cosy tables are dressed with smart white tablecloths. It is a charming little restaurant with classy touches not normally associated with a budget menu. The €12 lunch *menu* includes hearty traditional fare such as *magret*, *confit* and *entrecôte*. Our tender *entrecôte* in pepper sauce with steaming *frites* was cooked exactly as we had ordered it, and the berry salad dessert – a mix of cherries, cranberries, and raspberries in a custard cream – was perfect for summer (even if it appeared to have been made with frozen fruit). We made the mistake of ordering a cheap rosé which needed a little extra chilling to take the edge off; a temperature of around absolute zero might have helped.

La Potée des Halles
3 rue Etienne-Marcel, 1st (01.40.41.98.15). M° Etienne-Marcel. **Open** Mon noon-2.30pm; Tue-Fri noon-2.30pm, 7pm-midnight; Sat, Sun 7pm-midnight. **Prix fixe** €22.10 (dinner only). **Lunch menu** €14.30. **Credit** AmEx, MC, V.
The glorious tiled art nouveau decor of this purveyor of traditional fare made the camp atmosphere and soundtrack ('YMCA' and 'It's Raining Men') seem somewhat incongruous. Custard-yellow and leafy-green dominate, punctuated by such details as a painting of the female embodiment of beer. Though lunch is invariably busy, we arrived at 8.30pm on a Friday to find just two other couples. Still, the staff's welcome was friendly – the chef even emerged from the kitchen to greet us and illustrate the menu by pointing out what our neighbours were having. The food was all we'd been hoping for. Light, fresh smoked salmon with blinis and crème fraîche and a smooth avocado gratin with roquefort kicked off our meal pleasantly. *Boeuf bourguignon* came in a cast-iron pot, full of tender meat on the bone plus plenty of veg and broth. A slightly under-cooked chicken sautée was complemented by *sauce normande* (crème fraîche and mushrooms). Completely stuffed, we could only admire classic desserts like crème brûlée and *mousse au chocolat* from afar. The only unpleasant part of our meal was the bill: dinner prices have gone up but lunch remains a bargain.

2nd Arrondissement

Mimosa ★
44 rue d'Argout, 2nd (01.40.28.15.75). M° Sentier. **Open** Mon-Sat noon-3pm (evenings for private parties by arrangement). **Average** €14. **Prix fixe** €10, €12. **Credit** MC, V.
Hats off to Xavier Trauet and Thierry Soulat, the newly installed dynamic duo who have replaced Cedric Eng at this little gem. Xavier runs things out front with unflappable calm, warmly greeting his customers, many of whom are regulars. Thierry shops daily and cooks simple, thoughtful food with a Mediterranean bias. Deciding against *saltimbocca* (veal with prosciutto and wine) with grilled courgettes, we opted for a modestly titled *assiette froide*, which proved a real delight. The cold roast chicken and a blob of olive oil mayo, thinly sliced garlicky loin of pork, herb-strewn *tabouleh*, aubergine caviar, crisp rocket and carrot salad and a ripe tomato stuffed with yoghurty cucumber was heavenly at €10. This we had alongside a great culinary skill barometer – the omelette. Our *paysanne* was a triumph: loaded with potatoes and smoky bacon, sprinkled with chives, beautifully soft and served with green salad. Food to make you swoon and perfect with a quality *pichet* of chilled gamay. The salads are generous and good, too: a plentiful *niçoise* enlivened with oven-dried tomatoes; an *italienne* with farfalle pasta, bruschetta and ham; and a *pêcheur* with herring, smoked salmon, tarama and blinis. All familiar but executed with real flair. The wines are all supplied by nearby merchants Legrand Filles et Fils; the baguette is chewy and fresh and the service attentive.

La Petite France
14 rue de la Banque, 2nd (01.42.96.17.19). M° Bourse. **Open** Mon-Fri 8.30am-6pm; Sun 11am-6pm. **Average** €15. **Credit** AmEx, MC, V. **Wheelchair access**.
This airy and spacious place with sunflower-yellow walls, pale wooden tables and shelves stacked with Provençal produce is somewhat at odds with the lunchtime crowd of smartly besuited financiers from the nearby banks and Bourse talking gravely about the vertiginous drop in the markets. At lunch, choose from the blackboard *plats du jour* featuring dishes such as tuna steak in herb sauce served with a rice pilaf, and an interesting sounding *brandade* of smoked mackerel, or alternatively go for one of the many salads on the standard menu. You'll have no choice but the latter if, like us, you arrive late. The salads, nonetheless, were very enjoyable, if a little pricey at €10-€11. The *landaise* consisted of an intriguing mixture of duck breast, poultry gizzards and stewed pears on a crisp bed of green salad, including rocket, scattered with thin sticks of sweet gingerbread. The *antiboise* was more orthodox, with *tapenade* and mozzarella on organic bread served along with the salad; the accompanying sliced smoked chicken was disappointingly re-constituted. Also on offer, seafood salads and *salade minceur*. There were few desserts left by the time we reached that stage but bite-sized *cannellé bordelais* provided a decent finish.

3rd Arrondissement

Fontaines d'Elysabeth
1 rue Ste-Elysabeth, 3rd (01.42.74.36.41). M° Arts et Métiers. **Open** Mon-Fri noon-2.30pm, 8pm-midnight; Sat 8pm-midnight. Closed Aug. **Average** €15. **Prix fixe** €12. **No credit cards**.
It may be on a dusty side street sandwiched between the busy rue de Turbigo and rue du Temple, but this bistro, with its floral curtains and dark wood furniture, feels like the heart of the countryside – with cuisine to match. It also appears a very well kept secret among canny locals. The short menu, jotted down in blue felt-tip pen, tells of homespun cooking: no pretensions, no let-downs. From a range of mainly *charcuterie*-based starters, the potato mayonnaise salad with tomatoes and gherkins could not have tasted fresher – or more homemade. The *cassoulet* was marvellously succulent, with pieces of lamb simply melting off the bone. The avuncular chef, Jean Durand, popped out shortly before it was served to ask 'garlic?' and took the request seriously. The only dessert was *tarte aux pommes* but who's complaining when it's as crisp as this? A good bottle of Côtes du Rhône for €10 underlined the unbeatable value of this establishment.

4th Arrondissement

Bistro Beaubourg
25 rue Quincampoix, 4th (01.42.77.48.02). M° Châtelet. **Open** daily noon-2am. **Average** €10. **Credit** MC, V.
Don't go out of your way to come here, but if you happen to be at this end of the Marais and fancy getting away from the crowds, it's a safe

Right neighbourly Café de la Poste

bet. At night the place is bustling with 20-somethings, elbow-to-elbow at wooden tables, and you may have to wait a few minutes to be seated. Decor is fairly basic – hankies thrown over lightbulbs and a random collage of posters crowding the walls – but service is brisk and efficient and diners seem happy to be here. Go for the straight-up, no-frills dishes – it's not the place to be adventurous. We started with rather stringy leeks and wished we had ordered the rollmops, but a decent carafe of sauvignon washed them down well, and there was plenty of room left for a surprisingly good steak and chips. The *plat du jour* was disappointing – undercooked chicken legs, drowned in mushroom sauce, served on a stodgy bed of rice. Looking around it appeared most people knew the rules and had opted for fish or meat – if you do this, you won't begrudge spending around €15.

Café de la Poste
13 rue Castex, 4th (01.42.72.95.35).
M° Bastille. **Open** Mon-Fri noon-3pm, 7-11pm. Tea 3-6pm. Closed two weeks in Aug. **Average** €18. **Credit** MC, V.
The Café de la Poste is the kind of neighbourhood place everyone should be lucky enough to have around the corner. While the owner has changed since our last review, the cook has stayed on, and the new team seems a good match. The food is standard café fare with changing daily specials. At lunch a crowd of regulars takes over the small but airy dining room, decorated with paintings that change every three months. We kicked off with 'Oriental-style' anchovies, a pile of tangy marinated fish bathed in a creamy, spicy sauce, and three hefty chunks of the house terrine, served with *cornichons*. *Foie gras de canard maison* is also available for a very reasonable €6.90. A perfectly grilled steak with golden, puffy, round chips followed. We'll go back just for the chips; they're addictive. So many different bits of the duck (*confit*, smoked breast, and foie gras) littered the *landaise* salad that the greens and tomatoes seemed almost an afterthought. Everyone does a melting chocolate cake at the moment, and we have had our fair share of them, but this one didn't disappoint. It's worth straying off the main drag for a quick, good-value bite here.

La Canaille
4 rue Crillon, 4th (01.42.78.09.71).
M° Bastille or Sully-Morland. **Open** Mon-Fri 11.45am-2.15pm, 7.30-11.30pm; Sat 7.30-11.30pm. Closed one week in Aug.
Prix fixe €18.20, €23. **Lunch menu** €11-€13.50. **Credit** MC, V.
This bistro is a stalwart of the Parisian budget scene with its relaxed atmosphere, vast selection of wines and cooking that's more inventive than standard budget fare. Asian-inspired dishes (such as curried vegetables in coconut sauce) jostle alongside the more traditional options such as *entrecôte*, *magret de canard* and frog's legs. The chef's culinary flights of fancy, however, proved to be a little hit or miss. We generally had better luck with the less fancy dishes, although even simple dishes were sometimes executed with an odd twist. The *tournedos de cabillaud* consisted of small morsels of cod which were bizarrely baked in thick sheets of pork fat – which lent the fish an unattractive sheen and fatty taste. The glazed chicken thighs in a sweet ginger sauce were tastier, and served with good, fluffy basmati rice. Desserts were generally passable, such as an anodyne rhubarb tart served with a generous helping of thick crème fraîche, though the *aumônière* – orange-stuffed pancakes – was marred by a spectacularly bad caramel sauce of lumpy undissolved sugar doused with Grand Marnier.

Le Coupe Gorge
2 rue de la Coutellerie, 4th (01.48.04.79.24).
M° Hôtel-de-Ville or Châtelet. **Open** Tue-Thur noon-2pm, 7.30-11.30pm; Fri, Sat 7.30-midnight. Closed Aug. **Average** €15.
Lunch menu €11, €13. **Credit** MC, V.
This restaurant is reached through a little bar where a black enamel counter, bottles of liqueur and two barmen drying glasses set the classic scene. What differentiates it from your standard Parisian bar are the bundles of bottles curiously hung as lampshades and the hosts' jovial greetings as they lead you upstairs. Old kitchenware clutters shelves, 1930s radios rest on side cupboards and Martini posters adorn the walls here. It is simple bistro-style cooking but of an exceptional standard. We started with a deliciously moist and fragrant chicken terrine which arrived in an earthenware pot from which we helped ourselves. We followed it with duck *confit* with Port and *pommes dauphinoises*, and salmon trout with tarragon and saffron-scented rice. The duck was exceptionally tender, the potatoes wonderfully creamy and the salmon trout equally good. Generous portions of *île flottante* and tiramisu posed no problems as both were deliciously light. The wine list was as pleasant as the meal, ranging from €10 to €28 and straight-from-the-barrel *pichets* a bargain at €7.

Le Pavé
7 rue des Lombards, 4th (01.44.54.07.20).
M° Châtelet or Hôtel-de-Ville. **Open** Mon-Thur, Sun noon-2.30pm, 7.30-11pm; Fri, Sat noon-2.30pm, 7.30-midnight. Closed Christmas. **Average** €15. **Prix fixe** €10.52-€18.14. **Credit** MC, V.
Wheelchair access.
The kitsch decor of this little bistro once disguised an unexpected delight, but unfortunately the quality of the food has deteriorated so that the dining room is now one of the major attractions. Lots of red leather banquettes, wine bottles and brass set the conventional scene, hilariously offset by the mirrored ceiling (and, when we were there, fibre optic Christmas tree). The clientele was similarly mixed – gay and straight, locals and tourists. Staff were exceptionally friendly and the prices reasonable (we had the €18.14 set *menu*) so we were reluctant to admit that the food was only OK. Classic onion soup was edible, if a little tepid and drowned in cheese, while goat's cheese served with salad was stone-cold and wrapped in undercooked pastry. Mains of *ragout d'aiguillettes de canard aux légumes de saison*, and *pavé de cabillaud au pistou et pâtes fraîches* translated as 'overcooked duck in gravy dumped on boiled vegetables', and 'tasteless fish plopped onto overcooked pasta with a spattering of pesto'. Desserts – *tarte Tatin* and poached fruit tart– were better. Aside from the ceiling, the wine – a 1997 Château de Barbe – was the best thing about the meal.

Le P'tit Gavroche
15 rue Ste-Croix de la Bretonnerie, 4th (01.48.87.74.26). *M° Hôtel-de-Ville or Rambuteau.* **Open** Mon-Fri noon-3pm, 7-11.30pm; Sat 7-11.30pm; Closed at lunch in Aug. **Average** €15. **Prix fixe** €9.
Lunch menu €8. **Credit** MC, V
Named after a Victor Hugo character, Le P'tit Gavroche is the poster child for what we all suppose is the authentic French experience. It's like films of old-time Paris, of an era when the local bistro was an extension of the apartment. The atmosphere is a no-nonsense blend of vintage and tacky, with blaring '70s pop music ('Killing Me Softly With His Song') complementing a zinc bar and old posters depicting the ill-effects of alcoholism, an ironic comment given the freely flowing plonk (no bottle over €12.50). Where else in Paris can you get a three-course meal for €9? Sadly, there's a reason for this bargain: the food is dreadful. A mountain of blue cheese-walnut salad was more about quantity than quality, while the asparagus vinaigrette rated as merely passable. We thought we had ordered duck *au poivre* but the texture suggested it was beef. The salmon tasted off, and both plates were heaped with peas and beans which appeared to have come straight out of a tin. The middle-aged couple at the adjacent table seemed to have the right idea, moving from a bottle of red to two rounds of whiskey coffee. Le P'tit Gavroche is a heartbreaker: you want to love it, but the food doesn't love you back.

Le Temps des Cerises
31 rue de la Cerisaie, 4th (01.42.72.08.63).
M° Sully-Morland or Bastille. **Open** Mon-Fri 7.45am-8pm. Food served noon-2pm. Closed Aug. **Average** €12. **Prix fixe** €12.
Credit MC, V.
If we were Bastille locals, this would be a favourite. Not for the good-value three-course *menu* at €12 (consisting of salads, egg with mayonnaise, *saucisson*, chicken and chips, marinated fish, roasts, crème caramel and fruit tarts, of which nothing is spectacular), but rather for the cosy pleasure of a dining-out experience on a human scale. A warm greeting is dispatched by the flamboyantly moustached M. Vimad who is at the bar serving up Stella Artois beer on tap or loading cups in the dishwasher while Madame might be chatting with the regulars or helping the waitress clear off the tables. At the peak of the lunch hour, service reaches Olympic speeds. Neighbourhood regulars, old and young, complete the well-worn flea market ambience along with motley posters, browning photographs and original paintings and cartoons. Seating is tight; we were in a booth sharing a common breadbasket and water carafe with two fellow diners. The bar, open until 8pm, is ideal for a convivial pre-dinner beer and plate of cheese or *charcuterie*.

Le Trumilou
84 quai de l'Hôtel-de-Ville, 4th (01.42.77.63.98). *M° Hôtel-de-Ville.*
Open daily noon-3pm, 7-10.30 pm. Closed two weeks in Aug. **Average** €18.
Prix fixe €13.50, €16.50. **Credit** MC, V.
Wheelchair access.
Pale cream-coloured walls festooned with country crockery, copper pots and *sabots* (wooden clogs) lend a semi-rustic look to Le Trumilou, despite its location steps from city hall and a traffic-heavy *quai*. Part bar, mostly restaurant, with an ample terrace, Le Trumilou offers weighty dishes such as head-cheese pâté, country omelettes, rib steak, 'grandmother's chicken' and sausage tart. Lighter fare includes a chicory and blue cheese salad, and a delicate fricassée of *mousserons*, tiny and tender wild mushrooms sautéed in oil and herbs (the gritty bits reminding you of their earthy origins). We skipped the sea bass with fennel seed (a bit pricey) for the quail with raisins, slightly sweet and forming a dark sauce for a bowl of plain noodles. For dessert, try a classic *oeuf à la neige*, frothy egg whites in a pool of custard, or *pavé du Marais*: a crunchy biscuit sundae with coffee ice cream, hot fudge and whipped cream. Everything arrives on a separate platter or in a bowl, and the giant portions made us wonder if the dishes were meant to be devoured by two diners, not one.

5th Arrondissement

L'Ecurie ★
2 rue Laplace, 5th (01.46.33.68.49).
M° Maubert-Mutualité. **Open** Mon, Wed-Sat noon-3pm, 7pm-midnight; Tue, Sun 7pm-midnight. **Average** €20. **Lunch menu** €11.50. **No credit cards.**
Humble L'Ecurie is hidden on a village-like, tranquil square between rue des Ecoles and the magnificent St-Etienne-du-Mont church in the shadow of the Panthéon. In 1692 it was a stable but on a cloudless summer day its narrow pavement terrace became a superb location to sip the complimentary sangria and Calvados that began and ended a fine meal of grilled meat and country specialities. The Chenas Beaujolais arrived along with a parasol for our table, and we wondered if the cheery waiter had brought it to protect our heads or the wine from the sweltering sun. To start, a salad of walnuts and crumbled blue cheese, and tomato and red peppers *à la provençale* which reminded us why simple, fresh-off-the-grill food makes us so happy. A puny slice of saddle of lamb was nonetheless expertly cooked with rosemary and other herbs. Rump-steak with pepper sauce was more generous, and prepared as ordered, although both mains could have benefited from a more thoughtful dressing up than

Motherly fare at Chez Germaine

frites and a lettuce leaf. The chunky apple tart was moist and crisp while the banana *à la cendre*, topped with a pot of flaming rum, echoed the charcoal theme. Well-fed and warmed, we were ready to shoe a horse, and vowed to try the dungeon dining suite some grim winter's night.

L'Escapade

10 rue de la Montagne-Ste-Geneviève, 5th (01.46.33.23.85). M° Maubert-Mutualité. **Open** daily 11am-4pm, 7pm-midnight. **Average** €17. **Prix fixe** €17. **Credit** MC, V.

A sober night in L'Escapade must be hell, but then again we don't know anyone who has ever experienced one. The place in Paris most likely to remind you of drunken teenage mishaps, it's marvellous fun if you can suspend disbelief and taste for the length of a meal. A few cheap-skates attracted by the all-you-can-eat-for-€17 *menu* indulge in third helpings of beetroot cubes at the buffet upstairs, but downstairs is where it's at. In choking fog, gangs of boys and girls pissed up on the unlimited (and, predictably, pretty foul) wine flirt with each other over smelly cauliflower cheese and boiled eggs. The food really isn't the point, but it's really not that bad either. The *faux-filet* and the chocolate mousse are generally safe bets.

Le Jardin des Pâtes

4 rue Lacépède, 5th (01.43.31.50.71). M° Jussieu. **Open** daily noon-2.30pm, 7-11pm. **Average** €18. **Credit** MC, V.

If pasta conjures up images of Italy and tomatoes, think again. At the tiny 'pasta garden' just up the street from Jussieu, locals crowd around the wooden tables for unequivocally Parisian concoctions. The fresh pasta (€6.40-€12.05) is made, on the premises, from five different organic flours. We tried grainy chestnut noodles with strips of grilled duck, mushrooms and crème fraîche, and a rye pasta with ham, courgettes and onions in a white wine, comté and cream sauce. Next time we'll have buckwheat with chicken livers and prunes or the marine-themed barley with salmon and seaweed; there are also three vegetarian options. Plates are steaming and portions are mammoth; it's the perfect spot for some starchy winter warmth. We shared a plate of *crudités du jardin* (an exquisitely prepared salad of fine vegetable strips in a light lemon-mustard dressing) and a *tarte au chocolat*; if only we'd had room for the mouth-watering *clafoutis* as well. Wine is sold by the glass (€2.59) and there are some great organic juices (€2.13), coffee or a nerve-friendly, organic grain substitute. The dining room has an actual non-smoking section and the terrace was recently expanded.

Branch: 33 bd Arago, 13th (01.45.35.93.67).

Perraudin

157 rue St-Jacques, 5th (01.46.33.15.75). RER Luxembourg. **Open** Mon-Fri noon-2.30pm, 7.30-10pm. Closed two weeks in Aug. **Average** €24. **Lunch menu** €11.50. **No credit cards.**

Negative responses to the questions 'Do you serve on weekends?' and 'Do you take credit cards?' is often a decent measure of a bistro's *vieille France* authenticity (if such a thing can be quantified). At Perraudin, a slightly shabby, deep-red interior and mostly original fixtures transport you to the early 20th century, when the great-grandfather of the current owners began to sell food instead of coal. Despite being steps from the Panthéon in the heart of the studenty Latin Quarter, here the lunchtime scene caters mostly to old-timers who have found an adequate roost for unpretentious, standard fare with few flourishes. Stuffed scallops served on the half-shell, grilled steak and lamb get plopped on the checked tablecloths fairly soon after they've been ordered. An artichoke heart salad seemed assembled from tinned ingredients while the seafood terrine was a welcome change from heavier traditional starters. Without expecting a *tour de force*, you can't go wrong with the crispy, roast duck with green beans, or the cod fillet in a tangy sorrel sauce. The chocolate mousse, dense and almost chewy, takes no prisoners. In its attempt to capture the tastes and smells of French cuisine before it got all new-fangled, Perraudin might win you over. Or it might not.

6th Arrondissement

Marmite et Cassolette

157 bd du Montparnasse, 6th (01.43.26.26.53). M° Vavin or Raspail. **Open** Mon-Fri noon-2.30pm, 7-11pm. Closed Aug. **Average** €19. **Prix fixe** €14.50, €18.50. **Credit** MC, V. **Wheelchair access.**

About midway between Le Dôme and La Closerie des Lilas, Marmite et Cassolette holds its own in a humble, casual setting that's crying out for a makeover. A mirrored ceiling and the unfortunate bright green and yellow colour scheme lends the dining room a '70s lounge look, so it was a surprise to find such interesting and thoughtfully prepared dishes. Start with the cold vegetable salad, featuring carrots, aubergine and an intriguing celery seed flavour, or the wonderful custardy mussel and saffron gâteau. Barbecued pork with a sweet tomato sauce and noodles arrived in an iron pot (*marmite*), more a decorative flourish than utilitarian tool – the tender meat could not possibly have been cooked in the immaculate vessel. The standout was the *brandade de morue*. Often ordinary, here the cod-potato purée had been improved by topping it with juicy capers and not whipping it to textureless death. Profiteroles and a pool of raspberry sorbet and fruit made a happy ending to our meal. This fine-quality food deserved a much better setting.

Le Petit Saint-Benoît

4 rue St-Benoît, 6th (01.42.60.27.92). M° St-Germain-des-Prés. **Open** Mon-Sat noon-2.30pm, 7-10.30pm. **Closed** Aug. **Average** €16. **No credit cards.**

Like archaeologists, we examined the trim boards and wainscoting, whose layers of paint applied over the ages have obscured the original detail work. Other evidence, like the tiny tiled sink in the loo, a brazen refusal to take credit cards or reservations, and a bent coat hanger holding open the door on a balmy night, proves Le Petit Saint-Benoît's venerable presence in this otherwise moneyed quartier that has given in to fashion. Tables share baskets of bread; a handbell rings when the unadorned food is ready to be unceremonously plopped before you. You'll find all the old-school French favourites – hard-boiled egg and mayonnaise, rabbit terrine and plain vegetable soup for starters. A cod, onion and potato casserole was surprisingly moist, as was the roast chicken, which came with mashed potatoes and a fine gravy. Crème brûlée, fruit *clafoutis*, crumble and compote are among the classic desserts. If this bistro keeps serving its no-fuss, 'what do you expect?' budget fare in St-Germain, there is hope for civilisation.

Le Polidor

41 rue Monsieur-le-Prince, 6th (01.43.26.95.34). M° Odéon. **Open** Mon-Sat noon-2.30pm, 7pm-12.30am; Sun noon-2.30pm, 7-11.30pm. **Prix fixe** €18. **Lunch menu** €9. **No credit cards.**

If you think that a restaurant favoured by just about every guide book and cited as an exemplary model of traditional French cooking despite its near rock-bottom prices must be too good to be true, you're right. Polidor may indeed have become a Left Bank institution, and its prices may indeed be pretty reasonable (especially given the *quartier*), but it's hardly the pinnacle of excellent bistro cooking that it may once have been. Blame the guide books if you want, or the very uneven kitchen that has little to strive for since, regardless of product, lines of tourists and, yes, some loyal locals, stream through the door each night. Since we'd chilled considerably standing outside the door waiting for a table (don't even bother reserving, it's useless), we stuck with warming soups for starters. The *crème de lentilles* with a touch of foie gras was satisfying. Rich and potent, it put the humble little lentil in a whole new culinary category. A big bowl of orange-hued pumpkin soup was far less remarkable; chunks of the too-stringy squash almost ruined it. Mains were equally mixed. The guinea fowl with bacon and cabbage was prepared exactly as it should be; no culinary somersaults here, just chunks of meat falling off the bone to the warm embrace of a rich broth. A simple steak with shallot sauce was, on the contrary, swimming

Hip & Healthy

Crunch your way through a quick lunch

Health-conscious spots are offering speedy alternatives to the leisurely French lunch.

Bio.It

15 rue des Halles, 1st (01.42.21.10.21) Mº Châtelet or Les Halles. **Open** Mon-Sat 10am-10.30pm. **Average** €19. **Credit** DC, MC, V.

A combination lunch bar/delicatessen, Bio.It was recently set up by an association of Italian producers to showcase their quality, usually organic, produce. Intended to be the first of an international franchise, it has a smartly designed brochure which talks about 'the concept' and 'the dream', all of which seems a little out of place around Les Halles, where the typical choices are greasy kebab, or greasy kebab-*frites*. Here, fresh buffalo mozzarella and ricotta are flown in from Italy every fortnight. The restaurant works like a canteen: you take a tray and choose from a buffet in front of an open kitchen. Everything is homemade using quality seasonal produce, and is predominantly vegetarian. It's quite confusing for the first-timer – we didn't realise you could also have dishes made to order – but we were nonetheless happy with our choice of *antipasti* (the tuna was excellent), and plate of assorted hot dishes, including a fine mushroom risotto, penne with artichokes, and stuffed tomato and aubergine. The desserts, such as strawberry and custard tart, are fresh and delicious. Organic Italian wine is sold by the glass or bottle.

La Ferme Opéra

55-57 rue St-Roch, 1st (01.40.20.12.12). M° Opéra or Pyramides. **Open** Mon-Sat 8am-8pm. **Average** €11. **Credit** DC, MC, V. **Wheelchair access.**

La Ferme looks like an Ikea show barn, with empty milk jugs, cartoony cow posters, and wall-to-wall, floor-to-ceiling lightly stained wood. The hyper-clean self-serve section offers around 15 freshly made sandwiches, fresh fruit and vegetable drinks, mixed salads, refrigerated desserts such as fruit salads and chocolate mousse and hot lunch specials. There's also a small range of produce – milk, eggs, etc. – all from Ile-de-France. The comfortable dining area is filled with more wood and comfy wicker chairs. On our first visit, we realised as we were about to pay for our ridiculously loaded tray that we'd forgotten our money. We were bowled over when the serious young man suggested that we simply pay off our debt next time we came. A small miracle in Paris.

Nils

36 rue Montorgueil, 1st (01.55.34.39.49). M° Les Halles. **Open** daily 10.30am-10pm. Closed 25 Dec-2 Jan. **Average** €9. **Prix fixe** €6.50, €8.50. **Credit** MC, V.

Nils serves no-frills Danish fast-food in the most ordinary of atmospheres. Bottles of *glögg*, Scandinavian mulled wine, lingonberry jam and other Danish products fill the shelves, while an ample deli case faces customers, letting them point and pick from pre-assembled sandwiches and smoked fish plates. We tried the €3.80 *menu*'s bland *smygehuk* tomato-cheese sandwich and a Swedish curried chicken sandwich; the fish options may have been more flavourful. The *upptäck*, a generous cold plate of salmon, prawns, pickled herring, egg and sauces pleasantly surprised us with its flavour. Hit Nils during the busy lunchtime when turnover might be faster and the food perkier. A new branch is planned for May 2002 at 10 rue de Buci, 6th.

Cosi

54 rue de Seine, 6th (01.46.33.35.36). M° Odéon. **Open** daily noon-11pm. **Average** €10. **No credit cards.**

Oven-fresh flatbread is the speciality at Cosi, whose casual counter serves up far above-average paninis, plus soups, salads and desserts. Order downstairs, building your sandwich from ingredients such as tandoori chicken, grilled aubergine and mozzarella, or selecting from their opera-themed favourites (the *salmo* has salmon, ricotta and chives; the *perfide albion* stars roast beef, tomato, coriander and onion). Carry your tray to the two upstairs dining rooms, one happily smoke-free. The bread is crispy and chewy, not always the case with Paris paninis. Cosi has fast food far superior to that of most crêpe or pizza joints.

Bar à Soupes

33 rue de Charonne, 11th (01.43.57.53.79). Mº Bastille or Ledru-Rollin. **Open** Mon-Sat noon-3pm, 6.30-11pm. Closed Aug. **Average** €10 **Lunch menu** €8.40. **No credit cards.**

Once a prelude to a meaty main, soup has struck out on its own. Lighter eating habits mean that this bright, simply decorated soup bar has won a following among a *branché* Bastille set. The constantly changing selection includes such inventive soups as curried cream of courgette, carrot with coconut, and pumpkin *velouté* with bacon. Organic bread comes from Michel Moisan. There are also cheese and *charcuterie* plates to sate heartier appetites.

in grease and full of gristle. Order wisely and don't expect too much. The jovial and relaxed ambiance is still hard to beat.

7th Arrondissement

L'Auberge du Champ de Mars
18 rue de l'Exposition, 7th (01.45.51.78.08). M° *Ecole-Militaire.* **Open** Mon, Sat 7-10pm; Tue-Fri noon-2pm, 7-10pm. Closed Aug. **Prix fixe** €17. **Credit** MC, V.
Bilingual poster-sized menus listing the day's specials make it hard to miss this restaurant. Adjusting to its dim lighting, we spied two other customers having lunch in one of the corners. It was a bit lonely amongst the large plush sofas, plastic plants and brown walls, after they left and the Muzak grew annoying. We started with a thick helping of delicately flavoured scallop terrine, served with a light lobster sauce and garnished with red pepper. The same garnish showed up on another starter, the *salade de pignons*. Lettuce was doused with a tangy vinaigrette, the pine nuts a nice touch. Of the dozen main courses, we opted for the *blanquette de sole au Champagne*, a new take on a classic dish. The cream sauce was on the thin side, the rice was overcooked, and the by-now-inevitable red pepper garnish reappeared. From a dessert list that included crème brûlée and prunes with Armagnac, we opted for profiteroles, which didn't taste fresh and were drowned in too much chocolate sauce.

Au Babylone
13 rue de Babylone, 7th (01.45.48.72.13). M° *Sèvres-Babylone.* **Open** Mon-Sat 11.30am-2.30pm. Closed Aug. **Average** €18. **Lunch menu** €17.50. **No credit cards**.
What Au Babylone lacks in sophistication it almost makes up for with genuinely friendly staff and atmosphere. A lunchtime-only affair, the €17.50 *menu*, which includes a glass of wine or a bottle of beer, begins with a selection of cold starters: crudités swimming in dressing, rillettes, and egg-mayonnaise. *Plats du jour* included such rib-sticking favourites as roast chicken with stodgy purée, veal with cauliflower, and roast beef studded with whole cloves of garlic. The disappointing purée was the first sour note and there followed a few more: the Spartan loo (sink plus hole) without soap or hand-drying equipment; water with a bleach aftertaste; and bread that was rationed out four little bits at a time. But you're guaranteed to have a pleasant lunch if you concentrate on the good points (local banter, tradition, good value) and go to the loo before you come.

Chez Germaine
30 rue Pierre-Leroux, 7th (01.42.73.28.34). M° *Duroc.* **Open** Mon-Fri noon-2.30pm, 7-9.30pm; Sat noon-2.30pm. Closed Aug. **Average** €15. **Prix fixe** €12. **Lunch menu** €9. **No credit cards**.
There are discounts for pensioners and it got a rave review in a Japanese guidebook. These are two assumptions you could make after a glance into this modest dining room which seats about 30. Germaine herself was 'in the mountains' on our last visit but the budget dishes continued to steam out of the kitchen. Our starter of salad – a few giant leaves straight from the spinner with a measly splash of dressing – and hot *chèvre* on toast (has this ever disappointed?) were quickly followed by the mains: an *entrecôte de veau* with a creamed spinach sauce and liver with raspberry vinegar, served with steamed potatoes dressed in parsley. The ingredients were not as fresh as they could have been, but both pieces of meat were well tender and tasty. The desserts, chocolate cake and mousse, direct from the fridge, were an enjoyable, if rushed, end to the *menu* – the time between order and arrival was about five seconds. During peak hours, customers wait in the street while others, ushered in by well-meaning staff, colonise the tables of slow chewers. Charming and good value.

8th Arrondissement

Le Bistroquet
52 rue du Colisée, 8th (01.45.61.01.82). M° *Franklin D. Roosevelt or St-Philippe du Roule.* **Open** Mon-Fri 7am-10pm. Food served noon-2.30pm. **Average** €17. **Prix fixe** €11. **Credit** MC, V.
With tacky neon lighting, frayed Gainsbourg posters, ubiquitous photos of drunken escapades, and a throng of regulars crowding around the bar for a lunchtime glass of *rouge*, this place is rather out of keeping with the chic surroundings – only a stone's throw from the tourist-packed Champs-Elysées. Despite the decor, however, Le Bistroquet draws a crowd of suits for low-priced lunches. We skipped the starter (as instructed by the alarmingly frank waiter) and went straight to the main courses which ranged from staples such as rump-steak, to hamburger *à cheval* (topped with a fried egg) and *andouille* (tripe sausage). We opted for the *plat du jour*, which consisted of succulent morsels of pork in a dark gravy flavoured with fresh rosemary, and a *nordique*, one of the many salads on the menu, which was passable if a little plain and accompanied by suspiciously shredded smoked salmon. The amiable and rotund barmaid spoke in hushed tones about her favourite desserts and indeed the homemade *tarte Tatin* was rather good with oodles of accompanying cream, polished off with a couple of strong black coffees.

9th Arrondissement

Chartier
7 rue du Fbg-Montmartre, 9th. (01.47.70.86.29). M° *Grands Boulevards.* **Open** daily 11.30am-3pm, 6pm-10pm. **Average** €15. **Prix fixe** €12.20. **Credit** MC, V.
Chartier is the one remaining 19th-century workers' canteen in Paris that has kept not only its gorgeous mirrored interior but also its unfussy menu. 'Bouillons' like this used to feed workers all over Paris with restorative soup. But soup is no longer the main feature here. For €12.20, you get three courses (avoid the sausage, which matches the pink tablecloth), accompanied by a perfectly serviceable half-bottle of wine. Businessmen chomping their way through lamb chops and *frites*, teenagers ordering one starter each and tourists looking stunned by the noise – there's a seat for everyone at Chartier, and the waiters are miraculously unbothered by the glittering pandemonium around them. Cross the room to admire the decor, which still has the old napkin drawers for regular customers (today used for storing extra menus). The entire menu is reassuringly inexpensive, and our €12.50 bottle of Cahors was perfect to accompany the hearty meat and potato dishes on offer. Highlights included rollmops (pickled herring), generous green salads and the whole roasted fennel which accompanied a good pork plate. At only €1.80 for side dishes, you should spring for an order of *choucroute alsacienne*, and save room for that most traditional and bizarre of French desserts: puréed chestnuts with cream.

10th Arrondissement

Chez Papa
206 rue Lafayette, 10th (01.42.09.53.87). M° *Louis-Blanc.* **Open** daily 8am-1am. **Average** €15. **Prix fixe** €8.38. **Credit** AmEx, DC, MC, V.
There is one good reason to come to Chez Papa and its name is *boyarde complète*: a 'salad' (lettuce leaves numbering in the single digits) of potatoes, cantal, roquefort and cured ham served in an earthenware bowl/swimming-tub and crowned with two fried eggs. Sure, the potatoes seem reheated, the bread is often stale and the house wines smack of Tetra-pak, but who cares? The portion is comically big and costs €7.10. (Only one person in our midst, may he rest in peace, has been able to complete our Boyarde Complète Challenge: two in a one-hour sitting). Big bearded 'Papa' has never been spotted; his face adorns the menus and walls of all the branches of this south-west restaurant: simple open spaces (with lots of brown, wood, and cinema posters) that fill up quickly. A €8.38 *menu* is available until 9pm except on Saturdays (other branches have different *formules*), and there is a selection of pricier *à la carte* dishes (€10.67-€11.43), but that's beside the point. The Louis Blanc branch seems to serve up the most consistent *boyarde*: hangover cure or nightmare.
Branches: 29 rue de l'Arcade, 8th (01.42.65.43.68); 6 rue Gassendi, 14th (01.43.22.41.19); 101 rue de la Croix-Nivert, 15th (01.48.28.31.88).

Rôtisserie Ste-Marthe
4 rue Ste-Marthe, 10th (01.40.03.08.30). M° *Belleville or Goncourt.* **Open** Mon-Fri 12.30-2pm, 7.30-midnight. **Average** €10. Closed lunch mid July to end Aug. **No credit cards**.
In a neighbourhood full of dingy shops, funky bars and artists, this ragged-around-the-edges joint nevertheless packs them in, serving filling grub while filling the coffers for a good cause. Run by the Association Rôtisserie Ste-Marthe as a community restaurant at lunch, the kitchen is available in the evenings to groups raising funds for community, cultural and humanitarian projects. The house rules limit the price of starters to €3.05, main courses to €5.34 and desserts to €2.29. On a recent visit to the tightly-seated dining room, microscopic kitchen in full view, three women working for a children's educational charity in Morocco were hoping a full house would sample their Moroccan salad, chicken and olive *tagine*, and *délice au chocolat*. With priced-to-match house wines at around €4 for a half-litre, the food is entirely unpredictable – merely passable or happily satisfying – because the chefs change daily. But you can be assured of ample portions, and that your appetite will serve a higher purpose.

11th Arrondissement

Les 100 Kilos
2 rue de la Folie Méricourt, 11th (01.43.55.12.74). M° *St Ambroise.* **Open** Mon-Sat, noon-10pm. **Average** €17. **Lunch menu** €10.60. **No credit cards**.
With its shiny brass bar and handful of tables, this down-to-earth neighbourhood joint resembles dozens of others of its kind, except that here they serve dinner too. Ring ahead as they close if it's quiet: we arrived mid-week in July at 9.15 pm to find the chairs up and the shutters down but, unperturbed, we headed back the following night. Blackboards list specialities from the south-west and a limited selection of dishes are available from the exhaustive daytime menu. Single ingredient starters – carrot salad, hard-boiled eggs, *charcuterie* – were generous and really cheap at €3.10-€6.10. Our shared *petite assiette de saucisse sèche* was a flavourful pile, served with butter and baby gherkins, that we had trouble finishing on a sultry summer evening. We did well to save room. The *auvergnate* salad was a big bowlful with all the usual goodies: *jambon de pays*, cantal and potatoes (they were out of walnuts, but at €7.20 who's complaining?). The *aiguillette de canard, sauce vin de Cahors* was rather uninteresting – dry duck meat in a thick sauce, a misguided choice on a hot night. We drank the *vin du mois* – a light red Buzet 2000 from Comte de Belot – perfectly acceptable at €13. The only other customers were heavyweight locals who seemed to be doing more justice to the hearty regional dishes: *cassoulet* and *magret du sud-ouest*. Nobody lingered for long.

La Cheminée
7 rue Jean-Pierre Timbaud, 11th (01.49.23.06.76). M° *Oberkampf.* **Open** Mon-Fri noon-2.30pm, 7.30-11pm; Sat 7.30-11pm. **Average** €17. **Lunch menu** €8.40, €11. **Credit** MC, V.
It might not count as an essential restaurant on a tourist's itinerary, but if Paris is the place you call home you could do far worse than stop in for an inexpensive meal at this convivial little spot. Here, the friendly *patron* greets everyone who walks through the door with a handshake before merrily escorting them to their table. Such warmth certainly sets the tone of a meal and helps to compensate for the slightly too bright lighting and rather unremarkable decor (though the chairs were recently replaced). These things don't seem to be the point here. More expensive than most offerings on the menu, the beef fondue is almost too much fun to resist, but if you want to save a few euros and let someone else do your cooking, try one of the robust specialities, like steak tartare or chicken breast in cream sauce, all served with a choice of *frites* or green beans. Starting with a salad, like the poached egg and bacon number called the *lyonnaise*, instead of something heavier like escargots or a terrine, would compensate for the lack of vitamins in the overcooked green beans. Desserts are homemade, and if you ask nicely, the friendly waiter might even ladle a spoonful of chocolate sauce alongside your pear tart. Just like you might do at home.

Le Petit Keller
13bis rue Keller, 11th (01.47.00.12.97). M° *Ledru-Rollin.* **Open** Mon-Sat 7.30-11pm. **Prix fixe** €14. **Credit** MC, V.
If you're after a decent feed among the bars of Bastille – with money left over for a cocktail or two – it's hard to go wrong in this cheerful vintage bistro with its two Formica-furnished rooms. Seated in the back room, near the perilous spiral staircase leading up to the loo, we enjoyed the quiet atmosphere and efficient service. The restaurant is unfortunately no longer open at lunch, but for €14 you can have a three-course dinner (you can also order a main course alone for €10). The *menu* changes often; favourites are *magret* with peaches (for a small supplement) and apple crumble. Craving rib-sticking winter food, we started with a salad of *gésiers confits* (duck gizzards cooked in duck fat) and a thin slice of unremarkable duck terrine with sweet onion jam. A main of *boudin blanc* (fluffy veal-and-milk sausage) came charred black on one side but was tasty nonetheless; accompanying mashed potatoes nicely flavoured with parsley and a little star anise were sticky from having been overmixed. The *magret* in a sweet pink wine and peach sauce was cooked just right – rosé in the centre – and served with warming potato-and-cream gratin. Only the apple crumble truly disappointed: this was a sort of anti-crumble, with plenty of apple but no crumbs to be seen. Le Petit Keller is endearing for its understated decor – '50s before '50s was trendy – fresh ingredients and good intentions.

Le Temps au Temps
13 rue Paul Bert, 11th (01.43.79.63.40/ www.ifrance.com/restaurant75). M° *Faidherbe-Chaligny.* **Open** daily 8-11pm. **Prix fixe** €17. **Credit** MC, V.
This pocket-sized bistro decorated with clocks and watches all telling a different time is packed with a local crowd even on a Monday night. It doesn't take long to get the joke – the owner lives in a time zone all his own. If he tells you there'll be a table in ten minutes it probably means an hour, but you'll be offered a *kir* on the house and can spend the time looking at the satirical send-ups of *Libération* covers. The four-course €17 *menu* is good value and offers an unchanging choice of five starters, main courses and desserts with a cheese course. The warm foie gras on toast with salsify is a winner, the complementary flavours of the salsify and foie gras enhanced by a dribble of nut oil; from the main courses the *magret de canard* with a robust Port sauce was excellent both times we tried it and is further enhanced by crispy sautéed potatoes. Fillets of sole with *beurre blanc* are the only choice for non meat-eaters but got the thumbs-up – the sauce did not swamp the delicate flavour of the fish. A duo of quality cheeses followed but the jury is still out on the desserts: we enjoyed the *chaud-froid* of morello cherries but the *tarte Tatin* proved a disappointment. Wines are reasonable. Just one word of warning: towards midnight the owner gets obsessed with his CD collection (Bowie, Lou Reed, Iggy Pop) so don't expect to catch the last Métro.

Au Vieux Chêne
7 rue Dahomey, 11th (01.43.71.67.69). M° *Faidherbe-Chaligny.* **Open** Mon-Thu noon-2.30pm, 7.45-10.30pm; Fri noon-2.30pm, 7.45-11.30pm; Sat 7.45-11.30pm. Closed two weeks in Aug. **Average** €18. **Prix fixe** €18.30 (dinner only). **Lunch menu** €10.60. **Credit** AmEx, MC, V. **Wheelchair access**.
As newcomers, we received some inquisitive stares when we ventured into this unassuming bistro, which recently changed owners. Looks that seemed to ask, 'How did you know there was a restaurant here?' A reasonable question considering the rather drab exterior and off-the-beaten-track location. The interior is rustic – old tiles, playfully painted and papered walls,

simple wooden tables – and warm (they keep the ceiling fan going in winter). We expected our meal to be accompanied by a savvy jazz selection when we spied the giant mural, but the radio behind the bar was tuned into a top-40 station. Ridiculously cheap four-course *menus*, which change weekly, are sure to fill you up. Stick to the dishes that perform best in budget surroundings: lentil salad, *magret de canard*, *pièce de boeuf* and anything involving potatoes. Avoid the *andouillette*, salmon, and lasagne. 'A meal without wine is a day without sunshine' proclaims the menu and indeed many customers had rosy complexions before the second course. Homemade desserts such as crème caramel are good if not great, but the main event is the massive cheese platter. This generous tray of raw-milk gems and goats' cheeses with olive oil, fennel and cumin could easily serve as a meal in itself.

La Zygotissoire
101 rue de Charonne, 11th (01.40.09.93.05). M° Charonne. **Open** Mon-Thur noon-2pm, 7.30-11pm; Fri noon-2pm, 8-11pm; Sat 8-11pm. Closed three weeks in Aug. **Average** €27. **Prix fixe** €18.50 (dinner only). **Lunch menu** €13. **Credit** MC, V.

Locals know that for the past three years there's been an inspired chef at work in this bland-looking restaurant. His secret is a willingness to experiment, taking basics that usually feature on standard budget menus and adding a dash of imagination. Where an ordinary restaurant might do snails in garlic butter, the chef here dices the snails and wraps them in handmade ravioli, adding dollops of superb *aïoli* (garlic mayonnaise). The set *menu* offers a choice of three starters including the Burgundian *oeufs en meurette* and the more original beef *millefeuille*. The *menu*'s guinea hen arrived with medieval hints of nutmeg and clove. Quail stew was even better, with a generous serving of 'trumpets of death' – a favourite of mushroom connoisseurs, and excellent with poultry. The wine list is small, but it's easy to find something inexpensive and drinkable. An added pleasure is the bread, a yeasty whole wheat baguette variant made fresh on the premises. Try to save room for pudding, as the set *menu* includes whatever whimsy the chef has chosen for the day – it might be a simple warm apricot tart or a fantastical concoction of chestnuts, whipped cream and chocolate.

12th Arrondissement

... Comme Cochons ★
135 rue de Charenton, 12th (01.43.42.43.36). M° Reuilly-Diderot. **Open** Mon-Sat noon-2.30pm, 8-11.30pm. **Average** €27. **Lunch menu** €12.20. **Credit** AmEx, DC, MC, V.

There's nothing pig-like about the food on offer here other than the appetite it inspires and a decidedly gregarious banter between the area's slightly arty customers and friendly laid-back staff; it perfectly echoes the idiom '*être copains comme cochons*'. The corner space bursts with daylight, with a long banquette around the walls and changing exhibitions of artworks, while dishes are simple but appetising and reveal careful preparation. The lunch *menu* is a financial miracle offering three courses and wine. Vegetable tartare was a slightly grandiose name for crudités but well-presented and with rare inclusions like sliced fennel; a warm chicken liver mousse was light; and marinated herrings came with good waxy potatoes. Main courses change frequently depending on the market, but we've had roast sea bream with purée and sautéed courgettes, and roast chicken with spices rubbed into the skin. Desserts are of the variety you'd happily make yourself, perhaps chocolate cake or fluffy coffee mousse.

La Connivence ★
1 rue de Cotte, 12th (01.46.28.46.17). M° Ledru-Rollin or Gare de Lyon. **Open** Mon-Sat noon-2.30pm, 7.45-11pm; Sun noon-2.30pm. Closed Aug. **Prix fixe** €16.80, €21.35 (dinner only). **Lunch menu** €12.20, €15.25. **Credit** MC, V. **Wheelchair access**.

We ended up in this restaurant one fine August day only because Sardegna a Tavola next door was closed – but chef Pascal Kosmala so impressed us that our next visit certainly won't be accidental. La Connivence does an imaginative take on comfort food, in keeping with the warm burnt-orange and wood surroundings. Lunch choices are a little more limited than in the evening, but the dishes are just as complex. We settled on a blackboard special, the *terrine de la mer, sauce grelette* – a cool and light seafood concoction with a whipped cream sauce – and a lovely *fraîcheur de crevettes* from the *carte*, a prawn salad dressed with saffron sauce and peppery black nigella seeds. Main courses were meatier: tender chicken in a luscious cream sauce – saffron and nigella sneaked into this dish, too – all wrapped in crisp *brik* pastry and served with sautéed wild mushrooms, and veal medallions on tagliatelle noodles with foie gras sauce. These left us with room only for the quality sorbets, but larger appetites might opt for crêpes with candied orange or a chocolate Charlotte. Kosmala was admirably juggling the food and service single-handedly on our quiet lunch, but by September the restaurant was again buzzing – it's no wonder the name translates as 'in the know'.

L'Encrier
55 rue Traversière, 12th (01.44.68.08.16). M° Ledru-Rollin or Gare de Lyon. **Open** Mon-Fri noon-2.15pm, 7.15-11pm; Sat 7.15-11pm. Closed Aug. **Average** €20. **Prix fixe** €13 (dinner only), €14, €17.80. **Lunch menu** €10. **Credit** MC, V. **Wheelchair access**.

On a quiet street in the shadow of the swish Viaduc des Arts, this smallish restaurant with bare stone walls, wooden beams, tiled floor and relaxed, friendly service imparts a surprisingly designer feel, due largely to the open kitchen. It serves up some reliably good food at fair prices – and with this combination of atmosphere and decent, good-value eating, it's no surprise to find the place buzzing at most mealtimes. Suits predominate at lunch, with a cosier, more family-based crowd in the evening. The bargain €10 *menu* featured starters such as fromage blanc with grated radish, *potage de légumes* and a good lamb's lettuce salad with walnuts, apples and pieces of pink grapefruit. The mains included a chunky Montbéliard sausage with cabbage, well-cooked skate, and slightly dry kidneys redeemed by a tasty Madeira sauce. Desserts include standbys such as *mousse au chocolat* and the more inventive coconut tart, as well as a simple but refreshing fruit salad consisting entirely of oranges liberally dusted

Le Petit Keller: fun with Formica

with cinnamon. The staff are friendly and laid-back, and you'll find good wines around the €20 mark. Turn up early – the place is so popular they don't take reservations.

Le Pays de Vannes
34bis rue Wattignies, 12th (01.43.07.87.42). Mº Michel Bizot. **Open** 6.30am-8pm. Closed Aug. **Lunch menus** €9.15, €12.20. **Credit** MC, V.

Just the kind of neighbourhood restaurant you would like to find on your doorstep, the Pays de Vannes delivers much more than its café-like exterior promises. At lunch we found a jovial crowd of office workers tucking into hearty fare. The only tables left empty were a few inches from the loo doors so we were entertained throughout with a constant stream of visitors. This did not seem to bother anyone else at the other two tables near us and everyone got on with recounting the latest gossip while downing fair quantities of the so-so house wine. The crab cocktail was just the thing for a light lunch and featured a shower of shredded real crab, not the usual *surimi*, on a bed of crisp, freshly torn lettuce. The snowy-white flesh of our main course, melt-in-the-mouth *sole meunière*, came, at our request, with chunky, golden chips instead of the usual boiled or steamed spuds. We finished off this Breton-inspired meal with homemade *far breton*, a flan chock-a-block with plump, moist prunes light years from the often preferred dried-up version. This is a handy address if you find yourself in the neighbouthood.

13th Arrondissement

Chez Gladines
30 rue des Cinq-Diamants, 13th (01.45.80.70.10). Mº Corvisart. **Open** daily 9am-2am. **Average** €15. **Lunch menu** €9.50. **No credit cards.**

Chez Gladines is lucky enough to be in the Butte-aux-Cailles – a series of villagey streets that lie hidden among the huge housing blocks of the 13th, south of Place d'Italie. In this little oasis, you could almost pretend to be somewhere in the French Pays Basque as you're warmly welcomed at Chez Gladines, with its regional food, drinks and flag on the wall. Most diners go for the giant salads served in earthenware bowls with a choice of ingredients such as fried potatoes, *jambon de Bayonne* and just about any duck part you can imagine. Desserts such as the *gâteau basque* are reasonably priced although we suspected the *tarte du jour* of being the *tarte de la semaine*. This is a no-frills experience, but completely enjoyable: bare brick walls, paper-towel napkins, peeling menus, communal seating (*cohabitation des tables*, as they will inform you), and chaotic service (it was so busy during our visit that our friendly if slightly intense waiter went the whole evening with both his shoelaces untied).

Le Temps des Cerises
18 rue de la Butte-aux-Cailles, 13th (01.45.89.69.48). Mº Corvisart or Place d'Italie. **Open** Mon-Fri 11.45am-2pm, 7.30-11.30pm; Sat 7.30pm-midnight. **Average** €22. **Prix fixe** €10.98, €20.12 (dinner only). **Lunch menu** €9.15. **Credit** AmEx, MC, V.

It's hard not to like this relaxed Butte aux Cailles bistro where diners sit elbow-to-elbow at long wooden tables. Pony-tailed staff are friendly and good-humoured – perhaps unsurprisingly as they share in the profits created by this extremely popular place run as a workers' cooperative. Although the atmosphere may be lively, the standard of the cooking has in the past been a little unreliable, and this was again confirmed on our last visit. The duck pâté, which had a generous nut of foie gras in the centre, was under-seasoned and lacked the potent flavour we had been craving. A Caribbean-inspired house speciality, *accras de morue* (deep-fried salt cod and potato balls), was overcooked and rather bland, though the accompanying spicy tomato sauce did provide a tastier contrast. The *cassoulet* was more enjoyable, a piping-hot earthenware dish containing a meaty feast of ham, bacon, duck, and sausage that's easily a meal in itself. We also enjoyed the monkfish in a saffron-brightened seafood sauce, though it came with insipid over-boiled potatoes. As in many budget restaurants, the desserts were not great.

14th Arrondissement

Au Rendez-Vous des Camionneurs
34 rue des Plantes, 14th (01.45.42.20.94). Mº Alésia. **Open** Mon-Fri noon-2.30 pm, 7.30-9.30pm. Closed Aug. **Average** €17. **Prix fixe** €12. **No credit cards.**

Lying in one of the prettier parts of this *arrondissement*, Au Rendez-Vous des Camionneurs is a value-for-money locals' restaurant. The interior is warm and inviting, with French football as the central decorative motif, while outside a handful of rickety tables constitutes the terrace. Claude and Monique, who have run the place for many years, are helpful if a little scatty, coming to take our order no fewer than three times between them. The €12 *formule* can be a bit of a lottery. We started with rather greasy duck pâté and an intriguing-sounding dish, which turned out to be just a plate of sliced tomato. The main-course stew was delicious – tender, marinated veal in a rich, meaty sauce. However, a plate of bony anchovies swimming in brine was inferior, and not saved by its accompanying bowl of limp peppers. The portions are generous, and baskets of tasty homemade bread are regularly replenished. Polish it all off with a few glasses of good, cheap Côtes du Rhone.

15th Arrondissement

Café du Commerce
51 rue du Commerce, 15th (01.45.75.03.27). Mº Emile-Zola. **Open** daily noon-midnight. Closed 24 Dec. **Average** €20. **Prix fixe** €20. **Lunch menu** €10.55, €15.45. **Credit** AmEx, DC, MC, V.

The Café du Commerce is one of the most attractive budget restaurants in Paris. Three floors follow one another like square balconies around the open central atrium. A net is now in place at the top; its purpose is to keep out the sparrows but a few always manage to get through and amuse themselves and the restaurant's clients by darting from level to level in search of breadcrumbs – one was even so bold as to eat off our table. Founded in the 1920s as a *bouillon* (workers' canteen), it has all the charm the '20s and '30s had to offer. Especially engaging are the *trompe l'œil* paintings, both in the restaurant and on the walls of the surrounding buildings, visible through the open roof of the atrium. Traditional bistro nosh can be ordered *à la carte* or from the set *menus*. Grilled and raw salmon were both fresh and creatively seasoned, while the heartier dishes – steaks and *confits* served with steaming *frites* – left little to be desired, given the reasonable prices. If you have room, try the extravagant house dessert *la coupe Café du Commerce*: a mix of ice cream, Chantilly, raisins, bananas and hot fudge. It's understaffed and popular so arrive early or book.

Les Dix Vins
57 rue Falguière, 15th (01.43.20.91.77). Mº Pasteur. **Open** Tue-Sat noon-2.30pm, 7-11.30pm. **Prix fixe** €16. **No credit cards.**

'Ah, divin!' exclaimed my French guest, realising I was a little slow picking up on the play on words. Without invoking the supernatural, this is a good place to enjoy a very decent budget meal in the Montparnasse end of this *arrondissement*. The €16 blackboard *menu* is generously served by attractive young waitresses under Madame's vivacious eye. The freshly painted room, which features glass-topped tables that are apparently made of ancient wine racks, was cheerful and buzzing with lunchtime customers, most of whom seemed to be personal friends of the *patronne*. After nibbling on some rather miserable taramasalata toasts, we began with an excellent spinach, poached egg and bacon salad, and fine (though unseasonal) green asparagus with hollandaise sauce. The waitress advised us to try the *raie aux câpres*, plate-sized skate wings with a punchy butter, accompanied by a side serving of over-emphatic garlic mash. One of us finished up with some syrupy *poires au vin*, while the other made serious inroads into a whole round of first-rate camembert. With a bottle of reasonable Loire white and some change back from €50, we began to think that perhaps divine providence had played its role.

Au Métro
18 bd Pasteur, 15th (01.47.34.21.24). Mº Pasteur. **Open** Mon-Sat noon-3pm, 6-11pm. Closed Aug. **Average** €18. **Prix fixe** €18. **Credit** MC, V.

This little bar/bistro proudly wears its southwest colours on its sleeve, from the hearty *cassoulet* to the wall-to-wall rugby photos. With a tile floor reminiscent of the changing room of a public swimming pool, red paper tablecloths and a no-frills decor (paintings of sheep, basically), Au Métro is about good value in very simple surroundings: bring your own atmosphere. After-work drinkers gather around the bar quaffing cheap beer and going over the last Stade de France match while about ten tables accommodate diners – just us on this occasion. Our salads were large and fresh, the *magret de canard* was juicy and the accompanying roast potatoes were a garlicky delight. The *frites* that accompanied the roast chicken had been undercooked in an oil that needed changing but the bird itself was tender and, like everything else, huge. Basic desserts such as apple tarts and chocolate mousse are kept in the same display fridge as the Basque pâtés but this did not seem to affect their taste, for better or worse. The heavy portions are in sharp contrast with featherweight bill.

U Sampiero Corsu
12 rue de l'Amiral Roussin, 15th. No telephone. Mº Commerce. **Open** Mon-Sat 12.30-2.30pm, 6.30-9.30pm. **Average** €10.67. **No credit cards.**

You'll never visit another restaurant like it. Based on communist principles: 'From each according to his ability, to each according to his needs', here people out of work eat for free. Otherwise, those on a base salary of about €800 a month are charged a minimum of €6.85 – above that you pay what you can afford, for a (very) basic three-course meal. There was a choice of four starters – house salad, cucumber salad, pâté and terrine. Only three of the mains were available on our visit: *merguez*, roast chicken and 'paella Isabel'. For dessert, a choice of compote, yoghurt or camembert. A bottle of Corsican red cost €10.67. The less said about the food the better. The walls of the restaurant are covered with stirring phrases such as '*Branchez-vous sur la révolution*' ('Plug into the revolution') along with pictures of revolutionaries. Established in 1970 (31 years of service to the working classes!), this little restaurant seems to have lost most of its relevance. The couple who run it are getting old, and we don't know where communism stands on gender equality, but Monsieur read the paper while Madame took our order, cooked and served the customers – two curious German tourists and us – then did the dishes.

16th Arrondissement

Restaurant GR5 ★
19 rue Gustave Courbet, 16th (01.47.27.09.84). Mº Trocadéro. **Open** Mon-Sat noon-3pm, 7-11pm. **Average** €17. **Prix fixe** €20 (dinner only). **Lunch menu** €13.60, €16. **Credit** AmEx, MC, V.

Savoyard food is meant for mountain folk and hikers, fuel for yet another stretch of the *grande randonnée* (the GR5 is the long-distance footpath that winds through the Jura to the Alps). But then who said trekking around Paris wasn't exhausting? Tucked away amidst the chic boutiques of the 16th, this mock refuge (Chamonix posters, wooden skis, cow bells crowd the walls) and its genuinely warm welcome will transport you to more Alpine altitudes. Cheese

La Fourchette des Anges promises heavenly pleasures

and potatoes are the key ingredients. There's a good selection of fondues (€33.54 for two people) including the traditional *savoyarde*, and a *queyrassienne* with three cheeses, bacon and onions. If you don't want to share, try the *raclette valaisienne*, (all you can eat for €17.53), or one of the *tartiflettes* (€17.53). This cheese, potato and bacon concoction (choose between reblochon, vacherin or chèvre de chavignol) will give you the energy, if you can get up from the table, to climb Mont Blanc. The wines, too, are regional; our *pot* of Crépy, a light white, was pleasantly refreshing.

17th Arrondissement

La Fourchette des Anges
17 rue Biot, 17th (01.44.69.07.69). Mº Place de Clichy. **Open** Mon-Sat 7-11pm. **Prix fixe** €18.29, €22.87. **Credit** MC, V.
This little restaurant on one of Paris' newly hip streets, a stone's throw from the ever-bustling place de Clichy, promises almost heavenly pleasures at down-to-earth prices. Good-humoured and accommodating service, jasmine-scented air and eclectic decor set off to good effect the 12 or so comfortably spaced tables. This is a fine place to taste variations on French standards such as *cassolette de ravioles*, a rich, layered gratin of pasta, cheese and béchamel sauce, or a combination of spinach and scallops wrapped in crisp *brik* pastry and served in a pool of anise-infused cream. The menu changes every three months, but our chunky *boeuf au foie gras* more than justified the extra €3.81, the perfectly cooked beef moistened by a melting cascade of rich goose liver. Tender leg of lamb is equally subtle, fragrantly seasoned with just the right amount of thyme. An apple and Calvados *Charlotte* provides a light, almost ethereal ending to the meal, but if you like chocolate, don't even think of skipping the *fondant au chocolat*. This mound of chocolate cooked with a good dose of coffee and plenty of sugar is thicker and richer than the best fudge in the world. So sinful, in fact, that it makes you wonder if it's really an angel's fork – and not the devil's – that you've been holding all along.

18th Arrondissement

Chez Toinette ★
20 rue Germain-Pilon, 18th (01.42.54.44.36). Mº Abbesses. **Open** Tue- Sat 8-11pm. Closed Aug. **Average** €20.
No credit cards.
With its limited seating and even more limited opening hours, fabulous cuisine, discreet candle-lit atmosphere and ridiculously low prices, we were convinced that the owner and chef, Olivier Greco, is more public benefactor than businessman. We were greeted with a complimentary dish of mixed olives, small radishes and earthy wholemeal baguette that meant we hardly needed a starter. The beef carpaccio looked (and proved) too good to miss; a light sprinkling of nutmeg gave it a lovely spicy edge. Toinette, however, came into its own with the timeless Provençal mains heightened by the slightest of designer touches. A seasonal speciality on our visit was a sublimely aromatic *côtelette de marcassin*, baby wild boar cutlet smothered in wild mushrooms, bay leaves and coriander, complemented by a fruity Côtes de Thau red *vin de pays* recommended by the waiter. The baked chocolate and pear tart merited a full-page review to itself and the bill was so low we felt we had taken advantage of our host's generosity. Still, that makes a nice change. Reserve even on weekdays.

Le Relais Gascon
6 rue des Abbesses, 18th (01.42.58.58.22). Mº Pigalle. **Open** daily 11am-midnight **Average** €13. **Prix fixe** €12.50, €18.50.
No credit cards.
We left Pigalle's tourist sauciness and walked 200 metres up a side road to this haven of cheery southern hospitality. The decor is rustic, of the oak-beamed, tiled-floor rather than corn-dolly kind, and the service is attentive and speedy. A starter of 12 snails in garlic butter was fine if nothing special. As the owner himself admits, people don't come here for the starters, but rather for the speciality main course – the *salades géantes*. Though no-one will deny they are *géante* (they come in bowls the size of footballs), the claim to 'salad' status is more tenuous, a *salade fraîcheur* resembling nothing more than a delicious up-market fry-up. A thick layer of smoky bacon was covered with eggs, lashings of Parma ham, walnuts and sweet tomatoes and the whole thing was topped with a golden heap of thinly-sliced garlicky fried potatoes – the few lettuce leaves an afterthought. A chunky *bavette* was beautifully tender and draped in a delicate blue cheese sauce. A reasonably nice crème brûlée is probably the best dessert choice.

Le Rendez-Vous des Chauffeurs
11 rue des Portes Blanches, 18th (01.42.64.04.17). Mº Marcadet-Poissonniers. **Open** Mon, Tue noon-2.30pm, 7.30pm-11pm; Thur-Sun noon-2.30pm, 7.30-11pm. **Average** €20. **Prix fixe** €12. **Credit** MC, V.
Nothing here has changed over the past 80-odd years, and once you take your seat at one of the long tables, you'll understand why no-one's complaining. The inexpensive three-course *prix fixe* gives you a fair selection of dishes and even includes a pitcher of house wine, a completely drinkable one that goes so well with the traditional fare that we ended up ordering a second. We started with a simple fisherman's salad, the mayonnaise of the potatoes a good foil for the firm white fish, along with a plate of *saucisson sec*. The waiter duly unhooked the sausage from its traditional hanging place behind the bar, and sliced it up before us. Try to order a main dish with *frites*, as they're made fresh with wide potato slices. If you're feeling particularly hungry, order one of the substantial *à la carte* dishes, such as the lamb. Be sure to accompany your meal with the well-priced bottle of the month (€15), which sits enticingly on every table.

Au Virage Lepic
61 rue Lepic, 18th (01.42.52.46.79). Mº Blanche. **Open** Mon, Wed-Sun 7pm-midnight. **Average** €18. **Prix fixe** €14.48. **Credit** MC, V.
A snug hideaway, this restaurant is exactly what the neighbourhood's history demands: walls covered in music-hall posters and film star stills, tables with red- and white-checked table cloths, and a hugely moustached owner behind his traditional zinc bar. And, it all works beautifully. The food is good, the atmosphere cheerful. With only 24 seats, you're dancing with fate if you don't make a reservation. The two-course €14.48 *menu* is more than satisfying. We tried a sampling of the classics, starting with onion soup, cheesy as it should be, and a *gésiers de canard* salad – yes, warm duck gizzard salad, delicious if you are willing to try it. Our main courses – roast chicken, and tender pork with noodles – were exactly what we wanted.

20th Arrondissement

La Boulangerie ★
15 rue des Panoyaux, 20th (01.43.58.45.45). Mº Ménilmontant. **Open** Mon-Fri noon-2pm, 7.30-11.30pm; Sat 7.30pm-midnight; Sun noon-3pm, 7.30-11.30pm. **Average** €18. **Prix fixe** €18. **Lunch menu** €8.05, €11. **Credit** MC, V.
La Boulangerie offers just about everything you could ask of a restaurant: a warm setting in a former bakery (hence the name), exceptionally helpful waiters, and imaginative cooking at a very reasonable price. No wonder it's so popular with locals and American tourists who bravely venture beyond St-Germain. Opting for the €18 *menu*, we started with an intriguing *tatin de christophene*, a sweet, orange-spiked squash tart, and a smooth asparagus *bavarois* – refreshing with its cucumber coulis and hints of fennel and coriander. The *croustillant de grenadier* again showed the chef's creativity – a brandade-like potato and white fish purée wrapped in crisp *brik* pastry and served with a creamy Noilly butter sauce. Vermouth showed up again in the minty sauce for a lamb *brochette*, which was accompanied by rather too oily but thoughtfully spiced roasted aubergine, courgette and potato. We then chose a freshly made apple sorbet (for once an ivory colour rather than lurid green) with apple liqueur, and a lovely apple *sablé* served with the same sorbet and a blackcurrant coulis.

Chez Jean
38 rue Boyer, 20th (01.47.97.44.58). Mº Gambetta or Ménilmontant. **Open** Mon-Sat 7.30pm-12:30am. Closed Aug. **Average** €24. **Prix fixe** €15. **Credit** MC, V.
Step behind this unassuming facade to enter a bistro timewarp where the owner greets regulars by name, tables sport red-checked tablecloths and your meal is accompanied by the nostalgic sounds of a jazz guitar duo or accordionist. Diners pack Chez Jean knowing they can expect food that's as homely as the setting. Start your meal with one of the rustic, homemade *pâtés* or *terrines*. The Burgundy classic *jambon persillé* embeds rosy chunks of ham in a garlicky parsley aspic. Main courses include stuffed veal fillet with a woodsy wild mushroom sauce or nicely grilled salmon topped with toasted almonds. We passed on the tempting crème brûlée and chocolate mousse in favour of the chef's recommendation, a refreshing chilled strawberry soup with red wine and mint. Reserve on live music nights – Wednesday, Friday and Saturday.

Ma Pomme
107 rue de Ménilmontant, 20th (01.40.33.10.40). Mº Ménilmontant or Gambetta. **Open** Mon-Fri noon-2.30pm, 7.30-11.30pm; Sat, Sun 7.30-11.30pm. Closed two weeks in Aug. **Prix fixe** €20. **Lunch menu** €10, €13. **Credit** MC, V.
In the upper reaches of rue de Ménilmontant (bring oxygen just in case) you'll find one of the best value *menus* in Paris. Three beautifully presented courses are served in a slightly Conranised dining room where industrial galvanised steel meets solid wood tables and plaster mouldings. Service, though slightly erratic (one one occasion, they brought the main courses before the starters), is good-humoured. We started with carpaccio with parmesan – excellent meat which was rather swamped by a too-vinegary dressing – and an aubergine 'lasagne' which was faultless and impressive-looking on the plate: layered, lightly cooked aubergine with fresh anchovies and a salad with fennel and coriander. A duck *magret* with honey on tagliatelle had complex flavours in its sauce, including fennel, star anise and cinnamon. The *poêlée de poissons à la provençale* was mysteriously not pan-fried but cooked in foil – it was also undercooked, but after a few more minutes in the oven the flavours had blossomed. For desserts the *fondant au chocolat* was a firm cake rather than the *moelleux* variety, and came with an almond-flavoured *crème anglaise*. The short but well-chosen wine list is reasonably priced, and there are *pichets* too.

Cafe du Commerce, a capital address

Vegetarian

As meat-free cooking comes of age, purist restaurants remain trapped in a time warp.

You'd think that Paris would have a whole new breed of vegetarian restaurants in the wake of the mad cow crisis, which led to a series of food scares involving chicken, pork and even fish, but remarkably little has changed. Some, though admittedly not many, bistros and haute cuisine restaurants offer alternatives to meat (see p24, **Mad about cows**), but the hard-core vegetarian restaurants are having difficulty shedding their hippie image – not that most of them are even trying. A few exceptions are the creative **Le Potager du Marais** – though it does serve fish, the vegetarian dishes are imaginative and made with organic ingredients – the tiny Iranian restaurant **La Verte Tige** and the self-serve **Foody's**.

Cafés (see p104) remain ever-reliable bets for basic crudité sandwiches (beware eggs and tuna fish, though), salads and omelettes. Vegetarians often fare best, however, at international restaurants, particularly Far Eastern (p87), Italian (p93), Indian (p91) and occasionally North African (p99) ones.

Entre Ciel et Terre
5 rue Hérold, 1st (01.45.08.49.84/ www.entrecieleterre.com). Mº Les Halles or Louvre-Rivoli. **Open** Mon-Fri noon-3pm, 7-10pm; tea 3-6.30pm. Closed Aug. **Average** €23. **Prix fixe** €20.43 (dinner only). **Lunch menu** €12.34, €16.31. **Credit** AmEx, DC, MC, V.

A vegetarian oasis in a city known for it carnivorous appetite, Entre Ciel et Terre is not a typical Parisian restaurant: its dining room is packed but without a trace of smoke, staff are sincerely friendly and there is no Bordeaux on the menu (alternatives include soy milk, fruit juice and non-alcoholic beer). It's impeccably clean and the decoration is charming, even if it seems the result of a pre-school class project – cut-out hanging stars, Petit Prince inspired menu, paintings, and strange plastic objects hanging on the walls (they're for sale; that much is clear). The food is creative and fun: a vegetarian pâté, colourful *tabouleh* with fresh crudités and goat's cheese and tofu quiche appear under playful names such as 'entrée des étoiles', 'saveurs terrestres', and 'douceurs célestes'. Homemade desserts such as apple crumble and sinfully rich chocolate orange cake are the most conventional of the dishes and, coincidentally, the most enjoyable.

Foody's Brunch Café
26 rue Montorgueil, 1st (01.40.13.02.53). Mº Châtelet Les Halles. **Open** Mon-Sat 11.30am-7.30pm. **Average** €8.50. **Prix fixe** €7.65-€12.05. **Credit** MC, V. **Wheelchair access.**

This popular vegetarian fast-food café on the northern edge of Les Halles provides a welcome alternative to the standard greasy offerings in the area. The staff obviously take pride in what they do; on our visit the food was fresh and the place spotlessly clean. The simple canteen system involves taking a tray and choosing from a buffet of about ten salads, €4.45 for a small or €5.95 for a large. There's also soup of the day for €3.80, in our case a generous serving of delicious chilled gaspacho. Desserts included fruit salad, rice pudding and a variety of fromages blancs and compotes. The drinks were so good they were walking out the door, strings of teenagers opting for a large chilled glass of homemade lemonade or iced tea with mint or ginger rather than a Diet Coke. There are numerous *formules* available and everything can be taken away. The name might lead you to think that Foody's does brunch – oddly, though, it doesn't.

La Victoire Suprême du Coeur
41 rue des Bourdonnais, 1st (01.40.41.93.95). Mº Châtelet. **Open** Mon-Sat 11.45am-2.45pm, 6-10pm. **Average** €20. **Prix fixe** €16. **Lunch menu** €9, €10.40. **Credit** MC, V. **Wheelchair access.**

Probably the best vegetarian feast in Paris is hidden in this little Les Halles street. Run by devotees of New York guru Sri Chinmoy, this place is decorated in typical New Age style, complete with tinkling fountain. With a small but delicious menu, the space offers a calming haven to single diners as well as hip couples of all ages. Diners in the know check out the superb sweets table as soon as they arrive, to pace their meals. Our first course set a high standard with a perfectly-nuanced mushroom terrine. Other fine starters include the vegetable soup of the day and the cold tri-colour terrine: carrot, spinach, and leek served with a chive-yoghurt dressing. We drank tart organic cider; there is also organic sparkling white wine for an inexpensive, festive addition to your evening. The most exciting main dish, definitely one of the top veggie meals in the city, is the mushroom roast, sliced and served with blackberry sauce, lentils, potatoes and a delightful courgette curry. Compared to such a feast, the *prix fixe* menu is limited, with smaller servings. The seitan in Spanish pepper sauce needed perking up with the tabasco sauce, sesame seeds with sea salt, and brewers' yeast offered on every table. With raspberry tart in vanilla custard sauce and fabulous chocolate cakes distracting from more wholesome fare like apple compote, we knew to save space for dessert. We finished things off with a well-spiced *tchai* from an excellent range of teas.

Le Potager du Marais ★
22 rue Rambuteau, 3rd (01.44.54.00.31). Mº Rambuteau. **Open** Mon-Sat noon-3pm, 7-11pm. **Average** €17. **Prix fixe** €15. **Lunch menu** €10. **Credit** AmEx, MC, V.

A long, narrow dining room gives the impression of one communal table, not a bad sentiment given the socially minded ethos of the mostly vegetarian Potager du Marais. The menu claims 100 per cent organic ingredients, down to the wines, salt and pepper (though how could the extensive fish options, such as deep-ocean tuna, be verifiably organic?). Working steps above the usual plates of veggies and rice, the chef here turns out lovely fresh pastas, soups, and daily specials with quality ingredients and flavourful yet light seasonings. A grain and lentil soup and a plate of goat's cheese-honey toast began the meal on a simple yet pleasing note. For main dishes, try the stuffed tomato, the curried tofu penne, or a superbly soft and succulent cep ravioli with olive oil and herbs. The fish special, a giant tuna steak expertly grilled with a side of Provençal ratatouille (featuring some incredibly sweet onions), hardly left room for dessert, which the easy-going waiter reminded us was included in the *formule*. We mustered strength and chose the poached pear, which arrived upright and smothered in chocolate, and an unusual flower-scented crème brûlée. Our only complaint: the second course arrived moments after the first had been cleared, hardly giving us a chance to catch our breath. Never mind: we'll happily return with our vegetarian friends.

La Verte Tige ★
13 rue Ste-Anastase, 3rd (01.42.77.22.15). Mº St-Sébastien-Froissart. **Open** Tue-Sat noon-2.30pm, 7.30-10.30pm, Sun 12.30-4pm. Closed Aug. **Average** €20. **Prix fixe** €16.62 (evenings, Sat and Sun lunch). **Credit** MC, V.

Run by an Iranian couple who bring warmth to their service and creativity to their dishes, this vegetarian restaurant is in a class of its own. Unlike at most vegetarian restaurants, wine and beer are on the menu as well as more traditional fruit juices and teas – and there is even a smoking section. They have taken traditional Iranian dishes and subtracted the meat elements: this is true of the *espinada* – a spinach purée with fried onions, garlic and yoghurt that had just the right tang. *Albus*, a mix of yoghurt, fromage blanc, cucumber, raisins, nuts, dill and rose petals, reflects their interest in escaping the drab offerings that can be so prevalent in veggie establishments, and *viridis* – simply an avocado purée spread on toast – was sprinkled with pine kernels. Mains include a filling and varied vegetarian platter and couscous with tofu sausage – there is also a different €7.93 *plat du jour* each weekday. The €16.62 *menu* offering three courses is good value, and the caramelised date crumble was terrific. Unpretentious minty green walls and inverted basket lampshades do not seek to impress, but the friendly, open feel is fine for some relaxed, home-cooked health food.

Galerie 88
88 quai de l'Hôtel de Ville, 4th (01.42.72.17.58). Mº Hôtel de Ville. **Open** daily 10am-1am. **Average** €15. **No credit cards.**

The burgundy banquettes and Moroccan-influenced decor welcome new millennium twentysomethings in the mood for serious conversation and light food. Traffic rushes past without disturbing the superb view, best on a rainy day when the islands across the Seine are pure grey poetry. Snack plates are a good deal if you share. We enjoyed our Italian plate, which included fresh buffalo mozzarella, pickled artichoke hearts and sun-dried tomatoes, served with a basket of rye bread – a nice change from baguette, though it could have been fresher. Beware the surprise ingredient: a few slices of very red beef carpaccio which shocked the vegetarian among us as it wasn't listed in the description. However, the house guacamole and the lemon-flavoured Moroccan soup are vegan-friendly, and the best drink for a cold day is ginger juice, drunk hot or cool. It's a spicy, soothing concoction of ginger root, lemon juice and honey. If you need further comforting, there are always the dark chocolate brownies on the back counter.

Grand Appétit
9 rue de la Cerisaie, 4th (01.40.27.04.95). Mº Bastille. **Open** Mon-Thur noon-3pm, Fri noon-2pm. **Average** €10. **Prix fixe** €7.50-€15. **Credit** MC, V.

Adjacent to its sister natural foods shop, this nuts-and-bolts, wholesome place suffers from a sombre decor. Perhaps it's a central tenet of the macrobiotic philosophy not to disturb the eater with pleasant music or distracting art. Grand Appétit also takes 'self-service' to the extreme: you must hand-deliver your own bread basket, utensils, cup of water and murky tea, napkin and even placemat to your table. After examining the blackboard *menu*, we ordered at the dimly lit kitchen entrance, gathered our condiments – soy sauce, *gomasio* (toasted sesame and salt) and olive oil – and settled into our window seats overlooking a placid side street. The generous *grande assiette* arrived with rice and a wheat-like grain, tofu and bean sprouts, briny cabbage with radish, salty kelp and overcooked broccoli, most requiring extra zaps of spice. The pumpkin tart in a wholewheat crust should have been moister but had

Le Potager du Marais: a garden of delights for fish-eaters and vegetarians

Vegetarian

apparently dried out during reheating. The meal's highlight? Miso soup (€3 *à la carte*), a dark broth full of shredded carrot, onion, parsley and kelp. After tasting dessert, an odd, brown-coloured compote containing dandelion, we wondered if macrobiotic food needed to be this strange, and pondered what a Grand Appétit cooking class might be like.

Piccolo Teatro
6, rue des Ecouffes, 4th (01.42.72.17.79/ www.piccoloteatro.com) M° St-Paul or Hôtel de Ville. **Open** Tue-Sun noon-3pm, 7-11.30pm. **Average** €18. **Prix fixe** €14.50, €20 (dinner only). **Lunch menu** €8.20-€13.30. **Credit** AmEx, MC, V.
Piccolo Teatro offers both imaginative and imaginatively named vegetarian food, as well as a daily selection of soups, mains and desserts. This young and friendly joint is immensely popular with tourists and Anglo-Americans. We sipped tea and soaked up the atmosphere while waiting for our *tartare d'algues*, a seaweed salad that tasted nothing like the sea and a lot like olives, and was surrounded by an assortment of shredded raw veggies (carrots, cabbage, celeriac). A green salad disappointed with its lack of variety – batavia lettuce in a creamy sesame dressing – but it was delightfully fresh. Piccolo Teatro is best known for its filling gratins– earthy buckwheat grains mixed with tomato and courgette and topped with gruyère did not disappoint. Curried tempeh (soy-protein) was a real treat too, deliciously coated with a peanutty coconut sauce and served with perfectly steamed bulgur, but mismatched with the same cold shredded veggies that accompanied our starter. Since there was no more plum crumble to be had, we decided on a *moelleux aux poires* for dessert, but what should have been a gooey pear cake was bone-dry, hard, and served accompanied by a flavourless fruit compote. Do as we did: enjoy dinner, then cross over to the Ile St-Louis for two (or more) scoops of luscious Berthillon ice cream.

Le Grenier de Notre Dame
18 rue de la Bûcherie, 5th (01.43.29.98.29/ www.legrenierdenotredame.com). M° St-Michel or Maubert-Mutualité. **Open** Mon-Thur noon-2.30pm, 7.30-11pm; Fri, Sat noon-2.30pm, 7.30-11.30pm; Sun noon-3pm **Average** €20. **Prix fixe** €12.35. **Credit** MC, V.
Snugly located at the far end of Saint Michel's madness, this veggie standby boasts a macrobiotic menu that relys heavily on tofu creations reminiscent of the 1970s. We were disappointed to find the pleasant upstairs room closed (it opens only on busy nights), but we cheered ourselves up with a pitcher of good organic house wine; there's also an extensive fruit and vegetable juice menu. Things got off to a good start with fresh tofu, thinly sliced around a nest of seaweed. The 'cocktail selection' of salad was bland in comparison, with mung beans that had seen better days. It was cold in the little downstairs part of the restaurant, so we chose hearty hot dishes. The vegetable *cassoulet* turned out to be a simple, rather bland version of the Languedoc classic, made here with tofu, seitan, and soy sausage stewed with the traditional white beans, while the dense lasagne was heavy on tomatoes, with a bare hint of rosemary. We should have skipped dessert and stuck with our caffeine-free *café aux céréales*, as the house special chocolate cake turned out to be a skinny brownie drowning in an overwhelming orange sauce. In summer this place can fill up with people looking for hippie-style comfort food in a smoke-free environment.

Les Quatre et Une Saveurs
72 rue du Cardinal-Lemoine, 5th. (01.43.26.88.80). M° Cardinal-Lemoine. **Open** Tue-Sun noon-2:30pm, 7-10.30pm. Closed third week in Jul to third week in Aug. **Average** €22. **Prix fixe** €22. **Credit** MC, V.
Trudge uphill from the Seine to this brightly-painted restaurant and reward yourself with one of the excellent organic wines on the menu. The wine, along with fresh flowers, adds an elegant touch to this essentially West Coast environment (complete with uplifting art on the walls and advertisements for self-improvement courses on the way to the loo). Choices are limited but the daily special includes a fresh seasonally-inspired soup: we enjoyed squash soup made with a miso base. The next course, beautifully presented in a *bento* box, was a mild seitan stew with an assortment of fresh salads and grains. There's a sesame seed mixture and soy sauce for extra seasoning but even with these additions, our tofu and leek dish was bland. Our only real criticism, however, was the (French) tendency to overcook vegetables, which is very hard to forgive in a vegetarian restaurant. Good humour was restored with a hearty serving of the compote-like apple crumble, and an excellent anise tea. If you're a herbal tea aficionado, you'll find an interesting selection here.

Guen Maï
2bis rue de l'Abbaye, 6th. (01.43.26.03.24). M° St-Germain-des-Prés or Mabillon. **Open** Mon-Sat noon-3.30pm. Closed Aug. **Average** €19. **Credit** MC, V.
A rare haven for vegans, Guen Maï offers an Asian-influenced menu with two daily lunch specials. The address doubles as a health food shop, with most dishes available for take-away (the shop is open until 8.30pm, but the restaurant serves only lunch). A well-used juicer takes centre stage beside the cash register, so you can always just pop in for an energising drink. Feel free to ask for a combination that's not listed – they'll be happy to oblige. Tucked behind the shop, the restaurant is clean and bright, with a mostly-local clientele, and offers a comfortable environment for the single diner. Most days, the lunch special is a choice of soy or fish (usually eschewing dairy and wheat ingredients, Guen Mai does include trout and other fish on its menu). One of our favourites is the chewy seitan brochette, arranged with grains, salads and seaweed. The lunch plate makes a filling meal, nicely accompanied by an organic beer or by the speciality of the house, *mu* tea, a mixture of grains and ginseng. Choose your dessert carefully; when we visited recently, a tart made with dried apricots, raisins and prunes was a dry disappointment.

Verdibus
48 rue du Cherche Midi, 6th (01.40.49.06.17). M° Sèvres-Babylone. **Open** Mon-Sat noon-7.30pm (shop 10am-7.30pm). Closed 15 Jul-15 Aug. **Average** €18. **Credit** AmEx, MC, V.
This veg stand/eatery fills up during mealtimes with a rather expensive-looking crowd, which sits around Ikea glass-topped tables, chatting it up, perhaps eager to eat healthily after the previous night's indulgences. When they're done, some tables are shoved aside and the room reverts to a pricey produce stand. The focus at Verdibus is on fresh organic produce, both for sale and prepared as vegetarian fare in salads, quiches, and soups (though be warned that a minority of dishes are non-vegetarian). It's not a bad idea to have a veggie option in this upmarket neighbourhood, but we wished Verdibus would take a few more risks with its recipes and seasonings. The kitchen disappointed us with its carrot and cabbage *potage*, a mostly lifeless mélange, but the cold antipasti plate of marinated fennel, peppers and carrots, roasted to perfection, saved the first course. The mains were more reliable, but still fairly uninspiring: a tasty (but pasty) spinach gratin with poached eggs and a simplistic broccoli tart with whole-grain crust. An apple-pine nut tart tempted, but on our visit, it and the other desserts disappeared towards the end of lunchtime. You can always finish with a freshly squeezed juice such as carrot or tomato, order something to go, or pick up a head of lettuce as a souvenir.

Restaurant Haiku
63 rue Jean-Pierre Timbaud, 11th. (01.56.98.11.67). M° Parmentier or Couronnes. **Open** Mon-Fri noon-2.30pm, 7-10.30pm; Sat 7-10.30pm. Closed Aug. **Average** €19. **Credit** MC, V.
While Haiku's macrobiotic cooking philosophy may take its inspiration from the East, we were impressed with the international flavour of its menu. Daily specials ranged from an Alsatian pasta with emmental, onions and smoked tofu and a West-Indian avocado, salt-cod and chilli purée called *féroce*, to whole-wheat pasta with Italian-style sauces. We took a world tour, beginning with a tangy miso-coconut broth and a gigantic green salad loaded with grilled tofu, veggies, and pecorino cheese. Next came the not-so-ferocious avocado, served with, unfortunately, stale organic bread. The perfectly cooked Oriental brown rice was stir-fried with generous nuggets of courgette, carrot, tofu, and cashews. Pasta is made on the premises, but ours was overcooked and the ricotta, tomato and basil sauce lacked zing (and salt). Japanese green tea soothed our souls. Desserts are imaginative and mostly fruit-based. We chose mango mousse with coconut, but were tempted by freshly churned banana ice cream.

Aquarius
40 rue de Gergovie, 14th (01.45.41.36.88). M° Pernety or Plaisance. **Open** Mon-Sat noon-2.15pm, 7-10.30pm. Closed last two weeks in Aug. **Average** €15.24. **Lunch menu** €11. **Credit** AmEx, DC, MC, V. **Wheelchair access**.
The night we visited this popular and cheery vegetarian eatery we were greeted by a brood of loyal, wisecracking customers eager to include us in their jollity. Lots of friendliness from the serving team too. Our waiter, who appeared to be the owner, had lost his voice so was whispering – naturally we whispered back, which created a strange, not unpleasant, intimate atmosphere. The restaurant is basic, bright and cheery, and gives the impression of having expanded over time to accommodate an increasing demand. Each table comes with its own bottle of tamari and bowl of brewer's yeast along with the standard palette of seasonings. There are several impressive-looking salads on the menu, but we were in the mood for something heartier. We ordered the special of stuffed mushrooms on a bed of spinach for €10.51, which came drowned in a fairly tasteless and glutinous sauce. The portion was generous but the flavours were a bit dull. They got the vegetarian lasagne right, though. All the meals are served with good sourdough bread. About a third of the ingredients used are organic, and organic wine and cider are on the menu. They really go all out on the desserts: there were over a dozen on offer, ranging from fruit salad to a *fondant au chocolat*.

Au Grain de Folie
24 rue de La-Vieuville, 18th (01.42.58.15.57). M° Abbesses. **Open** daily noon-2.30pm, 7.30-11.30pm. **Average** €20. **Prix fixe** €8 (dinner only, before 8.30pm), €15. **No credit cards**.
Ideally, you should discover this spot by chance as you're wandering through the impossibly pretty streets of Montmartre. But if you're in the mood for homely vegetarian food, you might want to cheat and phone ahead because the restaurant is tiny. On a warm night it's a triumph to snag the only outside table. You won't take long in deciding on your meal since the selection is very limited, especially if you choose the set *menu* (at €8 before 8.30pm, it's hard to beat). The food is lovingly prepared in the small kitchen, and service is as it ought to be: cheerful, a little scatty but with its heart in the right place. The coarse and garlicky houmous makes a nice starter to whet the appetite and, if the weather's cool, order a hearty bowl of the *potage*, which varies according to which vegetables are in season. Main dishes come with salad, nicely-flavoured bulgur wheat and lentils, though the *curieuse*, a vegetarian tart surrounded by these accompaniments, was curiously dry. Goat's cheese or veggie stew were better choices. A good selection of organic wines is offered by the pitcher, along with Saison Dupont, a traditionally brewed organic beer. For dessert, go with a compote, made from seasonal fruit and served in a parfait glass.

JOE ALLEN
Since 1972
RESTAURANT BAR Terrasse

PARIS
NEW YORK
LONDON
MIAMI

Open daily noon-12.30am

30 rue Pierre Lescot, 1st
M° Etienne Marcel
Tel: 01.42.36.70.13
Fax: 01.42.36.90.80

International

Africa & Indian Ocean	**79**
The Americas	**81**
Caribbean	**84**
Eastern Mediterranean	**85**
Far East	**87**
Indian	**91**
Italian	**93**
Japanese	**96**
Jewish	**98**
North African	**99**
Spanish	**100**
Other International	**101**

ATHANOR

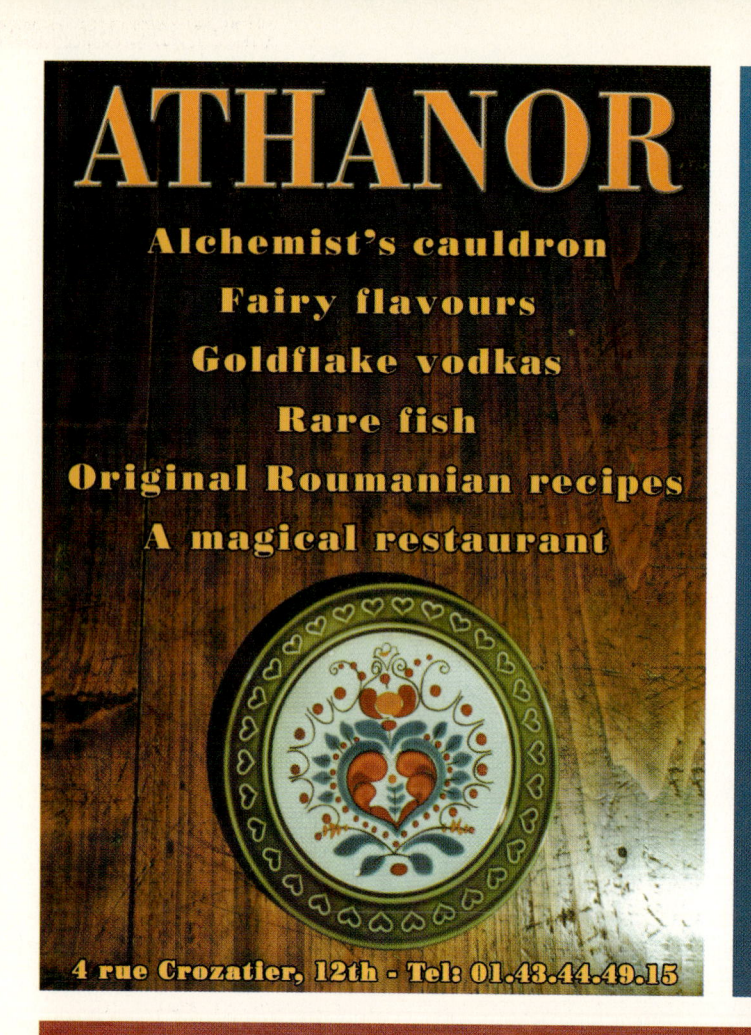

Alchemist's cauldron
Fairy flavours
Goldflake vodkas
Rare fish
Original Roumanian recipes
A magical restaurant

4 rue Crozatier, 12th - Tel: 01.43.44.49.15

Restaurant Ethiopia

For five consecutive years now, this Time Out favorite has managed to combine low prices with high quality

"One of the best places in Paris to discover this surprising cuisine"
Time Out Eating and Drinking Guide 1999

VEGETARIAN DISHES AVAILABLE

91 rue du Chemin Vert, 11th
Tel: 01.49.29.99.68. M° Voltaire or Père Lachaise

AU VILLAGE

Traditional Senegalese specialities

Come and discover "Yassa" (chicken or fish in a lemon and oignon marinade), "Tiéboudieune" (Senegal's national dish), "Mafé" (with beef or chicken with peanut sauce), and also Carribean specials such as acras, "boudin", traditional "Colombo" of kid.

Fantastic desserts: banana fritters, coconut "flan" or "thiakri" (millet semolina with milk, orange flowers and dried fruits)

Food served 7.30pm-midnight • Open until 2am

86 avenue Parmentier, 11th. M°Parmentier • Tel : 01.43.57.18.95
e-mail: auvillage@wanadoo.fr / Site: www.au-village.net

Africa & Indian Ocean

Tickle weary tastebuds with meaty *maffé*, fiery *féroce* and tangy *thieb'oudjen*.

The main immigrant populations in Paris either come from the Arabic-speaking former French colonies (*see p115*, **North African**), or Francophone West and Central Africa. Each country brings its own dishes to the table: from the ubiquitous *yassa* (citrus-soaked chicken) and *maffé* (groundnut paste served with meat) to the fish stew *thieb'oudjen* and *n'dolé* (bitter leaf sauce with smoked fish or chicken). In a region largely lacking green vegetables, grains, plantains and root vegetables mashed into a paste (such as *foufou*, made from cassava flour) compensate. The plate of meat with sauce complementing the side starch is the one common denominator (East Africa is represented by Ethiopian fare: fluffy *indjera* crêpes served with thick stews). Desserts aren't the focus – usually ice cream or a pineapple *flambée* suffices. Instead, the meal might be sweetened with kora or balafon music, or sincere service.

Au Coco de Mer ★

34 bd St-Marcel, 5th (01.47.07.06.64). M° St-Marcel or Les Gobelins. **Open** Mon 7.30-10.30pm; Tue-Sat 11.30am-2.30pm, 7.30-10.30pm. Closed two weeks in Aug. **Average** €37. **Prix fixe** €20.58, €25.92. **Credit** MC, V.

This cheerful little spot offers a trip to the Seychelles for the price of a Métro ticket. The atmosphere is decidedly festive and the food a tasty and reasonably authentic reprise of what you'd find on Praslin, one of the Seychelles. The front terrace is spread with fine white sand, while the ceiling in the yellow-painted main dining room is decorated with harmlessly ersatz palm crowns. Sample a *ti-ponch*, rum, lemon and cane syrup, while perusing the menu. Aside from the €20.58 *menu praslinois*, which offers chicken with saffron in coconut milk, lamb and aubergine curry, or sausages with *rougail*, a tomato and garlic sauce, the menu runs entirely to fish and shellfish, much of which is imported from the islands. Starters, rather more interesting than the main courses, include a delicious smoked swordfish carpaccio in a ginger, lemon and olive oil dressing, tuna tartare with fresh ginger, and dressed crab on a bed of avocado. Among the best main courses are the shark's meat curry, the octopus curry with chutney (the Seychelles have a large Indian population), and smoked tuna steak with a tangy barbecue sauce. Desserts include a pleasant frozen coconut cake with caramel sauce, passion fruit mousse or vanilla ice cream splashed with dark vintage rum. The €18.29 Côtes de Provence teams well with this cooking. Be sure to book, as it's especially popular on weekends.

Le Dogon

30 rue René Boulanger, 10th (01.42.41.95.85). M° République. **Open** Mon-Sat noon-3pm, 6.30pm-midnight. Closed one week in Aug. **Average** €23. **Lunch menu** €8.90. **Credit** MC, V.

The ground floor isn't much – an empty bar – but the second floor feels like a West African hideaway with its rattan ceilings, snake and leopard skins, and singer strumming his kora. A *bissap* (hibiscus flower juice) or zingy ginger juice, spiked or not, is a fine way to start as you mull over the diverse menu which mixes and matches dishes from Mali, Senegal, the Congo and the Ivory Coast. We settled on a moist prawn mousse (with a heartbreaking flourish of ketchup and mayonnaise) and the *assiette Dogon*, an unusual plate of okra, black-eyed peas, raw cabbage and bean sprouts. Salt cod fritters or stuffed pockets called *pastels* are more typical appetisers. Our neighbours went native – digging into their mains with their hands – while we used forks and spoons for our *foutou*, a mussel and prawn stew with *atieke*, a mashed root vegetable. The spicy chicken (*poulet spécial piment Dogon*), with a fresh, tomato-based hot sauce, was exceptionally juicy. We were licking our spoons after ice cream and the *mystère Congolais*, whose secret is revealed only to patrons of Le Dogon.

Ile de Gorée

70 rue Jean-Pierre-Timbaud, 11th (01.43.38.97.69). M° Parmentier. **Open** Mon-Sat 7-11.30pm. Closed two weeks in Aug. **Average** €22.87. **Credit** MC, V.

A fitting homage to the island just off Dakar's coast, this restaurant is an island of culinary excellence and conviviality amid a sea of ethnic restaurants and bass-thumping bars. Best to come early since a mix of locals quickly fills the small space, made all the more agreeable by the doting attention of the host and, on a good night, live kora music. Starters like *féroce*, an avocado, salt cod and manioc mixture with enough hot pepper to explain its name, or the just-fried salt cod fritters (*accras de morue*), could easily feed four so order conservatively. Slightly sweet and definitely smoky beef stew ladled on to deep-red *couscous sénégalais* makes its North African cousin pale in comparison. Similarly hued is Senegal's national dish, *thieb'oudjen*, a thick, though slightly dry, white fish in a piquant tomato and vegetable sauce. For dessert, pineapple, banana and mango fritters (*beignets éxotiques*) with intensely flavoured melon sorbet nicely round out the meal (and the belly). The wine list is short, with well-matched options for less than €15.

Au Petit Tam-Tam

137 rue Amelot, 11th (01.48.06.11.55). M° Filles du Calvaire or Oberkampf. **Open** Wed-Sat 8pm-dawn. Closed two weeks in Sept. **Average** €23. **Prix fixe** €18.29, €27.44. **Credit** MC, V.

Come to this cellar before 11pm and you will find yourself alone. It picks up the later it gets, as the band starts playing and diners become dancers. Service, as amiable and smiling as ever, has slowed considerably since our last visit – chances are you'll see no food for a good hour – and the minimal, hand-scrawled menu has been reduced with the change of chef. Skip the starters – small *boudin antillais* and lamb kebabs in a green *nene* sauce – and go straight to the main courses. The versatile green sauce went well with the tender sea bream, the only generous serving. Chicken *yassa*, more bone than chicken under the traditional onion and citrus sauce, left us hungry. Order the light, sweet fried plantains as accompaniment to everything but the *maffé* – lamb in peanut sauce which goes better with rice. Don't bother with dessert; just relax and enjoy the music.

Restaurant Ethiopia

91 rue du Chemin-Vert, 11th (01.49.29.99.68). M° Voltaire or Père Lachaise. **Open** daily 7pm-midnight. **Average** €16. **Prix fixe** €15. **Credit** AmEx, MC, V.

Wash your hands first: this food is consumed with *indjera*, a soft, spongy crêpe made of ground teff, an indigenous grain. Use the bread to grab little heaps of the *bäyyä anyätu*, the traditional Ethiopian meal (available here in ascending sizes). Our colourful meal for two (€30) arrived on a massive metal platter: chicken smothered in dark tomato sauce, whole hard-boiled eggs, curried beef, yellow split peas, spinach, and a tiny garden salad. After we'd licked that clean, we were presented with dollops of puréed orange lentils and sweet sautéed cabbage and carrots. When the gracious host, who served the entire restaurant single-handedly, inquired if we'd had enough to eat we opted for a third course of delicately spiced minced beef. These *à la carte* dishes cost €6 to €11 so if you want to try a few, order the *repas complet*.

Waly Fay

6 rue Godefroy-Cavaignac, 11th (01.40.24.17.79). M° Charonne or Faidherbe-Chaligny. **Open** Mon-Sat 8pm-12.30am. Closed one week in Aug. **Average** €23. **Credit** MC, V.

With minimalist decor – artfully distressed walls, subdued lighting, distant mood music, a few well-chosen objects – and utterly charming but unobtrusive staff, Waly Fay will lull everything but your palate into a total trance. From the first zap of ginger juice (wordlessly cut from our bill in apology for the previous week's lost reservation) to the final bitter shot of *fondant cocoa-café*, this is food with a punch, borrowed from West Africa, the Caribbean and, occasionally, France. The *accras de morue*, freshly fried salt cod fritters with spicy tomato chutney, and *boudin créole*, a spiced black pudding, were equally fiery and absolutely scrumptious. Chicken *yassa*, a West African standard stewed with onions and lemon, had just the right tang and its accompanying mound of plain steamed rice couldn't have been better. We were less convinced by the *n'dolé poisson fumé*, strips of a hardish, smoked fish blended with ground peanuts and wild, bitter spinach. Like everything else it was packed with flavour, but the predominance of bitter-smoke was, in the end, overwhelming. We couldn't imagine this food with wine – though La Volcanique from the Auvergne is a good buy at €12.50 – so we stuck to refeshing juices, ginger and bright red *bissap*.

Waly Fay: colonising French palates

Entoto

143-145 rue Léon-Maurice-Nordmann, 13th (01.45.87.08.51). M° Glacière. **Open** Tue-Sat 7.30-11pm. Closed two weeks in Aug. **Average** €19. **Credit** MC, V. **Wheelchair access.**

The Ethiopian food here challenges all but the heartiest appetites. You could order a three-course meal starting with *azifa* (a tangy lentil and lime mousse) or *yechuibra* (a heavy sauce smothering chickpea nuggets) but most likely a main alone will suffice. We ordered the *doro wott* (chicken cooked in its own fat, oregano and chillies) and the *végétarien*, served in little mounds on *indjera*, spongy bread used to scoop up the food. Salty spinach, sublime chickpeas, smooth yellow split peas, spicy chicken and hard-boiled egg, fresh aubergine, stewed courgettes and crumbled beef came prepared in spicy pastes. The *tedj*, a traditional honey wine, sweetly complemented all the flavours.

La Gazelle

9 rue Rennequin, 17th (01.42.67.64.18). M° Ternes. **Open** Mon-Fri noon-2pm, 7-11pm; Sat 7-11pm. Closed Aug. **Average** €38. **Prix fixe** €21.50, €24.50. **Credit** AmEx, DC, MC, V.

Whether to judge a restaurant by Western standards was our dilemma at La Gazelle. Its traditional cuisine from Senegal, Côte d'Ivoire and Cameroon challenged us. Should the *yassa*, a lemon and onion-based dish served with rice, have been topped with a prime cut of chicken, rather than the bony and fatty legs we received? Was the beef *n'dolé* overly salty and tough? The sauce of peanut and bitter leaf an acquired taste? Dishes had their merits in unusual sauces but left us thirsty. Admittedly, an apéritif of fresh juice and potent *punch Gazelle*, a brew of ginger, rum and spices, did not disappoint; nor did the starters of cod and prawn *beignets* with a spicy dipping sauce. Sides include chewy manioc, made with steamed cassava, tender plantains and the African starch staple, *foufou*. We wanted to love this schizophrenic place but considering the grand location, attentive service and high prices, we expected larger portions and more careful preparation.

Chez Aida

48 rue Polonceau, 18th (01.42.58.26.20). M° Barbès-Rochechouart or Château Rouge. **Open** Mon-Tue, Thur-Sun noon-midnight. Closed Aug. **Average** €11. **Credit** MC, V.

Motley paintings, travel posters and embossed copper scenes of village life create a Senegalese atmosphere. Reserved staff put on West African music for us and then brought over stunningly fresh, deep purple *bissap* and fresh ginger juices (also available with rum). The starter salad of avocado, prawns and greens was generous, while the fried crab *pastels* and their palm oil and onion relish reminded us of spicy Indian samosas. Crushed, oil-infused rice accompanied the *thieb'oudjen*, a powerful stew of carrots, manioc and white fish. A massive mound of chicken *yassa*, served with rice and a chilli pepper, struck us as one of the best versions we'd tasted. Oddly, no dessert was available on a quiet Sunday night.

Le Mono ★

40 rue Véron, 18th (01.46.06.99.20). M° Blanche or Abbesses. **Open** Mon-Tue, Thu-Sun 7-11.30pm. Closed Aug. **Average** €18. **Credit** MC, V.

Named after a river that crosses the south of Togo, Le Mono offers a refreshing break from typical West African cuisine with its variety of grilled fish and uncommon side dishes, served single-handedly by the easy-going host. The five different punches may knock you flat before the food; beware the powerful house lemon, ginger and rum concoction! Begin with stuffed crab, prawn fritters or *lélé*, tasty bean cakes smothered in tomato sauce, then launch into generous mains such as *akoboudessi*, a tomato-based mackerel and okra stew with an island of *pinon* (manioc paste) in the centre, or expertly grilled chicken with a hardy semolina cake called *akoume*. There are two plates for vegetarians plus other side dishes; fish lovers should try the sea bream, mullet, grouper, *capitaine* or *akpavi*, an African carp, cooked whole with *ablo* rice, tomatoes and onions. We were forgotten for a while but forgave all when the flaming pineapple finally arrived.

Brasil Tropical Montparnasse

Dinner – Performances
Gives you the new show
"YES BRAZIL"

Tuesday to Saturday from 8pm
Set menus from €50 during the week (drinks not included)
€70 & €85 on Fridays and Saturdays (drinks included)

36 rue du Départ, 15th - Reservations: 01.42.79.94.94

FAJITAS

MEXICAN RESTAURANT

"Miguel cooks deliciously fresh northern Mexican dishes with some southern specials among the starters(...) The signature fajitas with beef and chicken are a magnificent main."
Time Out Paris Penguin Guide 2002

OPEN DAILY NOON-11PM

15 RUE DAUPHINE, 6TH
M° ODEON / PONT NEUF
TEL: 01.46.34.44.69

SUSAN'S PLACE

Europe's Finest Chili! • 'Spécialité d'or' for Texas Nachos • Vegetarian Mexican Dishes

Susan will welcome you with Fajitas & a big Mexican starter for two with a **homemade Margarita**.
Try as well the delicious vegetarian dishes.
Don't miss Susan's excellent homemade desserts and the Mexican coffee...explosive!

51 rue des Ecoles, 5th (near bd St Michel). Tel: 01.43.54.23.22.
Open Tue-Sat noon-2.15pm, 7-11.30pm. Sun dinner only. Closed Mondays.

The Americas

If the French take on American fare seems skimpy, seek satisfaction south of the border.

There is no point in beating around the bush: Paris lacks convincing American restaurants. The closest you'll come to a decent hamburger is **Planet Hollywood** (the **Blue Bayou**'s are not bad either), and though many attempt to recreate the atmosphere of a big and boisterous US eatery, space is usually more cramped and portions smaller. Still, the Americans in Paris do attract a lively crowd of homesick expats and Parisians for their cocktails and copious brunches.

Fans of Latin American food will fare better. The best Mexican restaurants offer regional specialities: try sophisticated dishes at **A la Mexicaine**, **Anuhuacalli** and the newly-opened **Fajitas**. For a taste of Cuba, **El Paladar** serves up authentic atmosphere along with mounds of hearty food. At the ever-popular **Favela Chic**, you can move to the latest sounds while sipping potent Brazilian cocktails.

North America

Board Café Restaurant

8 rue Coquillère, 1st (01.40.28.97.98). M° Les Halles. **Open** daily 10.30am-2am. **Average** €25. **Prix fixe** €13.60, €18.60. **Lunch menu** €10.37. **Credit** AmEx, MC, V.

Claiming to be Paris' only 'extreme sports restaurant', Board is the Martha-Stewart-meets-Zen reincarnation of the former Chicago Meatpackers, whose new owners have taken fish-shaped lamps, big-screen TVs and demographic-straddling pop music (Beach Boys to Red Hot Chili Peppers) to new lows (though Tuesday and weekend Latino and funk parties liven things up). With endless surf and skateboard clips setting a frenetic pace, youthful staff scurry about the warren of rooms. Our awkward waiter had a charming habit of bowing after each encounter. Forgoing the starter/main tradition, the menu is curiously divided into 'medium', 'large', and 'extra large', each list corresponding to your cocktail-enhanced appetite. It's standard US-style bar fare – burgers, wings, nachos – plus oddball items like tagines, as well as grabs at Pacific Rim cuisine: Shanghai noodles, grilled fish and Hawaiian salad (grapefruit, prawns, coconut, palm hearts, avocado). The 'kemia board' was a plate of soggy, deep-fried squid, prawns, fritters and egg rolls. The tart key lime pie tasted mighty fine after that fat attack. We weren't sure who is targeted here – real surfers wouldn't set foot in this theme-park, though perhaps Board would be a fun tongue-in-cheek stop on a bar-hopping tour of Les Halles.

Joe Allen Restaurant

30 rue Pierre Lescot, 1st (01.42.36.70.13). M° Etienne-Marcel. **Open** daily noon-midnight. Closed Aug. **Average** €28. **Prix fixe** €18, €22.25. **Lunch menu** €12.20. **Credit** AmEx, MC, V. **Wheelchair access.**

This above-average, brick-walled American bistro, with siblings in New York and London, aims for a slightly more refined approach than the big Hollywood-inspired chains. Attentive bilingual staff deliver decent Stateside classics like Cajun chicken, sirloin steak and grilled tuna with some French touches. We enjoyed bread (and butter) before tender roasted vegetables and mozzarella arrived, along with an inventive salad topped with warm walnut-coated goat's cheese and cranberries. Grilled monkfish reminded us of sweet, buttery lobster, but the accompanying tomato sauce would have been better without the overpowering olives. Barbecued chicken remained moist beneath its average sauce, and we would have happily forgone the mayonnaise-laden coleslaw for more of those moist corn muffins. Vanilla ice cream came with chocolate chip cookies that made a decent stab at that fresh-baked flavour we miss so much. Joe Allen reminded us of cookouts back home.

Indiana Café

1 pl de la République, 3rd (01.48.87.82.35/ www.indiana-cafe.com). M° République. **Open** daily 9am-2am. **Average** €22. **Credit** DC, MC, V.

This restaurant sticks solidly to middle-of-the-road sports bar fare, reassuring homesick Americans (well-represented in the crowd), and attracting an international clientele with its large, reasonably-priced portions. Ketchup and A-1 bottles on every table, clichéd wall art evoking American Indians, and TVs in corners establish the ambiance. We ordered the mixed selection of Tex-Mex appetisers, which could have easily been shared among three or four, and found the guacamole, wings, nachos, and *taquitos* indifferently bland and the salsa tasteless. No sooner had that been whisked away than the waitress returned bearing two mini-mountains – our main courses. There were plenty of shoestring fries and the burgers were thick, juicy – and huge. Elegant it's not, but it's not expected to be, so it would be quibbling to complain that the blue cheese burger's sauce was watery and too strong or that the overdose of mayonnaise was unwelcome. If you have room for dessert, the two-inch-high cheesecake looked promising; or indulge in some of Ben & Jerry's most popular flavours (although, sadly, not Cookie Dough). Service was impeccable, friendly and very speedy. A good place if you're really hungry or want to have appetisers and drinks American-style.

Branches: 7 bd des Capucines, 2nd (01.42.68.02.22); 130 bd St-Germain, 6th (01.46.34.66.31); 235/237 rue du Fbg St-Honoré, 8th (01.44.09.80.00); 79 bd de Clichy, 9th (01.48.74.42.61); 14 place de la Bastille, 11th (01.44.75.79.80); 72 bd du Montparnasse, 14th (01.43.35.36.28).

The Studio

41 rue du Temple, 4th (01.42.74.10.38). M° Hôtel-de-Ville. **Open** Mon 7.30-11pm, Tue-Sun 12.30-11pm. **Average** €25. **Credit** AmEx, V. **Wheelchair access.**

The Studio's Renaissance exterior and its view onto an ancient cobbled courtyard housing a multi-storey dance school doesn't quite jibe with the salsa music, moody lighting and long bar lined with tequila bottles. But your first pitcher of slushy lime margaritas should stir up a hankering for the *nueva* Mexican grub happily delivered here. You could start off with chicken wings but most appetisers are stingy compared to the hefty mains, and you may not need them. We enjoyed the lightly fried spinach and cheese wrap, which arrived in bite-sized slices with rice and a piquant *chipotle* chilli sauce. Tasting a little pre-fab, the Phoenix chicken breast was a decent idea poorly executed – soggy pea, broccoli, cauliflower filling and the old onion rings on the side were a real put-off. Dessert is an event. Heralded by strange bells, whistles and hooting from the kitchen our *capricho* – a mountain of cinnamon ice cream, caramel sauce, whipped cream and sugared tortilla crisps that we were only too happy to scale – arrived at the table. Despite the cuisine's shortcomings, The Studio is worth visiting for its atmospheric terrace.

Buffalo Grill

1 bd St-Germain, 5th (01.56.24.34.49/ www.buffalo-grill.com). M° Jussieu. **Open** Mon-Thur, Sun 11am-11pm; Fri, Sat 11am-midnight. Closed 24 Dec. **Average** €15. **Prix fixe** €10.50. **Credit** MC, V.

The chilli con carne will not blow your head off, the burgers are not the plumpest in town and the rib marinade will not leave you begging for the secret recipe. What Buffalo Grill does have, however, is cheery service, a friendly, American-style atmosphere (pictures of cowboys and American Indians, a twang of country music, fringed, red lampshades and cosy booths) and something for everyone. While the emphasis is on steaks, ribs, burgers and Buffalo wings, there's also salmon in Béarnaise sauce, cheese and *tarte Tatin*. Admittedly, the mayonnaise on the complimentary salad was mildly mouth-puckering and the only garnish on the Texan platter was a moist towelette in a foil sachet but the Buffalo burger was satisfactory, the spare ribs lean and tender, and the chocolate brownies worthy of Grandma.

Branches include: 117 av du Général Leclerc, 14th (01.45.40.09.72); 15 pl de la République, 3rd (01.40.29.94.98); 36 bd des Italiens, 9th (01.53.24.19.15).

The Chicago Pizza Pie Factory

5 rue Berri, 8th (01.45.62.50.23). M° Georges V. **Open** daily noon-1am. **Average** €24. **Prix fixe** €16.80. **Lunch menu** €9.30-€12. **Child's menu** €8.50. **Credit** AmEx, MC, V.

Factory is the operative word here: deep-dish pies, salads and nachos churned out with little regard for originality or quality. An enormous Chinatown chicken salad plate had a vaguely pleasing peanutty taste but the oversweet dressing was laid on too thick. Puffy garlic bread soaked up its grease like a sponge (and tasted a bit like one). The pizza itself arrived in an unattractive, well-scorched pan. A dense vegetarian pizza's crisp crust seemed inviting at first, and the roasted aubergine, red pepper and courgette tasted fresh. After the second slice, however, its molecular structure transformed into something closer to a gooey doorstop. It is against our religion to leave a dessert half-eaten, but we made an exception after being served a shamelessly inedible apple pie (not rescued by a plop of vanilla ice cream). Perhaps this place appeals to dazed Champs-Elysées shoppers, but they would be wiser to hit any number of better, non-chain pizzerias than risk the cheesy fires of this inferno.

Planet Hollywood

76-78 av des Champs-Elysées, 8th (01.53.83.78.27/www.planethollywood.com). M° Franklin D. Roosevelt. **Open** daily noon-1am. **Average** €23. **Lunch menu** €13.57. **Credit** AmEx, DC, MC, V. **Wheelchair access.**

The waiters look pubescent and perform slowly under stress. The crowd mixes weary tourists with Parisians who enjoy a good joke. Our neighbours included a young British couple alternately sipping Coke, beer and white wine, and a female-VIP type dining with her mobile phone and absentmindedly picking at what looked like a sampler plate of eight desserts. Welcome to Planet Hollywood. You might start with a fresh, creative cocktail, such as a frozen mango mojito or a non-alcoholic fruit smoothie, then launch into the tasty and gigantic grilled Cajun shrimp with mustard. Eschewing ribs, bacon cheeseburgers and onion rings, expect the worst – and then be pleasantly surprised by the sizzling *fajitas* served with a massive plate of raw garnishes, including super-juicy giant mushrooms. The Asian chicken salad is a formidable mountain of salad to be sure, but the cold chicken strips are stacked like kindling and almost as dry. American-style desserts abound; do not finish off the evening with a very boozy and gloppy bread pudding with vanilla ice cream. If you enjoy dining to the racket of car chases and explosions, under the ever watchful gaze of a prosthetic severed dog's head (from the film *Pet Sematary II*), Charlie Sheen's *Platoon* trousers and other props, costumes and celebrity shots, Planet Hollywood is for you.

Hard Rock Café

14 bd Montmartre, 9th (01.53.24.60.00/ www.hardrockcafe.com). M° Grands Boulevards. **Open** daily 11.30am-2am. **Average** €23. **Children's menu** €5.95. **Credit** AmEx, DC, MC, V. **Wheelchair access.**

Many have spent the better part of two decades deprogramming themselves from the 1980s, but if you're the nostalgic type, the Hard Rock Café delivers a cryogenically-thawed formula of music and food. Housed in a redone theatre dressed with pop memorabilia, music videos and red-checked tablecloths, the emphasis is on burgers, barbecues, beer and lightning-quick service with a smile. Not only do you have to tolerate below-par food but also self-serving 'Save the Planet' sloganeering on the menus and walls. The insubstantial Santa Fe spring rolls starter contained a bland mush of chicken, spinach and monterey jack cheese. Sugary fries and inedible baked beans partnered an industrial-quality pork sandwich, processed smooth enough to eat with a straw. A passable veggie burger was inexplicably served with two baked potatoes. An overpowering chocolate brownie with vanilla ice cream struck us as too little (or too much) too late.

Blue Bayou ★

111-113 rue St-Maur, 11th (01.43.55.87.21). M° Parmentier or St-Maur. **Open** Mon-Sat noon-2pm, 7.30pm-midnight; Sun 11am-5pm (brunch). **Average** €26. **Prix fixe** €12-€26. **Credit** MC, V.

The Blue Bayou is adamantly not American. 'We're a Cajun restaurant', a waitress told us politely but firmly on the phone. To reinforce the point, Coca Cola is not even served – we settled for lemonade and beer. The decor backs up the Cajun claim: dead animals on the walls (rather callously displayed next to traps), mining lights, chilli peppers, twiggy chairs and what appears to be a real, though not living, alligator. What makes the Blue Bayou more authentically American than many pretenders, though, is size. The dining room feels airy and spacious, and portions are satisfyingly unfinishable. In the heart of the Oberkampf bar scene, this restaurant is busiest in the evenings and for its hangover-bustin' Sunday brunches (€12), which are less impressively fresh than they used to be. We stopped in for lunch and in true Louisiana spirit we ordered the jambalaya, a hearty plate of nicely spiced sausage, chicken, peppers and rice. We also couldn't resist a Baton Rouge burger, whose juicy meat had a pleasing hand-shaped look even if the bun didn't – but pre-fab bread can hardly be considered a crime in a hamburger. This was served with a creamy potato gratin, quashing any French fry fantasies. Desserts are not the strong point, so you might want to finish off your meal with a game of billiards downstairs.

Latin America

A la Mexicaine ★

68 rue Quincampoix, 3rd (01.48.87.99.34). M° Rambuteau or Les Halles. **Open** Mon 8-11pm; Wed-Sat noon-3pm, 8-11pm. **Average** €23. **Prix fixe** €23, €45. **Lunch menu** €15. **Child's menu** €12. **Credit** AmEx, MC, V. **Wheelchair access.**

Anyone who knows and loves Mexican food will come away from this charming cantina grateful to Yurira Iturriaga, the fiery proprietor who leads a one-woman crusade against the tide of Tex-Mex mediocrity in Paris that obscures how sophisticated and delicious real Mexican food can be. The amber painted walls, hung with Iturriaga's collection of Mexican ceramics, help pull a crowd of regulars who know how good the food is. The tacos are made from scratch, which you would expect in a restaurant founded by a woman who used to be director of the Mexican Cultural Centre in Paris and who is also a journalist for one of the country's leading opposition papers. Beyond the superb guacamole, come here for tacos stuffed with cheese or chicken, marinated pork with black beans, chicken *pipau*, and all of the dishes made from delicious Argentine beef. Finish with the rich cake made from chocolate, maize flour and eggs, and do try some Mexican wine.

Anahi
49 rue Volta, 3rd (01.48.87.88.24). M° Arts et Metiers. **Open** daily 8pm-midnight. Closed 15 Aug, Christmas and New Year. **Average** €40. **Credit** MC, V.

Anahi is one of those insider addresses. Tucked in an unprepossessing part of the Marais, the only thing that distinguishes it from its neighbours is that Anahi looks like the building most likely to fall down – the exterior isn't so much distressed as severely traumatised. Members of the in-crowd are greeted cheek to cheek by the owners in the stylishly stark interior. In this former butcher's shop the white tiling is interrupted by a few black and white photos and bottles of South American liquor, which contrast nicely with the faded art deco ceiling. Based on its appearance you would expect this restaurant to be costly. With prices like these you would hope that the food would be, at the very least, palatable. Sadly the price lived up to expectations and the food didn't. We started with *soupa veiras*, a rather thin saffron soup with scallops, and *jamón*, as described, a very large plate of (unexceptional) ham. The biggest disappointment of all, however, was the Argentine steak. Served on a wooden board with a green side salad, the steak was much thinner than anticipated and was neither tender nor tasty. It was hard to see what the €22.10 was for. The chicken marinated in lemon was tough, the lemon sauce had hardened and the accompanying pineapple chunks looked like escapees from a take-away pizza. Anahi is friendly and the atmosphere is relaxed, and for those with a passion for South American wines it's almost worth a detour.

Anuhuacalli
30 rue des Bernardins, 5th (01.43.26.10.20). M° Maubert Mutualité. **Open** Mon-Sat 7-11pm; Sun noon-2pm. Closed Aug. **Average** €29. **Credit** MC, V.

Regarded by many as the best Mexican restaurant in the capital, Anuhuacalli doesn't trumpet its origins with displays of sombreros and fake cacti. Rather, as befits a restaurant that is serious about food, the decor is elegant and low-key, putting the interest squarely on the the regional specialities dished up by the kitchen. Start with *sopa Azteca*, a rich tomato soup with a smoky pork base, chilli, cheese, and a layer of corn chips, or *cazuela de huevos*, a just-baked egg in a broth of peas, corn, cactus, mushrooms and sour cream. Mains include *tamales*, burritos and excellent *enchiladas verdes*, stuffed with chicken (or beef), covered with a spicy green *tomatillo* sauce and baked with a layer of cheese. Also on offer is the Pueblan classic *mole poblano*, turkey cooked in a sauce containing 20 or more seasonings, including chocolate. Mexican restaurants stand or fall on their *mole* and Anuhuacalli's is top-notch: thick, dark and expertly spiced. Also good is the Yucatan *cochinita pibil* – marinated pork cooked in banana leaves. For dessert, bypass the crème caramel with cinnamon and try ice creams or sorbets with a punch: lemon and pineapple with lashings of tequila.

Botequim
1 rue Berthollet, 5th (01.43.37.98.46). M° Censier Daubenton. **Open** Mon-Sat noon-2pm, 8-11.30pm; Sun 8-11.30pm. **Average** €30. **Credit** MC, V.

In the Carioca slang spoken with pride in Rio de Janeiro, *botequim* refers to a small, scruffy neighbourhood bar or restaurant serving food in a casual, no-fuss atmosphere. Import such a concept to Paris and it's bound to get dressed up a bit. The mood is lightened by jovial groups of not-too-young, not-too-old French, leisurely enjoying the excellent food. Follow their lead and start your meal with a caipirinha, a potent cocktail made with fresh lime, lots of sugar and Brazil's liquid passion, cachaÿa. Mains are huge but if you want a starter, try the *panaché*, a sampling of well-prepared Brazilian snacks, or the fluffy *aipo*, a celery mousse topped with a tangy prawn-flavoured dressing. As a main, there really is no avoiding the superb *feijoada*, Brazil's national dish made from several cuts of fresh and salted meats stewed with black beans and served up with rice, garlicky sautéed greens, orange slices and a grainy manioc flour called *faraofa*. Lighter, but just as good, the *camarao en moqueca* is a modified (possibly improved) traditional Bahian stew of succulent prawns, coconut milk and coriander. A varied selection of *quindim* and *pudim*, Brazilian confections made with coconuts and eggs, promise to seduce your sweet tooth.

El Palenque
5 rue de la Montagne-Ste-Geneviève, 5th (01.43.54.08.99). M° Maubert-Mutualité. **Open** Mon-Sat 12.30-2.30pm, 8-10.30pm. Closed Aug. **Average** €40. **No credit cards.**

El Palenque has long prided itself on serving some of the best beef in Paris, imported straight from the clean grass of the Argentine *pampa* (reassuring in these days of mad cow). As good as the beef is, its perfection relies upon the extraordinary grill and the gifted hand that oversees it, perfectly recreating the charred flavour of a barbecue. Whet your appetite with a zingy Peruvian pisco sour, made with fresh lime juice, and bear down for the *parillada completa* for two, a wealth of grilled meats including *morcilla* (black pudding), *chorizos criollos* (Argentine sausage), *molleja* (sweetbreads), *riñon* (kidneys) and *asado de tira*, a cut of meat which resembles but far exceeds the more pedestrian short rib. Accompanied by a light green salad, the meal would still be incomplete without a portion of vinegary *palmitos*, hearts of palm, or savoury, cold corn pancakes, *torrejas de choclo*. The superb flan *con dulce de leche* promises to send you over the edge, pairing a dense egg pudding with a good-sized dollop of the cherished condensed milk sweet.

Mexi & Co
10 rue Dante, 5th (01.46.34.14.12). M° Cluny-La-Sorbonne. **Open** daily 10am-midnight. Closed Christmas and New Year. **Average** €15. **No credit cards.**

Handkerchief-sized Mexi & Co has a ceiling heavy with south-of-the-border paraphernalia (*piñatas*, Sol-beer-bottle chandelier, and spice packets galore) and walls groaning with Americana munchies (cranberry juice, peanut butter and cookies). Stick with perennial favourites: guacamole, nachos and basic burritos (sold out on our visit) rather than fancy fare such as the vegetarian special of poorly heated carrot and cheese, peas, beans and coriander and a watery coconut sauce in a mushy spinach tortilla. For sweet tooths, there are brownies, a sugary pecan pie and ice cream. Help yourself to Mexican beer and Latino wine from the fridge. Low prices, friendly staff and the jumble-shop atmosphere encourage a young, friendly French-American crowd. Munchkin stools and tables skirt the walls and a communal breakfast bar with high chairs takes up centre space.

La Casa del Habano
169 bd Saint Germain, 6th (01.45.44.33.56). M° St-Germain-des-Prés. **Open** (restaurant) Mon-Sat noon-2.30pm, 7.30-11.15pm. **Average** €38. **Prix fixe** €22.87. **Credit** AmEx, DC, MC, V.

Throw the keys of your Porsche Carrera 912 or BMW Z3 roadster to one of the parking boys and step into a man's world. After all, it takes a lot of puff to master a complex, 235mm-long, Monte Cristo A. If you need practise, the easy option is to join the cigar club which meets in a private room on the second floor. The elegant cedar-wood bar on the ground floor, open to everyone, serves racy rum-based cocktails such as the Cuba libre, rum Alexander, mojito and the Ernest Hemingway special; but if you prefer to keep your head while savouring a double Corona, stick to the excellent coffee. The most satisfying moment to light up, though, has to be after an excellent meal, which is why owner Louis-Gérard Biret offers a sleek, air-conditioned dining area beyond the bar. Meat is the big draw: our lush *rumsteack d'Uruguay*, too big for the plate, resembled a map of the country, while the superbly tender *entrecôte poêlée* suits less intrepid appetites. Side dishes of potatoes mashed with goose fat, fresh spinach and fat chips, along with a mellowing bottle of St-Emilion left us happily sated on the immaculate leather banquette.

Fajitac ★
15 rue Dauphine, 6th (01.46.34.44.69). M° Odéon. **Open** Tue-Sun noon-11pm; Mon 7-11pm. **Average** €24. **Prix fixe** €18.50. **Lunch menu** €9 (Tue-Fri). **Credit** AmEx, MC, V.

A Mexican/American husband-and-wife team run this colourful new restaurant in St Germain, but there is very little Tex in the Mex; slim, quietly spoken Amy who does the front of house is as far from a brash Texan as you could find. Miguel cooks deliciously fresh northern Mexican dishes with some southern specials among the starters. The *ceviche* – fish marinated in lime – with *sauce caraïbe* was no longer available when we ordered, but the *cocktail de cameroñes* recommended in its place almost made up for it with its tangy lime sauce and liberal sprinkling of fresh coriander over tiny, firm and tasty prawns. The guacamole got the thumbs-up for its homemade consistency and the addition of small tomato pieces. For mains we chose the signature *fajitas* with beef and chicken and a chicken burrito, both flavourful and pleasingly light. Miguel is a champion of the *fajita*'s untapped potential. In an effort to hook the French he has devised the mini-wrap – miniature *fajitas* with wildly adventurous fillings including tandoori chicken. Lightly fried, they make a fine take-away lunch and a selection of them can be ordered as a main. They also feature as puddings – the banana and caramel one is ambrosial. The drinks list includes South American wines that are expensive by French standards but there is a small selection of cheaper French ones, a choice of Mexican beers and excellent cocktails including a frozen margarita which, though it comes out of a machine, is made from fresh ingredients.

Arriba Mexico
32 av de la République, 11th (01.49.29.95.40). M° Parmentier or République. **Open** daily 10.30am-2.30pm, 6.30pm-1am. **Average** €20. **Prix fixe** €21.34-€39.64. **Lunch menu** €8.99. **Credit** AmEx, MC, V.

Certainly the average Mexican family would not actually wear colourful straw sombreros while at the dinner table but, then again, they probably wouldn't drink margaritas by the

There's no shortage of Brazil nuts at Favela Chic

pitcherful (€31.25), either. What we have here is a fun theme restaurant which uses surprisingly fresh ingredients in its plentiful offerings. Standard mains like burritos, *tostadas, fajitas, enchiladas, quesadillas, flautas* and tacos are available (most €10.67), but more unusual fare includes a Mexican *ceviche* (salmon marinated in lime juice) and the vegetarian *galetta*, which takes the French-like crêpe further with tomato, cheese, cactus and spicy *pico de gallo*. *Parilladas* are grilled meats, and the *tacos mole* use unsweetened cocoa as the base of a dark sauce to accompany a tender chicken filling. Margarita pie or flan make fine finishers, if you haven't already overdosed on Mexican wine or beer, not to mention that not-yet-empty pitcher. Oh, on your way out, don't forget to return your hat.

El Paladar
26bis rue de la Fontaine au Roi, 11th. (01.43.57.42.70). M° *République or Goncourt.* **Open** *Mon-Sat 8pm-2am.* **Average** €27. **Credit** MC, V.
Grafitti-covered pink and aqua walls and wooden tables set the tone at this four-year-old Cuban outpost (customers are encouraged to add their scribbles). Despite El Paladar being out of Cuban beer and mineral water (the host offered us 'Château de Paris' tap water as consolation), the outgoing staff was happy to explain the regularly-changing menu of Cuban food borrowing from the fried and stewed schools of cooking. *Yuca con mojo*, sautéed manioc with onions and garlic, proved oily but nonetheless delicious, and *tostones*, batter-fried plantains, were surprisingly light and crispy. Main dishes include pork, chicken, fish and an impressive load of veggies and eggs, the *arroz a la cubana*. We sampled *pavo saltiado* – stewed turkey and potatoes seasoned with bay leaves – and a *pollo pio-pio*, chicken fried in citrus. The *pescado guisado* fish struck the only false note with its oddly muddy sauce of tomatoes, garlic, onions, potatoes and peppers. Overall the dishes had substance and character. The *flan maison*, a stupendous sugar-soaked coconut custard, ended the meal on a high note.

Favela Chic ★
18 rue du Fbg-du-Temple, 11th (01.40.21.38.14/www.favelachic.com). M° *République.* **Open** *Mon-Sat 8pm-2am.* **Average** €28. **Credit** MC, V. **Wheelchair access**.
Holy chic, this place is popular. Hidden down an alley that's home to an array of start-ups, this Brazilian cantina-cum-nightclub has hit a nerve judging by the crowds of people downing cocktails by the bar and feeding elbow-to-elbow on rows of wooden benches and tables. The shabby chic decor comprising bouquets of foliage and flowers, exposed heating/cooling ducts, industrial walls, distressed furniture (and clients to match) might have a thrown-together feel but no doubt careful planning is behind it. A tiled open kitchen means you can check out the cooking action and, like the music, it's furious. We waited no time at all for caipiroskas (vodka with crushed limes) and tapas of fried manioc chips, cheese puffs and fish fritters with a creamy dip. *Pasta de Itacaré*, pasta with prawns and cherry tomatoes in a creamy coconut sauce, tasted fine despite an avalanche of parmesan. *Liberdade de San Paolo*, grilled smoked chicken with grilled mango, onion and ginger confit, puréed pumpkin and peanut rice, also worked well. A dense *chocococo fondant* finished us off. Though prices seem to have crept up, conversation is nigh impossible, and smoke gets in your eyes and food, the party shows no signs of flagging.

Taco Loco
116, rue Amelot, 11th (01.43.57.90.24). M° *Filles du Calvaire.* **Open** *Tue-Sat noon-4pm, 7pm-midnight; Mon 7pm-midnight. Closed two weeks in Aug.* **Average** €17. **Credit** MC, V. **Wheelchair access**.
Because we know from long experience that finding tasty, authentic Mexican food in Paris is a challenge, we didn't expect much. But neither did we expect to be so disappointed by Taco Loco. The guacamole and homemade tortilla chips were decent, but the *tostados* – crispy corn tortillas topped with a choice of beans, chicken or beef with lettuce, sour cream and tomato – were swimming in a pool of water. This defeated the purpose of the *tostado*, which should be brought to the mouth by hand and explode in a thunderous crunch. The *enchiladas verdes* were nicely tangy but meagerly filled with boiled chicken. Slopped together on the plate and coated with shredded emmental, they demonstrated a singular lack of imagination, especially given that better substitutes for Mexican cheese are readily available in France. We fared no better with *enchiladas mole*. The complex Mexican *mole* sauce lacked depth and tasted strongly of vinegar. Both plates came with boiled rice, re-fried beans and salad. The house margarita had strong lemon overtones and not much tequila flavor, and the plastic bottle of mineral water served at a restaurant price did not impress. Taco Loco is not meant to be sophisticated, but regrettably it shows scant respect for Mexico's varied and delicious cuisine.

El Bodegon de Pancho
8 rue Guy-Môquet, 17th (01.53.31.00.73). M° *Brochant.* **Open** *Tue-Sun noon-2am. Closed 24 Dec-4 Jan.* **Average** €12. **Prix fixe** €10.70. **Credit** MC, V.
Half-bar, half-restaurant and a meeting place for the neighbourhood's expanding Colombian population, this place fills early with gregarious young men and a few couples looking to speak Spanish, drink some beer, listen to salsa and *ranchera* music and play a few rounds of *sapo*, an impossibly difficult Andean game that involves trying to toss little metal discs into a bronze frog's mouth. Without gourmet pretensions, the fare consists of everyday dishes relished for their hearty simplicity. A few *empanadas*, hot potato and corn fritters filled with lightly curried ground beef and onions, pair off perfectly with a cold beer, and tide you over while you wait for a main course. The enormous *bandeja paisa* features various cuts of pork, curry-flecked red beans, fried eggs, rice, salad and a small piece of bland hominy-based Colombian bread that takes on a whole new life when you dip it into beans. For dessert, the *aborrajado* successfully marries fried green banana and guava paste with a salty sliver of Andean cheese to remind you, if you've somehow forgotten, that you have travelled to a world far, far away from Paris. Happy and full, you may feel reluctant to leave.

Go spice skating at tiny Mexi & Co

Caribbean

Sample the sizzling cooking and cocktails of the French Caribbean. The isles have it!

Paris has a sizeable community of some 200,000 people from the French *Antilles* – many came to study and stayed to work. Similar to African cooking, French Caribbean specialities show an Asian influence – as in *colombo*, the *antillais* take on curry. A meal generally starts with a rum-based *ti ponch* and salt cod fritters (*accras*), continues with grilled fish or a hearty stew and ends with fresh fruit or ice cream.

La Paillotte des Iles ★
16 rue Thorel, 2nd (01.45.08.58.22). M° Bonne Nouvelle. **Open** daily 12.30-2.30pm, 7.30pm-midnight. **Average** €20. **Prix fixe** €19.80-€32. **Lunch menu** €10.50-€15. **No credit cards**.
'Ooh all that's missing is the sea,' as the old Wham! song goes; but don't worry, there are wall-to-wall murals of it, plus sand-coloured velvet banquettes, vibrant yellow tablecloths and fake roses complete with remarkably realistic dew drops. Our waitress was adorable as she tried to explain the extensive *à la carte* menu. In the end we opted for the €32 menu, which included a house apéritif – a kind of planter's punch, distinctly medicinal but in a nice way – and half-bottle of decent rosé. The meal got off to a great start with a salad of sweet potatoes which was more about delicious fresh crab meat, prawns, crisp green salad and a creamy herb sauce, and spicy *accras de morue*, salt cod fritters. Our mains were a *colombo de capitaine*, a meaty, big-boned fish lightly curried with tangy herbs and served with fluffy rice and a pot of red beans in thick gravy, and *maffe*, an African dish of tender lamb stewed in a peanut sauce that can only be described as ambrosial. Sadly the *tourment d'amour* (a kind of gâteau) was replaced by a banana *flambé* (more medicinal rum). On weekends there is a disco dance floor downstairs.

Le Marais-Cage
8 rue de Beauce, 3rd (01.48.87.31.20). M° Temple. **Open** Mon-Fri noon-2pm, 7-10pm; Sat 7-10pm. **Average** €28. **Prix fixe** €16-€29. **Lunch menu** €14, €21.50. **Credit** AmEx, DC, MC, V.
Instead of trying to evoke the Caribbean with a neo-tropical decor, Le Marais-Cage is content to spirit you away on the strength of its cooking – and since the food is vividly seasoned and delicious, it works. The €29 *menu* is a good buy: a cocktail – rum with lime or a planter's punch – some of the best *accras* (salt cod fritters spiked with Cayenne pepper) in town, two generously served courses, plus dessert or coffee. Start with the *féroce martiniquais*, a pleasant mash of avocado, salt cod and Cayenne pepper, or the gratin of christophene squash, and then try the succulent *colombo de porc*, chunks of pork stewed in a rich, oniony sauce, or the shark *court-bouillon*, a thick slice of shark in a sweet sauce of tomatoes, onions and peppers with bay leaf. All main courses come with rice and red beans, and desserts run to sorbets and crêpes flamed in rum. The wine list is pricey and a bit drab, but the red Menetou-Salon goes well with this food.

La Table D'Erica
6 rue Mabillon, 6th (01.43.54.87.61). M° Mabillon. **Open** Tue-Sat noon-2pm, 7-11pm; Sun, Mon 7-11pm. Closed Aug. **Average** €38. **Prix fixe** €22.70. **Lunch menu** €10.37. **Credit** AmEx, MC, V.
A tiny walkway leads to this multi-level Creole hideaway whose diverse menu lets you dive headfirst into Caribbean classics such as octopus stew, prawns in coconut milk, West Indian *cassoulet*, lime-marinated fish and other chicken, beef and seafood dishes. The *féroce d'avocat* combined cod, manioc and avocado in a tasty paste, though we wish we'd been given more than one cracker. A fresh, cold crab and papaya salad was tossed in a light dressing that accentuated the crab. Both starters hinted at what quality the kitchen might produce on a more focused night. What should have been the star dish, a €27.44 lobster *à la Créole*, was a tragedy, its flesh scant, rubbery, and cold, its pre-split body stuffed with bland veggies. The tepid, soggy, and bony 'island fish' was only salvaged by hot pepper sauce. We left feeling disappointed, not in the mood to risk dessert.

Le Flamboyant
11 rue Boyer-Barret, 14th (01.45.41.00.22). M° Pernety. **Open** Tue 8-10.45pm; Wed-Sat noon-2pm, 8-10.45pm; Sun noon-2pm. Closed Aug. **Average** €24. **Lunch menu** €11. **Credit** AmEx, MC, V.
No detail is neglected here: vivid decor, clairvoyant service, and patient explanations by both the waiter and chef of intriguingly named menu items such as *blaff*, *blanc manger* and *igname* (a poached fish, coconut pudding and root vegetable, respectively). We nibbled on complimentary cod *beignets* as we scanned the extensive menu. Avoiding decisions, we settled on the *assiette composée* (€13), a two-person sampler of tartlets filled with avocado, crab, fish and aubergine and accompanied by an island-inspired black pudding. Main dishes took our breath away: Haitian chicken in succulent coconut curry, and the lime-infused *blaff*, both accompanied by perfect white rice and gravy-laden red beans. By the end of our near-perfect meal, we had been invited into the kitchen and felt like one of the family.

Island spice at Le Flamboyant

Eastern Mediterranean

Wrap your tongue around regional specialities and you might even learn to love *Isnat*.

The Latin Quarter and rue Mouffetard abound with Greek joints which entice tourists with cheap set *menus*. If you're craving something a little more adventurous, though, Paris has plenty to offer – from Lebanese *Isnat* (hot or cold tongue) to Kurdish *kavourma* (spicy beef and pepper stew). **Mavrommatis** and its more casual offspring **Les Délices d'Aphrodite** have long set the standard for Greek gastronomic excellence in Paris, while the 15th *arrondissement* harbours the city's most authentic Lebanese food, thanks to a wave of immigration in the 1980s.

Les Délices d'Aphrodite ★

4 rue de Candolle, 5th (01.43.31.40.39) M° Censier Daubenton. **Open** Mon-Sat noon-2.30pm, 7-11.30pm. **Average** €28. **Lunch menu** €14.30, €14.60. **Credit** MC, V.

The relaxed, friendly atmosphere and delicious food at this very good and extremely well-run Latin Quarter Greek is likely to incite an urgent desire to travel to Greece itself in search of more of same. Owned by the Mavrommatis brothers, who also run nearby Mavrommatis, this simple dining room with framed pictures of Greece, blue upholstery and an ivy trellis overhead is very popular with a diverse crowd of arty locals, resident Greeks and tourists. What really pleases here is the authenticity of the details and the great produce, plus the buzz of people having a good time over good food. We loved first courses of grilled feta and halloumi cheese, brightened with very aromatic oregano and served with a pleasant and well-dressed salad, and flavourful *spanakopita*, a flaky pastry stuffed with spinach and also served with salad. Main courses of *pastitsio* (pasta, ground pork, tomatoes and béchamel sauce) and *keftedes*, airy deep-fried balls of ground lamb served with diced courgettes and carrots in tomato sauce, were wonderful, too. Not too keen on retsina, we went with the Nemea, a red from the Peloponnese region that teamed perfectly with this food, and lingered over flaky baklava and coffee well into the night without feeling that anyone was edging us towards the door. A perfect night off from French food, but come with a hearty appetite, as portions are generous.

Mavrommatis

5 rue du Marché des Patriarches, 5th (01.43.31.17.17). M° Censier Daubenton. **Open** Tue-Sun noon-2.30pm, 7-11pm. Closed Aug **Average** €37. **Prix fixe** €27.45. **Credit** MC, V.

Two hundred metres and a world away from the pushy moussaka boys of the rue Mouffetard, here is an embassy for a refined and cultivated Greece where there's no 'Greek salad' on the menu and nothing is painted white and blue. It seems magical that something as creamy as houmous can come from something as inauspicious as a chickpea and our starter was a good contrast of richness and lemony zing. To follow, we chose a leg of lamb, cooked slowly after the 'style of the resistance fighters of 1821'. Good name but a bit dry. Or maybe that's how resistance fighters liked their lamb back then. In any case, sexily juicy and dusted with cumin and cinnamon, the *steftalia* sausages were much more interesting and well-accompanied by what is probably the best retsina you can find outside Greece, Kourtaki from Attica. The milk cream with orange flower water was good but their Greek coffee is out of this world.

La Voie Lactée

34 rue du Cardinal-Lemoine, 5th (01.46.34.02.35). M° Cardinal-Lemoine **Open** Mon-Sat noon-2.30pm, 7-11pm. Closed Aug. **Average** €17. **Prix fixe** €14-€17. **Lunch menu** €9.50, €12. **Credit** MC, V.

The French translation of Milky Way somehow has more culinary overtones than its English equivalent, and this Turkish restaurant makes for a relaxing evening out. The room is pleasantly decorated and refreshingly separate from the take-away branch of the same name around the corner in the rue des Ecoles. We began our meal with the hors d'oeuvres buffet,which can also be ordered as a main course for €8.40, or as a part of the wide choice of *menus*. The salads were remarkable not for their sophistication but for their freshness, and all the dishes were kept well topped-up. We were drawn to the various types of meatball mains: the pistachio and aubergine version and the thyme-flavoured *boulettes à la nomade*, served on a bed of vegetables, were particularly delicious. Ditto for an indigenous red wine, recommended by the ever-attentive waiter.

Meze about at Fakhr el Dine

Fakhr el Dine

3 rue Quentin-Bauchart, 8th. (01.47.23.44.42). M° George V or Alma-Marceau. **Open** daily 11.30am-3.30pm, 7.30-11.30pm. **Average** €25. **Prix fixe** €23, €26. **Lunch menu** €19. **Credit** MC, V.

It may sound like a nasty Middle Eastern insult, but Fakhr el Dine was in fact an 18th century Lebanese independence fighter who got his throat slit by the Ottomans for his trouble. As did all his family. So have a shot of raki and water to the memory of poor old Fakhr as nibbling on a slice of marinated turnip and pretending you might choose anything other than the *meze*. As it turns out, the *meze* is an excellent choice. The high points were the *baba ghanouj* (aubergine purée), which was unctuously delicious thanks to the judicious use of sesame seeds and its smoky aroma. And who would have thought a very basic-looking brown ball of minced meat (*kafta naye*) could be so light and subtle of taste? The *meze* low point was probably the chicken wings. If you're a wine-drinker, there is an excellent, silky red from the Bekkar Valley, or if you prefer beer, try a bottle of the malty Almaza. To round things off we went for a plate of sticky Lebanese pastries, excellent with a couple of cups of good, strong, black coffee. Service, aside from being well-informed on the socio-political situation of contemporary Lebanon, is friendly and attentive. And the decor? Elegant, in a slightly white-piano kind of way.

Kibele

12 rue de l'Echiquier, 10th (01.48.24.57.74). M° Bonne Nouvelle or Strasbourg-St-Denis. **Open** Mon-Sat 7-11.30am. **Average** €30. **Prix fixe** €12, €14. **Lunch menu** €9. **Credit** AmEx, MC, V.

Turkish friends raved about this restaurant, and we weren't disappointed, beginning with the first course sampler of taramasalata, stuffed vine leaves and other Middle Eastern favourites. *Borek* was just right, the pastry light and flaky, the goat's cheese melting inside. A favourite main course is the classic *eli nazik*. If you have a Turkish grandmother you might quibble over the details, but we found the traditional combination of garlic-laced yoghurt, aubergine purée and lamb delicious. In the *yogurtlu tavuk*, one of the *prix fixe* options, chicken stands in for lamb for a milder effect. Desserts offer no surprises. The cinnamon-laced rice pudding is typically Turkish, although those who prefer intense sweetness might opt for baklava. Linger chatting over Turkish tea or coffee, or follow the music downstairs. From Tue-Sat Kibele holds Turkish and other world music concerts in its stone cellar.

Zagros

21 rue de la Folie-Méricourt, 11th (01.48.07.09.56). M° Richard-Lenoir or St-Ambroise. **Open** Mon-Sat 12.30-2pm, 7.30-11.30pm. **Average** €18. **Prix fixe** €16, €22.50. **Lunch menu** €10.50. **Credit** MC, V.

In a city with a rapidly growing immigrant population, modest little restaurants that dish up the culinary traditions of their native lands with love and pride in lieu of fanfare compete with more pretentious spots. Zagros is certainly one of those places. If you were to walk by this two-roomed, trattoria-style restaurant in the middle of the afternoon, you'd never imagine how lively it gets at night when neighbourhood denizens congregate to sample the Kurdish cooking here. The *assiette Zagros* features items that sound like standard fare at any number of Greek or Turkish restaurants, but rarely will you find taramasalata so silky or aubergine salad so zestful and fresh. The rest of the fare is also robustly flavoured, with kebabs dominating the menu under different guises and with different sauces. Splash them with plenty of the well-seasoned yoghurt that the friendly servers are only to happy to replenish and you will understand why everyone here looks so happy. How could they not be?

El Bacha

74, rue de la Croix-Nivert, 15th (01.45.32.15.42). M° Commerce. **Open** Mon-Fri noon-3pm; 6-11pm, Sat 11am-3pm; 6-11pm. **Average** €17. **Prix fixe** €7.50-€17. **Credit** MC, V.

The window dressing of lamb on a giant revolving spit and the dilapidated decor – including faded photos of pre-war Beirut, dusty plastic flowers and pink walls– didn't inspire us, and, admittedly, our meal started off somewhat shakily with bread-in-a-bag and unappetising appetisers. But the starters which followed were very enjoyable: houmous with a swirl of olive oil; *caviar d'aubergine* with a subtle nutty, smoky taste; crunchy felafel served with tahini sauce; and a great *tabouleh* with swathes of fresh parsley, tomatoes and firm bulgur wheat, tossed with a zesty vinaigrette. Though the starters were sufficient for a full meal, we couldn't resist something from the grill: chicken in a citrus sauce with tomato-flavoured bulgur wheat. We finished up with an excellent baklava oozing with syrup and soaked up the lively local atmosphere.

Mazeh

65 rue des Entrepreneurs, 15th (01.45.75.33.89). M° Charles-Michels or Commerce. **Open** Tue-Sun 11am-10pm.Closed last three weeks in Aug **Average** €18. **Prix fixe** €14.80-€16.80. **Credit** MC, V.

Four plastic tables against one wall, once-white paint, and metal appliances make up the decor of this Iranian restaurant. The owner's genuine warmth adds charm, but the list of lamb kebabs and sandwiches tacked to the wall doesn't look promising. Tip: talk to the owner about possibilities, and don't hesitate to show an interest in Iranian cuisine. Centre of a catering business, this restaurant holds more than meets the eye. Though it was nowhere on the menu, we found ourselves starting with a sampler of regional products accompanied by *lavach*, a paper-thin bread. Here there were no surprises, just exceptional quality. A chicken and olive salad, held together by the house mayonnaise, was perfect. The *chirazi* salad resembled tomato-cucumber salads common in Greek and Turkish restaurants but here the freshness tingled. Mazeh's own yoghurt turned the typical yoghurt, mint, and cucumber salad into something memorable. Our neighbours' lamb kebabs looked delicious, but we tried the *coquelets*, young and tender cockerel grilled kebab-style. We particularly liked the lemon and saffron combination, although the *coquelets* marinated in white wine and basil deserve a mention. While the building blocks of the meal were simple, little details such as the best rice we've had in Paris make this place a real find, particularly for the price. And, while the physical environment is far from beautiful, we would be hard put to find a more generous welcome. For an improvement in decor, try the takeaway.

Restaurant Al Wady ★

153-155 rue de Lourmel, 15th (01.45.58.57.18). M° Lourmel. **Open** daily noon-3pm, 7-midnight. **Average** €25. **Lunch menu** €9.91, €12.96. **Credit** AmEx, MC, V.

We didn't have the courage for lamb's brain or the *Isnat* (tongue served either hot or in a salad), so there were just 47 appetisers left to choose from. After half an hour of concentrated study we settled on a *meze* lunch of just five, vetoed the main courses (steel platters laden with fish or grilled meats and big bowls of fresh, uncut vegetables), and sat back in anticipation. The decor – resolutely old-fashioned 'fine dining' – bode well, as did the distinctly Middle Eastern clientele; and we weren't disappointed. Armed with a plateful of soft, warm pitta, we went straight for Al Wady's *spécial moutabal* (€6.10), a delicately smoked aubergine caviar crowned with walnuts and juicy red pomegranate seeds. Like the *chankaliche*, chunks of mild goat's cheese and tomato tossed with an array of tantalising spices, it was outstanding. A silky *hommos bayrouti* (€5.33), chickpeas puréed with tahini, lemon and parsley, rounded out our selection of dips and made a tasty, if unconventional, sauce for the *fatayer sabanich* (airy spinach fritters). Last but not least was the *fattouche* salad; coarse lettuce with chunks of cucumber, radish, red pepper and lightly fried pitta, laced with lip-puckering chilli and lemon; all guaranteed to cleanse the palate. The wines are Lebanese, the coffee is dark and thick, and for dessert there are stacks of honeyed pastries. If you have a hankering to visit Beirut, consider instead taking the Métro to the 15th and working your way down the menu of this thoroughly enjoyable restaurant.

Tibetan Restaurant

[Open from 12pm-2.30pm and 7pm-11pm
Closed Sunday]

tel: 01|47|00|90|18| mobile: 06|12|97|87|54

Norbulinga

Norbulinga welcomes you to discover real traditional Tibetan food with its typical decoration and cheerful atmosphere

Bus 56. 96. 20. 65
Ⓜ Filles du calvaire
Ⓜ Oberkampf

118 | rue | Amelot | 75011 | Paris

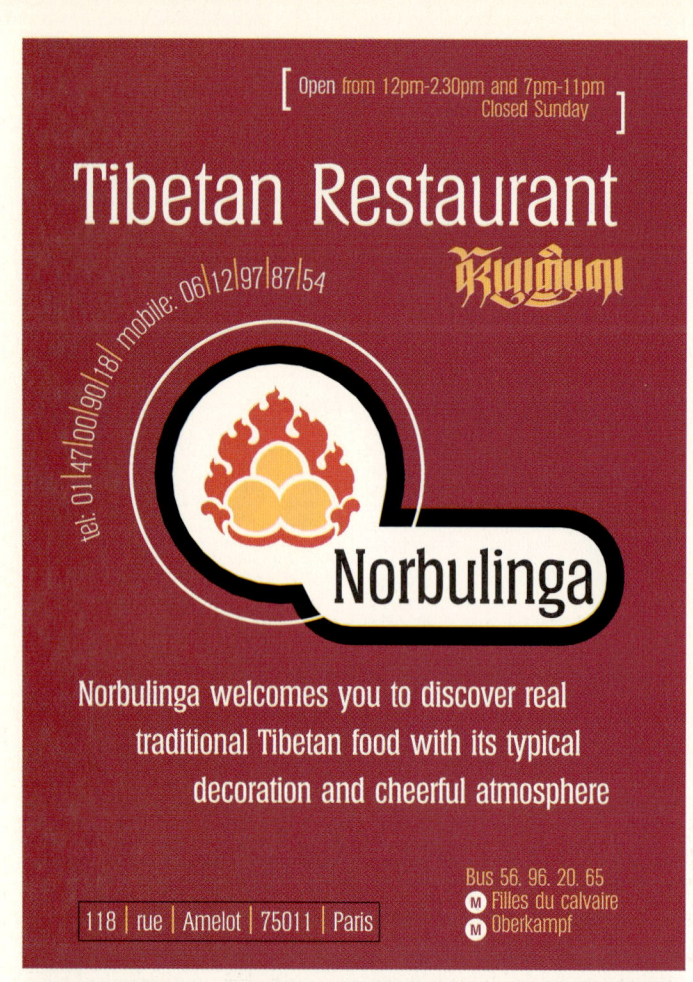

GANDHI-OPÉRA
INDIAN RESTAURANT

Owner Sunilseth and Chef Kuldip Singh guarantee to bring you authentic Indian cuisine.

Savour wonderful, aromatic dishes including *machi tikka* (marinated, spit-roasted fish), mixed grill tandoori, *murgh pudina* (chicken marinated in fresh mint and roasted in a wood oven), *chota jheenga* (gently spiced shrimp fritters), *ghosh vindaloo* (lamb flavoured with twenty spices) and jheenga azam (gambas with cashew nuts and mild spices).

Vegetarian dishes available, excellent wine list (including Indian specialities)
'Best classical Restaurant of Paris 2001' *Zurban* - Gold Medal 2001

13 rue St-Augustin, 75002 Paris - M° Opéra/Quatre Septembre
Tel: 01.47.03.41.00 / Fax: 01.49.10.03.73
Open daily noon-2.30pm & 7pm-11.30pm

Komodo
RESTAURANT

A surreal voyage through Asia with the best recipes from Thailand, China, Japan, Vietnam and India

16 RUE DU DRAGON - PARIS 6th
M° St Germain des Prés - Open daily except Sun and Mon lunch
Tel: 01.45.48.49.49 - Fax: 01.45.49.19.66

Jardin de L'Inde
Indian & Pakistani Specialities

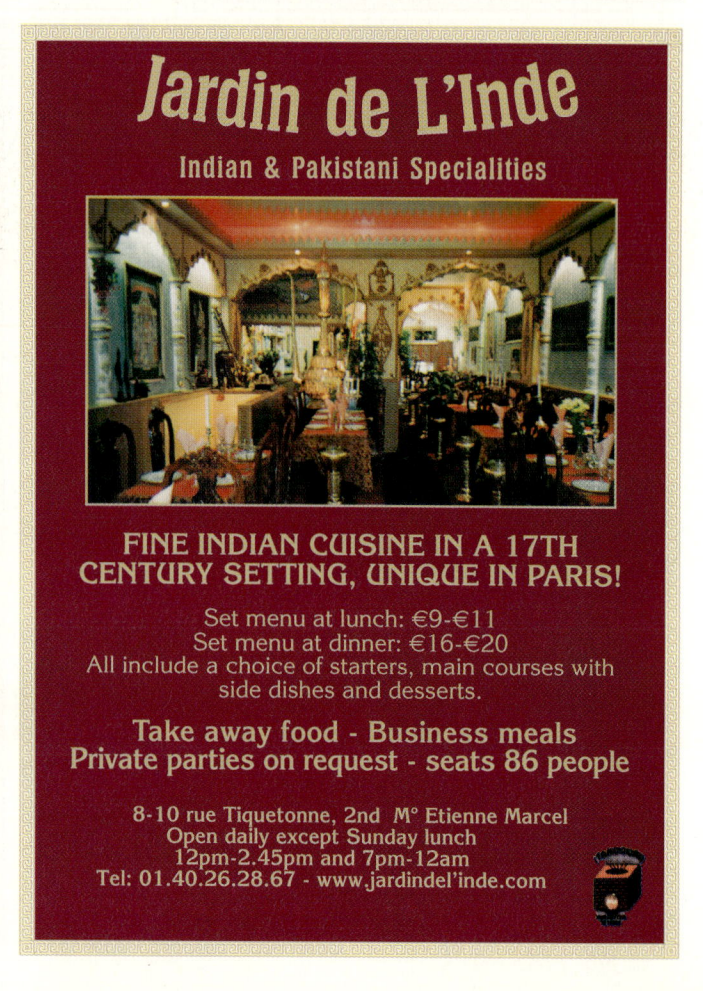

FINE INDIAN CUISINE IN A 17TH CENTURY SETTING, UNIQUE IN PARIS!

Set menu at lunch: €9-€11
Set menu at dinner: €16-€20
All include a choice of starters, main courses with side dishes and desserts.

**Take away food - Business meals
Private parties on request - seats 86 people**

8-10 rue Tiquetonne, 2nd M° Etienne Marcel
Open daily except Sunday lunch
12pm-2.45pm and 7pm-12am
Tel: 01.40.26.28.67 - www.jardindel'inde.com

Far East

Take a wok on the wild side to unearth true Asian treasures in Paris.

Paris can be a frustrating place for Far Eastern flavour fanciers. The 13th *arrondissement* around tower-block Porte de Choisy – the closest thing Paris has to a Chinatown – is the obvious place to start with its vast Hong Kong-style eateries and smaller noodle houses specialising in Vietnamese *pho*. But some of the best Asian restaurants lurk in unexpected neighbourhoods: **Kambodgia** is a sultry haunt near the Champs-Elysées, **Baan Boran** serves stunning Thai food near the Palais-Royal and **Chen** wows expense-account diners in a shopping centre underpass in the 15th. Belleville is also a good place to seek out Chinese and Vietnamese food, if you're willing to take your chances: the noodle house **Duong Huong** and the popular, canteen-style **Lao Siam** are good bets.

Cambodian

La Mousson

9 rue Thérèse, 1st (01.42.60.59.46). M° Pyramides ou Palais Royal. **Open** Mon-Sat noon-2.30, 7.15-10.15. **Average** €23. **Prix fixe** €15.10, €19.10. **Lunch menu** €11.60, €16. **Credit** MC, V.

Everyone looks happy in this compact dining room, and it's no wonder – the setting is warm with stone walls, bamboo and giant origami birds, the service is thoughtful and the food freshly prepared. The tiny cook, known to her faithful customers as Lucile, moved to Paris in 1975 and has been recreating Khmer flavours ever since. Won ton soup, though originally a Chinese dish, is prepared here in the Cambodian way with lettuce and prawns in a subtle broth. A chicken soup was bolder and spicier, with corn, bamboo shoots, kaffir lime leaf, fish sauce, ginger and zingy chilli. The waiter pointed us to the most authentically Cambodian main courses: *amok*, a soothing steamed fish dish made with coconut milk, galangal, lemongrass, lemon zest and kaffir lime leaf, and giant prawns in their shells with a mild tomato and chilli sauce. Feeling adventurous, we ordered the *ta peir* – fermented black rice – for dessert, an acquired alcoholic taste. Our waiter also urged us to try the steamed coconut cakes, which, though white and rather bland-looking, proved memorably squishy and sweet. It's no wonder this restaurant has such a loyal following of office workers at lunch and locals at dinner, despite its discreet location.

Le Cambodge

10 av Richerand, 10th (01.44.84.37.70). M° Goncourt or République. **Open** Mon-Sat noon-2.30pm, 8pm-11.30pm. Closed one week in Aug. **Average** €16. **Credit** AmEx, MC, V.

This bright spot on the often dull Paris Asian food scene offers enchanting Cambodian rice and noodle dishes, with prices that are scaled to the modest surroundings. Steps from the Canal St-Martin, Le Cambodge has a no-nonsense atmosphere coupled with an unusual self-ordering system. The waiter negotiates the cramped dining room and brings over a pen and slip of paper with the menu; it's up to you to write legibly and hand over your order. Every dish presented by the elderly Cambodian co-chef invited hungry stares: *natin*, a pork and prawn soup, creamy curries, and *ban hoy*, an Angkorian build-your-own picnic. The prawn soup combines rice noodles with a subtle broth, while the fish salad heaps up bean sprouts, red pepper, fresh mint leaves and marinated fish drenched with a tangy dressing. The various *bo bun* dishes juxtapose hot and cold, garden-fresh ingredients. The *riz cantonnais à la Cambodge* is a stand-out: prawns and chicken on a bed of reddish fried rice. No afters at Le Cambodge, just an iced coffee or tea, but they do a cost-per-person bill which kindly eliminates taxing mental gymnastics.

Kambodgia

15 rue de Bassano, 16th (01.47.23.08.19). M° George V or Charles de Gaulle-Etoile. **Open** Mon-Fri noon-2pm, 7.30-10pm, Sat 7.30-10.30pm **Average** €49. **Lunch menu** €18, €23. **Credit** AmEx, MC, V.

This excellent Indochinese restaurant tucked down a flight of stairs not far from the Arc de Triomphe is an ideal spot for a tête-a-tête, if you don't mind the stiff prices. Low lighting, teak flooring, plants and woven bamboo wall-coverings effectively disguise the basement setting, and solicitous, soft-spoken service makes it easy to relax, although some background music might have masked the tedious monologue from a nearby politically far-right-leaning woman in the midst of a divorce. We promptly forgot her woes, however, with the arrival of delicate steamed ravioli stuffed with roasted duck, delicious deep-fried beef and basil-stuffed crêpes, and a nicely seasoned Laotian salad of chicken with sesame. Main courses of sea trout steamed with ginger in a banana leaf and prawns sautéed with garlic and black pepper were also first-rate, as were bean sprouts sautéed with garlic flowers. Tempting desserts included a delicate flan made with sweet corn in a tapioca sauce, and roasted mango.

Chinese

Chez Vong ★

10 rue de la Grande Truanderie, 1st (01.40.26.09.36). M° Etienne-Marcel. **Open** Mon-Sat noon-2.30pm, 7-11.30pm. **Average** €46. **Lunch menu** €23 (Mon-Fri). **Credit** MC, V.

In this inauspicious address, around the corner from the Saint-Denis porn shops, is an elegant Cantonese restaurant whose rooms are lined with green porcelain bamboo. The staff glide past in satin waistcoats and delicate music combines with the sound of falling water from a small fountain. Well-spaced tables are set with lion-shaped chopstick holders, and while the trilingual menu holds no surprises, what makes the food special is the chef's commitment to authentic ingredients. There are no shortcuts here: the seafood salad is generously heaped with real, freshly shredded crab, mushrooms and jellyfish strips have exactly the right consistency, and even simple dumplings contain firm whole prawns. To contrast with the fine sizzling fish plates, choose at least one duck dish, such as the crispy-skinned Five Spice duck. Order steamed rice wrapped in a lotus leaf as an accompaniment. With modest servings that invite sharing, this is an excellent place to sample traditional ingredients you might otherwise hesitate over. Dessert is less important, though of the classic options, the sesame-covered nougat is a nice conclusion.

Mirama

17 rue Saint-Jacques, 5th (01.43.54.71.77). M° St-Michel. **Open** daily noon-10.45pm. **Average** €22. **Credit** MC, V.

There are few things better on a cold winter's night in the Latin Quarter than a bowl of steaming prawn dumpling soup – even if you have to queue for the privilege. This is a popular haunt, well known to local student-types and budget-conscious tourists alike, but we reckon the Mirama's straightforward, well-priced cuisine is worth waiting for. Chinese *canards* can be pretty scrawny creatures, involving hours of mucking around with unlikely-looking bones, but our caramelised water-fowl was plump, well-proportioned and pleasantly crispy on the outside. A couple of bottles of sweet Chinese Tsing-Tao beer put us in the mood for more so we got a big plate of Chinese greens. A good place for eats with friendly, polite staff.

Le Chinois

3 rue Monsieur le Prince, 6th (01.43.25.36.88) M° Odéon. **Open** Tue-Sat noon-2pm, 7.30-10.30pm. **Average** €24. **Lunch menu** €13.72. **Credit** AmEx, MC, V.

There's nary a plastic Buddha in sight at this stylish new Chinese restaurant tucked away in striking stone-vaulted dining room just steps from the Odéon. Instead, dark wood tables and chairs, red walls, soft lighting and a huge antique chest of drawers create contemporary Sino chic in a welcome departure from the non-descript decors that characterise Asian restaurants in Paris. And, if the menu is rather classic, the food is quite good and reasonably priced. Start with an assortment of *dim sum*, steamed ravioli stuffed with pork, prawns and pork, and prawns and vegetables, a delicate salad of crisp vegetables garnished with chicken or crab, or spicy Pekinese soup. Then try the Peking duck for two, Szechuan-style pork and aubergines, or steamed fish with ginger and chives. The noodles with duck and mushrooms or with prawns, scallops and squid are fine one-course feeds, and the coconut fritters make an original dessert. Wine is served by the glass.

New Nioullaville

32 rue de l'Orillon, 11th. (01.40.21.96.18). M° Goncourt or Belleville. **Open** daily 11.45am-3.00pm, 6.45pm-1am. **Average** €15. **Lunch menu** €5.79-€10.37. **Credit** AmEx, MC, V. **Wheelchair access.**

In the heart of Belleville's Chinese community, the New Nioullaville is a spacious 500-seat restaurant, with separate open kitchens for the different specialities that fill the encyclopaedic menu. Just as we were ploughing through the infinite possibilities, a waitress arrived with a trolley of langoustine and pork *beignets*. Happy to avoid decision-making, we tucked into the greasy but tasty fritters while discussing our next move. In the end we plumped for a vibrant combination of garlic, ginger and tofu complemented by a sizzling platter of seafood, with some above-average fried rice. A cocktail of various dried fruits in a pleasantly under-sweetened juice proved refreshing. The other diners included a good number of Asian families – always a sure sign of authenticity – enjoying a midweek, late evening feast in a relaxed, child-friendly atmosphere. The service was unusually friendly and remarkably efficient and our Bandol rosé was a class act in keeping with our meal.

Le Président

120-124 rue du Fbg-du-Temple, 11th (01.47.00.17.18). M° Belleville. **Open** daily noon-2.30pm, 6pm-2am. **Average** €18. **Lunch menu** €9, (Mon-Fri). **Credit** AmEx, DC, MC, V.

If you believe that bigger is better, then Le Président's cavernous dining room, its garishly resplendent reception area and its book-length menu of Chinese and Thai specialities will delight. Be warned, however; things are not as good as they are cracked up to be at this super-sized eatery. Our meal began rather poorly with an assortment of dry and undesirably stiff steamed pork and prawn dumplings culled from a rolling cart of ostensibly fresh *dim sum*. A few bamboo-shoot-wrapped prawn *rouleaux* in a light oyster sauce proved much better, warmer and gentler on our teeth. Mains were equally inconsistent. *Broccolis aux seiches* turned out to be a plate of undercooked broccoli so radically oversauced and a handful of over-cooked squid so untenably chewy that we had to send it back. In its place, we were quite pleased with the savoury grilled quail with salt and pepper and delicate prawns in (fragrant) fermented black bean sauce. Those looking for a taste of Asia in Paris might do well to head deeper into the neighbourhood to a number of smaller, more welcoming restaurants.

Wok

23 rue des Taillandiers, 11th (01.55.28.88.77). M° Bastille or Ledru-Rollin. **Open** Mon-Sat 7.30pm-11pm, **Average** €19. **Prix fixe** €15.50-€19. **Credit** MC, V.

Frosted glass, polished pine and chrome. What might sound like a Swedish hotel bathroom is, in this case, the Spartan interior of a Chinese restaurant. Fortunately, as you breathe in the aromas of soy and fresh ginger drifting over from the flaming woks in the back corner, you realise that the similarity ends there. The owner cheerfully admits that he was inspired by London restaurants such as Wagamama. The menu has a number of trans-Asian dishes ready to order but most of the customers (a mix of young professionals and Bastille locals) prefer the self-serve option: given a bowl half-filled with egg or plain noodles, you fill the top half with your choice of ingredients from the buffet: marinated duck, prawns, salmon, bean sprouts, pineapple – don't be shy to pile it high as the volume reduces during cooking. A list of suggested combinations is posted and the stoic chefs will help with sauce and spices if you ask. If you're really hungry, you might want to try the menu *aller-retour* which includes two trips to the wok, although our server talked us out of ordering it. We had the caramelised fruit salad for dessert but its bitter aftertaste made us wish we'd got ice cream instead.

La Chine Masséna

Centre Commercial Masséna, 13 pl de Vénétie, 13th (01.45.83.98.88). M° Porte de Choisy. **Open** Mon-Thur 9am-11.30pm; Fri-Sun 9.30am-1.30am. **Average** €15. **Lunch menu** €8, €10. **Credit** MC, V. **Wheelchair access.**

Flanked by three Chinatown apartment towers, and true to its chopstick wrappers which read 'For banquets, receptions, marriages and business dinners', this 500-seater with stage and dance floor is a mainstay for Chinese and Cambodian community events. Saturday night around 8pm, we had just ordered from the extensive Chinese, Thai and Vietnamese menu when the lights dimmed, and a shy newlywed couple had their first dance to a plaintive Chinese song. Misty-eyed, we applauded as the band then kicked off the show. The performance ranged from Chinese pop to Dalida, Elvis, Doris Day and Cher and soon there were more than 50 people doing the hustle in quasi-unison as the singer belted out *Stand By Me*. We ate heartily and enjoyed the spectacle, since conversation was nearly impossible. The sour prawn soup, with its twist of crab, pineapple and tomato, was a treat. Soy-marinated ginger and chives covered the lightly battered and fried chicken, and the mixed *rôtisserie* plate included crisp-skinned Peking duck and sweet roasted pork belly. Cambodian dancing had begun when we noticed that our rice and one of our platters had never arrived. We didn't mind, though, and left the party in high spirits. Book on Friday and Saturday nights.

Tricotin

15 av de Choisy, 13th (01.45.84.74.44). M° Porte de Choisy. **Open** daily 9.30am-11.30pm. **Average** €15. **Credit** MC, V.

At the far end of Chinatown's main strip is a rare gem, as appealing to the palate as it is easy on the pocket. Canteen-style tables teem with families, students and couples feasting on a colourful and steaming array of Chinese, Thai, Cambodian and Vietnamese delicacies. Decor is minor since the food itself is the mesmerising star of these festivities. A peek into the kitchen reveals chefs in white uniforms preparing food in rhythmic unison. A whopping 15 people wait patiently for seats as waiters whiz by with armfuls of dumpling soup and side orders of bean sprouts and lemon, assorted platters, *dim sum* in bamboo steamers, and exotic drinks such as sweet red beans in coconut milk. Each item appears more mouthwatering than the previous as you attempt to find it on the raggedy menu with its eye-rubbing bargain prices. We marvelled that such delicious, inexpensive and speedily-made dishes could also be so beautifully presented. Marinated lemon slices and a spinkle of spring onions topped the tender chicken legs, and the sliced beef and Chinese cabbage came atop a disc of fried noodles. Desserts include banana tapioca, ginger candy and fruit ice cream. Booking is recommended, especially for larger groups.

Chen
15 rue du Théâtre, 15th (01.45.79.34.34).
Mº Charles Michels. **Open** Mon-Sat noon-2.30pm, 7.30-10.30pm. Closed two weeks in Aug. **Average** €76. **Prix-fixe** €75. **Lunch menu** €39.64. **Credit** AmEx, MC, V.
Beyond its unlovely location in a dark, fume-filled underpass, the real mystery of this highly rated Chinese restaurant is why a chef as talented as Shanghai native Fung Ching Chen, allows his superb cooking to be held captive to such pushy and unpleasant staff. The moment that one of us decided to order the set-priced but still pricey lunch *menu* we sensed the waiter's impatient disdain and an attempt to order a bottle of Muscadet, one of the few affordable bottles on a boldly over-priced wine list, brought the scornful warning that 'it's not very good' (it was just fine). In the end, this place does quite well off corporate expense account types and high-ranking government officials dining out in style, plus a certain intrepid clientele that's attracted by star ratings – and so had little use for the likes of us. The meal, though, was delightful – in culinary terms anyway. Chen proudly announces on the menu that he works with only the finest French produce, much of it *appellation d'origine contrôlée*, including Bresse chicken, and it's his mastery of Chinese technique, applied to spectacular Gallic produce, that makes this a fine restaurant. Star dishes include elegant Eurasian starters like courgette flowers stuffed with crab mousse in a sauce of fresh crab meat, a nod perhaps to Roger Verger, and frogs' legs sautéed in salt and Szechuan pepper, plus main courses like rock lobster in ginger and spring onion sauce and Peking duck in three services – the roasted skin with spring onions on rice pancakes spread with a jam of roasted figs and mango, the bird's meat with bamboo shoots and other vegetables and, finally, a small bowl of earthy duck bouillon. Even the desserts are good, including the enticingly bizarre *tan yuang aux fleurs de laurier*, gummy rice dumplings stuffed with sugar and bay leaf in a 'broth' infused with laurel flowers. If you love Chinese food and someone else is paying, this is a good spot; otherwise, there are places in the 13th where you'll be happier. You could also try the well-reputed Le Bonheur de Chine (2-6 allée Aristide-Maillol, 92500 Rueil-Malmaison/01.47.49.88.88), run by Chen's brother.

Salon de Thé Wenzhou
24 rue de Belleville, 20th (01.46.36.56.33).
Mº Belleville. **Open** Mon-Wed, Fri-Sun 10.20am-9.30pm. **Average** €11.
No credit cards.
Most France-bound Chinese immigrants have hailed in recent years from the coastal city of Wenzhou, but despite a sizeable expatriate community in Paris, few restaurants serve authentic Wenzhou-style cuisine. This one does, though on a modest scale: the welcoming Xu family offers the Chinese equivalent of a corner bistro, with soup noodles, dumplings and stir-fried dishes. A house speciality is *guotie* (pot stickers), plump pork-filled dumplings that are first steamed in a covered pan and then fried as the water evaporates, leaving one side golden brown. These are traditionally eaten with a little black vinegar and chilli oil (both on the table), but one can safely experiment with the other sauces offered, too. Ditto the very good *xiaolong bao*, or dragon dumplings (wheat flour wrappers filled with spiced minced pork and bamboo shoots), served in a bamboo steamer. The decor is functional but exudes an unpretentious charm.

Sinostar
27-29 av de Fontainebleau, 94270
Le Kremlin-Bicêtre (01.49.60.88.88).
Mº Porte d'Italie. **Open** Mon-Thur noon- 3pm, 7pm-midnight; Fri-Sun noon-3pm, 7pm-2am. Closed Mon in July and Aug. **Average** €15. **Prix fixe** €21.50. **Lunch menu** €12. **Credit** MC, V. **Wheelchair access**.
Just beyond the 13th *arrondissement* lies this 650-seat Hong Kong-style family restaurant featuring Cantonese and Téo-Chew cuisine. The English-subtitled menu has shark-fin soup, frogs' legs, pork tripe, crayfish, carp-fish head, pigeon, and next to our table was a tank housing two turbot, one of which was fished out midway through our meal. We started with a jellyfish salad and then moved on to mains, which upheld the Cantonese reputation for subtly harmonising different flavours: the stewed chicken with soft, sweet chestnuts, the ginger beef sautéed with pineapple slices served in a pineapple half-shell, and the prawns and mango slices in a nest of fried noodles. Around 9pm, the band kicked off. At first, the dance floor was slow to fill as a bold teenage girl did tango steps with her grandma and the singer crooned *Black Magic Woman*. The minimum order is €25 per person for seats in the dancing section and reservations are recommended for weekend nights.

Indochinese

Au Coin des Gourmets
5, rue Dante, 5th (01.43.26.12.92). Mº Cluny-La Sorbonne. **Open** daily noon-2.30pm, 7-10.30pm. **Average** €22. **Prix fixe** €26 (Mon-Thur). **Lunch menu** €11.25 (Mon-Fri). **Credit** MC, V.
This friendly Asian restaurant serves unusual food from Indochina (Cambodia, Vietnam and Laos). The menu offers a dazzling array including spicy soups, warm salads, rice dishes, Asian ravioli, savoury pancakes and curries. We started with soups and enjoyed two quite exquisite dishes: a sweet and tangy prawn and tomato soup flavoured with tamarind, and a thick, tasty fish soup of cod in a coconut and Thai red curry sauce with fine vermicelli and *al dente* courgettes. The small *pomme d'amour* ravioli offered a lighter starter of appropriately dainty prawns steamed in a sweet yellow egg yolk batter. For our main course we tried the house speciality *amok cambodgien*, delicately cooked cod in a luxuriant coconut sauce lightly perfumed with lemongrass and baked in a giant banana leaf. The *banh xeo*, a Vietnamese pancake packed with soy beans, prawns and pork, and accompanied by sprigs of fresh mint, was original though somewhat less flavourful than the other dishes. Finish off with a number of tempting desserts such as stewed lychees or baked bananas with marinated ginger.

Indonesian

Djakarta Bali
9 rue Vauvilliers, 1st (01.45.08.83.11).
Mº Louvre-Rivoli. **Open** Tue-Sun 7-11pm. **Average** €26. **Prix fixe** €16-€41. **Credit** MC, V.
This superb Indonesian restaurant, with its pretty decor, gracious service and generously spaced tables, offers a splendid opportunity to discover the elegant, subtle and relatively little-known cuisine of the various islands that make up the Indonesian archipelago. If you think you know Indonesian cooking from having had a *rijsttafel* in Amsterdam, you will be surprised to find that this sincere and flavourful home cooking has nothing at all in common with the deracinated dishes that dominate most Dutch menus. The Hanafis, a brother and sister team, make dinner here seem like an invitation to their house. Start with the *soto ayam*, a delicious and delicate soup of chicken broth, rice noodles and vegetables, and then follow with several other starters to be shared: *lumpia*, fried homemade spring rolls filled with chicken, noodles and prawns served with a fresh peanut sauce; or *saté daging*, beef on skewers with peanut sauce. Outstanding main courses include *rendang daging*, tender slices of beef in coconut milk seasoned with Indonesian herbs, and *ayam jahe*, caramelised chicken in ginger sauce, accompanied by *nasi goreng* – Indonesian-style fried rice with tiny prawns and chicken. The white Domaine la Croix Belle le Champ de Lys, a Côtes de Thongue, complements the food beautifully. Finish with a *coupe kolak*, banana and jackfruit in coconut milk.

Korean

Han Lim ★
6 rue Blainville, 5th (01.43.54.62.74).
Mº Place Monge. **Open** Tue-Sun noon-2.30pm, 7-10.30pm. Closed Aug. **Average** €19. **Lunch menu** €13.50. **Credit** MC, V.
This family-run restaurant, long a favourite of the Asian expatriate community, is a well-kept secret in the bustling Latin Quarter. The Han family serves homestyle fare amid modest surroundings with strikingly authentic details such as lidded metal rice bowls and traditional spoons and chopsticks. Little has been altered to suit French tastes or dining style. There are no pre-selected dinner *menus* and the plates arrive in the order that they are ready. The service is attentive and fast, so you'll have no difficulty making it to that after-dinner film. The highlight of our meal was the *panchan*, small bowls of assorted vegetable side dishes that came with the tableside grilled beef barbecue or could be ordered separately. Grazing over mounds of steamed spinach laced with sesame oil and tangy *kimchee* cubes (made here with white radish fermented in hot peppers) lies at the heart of a satisfying Korean meal, and this place delivers. Marinated squid with onions was delectable. We also loved the *bibimbap*, a medley of vegetables, fried egg, meat and rice mixed with a dollop of sweet hot sauce. Korean beer (OB) or *soju* (rice vodka) are the ideal accompaniments to this garlic-based cuisine. Booking is advised.

Gin Go Gae
28 rue Lamartine, 9th (01.48.78.24.64).
Mº Cadet. **Open** Mon-Sat noon-2.30pm, 7-11pm; Sun 7pm-11pm. **Average** €15. **Lunch menu** €10. **Credit** MC, V.
The family-run Gin Go Gae offers an authentic Korean experience. Dad, whose wizened face cries out to be painted, runs the show with a mimimum of words and gestures, while Mum works with lightning speed in the kitchen and their son explains to newcomers how to tackle the food (speaking English is an advantage, as his French is limited). After contemplating such mind-boggling specialities as beef tripe cooked on a stone and fritters of *kimchee*, the fiery fermented cabbage, we opted for beef grilled at the table (*bulgogi*) and strips of raw salmon on a heap of thinly sliced cabbage. Junior supervised our cooking of the marinated beef with onions on a dome-shaped cast-iron pan, adjusting the heat when necessary. Small dishes of *kimchee*, bean sprout salad and spinach with sesame seeds accompanied the beef. We were shown how to wrap these in paper-thin sheets of seaweed with a little rice to make a kind of Korean sushi. The salmon provided a fresh counterpoint.

Korean Barbecue
22, rue Delambre, 14th (01.43.35.44.32)
Mº Vavin **Open** daily noon-2pm, 6.30-11pm **Average** €25. **Prix fixe** €18.90-€26.68. **Lunch menu** €9-€14. **Credit** MC, V.
All of the tables in the elegant front room were taken on the Monday night we visited, but we were quickly ushered to the cosier back room. The grill in the middle of each table and the extractor hood hanging at eye level mean business; you come to eat, not to gaze longingly at your dinner partner. No matter, for once the meal arrives, distractions become annoying. Although there is an ample choice of *menus*, we ordered *à la carte*. After a rich broth laced with sesame oil, offered by the house, we shared deep-fried and grilled dumplings, both filled with subtle combinations of minced meat and vegetables, and served with soy-based dipping sauces. Next came an impressive plate of sashimi, hefty chunks of salmon, tuna, mackerel, and a mullet tartare with ginger and spring onion. Our marinated rib steak (we took a small portion of the leaner *noix d'entrecôte*, but you might prefer well-marbled ribsteak or tongue) arrived soon after. Served with *bibimbap* (rice topped with strips of omelette, bean sprouts,

Eat, drink, man, woman at Chez Vong

Malaysian

Chez Foong
32 rue de Frémicourt, 15th (01.45.67.36.99). M° La Motte-Picquet-Grenelle or Cambronne. **Open** Mon-Sat noon-2.30pm, 7-11pm. Closed July 21-Aug 26 **Average** €25. **Prix fixe** €14.50, €15 (Mon-Thur). **Lunch menu** €9.60 (Mon-Fri). **Credit** MC, V.

There aren't many Malaysian restaurants in Paris and this one is well worth the trek to this less-than-exotic part of the 15th *arrondissement*. There is a bewildering array of choices on the main menu, but the best bet is to go for the great value *prix fixe*. We started off with the *potage chinois*, a spicy chicken soup with slivers of tasty black Chinese mushrooms. This contrasted nicely with the *beignets de légumes*, crisply fried vegetables with the magical addition of a mysterious and flavoursome peanut sauce at once both sweet and savoury. The main courses spanned a variety of seafood, red meat and poultry dishes; we enjoyed the chicken cooked in soy sauce and lemongrass, served with sugary caramelised onions. Though the lamb, beef and chicken *brochettes* were unremarkable in themselves, they were accompanied by a rich satay sauce made with shallots, garlic, tamarind, lemongrass and ground peanuts. Two good desserts – *pâtisseries malaises*, small cigar-shaped pancakes stuffed with coconut and drizzled with a honeyed sauce, and a crisp, amazingly light pineapple fritter – rounded off the meal.

Thai and Laotian

Baan-Boran ★
43 rue Montpensier, 1st (01.40.15.90.45). M° Palais Royal. **Open** Mon-Fri noon-3pm, 6pm-1am; Sat 6pm-1am (last orders 11.30pm) **Average** €30.49. **Lunch menu** €11.50. **Credit** AmEx, DC, MC, V.

Night owls and fans of Thai food will be delighted by this reasonably priced new spot across the street from the Palais-Royal. With its soft lighting, flower arrangements and gentle service, it is a great destination at the end of a fraught day, and has become popular with an arty crowd of locals. The two Thai women in the kitchen come from the north and centre of the country, and they specialise in traditional, family-style regional dishes as opposed to the royal Thai cuisine often found overseas. Their cooking privileges fresh herbs, in particular basil, lemongrass, garlic and ginger, as found in starters like the *larb neva*, a salad of beef marinated in lemon with shallots, onions and mint, and *tom khaa kai*, spicy chicken soup made with coconut milk. A pictogram system rates the heat and spice in each dish, so that delicate palates are spared, but it would be a shame to pass up the excellent red chicken curry or *saikkoh isan*, little pork and garlic sausages from northern Thailand that are served on a bed of salad. If you prefer something savoury but less spicy, try the grilled chicken with green papaya salad, or shellfish cooked in a banana leaf with coconut milk. Unusually, there is also a list of 'light' dishes prepared without sugar or added fat, including grapefruit salad with dried prawns, braised crab and fish steamed with herbs. All dishes here are prepared without MSG and, in addition to Thai beer, several interesting foreign wines are available.

Bali Bar
9 rue St-Sabin, 11th (01.47.00.25.47). M° Bastille. **Open** Mon-Sat 7-11.30pm. **Average** €36. **Prix fixe** €38.11. **Credit** DC, MC, V. **Wheelchair access**.

If you like the Blue Elephant, Paris' most fashionable Thai, chances are you'll love the lesser-known Bali Bar. The atmosphere is similarly lush, with red walls, tropical plants, Indonesian carvings and spacious seating, prices are lower and the food is at least as good – not surprisingly since the chef, Oth Sombath, made his name at the Blue Elephant. After a potent Jakarta Post cocktail (Cythera plum, lime, marakuja, white and dark rum and apricot syrup), we started with a basket of steamed pork and prawn dumplings, which were unusual only for their lightness and fresh flavours. *Kaeng peg* (red duck curry) was presented French-style, with the slices of duck breast fanned out on a plate, but the flavours were distinctly Thai: pineapple, grapes, pea-sized aubergines, aniseedy Thai basil and gutsy but not overwhelming chilli. More recognisably Thai was the *yam neua*, a spicy salad of rare beef, shallots, mint and coriander. As the restaurant filled up service started to fray around the edges – we had nearly finished our mains before the rice arrived (after several reminders) and had a long wait for our bill. But the waiters' good manners – along with the chef's obvious sincerity when he asked if we'd enjoyed our meal – made us forgive this flaw.

Blue Elephant
43 rue de la Roquette, 11th, (01.47.00.42.00). M° Bastille. **Open** Mon-Fri noon-2.30, 7pm-midnight; Sat 7pm-midnight; Sun noon-2pm, 7-11pm. **Average** €43. **Prix fixe** €44. **Lunch menu** €18.29. **Credit** AmEx, DC, MC, V.

Hectares of teak walls, Buddhas and exotic plants dispatch diners to a 'virtual' Thai village in the heart of busy Bastille, and the authenticity extends to the food. Thai spices, herbs, fruit, vegetables and flowers are flown in from Bangkok markets and with them chef Nopporn Siripark creates dishes such as prawn and lemongrass soup, salmon soufflé in banana leaves, and jasmine tart. Thai fish cakes and *yam pomelo* (shredded grapefruit, chicken, and prawns doused in fish sauce and chilli, and topped with a fried hard-boiled quail's egg) make for good, traditional starters. The heat factor is indicated by one, two or three (red) elephants. The 'three elephant' green chicken curry with Thai aubergine is nice and spicy but not so hot as to cause meltdown. Less fiery is Bangkok fish – fried fillets with a sweet and sour sauce and julienned vegetables. To wash it down, a spicy Gewurztraminer is just the thing. For dessert, try the fresh Thai mango or banana sorbet flavoured with Mekong whiskey. The place was buzzing and service was correspondingly swift.

Khun Akorn ★
8 av de Taillebourg, 11th (01.43.56.20.03). M° Nation. **Open** Tue-Sun noon-2pm, 7.30-11pm. **Average** €35. **Credit** AmEx, MC, V.

The first time we ate at Khun Akorn – a restaurant with branches in Bangkok and London – we loved the elegant surroundings and gracious service, but craved more spice. Now the kitchen appears to have let loose. Our waiter's eyes lit up when we told him that we liked our food spicy; we later realised that it might have been wise to order one or two milder dishes, for balance. Still, we had no complaints about the assertive cooking, fiery enough to light up the palate but not at the expense of other, more subtle flavours. A classic prawn soup, *tom yum koong*, was scented with lemongrass and kaffir lime leaves, while *som tam*, a salad of green papaya with dried prawns, carrot and peanuts, was refreshingly tangy. Both mains successfully combined sweet and spicy: a duck curry with grapes, pineapple, lychees and pea-sized aubergines, and seared scallops with Thai basil. By this time, a burning sensation was travelling from our throats down to our arms in a surprising but not entirely unpleasant way. We had two kinds of rice to soothe our palates: the sticky Thai version and scented white rice. Pineapple sorbet further cooled us off. There is a decent selection of wines, including our Tavel rosé, but watch out for overpriced apéritifs. And fear not: mild dishes are available 'for soft tongues'.

Sawadee
53 av Emile Zola, 15th (01.45.77.68.90). M° Charles Michels. **Open** Mon-Sat noon-2.30pm, 7-10.30pm, Closed two weeks in Aug. **Average** €27. **Prix fixe** €19.50-€28.80. **Lunch menu** €12.95. **Credit** AmEx, MC, V.

Pockets of golden Buddhas, glittering elephants and deep red walls recreate Thailand on a residential corner. And there's a touch of Bangkok street madness with waiters scurrying from crowded table to crowded table and noise levels rising as the evening progresses. The surroundings are pleasant, the service is assured and the menu promises much. Although Sawadee is consistently rated as one of the best Thai restaurants in Paris, on our visit the heat wasn't on; dishes arrived lukewarm and the spice element was sadly lacking. A green chicken curry had none of its customary fire while mixed satays and chicken wings stuffed with pork were almost stone-cold after being set down; so too the overly sweet, oil-drenched *meekrob* (crispy noodles). We fared better with flavourful *tod man pla* (fish cakes), still sizzling on arrival, prawns with basil, and *pad thai* (stir-fried rice noodles). Curiously, the food lacked the rich aromas and piquancy generally associated with Thai cuisine.

Lao Siam
49 rue de Belleville, 19th (01.40.40.09.68). M° Belleville. **Open** daily noon-3pm, 7pm-11.30pm **Average** €18. **Credit** MC, V

Lao Siam doesn't serve the best Thai food in Paris, but the prices are reasonable and it's located in a vibrant part of Paris that many visitors miss. A mixed local clientele in the non-smoking dining area is surrounded by Buddhas, ceramic geese, pensive elephants, and Thai landscapes. Smokers are relegated to a small, crowded section in the back separated from the front by an aquarium. The menu – dispensed with by hard-core regulars – is charmingly cryptic, beginning with starters and mains, followed by more starters and another list of mains. Our waiter, whose manner was stoic bordering on military, was reticent when asked about the chef's specialities. 'Anything with duck, beef, or prawns', was his reply. With our choices insignificantly narrowed, we ordered the spicy, overdressed Thai salad: a violent mix of lemongrass, fresh coriander, mint, peanut oil, shallots, onions, and onions (did we mention the onions?). Main dishes were more carefully prepared. Sautéed beef with red peppers, bamboo shoots and whole peppercorns was tasty, if slightly cool on arrival. All the mains, except the coconut-based ones, come at a uniform level of spiciness – a shock for some delicate French palates, but tame by Thai standards. Stick to the fresh fruit and sorbets of the dessert menu; the Thai chocolate mousse cries beware while the 'Mystery' pudding should remain one.

Krung Thep
93 rue Julien-Lacroix, 20th (01.43.66.83.74). M° Belleville or Pyrénées. **Open** daily 6-11pm **Average** €18. **No credit cards**.

Last year we referred to this Thai restaurant, discreetly located on a Belleville side street, as a jewel-in-the rough. Unfortunately, it seemed more like a trinket on our last visit, and we were somewhat bewildered by the fact that at least four groups of hungry eaters were turned away for lack of room before we had finished our meal. Thai steamed mussels were just that: steamed mussels with a sprig of Thai basil plopped on top. While lacking any distinctive touch, the shellfish were at least light and puffy, in contrast with our overpriced, leaden and flavourless fish cakes. We eagerly lapped up the shallot and coriander sauce that accompanied them in order to liven things up. Our main dishes also suffered from oil overkill. Roast duck in coconut curry (by no means a light dish, we admit) came loaded with duck skin and fat, and held only two meagre strips of meat. *Pad thai* was gummy, greasy and tepid. The only winners were the nicely spiced pork with ginger and black mushrooms, the aromatic sticky rice and the icy Chinese beer.

Tibetan

Pema Thang
13 rue de la Montagne Ste-Geneviève, 5th (01.43.54.34.34). M° Maubert-Mutualité. **Open** Mon 7-10.30pm, Tue-Sat noon-2.30pm, 7-10.30pm; **Average** €16.50. **Prix fixe** €13-€17. **Credit** MC, V.
If you're looking for a subtly romantic meal with vegetarian options, this candle-lit restaurant filled with Tibetan photographs and fabrics should be on your list. By the time we had finished perusing the menu (which thoughtfully includes English explanations), we had been lulled by the chanting on the stereo and were in the mood to appreciate the subtle flavourings of little-known Tibetan food. We began with *tsampthuk*, a porridge soup of barley flour, very salty and buttery, two flavourings that seem to feature frequently (even the tea comes with salted butter). For less adventurous souls, there's *pema thang*, a comforting cream soup with roast tomatoes and coriander. We shared a perfectly-cooked *shadré* lamb curry and a sesame-flavoured tofu *tseldremoug*, which was a little rubbery. The relaxed crowd of locals and tourists all seem willing to try the buttery house tea, as we did. The tea might be an acquired taste, but we happily lingered over our warm rice pudding and apricot compote.

Vietnamese

Restaurant Pho
3 rue Volta, 3rd (01.42.78.31.70). M° Arts et Métiers. **Open** Mon-Sat 10am-4pm. Closed Aug. **Average** €11. **No credit cards**.
It's hard to find a better-value meal than *pho*, the giant Vietnamese noodle soup. One of our favourites among the many *pho* restaurants in Paris is this popular 32-seat establishment located on the ground floor of one of the oldest buildings in the northern Marais. The restaurant offers only three regular dishes and two weekly specials, in a choice of medium or large portions. All are good, but the *bo bun* – rice vermicelli with spring rolls, sautéed beef slices, fresh mint, peanuts and bean sprouts, all garnished with the traditional fish-sauce-based dressing – is full of contrasting textures and perfectly spiced. If wheat egg noodles are your thing, they come in a broth with roast duck slices, coriander and bean sprouts. Quality and freshness never lag, making this an enduring favourite with locals. Service is fast and always polite, seating is elbow-to-elbow and you may have to share a table but if you're not in the mood, you can always order takeaway.

Thuy Long
111 rue de Vaugirard, 6th (01.45.49.26.01). M° St-Placide. **Open** Mon-Thur 11am-8pm, Fri-Sat 11am-9pm. **Average** €11. **Prix fixe** €9-€10.60. **Lunch menu** €8.40. **No credit cards**.
This minuscule Vietnamese canteen turns out copious and delicious house specialities to a mostly lunchtime and takeaway crowd, though you can stop by to have a bite at any time of the day. For €8.40, you'll get three crispy *nems* or prawn ravioli, a wide choice of mains – such as a bowl of steaming, beefy *pho*, or a slow-cooked meat or fish dish – as well as a dessert. The menu offers some unusual northern and southern Vietnamese alternatives, including divine stuffed chicken with onions, coriander and lemongrass, which came served in thin, boneless slices atop shredded cabbage, carrots and cucumber. The *bo bun*, prepared before your eyes in the tiny kitchen, is top-notch, covered in lemongrassy sautéed beef and slivers of carrot. Desserts such as banana-coconut cream and a tapioca pudding round things off nicely. The dirt-cheap prices and down-to-earth service make Thuy Long a welcome stop in the pricey, restaurant-chain wilderness of Montparnasse.

Dong Huong
14 rue Louis-Bonnet, 11th (01.43.57.18.88). M° Belleville. **Open** Mon, Wed-Sun noon-11pm. Closed Aug. **Average** €12.20. **Credit** MC, V.
With a packed bin of plastic chopsticks, a fresh bottle of Sriracha hot chilli sauce and Good Fortune toothpicks by our side, we pounced on the two-page menu. The other customers, mainly groups of Vietnamese friends on a Saturday night out, skipped the starters, *prix fixe* dinners and English translations. Our dishes arrived haphazardly, creating a homely feast. We were delighted with the prawn and onion in their crunchy fried noodle shell, the steamed pork and cellophane noodles rolled in floppy rice ravioli skins sprinkled with ground beef and dried onions, the extra-crispy mini spring rolls, and grilled chicken laminated with pork sauce. Soups are also popular: try the healing free-range chicken with rice noodles or a spicy *saté* version. We finished with a warm banana tapioca with sesame seeds and *xinxa hotluu*, a sweet drink with gelatine, lotus and lychees.

Kok
129bis av de Choisy, 13th (01.45.84.10.48). M° Tolbiac. **Open** daily 9am-midnight. **Average** €9. **No credit cards**.
The decor is dismal and the service phlegmatic, but the food is cheap, filling and available from dawn to midnight. Craving that Vietnamese cure-all, *pho*? This is your place. Every table is set with chillies, lemon wedges and varied sauces. Sit down and a plate of bean sprouts, fresh mint and basil appears immediately. You're best off ordering one of the soups; beef is always available, but after 6pm your options become more interesting, with chicken or seafood *pho*. The big bowls of soup make a meal by themselves; tear up the mint and basil, throw in some chillies and bean sprouts, maybe some hot sauce, and tuck in. Order a Tsing-Tao beer, and your meal will still cost less than €10. The translucent pork-filled ravioli make a nice starter if you're sharing, but don't order the 'petite pizza', a disastrous experiment in fusion cuisine. For dessert, rev yourself up with a super-strong Vietnamese iced coffee, sweetened with condensed milk. Or, if you're feeling daring, try a lotus grain tea, served iced with lychees, preserved plum and lotus.

Kim Ahn ★
49 av. Emile Zola, 15th (01.45.79.40.96). M° Charles Michels. **Open** Tue-Sun 7.30-11pm. **Average** €38. **Prix fixe** €34. **Credit** AmEx, MC, V.
In this new location, yellow, olive and imperial-red fabric panels and rich mahogany-coloured wood have replaced the bamboo and wicker of the old address, and while prices, as before, are a tad hefty, the new upmarket decor now gives fair warning. Caroline Kim Ahn's servings aren't copious – just two ravioli or spring rolls as a starter – instead she emphasises quality and authenticity over quantity. The spring rolls bursting with chicken, prawns, vermicelli and Vietnamese mint were standouts. Mains of lacquered, sliced duck with a sweet orange and soy sauce, and *langoustines caramelisées*, two giant prawns (working out at a weighty €13.72 a piece) in a sticky combo of onions, sugar, soy and fish sauces showed refined, careful cooking. Plain steamed rice rather than fried is the best accompaniment. Fresh tropical fruits such as mangostan, a plum-brown fruit with a marshmallowy white centre and a taste akin to a sweet mini banana, are good bets for dessert.

Thu Thu
51bis rue Hermel, 18th (01.42.54.70.30). M° Jules-Joffrin. **Open** Tue-Sun noon-2.30pm, 7-11pm. Closed two weeks in Aug. **Average** €15. **Prix fixe** €21.34 (dinner). **Lunch menu** €6.86. **Credit** MC, V.
It's easy to pass by tiny Thu Thu, but succulent Vietnamese cuisine awaits those who push open the door. Dishes are out of the ordinary and highly authentic. A steamed vegetable dumpling turned out to be a plate-sized, rice-flour ravioli filled with fresh vegetables and topped with crunchy fried shallots, bean sprouts and coriander sprigs. Prawn and crab meat on a sugar-cane skewer came with piles of fresh lettuce, herbs and rice-paper wrappers. Staples such as *bo bun* and *pho* don't disappoint either, while the house speciality – beef cooked seven ways – is a unique (and very filling) experience for meat lovers. The waiter-owner is happy to explain the more complex creations, and his mother – the chef – will gladly prepare specialities from her native region. Even desserts are excellent: a baked banana with coconut milk and tapioca goes down a treat. Book ahead; it fills up fast.

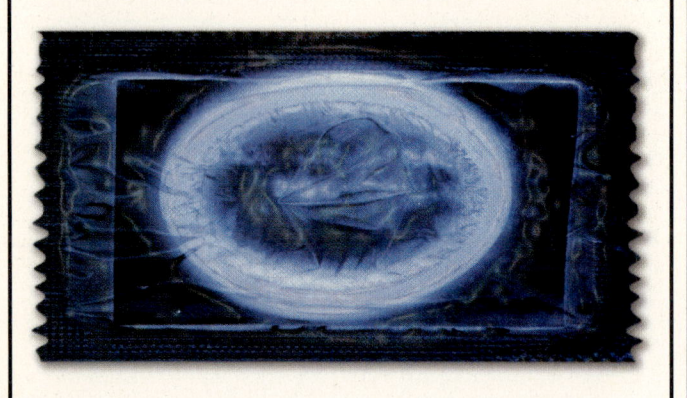

A CONDOM IS STILL THE BEST WAY TO PREVENT H.I.V.

AIDES

WISHES YOU THE BEST "TIME OUT" IN FRANCE.

espace offert par le support

AIDES
Tour Essor – 14 rue Scandicci
92508 Pantin Cedex
Tel: (0)1.41.83.46.46
Fax: (0)1.41.83.46.49

www.aides.org

Indian

As quality creeps slowly up, the Eurostar is no longer the only answer to a curry craving.

If you're pining for a palate-searing vindaloo, Paris is not the ideal place to look. Then again, fiery spices don't sum up Indian cooking: it can also be much more subtle. In the better restaurants, such as **Gandhi-Opéra** and **Kirane's**, you'll find the spicing well-balanced without being overwhelming – you can always ask the chef to turn up the heat. Frequently run by Pakistanis, 'Indian' restaurants in Paris usually favour tandoori cooking. Wander the streets around the Gare de l'Est for authentic south Indian food in modest restaurants such as **New Pondichery**. Oddly, restaurants run by Sri Lankans shy away from local specialities; **Ganesha Corner** is an exception.

Gandhi-Opéra
66 rue Ste-Anne, 2nd (01.47.03.41.00/ www.restaurant-gandhi.com). M° Quatre-Septembre. **Open** Mon-Sat noon-2.30pm, 7-11.30pm; Sun 7-11.30pm. **Average** €27. **Prix fixe** €23, €27.50 (dinner only). **Lunch menu** €11-€19.70. **Credit** AmEx, DC, MC, V.
Gandhi has a plush look with comfy red chairs, white tablecloths, a shiny black bar and tasteful Indian paintings. On a Saturday night, it was full of the young professionals who inhabit these parts. The menu lists an extensive selection of north and south Indian specialities, including tandoori grills and biryanis. Apéritifs are reasonably priced, including Champagne at €5.34 a glass, and the wine selection could compete with that of many French restaurants – we chose a half-bottle of Guigal Côtes du Rhône for €11. A standout starter is the *murgh pudina*, marinated, grilled chicken which is green on the outside and red within (don't let the colour put you off). *Machli Goa* was a delectable, not-too-spicy fish curry made with coconut, while a lamb dish, *gosht baingan*, was seductively scented with coriander and cardamom. We also tried the gutsily spiced chickpea curry and a freshly baked *paratha* – much like a nan but layered and buttery. **Branch**: Gandhi, 54 av Edouard Vaillant, 92100 Boulogne (01.47.61.05.04).

Yugaraj
14 rue Dauphine, 6th (01.43.26.44.91). M° Odéon or Pont-Neuf. **Open** Tue-Sun noon-2pm, 7-11pm. Closed Aug. **Average** €37. **Prix fixe** €28-€48. **Credit** AmEx, DC, MC, V.
With its wonderful collection of Hindu statuettes and colonial teak furniture dating from as early as the 18th century, this luxurious restaurant clearly echoes the antique shops that cram the area. Being vinophiles, however, we were impressed by the wine list from which we chose what we consider to be one of France's best bottles – a lush Rosé des Riceys from Morel whose chocolate and spice bouquet provided the perfect foil to fiery food. It took us some time to wade through the small-print encyclopaedic explanations of each dish but we finally settled on the sampler starter with various spiced (and unspiced) tidbits: fried fish cubes, chicken kebabs and *bhajis* served with a selection of colourful sauces and chutneys. Our tandoori-baked cheese nan was delicious but the plain one was well, rather plain, and a little greasy. The highlight of our meal: two delectably plump, free-range Vosges quails, the legs fried and medium-spiced and the wings bathed in a creamy sauce of spice, herbs and raisins. We mopped up every last morsel. Our other main course, the *ghost rada*, featured chunks of lean lamb prepared in a fragrant mixture of fenugreek, ginger and garlic. Desserts were nothing special; the stars were the wine list and Moghul main courses.

Kastoori
4 pl Gustave Toudouze, 9th (01.44.53.06.10). M° St-Georges. **Open** Mon 6.30-11.30pm, Tue-Sun 11.30am-2.30pm, 6.30-11.30pm. **Average** €16. **Prix fixe** €13 (dinner only). **Lunch menu** €8. **Credit** MC, V.
A tabla soundtrack and colourful throws and cushions on the banquettes give this restaurant a cosy feel. In summer, diners spill onto the leafy terrace with its parasols and cotton lanterns. The Indian chef cooks satisfactory food, served in sparkling zinc and copper dishes at a very reasonable price; the four-course *menu* is stunning value at €13. The chicken tikka, saffron basmati rice and *baingan bartha* (aubergine curry) were the highlights of our meal while the chef's 'special tandoori', though copious and good value (€8), was dry rather than special. Popular among French customers is the mild *moglaï* lamb cooked with plenty of crème fraîche, almonds and raisins. The strong, velvety and exotic Goa milkshake (pineapple, mango and papaya) was a sumptious end to our meal – just a shame it wasn't chilled. While alcohol is not available, the relaxed staff will happily direct you to a nearby shop, and there is no corkage charge.

Ganesha Corner ★
16 rue Perdonnet, 10th (01.46.07.35.32). M° La Chapelle. **Open** daily 11am-10pm. **Average** €7. **Credit** MC, V.
Who could resist a Sri Lankan fast food restaurant that also has its own wood-burning pizza oven? Settled into the spanking clean dining room, which boasts ceiling mouldings and fresh yellow paint, we admired the speed of the cooks at work behind the counter. The menu is limited – just three daily specials, to be precise. We chose vermicelli noodles formed into flat cakes, topped with three of the freshest and most punchily spiced curries we've tasted in Paris: spinach with fennel seeds, carrot and turnip with mustard seed, and cabbage with red lentils and potent spices. Yet another vegetable stew with potatoes was served for ladling over the top. This meal left us only €5.34 poorer and sadly too full to splurge on the sweet cakes on display. In the evenings the oven turns out Italian-style pizzas, though the cooks sometimes can't resist spicing them up.

New Pondichery
189 rue du Fbg-St-Denis, 10th (01.40.34.30.70). M° Gare du Nord. **Open** daily noon-10.30pm. **Average** €10. **Prix fixe** €6.60, €8. **Credit** MC, V.
Here is a real taste of southern food in a setting much like one you might find in the former French colony referred to in the restaurant's name. This is the only place in the capital where we have come across *idli*, a fat, spongy cake of rice and lentil flour, and, just like in India, it arrived with a spicy red paste and coconut chutney. Another starter worth trying is the doughnut-shaped *vadai*, a spiced lentil fritter that's served warm. Move on to the filled crêpes (*dosai*) or the biryani, both typical of southern India. Huge *dosai* come with vegetable and/or meat fillings and a yellow stew (*sambar*), to be scooped up by hand with pieces of the pancake. Also try the the chicken biryani and its succulent sauce which you spoon on yourself. Ridiculously cheap *menus* are available, but what's the point when you can assemble your own meal for less than €8? No alcohol, but the *lassis* are particularly good.

Shalimar
59 Passage Brady, 10th (01.45.23.31.61). M° Strasbourg-St-Denis or Château d'Eau. **Open** daily noon-2.45pm, 7pm-11.45pm. Closed 1 May. **Average** €16. **Prix fixe** €16. **Lunch menu** €7.93, €8.38. **Credit** MC, V. **Wheelchair access**.
Two details make this a solid address among the chaotic Passage Brady options. First, there's the colour scheme of papaya-hued walls, embroidered hangings of elephants, and the complimentary pale-blue cocktails. Then there's the cheerful chef in the window, making fresh Indian breads. Since much of the food on the strip seems to emerge from microwave hell, it's a relief to have some proof of authenticity before ordering. Circumspect selection is wise so stick with meaty basics. We were impressed with the flavourful *murgh tandoori*, carefully spiced chicken, and the various breads did the chef proud. An excellent house special is the *tandoori Shalimar*, nan bread studded with pistachios and almonds. Though ample, the vegetarian curry was under-spiced. Service began to degenerate as the restaurant grew crowded and our polite but harassed waiter had a command of neither French nor English, which led to confusion over our orders. Best to ignore such trifles, and replace dessert with a simple milky Punjabi tea.

Coffee India
33-35 rue de Lappe, 11th (01.48.06.18.57/ www.coffee-india.com). M° Bastille. **Open** daily 11am-2am. **Average** €16 (dinner only, Mon-Thur), €25. **Lunch menu** €9. **Credit** AmEx, DC, MC, V.
You might be tempted to think the worst of this restaurant, which after 10pm becomes a bar and lounge with 'electro-massala' music by DJ Soundar and DJ Ganesh. The decor is beautiful in a Buddha Bar kind of way – soft orange, purple and green walls with wicker chairs, Indian-style paintings and curvy lanterns – but in Paris this can bode ill for the food. Then comes the surprise: the menu is short and admittedly expensive, but the dishes are both imaginative and fun to eat. We started with a standard, meat-filled samosas, which here came hot and crisp on a round of fresh banana leaf with three sauces laid out like paint on a palette. A 'Kerala' salad of shredded crab was light and sweet with tropical fruit. Feeling nostalgic for south India we ordered the *masala dosa*, which came in a bowl the size of a sink – two long crêpes with a tender beef curry (south Indians do occasionally eat beef) and vegetable stew called *sambar*. The *murgh Hyderabad*, a slightly hot vegetarian curry with peppers and potatoes, arrived in a small, sizzling pan with *dosai* on the side. In a tribute to India's colonial past, you can also order fish and chips and English-style desserts. Skip the gutless masala tea.

Kirane's ★
85 av des Ternes, 17th (01.45.74.40.21). M° Porte Maillot. **Open** Tue-Sat noon-2.30pm, 7-11pm. **Average** €38. **Prix fixe** €27, €30.50 (dinner only). **Lunch menu** €12.50, €15.50. **Credit** AmEx, DC, MC, V.
Kirane, the head chef here, was born in Bombay of a long line of restaurant owners. She has been mixing spices since the age of five and it shows. We could find no fault with any of the dishes. The decor is fairly sober; for once the emphasis is on the food rather than Ganesh. We kicked off by sharing a mixed tandoori featuring juicy chunks of chicken, fat prawns, moist salmon and succulent pieces of lamb. This was accompanied by pillowy nans and eight sauces, ranging from tongue-curlingly fiery to cooling, creamy mint. A main course of lamb *rogan josh* was a masterpiece of finely balanced spices while royal salmon *hara* was an attractive coral wedge of grilled, marinated fish in an aromatic green sauce. We ended our meal with fruit salad and a heavily pistachioed *kulfi*. Attentive service from Kirane's husband and smiling waiters only added to our pleasure.

Shah Jahan
4 rue Gauthey, 17th (01.42.63.44.06). M° Brochant. **Open** daily noon-2:30pm, 7-11.30pm. **Average** €20. **Prix fixe** €18, €20. **Lunch menu** €8.50, €20. **Credit** AmEx, DC, MC, V. **Wheelchair access**.
Named after the ruler who built the Taj Mahal, this Indo-Pakistani restaurant may not be as architecturally glorious as its namesake might have liked, but the staff's courtesy coupled with our very tasty meal made us feel like royalty. Starters of the standard fried and grilled variety are served with fresh coriander and yoghurt sauce, sweet banana chutney and lime pickle. We opted to order *à la carte* and to share the €20 *menu*, which comes with bread, rice, a drink and dessert. We used the stuffed *paratha* loaded with morsels of curried potato and sweet peas to lap up our *dahl sag* – dark green spinach purée dotted with green whole lentils. Chunks of flavoured lamb worked well with the mild aubergine purée and if the chicken in our biryani was slightly dry, at least it had been grilled in the tandoor oven before being added to the saffron rice, almonds and peas. Scoops of rose petal and pistachio ice cream sweetly topped off our evening.
Branches: Les Jardins de Shah Jahan, 15th (01.47.34.09.62); Le Palais Shah Jahan, 15th (01.45.78.21.07).

Great breadside manners at Gandhi-Opéra

Chiaro di Luna

Traditional Italian cuisine

8 rue de Jouy, 4th. M° St-Paul
Tel: 01.42.78.38.66

Open Mon-Sat noon-2.30pm, 7.30pm-11.30pm

Le Perron

L'italianissimo de Saint-Germain

6 rue Perronet, 7th - Tel: 01.45.44.71.51
Metro & Parking: Saint Germain des Prés

Open daily 12.15pm-2.15pm, 7.45pm-10.45pm
Closed Sunday

IL VICOLO

It's plain Parisian cheek to defy Italian chic...

34 rue Mazarine, 6th.
M° Mabillon or Odéon
Tel: 01.43.25.01.11

"The best of Italy in Paris" – Elle (2001)

Italian

Paris' Italian battalion pass the pizza, pasta and pesto test with (buon) gusto.

Though pasta and pizza now easily rival couscous in Paris as alternatives to *steak-frites*, convincing Italian food remains surprisingly hard to come by – and, when quality is high, the price might leave you feeling a little shell-shocked. Still, if you know where to look, this city offers something for everyone: real Neapolitan pizzas at **Alfredo Positano**, cheerful bowls of pasta at **Gli Angeli**, lush Venetian risotto at **L'Osteria**, hard-to-find regional ingredients at **Sardegna a Tavola**, and stargazing at the ever-fashionable **Le Stresa**. Also worth seeking out are **Il Baccello**, whose inventive chef uses mostly organic ingredients, and the classic but classy new **Brasseria Italiana** in St-Germain.

Il Cortile
Hôtel Castille, 37 rue Cambon, 1st (01.44.58.45.67). Mº Concorde. **Open** Mon-Fri noon-2.30pm, 7.30-10.30pm. **Average** €55. **Lunch menu** €42. **Credit** AmEx, DC, MC, V. **Wheelchair access.**

The smart Il Cortile sits in one wing of an upmarket hotel, where it attempts to recapture Italy in a courtyard with a roaring fountain, neo-Tuscan *trompe l'oeil* stucco and outdoor tables under large parasols. The main lures are Alain Ducasse who supervises (from afar) its Franco-Italian cuisine and the excellent, if expensive, Italian wine list. Serious grey-clad waiters ration out olive bread, *pain de campagne* and fragments of *focaccia* for dipping in olive oil to an international clientele who probably barely notice which city they are in. Starters included *porchetta di canoglio al rosmarino*, cold slices of rosemary-infused, stuffed, rolled rabbit with mustard sauce, and a rather insipid tomato and mozzarella bruschetta. Spit-roast lamb with aubergine was competent; fresh cod with black olive butter, green asparagus, black olives, and a dollop of a dense green, garlic and parsley sauce was light and pleasant if of indiscernible geographic origin. That's the problem here: the overpriced food is short on Italian charisma. Perhaps we should have had the pasta or risotto – crab and lobster cannelloni and risotto with frogs' legs or *girolles*. Beware if you go for the full *antipasti*, *primo* and *secondo piatti* and dessert: the bill will soar into the stratosphere.

La Bocca
59, rue Montmartre, 2nd (01.42.36.71.88). Mº Sentier or Etienne Marcel. **Open** daily noon-2am. **Average** €25. **Credit** MC, V.

Both the decor and the clientele of La Bocca have a casually hip, lived-in look, and the seasonally-based Italian food is a good match. Perch on the tiny terrace on a fine day, or if the weather's iffy, drop down at a pretty tiled table inside and peruse the blackboard menu. An *antipasti* plate of grilled aubergine, courgette, peppers, mushrooms, artichokes and sweet onions makes for a generous shared starter, then it's on to a daily pasta or fish special. Both *linguine Siracrusa* with garlic, chilli, basil and dried tomatoes and kingfish rolls stuffed with tomato and basil were excellent. A plate of raspberries with orange segments made for a fine conclusion. For Italian wine lovers there's premium Brunello at €45 a bottle and Montepulciano d'Abruzzo for less than €15 a bottle. A pitcher of summery rosé is a cheaper alternative. The espresso is top-notch, aided no doubt by the turn-of-the-century Victoria Arduino coffee machine.

Il Buco
18 rue Léopold Bellan, 2nd (01.45.08.50.10). Mº Sentier. **Open** Mon-Fri noon-2.30pm, 8-11pm; Sat 8-11pm. Closed two weeks in Aug and in Dec. **Average** €30. **Credit** AmEx, MC, V. **Wheelchair access.**

Il Buco looks like just the kind of trattoria you might find hidden in an Italian back street: long and narrow, with ochre walls, wooden tables and a minuscule terrace. The waiters' Italian accents keep up the illusion, as does the handscrawled blackboard menu. Most people were ordering pasta only – we should have taken the hint, as starters were practically a meal in themselves. Tender, thinly sliced speck ham came on a heap of lentils seasoned simply with olive oil, lemon juice and bland diced tomato, while bruschetta was a satisfying serving of three bread slices topped with classic tomato, flat parsley and olive oil, with a side salad. During the lunchtime rush (reservations are essential) we had time to work up a second appetite before the pasta. Bonbon-shaped pasta filled with ricotta and spinach came with a sweet tomato sauce scented with basil – nice, if not revolutionary. The gigantic serving of fusilli with a creamy porcini sauce looked appetising but proved overly rich and unfinishable. We couldn't resist gelato, and the blackcurrant version was outstanding; coffee parfait was another good choice. Our only real complaint was the overwrought service; lunch took a good two hours.

Gli Angeli
5 rue St-Gilles, 3rd (01.42.71.05.80). Mº Chemin-Vert. **Open** daily noon-2.30pm, 8-11.30pm. Closed Aug. **Average** €34. **Credit** MC, V.

Locals, business people and in-the-know tourists head to Gli Angeli, steps from the fashionable place des Vosges, for traditional Italian cooking in a laid-back setting. Diners are greeted with a warm *buon giorno* at this classic trattoria with stone walls, well-spaced tables and a menu of lovingly executed regional classics. One of our group waxed lyrical about the peppery garlic tomato sauce ladled over a starter of slow-cooked mussels, and mopped it all up with crusty baguette. Our waiter warned him not to fill up on bread and when our mains arrived we understood why. As copious as it was delicious, the *taglierini* with shaved parmesan and rocket was creamy and intense. A massive, perfectly cooked steak with 'sweet and sour' sauce was swathed in a rich, meaty broth with a hint of balsamic vinegar and lots of cracked pepper. Seared tuna covered in crushed basil atop tomato coulis looked fresh and elicited 'oohs' and 'ahs' from a neighbouring diner. Though stuffed, we licked up every last bit of tiramisu, with gooey mascarpone and espresso-doused biscuits, and a *semi-freddo* of homemade vanilla ice cream with candied fruit. The all-Italian wine list covers the main regions and starts at €4 for a carafe of house red; the €26 Rubesco our waiter recommended went down a treat. Gli Angeli's reasonable prices, friendly service and well-crafted cuisine are no secret, so book.

L'Osteria
10 rue de Sévigné, 4th (01.42.71.37.08). Mº St Paul. **Open** Mon 8pm-10.30pm; Tue-Fri 12.30-3pm, 8-10.30pm. Closed Aug. **Average** €50. **Credit** DC, MC, V.

Although Tony Bianello is renowned for his risottos, any dish the Venetian magician conjures up in his tiny kitchen is likely to be first-class. L'Osteria means a casual place to eat but don't be fooled, there is nothing random about the freshness of the ingredients or the inventiveness and precision of the cooking. Still, the regular clientele are studiedly blasé: sleek young businessmen gabble on mobiles, urban warriors paint their lips between courses and bookish types plunge into highbrow dialogues seemingly oblivious of the aromas tickling their noses. Quite prepared to be ostracised for our too-evident appreciation of the chef's skills, we tucked into fat slices of buffalo mozzarella with beefy tomatoes (the kind that actually have taste) loaded with olive oil and fresh basil, and exquisitely constructed *oeufs aux truffes*. We picked *seppie al nero con polenta* and *osso buco alla gremolata* from the simple parchment menu, which changes daily. Squid cooked in its own ink melted in the mouth, while the polenta soaked up the black sauce like a featherweight sponge. The tender veal knuckle was breathtakingly succulent, filled to the brim with herb-scented marrow. Our desserts, pears in red wine fragrant with cinnamon, and tiramisu were irreproachable. The downside is the close proximity of the tables in the spartan dining area; try for a table for two next to the tiny bar and you will have peace on one side at least. Bypass the astonishingly bland vini dell'Osteria table wine in favour of the Badie a Coltibuono Chianti Classico 1997.

Alfredo Positano ★
9 rue Guisarde, 6th (01.43.26.90.52). Mº Mabillon. **Open** Mon-Sat noon-2.30pm, 7-11.30pm. Closed Aug. **Average** €38. **Credit** MC, V.

They don't take bookings on Saturday nights at this nondescript trattoria and, although tables turn over astonishingly fast, by 8pm the queue stretches out the door. And it's clear why. From a menu that features pizza, pasta and a small selection of meat and fish main courses, we started with excellent *antipasti di verdura* – grilled courgettes, aubergines and mushrooms, glistening artichokes and plump butter beans. Although our neighbours and their children – this is an ideal family restaurant – were tucking into delicious looking *penne all'arrabiata*, risotto with white truffles and *gnocchi alla Sorrentina*, we were here for the pizza. The *manou*, named after the laconic *pizzaiolo* himself, is properly made – tomato sauce, mushrooms, capers and mozzarella. But the *napolitaine*, the stripped-down quintessence of pizza, left us in awe: thin, crunchy dough – the kind with those big air pockets that look like volcanoes – straight out of the wood-fired oven, all charred base and yeasty aroma, smeared with tomato, oregano, garlic, fresh basil, anchovies and no cheese. Service is straightforward, tables are cramped, wine is decent and the tiramisu carries the endorsement of superchef Joël Robuchon. If you love pizza, join the queue.

La Brasseria Italiana
81 rue de Seine, 6th (01.43.25.00.28). Mº Odéon or Mabillon. **Open** Tue-Sun noon-2.30pm, 8-10.45pm. **Average** €47. **Lunch menu** €16.50-€22.95. **Credit** AmEx, MC, V.

Though this new Italian restaurant puts another nail in the coffin of what used to be a thriving street market, given the galloping fashionisation of St-Germain it's at least a relief that this former fishmonger has become a restaurant rather than yet another wannabe-hip clothing store. And considering the often mediocre quality of Italian cooking on the Left Bank, this new place is welcome, since it's clear from the moment you arrive that it's a serious restaurant. Settling into the attractive room, decorated with cast-iron lamps with jewel-toned shades, we enjoyed complimentary appetisers of liver paste, aubergine caviar and carrot purée with fresh coriander served with croutons, and were similarly impressed by *antipasti* of grilled vegetables (aubergine, cour-

Positively the best pizza at Alfredo Positano

GAUDIUM

Ristorante Italiano

76 rue Mazarine, 6th. M° Odéon
Tel: 01.43.25.63.40
Open Mon-Sat, noon-3pm and 7pm-11.30 pm

Piccolo Teatro
VEGETARIAN RESTAURANT

Open daily noon-3pm, 7pm-11.30pm
6 rue des Ecouffes, 4th. M° St Paul - Hôtel de Ville
Tel: 01.42.72.17.79

www.piccoloteatro.com

---

gette, pepper, spring onion) with scamorza cheese, and courgette flowers stuffed with herbed ricotta (though the heavy breading rather overwhelmed the delicate flowers and the cheese stuffing). *Primi* of risotto with nettles, a wonderful old-fashioned mid-summer's dish, and linguine with *girolle* mushrooms and bacon were excellent, as were tiramisu and *torta della nonna* (granny's tart), one of the homeliest Italian desserts, with a shortbread crust and jam filling. Wonderful, if pricey, Italian wines, plus excellent service and an interesting crowd make this place worthwhile.

Chez Bartolo
7 rue des Canettes, 6th (01.43.26.27.08). M° Mabillon or St-Germain-des-Prés. **Open** Tue-Sat noon-2.30pm, 7-11.30pm; Sun 7-11.30pm. **Average** €40. **No credit cards.**
Having known this eternally stylish St-Germain Italian for many years, we can authoritatively state that this crowded, casual restaurant decorated with framed illustrations of an erupting Vesuvius remains extremely consistent – the food is dependably good, the bill is always too high, and the service sullen. That said, we always come away saying that if it weren't so pricey, we'd come often. The food is often leagues better here than at other Paris Italians, as seen in a brilliant starter salad of sautéed prawns on baby spinach and mixed herbs dressed with a vinaigrette that included the pan drippings of the prawns. Ditto a carpaccio of *bresaola* on a bed of rocket and green beans. *Tagliolini* with small squid in tomato sauce was excellent, while that Neapolitan classic of spaghetti with *vongole* flopped – instead of the fingernail-sized clams served in Italy, this version used large, tough ones. Almost no-one bothers with dessert here, but the tiramisu is good. Sardine seating notwithstanding, this is a place where you end up lingering, since the mixed crowd is attractive and interesting, and the wood-fired pizza oven creates a homely atmosphere.

Le Perron
6 rue Perronet, 7th (01.45.44.71.51). M° St-Germain-des-Prés. **Open** Mon-Sat noon-2.30pm, 7.30-11pm. Closed two-three weeks in Aug. **Average** €30.50. **Credit** AmEx, MC, V.
Anyone who doubts the existence of St-Germain *d'après*, now that fashion victims rather than intellectuals crowd the 'literary' cafés, will be reassured by this restaurant. It brims with local intelligentsia, including journalists and editors from nearby publisher Gallimard, *gauche caviar* lawyers and, if we must talk fashion, Yves Saint Laurent's business partner Pierre Bergé. Not that anyone cares who their neighbours are here; what attracts regulars is the serious cuisine, the delightful intimacy, especially the opera-box alcoves on the mezzanine, and the relaxed hospitality of the Sardinian owner and his staff. Although the *carte* hardly changes, the dishes are consistently good and the seasonal *plats du jour* always imaginative. Enticing first courses include *vongole in umido*, a dish of lightly sautéed clams; *salsicce abruzzese alla griglia*, sausages marinated in wild fennel; and *antipasto del Perron*, sun-dried tomatoes, courgettes, aubergines, small mushrooms and endives baked to melting point in extra-virgin olive oil. Densely-flavoured risottos are a feast, especially the devilish-looking *risotto del scrivano*, squid in its own ink. The chef has an assured touch with veal dishes such as *scaloppine alla valdostana*, succulent veal escalopes piled with Italian ham and mozzarella. For afters, opt for Italian cheese or homemade tiramisu. Stick to Le Perron's Sardinian house red Argiolas Costera 1998; its vanilla and blackcurrent bouquet has an uncanny way of loosening writers' block.

Le Bistrot Napolitain
18 av Franklin D. Roosevelt, 8th (01.45.62.08.37). M° Franklin D. Roosevelt. **Open** Mon-Fri noon-2.30pm, 7-11pm; Sat noon-2.30pm **Average** €28. **Credit** AmEx, MC, V.
There is nothing new or overtly fashionable about Le Bistrot Napolitain – which, around the Champs-Elysées, makes it very refreshing indeed. A bastion of straightforward southern Italian fare for the past 15 years, this crowded and smoky bistro attracts a lively, unselfconscious set. Once you've been squeezed into the banquette, sit back and enjoy the scenery – diners tucking into big plates of ham, fried red mullet or carpaccio, the *pizzaiolo* toiling before his oven, waiters dashing around bearing big plates of pasta. Though many people had come for a full Italian feast, we stuck to the pizzas, reputed to be among the best in town. Indeed, the crusts were thin and crisp with big air pockets, though the *margarita* topping was slightly bland – we preferred the rocket and fresh tomato version, which we drizzled with olive oil. At around €12, pizzas are pricey – not surprising in this area. We skipped dessert and downed the last drops of our decent Tuscan rosé.

Il Sardo
11 rue de Treilhard, 8th (01.45.61.09.46). M° Monceau or Miromesnil. **Open** Mon-Sat noon-2.15pm, 7.30-10.30. **Average** €37. **Credit** AmEx, MC, V.
Originally in a crowded but convivial space on the noisy rue de Clichy, this Sardinian restaurant made an upwardly mobile move in mid-2001 to a larger, more comfortable and duller space in a wealthy but rather sad corner of the 8th. Something has gone missing in this new setting with its exposed stone wall and rather awful faux-Estruscan frescoes. The food is still quite good – first courses of grilled baby squid on salad, and artichoke with rocket and treviso were delicious. *Malloredus* – tiny pasta shells – served with big hunks of sausage and tomato sauce was excellent. Not so the over-priced linguine with bit-pieces of prawns and veg and a stingy sauce. The owners seem keen to cash in on their reputation in a richer neighbourhood and are obviously counting on the money-bags not to know better. We finished up our delicious Sicilian Merlot with some gorgonzola and parmesan in lieu of dessert, and tarried over superb coffee with complimentary shots of mirto, the potent myrtle-berry liqueur.

Le Stresa ★
7 rue Chambiges, 8th (01.47.23.51.62). M° Alma Marceau or Franklin D. Roosevelt. **Open** Mon-Fri noon-2.30, 7.15-10.30pm. Closed Aug, Christmas. **Average** €75. **Credit** AmEx, DC, MC, V.
The Faiola brothers have run this perennially fashionable haunt for years and people just keep coming back for the impeccably fresh food and the welcome. The walls testify to the restaurant's link with *le gratin de Paris*: sculptures and photos by César, collages and personally signed pix by Peter Beard. On our visit the venerable Jean-Paul Belmondo and footballing prince Emmanuel Petit were 'ciaoing' down while a Dolce & Gabbana-clad photographer was showing off her latest snaps of Sean Connery. The menu, too, is full of classics: mozzarella and tomato pizza, sole with lemon, spinach ravioli and tiramisu. Mixed antipasti with fresh artichoke, roasted chilli, asparagus and aubergine salad and the spaghetti with small clams are excellent starters. Also good is the fiery *spaghetti à la Jean-Paul Belmondo* (yes, he ordered it, too) bathed in chilli, tomato, olives and garlic, as well as simple pan-fried veal with lemon and a mound of emerald-green spinach. Finish with forest-berry gelato.

I Golosi
6, rue de la Grange-Batelière, 9th (01.48.24.18.63). M° Grands Boulevards or Richelieu-Drouot. **Open** Mon-Fri noon-2.30pm, 7.30-midnight; Sat noon-2.30pm. Closed Aug. **Average** €30. **Credit** MC, V.
The warmth of Italy permeates every corner of this bistro-cum-food and wine shop, from the sun-dried tomatoes and sun-kissed wine to the welcoming handshake of the elfin Venetian patron. The menu changes weekly, showcasing seasonal ingredients and northern Italian flair; you might find a warm aubergine *timbale* flavoured with cumin accompanied by a fat, whole roasted tomato; salad of octopus, fennel and potato drizzled with vinaigrette, calamari stuffed with Swiss chard, or simmered veal with white radish – all attractive, satisfying dishes. Venice's favourite dessert, tiramisu, lived up to its pick-me-up name while a bottle of Tocai Rosso at €16 completed the Italian experience – or try one of the wines by the glass. Upstairs is colourfully modern, downstairs is more straightforward bistro-shop style, but wherever you sit it's service with a smile.

Italian

Pizza Milano
30 bd des Italiens, 9th (01.47.70.33.33). M° Opera. **Open** daily 11.30am-12.30am. Closed Christmas eve and Christmas lunch. **Average** €15. **Credit** AmEx, MC, V. **Wheelchair access**.

Among the area's chain restaurants, this place stands out – its low-key decor and low lighting contrast with the plastic Americana that prevails elsewhere and the food is decently priced and good. The continental branch of the successful UK-based Pizza Express chain, Pizza Milano is a perfect eat-on-the-run or late-night option. We were pleased with the prompt, friendly service and the standard of our starters – a delicious *insalata caprese* (mozzarella and tomatoes with basil dressing) served with hot pizza-crust balls and a green salad. Pizzas were nicely topped, too – the *siciliana* is strewn with artichoke hearts, black olives, anchovies, ham and mozzarella and the *calabrese* is a tomato and mozzarella pizza sprinkled with parmesan shavings and fresh rocket when it comes out of the oven. Doubtless encouraged by the low lighting and proximity of the tables, people chat back and forth.

Da Mimmo
39 bd Magenta, 10th (01.42.06.44.47). M° Jacques-Bonsergent. **Open** Mon-Sat noon-2.30pm, 7.30-11.30pm. Closed Aug. **Average** €32. **Lunch menu** €21.35. **Credit** MC, V.

The wood-fired brick oven just inside the door glows invitingly as the old *pizzaiolo* in regulation vest and paunch pummels a huge mound of dough. The centrepiece display groans under the weight of homemade *antipasti*: glistening *carciofi* (globe artichokes), jars of preserved mushrooms, whole sea bream and red mullet, a knuckle of *prosciutto* and a wedge of *parmigiano reggiano*. Charming waiters deliver beautiful food on huge white plates. For a moment, you could be in Napoli … then you see the prices. Most pasta dishes cost €13.71 to €18.29, although we were offered *bigoli* with *chanterelles* and summer truffles at €39.63! Fish, cooked on the bone and sold by weight, costs from €10.50 to €30.50 per person and a large bottle of mineral water will set you back €6.85. Admittedly, the vegetable *antipasti* are terrific and the lunch *menu* – bruschetta with tomato, basil and mozzarella (excellent), a quarter litre of wine, choice of pizza (surprisingly average) and coffee or dessert – is good value. The clientele, with its sprinkling of Jake Lamotta lookalikes and likely 1960s film stars, is fascinating.

Sardegna a Tavola ★
1 rue de Cotte, 12th (01.44.75.03.28). M° Ledru-Rollin. **Open** Mon 7.30-11.30pm, Tue-Sat noon-2.30pm, 7.30-11.30pm. Closed Aug. **Average** €37. **Credit** AmEx, MC, V.

This sunny Sardinian restaurant impressed us when it opened in late 1999 and it has only improved. The husband-and-wife owners have dressed up the decor: discreet lighting and colour photos of a bearded 96-year-old dancer from their native village, sea-blue ceiling beams, braids of garlic and chillies and, more alarmingly (during game season), hares and hams, as well as shelves filled with Sardinian wine, olive oil, pasta, salt and rice. Our lunch started with thinly sliced *charcuterie* and chunky vegetables – fat beans, aubergines cooked with wine, roasted peppers, courgette and cauliflower. Then came hearty ravioli stuffed with ricotta and mushrooms in thick, tomato-mushroom sauce, and farfalle pasta with a typically Sardinian combination of mint, crushed almonds, fresh (though mild) chilli pepper and plenty of olive oil. The house wine, served by the carafe, is delicious.

Il Baccello
33 rue Cardinet, 17th (01.43.80.63.60). M° Wagram. **Open** Tue-Sat noon-2.30pm, 7.30-11pm. Closed three weeks in Aug. **Average** €34. **Prix fixe** €34 (dinner only). **Lunch menu** €15.50-€30. **Credit** AmEx, DC, MC, V.

Chef Raphaël Bembaron has an impressive culinary pedigree – Lucas Carton in Paris, Enoteca Pinchiorri in Florence, and Joia, the superb gourmet vegetarian restaurant, in Milan. It's the latter that the chef says has had the largest impact, and he cooks with as much organic produce as possible. Willow-green walls, spot-lit ceramics, industrial grey carpeting and polished mahogany give this snug dining room a Milan-meets-Tokyo-style, but the plump black olives and whole-wheat bread tell you that you're going to get the best of the boot. Starters of whole-wheat *papardelle* with wild mushrooms and chickpea soup garnished with *pancetta*-wrapped langoustines were superb, as were main courses of risotto cooked with Barolo wine and garnished with duck breast and aged mimolette cheese, and langoustines on toothpicks with almond-stuffed olives on spelt and broccoli in pumpkin coulis. For dessert, go for the almond-flavoured *panna cotta* in prune sauce or the highly original *gelée*, two aspics of fruit brandy. The wine list is small but interesting.

Paolo Petrini
6 rue du Débarcadère, 17th (01.45.74.25.95). M° Argentine or Porte Maillot. **Open** Mon-Fri noon-2pm, 7-10pm; Sat 7-10pm. Closed three weeks in Aug. **Average** €40. **Prix fixe** €29.50 (dinner only). **Lunch menu** €20. **Credit** AmEx, MC, V. **Wheelchair access**.

Catering to locals in a bourgeois neighbourhood, this restaurant wouldn't win any prizes for value, but the authentic fresh pastas, grilled meats and homemade desserts are top-notch. The €29.50 *menu*, while not as tempting as the *carte*, began well with a bowl of melt-in-your-mouth *gnocchi* tossed with tomato and basil sauce and smothered in freshly grated parmesan. Rabbit stuffed with artichokes was less exciting. From the *carte*, a €14 plate of *antipasti* – miniature stuffed peppers, grilled aubergines, artichokes and spring onions doused in olive oil – was copious. A main of grilled rib steak with fresh herbs, olive oil and roasted cherry tomatoes was perfectly cooked but pricey at €26. Pastas shine, as does the risotto with wild asparagus, fresh lima beans and garden peas, which solicited raves all round. Also good was the coconut tiramisu.

Chez Vincent
5 rue du Tunnel, 19th (01.42.02.22.45). M° Botzaris. **Open** Mon-Fri noon-2.30pm, 8-11pm; Sat 8-11pm. **Average** €34. **Prix fixe** €32, €35. **Credit** AmEx, DC, MC, V.

Don't let the name fool you: Chez Vincent (Casa Cozzoli) is a no-nonsense haven for aficionados of down-home *cucina Italiana* and it's always packed. The atmosphere is cosy and convivial with friendly and helpful staff, an open kitchen in the back, and the theatrical Vincent continuously anointing *antipasti* with a vigorous sprinkling of olive oil, lemon and herbs. (To mark the second sitting, he blows his air horn and serenades the crowd.) A full-course dinner can be pricey, but generous portions and lots of extras make it good value. The tasting *menu* is great at €35 (€32 without meat), with ample fare for two: fresh and succulent seafood (juicy calamari, sardines, anchovies and meaty gambas); a tiny aubergine gratin; tender beef carpaccio; a trio of contrasting pastas (tomato, pesto, and *quatro formaggi*); all topped off with tiramisu and gelati.

Indoor fireworks: the art of the pizzaiolo

Da Mimmo has a burning passion for pizza

Though the exact origins may be disputed, it is universally accepted that the true home of pizza is Naples. Neapolitans are so fiercely protective of the quality of their pizza that since 1997, *pizza napolitana* has carried DOC status (similar to AOC in France). Luckily, however, *la vera pizza napolitana* can be produced anywhere in the world, providing certain essential criteria are met.

According to the Associazzione di Vera Pizza Napolitana, pizza dough should only be made from flour, water, salt and natural or brewer's yeast. (Dough made with natural yeast has a characteristic sourdough taste, but is more of a challenge to produce, particularly in the summer, when outside temperatures soar.) The dough must be handled lightly, which precludes the use of industrial-strength mixing machines; rolling pins and frisbee-style antics are also a definite no-no. Pizza-making is serious business.

There are three 'classic' toppings but tasteful variations are permitted. Marinara, also known as *napolitana* or *romana*, is so called because its ingredients of tomato, garlic, oregano and olive oil could be carried on voyages by the sailors of Napoli. This is the simplest, purest expression of the *pizzaiolo*'s art, and is therefore the test of a good pizzeria.

If you want cheese, ask instead for a *margarita*. This delicate combination of tomato, fresh basil and buffalo mozzarella – or more commonly fior di latte, its denser cow equivalent – was 'invented' in 1889 in honour of Italy's queen (the red, white and green supposedly represent the Italian tricolour). When you're really hungry, try a pizza *ripieno*, or *calzone* (meaning trouser leg), where the dough is filled with ricotta, fior di latte or mozzarella and salami, folded and baked.

The pizza has to be placed directly on the stone floor of a dome-shaped, brick-built, wood-burning oven, heated to 400°C. At this temperature, the topping fuses in a matter of seconds (it takes around 90 seconds to cook a *margarita*), while the dough around the outside puffs up like a feather pillow. Naples may have the edge thanks to the quality of the local ingredients – sun-ripened (albeit tinned) San Marzano tomatoes; pungent basil and garlic; pure, volcanically filtered water (chlorinated tap water can kill the yeast in the dough) and bountiful walnut and oak to fire the oven. But, if you look hard enough, it is just possible to find near-authentic pizza in Paris.

Da Mimmo, with its check tablecloths, and cheeky Neapolitan waiters, makes a reasonable stab at it but perhaps the best in Paris is at Alfredo Positano. Tuck into a *marinara*, with its light, yeasty dough, thin layer of tomato sauce, generous sprinkling of oregano and a couple of (unorthodox) anchovies, and you'll understand why the queue usually stretches out the door.
Neil Haidar.

Japanese

Satisfy a yen for sushi or noodles, or splash out on a refined *kaiseki* meal.

Sushi-to-go spots have sprung up all over Paris, reflecting the sudden popularity of Japanese food. But any sushi chef worth his *wasabi* knows that the only raw fish worth eating is freshly prepared, not sealed in plastic and stored in a supermarket fridge. Fortunately, Paris has a growing number of serious sushi restaurants, especially in the Japanese enclave of rue Ste-Anne. Also well-represented are other specialities such as *ramen*, *shabu-shabu*, *yakitori* and even refined *kaiseki* cuisine. The Paris opening of Nobu has made a particular splash (*see p51*, **Trendy**).

Kinugawa ★
9 rue du Mont-Thabor , 1st (01.42.60.65.07). M° Tuileries. **Open** Mon-Sat noon-2.30pm, 7-10pm. Closed 23 Dec-7 Jan. **Average** €60. **Prix fixe** €86-€108 (dinner only). **Lunch menu** €26, €52. **Credit** AmEx, DC, MC, V.

If Japanese restaurants had the same mass appeal as football clubs, you wouldn't be able to step out of the house without seeing people in Kinugawa scarves and Kinugawa tracksuits on every other corner. Its fan base includes dozens of household names, and little wonder. Everything here breathes excellence, from the decor – deep carpets, glossy tables and colourful wall panels (a far cry from the usual *nihon-no* pale wood minimalism) – to the the crockery and gentle, assiduous service. The food follows the highly refined *kaiseki-ryori* tradition, embodying the quintessential Japanese virtues of *wabi* (simplicity) and *sabi* (unstudied elegance): put differently, it's not (only) what you do, it's how you do it. You can order *à la carte* or choose from a range of *menus*: at a recent meal here we opted for the €86 *menu*, which brings nine courses plus dessert. Describing the rapture each dish brought us could fill pages, so let this simple phrase suffice: for the space of a meal, we were in heaven. From the classic (but stunningly fresh) sashimi to the original lime-scented fish consommé served in a small earthenware kettle with tiny matching bowls, via grilled fish, a vegetable *pot au feu*, salad with dressing, superbly light tempura, the fluffiest rice and wonderful miso soup, every new presentation, every fascinating combination of texture and flavour had us swooning with delight. Even the wine – the dry house Bordeaux – was a joy.
Branch: 4 rue St-Philippe-du-Roule, 8th (01.45.63.08.07).

Laï Laï Ken
7 rue Ste-Anne, 1st (01.40.15.96.90). M° Pyramides. **Open** Mon-Sat noon-10pm; Sun 6-10pm. **Average** €14. **Prix fixe** €13. **Credit** AmEx, MC, V.

The last Japanese restaurant on the rue Ste-Anne before the avenue de l'Opéra is one of the most reliable eateries in town. LLK certainly doesn't aim for the culinary stratosphere, yet it's pretty much unbeatable in the 'homely, flavourful and affordable' category: we've been going there regularly for five years now, and it hasn't disappointed once. The service is pleasant and attentive and the surroundings clean and low-key. *Ramen* – noodle soup laden with bamboo shoots and pork slices – is the way to go; otherwise, take your pick from an extensive menu which features such well-made and generous dishes as stir-fried beef with green peppers, fried rice or more exotic numbers like jellyfish. Above all, don't miss the sublime *age gyoza*, deep-fried pork and garlic dumplings in a crispy rice pastry wrapper, preferably accompanied by large cans of Asahi beer. You know the food is authentic when you see so many Japanese diners – this is a place that can easily become a regular destination.

Takara ★
14 rue Molière, 1st (01.42.96.08.38). M° Palais-Royal. **Open** Tue-Fri noon-2.30pm; Sat, Sun 7-10.30pm. Closed three weeks in Aug, two weeks in Dec. **Average** €60. **Prix fixe** €46-€59. **Lunch menu** €19-€42. **Credit** MC, V.

The name means 'treasure', and if that's not enough to convince you, take a look inside. Although the elegant decor – Japanese artwork, dark wood and a colour scheme of creams and dark blues – discreetly but unmistakably whispers 'class', there's nothing stuffy about this place: in fact, you'll rarely see normally restrained Japanese diners (including salarymen) so clearly enjoying themselves. We went for the *shabu-shabu* set meal (€59 per person), which began with sublime *amuse-bouches* of angler fish liver terrine, served with crushed radish in tangy *ponzu* (vinegar and soy sauce). Next came ten pieces of sashimi which, as well as being flawlessly fresh and well presented, were served with exquisite, delicately flavoured (and, in Paris, very rare) *shiso* leaves. Then we were served *chawa-mushi*, a marvellous, steamed egg custard flavoured with fish stock and containing shitake mushrooms, gingko tree nut and pieces of chicken and prawn. The centrepiece of the meal, the *shabu-shabu*, consisted of beef and vegetables – Chinese cabbage and *konomono* (edible chrysanthemum leaves) – dipped in a large pan of boiling stock above a gas burner. Delicious coconut ice cream with red bean jam and grilled *hojicha* tea concluded the meal. The tableware was as refined as the service by attentive, kimono-clad waitresses and a twinkly-eyed waiter. After an excellent hot sake we left feeling restored and utterly jubilant.

Zen
18 rue du Louvre, 1st (01.42.86.95.05). M° Louvre-Rivoli. **Open** Tue-Sat noon-2.30pm, 7-10.30pm; Sun 7-10.30pm. Closed first two weeks in Aug. **Average** €45. **Prix fixe** €24-€60. **Lunch menu** €12.50-€35. **Credit** AmEx, MC, V.

Zen has been open for 12 years, in its rather inauspicious location beneath a detective agency, serving some of the best sushi in town to a mostly Japanese clientele in a plush, soundproofed, air-conditioned decor. Portions seemed slightly smaller since our previous visit, but quality was as high as ever. We chose the 'superior' sushi selection with tempura, which began with bean-sprout salad drizzled with a sesame dressing, then pieces of pickled cucumber and turnip (fascinatingly soft and crunchy at the same time) and steaming *miso* soup laden with tofu chunks and seaweed. The centrepiece of the meal was the first-class sushi served on frosted-glass plates – 12 pieces of perfect fish (tuna, salmon, sea bream, squid and raw prawns among others) atop immaculately moist rice. Green-tea ice cream with red bean jam finished off the meal, during which our attentive Japanese waiter had kept us smiling with discreetly wry remarks. The wine list is pricey – we suggest that you stick to the very drinkable house white.

Aki
2 bis, rue Daunou, 2nd (01.42.61.48.38). M° Opéra. **Open** Mon-Fri noon-2.30pm, 7-11pm; Sat 7-11pm. Closed three weeks in Aug. **Average** €38. **Prix fixe** €28.50-€58.50. **Lunch menu** €14.50-€18. **Credit** AmEx, MC, V.

After several incarnations this two-level space

MIYAKO
Japanese restaurant

Home delivery - Take away

Sushi - Sashimi - Yakitori

Recommended by several guides

Reserve at lunch time!

121 rue de l'Université, 7th.
M° Invalides
Tel: 01.47.05.41.83 - Fax: 01.45.55.13.18
Closed Sat lunch and Sun all day
Closest parking "La Tour Maubourg"
45 quai d'Orsay, 7th

has resurfaced as a stylish Japanese restaurant, providing a refreshing contrast to the more pared-down approach of the many nearby noodle houses. Red velvet chairs, soft lighting, gold walls and dark wood tables set the seductive tone — the only flaw being the tables' chunky pillar design, which leaves you wondering what to do with your knees. At lunch, the obvious choices are the *bento* box or a more elaborate *menu* which features similar ingredients presented separately in larger quantities. Chef Terazaki Toshiyuki is trained in the refined *kaiseki* tradition and it shows in the presentation: sashimi came elegantly arranged on a leaf atop a square bamboo board on a bed of ice, while tempura arrived in a porcelain basket perched on a pedestal. Though the sashimi and sushi were impeccably fresh, we would have liked to see more variety beyond salmon, tuna and sea bream — the chef is obviously playing it safe with his mostly French clientele. The *bento* box was the better choice for a quick meal — it also included rice moulded into a crescent shape, rather nondescript grilled salmon and chicken, and spinach in a nice peanut dressing. Few people ordered desserts, but we were pleased with our matcha tea ice cream topped with sweet red beans, and light banana fritters with mango sorbet. We hope that over time Toshiyuki will feel freer to let his creativity loose.

Isse
56 rue Ste-Anne, 2nd (01.42.96.67.76). M° Pyramides. **Open** Tue-Fri noon-2pm, 7-10pm; Sat 7-10pm. Closed three weeks in Aug. **Average** €60. **Lunch menu** €22.87, €30.50. **Credit** MC, V.

This is upmarket Japanese cuisine, and as much a cultural as a culinary experience. You might want to preface your meal with a trip downstairs to the loo, if only to wash your hands – a dainty rock garden and a pebble-filled basin have an oddly calming effect. A few tables on the ground floor share space with a typical sushi bar, where you can admire the chef's prowess with a sharp instrument. Upstairs a small dining room feels like a first-class cruiser cabin: low ceiling, blond wood panelling, a deep-blue sea of carpeting. Service is sumptuous, almost sensual – very Japanese. A large selection of sushi and sashimi is reassuringly incomplete – only the freshest sea fare will make it you your table, dusted with *wasabi* and served with an excellent pickled ginger that has not, as is usually the case, been dyed pink. Appetisers range from a variety of unusually pungent miso soups to lightly stir-fried seasonal vegetables. A main-course crab dish was nicely set off by fresh ginger, *mirin* (sweet rice wine) and a hint of peppers. All good, but not exceptional – even a bit disappointing for the price. Also, given the every-detail-counts nature of Japanese cuisine, a surprising number of lapses: disposable chopsticks, no hand towels and insufficiently warm sake.

Isami
4 quai d'Orléans, 4th (01.40.46.06.97). M° Pont Marie. **Open** Tue-Sat noon-2pm, 7-10pm; Sun 7-10pm. Closed three weeks in Aug. **Average** €30. **Prix fixe** €24.50-€27.45. **Credit** MC, V.

Seating just 30 diners, this tiny place on the Ile St-Louis is a fine example of the Japanese gift for miniaturisation – and booking is essential. The clean, unassuming decor and heavy linen tablecloths and napkins added a note of understated stylishness to our meal, which started with whelks and chunks of monkfish liver. We were asked by the hostess if we had aversions to any type of fish, and we asked her to lay on the full works – which, here, means sea urchin, octopus and cuttlefish as well as the more usual salmon, tuna and halibut, all served on traditional wooden boards. The fish is pleasingly fresh, and if you go *à la carte* you can choose individual sushi and sashimi pieces, as well as a variety of fish, vegetables, omelettes or combinations thereof, rolled up with rice inside seaweed.

Japotori
41 rue Monsieur-le-Prince, 6th (01.43.29.00.54). M° Odéon. **Open** daily noon-3pm, 6-11.45pm. Closed 24, 25 Dec. **Prix fixe** €5.49-€14.48. **Credit** MC, V.

Low prices draw a young, lively crowd every night to this popular joint specialising in *yakitori* (Japanese-style kebabs), and at weekends it gets completely packed. Don't be surprised to see people queuing up outside, and be prepared to do the same. The *menus* feature *yakitori* in varying styles and number – the top price brings eight, which add up to a filling meal. All *menus* include rice and soup containing thin slices of onion and mushroom; the *yakitori* are brought to the table in batches of two or three – duck, chicken, molten cheese wrapped in a thin slice of beef, whole grilled mushrooms, meatballs and pork. A tiny cup of sake tops it all off at the end. Fun, filling and just about unbeatable value.

Tsukizi
2bis rue des Ciseaux, 6th (01.43.54.65.19). M° Mabillon. **Open** Tue-Sat noon-2.30pm, 7-10pm; Sun 7-10pm. Closed three weeks in Aug. **Average** €30. **Lunch menu** €15. **Credit** AmEx, MC, V.

A reverential hush hung over the tables in this tiny sushi restaurant when we came for lunch, as well-to-do, mainly European connoisseurs concentrated on their food in a traditional decor of wooden lattice screens and dark wooden tables. We sat at the counter, the ideal vantage point from which to watch the Japanese chefs at work – one concentrating on sashimi, the other on sushi – as they sliced up various types of fish with impressive dexterity. After ten minutes observing them making up selections for other tables we had developed a ravenous hunger. Finally it was our turn, and our sushi and sashimi *menus* were set before us. Although the fish was undeniably good, it's not amazing value (the St-Germain location pushes the price up): €24.50 only buys you nine pieces of sushi, and a similar quantity of sashimi. Still, the experience was pleasingly authentic, and some of the customers were clearly regulars. It just was a shame that the (non-Japanese) waiter should have been so unfriendly – the only off-note in an otherwise good meal.

Yen ★
22 rue St-Benoît, 6th (01.45.44.11.18). M° St-Germain-des-Prés. **Open** Mon 7.30-11pm, Tue-Sat 12.30-2.30pm, 7.30-11.30pm. Closed two weeks in Aug. **Average** €46. **Lunch menu** €18.29, €30.49. **Credit** AmEx, MC, V. **Wheelchair access**.

The rue St-Benoît no longer swings to the rhythm of jazz like it once did, but one welcome addition to this increasingly fashion-minded area is Yen. Though the upstairs dining room's ancient beams show we are indeed in St-Germain, the minimalist but comfortable beige and blonde wood decor feels convincingly Japanese – a sensation reinforced by the great majority of Japanese diners and staff (our exceptionally helpful French waitress was able to explain the menu in detail). The menu is divided into appetisers, starters and the speciality of cold or hot *soba* (buckwheat noodles). Prompted by the waitress, we started with an unusual tongue-teaser of *soba miso*, a tantalising mix of sweet *miso* and grilled buckwheat grains cooked and served on flat wooden spoons. Moving straight on to noodles, we ordered the *ten seiro* – cold noodles in a basket with a side order of fluffy vegetable and prawn tempura – and a hot noodle soup with strips of duck breast. Eating the noodles is a slightly complex procedure which staff will be happy to explain – suffice it to say that we emerged feeling invigorated. Just as soothing, the potent orange-scented soup broth was so good that we slurped it straight from the bowl – 'the chef will be pleased', our waitress assured us. We indulged in ice creams made with green tea and, more unusually, ginger to finish off a meal that we can't wait to repeat.

Jipangue
96 rue La Boétie, 8th (01.45.63.77.00). M° St-Philippe-du-Roule. **Open** Mon-Fri noon-2pm, 7-11pm; Sat 7-11pm. Closed 13 Jul-14 Aug. **Average** €30. **Prix fixe** €17.50-€34.50. **Lunch menu** €13.70-€14.50. **Credit** AmEx, MC, V.

Just a short walk from the Champs-Elysées, Jipangue is hardly in prime Japanese restaurant territory, but its decor is authentic enough. Sushi is served on the ground-floor dining room, with its clean, pale surfaces and plenty of wood; but you should head upstairs for *sukiyaki*, which, despite being probably the best-known Japanese meat dish is, in Paris, difficult to find. On the first floor, amid mirrrors and plush red trimmings, each table of four features a large round hotplate sunk into the centre. The waitress ceremonially lifts its cover, lights the gas and puts a piece of beef fat to sizzle on the hot plate, before bringing on plates of raw, gossamer-thin beef and vegetables (or shellfish) that you cook yourself and dip in soy sauce before eating. On the evening of our visit, the clientele was a slightly odd mix of Japanese expense-account businessmen and a smattering of T-shirt-and-shorts tourists from Eastern Europe.

Kifuné
44 rue St-Ferdinand, 17th (01.45.72.11.19). M° Argentine. **Open** Mon 7-10pm; Tue-Sat noon-2pm, 7-10pm. Closed two weeks in Aug, two weeks in winter. **Average** €35. **Lunch menu** €23.50. **Credit** MC, V.

Well beyond the Japanese heartland of rue Ste-Anne is a surprisingly isolated Japanese haunt; when we called Kifuné for a dinner reservation, they answered the phone in Japanese and seemed surprised to hear French. The sleepy street is not very easy to find but that doesn't stop this small, understated restaurant (it looks like a converted café) from filling up with an entirely Japanese crowd — we were the only westerners. Watching the chefs at work it was clear that they weren't fooling around: many of those around us were ordering the *futo maki* (inside-out seaweed rolls). We started with a sublime crab and prawn salad — real crab claws with squeaky fresh prawns and ever-so-thin marinated cucumber slices — and miso soup with clams. Always a good test of a Japanese restaurant, the broth was richly flavoured — we lapped up every drop. Sushi and sashimi are expensive here — a 'special' sushi assortment, presented on a wooden board, featured nine pieces, including raw prawn and tender squid, and cost €27.50. Still, we don't mind paying for quality fish and this was very respectable, with service and atmosphere to match. Green tea ice cream here is fine, not great — more exciting is the Japanese-style fruit salad with ice cream, with a tiny glass of syrup for pouring over top.

Takara: a Japanese experience to treasure

Jewish

Beyond bagels and lox: dig into crunchy felafel, steaming couscous or juicy meats.

Jewish food in Paris takes many forms. The ancient rue des Rosiers in the Marais, with its incongruous mix of fashion boutiques and felafel joints, is still the best place to try the cooking of Ashkenazi Jews from eastern and central Europe. Restaurants open and close at a dizzying rate, but the best of the bunch have long been **Chez Marianne** and **L'As du Fallafel**. Along the rue du Faubourg-Montmartre and the rue Richer, a cluster of simple restaurants run by Sephardic Jews from North Africa offer fresh Tunisian salads and juicy grilled meats. The multicultural Belleville also has a number of thriving North African Jewish restaurants, packed with authentic atmosphere. Though bagel shops are popping up all over Paris, this is not what the city does best.

L'As du Fallafel ★
34 rue des Rosiers, 4th (01.48.87.63.60). Mº St-Paul. **Open** Mon-Thur, Sun 11am-midnight; Fri noon-sunset. **Average** €8. **Credit** MC, V.
'Often imitated, never equalled,' says a sign in the window, and indeed L'As du Fallafel has something to brag about. Formerly an ordinary-looking shop which sold exceptional felafel at a small counter, L'As has morphed in the past few years into a noisy and exuberant New York-style eatery. The tables are packed close together, the plates and forks are plastic, yet a meal here is a great all-around dining experience, with the cooks and fellow diners as entertainment. Half-a-dozen kitchen staff throw freshly-fried felafel into pitta pockets at lightning speed while, a few tables away, a regular works her way through one of the gargantuan sandwiches while talking on her mobile phone. You can order other things – *shawarma* (shaved lamb), *frites* – but felafel is what it's all about. Don't miss out on the *spécial*, which comes with extras of sautéed aubergine and a dollop of houmous; hot sauce is on the table for those who dare. Freshly-squeezed orange or carrot juice makes a fine accompaniment. Though the queue for take-away felafel outdoors is an enjoyable ritual, it's well worth paying a little extra more to sit at a table and soak up the atmosphere.

Chez Marianne
2 rue des Hospitalières-St-Gervais, 4th (01.42.72.18.86). Mº St-Paul. **Open** daily 11am-midnight. **Average** €15. **Credit** MC, V.
Smack dab in the middle of it all, Chez Marianne has long set the standard by which all other Jewish restaurants in Paris are judged. To escape the hordes, the second dining room just down the street (accessible only after 'checking in' at the main restaurant) boasts the same beamed ceilings and stone walls but not quite the same hustle and bustle. The *assiettes composées*, plates of four to six Middle Eastern and central European Jewish specialities, are the best way to go. Here they are served with baskets of astonishingly delicate pumpernickel and rye bread. From the long list of choices, the houmous and *tahini* should not be missed. Equally enticing deli classics such as pastrami or creamed herring are rich and salty, and the superbly executed chopped liver with onions would make any Jewish grandmother proud. Slightly blander and less fresh were the *tabouleh* and stuffed grape leaves. To accompany your meal, try the full-bodied Israeli lager, Maccabee. And, if you still have room, order the *vatrouchka*, a chunk of surprisingly light cheesecake.

Jo Goldenberg
7 rue des Rosiers, 4th (01.48.87.70.39). Mº St-Paul. **Open** daily 8.30am-midnight. **Average** €18. **Credit** AmEx, DC, MC, V.
Long-established restaurateur Jo Goldenberg was charged in 2001 with some alarming hygiene infractions (*see p33*, **Bistros**), but his landmark restaurant remains open and still attracts a crowd. This multi-purpose Jewish food emporium lets you snack, order a meal, grab take-out pastries or select deli items no matter the time of day. Soups such as *borscht*, *krupnik* (mushroom barley), matzoh ball (with chicken broth), as well as blinis, smoked fish, caviar, stuffed peppers, potato *latkes* and daily specials such as roast turkey breast or stuffed cabbage fill out a long list of kosher and Eastern European favourites. Our cured salmon was top-notch, creamy and tender while the beef-and-tomato-stuffed aubergine, surrounded by three types of grains including a semolina pasta (*ferfel*), was filling rather than elegant. In the off-hours between lunch and dinner locals sit amiably chatting over lemon or mint tea and a very crispy, flaky, buttery, warm apple strudel doused in cream.

Pitchi Poï
7 rue Caron, 9 pl Marché Ste-Catherine, 4th (01.42.77.46.15). Mº St-Paul. **Open** daily 10.30am-3pm, 6-10.30pm. Sunday brunch noon-4pm. **Average** €24. **Prix fixe** €18.14. **Credit** AmEx, DC, MC, V.
Set on one of the most picturesque squares in Paris, Pitchi Poï bills itself as a '*blinisserie*', though you'll discover not only blinis but a variety of Eastern European, Mediterranean and Jewish choices on the short menu. Zipping from party to party, our waitress was cheery under pressure, attending to every request speedily and with a broad smile. Our aubergine caviar and houmous struck us as bland and a tad meagre, though we warmed to the deep red *borscht*, freshly made and served with potatoes on the side. We sampled an impressive slice of fish pie (*coulibiac*) – rice, spinach and salmon in a doughy wrap with saffron sauce – and *datcha*, a slab of smoked salmon with jacket potato and garlic crème fraîche. Our too-sweet, slightly soggy strudel made us wish we'd chosen differently; still, you could do a lot worse than spend an hour or two at Pitchi Poï.

Les Ailes
34 rue Richer, 9th (01.47.70.62.53/ www.lesailes.fr). Mº Cadet. **Open** daily noon-2.30pm, 7-11.30pm. **Average** €34. **Credit** MC, V.
This kosher Tunisian, the best-known in the area, packs in the locals with generous portions served at breakneck speed. We barely had time to sit down before half a dozen appetising little dishes (called *kamie*) of spicy pickled vegetables, olives and nuts arrived and were then whisked away to make way for starters we had ordered just minutes before. Judging from everyone's plates, the main attraction is the charcoal grill. *Entrecôte*, lamb chops, *merguez* (spicy lamb sausage), chicken skewers and liver come as accompaniments to a homely couscous, or loaded on big platters as meals in themselves. Fish include whole sea bream, tuna, red mullet and salmon. All arrived juicy and well-charred but without the slightest seasoning. Lemon, salt and *harissa* (garlic, oil and red chillies) are on hand, but we expected a bit more finesse for dishes that approach €23 without accompaniments (an additional €3). Dessert was a wonderful honey-flavoured sabayon with rich sponge cake and fresh strawberries. Our €16 Bordeaux was a bargain on an otherwise pricey list.

Patrick Goldenberg
69 av Wagram, 17th (01.42.27.34.79). Mº Ternes. **Open** daily 9am-11pm. Hot food served noon-3pm. **Average** €23. **Prix fixe** €21.34. **Credit** MC, V.
Over the course of several generations, the Goldenberg family has made its way from Odessa to Paris' swanky 17th *arrondissement* via Bucharest, Sofia and Istanbul. Drawing upon a wealth of family recipes, Jo Goldenberg's nephew Patrick offers five nation-specific menus, each honouring a particular tradition of Jewish cooking. We paired the Russian *harengs gras* with the Romanian main course of *mittité*, and strudel. The large herring fillet was perfectly marinated but it might have been better teamed with a crisp Russian vodka than with the pungent *swica*, a Romanian prune *eau de vie*, that we chose. *Mittité* consisted of minced beef seasoned with spices too foreign for our palates to identify, and grilled to perfection – crispy on the outside and deep pink on the inside. A triumphant finish, the apple and nut strudel arrived steaming hot, fresh from the oven. Less elaborate, but equally traditional, and a meal unto itself, the triple-decker pastrami sandwich was faultless.

Benittah ★
49 quai de Seine, 19th (01.40.05.99.00). Mº Riquet. **Open** Mon-Thur, Sun noon-2.30pm, 6.30-midnight; Sat sunset-midnight. Closed two weeks in Aug. **Average** €28. **Credit** MC, V.
Benittah is a gem in the rough, a superb Israeli/Jewish eatery in a neighborhood with a feeble culinary endowment. This spotless corner restaurant is separated from the Canal Saint Martin by towering leafy trees and in good weather a wide pavement accommodates diners ten-deep. Service is attentive and charmingly informal, and always under the watchful supervision of the owner. Your table is laden with house delicacies – giant lemon-marinated green olives, coriander-cucumber-tomato salad, and spiced boiled almonds – even before you see a menu. Sublime kebabs of grilled lamb, duck, kidneys, liver, meatballs and spiced sausages (*merguez*) are a must. The green beans and fish alone are worth the trip though rarely is everything on the menu available. It would be criminal to leave without sampling the homemade sabayon, an eggy ice cream-like concoction with pistachios. This is a family restaurant in a way that doesn't prevent the rest of us from enjoying our meals. Everything at Benittah is kosher in every sense.

Maison Benisti
108 bd de Belleville, 20th (01.46.36.87.88). Mº Belleville. **Open** Tue-Sun 8am-10pm. **Average** €11. **Credit** V.
A hybrid bakery, deli, sandwich shop and restaurant, Benisti rises to the challenge of feeding hungry Tunisian and Jewish families in this North and West African and Asian neighbourhood. The bright lighting in the dining area highlights the clash of Moorish tiles with blue and white-checked tablecloths and stained, green plastic lawn furniture. But forget the no-frills atmosphere, think cheap and heaps. Choose from snacks or *petite faim* options such as *brik* pastry filled with tuna and mashed potato or a bulbous carrot and egg sandwich. If you've got a *grande faim*, then one of a half-dozen decent pizzas or the familiar and generous felafel plate with carrot, cucumber and cabbage salads should hit the spot. Weeknights are fairly dead while weekend lunchtimes are full chaos with folks ordering at the counter and toting their steaming couscous or Tunisian sandwiches back to their tables. Finish with a toasted coconut mound or one of the almond-flour horns dusted with sugar.

L'As du Fallafel: heavenly food off lowly plastic plates.

North African

Push through Paris' kilim curtains to discover oases of Maghreb flavours.

In recent surveys on their eating habits, the French have consistently declared the North African staple couscous to be among their favourite dishes, a close runner-up to the eternal *steak-frites*. The most obvious explanation for the popularity of North African food is immigration: today, the Paris region counts about 200,000 Algerians, 130,000 Moroccans and 48,000 Tunisians, without considering the second or third generations.

A little vocabulary will go a long way in Maghreb restaurants: couscous refers to steamed semolina but also to a complete dish, usually served with vegetables in broth and meat; Moroccan tagines are sweetened stews cooked in cone-shaped clay dishes; *briouates* are triangular pastries, variously filled; *méchoui* is spit-roasted lamb hacked into pieces and served in giant hunks. Another Moroccan speciality is *pastilla*, meat (usually pigeon) wrapped in crisp pastry and sweetened with sugar and cinnamon.

404
69 rue des Gravilliers, 3rd (01.42.74.57.81). M° Arts et Métiers. **Open** Mon-Fri noon-2.30pm, 8pm-midnight; Sat, Sun noon-2.30pm (brunch), 8pm-midnight. Closed at lunch and Sun in Aug. **Average** €27.
Lunch menu €17 (Mon-Fri); brunch €21 (Sat, Sun). **Credit** AmEx, DC, MC, V.
The Moroccan treats here definitely take a back seat to the setting and, on weekends, the party vibe, which gets cranking as you order your first course. Lest you forget, 404 is a restaurant (the open kitchen reminds you of that) with great atmosphere: low tables, cushioned benches along the walls, dark beams and palm frond shadows cast from feathery candlelight and metal lanterns. We found the mushroom-prawn and cheese-potato-mint *briouates* (little pastries) a let-down given the promising build-up and price; likewise, the couscous and tagines are hit-or-miss. The chicken tagines – one with pear, the other with preserved lemon and olives – impressed us, while the vegetarian version lacked intensity. Grilled *daurade* (sea bream) was overcooked and its side rice and veggies bland, suggesting 404's flair does not extend beyond the meaty, more traditional dishes. Desserts redeemed: try the mini *crêpe Berbère* with honey and nuts, and an outstanding sweet mound of semolina called *saffae*, topped with toasted almonds. By meal's end, the house music makes conversation nigh impossible, though the politeness and infectious energy of the grooving staff, dressed in skin-tight gold and black tops, make it hard to fault their mood. Reservations, and a day-of follow-up calls to confirm, are required.

Chez Omar
47 rue de Bretagne, 3rd (01.42.72.36.26). M° Arts et Métiers. **Open** Mon-Sat noon-2.30pm; Sun 7pm-midnight. **Average** €27. **No credit cards**.
Affluent and arty thirtysomethings continue to crowd into Chez Omar. It's an old formula, but a good one: the traditional bistro setting exercises a sentimental charm; the waiters are cheekily frenetic; the couscous and vegetables seemingly limitless. But, before you launch into your grilled lamb *brochette*, your enormous barbequed *méchoui* (grilled lamb) or your spicy *merguez* sausage, beware. Something has gone slightly awry at this Algerian institution. It may look as good as it always did, but on a recent visit, the quality of the meat seemed to have slipped – what was always exquisite is now, sadly, merely satisfactory. Having said that, the portions (especially the Royale, which could feed a family of four) are still enormous. The same generosity extends to the delicious Algerian pastries – although anyone who is still eating at that stage quite frankly deserves a standing ovation. Make sure you finish with a mint tea – it's delicious and aids digestion. Prepare to prop up the bar (Chez Omar doesn't take reservations), and to be rather more intimate with your neighbours than you might have anticipated.
Branch: Café Moderne, 19 rue Keller, 11th (01.47.00.53.62).

L'Atlas
12 bd St-Germain, 5th (01.44.07.23.66). M° Maubert-Mutualité. **Open** Tue-Sun noon-2.30pm, 7.30-11pm. **Average** €38.
Lunch menu €15 (Mon-Fri).
Credit AmEx, DC, MC, V.
Steps from the Institut du Monde Arabe, Atlas is the kind of place where a man dressed in a tall chef's hat takes your order, and on your way to the beautiful loo, no fewer than three waiters back away to let you pass. Reading the huge menu, it's immediately clear that Atlas is all about fusion takes on the Moroccan food routine, with inventive tagines (€20-€22) that feature grouper, saffron and mango; delicately seasoned sea bass and fennel; and even calf's brains. Starters include smoked fish with salad, and a memorable aubergine purée and artichoke salad. The bran and mint soup (*soupe de son*) may be the most unusual choice: blandish, but oddly soothing. Meatless couscous is a refined version of the average standby, with a clear broth and plenty of veggies. Glazed pigeon with dates struck us as too sweet, while the pigeon and wild mushroom tagine had been superbly roasted in its clay pot to bring out its spirited flavours. For dessert, the *assiette gourmande* mixes French faves such as ice cream with little Maghreb pastries. This is an over-the-top Moroccan wonderland, whose elaborate tiling and arabesque plasterwork tricks you into thinking you're in a royal palace and not in the Latin Quarter. Almost.

Ziryab
Institut du Monde Arabe, 1 rue des Fossés-St-Bernard, 5th (01.53.10.10.20). M° Jussieu. **Open** Tue-Sun noon-3pm. **Average** €45.
Credit AmEx, MC, V. **Wheelchair access**.
Ziryab was the name of a ninth century musician, who invented the five-string Arabic lute, and was generally known as a sophisticated chap who liked his food. For this reason the restaurant on the top floor of the Institut du Monde Arabe bears his name. As our first courses took 20 minutes to arrive we had plenty of time to enjoy the spectacular view looking down-river towards Notre-Dame. Despite the North African music, the atmosphere is more akin to an upmarket lounge in an international airport than a café in the casbah – as is the menu, which offers a number of 'Mediterranean' dishes which would be more at home in a hotel dining room. We eventually began our meal with an unusual seafood *brik* and a selection of *briouates*, delicately stuffed samosa-style parcels, both served with an exotic herb salad. Couscous *méchoui* was notable for the freshness of the vegetable broth, which included nicely firm red peppers, aubergines and courgettes. The lamb, though, was rather over-charred and the couscous grain not outstanding. We ordered a seafood *pastilla* and ended up with a tasty quail and almond version of the pastry, but once the mistake had been noticed, the headwaiter brought an extra dish of fish poached in a pungent coriander-heavy broth. With the last drops of the excellent Moroccan Ksar rosé, we enjoyed a vanilla cream flavoured with orange water, served on a sugared disc of filo pastry; in this dish tradition and innovation came together successfully. High-tech Moroccan with a view over Paris was well worth our €91.46 bill for two.

Wally le Saharien
36 rue Rodier, 9th (01.42.85.51.90). M° Notre-Dame-de-Lorette or Anvers. **Open** Mon 7.30-10.30pm, Tue-Sat 11.30am-2pm, 7.30-10.30pm. Closed Aug. **Average** €23 (lunch only). **Prix fixe** €40.40 (dinner only).
Credit MC, V.
Ouali Chouaki, a ponytailed Berber from Djanet, is a couscous aristocrat. In a city spoilt for choice, his grains, light as angel's breath, are unrivalled. Dinner here, comfortably tucked in a carpet-clad corner, is a ritualised affair. There's no menu, no choice, but enough flavour to satisfy even the most Sahara-weary palate. A meal might begin with *harira* (spiced up with a teasing array of mint, coriander, fennel, pimento and cinnamon); a delicate pigeon *pastilla*, served rather unusually like a sugar-dusted spring roll; and finally a giant sardine, stuffed with garlic and parsley. All just a prelude to the pink and unimaginably tender lamb *méchoui*. Each plate of lamb is served with roughly spiced *merguez* and a mound of airy couscous (seconds optional). If you still have room, there is mint tea and a platter of elegant, nut-laden pastries. Wine is extra, but the Maghreb selection is reasonably priced. A small *traiteur* next door stocks enough ingredients (including pre-made *pastillas* and mountains of mouthwatering desserts) to allow you to try the Algerian campfire experience at home. Wally also serves lunch, with a more conventional – but no less tasty – menu offering both tagines and couscous.

L'Homme Bleu ★
55bis rue Jean-Pierre Timbaud, 11th (01.48.07.05.63). M° Couronnes or Parmentier. **Open** Mon-Sat 7.30pm-1am. Closed Aug. **Average** €23. **Credit** MC, V. **Wheelchair access**.
Pop into this restaurant on a weekend without a reservation and you can expect to wait all night to be seated. Squeezed between the open kitchen where cheerfully humming chefs prepare your meal and the crowded zinc bar near the door, the upstairs dining room is more entertaining than the well-ventilated cellar. Fresh and lavishly prepared, the exquisite cooking doesn't depart radically from Maghreb standards, but treats traditional dishes with aplomb. Our tastebuds cried out thankfully at the arrival of the tender prawns with garlic and coriander, *timâmucin yeqlin*, and the *kefta mqetfa*, richly seasoned, grilled ground-beef skewers, that we'd selected from an inviting list of cold and hot appetisers. A main course of *tagine ilhman lahlou* paired lean lamb chunks with sticky prunes in a cinnamon-based sauce studded with almonds. The scent alone was divine. Less exotic, the *seksou n inebgi*, a mixed meat couscous, was enormous. The broth, often an all-too-bland vehicle for sodden vegetables, was light and aromatic and the vegetables firm and perfectly cooked. For dessert, we savoured sublimely sweet honey-and-nut Tunisian pastries hand-picked from a roving tray, and long thin glasses of mint tea served from a decorative silver pot.

More of anything? Moor of everything at Le Mansouria

Le Mansouria

11 rue Faidherbe, 11th (01.43.71.00.16). M° Faidherbe-Chaligny. **Open** Mon, Tue 7.30-11pm; Wed-Sat noon-3pm, 7.30-11pm. Closed 12-20 Aug. **Average** €46. **Prix fixe** €29, €44. **Credit** MC, V.

On a Monday night Le Mansouria was packed, a sign of its unflagging popularity. Mysteriously, though, the plush front room to the right of the entrance, furnished with cushy red-and-gold Moroccan-style banquettes, was kept entirely empty while only the plainer bistro-style room was used. Seated at a tiny table next to a looming pillar, we asked to be moved and promptly were. Dishes were familiar to us from our last visit: 'bride's fingers' (crisp cylindrical pastries filled with spicy prawns), 'veiled couscous' and *mourouzia*, a mysterious-sounding 12th-century lamb recipe. We started with the unpronounceable *r'raif*, a thin layer of minced meat and onion folded into crisp crêpes, and a refreshing salad of chopped herbs with tomato. Then the mains engulfed our small square table: couscous striped with cinnamon over chunks of chicken with sweet onions, raisins and almonds, and a truly medieval-sized hunk of lamb in a thick, honey-sweetened yellow sauce intriguingly flavoured with the 27-spice mix *ras al hanout*. Utterly stuffed, we finished our meal with sweet mint tea. The €44 *menu* includes eight starters, a main course, dessert, wine and mint tea, but must be ordered three to four days ahead. Though the standard of cooking is still high, the couscous was slightly lumpy this time and we would love to see Hal introduce more regional dishes from her travels around Morocco.

Restaurant des 4 Frères

127 bd de Ménilmontant, 11th (01.43.55.40.91). M° Ménilmontant. **Open** Mon-Thur, Sat, Sun noon-4pm, 6-11pm; Fri 3-11pm. **Average** €9. **Credit** MC, V.

Run by four genial Algerian brothers, this humble neighbourhood joint serves up stunningly cheap heaps of fluffy couscous. Extended families and couples crowd the cramped tables, but once we dipped our spoons into the chunky chickpea soup and sampled the simple salads (egg, onion, beetroot, lettuce), the food fight at the next table seemed part of the fun. Don't even think about finishing your vat of *couscous maison* (€6), available with crisp, grilled beef, chicken, lamb or veal. Daily specials round out the mysterious menu, which appears partly on two blackboards and partly in the waiter's head. It must pay to be a regular: then you'll know to order the omelette with *frites*, or to ask for a bottle of olive oil to bathe your basic baguettes. No alcohol is served; you're not allowed to bring your own, and there's no dessert. But, for purists with a hankering to stuff themselves silly with couscous, brochettes and tangy sauces, this is heaven.

Le Souk

1 rue Keller, 11th (01.49.29.05.08). M° Ledru-Rollin or Bastille. **Open** Sat, Sun noon-.2.30pm, 7.30pm-12.15am; Tue-Fri 7.30-11.45pm. **Average** €27. **Credit** AmEx, MC, V. **Wheelchair access.**

When you push back the kilim that curtains the entrance to the Souk, the richly-coloured carpets, cut-work lanterns, mosaic tables, and djellaba-clad waiters will transport you straight to Oran (the Souk is Algerian-owned). Add the waft of smouldering herbs and the sizzle of piping-hot tagines and your tastebuds know they're in for a treat. We went straight for the *pastilla*, layers of *brik* pastry, pigeon and ground nuts, dusted with sugar and cinnamon; it was a little dry, but the subtle blend of meat and sweet was perfect. Innovative tagines include our favourite *jebli*, rabbit with sweet potatoes, and the honey-lashed *canette* (meaty duckling) with super-sweet figs and apricots. There are also huge *brochettes* of tender lamb, *kefte*, chicken and an impressive array of airy couscous. Try to leave space for dessert, such as the almond *pastilla* or *crêpe berbère*, and a pot of mint tea. The Souk is fashionable and always full; there are two sittings for dinner and you must book ahead.

Taninna

14 rue Abel, 12th (01.40.19.99.04). M° Gare de Lyon or Ledru Rollin. **Open** daily 5pm-2am. **Average** €26. **Credit** MC, V. **Wheelchair access.**

We'd arrived too early to eat. Rather than pitching us back into the cold night, our welcoming host Youcef gave us the royal tour of Taninna. After seeing his upstairs art gallery/cultural space, with its own stage and bar, we sat together in a bar-side nook and chatted about blues music over mint tea and dates until the chef was ready to take our order. We admired the star-lit ceiling and dreamy murals of rural Algeria, unprepared for Taninna's exceptional take on the tagine-couscous routine. Fresh-from-the-oven flatbread warmed our stomachs before the *pastilla* arrived, a crisp pastry-wrapped pie stuffed with chicken, egg, coriander, flower water and cinnamon and sprinkled with icing sugar. The *adebsi n taninna* sampler plate gave tastes of several starters, including aubergine purée and *cakcuka*, a stewed sweet pepper dish. Our chicken, dried fruit, almond and pear tagine was as exquisite as the barley couscous, which Youcef advised must be drizzled with his fragrant Algerian olive oil. Called *ameqful n temzin*, the fine barley came mixed with vegetables and accompanied by a selection of juicy grilled meats. The giant portions left little room for sweets, though we accepted a traditional pastry. No doubt, we were in the hands of a master, someone eager to share his unique world of food, music, and tradition.

Au P'tit Cahoua

39 bd St-Marcel, 13th (01.47.07.24.42). M° St-Marcel. **Open** Mon-Thur noon-2pm, 7.30-11pm; Fri, Sat 7.30-11.30pm. **Average** €25. **Prix fixe** €25. **Lunch menu** €11. **Credit** MC, V.

The minute you cross the doorstep of this lush Moroccan oasis you are struck by the aroma of exotic spices. Open-work lanterns hang from the ceiling and adorn the mustard-laquered walls. Brightly printed banquettes line two sides of the dining room, and the bar opposite, like the tabletops, is covered with bright mosaic. The effect is crazy yet balanced and utterly magical, and kids love this place as much as the trendies who pack in on weekends. The fare is every bit as enchanting. The crisp triangular *briouates* stuffed with feta and mint tasted brilliant and the *choppe*, a fried potato cake with prawn, was deliciously spicy, while the soggy sardine fritters proved the only sour note in our meal. Next time we'll skip starters, so copious and satisfying was the house couscous: a huge soup basin of fragrant broth, a bowl of raisins and chickpeas, another of steaming semolina and a sizzling metal plaque with two nicely charred *merguez*, a steak-sized *kefta* and a luscious, glistening shoulder of *méchoui*, all tasting even better than they looked on the colourful crockery. Take your time, and savour the last moments over sweet mint tea before staggering back out into the real world.
Branch: 24 rue des Taillandiers, 11th (01.47.00.20.42).

Timgad ★

21 rue Brunel, 17th (01.45.74.23.70). M° Argentine. **Open** daily noon-2.15pm, 7.30-11pm. **Average** €38. **Credit** AmEx, DC, MC, V.

Everything about Timgad exudes class, from the artisan-crafted stone wall decorations to the tuxedoed waiters and silver serving dishes. This grande dame of Moroccan restaurants has its accolades framed on the wall, but the food speaks for itself. On arrival you will be seated in the lounge area and presented with a tray of *kemia* (appetisers) including spicy carrots and fat olives. Starters include *briks* (various fillings in a crisp crêpe-like shell) and delicious salads – we enjoyed the warm, garlicky *zaabuk* (puréed aubergine) and a refreshing *salade marocaine* of chopped tomatoes and onions in a lightly spiced vinaigrette. The menu is divided into couscous, tagines and grilled meat dishes, but our eyes immediately fell on the pigeon *pastilla* for two. Its 25-minute preparation time was not a problem given the size and quality of the starters. The wait is worth it for this heavenly dish – tender pigeon mixed with chopped almonds, encased in delicate pastry lightly sprinkled with icing sugar and cinnamon. Mint sprigs that melted under the pastry tempered the sweetness and a delicately flavoured gris de Gerrouane proved a good choice of accompanying wine. Dessert was out of the question, but the table next to us enjoyed a tantalising three-tier platter of North African cakes while we drank our mint tea.

Spanish

Seductive *jamóns* and sprightly paellas will have you stamping your feet for more.

Parisians have been slow to catch on to the tapas habit. But, as the popularity of the pocket-sized **La Plancha** and **Caves Saint Gilles** attests, they are starting to embrace the Spanish way of eating. **Fogon Saint-Julien** specialises in authentic paellas, while **La Catalogne** offers the Catalan version. If it's guitar plucking and flamenco dancing you're after, visit **Las Ramblas**.

Caves Saint Gilles

4 rue St-Gilles, 3rd (01.48.87.22.62). M° Chemin Vert. **Open** daily noon-2pm, 8-11.30pm. **Average** €20. **No credit cards.**

Caves Saint Gilles can feel a little frenzied but then so can tapas bars in Spain. That's what makes this colourful restaurant so popular with *branché* Parisians and Spanish expats alike: both the food and the boisterous atmosphere, complete with sport on the telly, are reminiscent of the real thing. What differs is the price, often twice what you might pay in Spain. Of the tapas from the *plancha*, the best are the *chipirones con su tinta*, tender baby squid grilled in a garlicky sauce made from their own ink, and *gambas*. The *ensaladilla de pulpo* is even better, its chunks of chewy octopus swimming in a perfectly balanced vinaigrette. If you can afford it, slices of the famous *jamón pata negra* will forever blind you to other ham. The *tortilla* almost measures up to Spanish standards and the deep-fried calamari are unusually light. Any of the well-selected but pricey reds from the Rioja or Navarra regions would go well. Desserts are simply fantastic, especially the *crema catalana*, whether served at room temperature or frozen over a disc of vanilla ice cream in the *copa de crema helada catalana*. That, they do even better than in Spain.

Fogon Saint-Julien ★

10 rue St-Julien-le-Pauvre, 5th (01.43.54.31.33). M° St-Michel. **Open** Mon-Fri 7pm-midnight; Sat, Sun noon-2.30pm, 7pm-midnight. Closed one week in Sept. **Average** €30. **Prix fixe** €28, €37. **Credit** MC, V.

If you can't head for the Med, you can still dine like the holiday-making throngs in Spain. In fact, when it comes to Spanish cooking, you'll probably eat far better at this little Iberian restaurant than in most major Spanish resorts. Alberto Herraiz, the chef-owner, is serious, hard-working and friendly, which is why this place is also the most popular in Paris for the city's resident Spanish community. Start with an assortment of tapas – it depends on what Herraiz has found in the market, but often includes a tiny cup of gazpacho, *jamón pata negra* (sublime Spanish ham) and a salad of sea snails, clams and potatoes dressed in olive oil. Then choose your rice – paella is the house speciality and comes in six different cooked-to-order versions. Our favourite is the black rice prepared with squid's ink and garnished with squid, clams and morsels of fish, but the best way to eat here is to come in a group and order several different versions to share.

La Catalogne

4-6-8, cour du Commerce Saint-André, 6th (01.55.42.16.19/www.catalogne.infotourisme.com). M° Odéon. **Open** Tue-Fri noon-3pm, 7-11pm; Sat noon-3pm; 7-11.30pm; Sun noon-3pm. **Average** €18. **Prix fixe** €17.53. **Lunch menu** €10.37. **Credit** MC, V.

La Maison de Catalogne tourist office houses both a lively, loud tapas bar and a more sedate (and expensive) restaurant. Unfortunately, you can't book for the tapas bar downstairs and it's packed almost every night after 9pm. Here, though, Spain reigns with tapas of fried calamari, *patatas bravas* (fried potatoes in a spicy sauce), *tortilla*, marinated red peppers, mussels in white wine, broad beans, asparagus and ham in mint oil, and mini tuna kebabs. Then it's on to Catalan paella with mussels, cockles, prawns and chicken, rice coloured black with squid ink, or *fideuà* – chopped, fried vermicelli with seafood and a pot of garlicky mayonnaise to spoon over it. Finish with *crème catalane*, their seriously wobbly take on crème brûlée.

La Plancha

34 rue Keller, 11th (01.48.05.20.30). M° Bastille. **Open** Tue-Sat 6pm-2am. Closed one week in Aug. **Average** €27. **No credit cards.**

Arrive early and you might find this tapas bar uncharacteristically quiet. Come at night and you'll have trouble squeezing into the place, which offers an authentic whiff of Spain with colourful tiles, bullfighting on telly and giant hams hanging from the ceiling. Though there are probably menus, most people trust the advice of the *patron*, a jokey Basque exseminarian. We nibbled on thinly sliced serrano ham, crunchy calamari fritters, grilled, marinated red peppers and mushrooms sautéed with garlic. All quite convincing, but we couldn't help feeling that prices were a little high, especially with sangria at €10 for a medium-sized pitcher. Still, when the place is hopping the atmosphere justifies the prices.

Las Ramblas

14 rue Miollis, 15th (01 47 83 32 98). M° Cambronne or Ségur. **Open** Mon 9am-4pm; Tue-Sat 9am-2am. Closed Aug. **Average** €25. **Prix fixe** €19 (Mon-Thur). **Credit** MC, V.

The time-warp decor of Las Ramblas – large television set and assorted sporting trophies – is authentically Spanish, as is the hearty food, which includes starters such as *chorizo*, *jamón serrano*, and a pile of crisp fried calamari. With the first-rate Rioja we paired a rustic rather than refined paella of mussels, rabbit, chicken calamari and langoustines. Our flagging appetites kept us from the homemade tart; instead we opted for manchego cheese served with sweet quince jelly. On Fridays and Saturdays this restaurant offers live guitar music and occasional flamenco dancing. Midweek it moves at a more leisurely pace, attracting families and sports-minded Spaniards.

Latin life at La Catalogne

Other International

Think global, eat local. Every cuisine – from Afghan to Swedish – has its ambassador.

Afghan

L'Afghani
16 rue Paul-Albert, 18th (01.42.51.08.72). M° Château-Rouge. **Open** Mon-Sat 8pm-midnight. **Average** €15. **Credit** MC, V.
If you know nothing about Afghan food, as in our case, this is an inexpensive introduction to a spicy cuisine that combines meats, beans, pastas and vegetables. Start with 'the door', a cucumber, yoghurt and mint drink, then move on to mostly veggie-based starters, such as the irresistible *gol-ê-karam* (cauliflower fritters in a piquant sauce). The *shorwa* soup reminded us of minestrone; we wished we had ordered the aubergine *frites* because our mains were also bean-based. *Ashak* is a plate of tender leek and lentil dumplings, red beans, chickpeas, garlic and yoghurt, while *ashe* combines beans, noodles, mint and a fabulous drizzle of clarified butter. Other dishes star lamb or veal. For dessert, try the *halwa* (toasted crumble and almonds) or *firni* (a cardamom flan). Large parties can reserve the cushioned basement room for a right royal treat. Although not nearly as daunting as the rugged Afghan peaks, a hike up the nearby steps to Sacré-Coeur is a fitting post-meal conclusion.

Australian

Bennelong ★
31 bd Henri IV, 4th, (01.42.71.07.71). M° Bastille or Sully-Morland. **Open** Tue-Fri noon-3pm, 7.30-10.30pm; Sat 7.30-10.30pm; Sun 7.30-10pm. **Average** €40. **Prix fixe** (dinner only) €28.95-€38.10. **Lunch menu** €20. **Credit** AmEx, MC, V.
Jean-Paul Bruneteau is a wizard of Oz and France – he was born in the Vendée but spent some 30 years in Australia where he pioneered the use of Australian 'bush' foods in his restaurants. Opt for the smoked emu salad followed by fillets of tender, just-cooked kangaroo and you'll be munching your way through the Australian coat of arms. If that's a tad too authentic, dip into the other mod-Oz and Mediter-Asian dishes: delicate slices of calamari bathed in 'marmalade' (a sweet orange sauce), a punchy, finely balanced Thai chicken curry or a beautifully cooked *daurade* (sea bream) with a side of crisp, steamed veggies. Finish off with Australia's national dessert, Pavlova. Bruneteau's is a pretty pyramid of meringue, cream and red berries, circled by raspberry coulis and topped with threads of chocolate. A full vegetarian menu is offered on Sunday nights. The decor is contemporary: warm plums and purples, including an eye-catching throne-like chair.

Finnish

Au Soleil de Minuit
15 rue Desnouettes, 15th (01.48.28.15.15). M° Convention. **Open** Tue-Sun noon-2pm, 7.30-10.30pm. **Average** €37. **Prix fixe** €21 (Tue-Thur, Sun), €29.50. **Credit** AmEx, MC, V.
The cuisine of Finland shines in this austere, blue-and-white-accented dining room which radiates Scandinavian simplicity. It's sleek right down to the silverware and service. A cool, creamy cucumber *velouté* accompanied an eye-catching assortment of smoked lake and ocean fish. We passed on the elk and reindeer steaks for the crispy pan-fried sea bream with pesto and carrot purée, and the lovely *lavaret*, a freshwater fish accompanied by tiny mushrooms and steamed greens. The short, elegant menu was enhanced by desserts such as the *bavarois*, a wedge of chunky chocolate, coconut and raspberry. The €29.50 'tour de Finlande' is a fine way to sample several fish and meat dishes. Wash it all down with a Lapland beer or a *kir royal finlandais*, a wild potion of Champagne and Arctic blackberries.

Global

Hélices et Délices ★
8 rue Thénard, 5th (01.43.54.59.47). M° Maubert-Mutualité or RER Cluny La Sorbonne. **Open** Tue-Sat noon-2.15pm, 7.45-10.15pm. **Average** €24.40. **Lunch menu** €12.96. **Credit** AmEx, MC, V.
Christine Daynac has created a hybrid restaurant/lecture space that combines her passions for international food and travel. Hélices et Délices (literally, 'propellers and delights') offers themed dinners with guest speakers in the basement, or you can eat in the elegant main-floor dining room with its photo displays and inspiring travel magazines. Our two affable hostesses served us a house apéritif that combined *crémant*, a sparkling wine, with a tea-based syrup. We passed on an intriguing camembert, snail and jacket potato starter for the spinach soup garnished with parmesan and hunks of spice bread, and a daring smoked salmon and mango dish. The mackerel fillet spiced with cardamom, and a skewer of sesame chicken over a bed of buttery mashed potatoes, retained their flavours and juices. We opted for the hot, dense *moelleux* which oozed like a chocolate volcano and came with an irresistible comfort food touch: a glass of milk to wash it down. The menu changes every six weeks.

Hungarian

Le Paprika
28 av Trudaine, 9th (01.44.63.02.91/www.le-paprika.com). M° Anvers. **Open** Mon-Sat noon-2.30pm, 7.30-10.30pm. **Average** €30.49. **Prix fixe** €27.44 (dinner only). **Lunch menu** €12.20, €22.87. **Credit** AmEx, MC, V. **Wheelchair access**.
Whether you're sitting on this very good Hungarian restaurant's spacious terrace or in the old-fashioned dining room you're as likely to hear Polish, German and other Eastern European tongues as French: Le Paprika plays club-canteen for the city's not insubstantial Eastern European population. Young and old rub elbows; an appealing old-world *bonhomie* prevails. Ordering *à la carte* is a bit expensive so try the good-value menus, which include starters of paprika-spiked cheese, thin slices of the famous salami, crêpes filled with finely ground veal, or poached egg with crayfish. Savoury main courses include tender goulash served with *spätzle* (nubby egg noodles), pepper stuffed with rice and veal in a tangy tomato sauce, duckling roasted in cabbage or sautéed foie gras. Desserts are delicious, too, including the *crêpe Gundel* filled with powdered walnuts and served with chocolate sauce and whipped cream, or an apple strudel. Finish off with one of Hungary's fine Tokaj dessert wines.

Polish

Mazurka
3 rue André-del-Sarte, 18th (01.42.23.36.45). M° Anvers or Château Rouge. **Open** Mon, Tue, Thur-Sun 7pm-midnight. **Average** €23. **Prix fixe** €17.53. **Credit** AmEx, MC, V.
This endearing red velvet restaurant, nestled in the foothills of Montmartre, oozes Krakovian hospitality and charm. The menu revolves around standard Polish fare, homemade and elegantly prepared. Serenaded by a duo crooning Polish (and sometimes Russian) folk songs, we started off with a cold Okocim beer and the berry-infused house cocktail, followed by a salmon and shark blini platter. The ruby-red beetroot *borscht* accompanied by a delicate minced meat pastry is a must. The sole Pole among us confirmed that the main dishes, silky *pierogi* stuffed with potatoes, cheese and buttery onions, as well as the *bigos*, sauerkraut stewed with meat, were as good as mum's. Pickled herring, stuffed cabbage and sausage *flambé* also rang true. No Polish dinner is complete without some poppy-seed gâteau and cheesecake-like *sernik*, both excellent here. Sit back and enjoy the music over a generously sized coffee served in a brass pot with an icy-smooth shot of honey vodka on the side.

Portuguese

Vasco da Gama
39 rue Vasco de Gama, 15th (01.45.57.20.01). M° Lourmel. **Open** Tue-Sun noon-3pm, 7.30-11.30pm. **Average** €30. **Lunch menu** €10. **Credit** MC, V.
This Portuguese seafood den is decked in a seafaring theme, with murals of salty locals and dusty wooden ship models. The favoured fish at Vasco da Gama is *morue* (salt cod), prepared about ten different ways in stews, grilled, or pan-fried. You'll also find squid and giant *gambas*, as well as Portuguese *cassoulet* and dishes heavy on pork and beef. We split an expensive *gambas vasco* (€18.14), a half-dozen bright orange whole prawns floating in a pond of smoky cream sauce, a mess to eat with fingers but delicious. The mains were less to our liking: a cod steak roasted over a wood fire was moist, and the side potatoes buttery, but the flesh was incredibly salty. Likewise, the simple and filling fish stew was chock-full of cod and potatoes but despite the abundant broth it still managed to parch us. Other plates seemed to be only a slight variation on the same theme. A sweet rice pudding, the *arroz doce com canela* and the slightly sparkling white *vinho verde*, Casal Garcia, were pleasing if not refined.

Romanian

Doïna
149 rue Saint-Dominique, 7th (01.45.50.49.57). M° Ecole-Militaire or RER Pont de L'Alma. **Open** Tue-Sun noon-3pm, 6pm-midnight. **Average** €23. **Lunch menu** €12. **Credit** AmEx, MC, V.
Practically under the skirts of the Eiffel Tower, this Romanian restaurant attracts an expat crowd eager for solid home cooking. While the host makes a point of greeting each table personally (except, strangely, us), candles, quaint scenes of Bucharest and blaring Romanian folk and pop music add to the mood. Vivid bowls filled with pickled cauliflower and peppers go well with the local wine Murfatlar, a sweet and fruity pinot noir. We passed on the tripe salad and herring plate to sample the comforting corn polenta sprinkled with a tangy cheese, then dived right into our main dishes. An aubergine moussaka made with plenty of finely minced beef proved rib-stickingly satisfying. The fried *sandre* (pike-perch) came with capers and boiled potatoes but we found the batter greasy. Great wooden boards laden with vegetables and grilled, minced meats (*mititei*) are other filling options. Watch your head on the way down to the loo or you'll knock yourself unconscious before you get a chance to sample the *torte Bucharest* which, true to its Eastern European roots, ended the meal with a sweet chocolate-and-Chantilly flourish.

Russian

Dominique
19 rue Bréa, 6th (01.43.27.08.80). M° Vavin. **Open** Tue-Sat 7.30pm-1am (bar/boutique Tue-Sat 11am-1am). **Closed** late July-late Aug. **Average** €50. **Prix fixe** €40, €55. **Credit** AmEx, DC, MC, V.
Pass straight through the front bar and deli (which serves more casual food) to the back dining room with its mix of 1920s decor, backlit wooden panels and painted folkloric carvings for typical fare like smoked fish, *borscht* and *pirojok* (beef-stuffed pastries). *Zakouski* is a good place to start: a salad plate which may include salmon or pork pâté, piquant aubergine and red beans, *kasha* or a cucumber-apple-egg-dill rémoulade. Relatively frugal diners can opt for one of the €40 *menus* while those who prefer more choice can try the *à la carte* options such as roasted sturgeon, honey-fried salmon, grilled lamb with dried fruit and cold onions, and a nut-and-coriander marinated chicken. The spectacular apple strudel was hot and crisp, and the cheesecake modest but densely satisfying. Chilled vodka, first-rate caviar (at €69 a pop) and old-time Russian songs could make you believe you're a Russian expat holed up against the cold, in style.

Swedish

Gustavia
26-28 rue des Grands-Augustins, 6th (01.40.46.86.70). M° Odéon or St-Michel. **Open** Mon 7.30-10pm, Tue-Sat noon-2pm, 7.30-10pm. **Average** €22. **Prix fixe** €14 (dinner only). **Lunch menu** €12.20. **No credit cards**.
If it's fish you're after and the world-class catch down the street at Jacques Cagna is out of your price range, stop in at this soothingly Nordic café. A perfect lunch, the *assiette Gustavia* presents a delicate but filling sampler plate of three kinds of herring (marinated in mustard, cream and vinegar), three kinds of salmon (poached, smoked and preserved in dill) and a delightful dollop of *skagen*, a prawn salad topped with plump and juicy fish roe. Each bite is better than the last and it's hard to say which sample wins. Service is smiling and unobtrusive, making this haven of Swedish gastronomia an ideal place for a friendly, fast meal in St-Germain.

Finnish your food at Au Soleil de Minuit

Café Oz   The Australian Bar

for fine Australian wines, ice cold Australian beers and a warm Australian welcome!

www.cafe-oz.com

now open every day opposite the Moulin Rouge from 3pm - 2am
1 rue de Bruxelles, Paris 9th Métro Blanche

and still, of course:
18 rue Saint Denis, Paris 1st Métro Châtelet
184 rue Saint Jacques, Paris 5th RER Luxembourg
33 place Louise de Bettignies, Lille

On the Town

Cafés	**104**
Bars & Pubs	**117**
Tea Rooms & Ice Cream	**127**
Wine Bars	**129**
Eating & Entertainment	**133**
Gay & Lesbian	**134**
Clubs	**135**
Shops & Markets	**137**
Home Delivery	**141**
Learning & Tasting	**143**

Cafés

From literary lairs to fashion plates, we spill the beans on the Paris café scene.

Along with your *café crème*, Paris cafés serve up a huge slice of city life. Plonk down and enjoy the scenery – from glossy young urban guerillas to unkempt ageing academics, from tortured blonde trophies to feral philosophers and almost every species in between. Add a glass of red, a cheesy *croque monsieur*, a wedge of *tarte Tatin*, and a waiter with no intention of hurrying you along and it's pretty much heaven to the power of ten.

Most cafés offer light meals and many serve hot food, especially at lunch, which is often both better value and quality than many a budget restaurant. Remember that you generally pay less standing at the bar than at a table inside, and more on a terrace. Prices can be gulp-inducing in some famous tourist haunts. Many cafés, like bars, put prices up by €0.30 or €0.50 after 9pm or 10pm.

1st Arrondissement

Bar de l'Entr'acte
47 rue Montpensier, 1st (01.42.97.57.76). M° Palais Royal. **Open** Tue-Fri 10am-2am; Sat, Sun noon-midnight. Food served Tue-Fri noon-3pm, 7.30-11pm; Sat, Sun 1-7.30pm. **Beer** 25cl €2.29. **Credit** AmEx, MC, V.
Lurking inconspicuously on a side street near the Palais-Royal is this centuries-old café, formerly known by many other names – La Pissotte, for one. Its sprawling terrace looks like a jumble sale, with all manner of abandoned curios serving as furniture. Finding a table can be tricky during peak hours as this casual drinking hole is popular with theatregoers and the local boho chic. We were served caustic beer from Quebec by a bartender younger than many of the bottles of whisky behind him (dad must have been on a break). The *jardin d'hiver*, a cellar done up with theatre scenery and red curtains, is best visited after several drinks in the amicable atmosphere upstairs.

Café Marly ★
93 rue de Rivoli, cour Napoléon du Louvre, 1st (01.49.26.06.60). M° Palais Royal. **Open** daily 8am-2am. Food served daily noon-1am. **Beer** 25cl €5. **Credit** AmEx, DC, MC, V.
Opened in 1994 as part of the Grand Louvre project, Café Marly is another Costes brothers success (they're the pair behind Café Beaubourg, Hôtel Costes, Georges and others). The terrace is beautiful, ensconced in the stone balcony of the Louvre's Cour Napoléon with a privileged view of the glass pyramid. The snappily-dressed waiters glide between tables delivering gazpacho, club sandwiches and €90 sevruga caviar to pods of summer-spectacled customers who sip cocktails (€10) and crane their necks to confirm celebrity spottings. The lush interior, designed by Olivier Gagnaire, is also worth a visit. The lower-end wines – €4-€8 a glass – are hit-or-miss.

La Coquille
30 rue Coquillière, 1st (01.40.26.55.36). M° Les Halles. **Open** Mon-Sat 7am-10pm. Food served Mon-Sat noon-3.30pm. **Beer** 25cl €1.60-€1.80. **Credit** MC, V.
This down-to-earth, vintage '50s shoebox café is a local favourite. Its one-table 'terrace' is usually taken, so expect to end up inside (a high ceiling and mirrors make it seem bigger). Maria, the friendly woman behind the bar, is not quite a beer connoisseur – she asked us to explain the difference between a *blonde* and a *blanche* – but she more than makes up for it with a good selection of dirt-cheap wines, €1-€1.50 a 7cl glass. The budget food, served up fast and fresh, runs from *entrecôtes* to giant salads (the *salade coquille* is particularly nice). Admire the Portuguese owner's gravy boat collection as you sip a glass of *vinho verde*.

Papou Lounge
74 rue Jean-Jacques Rousseau, 1st (01.44.76.00.03). M° Etienne-Marcel or Les Halles. **Open** Mon-Sat 10am-2am; Sun 5pm-midnight. Food served Mon-Sat noon-4pm, 7pm-midnight; Sun 7pm-midnight. **Beer** 25cl €3.05. **Credit** MC, V. **Wheelchair access**.
An eclectic menu, comfortable terrace and excellent €6.10 cocktails – the white Russians and whisky sours are expertly prepared – are good reasons to stop into Papou. The interior is decorated with masks, carvings, and black-and-white tribal photographs; Christmas lights create a warm atmosphere around the wood bar, making it a difficult place to leave.

Le Zimmer
1 pl du Châtelet, 1st (01.42.36.74.03). M° Châtelet. **Open** daily 8am-1am. **Average** €22.87. **Prix fixe** €15. **Credit** AmEx, MC, V.
Its 1896 interior reworked by flamboyant designer Jacques Garcia, Le Zimmer is now a

Café Le Nemours
2 pl Colette, 1st (01.42.61.34.14). M° Palais Royal. **Open** Mon-Fri 7am-1am; Sat 8am-1am; Sun 9.30am-9.30pm. Food served all day. **Beer** 25cl €2.30-€3.51. **Credit** MC, V.
The main attraction of the Nemours is a seat on the terrace under the elegant colonnades of the Palais-Royal. During the day, it attracts top-brass civil servants from the neighbouring Conseil d'Etat, refuelling shoppers and thesps taking a break from rehearsals at the nearby Comédie Française. But it is transformed in the early evening when a lively group of locals gathers around the bar talking animatedly about issues of the day such as the rising price of *baguette* and this year's Beaujolais.

Café Ruc
159 rue St-Honoré, 1st (01.42.60.97.54). M° Palais Royal. **Open** daily 8am-2am. Food served daily 11am-1am. **Beer** 25cl €5.05. **Credit** AmEX, DC, MC, V.
The decor of this Costes brothers café is chic: crimson velvet banquettes, soft lighting from satin-shaded lamps, all presided over by suavely dressed waiters. Lulled by the languorous jazz soundtrack this place is a relaxed haven. The relatively simple cuisine is elegantly executed and ranges from caviar or oysters to fluffy omelettes and towering club sandwiches, plus hot specials. The house speciality, a giant chocolate éclair named in honour of Madame Ruc, looked – like its namesake, apparently – very impressive.

Le Comptoir
37 rue Berger, 1st (01.40.26.26.66). M° Châtelet. **Open** Mon-Thur, Sun noon-2am; Fri, Sat noon-3am. Food served noon-3pm, 7pm-midnight. **Beer** 25cl €3.81. **Happy Hour** Mon-Fri 6-8pm. **Credit** MC, V.
This café-restaurant is a swish Moroccan-inspired haven from the bustle of Châtelet. Crisply dressed waiters deliver soothing mint tea to shopaholics reclining in the velvet-backed chairs after a spot of retail therapy on the rue de Rivoli. Designer-clad couples take advantage of the candlelit ambience for a spot of early evening smooching. Trendies discuss plans for the night ahead over mysteriously-named and potent cocktails. Food is expensive and minimalist but it is pretty obvious that this place is devoted to style and not gastronomy.

hushed, opulent, hoping-to-be-hipper spot. Red velvet curtains, plush chairs and dangling fringes create a posh hotel lobby/Orient Express atmosphere, the decorative plaster ceiling remaining intact (though piped-in soft pop music is slightly incongruous). The bored-looking but efficient waiting staff lingers about, staring plaintively at lively place du Châtelet through the Zimmer's generous windows. *Choucroute* (sauerkraut) and tartare are the more hearty specialities; between mealtimes, opt for a classic French snack such as a *tartine* (open-faced sandwich) of bacon and goat's cheese, or one of their new-fangled cold platters such as the chicken and apple curried Indian salad. Decent profiteroles represent Zimmer's solid, traditional desserts.

2nd Arrondissement

Le Café ★
62 rue Tiquetonne, 2nd (01.40.39.08.00). M° Etienne-Marcel. **Open** Mon-Sat 10am-2am; Sun noon-midnight. Food served daily noon-midnight. Closed one week in Aug. **Beer** 25cl €3-€3.50. **Credit** MC, V.
A young and hip crowd is drawn to this café which buzzes with loud and funky music, matching its customers' attitude. The interior looks like a fusion between Ali Baba's cavern and an explorer's attic, filled with African statuettes, antique globes, Lenin bust, and browning maps of exotic locations. Despite the unusual decor, the food is somewhat less adventurous, consisting of generous salads, plates of smoked fish and *plats du jour* of salmon tagliatelle or quiche lorraine. Drinks are reasonably priced and standard; the only concession to exotica was a bottle of 'Famosa' Guatemalan beer. The chronically overworked waiter was amazingly polite and efficient.

Le Dénicheur
4 rue Tiquetonne, 2nd (01.42.21.31.01). M° Etienne-Marcel. . **Open** Tue-Thur 12.30-3.30pm, 7pm-midnight; Fri, Sat 12.30-4pm, 7pm-2am; Sun 12.30-4pm, 7pm-2am. Food served all day. Closed two weeks in Aug. **Beer** 25cl €2.60. **No credit cards**.
The row of garden gnomes standing to attention in the window give the game away: Le Dénicheur doesn't take itself too seriously. Even better, just a street or so away from the tourist-fleecing joints of Les Halles, it's a place where you can pick up a very affordable light lunch or supper. The lunchtime *menu* at €7.70 could include a huge plate of very fresh salad followed by a crunchy homemade apple crumble. There's also a Sunday brunch worth catching at €13. The decor – bright blue paint, jumble on the walls, a chalk-scrawled tribute to (who else?) Kylie – creates a kitsch charm that the cheek-by-jowl seating arrangement in this tiny café only enhances.

Lézard Café
32 rue Etienne Marcel, 2nd (01.42.33.22.73). M° Etienne-Marcel or Les Halles. **Open** Mon-Sat 9am-2am. Food served Mon-Sat noon-5pm. **Beer** 25cl €2-€2.80. **Credit** MC, V.
The pleasant summer terrace remains an excellent place to sit, sip and people-watch. During the winter, the customers, what's left of them, move to the sparse interior. A barn floor,

Come out of your shell at La Coquille

The best For Food

Café Ruc (1st)
Formidable éclairs.

Le Dénicheur (2nd)
Salad days.

L'Escale (4th)
A slice of local life on the Isle.

Granterroirs (8th)
Luxury deli fare.

Au Dernier Métro (15th)
Don't miss it.

Bar du Marché: the *flâneur*'s approach to market shopping

exposed pipes and beams, and a decor that consists of... a blue painting: the Lézard relies on the customers for its good looks. A close-knit bunch of regulars sporting trendy tattoos and shiny trainers conglomerates around the bar (where you have to order your drinks). Cheapish beer and a modest selection of cocktails are served with the few rudimentary supplies.

Au Vide Gousset
1 rue Vide-Gousset, 2nd (01.42.60.02.78). *Mº* Bourse. **Open** Mon-Fri 8am-8pm. Food served all day. Closed Aug. **Beer** 25cl €1.98-€2.90. **No credit cards.**
A stone's throw from the elegant place des Victoires, this café-*tabac* is light years away in style and outlook. It's the archetypal down-at-heel smoke-filled Parisian café, complete with battered tables, shiny crimson banquettes and hideous '70s lights. Nonetheless, the café does a brisk trade and attracts a diverse clientele of expensively perfumed professional shoppers, stockbrokers from the Bourse, caffeine addicts, Gitane-smoking barflies and even, on our last visit, a smartly blazered man accompanied by his headscarf-wearing dog. Simple but pricey food is served at lunch: plates of *charcuterie*, *croques Poilâne*.

3rd Arrondissement

L'Appartement Café
18 rue des Coutures-St-Gervais, 3rd (01.48.87.12.22). *Mº* Filles du Calvaire or St-Paul. **Open** Mon-Fri noon-2am; Sat 4pm-2am; Sun noon-midnight. Food served Mon-Sat 12.30-3pm, 7pm-midnight; Sun 12.30-4pm, 6pm-11.30pm. **Beer** 25cl €3.81. **Credit** MC, V.
This cosy café across from the Picasso museum is decorated like the front room of an eccentric friend with a drinking problem. Board games, comfy leather and velvet armchairs, and a heaving pile of books and magazines are easy surroundings in which to while away an afternoon. All the comforts of home with, of course, a bill. Drinks are a little pricey but will keep you fuelled for longer than most.

Le Baromètre
17 rue Charlot, 3rd (01.48.87.04.54). *Mº* St-Sébastien-Froissart. **Open** Mon-Fri 7am-9pm. Hot food served Mon-Fri noon-3pm. Closed 25 Dec-2 Jan. **Beer** 25cl €1.80-€2.30. **Credit** MC, V.
The Marais art-gallery crowd and assorted locals unwind over a variety of Alsatian, Beaujolais and other wines bought direct from the producers at this charming corner café. Lilacs, lace curtains and a hunting horn add a distinctly rural feel and lunchtime *plats du jour* are often regional dishes. Lighter fare includes salads, *croques* and open sandwiches.

Web Bar
32 rue de Picardie, 3rd (01.42.72.66.55/ www.webbar.fr). *Mº* République. **Open** Mon-Fri 8.30am-2am; Sat 11am-2am; Sun 11am-midnight. Food served Mon-Fri noon-11pm; Sat, Sun noon-4pm. **Beer** 25cl €2.80. **Credit** MC, V.
The *net-plus ultra* of Paris cyberspace is far more than just a computer nerd's hangout. Industrial vibes intensify as you pass through its wicker-chaired terrace, mellow-lit bar slamming with speed chess, and the impressive triple-height atrium (a former silversmith's atelier). Web activities go beyond prosaic e-mails to live web painting and online DJ links. A cultural all-rounder, with multimedia poetry nights, concerts and art exhibitions.

4th Arrondissement

Baz'Art Café
36, bd Henri IV, 4th (01.42.78.62.23). *Mº* Sully Morland or Bastille. **Open** daily 8am-midnight. Food served all day. **Beer** 25cl €3.70-€4. **Credit** AmEx, MC, V.
This light, airy and very spacious café attracts everyone from the late night opera crowd to locals and tourists. Baz'Art offers good-quality café fare and a relaxed, stylish atmosphere in which to linger. The sandy yellow walls, red velvet chairs, heavy iron chandeliers and jazzy soundtrack make a pleasant backdrop and the service couldn't be friendlier. Plenty of market-fresh salads and great-value Sunday brunches from €16.76 to €19.05.

Bricolo Café
Basement of BHV department store, 52 rue de Rivoli, 4th (01.42.74.90.00/ www.cyberbricoleur.com). *Mº* Hôtel-de-Ville. **Open** Mon, Tue, Thur, Sat 9.30am-7pm; Wed, Fri 9.30am-8pm. Snacks served noon-7pm. **Beer** 25cl €2.21. **Credit** AmEx, MC, V. **Wheelchair access.**
This small, funky café is hidden in the basement of department store BHV, at the very back of the DIY/hardware section. Its design evokes a workshop somewhere in the American mid-west, complete with period tools and a blues track in the background. There's a range of light snacks and desserts on offer. But, the real attraction must be Bricolo's free daily DIY masterclasses, from the mysteries of bicycle maintenance to how to plumb in your washing-machine, at 12.30pm or 4pm. Reputed to be one of the hottest singles hang-outs in town.

Café Beaubourg
43 rue St-Merri, 4th (01.48.87.63.96). *Mº* Hôtel-de-Ville or RER Châtelet-Les Halles. **Open** Mon-Fri 8am-1am; Sat, Sun 8am-2am. Food served daily 8am-midnight. **Beer** 25cl €5. **Credit** AmEx, DC, MC, V.
After passing through the plush red velvet curtains, you might have lots of time to take in the post-modern interior, as the service seems to spring from the same minimalism that spawned the bare concrete walls. The waiters, dressed in tailored black suits (the Costes brothers' standard), are better-dressed than most clients. No small feat as this dimly-lit hang-out which, like its sibling restaurant Georges atop the Centre Pompidou, is frequented by the rich and the beautiful – a fact that's reflected in the fairly high prices.

Café des Phares
7 pl de la Bastille, 4th (01.42.72.04.70). *Mº* Bastille. **Open** daily 6.30am-4am. Food served all day. **Beer** 25cl €2.20-€3.20. **No credit cards.**
The late Sorbonne lecturer Marc Sautet established the continuing tradition of Sunday morning philosophy talks (11am) here. The aim was to return philosophy to its rightful place in life, and it started a boom in philo-cafés across the city. You can ponder the very essence of the menu on the pavement terrace slap-bang on place de la Bastille. And, if freedom is having infinite choice, as the Existentialists believed, then the menu is liberating: *croques*, salads, international dishes, breakfast and brunch.

Café du Trésor
7-9 rue du Trésor, 4th (01.42.71.78.34). *Mº* Hôtel-de-Ville or St-Paul. **Open** daily noon-2am. Food served Mon-Fri noon-3pm, 7.30pm-midnight; Sat 12.30pm-2am; Sun 12.30pm-12.30am. **Beer** 25 cl €3.81. **Credit** MC, V.
With a pedestrian impasse almost to itself, Le Trésor has one of the bigger Marais terraces and the kids dig it. This is the ideal spot to accommodate a large group of friends with whom you do not want to speak. Knowing grins and eyebrow theatre will have to do as the music is often pumping, even when customers number in the single digits. Drinks are pricey but they tend to go far. Some little nooks and crannies are comfortable and private.

Columbus Café
25 rue Vieille-du-Temple, 3rd (01.42.72.20.25/www.columbuscafe.com). *Mº* Hôtel-de-Ville or St-Paul. **Open** Mon-Thur 7am-8pm; Fri, Sat 7am-11pm; Sun 7am-9pm. Snacks served all day. **Credit** MC, V.
This chain of Seattle-style coffee shops does a brisk business with the usual line-up of watchamaccino-in-cardboard-cup coffees as well as offering baked goods. Coffee murals, sauna-like panelling and faux-grain wooden tables toil to remind you that you are, if fact, in

CAFE PUCE
BAR • RESTAURANT

This new restaurant in the exciting 11th arrondissement of Paris invites anglophones to come and taste its traditional and inventive cuisine.
Average price: € 23 Sunday brunch

68 avenue de la République, 11th - Tel: 01.43.58.03.03 - M° Saint Maur

---

Le Centre Ville CAFE

"Your village cafe in the heart of Paris"

57 rue Montorgueil, 2nd. M° Les Halles/Sentier - Tel: 01.42.33.20.40
www.lecentreville.fr • e-mail: info@lecentreville.fr

AU BOUQUET SAINT-PAUL
OLD STYLE WINE BAR & RESTAURANT

The best "Croque-Poilane" in the centre of Paris!
Come and taste our traditional French cheeses & wines.
OPEN DAILY FROM 7am to 2am

85 rue Saint Antoine, 4th - M° Saint Paul - Tel: 01.42.78.55.03
www.paris-zoom.com

La Perla BAR

Tequila, Rum and Mexican food since 1976

26 rue Francois Miron, 4th. Tel: 01.42.77.59.40
London: 28 Maiden Lane, WC2. Tel: 0207 240 7400
London: 803 Fulham Road, SW6. Tel: 0207 471 4895
London: 11 Charlotte Street, W1. Tel: 0207 436 1744

CAFE PACIFICO

SYDNEY
95 Ridley Street
Tel: 02.9360.3811

Fresh, homemade **MEXICAN** *food since 1976*

Large range of tequila and cocktails

LONDON
5 Langley Street, WC3
Tel: 0207 379 7728

50 BLVD MONTPARNASSE, 15TH
TEL: 01.45.48.63.87

AMSTERDAM
Warmoesstraat 31
Tel: 6242911

a coffee shop. The mezzanines are peaceful and the non-smoking areas are respected.
Branches include: 21 rue Soufflot, 5th (01.43.25.41.41); 24 rue St-André-des-Arts, 6th (01.56.24.08.64).

L'Escale ★

1 rue des Deux-Ponts, 4th (01.43.54.94.23). M° Pont-Marie. **Open** Tue-Sun 7.30am-9pm. Food served Tue-Sun noon-3pm. Closed three weeks in Aug. **Beer** €1.75-€3.35. **Credit** MC, V.

With an idyllic Ile St-Louis location and grumpy regulars reading *L'Equipe* at the counter, L'Escale remains a real neighbourhood café/wine bar. Its decor of wall-mirrors and check tablecloths includes a blackboard menu displaying the day's specials: there is no *prix fixe*, but a meal will cost between €9.95-€11.45. Expect all the veg to be cooked in olive oil and garlic, and the small portions of meat to be tender. The service is personal and unrushed (and good humoured, the owner not batting an eye when a luncher asked for a steak tartare 'well done, as usual'). The excellent *vin du mois* is a bargain at €14.50 a bottle.

L'Etoile Manquante

34 rue Vieille-du-Temple, 4th (01.42.72.48.34/ www.cafeine.com). M° Hôtel-de-Ville or St-Paul. **Open** daily 9am-2am. Food served daily noon-1.15am. **Beer** 25cl €2.44-€3.20. **Credit** MC, V.

Xavier (Petit Fer à Cheval) Denamur's artwork-filled endeavour is worth a visit even if you only use the loo. As you relieve yourself an electric train circulates beneath a large photograph of a block of flats by night. Then don't forget to smile as you wash your hands and see yourself recorded on the screen reflected in the mirror, along with images of science (fact) and science (fiction), all part of a theme on thresholds between known and unknown worlds. Make sure you stay on for a drink, especially on a hot, sticky evening when the Zoncajito cocktail (a thirst-quenching mix of *citron pressé*, lemonade and fresh mint) comes into its own.

Le Flore en l'Isle

42 quai d'Orléans, 4th (01.43.29.88.27). M° Hôtel-de-Ville or Pont-Marie. **Open** daily 8am-2am. Food served daily 11am-midnight. **Beer** 33cl €5.50. **Credit** MC, V.

One of the bigger café-brasseries on Ile St-Louis, Le Flore en l'Isle is particularly popular on hot summer afternoons as the dessert menu includes ice creams and sorbets from the famous *glacier* Berthillon. The rest of the rather expensive menu consists of dressed-up, mostly meaty traditional fare. Our *tagliatelle aux deux saumons frais* was piping hot and generous, but, at €15, a bit steep. Dark wood panelling and obscure classical music create a sombre atmosphere inside, but most customers come to enjoy the terrace with its excellent views of the spidery apse of Notre-Dame.

L'Imprévu Café

7-9 rue Quincampoix, 4th (01.42.78.23.50). M° Hôtel-de-Ville or RER Châtelet-Les-Halles. **Open** Mon-Sat noon-2am; Sun 1pm-2am. **Beer** 25cl €3-€4. **Credit** AmEx, DC, MC, V.

Half-way between the edgy *banlieue* vibe of Les Halles and the gaudy tourist mêlée around the Centre Pompidou, this café is worlds apart from both. Cluttered with battered but super-comfy sofas and leopard-skin easy chairs, it exudes a relaxed and stylish charm and offers friendly, laid-back service. There's a wide choice of exotic cocktails, ranging in strength from those earmarked for *les chérubins* and *les jeunes filles* to those reserved for *les machos* and *les durs*. The back, with its tented ceiling and fluorescent Arabian Nights mural, feels rather like hanging out in the living-room of a schizophrenic Moroccan – actually a lot of fun.

Au Petit Fer à Cheval

30 rue Vieille-du-Temple, 4th (01.42.72.47.47/www.cafeine.com). M° Hôtel-de-Ville or St-Paul. **Open** daily 9am-2am. Food served noon-1am. **Beer** 25cl €2.59-€3.35. **Credit** MC, V.

A Marais institution, the vintage horse-shoe-shaped bar attracts local drinkers while the windowless chamber in the back – not a place for the smoke-sensitive – attracts, well, the same people, when they're hungry. The decor is charming: antique wall clocks, blackboard menus and murals of musical instruments. Service is always friendly and always rushed – expect the occasional mix-up. The *salade du Petit Fer à Cheval* is a hearty number with warm *chèvre* on toast, duck breast and blue cheese.

Le Petit Marcel

65 rue Rambuteau, 4th (01.48.87.10.20). M° Rambuteau or RER Châtelet-Les Halles. **Open** Mon-Sat 7am-midnight. Food served all day. Closed first three weeks in Aug. **Beer** €1.90-€2.90. **No credit cards.**

This little bar comes from the Parisian school of authentic faded charm. You sit on old wooden chests beneath a cracked painted ceiling and gaze through decorated window panes as the lunches sizzle in the corner kitchen. The welcoming waiter will run through the day's offerings on the blackboard menu and suggest a suitable wine. Three *plats du jour* (€8.50-€10) are marked next to the good range of steak dishes (like the succulent *pavé* in pepper sauce), omelettes, pastas and salads, all prepared by an impossibly French chef.

5th Arrondissement

Café de la Nouvelle Mairie ★

19-21 rue des Fossés St-Jacques, 5th (01.44.07.04.41). RER Luxembourg. **Open** Mon, Wed, Fri 9am-8pm; Tue, Thur 9am-10pm. Food served Mon, Wed, Fri noon-3pm; Tue, Thur noon-3pm, 8-10pm. **Beer** 25cl €2.80. **No credit cards.**

Away from the Anglophone sports-screen theme pubs of the area, this is a low-key haunt with bags of natural style. Energetic waiters work the dark wood, chrome-topped bar, occasionally zipping across the room to serve up delicious French fare: quiches, salads and soups and a couple of hearty *plats du jour*. Blackboard wine lists, hanging lamps, old maps and grey-green walls lend real warmth to the room full of thinkers, workers and diners. Weather permitting, the windows open onto the pavement tables and the chatter and jazz float out into the quiet street.

Café de la Poste

7 rue l'Epée-de-Bois, 5th (01.43.37.05.58) M° Place Monge. **Open** Mon-Fri 8.30am-midnight. Food served noon-2.15pm. Closed two weeks in Aug. **Beer** 25cl €1.90-€2.30. **No credit cards.**

The atmosphere in this filthy-floored blues café is epitomised by the painting on the back wall of an old man in beret and string vest reaching for his glass of wine. It's a real local's hangout – think the set of *Cheers* except less classy and with a tipsy landlady. However, if you can brave the piercing stares of the *habitués*, the wine is good and cheap and comes in various sizes. The merlot is especially nice and costs only €1.05 for the smallest glass. The music is supplied by Ella and Charlie and the service is efficient if a little slurred.

Café Delmas

2-4 pl de la Contrescarpe, 5th (01.43.26.51.26). M° Place Monge. **Open** Mon-Thur, Sun 7am-2am; Fri, Sat 7am-4am. Food served Mon-Thur, Sun 9am-midnight, Fri, Sat 9am-1am. **Beer** 25cl €3.96-€4.73. **Credit** MC, V.

Reopened and renamed a couple of years ago, this café has gone a bit upmarket, with a posh new menu and a funky polka-dotted interior crammed with comfy leather armchairs. Its terrace dominates the pretty little *place* with an erratic fountain and stunted trees. It's the ideal place to people-watch during the day or go for a drink to start or finish off the evening and the service is attentive and quick. The food, however, is expensive and, apart from the grilled *faux-filet*, rather disappointing.

Le Comptoir du Panthéon

5 rue Soufflot, 5th (01.43.54.75.36). RER Luxembourg. **Open** Mon-Sat 7.30am-1am; Sun 9am-7pm. Food served Mon-Sat 11am-11pm; Sun 11am-7pm. **Beer** 25cl €1.80-€2.50. **Credit** MC, V. **Wheelchair access.**

This café has been stylishly renovated with contrasting dark wood and crimson velvet furniture, funky coloured walls and abstract art. Despite the modish interior it is first and foremost a student hang-out. But don't expect to discover young radicals here – the bourgeois, well-dressed students are more likely to be discussing *affaires du coeur* or the PSG score sheet than engaging in political discourse or organising the next demo. Venture onto the terrace outside and you'll swap Marlboro fumes for pollution, but this is more than compensated for by the stunning view of the Panthéon, the Law Faculty and the Mairie du Vème.

Le Rallye

11 quai de la Tournelle, 5th (01.43.54.29.65). M° Jussieu. **Open** Mon-Fri 7am-2am; Sat, Sun 9.30am-2am. Closed 23 Dec. **Beer** 25cl €1.70-€2.30. **No credit cards. Wheelchair access.**

On the Seine, next door and in stark contrast to the Tour d'Argent, Le Rallye is an animated crossroads of local characters and taxi drivers who stop in to drink a quick *demi* at the bar, stock up on Lucky Strikes and cultivate their eccentricities. The terrace floor is covered with cigarette butts and roving dogs. The inside is a shrine to Tintin with a few model planes thrown in for good measure. With most of the tourists scared away you can enjoy a cheap beer and a slice of authentic Parisian life.

Le Reflet

6 rue Champollion, 5th (01.43.29.97.27). M° Cluny-La Sorbonne. **Open** daily 10am-2am. Hot food served noon-midnight. **Beer** 25cl €1.90-€2.60. **Credit** MC, V.

Across from the arthouse cinema of the same name, Le Reflet is a temple to film. Black-and-white photos of stars past and present hang from the walls. Lights hanging from a tubular steel rigging create an atmosphere that attracts black-clad philosophy students eager to practice their interview gestures while deconstructing the film. The service can be hazy, but is always friendly. Cheap beer and food and good music make a visit here always worthwhile.

Tabac de la Sorbonne

7 pl de la Sorbonne, 5th (01.43.54.52.04). M° Cluny-La Sorbonne/RER Luxembourg. **Open** daily 6.30am-2am; Nov-Mar 6.30am-11pm. Closed Christmas and New Year. **Beer** 25cl €3.35. **No credit cards. Wheelchair access.**

Even if the competition between *tabacs* were not strictly regulated, the Tabac de la Sorbonne would probably do a roaring trade. It's the cigarette supplier to most Sorbonne students, as well as a pleasant terrace meeting spot; its reasonably priced omelettes, *croques* and *plats* are doled out by efficient moustachioed waiters. The interior becomes obsolete in the summer when the terrace reigns supreme. On our last visit, a leather-clad smoothie was been interviewed over coffee by French television on the rigours of modern student life – the café chosen as the natural site for such a discussion.

Le Verre à Pied

118bis rue Mouffetard, 5th (01.43.31.15.72). M° Censier-Daubenton. **Open** Tue-Sat 8.30am-9pm; Sun 9am-2.30pm. Food served Tue-Sun noon-2.30pm. **Beer** 25cl €1.90-€2.80. **No credit cards.**

The buzz of rue Mouffetard can wear you out – thankfully there are places like this where you can slow down with a cold drink. Le Verre à Pied, open since 1870, has such a timewarp feel that its long bar recently featured in the film *Le Fabuleux Destin d'Amélie Poulain*. Locals and street performers crowd in at the small tables for homely fare as the market shuts down for lunch; there is usually just one hot special but the *patronne* can be persuaded to whip up a salad.

6th Arrondissement

Bar de la Croix-Rouge

2 carrefour de la Croix-Rouge, 6th (01.45.48.06.45). M° Sèvres-Babylone. **Open** Mon-Sat 6am-10pm. Food served all day. **Beer** 25cl €3.20-€4.26. **No credit cards. Wheelchair access.**

Occupying a plum position a short walk from the Bon Marché, the Bar de la Croix-Rouge is at the heart of shopping Mecca. It's an ideal place to stop mid-spend for a quick expresso or *kir*, as the beautiful ones stroll past. On a sunny afternoon, you'd be hard-pushed to bag one of the pavement tables on the compact terrace. The dark brown interior is fairly cramped, but buzzing, and the simple food is good value, particularly given the modish location. Choose from a range of cheese or cold meat platters or one of the deservedly famous *tartines* made with *pain Poilâne*.

Café **Society**

South African rugby international Pieter De Villiers has been a prop on the Stade Français team since the 1995/96 season. Rugby players in France are known for their love of meaty south-western cuisine and De Villiers is no exception, having grown up in 'barbecue country'. But he also enjoys experimenting with Italian cooking at home and learned to make Thai curries during a holiday near Chiang Mai. So important is food to De Villiers that he recently opened a restaurant in the Parc des Princes, ***Le Stade*** *(2 rue du Commandant Guilbaud, 16th/ 01.40.71.33.33).*

One of my favourite new discoveries in Paris is the **No Stress Café**, which is near where I live. It has a modern decor, the food is excellent and you can even have a massage, though I might try the oxygen instead! When I want a good steak I go to the **Maison de l'Aubrac** (*see p45*, **Brasseries**), a 24-hour place off the Champs-Elysées. The owner is a former Stade Français player and has his own farm which supplies the meat. Last time I had the *côte de boeuf* for two with *aligot* and had a feast of a time. They don't have Bordeaux on the wine list as they want to introduce the consumer to some other French jewels. I also like **La Régalade** (*see p13*, **Bistros**), run by another rugby enthusiast, Yves Camdeborde. You can ask for a tasting menu and they'll bring you several small courses. A classic for rugby fans is **Le Métro** (*see p67*, **Budget**), a little place where you can drop in to watch a match or after the match. They serve very good, rustic south-western food. **Barfly** (*see p117*, **Bars & Pubs**) is a place where I go with other rugby players to enjoy a good meal and watch *les branchés* coming and going. Their brunch must be one of the best-value meals on the Champs-Elysées. I also like the Latin atmosphere at the **Barrio Latino** (*see p117*, **Bars & Pubs**), but for a group it's best to reserve a table. A cosy little hideaway I've discovered is **Pub the Shebeen** (7 rue Tournefort/01.45.87.34.43), in a cellar just off rue Mouffetard. The bartender Earl is South African and gives the place great African atmosphere.

FUSION IN PARIS
COCOA CAFE

Friendly service, delicious cocktails, and a successful cuisine that is a fusion of worldly influences. A delightful alternative to traditional French dining, to be enjoyed in a cosy, home-like atmosphere with the cool sounds of lounge music in the background.

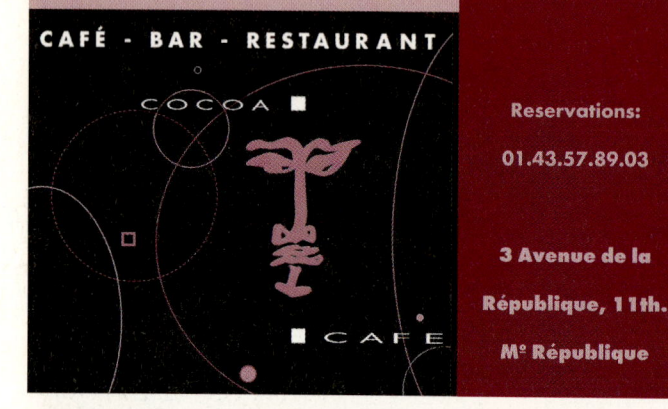

CAFÉ - BAR - RESTAURANT
COCOA CAFE

BAR & CAFÉ
Serving from
11.30-2am Mon-Sat

RESTAURANT
Lunch noon-2.30pm
Dinner 8-11pm

Reservations:
01.43.57.89.03

3 Avenue de la République, 11th.
M° République

DUPONT

Cocktails - pints - salads
open-faced - sandwiches

DUPONT Café
198 rue de la Convention, 15th
Tel : 01 45 32 95 65
Metro : Convention
www.dupont-cafe.com

---

la fourmi café
open daily 9am-2am

74, rue des Martyrs • 18th • M° Pigalle • Tel: 01.42.64.70.35

Café Cassette sums up the café restaurant of my dreams.

Here, in our cosy and comfortable restaurant and its up-to-date interior, you'll enjoy our typically Parisian brasserie menu, where products and recipes are rooted in tradition.

Wishing you a most pleasant meal...

CAFÉ CASSETTE

73 rue de Rennes, 6th
01.45.48.53.78
www.cafecassette.com

Bar du Marché
75 rue de Seine, 6th (01.43.26.55.15).
Mº Odéon. **Open** daily 7.30am-2am.
Food served daily 9am-6pm. **Beer** 25cl
€2-€3.50. **Credit** MC, V.
Bar du Marché is the perfect place to contemplate what you want to make for dinner; you'll find all the ingredients you need in the market street rue de Buci. Then again, once you get a table here you might as well hang on to it as the high standards of food and service have kept it popular with both locals and visitors. If laziness strikes, ask one of the flat-capped, overalled waiters for one of the excellent omelettes. On your way home you can always grab a delectable pastry from Carton, the bakery a few doors down.

Café de Flore
172 bd St-Germain, 6th (01.45.48.55.26).
Mº St-Germain-des-Prés. **Open** daily
7am-1.30am. Food served all day. **Beer** 40cl
€6.50. **Credit** AmEx, MC, V.
The haunt of the Surrealists in the 1920s and '30s is smokier and, strangely, both rougher and more genuinely stylish than Les Deux Magots nearby (yet prices are similarly steep, if not fractionally higher; a coffee costs €4), with a perpetual buzz and insouciant yet genuinely charming waiters. Although it has had no shortage of illustrious customers – Dali, Miró, Breton and Eluard were regulars, while Picasso met muse and model Dora Maar here in 1937 – the Flore's internationally spun crowd still contains its share of authentic Parisian writers, intellectuals, filmmakers and artists (Bernard-Henri Lévy and Eric Rohmer are regulars and we spotted Frédéric Beigbeder being interviewed on the terrace).

Café de la Mairie
8 pl St-Sulpice, 6th (01.43.26.67.82).
Mº St-Sulpice. **Open** Mon-Sat 7am-2am.
Food served all day. **Beer** 25cl €2.10-€3.60.
No credit cards.
This very ordinary-looking little bar justifies its chic location with the perfect leafy pavement terrace to take a break from your wanderings and whet your whistle in the dappled sunshine. Most of the genteel crowd is too busy reading newspapers or gazing at the mighty St-Sulpice church and its lion-guarded fountain to watch the inhabitants of this *quartier* saunter by on their way to Yves Saint Laurent and Christian Lacroix just next door. A traditional range of food and snacks is served all day by the polite staff, so you can re-fuel before a stroll in the Luxembourg – but avoid the grotty loo.

Les Deux Magots
6 pl St-Germain-des-Prés, 6th
(01.45.48.55.25/www.lesdeuxmagots.com).
Mº St-Germain-des-Prés. **Open** daily 7.30am-1.30am. Food served all day. Closed one week in Jan. **Beer** 25cl €5.20-€5.50. **Credit** AmEx, DC, MC, V. **Wheelchair access.**
This is the epitome of the Paris literary haunt (since 1933, it has been awarding its own literary prize). Find out what its name means by reading the blurb on the menu. Dishes include the usual suspects – *charcuterie* and *rosbif froid* – as well as more indulgent foie gras and sevruga caviar. This is one of the few cafés in Paris, as staff won't hesitate to inform you, where wine by the glass is served from the bottle in front of you. With past regulars such as Sartre and de Beauvoir, Picasso, Verlaine and Hemingway, this was *the* place to have an Existential crisis; now, however, it's perhaps better suited for a financial one.

Les Editeurs ★
4 carrefour de l'Odéon, 6th (01.43.26.67.76/
www.lesediteurs.fr). *Mº Odéon.* **Open** daily
8am-2am. Food served daily noon-2am.
Beer 25cl €4.20-€4.50. **Credit** AmEx, MC, V.
Like so many places in St-Germain, the former Chope d'Alsace has gone modern, shedding its endearing winstub decor for a plush red velvet interior. Unlike so many places, though, Les Editeurs seems comfortable in its new clothes – this is a great spot to sip an apéritif and watch the world go by. You don't need to be feeling sociable to come here; the shelves are stacked with books from nearby publishers, which customers are free to peruse. Should hunger strike, you can order *choucroute* – a tribute to the café's former life – or lighter dishes such as a club sandwich or roast cod.

Painting the town rouge *at La Palette*

M's Coffee Room
71 rue du Cherche-Midi, 6th
(01.45.44.20.57). *Mº St-Placide.*
Open Mon-Sun noon-7pm, Sun 11am-7pm.
Food served all day. **Beer** 25cl €4.
Credit AmEx, MC, V.
If you're crying out for scrambled eggs on a Sunday morning this laid-back establishment is the business. Inside you'll find a comfortable place to while away an afternoon playing board games and lounging in the leather armchairs surrounded by clubby paraphernalia. The weekday €12.50 *menu* offers dishes such as *parmentier de canard* and salads. A collection of silver teapots comes into play in the afternoon. The weekend all-day brunch, though expensive at €19, includes freshly squeezed juices, scrambled eggs, smoked bacon, salmon and pastries.

La Palette
43 rue de Seine, 6th (01.43.26.68.15).
Mº Mabillon or Odéon. **Open** Mon-Sat 8am-2am. Food served Mon-Sat noon-3pm. Closed Aug. **Beer** 25cl €1.83-€3.81. **Credit** MC, V.
Located behind the Ecole des Beaux-Arts and on a street lined with private galleries, it's no wonder that La Palette has fallen in line with the neighbourhood. Not surprisingly, a good part of the clientele consists of gallery owners or frequenters. The atmosphere on the large, popular terrace is slightly reserved during the day. At night, however, things can get downright wild. Take the occasionally surly service with a grain of salt.

Au Petit Suisse
16 rue de Vaugirard, 6th (01.43.26.03.81).
Mº Odéon. **Open** daily 7am-11pm. Food served all day. **Beer** 25cl €2.90-€3.51.
Credit MC, V.
Named after Marie de Medici's Swiss guards, the compact Au Petit Suisse has an enviable location next to the Jardins du Luxembourg. For those who don't live on coffee and cigarettes alone, the bilingual menu offers a range of predictable but generally decent food, served by old-school waiters. There is a wide selection of beers on tap, which draw in the students (many of these take advantage of the big tables in the mezzanine to pore over drifts of note paper). Be warned, it can get very smoky in winter.

Le Rostand
6 pl Edmond-Rostand, 6th (01.43.54.61.58).
RER Luxembourg. **Open** Mon-Thur, Sun 8am-midnight; Fri, Sat 8am-2am. Food served all day. **Beer** €4-€4.50.
Credit AmEx, DC, MC, V.
The large, heated terrace looking onto the Luxembourg gardens is the Rostand's main draw. During rush hours, however, it's best enjoyed with earplugs and a gas mask. The inside, done up a few years ago, is classy and clean with Orientalist paintings, long mahogany bar, wall-length mirrors and polished brass fixtures. Food is limited, but there's a wide selection of beers, whiskies and cocktails.

Le Select
99 bd du Montparnasse, 6th
(01.42.22.65.27). *Mº Vavin.* **Open** daily 8am-3am. Food served all day. **Beer** 25cl €3.30-€4.60. **Credit** MC, V.
As the setting of events in scores of memoirs and biographies of writers such as Hemingway and Fitzgerald, you might think Le Select would have little need to blow its own trumpet. We left with our ears ringing: this '*bar américain*' is swimming in its own nostalgia. The better part of the present-day atmosphere is created not by philosophical diatribes but by the smoke from expensive cigars. The food is better-priced than the drink (though the €10.40-€11 cocktails are excellent). We fattened up on cheese and some excellent Bordeaux.

Au Vieux Colombier
65 rue de Rennes, 6th (01.45.48.53.81).
Mº St-Sulpice. **Open** Mon-Sat 8am-midnight; Sun 11am-8pm. Food served daily noon-10pm. **Beer** 25cl €2-€3. **Credit** MC, V.
With a long, deeply varnished wood bar, teardrop chandeliers and other art nouveau touches, Aux Vieux Colombier attracts a cross-section of the area. Making colourful cocktails and serving cheapish beer and refreshing snacks with blinding speed, the young staff are friendly and efficient. Although it can get quite smoky, and you may find your elbows sticking to your table, theses are small trade-offs for the vibrant atmosphere. Full-wall mirrors combat any feelings of claustrophobia in the small room and create lovely reflections when the candles come out at dusk.

7th Arrondissement

Bar Basile
34 rue de Grenelle, 7th (01.42.22.59.46).
Mº Rue du Bac or Sèvres-Babylone.
Open Mon-Fri 7am-9pm, Sat 7am-7.30pm.
Food served Mon-Sat noon-5pm. **Beer** 25cl €2-€2.50. **Credit** V.
Dowdy and down-at-heel from the outside, Bar Basile is awash with vibrant colours within. Shocking pink and lurid orange clash with yellow, turquoise and electric blue, giving the overall impression of a '60s diner crossed with a school canteen. A favourite hangout of Sciences-Po students and local businessmen roughing it a little, this place is jam-packed at lunch, when it serves a range of filling *plats*. Don't miss the sausage and lentil salad.

Café Le Dôme
149 rue St-Dominique, 7th (01.45.51.45.41).
RER Pont de l'Alma. **Open** Mon-Sat 7am-2am.
Food served all day. **Beer** 25cl €1.83-€3.05.
Credit MC, V. **Wheelchair access.**
The Eiffel Tower's upper half is just visible from the south section of this café's comfortable terrace, at its best in early evening. Sitting outside, you feel properly ensconced as you are separated from the pavement by flower-box ramparts, making it easier to see than be seen. The postcard rack and quadrilingual menus give away who makes up most of the clientele, but the lively conversation around the bar and friendly service create a personal, unpretentious atmosphere. Good *plats*, crêpes and view.

Café des Lettres
53 rue de Verneuil, 7th (01.42.22.52.17/
www.cafedeslettres.com). *Mº Rue du Bac.*
Open Mon-Sat 10am-midnight; Sun noon-4pm. Food served Mon-Sat noon-11pm; Sun brunch noon-4pm. Closed two weeks at Christmas. **Beer** 25cl €4.57. **Credit** MC, V.
Café des Lettres has a moody feel, with dark furniture, deep turquoise and maroon coloured walls, deeply meaningful abstract art and a heavy Gauloise-pervaded atmosphere. There is even likely to be the odd brooding intellectual as the salon is used by the neighbouring Maison des Ecrivains for literary discussions and novel-reading sessions. Contrastingly airy, the courtyard is a good place to drop in for an espresso on a summer's afternoon. On our last visit, the mostly-Scandinavian food was of disappointing quality for the price, which reflects the swish location. We tried the *lax-pudding*, a bizarre dish of mashed potato and (rather dry) salmon, and *tentation de Jansen*, a tastier mixture of creamed potatoes and anchovies.

Café du Marché ★
38 rue Cler, 7th (01.47.05.51.27). *Mº Ecole-Militaire.* **Open** Mon-Sat 7am-midnight; Sun 7am-5.30pm. Food served Mon-Sat 11.30am-11pm; Sun 11.30am-3pm. **Beer** 25cl €1.90-€2.50. **Credit** MC, V. **Wheelchair access.**
You don't expect to find a relaxed place like this sandwiched between the Eiffel Tower and Invalides. The inside may be scruffy ('70s mosaic-tiled floor littered with debris) and there's always a group of regulars who look as if they are surviving on a nicotine and liquid diet, but this just proves that it is not an ordinary, sedate 7th *arrondissement* establishment. With friendly young staff, it's a convivial place to stop off during tourist duties to have a cheap drink or to enjoy one of the copious *salades composées* (€8) or daily specials from the blackboard menu (€9.50). Located in a market street, the café also provides a good vantage point for a spot of people-watching.

La Frégate
1 rue du Bac, 7th (01.42.61.23.77/
www.la-fregate.com). *Mº Rue du Bac.*
Open daily 7am-midnight. Food served daily 11.30am-11.30pm. **Beer** 25cl €3.60-€3.90.
Credit AmEx, MC, V.
Next to the Musée d'Orsay, with a view over the Seine to the Louvre, there's plenty to look at from the orderly terrace here (important, as

LE TROISIEME BUREAU

RESTAURANT/CAFÉ BAR

Open Mon-Sat 7am-2am, Sundays 10am-2am
Sunday brunch noon-3pm

74 rue de la Folie Méricourt, 11th M°Oberkampf

letroisiemebureau@hotmail.com

CUBAN-BAR-RESTAURANT

SMOKING ROOM with a cellar of Havana cigars **HORAS LOCAS**

COCKTAILS Cerveza de la Casa

CUBAN DISHES and Tapas

happy hours 5pm-7.30pm

CUBANA Café — BAR - RESTAURANT
47, rue Vavin 75006 Paris
Téléphone 01 40 46 80 81

WWW.CUBANACAFE.COM

SAT & SUN BRUNCH

47 RUE VAVIN, 6TH. M° VAVIN. OPEN DAILY 11AM-3AM. TEL: 01.40.46.80.81

traffic on quai Voltaire can swallow conversation). The interior has been immaculately revamped with engraved metallic café tables and lovely curving bar at the front and a second room with larger restaurant tables, more accommodating for the fish-focused menu. The cherub-painted ceiling is unique and the loos among the nicest we've seen in a Paris café.

8th Arrondissement

Atelier Renault
53 av des Champs-Elysées, 8th (01.49.53.70.00). M° Franklin D. Roosevelt. **Open** daily 8am-2am. Food served daily noon-12.30am. **Beer** 25cl €4. **Credit** AmEx, DC, MC, V.
Brand-conscious consumers were in seventh heaven when Renault opened L'Atelier Renault after a total revamp of the former Pub Renault. Renowned chef Jean-Pierre Vigato has devised a modern international menu (Moroccan-glazed roast lamb, caramelised chicken breast with gnocchi, spicy scampi with Chinese ravioli) or you can stop by anytime for snacks and ice cream sundaes. Upstairs, American elm, glass and steel provide surroundings that take their cue from a ship's cabin. There's a bar with armchairs and low tables, while five footbridges crossing the space give the 200-seat restaurant views over conceptual cars below and genuine traffic (jams) on the avenue.

Bar des Théâtres
6 av Montaigne, 8th (01.47.23.34.63). M° Alma-Marceau. **Open** daily 6am-2am. Food served all day. **Beer** 25cl €2.20-€5.10. **Credit** AmEx, MC, V.
Nestling between Valentino and Emanuel Ungaro on avenue Montaigne, bang opposite the Théâtre des Champs-Elysées, this popular bar/café has a location to die for. It's always buzzing in the evenings after the curtain falls, and attracts a steady daytime stream of trendy fashionistas. Yet Bar des Théâtres couldn't be less pretentious. Its cosy, informal atmosphere and service are reflected in the simple, though pricey brasserie-style fare served in the traditional café area or the slightly more formal restaurant section.

Granterroirs ★
30 rue de Miromesnil, 8th (01.47.42.18.18). M° Miromesnil. **Open** Mon-Fri 8.30am-8pm. Food served all day. Closed three weeks in Aug. **No beer**. **Credit** AmEx, V, MC. **Wheelchair access**.
Welcome to snack-time, luxury-style. This gourmet delicatessen-cum-café is always packed out at lunchtime with gaggles of local office workers. It's possible to book before 12.30pm, but after that it's first come, first served. Don't be deterred – even if you have to be shoe-horned onto the benches alongside the two large picnic tables. The *assiette italienne* arrived as a huge serving of sun-dried tomatoes, aubergines, mushrooms, Italian ham, shaved parmesan, basil, olives, courgettes and artichokes, accompanied by a very fresh rocket and mint salad. Afterwards, the choice was a sensational *tarte aux fraises*, the largest *crème caramel* we had ever seen or an exotic range of *glaces artisanales*. Earl Grey sorbet anyone?

Handmade
19 rue Jean-Mermoz, 8th (01.45.62.50.05). M° Franklin D Roosevelt or Miromesnil. **Open** Mon-Fri noon-3pm. **Beer** 25cl €3. **Credit** MC, V. **Wheelchair access**.
Englishman Hugh Wilson has created a temple to chic just off the Champs, with a perfectionism that borders on obsession. Stone floor, pale wood tables and minimalist white walls set the tone, while help-yourself packs of homemade sandwiches (true Brit faves include cheddar and chutney or coronation chicken), inventive mini-salads, water and fruit juice are all carefully packaged, and tea is imported direct from Delhi. You can tell the flapjacks have cool – Wilson now supplies Colette.

Le Petit Bergson
10 pl Henri-Bergson, 8th (01.45.22.63.25). M° St-Augustin. **Open** Mon-Fri 11am-3pm. Food served all day. **No beer**. **Credit** MC, V.
Le Petit Bergson's main selling-point is its fabulous location – on the corner of one of the prettiest squares in Paris, with a view over a small park and the back of the St Augustin church. At lunch the terrace is packed with local office workers enjoying a selection of *formules*, which start at €11. A free fruit juice or *kir* is offered to those who have to wait for a table, and the service is friendly. The food is mainly salads, quiches and pies, but there are a few hot dishes as well. The owner bustles in and out being jovial but you may have to wait a while for your bill because he keeps stopping to have a drink with his mates at the bar.

9th Arrondissement

P'tit Creux du Faubourg
66 rue du Fbg-Montmartre, 9th (01.48.78.20.57). M° Notre-Dame-de-Lorette. **Open** Mon-Sat 7.30am-7.30pm. Food served all day. Closed mid-July-mid-Aug. **Beer** 25cl €1.80-€2.20. **Credit** MC, V.
What you see is absolutely what you get at the P'tit Creux du Faubourg. Perched on a busy corner, the café is a magnet for locals and passers-by. The tattered menu may look as though it's launched a thousand lunches, but the €8, €9 or €10.35 no-frills *formules* on offer are very good value. The main course of chicken in a creamy sauce was excellent, the accompanying peas mixed with chopped ham, onions and oregano an unexpected twist. The fruit salad which followed couldn't have been fresher – not a tinned cherry in sight. Service was brisk and efficient. The P'tit Creux du Faubourg is a great place to pop into for a quick bite if you're in the neighbourhood.

10th Arrondissement

Chez Prune ★
71 quai de Valmy, 10th (01.42.41.30.47). M° République. **Open** Mon-Sat 7am-2am; Sun 10am-2am. Food served daily noon-3pm; snacks 6.30-11pm. **Beer** 25cl €2-€2.50. **Credit** MC, V.
Bang in the heart of bobo (bohemian bourgeois) heaven, Chez Prune has become a magnet for local creative types. The black turtlenecks are many and the beards are complicated; bindis, headscarves and Birkenstocks abound. If Oberkampf has become a little too mainstream, then this vibrant Canal St-Martin hotspot may be just the place for a *pastis* or a well-cooked lunch. Everyone seems to know each other, but it's far from cliquey: as long as you look suitably street and have a screenplay to talk about you'll fit right in.

Le Grenier Voyageur
3 rue Yves-Toudic, 10th (01.42.02.25.50). M° République. **Open** Mon-Fri 7.30am-2am; Sat, Sun 5pm-2am. Snacks served daily 7pm-10.30pm. **Beer** 25cl €2-€2.45 **Credit** MC, V.
A young and friendly couple take care of this café just off the Canal St-Martin, one of the latest groovy areas. A comfortable bar on entering, it segues into a low-key restaurant decorated in warm, earthy tones. The place filled up over the course of our meal with what looked like locals wandering in for a cheap and cheerful dinner. The volume of salads coming out of the kitchen indicated that only the unenlightened ventured past them – indeed, the hot dishes we ordered were sub-par. Dessert was apple pie, not homemade (in this case, probably a good thing) and garnished with a froth of cream from a can. Friendly service is just not enough to counter the weakness in the kitchen here – stick to the cosy bar and, if you absolutely must eat, take your lead from the locals and order a salad.

Jemmapes
82 quai de Jemmapes, 10th (01.40.40.02.35). M° Château Landon. **Open** daily 10am-2am. Food served all day. **Beer** 25cl €2-€3. **Credit** AmEx, MC, V.
Perched alongside the Canal St-Martin, Jemmapes' outside tables give you a bird's-eye view of the local trendoids at play. During the day, the studiedly scruffy interior has a laid-back air: you could almost imagine yourself in a tapas bar in a Madrid back street. At night the café comes into its own: smoky, noisy and filled with a youngish crowd, with the tourists who drop by during the day long gone. The day we turned up the service fell foul of a domestic spat, much to the amusement of the punters. The salads, when they eventually arrived, were generously proportioned and – at €7.35 – pretty good value.

Le Petit Château d'Eau
34 rue du Chateau d'Eau, 10th (01.42.08.72.81). M° République. **Open** Mon-Fri 9am-9pm. Food served Mon-Fri noon-3pm. Closed Aug. **Beer** 25cl €2. **Credit** MC, V. **Wheelchair access**.
A gem of a café on an otherwise grim street, this place oozes relaxed, classy charm. The high-ceilinged main room is stacked with flowers and dominated by a large circular bar around which regulars perch to knock back cheap glasses of Beaujolais and Bordeaux. The barman's seven-year-old son ferries orders and glasses back and forth, breaking hearts with his cuteness and avoiding spilling drinks by the narrowest of margins. Perfect for a lunchtime omelette or an early-evening *demi*, and a good place for meeting friendly locals.

11th Arrondissement

Ba'ta'clan Café
50 bd Voltaire, 11th (01.49.23.96.33). M° Oberkampf. **Open** daily 7am-2am. Food served daily 11am-1am. **Beer** 25cl €2.15-€2.75. **Credit** MC, V. **Wheelchair access**.
The Ba'ta'clan café, next door to the theatre of the same name, attracts a varied clientele, from intellectuals catching up on their Kant to suited businessmen. The open-plan bar spills out onto a huge terrace, which starts to get really busy around 11pm. Inside, big leather armchairs make for a cosy evening's drinking under the watchful gaze of a slightly pervy statue of a Greek god. Psychedelic paintings, heavy metal chandeliers and fairy lights complete the ensemble. A wide range of food is on offer, a cut above the usual offerings, and *pots* of wine are cheap and plentiful.

Le Bistrot du Peintre
116 av Ledru-Rollin, 11th (01.47.00.34.39). M° Ledru-Rollin. **Open** Mon-Sat 7am-2am; Sun 9am-midnight. Food served Mon-Sat noon-midnight; Sun noon-5pm. Closed 25 Dec. **Beer** 25cl €1.80-€2.60. **Credit** DC, MC, V.
Founded in 1902, this is a fine example of a sophisticated, well-restored art nouveau café, with luscious carved wood, painted vineyard scenes, frosted-glass partitions, tall mirrors and a long zinc bar. The cooking is generally impressive, pulling in a crowd of Bastille regulars. Hot dishes such as *pot-au-feu, confit de canard* or baked sea bream change daily, while Salers beef, salads and plates of *charcuterie* are always available, along with good wines.

Café de l'Industrie
16 rue St-Sabin, 11th (01.47.00.13.53). M° Bastille. **Open** Mon-Fri, Sun 10am-2am. Food served noon-1am. **Beer** 25cl €2-€3. **Credit** MC, V.
A frenetic atmosphere prevails in this high-turnover hangout where super-efficient waiters provide charming service to the sound of soul music classics. A noisy, boisterous party of a café with elegant decor, it offers a respite from the tinselly tourist spots of the neighbouring rue de Lappe. The menu is original (try the red peppers with apricot jam) but doesn't always quite hit the mark (the steak tartare is an unseasoned lump of minced meat). Choose from an intriguing collection of rum punches.

Extra Old Café
307 rue du Fbg-St-Antoine, 11th (01.43.71.73.45). M° Nation. **Open** daily 7am-2am. Food served daily 11.30am-3pm, 6pm-midnight. **Beer** 25cl €2-€2.30. **Credit** MC, V.
The faded grandeur of a 19th-century salon provides the setting for a funky glass-fronted

Chez Prune: bobos, bindis and beards galore

On en oublie d'aller ailleurs*

amnésia
café
42 rue vieille du temple, 4th Paris • 01 . 42 . 72 . 16 . 94

Open daily from 11am to 2am

* you'll forget to go somewhere else

spot patronised by the cream of Nation's café society. Cocktails don't feature on the menu, but the T-shirted staff will knock up a mean margarita or mojito if you ask them to. Idiosyncratic little touches abound, like the rose-garden toilets and the wall-sized doll cabinet stuffed with toys and records. The music is rock and roll, the terrace is heated, and bottles of wine start at €11.

Le Kitch
10 rue Oberkampf, 11th (01.40.21.94.14). Mº Oberkampf. **Open** Mon-Fri 10am-4pm, 5pm-2am; Sat, Sun 5pm-2am. Food served Mon-Fri noon-3pm, 8pm-midnight; Sat, Sun 8pm-midnight. **Beer** 25cl €1.50-€2.30. **No credit cards**.

The name is not an empty promise: children's plastic furniture (some of which we couldn't fit into, or out of), marbles (as in the round ones you play with), murals and outcrops of chicken wire provide plenty of conversation-starters. The beer is well-priced, the inventive cooking is reliable and the atmosphere unpretentious.

Morry's
1 rue de Charonne, 11th (01.48.07.03.03). Mº Ledru-Rollin. **Open** Mon-Sat 8.30am-7.30pm. **Average** €2.60-€5.80. **Credit** AmEx, MC, V.

This is not the only bagel place in Paris, but Morry's is an especially handy spot for a quick bite around the Bastille. The cheapest bagel, at €2.60, is the cream cheese version, but you can also splash out with the €5.80 Grand Central, layered with bacon, turkey, cheddar cheese and salad. We also like the vegetarian: salad leaves, cheese, guacamole and sundried tomato. The tiny beamed interior is pleasant, and Morry squeezes a few tables on to the pavement in summer.

Pause Café
41 rue de Charonne, 11th (01.48.06.80.33). Mº Ledru-Rollin. **Open** Mon-Sat 7am-2am; Sun 9am-8.30pm. Food served daily noon-5pm, 7-11pm. **Beer** 25cl €1.85-€2.60. **Credit** AmEx, MC, V.

Voted best café in France by a glossy book on European cafés, the jazzy Pause Café – made famous in its pre-expansion days by a role in the film *Chacun cherche son chat* – has a lot to live up to. On recent visits service has been in keeping with the name – mime school graduates have the best chance of getting a waiter's attention. Still, the setting remains funky and bright thanks to the picture windows and the kitchen makes an effort with hot specials, a selection of filling *tourtes*, and goat's cheese in *brik* pastry with sweet sautéed pears. Seats on the heated terrace are coveted even in winter.

12th Arrondissement

Chez Gudule
58 bd de Picpus, 12th (01.43.40.08.28). Mº Picpus. **Open** daily 7.30am-1.45am. Closed Christmas. **Beer** 25cl €2-€2.50. **Credit** MC, V.

Sister-ship of the boho-trendy Chez Prune café on the canal St-Martin, Chez Gudule is an oasis of jazz and houmous in a neighbourhood otherwise dominated by filling stations and temp agencies. The choice of three platters – meat, Mediterranean dips or crudités – and pastel decor is lifted straight from its sibling. What is different is the crowd: a mellowed-out mix of young adults. The service is similarly laid-back but efficient – our waiter swam through the trash to find a receipt that we had forgotten to ask for. The bread is divine.

Roller Café ★
50 bd de la Bastille, 12th (01.43.46.55.22). Mº Bastille. **Open** daily 7am-2am. **Beer** 25cl €2.15-€2.75. **Credit** MC, V. **Wheelchair access**.

A roomy, glass-fronted café perched on a boulevard down which the Parisian skaters frequently take their Friday night hurtle, the Roller Café is cashing in on the current craze for blading and boarding. With a funky logo and flashy, themed menus it gives the impression of wanting to become a chain. This would be good news – the service is chummy, the freshly-squeezed fruit cocktails zingy and the list of €3.80 snacks (including guacamole with tortilla chips and aubergine caviar with pitta bread) tempting. The decor is artistic graffiti and neon, and hats, T-shirts and skaters' umbrellas are on sale. Stop in for a 'roller breakfast' with pancakes and lashings of syrup.

T pour 2 Café
23 cour St-Emilion, 12th (01.40.19.02.09/ www.tpour2cafe.com). Mº Cour St-Emilion. **Open** daily 11am-midnight. Snacks served all day. **Beer** 25cl €3.10. **Credit** AmEx, MC, V.

This fashionable modern café (bar/restaurant at lunch and in the evening) offers a vast selection of teas and coffees ranging from the traditional (lapsang souchong) to the exotic (*Guadeloupe bonifieur*) and the just plain amusing (*grand jasmin monkey king*). The atmosphere is relaxed – big comfy chairs, mugs of coffee and Fashion TV and M6 playing in the background. There is a selection of light foods including desserts, sandwiches and expensive salads (around €12).

Le Viaduc Café
43 av Daumesnil, 12th (01.44.74.70.70). Mº Ledru-Rollin or Gare de Lyon. **Open** daily 9am-4am. Hot food served noon-3pm, 7pm-3am. **Beer** 25cl €3.05. **Credit** AmEx, DC, MC, V. **Wheelchair access**.

Occupying two lofty arches beneath the swish Viaduc des Arts, Le Viaduc becomes a full-blown restaurant at lunch (average €22.87), serving modish, contemporary cooking (*croustillant de cabillaud aux courgettes*, choco- late tart, etc) to suits and style-conscious hipsters. If you're not a regular, the unique setting and pretty good food can be let down by occasionally aloof service, but it's nonetheless a fine place for a sophisticated apéritif or nightcap. Jazz brunch on Sunday.

13th Arrondissement

La Route du Cacao
Quai de la Gare, 13th (01.53.82.10.35/ www.larouteducacao.com). Mº Quai de la Gare or Bibliothèque. **Open** Mon-Fri, Sun 10am-7pm (lunch served noon-3pm). **Hot chocolate** €4.88. **Credit** MC, V. **Wheelchair access**.

Next to the Batofar, a floating nightclub, this *péniche* specialises in a different type of decadence: chocolate. Each of the six hot chocolate variations is made to order, and puts to shame the anaemic mixtures served in most cafés. We tried the misleadingly named *caramel* (melted chocolate in milk spiced with cinnamon), before sampling a rich *coupe* of banana and coconut ice cream with thick chocolate sauce. Chocolate chip cookies made on the premises appeared with our order, and there are several sweet specials daily. The rather functional decor features benches upholstered in carpet, but is made up for by the view of the sun setting over the Seine.

Au Soleil d'Austerlitz
18 bd de l'Hôpital, 13th (01.43.31.22.38.). Mº Gare d'Austerlitz. **Open** Mon-Fri 6am-9.30pm; Sat 6am-4pm. Food served Mon-Fri noon-10pm; Sat noon-4pm. Closed Aug. **Beer** 25cl €2-€3.20. **Credit** MC, V.

At the foot of a greying 20s-style apartment block and looking out over the Austerlitz station and a busy main road, this is a café whose charm is by no means obvious. However, if you're in the area, a lunchtime visit is worthwhile simply to enjoy the entirely untouristy, gruffly French atmosphere. Hearty career waiters shepherd customers through standard fare plus daily specials, which come with potato gratin or salad. For dessert there is a big selection of pricey but pleasant tarts and pies. One gets the impression that neither the decor nor the staff has changed for the past 30 years.

14th Arrondissement

Le Cadran
38 rue Raymond-Losserand, 14th (01.43.21.69.45). Mº Pernéty. **Open** Mon-Sat 7am-9pm. Food served Mon-Sat 11.30am-2.30pm. **Beer** 25cl €1.80-€2.10. **No credit cards**.

Behind a sparkling green facade lies a beautifully prosaic slice of old Paris. Its mosaic floor and zinc bar emerge occasionally from the requisite cigarette fug as a gang of regulars downs *apéros* at the bar, and all ages head to the second room for lunchtime sustenance. He mans the bar; she waddles to and from the kitchen, bearing plates laden high with the *plat du jour*, perhaps rosy, roast lamb and green beans. The fruit tarts, fresh from the oven, are winners. Happily oblivious to trends.

Café de la Place ★
23 rue d'Odessa, 14th (01.42.18.01.55). Mº Edgar-Quinet. **Open** Mon-Sat 7.30am-2am; Sun 10am-11pm. Food served Mon-Sat 11am-1am; Sun 11am-10pm. **Beer** 25cl €3.50. **Credit** MC, V.

This pavement café overlooking the place Edgar-Quinet is a much classier option than the glitzy places two minutes' walk away on the boulevard du Montparnasse. Inside it has a warm feel with a wood-panelled interior, vintage Ricard jugs and battered 1950s ads. There is also a vast selection of wines on offer. The real draw, however, is the lively terrace, a perfect location for a summertime *apéro*. The food is of reasonable quality if a little over-priced, ranging from salads or sandwiches to more hearty options such as Auvergnat *charcuterie*.

La Chope Daguerre
17 rue Daguerre, 14th (01.43.22.76.59). Mº Denfert-Rochereau. **Open** Mon, Sun 7am-8pm; Tue-Sat 7am-midnight. Food served noon-3pm, 6.30-11pm. **Beer** 25cl €2-€3.70. **Credit** MC, V.

Snack with the fashion pack

Antoine et Lili Café: sweet and syrupy

In this capital of both fashion and café culture, it's only surprising that the new crop of fashion cafés has taken so long to arrive. It could be argued that serious size-ten fashionistas can't be interested in eating, but at the very least they provide the perfect backdrop to admire and be admired.

The **Colette Water Bar** (213 rue St-Honoré, 1st/01.55.35.33.90) is the place to cast a critical eye on fashion's victims. Light, modern lunches can be washed down with one of more than 80 designer mineral waters (€1.22-€5.34). Unlike the prescriptive vision on offer upstairs it is surprisingly friendly, communal tables placing everyone in a very un-minimal proximity. Equally good for eavesdropping with its thigh-by-thigh seating is the **Armani Caffe** (149 bd St-Germain, 6th/ 01.45.48.62.15), home to lots of chic types pushing salad leaves around their plates. Deliberately avoiding the minimal chic of Colette and Armani is Joseph's new venture, **Joe's** (277 rue St-Honoré, 8th/ 01.49.27.05.54). The moulded plastic furniture, orange lacquer and coloured fluorescent lighting all create a '60s feel, while the designer food remains firmly in the present: sushi, carpaccio and slimline salads, all at designer prices. **Barbara Bui Café** (27 rue Etienne-Marcel, 1st/ 01.45.08.04.04) attracts a similar set of hip young things. Here you can munch on a honey and soya chicken kebab or Oriental-style salad while watching killer heels being tapped to the latest in jazz-funk.

Smaller boutiques are also turning their shops into spaces to spend time as well as money. One of the most attractive of these is **Honoré et sa Cantine** (38 rue Madame, 6th/01.45.48.96.86), which is unlike any canteen you'll have encountered before. Each formica table has its own toaster (soup and sandwiches are the order of the day) and your neighbours are the pretty people of St-Germain. Annick Lestrohan's stylish street-wear and accessories in gentle tones fill the rails.

Taking kitsch to its exuberant extreme is the canal-side **Antoine et Lili Café** (95 quai de Valmy, 10th/01.40.37.41.55). Plastic chandeliers, floral prints, leopardskin and row upon row of different coloured syrups are matched by an eclectic menu and crowd. Mediterranean-inspired dishes include tortilla, tapas and artichoke salad.

Though just a street away, the tiny **Purple** boutique and café (9 rue Pierre-Dupont, 10th/ 01.40.34.14.21) is a million miles away conceptually. There are just two Judd-like tables at which you can sip at miso soup or a *fluide floral*, a mix of rice milk and violet extract. On the single rail hang pieces from designers such as duo Bless and Susan Ciaciolo. *Phoebe Greenwood.*

footsie

La Bourse des Boissons

footsie
A unique bar, a unique atmosphere... An elegant setting for lunch, dinner, or drinks; the music here gets funkier as the hours pass and the 'stocks' plummet and rocket.

footsie
A unique concept in France. Drink prices are set according to consumption, just like at the stock-market

Your drink could well bring on a recession

12 rue Daunou, 2nd - Tel: 01.42.60.07.20
Open weekdays from 12pm - 2am and until 4am Fri and Sat - Trading starts at 6pm

---

What's on this week in Paris?

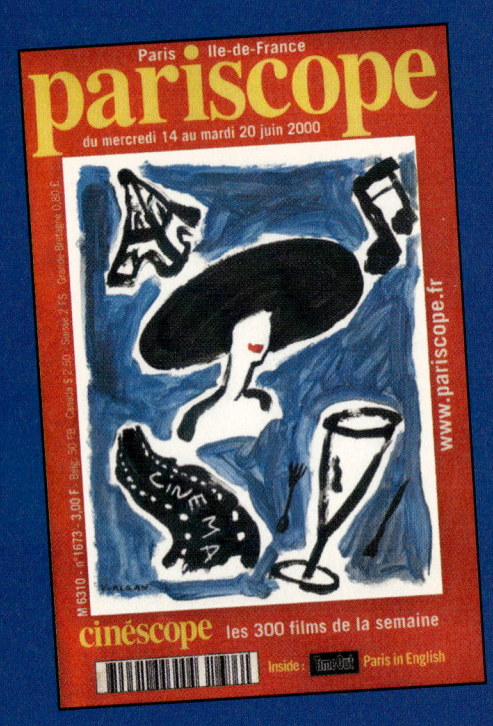

Every week inside **Pariscope** (€0.40 at all Paris-area newsagents) you'll find the English-language supplement **Time Out** *Paris*, six pages of essential arts and entertainment events, plus the hottest spots for going out.

Time Out *Paris*
100 rue du Fbg-St-Antoine
75012 Paris
Tel: +33 (0)1.44.87.00.45
Fax: +33 (0)1.44.73.90.60
editors@timeout.fr

Now on sale from Wednesday morning at WHSmith Waterloo.

Rue Daguerre positively drips with cafés from the humblest plastic *tabac* to nouveau design velour. La Chope falls somewhere between the two, but is the rendezvous of choice for locals. Recently spruced up with dark wood, new chairs and glowing red lamps, this is a place to skulk inside over an *apéro*, or sun on the terrace absorbing the sights, sounds and smells of the market. Food is fresh and generous, with big salads and blackboard suggestions such as chicken with morels or five-pepper steak.

L'Entrepôt
7-9 rue Francis-de-Pressensé, 14th (01.45.40.60.70). M° Pernéty. **Open** Mon-Fri, Sun 11.30am-2am; Sat 5pm-2am. Food served Mon-Fri, Sun noon-2.30pm, 7.30pm-midnight; Sat 7.30pm-midnight. **Beer** 25cl €2.44-€3.51. **Credit** AmEx, MC, V.
This converted paper warehouse has something for every taste: a restaurant with leafy outdoor courtyard, an independent arts cinema, and a café. The ceilings are high and the matt black walls are covered in film posters. You can chill out on the couches and listen to music (often jazz) several nights a week, philosophy discussions or the occasional salsa night. A small charge for music is tagged on to each drink.

15th Arrondissement

Au Dernier Métro
70 bd de Grenelle, 15th (01.45.75.01.23/www.auderniermetro.com). M° Dupleix. **Open** daily 6am-2am. Food served daily noon-1am. **Beer** 25cl €1.90-€2.60. **Credit** AmEx, DC, MC, V.
Arrive early at this gem of a café, as the few tables tend to be permanently occupied by café philosophers and smart twentysomethings *entre amis*. Colourful paintings and old advertising hoardings line the walls and the bar has designated elbow space for each of the *habitués* with corresponding floor space for their dogs. You're likely to end up talking to the guy next to you about his broken heart or your plans to change the world. The enormous salads and *plats du jour* are always good choices.

No Stress Café
27 rue Balard, 15th (01.45.58.45.68). M° Javel. **Open** Mon-Fri 10am-2am; Sat, Sun 8pm-2am. Food served Mon-Fri noon-2.30pm, 8.30-11pm; Sat, Sun 8.30-11pm. **Beer** 25cl €2.80. **Oxygen** 8l bottle €23. **Shiatsu massage** €7.62. **Credit** MC, V.
Although the adverts for massages and other stress-relieving activities may suggest an upmarket St Denis-style 'massage parlour', this is in fact a bona fide chill-out zone. The tense exhibitionist in you can be treated to a ten-minute shiatsu massage (fully clothed), which takes place on an weird-looking chair in the centre of the room. Should pollution levels be at the root of your stress, then the slightly more bizarre option is to inhale oxygen-in-a-can *à la* Michael Jackson. Alternatively, relieve stress the orthodox way by having a few beers or cocktails at the bar, or indulging in the popular food.

Le Roi du Café ★
59 rue Lecourbe, 15th (01.47.34.48.50). M° Sèvres-Lecourbe. **Open** daily 7am-2am. Food served until 11.30pm. **Average** €11.50-€15. **Beer** 25cl €1.90-€2.75. **Credit** MC, V. **Wheelchair access**.
This is the perfect address for a lazy, warm summer evening when you're not in the mood for Montparnasse. If you choose your seat carefully, you'll be treated to a gorgeous sunset, with periodic glittering reflections from the Eiffel Tower. The range of liquor behind the bar, presided over by a head waiter with a huge moustache, means you'll never run out of fancy drinks to try, but the real reason for hanging out here is the worn art deco elegance. The kitchen serves a decent selection of basics, especially useful outside normal mealtimes.

16th Arrondissement

Café Antoine
17 rue La Fontaine, 16th (01.40.50.14.30). RER Kennedy-Radio France. **Open** Mon-Sat 7.30am-11pm. Closed two weeks in Aug. Food served Mon-Sat noon-3pm, 7-10.30pm. **Beer** 25cl €2-€3. **Credit** AmEx, DC, MC, V.
Hector Guimard slipped this tiny café into one of his famous art nouveau apartment blocks, with a view over a small but classy food market on Tuesdays and Fridays. Inside is a strawberries-and-cream idyll of days gone by: roses on the tiles, a painted-glass ceiling and blowsy scenes of horseracing and rowing. An excellent Italian espresso comes on a tiny tray with a chocolate coin; they also do hot chocolate and mulled wine, while tiny blackboards announce tempting, if pricey, foie gras, *poulet à la normande*, steaks and *charcuterie*. Adorable.

Le Totem ★
Musée de l'Homme, 17 pl du Trocadéro, 16th (01.47.27.28.29). M° Trocadéro. **Open** daily noon-2am. **Beer** 25cl €4.30. **Credit** AmEx, DC, MC, V. **Wheelchair access**.
Two giant totems from British Columbia give the café its name, while a panorama of the Eiffel Tower provides a spectacular view. A chic mix of branché *bourgeoisie*, tourists, businessmen and celebrities meets at the well-stocked bar. Contemporary French food is served at lunch, while at night it's best to reserve for adventurous dinner fare.

18th Arrondissement

Chez Camille
8 rue Ravignan, 18th (01.46.06.05.78). M° Abbesses or Pigalle. **Open** Tue-Sat 9am-1.30am; Sun 11am-8pm. Closed Aug. **Beer** 25cl €1.80-€2.50. **No credit cards**.
This is a more down-to-earth café than we could have hoped to find on the *butte* Montmartre, complete with chess players (including the waiter, which didn't speed up service), a lovely old clock, zinc bar and tipsy pick-up artist. Perched on the tiny terrace, you can rest your elbows on a narrow wooden counter and feast your eyes on a panoramic view to the left, a bucolic square to the right, while soaking up a rare slice of Montmartre bohemia.

Le Chinon ★
49 rue des Abbesses, 18th (01.42.62.07.17). M° Abbesses. **Open** daily 7am-2am. Food served daily 11am-11.30pm. **Beer** 25cl €1.80-€3.10. **Credit** MC, V.
Many of the bars and restaurants in Montmartre are filled entirely with tourists, but in this stretch of the road the atmosphere is more Parisian. With trendy tables and chairs worthy of a collector, this café can almost be forgiven for serving watery-tasting wine, such as our vieilles vignes Chinon for €10.40 a tiny carafe. As long as you stick to coffee or beer you should be fine, especially if you follow the lead of the mostly-French clientele and avoid eating here (watching the bartender eat pasta should just about put you off anyway). Simply meet your friends here for beer and appreciate the renovated loo before you head back out into the madness of the street.
Branch: Le Troisième Chinon, 56 rue des Archives, 4th (01.48.87.94.68).

L'Été en Pente Douce
23 rue Muller, 18th (01.42.64.02.67). M° Château Rouge or Anvers. **Open** daily noon-1am. Closed Christmas and New Year. Food served noon-3pm; 7-11.45pm. **Beer** 25cl €3. **Credit** MC, V.
Location, location, location – that's what it's all about here. The wine hasn't improved since last year, the food is less than ordinary and the waitresses are a trifle tetchy... but, nestled as it is half-way up the slope leading to the Sacré-Coeur and overlooking a park, none of this is affecting business. Inside is a charming, typically French art nouveau dining room, and outside is a large terrace crammed with tables and chairs. Those lucky enough to get a seat outside become a captive audience for the stream of fiddlers, tap dancers, accordion players etc. capitalising on the spirit of goodwill and generosity brought on by the glorious setting (to which the staff have apparently become immune).

Le Sancerre
35 rue des Abbesses, 18th (01.42.58.47.05). M° Abbesses. **Open** daily 7am-2am. Food served all day. **Lunch menu** €11.50. **Beer** 25cl €1.70-€1.80. **Credit** MC, V.
Bohemia is alive and well in this fashionably disheveled café on the slopes of Montmartre. Don't let the scruffy appearance of the staff or the premises fool you. Service is efficient and professional, and the kitchen crew serves up an appetising selection of omelettes, salads and sandwiches. The beverage menu offers an extensive choice of wines or whiskies and good quality beers. On busy evenings, bypass the competition for terrace seats and sit just inside the sliding doors. The people-watching is just as good, and best of all, you're less likely to be jostled by the hordes of sightseers clogging the narrow pavement.

19th Arrondissement

La Kaskad'
2 pl Armand-Carrel, 19th (01.40.40.08.10). M° Laumière. **Open** daily 9am-1am. Food served daily until 11pm. **Average** €15.10-€18.20. **Prix fixe** €24.40. **Lunch menu** €21. **Beer** 25cl €2.50-€3.60. **Credit** MC, V. **Wheelchair access**.
Since our last visit, La Cascade café has morphed into the more upmarket La Kaskad'. Stylish upholstered banquettes and armchairs have replaced the nautical decor and the kitchen has jumped on the fusion food bandwagon. A new menu offers tapas-style starters and main dishes that incorporate influences from around the globe. At €10.40 the hearty salads (in summer) are a budget-conscious diner's delight. One salad easily makes an entire meal. In winter, salads make way for the 'brasserie de luxe' menu.

Le Rendez-vous des Quais
MK2 sur Seine, 10-14 quai de la Seine, 19th (01.40.37.02.81). M° Stalingrad or Jaurès. **Open** daily noon-midnight. Food served daily noon-midnight. **Beer** 25cl €2.74-€3.81. **Credit** AmEx, DC, MC, V. **Wheelchair access**.
On a lazy afternoon, you can easily while away hours watching the barges and tour boats from your table at this relaxed café on the esplanade of the Bassin de la Villette. Food-loving film buffs can't miss with the €22.71 *menu ciné*, which includes main course, dessert, beverage, coffee and a ticket to the adjoining MK2 cinema. The food is a cut above typical café fare, and desserts tend towards the rich and gooey, like the sumptuous chocolate tart with *dacquoise* sponge cake crust.

20th Arrondissement

Le Soleil
136 bd de Ménilmontant, 20th (01.46.36.47.44). M° Ménilmontant. **Open** daily 9am-2am. **Beer** 25cl €1.52-€2.29. **No credit cards**.
Aptly named, as the terrace catches most of the afternoon sun, this brightly lit café is a standby for local artists, musicians and hipsters and always an interesting place to strike up a conversation. It's totally unexceptional inside, but you want to be outside anyway. No food.

Charli's pub 15

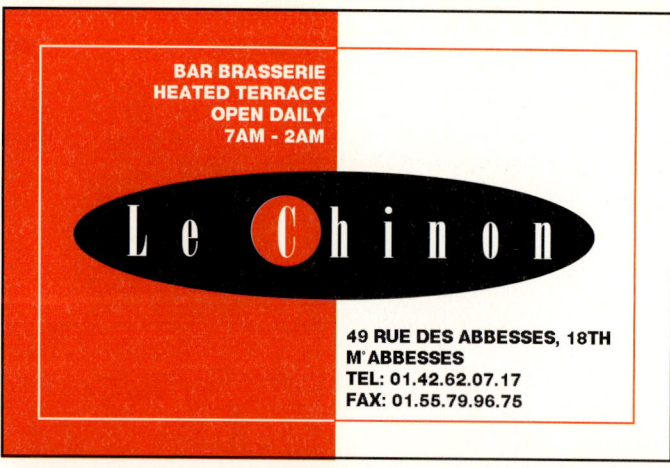

PINTS AT 4€ all week all night

STUDENT NIGHT every wednesday

LADIES NIGHT every thursday

DJs every Friday & Saturday

BASTILLE
24, rue Keller
75011 Paris
France

+ 33 (0) 1 48 07 80 99

Tuesday - Saturday
5:00 pm - 2:00/5:00 am

charlis_pub@hotmail.com

**BAR BRASSERIE
HEATED TERRACE
OPEN DAILY
7AM - 2AM**

Le Chinon

49 RUE DES ABBESSES, 18TH
M° ABBESSES
TEL: 01.42.62.07.17
FAX: 01.55.79.96.75

In a seventies Style Decor, Bar Brasserie Le chinon III
Food Served Lunchtimes and evenings...
Sunday Brunch

(Group bookings possible)

3 Le troisième Chinon

56 RUE DES ARCHIVES, 4TH
TEL: 01.48.87.94.68

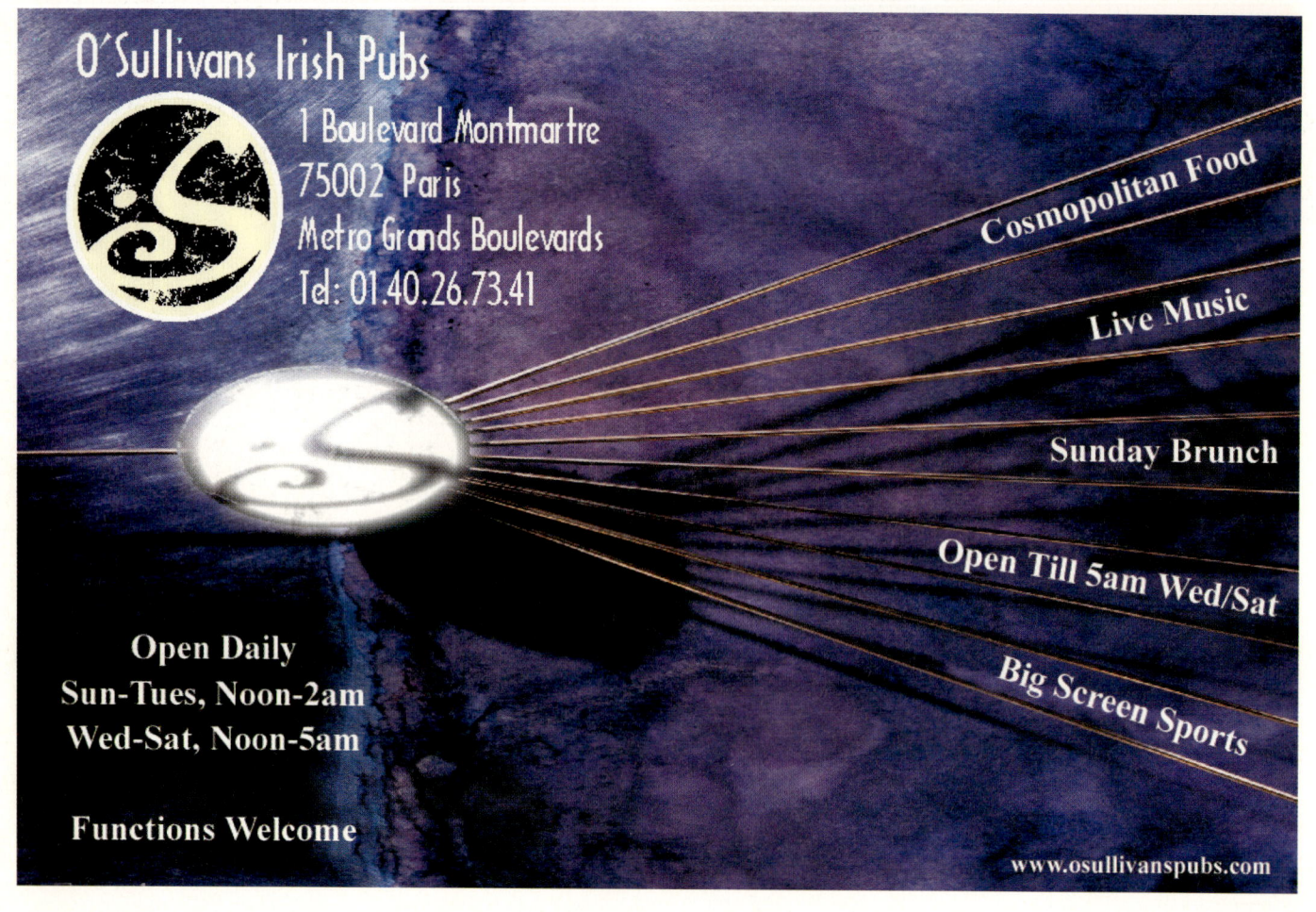

O'Sullivans Irish Pubs

1 Boulevard Montmartre
75002 Paris
Metro Grands Boulevards
Tel: 01.40.26.73.41

- Cosmopolitan Food
- Live Music
- Sunday Brunch
- Open Till 5am Wed/Sat
- Big Screen Sports

Open Daily
Sun-Tues, Noon-2am
Wed-Sat, Noon-5am

Functions Welcome

www.osullivanspubs.com

Bars & Pubs

Find a message in a bottle plus other high-spirited flotsam in Paris watering holes.

Paris has a definite generosity of spirit, or rather spirits. If you fancy a capricious caipiroska, an overly adult martini, a lethal vodka jelly, or simply a fish bowl full of beer or wine, the city has a bar for every palate and pocket. You can get low-down and dirty in betting (PMU) *bar-tabacs*, lament the state of your football or cricket team with like-minded folk in expat outposts, flirt with the French in *branché* bars or glide into some bubble and sleek hotel bar.

Oberkampf and its surrounding streets remain the focus of bar activity; but despite the many imitators that have now sprung up – with requisite distressed walls and flea-bitten furniture – the pioneers remain the classics. The Canal St-Martin is also buzzing, but perhaps the most exciting news is the Seine nightlife scene (see *p123*). See **Trendy** (*p67*) for fashionable restaurants that double as bars, such as **Man Ray** and **Cabaret**.

1st Arrondissement

Café Oz
18 rue St-Denis, 1st (01.40.39.00.18/ www.cafe-oz.com). M° Châtelet. **Open** Mon-Thur, Sun 3pm-2am; Fri-Sat 3pm-3am. **Beer** 25cl €3.50. **Happy hour** daily 6-8pm. **Credit** MC, V. **Wheelchair access**.
This Aussie watering-hole feigns an outback-style interior with wood-shack decor, stuffed croc, and Aboriginal motifs. But the beer is cold and authentically Australian, and the crowd lively. At the weekend, things can get noisy and boisterous as hoards of thirsty Antipodeans empty pints of VB at the bar and DJs pump out didgeridoo-inspired tunes.
Branches: 184 rue St-Jacques, 5th (01.43.54.30.48); 1 rue de Bruxelles, 9th (01.40.16.11.16).

Flann O'Brien's
6 rue Bailleul, 1st (01.42.60.13.58/ www.irishfrance.com/flannobrien). M° Louvre-Rivoli. **Open** daily 4pm-2am. **Beer** 25cl €3.40. **Happy hour** Mon, Tue, Thur-Sun 4-8pm; Wed 4pm-2am. **No credit cards. Wheelchair access**.
If you're of the mind that one Irish pub is pretty much the same as the next, order a pint of Guinness here. When it arrives a full five to six minutes later, you'll understand why Flann O'Brien's is a cut above the rest. Competition on the pool table is fierce, but the live Irish band keeps the atmosphere congenial. The pub also boasts a satellite feed for Irish sporting events, featuring weekly hurling matches during the season (if you don't know, you probably aren't interested).

Le Fumoir ★
6 rue de l'Amiral-de-Coligny, 1st (01.42.92.00.24/www.lefumoir.com). M° Louvre-Rivoli. **Open** daily 11am-2am. Food served daily noon-3pm, 7-11pm. Closed one week in Aug. **Beer** 25cl €4. **Cocktails** €9-€10.50. **Happy hour** daily 6-8pm. **Credit** AmEx, MC, V. **Wheelchair access**.
Everything from the oil paintings to the brushed-metal light fixtures at Le Fumoir is so impeccably integrated that even the bar staff seem to have been included in the interior decorator's sketches. A sleek crowd sipping martinis or browsing the papers at the bar gives way to young professionals in the modish restaurant (well-designed, modern dishes such as tuna tartare or warm squid with artichokes). The real pearl, however, is the 3000-book library. Although many of the best are reserved for consultation on site, there's a worthwhile swap session every afternoon.

2nd Arrondissement

Café Noir
65 rue Montmartre, 2nd (01.40.39.07.36). M° Sentier. **Open** Mon-Fri 8am-2am; Sat 4pm-2am. Food served Mon-Fri noon-3pm. **Beer** 25cl €2.15-€3. **No credit cards**.
This bar, with its tacky and tatty decor, lives a contrasting double life. It is a busy lunchtime venue for the Sentier's rag trade workers and *Le Figaro* journalists who bask on the sunny terrace to enjoy solid if unexceptional French classic bistro fare such as roast chicken, savoury *tourte* or pasta. In the evenings it's a quieter bar which, despite claiming to have been a celeb haunt in the past, is mainly frequented by those famous in their own minds – aided by ample liquid.

The Frog & Rosbif
116 rue St-Denis, 2nd (01.42.36.34.73/ www.frogpubs.com). M° Etienne-Marcel or RER Châtelet-Les-Halles. **Open** daily noon-2am. Food served daily noon-11pm. **Beer** 25cl €3.80. **Happy hour** Mon-Sat 6-8.30pm. **Credit** MC, V.
This pub is one of the best English boozers in Paris with wooden pews, blackboard ads for classic themed nights, and a good selection of house-brewed beers with names such as Dark de Triomphe and Parislytic. These are served up to a mixed crowd of rotund expats, tourists whose idea of a holiday consists of downing pints in an English pub abroad, and local French drinkers gingerly sipping pints. All in all, this is good place to head for if you are nostalgic for pub atmosphere.
Branch: Frog at Bercy Village, 25 cour St-Emilion, 12th (01.43.40.70.71).

Harry's New York Bar
5 rue Daunou, 2nd (01.42.61.71.14/ www.harrys-bar.fr). M° Opéra. **Open** daily 11am-3am. **Beer** 25cl €5.20-€6.40. **Cocktails** €9.15-€13.25. **Credit** AmEx, DC, MC, V.
Harry's claims to have invented the Bloody Mary. We'll let them and the King Cole bar in New York fight it out, but it has certainly been the origin of some bloody awful hangovers, memory gaps and serious indiscretions. The long bar is full of vodka veterans as cocktails are taken very seriously here. The dry martini is particularly impressive but everything on the long list is expertly mixed. White-coated waiters engage in jokey banter with a lively crowd of tourists, local businessmen and American alumni. If you can avoid the bar bores, Harry's is a great place to go for a kill-or-cure hair of the dog. Just don't ask for a soft drink. Ever.

La Jungle
56 rue d'Argout, 2nd (01.40.41.03.45). M° Sentier. **Open** Mon-Thur 10am-2am; Sat, Sun 4pm-2am. Food served Mon-Thur noon-2pm, 7pm-midnight; Sat, Sun 7pm-midnight. **Beer** 25cl €1.83-€2.74. **Credit** AmEx, DC, MC, V.
Potent cocktails, a cool African soundtrack and a relaxed summer terrace make this bar a fun location for afternoon drinks. Inside the minute bar things get a bit more seedy, with dusty African memorabilia, plastic palm trees wilting under the heat and a colourful crop of regulars who look as though they have been through all the 50-plus cocktails in one sitting. In our experience, the African-inspired food is best avoided. Stick to the cocktails.
Branch: La Jungle Transatlantique, 15 rue d'Aboukir, 2nd (01.45.08.54.17).

Somo
168 rue Montmartre, 2nd (01.40.13.08.80). M° Grands Boulevards or Bourse. **Open** daily 11.30am-2am. Food served Mon-Fri noon-3pm, 7-11pm; Sat 7-11pm; Sun noon-4pm, 7-11pm. Happy hour daily 6-8pm. **Beer** 25cl €3.5. **Cocktails** €8.50. **Credit** MC, V.
Opened by the gang behind the Lizard Lounge, Stolly's and the Bottle Shop, the upmarket Somo feels a little out of place among the area's tacky theme bars and kebab stands. But we suspect there is method behind this apparent madness. Somo has a New-York-loft feel, with an exposed concrete effect and a cool mezzanine for surveying the scene. Sip a 'chic blonde' or try one of the potent Champagne cocktails, such as the aptly named lush (with Cognac and a sugar cube soaked in Angostura bitters).

Le Tambour
41 rue Montmartre, 2nd (01.42.33.06.90). M° Les Halles. **Open** daily 24 hours. Food served daily 8pm-2am. **Beer** 25cl €1.80-€2.60. **Credit** MC, V.
The 1st *arrondissement* is hardly lacking in all-night bars, but this place is a welcome alternative to the generally tacky Châtelet boozers. The strange Alpine chalet-style exterior is matched by an equally odd interior of flea market bric-a-brac, including a vintage 'find your destination' Métro map which handily aids in orienteering back to *chez soi* after a skinful of cheap *demis*. Despite the dog-eared novels and the classical statuettes on the shelves, this is not the home of the intellectual elite: although many of the drinkers have strongly expressed opinions, they are not often of the coherent sort. In the early evening, this place is transformed into a bistro of reasonable price and quality, in the steak and chips vein.

3rd Arrondissement

L'Art Brut
78 rue Quincampoix, 3rd (01.42.72.17.36). M° Rambuteau. **Open** daily 5pm-2am. Snacks served all day. **Beer** 25cl €2-€2.30. **Credit** AmEx, DC, MC, V.
Dim light from a tin bathtub hung from the ceiling, exposed stone walls and dark wooden tables, benches and chairs create a slightly gloomy effect – offset by the laid-back clientele deep in books and intellectual conversation. Rough and ready details abound, from the scrap-metal facade and the huge ventilation duct, to various pieces of chunky *art brut* on the walls. Staff are friendly, but the clients are so clearly regulars that you might feel like an intruder.

4th Arrondissement

The Auld Alliance
80 rue François-Miron, 4th (01.48.04.30.40). M° St-Paul. **Open** Mon-Fri 4.30pm-2am; Sat, Sun noon-2am. **Beer** 25cl €2.80. **Happy hour** Mon, Tue, Thur-Sun 4.30-8pm; Wed 4.30-9pm. **No credit cards**.
Named after a 13th-century treaty agreed between the Kings of France and Scotland 'to do battle against the King of England', this pub now bonds the two nations over the biggest collection of Scottish Single Malt Whisky in France, and Irn Bru for the initiated. Refreshingly for a theme pub you will hear a lot of French, as well as regular bursts of live bagpipe. It's packed during sports matches and there's an eclectic mix of live music on Friday afternoons. The Celtic decor is largely understated, except for a rather gloomy stag's head.

La Jungle boogies to an African beat

RESTAURANT — ENGLISH PUB

BIG BEN PUB

Open daily

Pub food available every evening

Lunch menu from 11am
Salads, burgers, plat du jour

Live Rugby & World CuP on big screen T.V.

207 av Charles de Gaulle 92200 Neuilly
M° Pont de Neuilly
01.47.47.44.44

The Silver Goblet pub

Paris' original Irish pub

Open daily from 6pm till late
11 rue du Cygne, 1st. M° Etienne Marcel

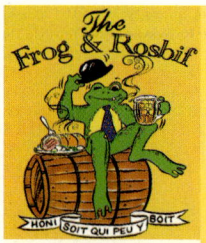

LE BAR DES FERRAILLEURS

Slide Sport — Free steel

Ti-Punch – Mojito
Caïpirina – Long Island
Frozen Margarita €5.50
before 10pm

Cheaper prices before 10

COOL JAZZ – CLASSICS
DEEP HOUSE – TECHNO

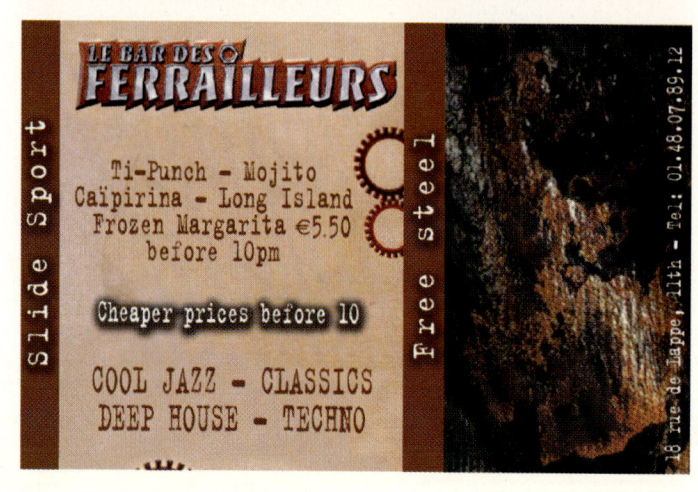

18 rue de Lappe, 11th – Tel: 01.48.07.89.12

FrogPubs
www.frogpubs.com

The Frog & Rosbif
116 r St Denis
M° Etienne Marcel
tel: 01.42.36.34.73

The Frog & Princess
9 r Princesse
M° Mabillon
tel: 01.40.51.77.38

The Frog at Bercy Village
25 cour St Emilion
M° Cour St Emilion
tel: 01.43.40.70.71

The Frog & British Library
114 Ave de France
M° Bibliothèque
tel: 01.45.84.34.26

Great Food
Live Sport
Happy Hours
Friendly Staff

..and of course
Cracking
Micro-Brewed Beers
served in the legendary
Big Jugs!!

Chez Richard

37 rue Vieille-du-Temple, 4th (01.42.74.31.65). M° Hôtel-de-Ville or St-Paul. **Open** daily 6pm-2am. Food served daily 8pm-midnight. Closed two weeks in Aug. **Beer** 25cl €3.70. **Cocktails** €7-€10. **Happy hour** daily 6-8pm. **Credit** AmEx, MC, V.

A real gem that pulls in a mix of first-daters, people looking for a quiet night out and pre-party gangs gathering strength. The long squishy bar begs elbows and pissed philosphising, while the friendly staff, well-mixed cocktails and perfectly chilled Champagne bring Chez Richard close to bar heaven.

Les Chimères

133 rue St-Antoine, 4th (01.42.72.71.97). M° St-Paul. **Open** daily 6.30am-5.30am. Snacks served daily 7.30pm-2am. **Beer** 25cl €1.70-€3.85. **Happy hour** Mon-Fri 6-9pm; Sat, Sun 3-9pm. **Credit** MC, V.

With its neon lights, fake Americana, MTV monitors and karaoke evenings, this bar in the hectic couth-side of the Marais is by no means the epitome of Parisian sophistication. But if you're looking for a lively atmosphere, reasonably priced drinks (knockdown happy hour prices and Wednesday 10pm-midnight promotion) and long hours, then it's ideal. Be warned, arrive after midnight and the karaoke kicks in. It's then that you are likely to witness an (authentically) out-of-tune version of one of Johnny Hallyday's eminently forgettable '70s hits, or, better still, an (authentically) slurred Gainsbourg number.

Les Etages

35 rue Vielle-du-Temple, 4th (01.42.78.72.00). M° Hôtel-de-Ville or St-Paul. **Open** Mon-Fri 3.30pm-2am; Sat noon-2am; Sun 11am-2am. **Beer** 25cl €3.20-€4. **Cocktails** €7-9. **Happy hour** daily 3.30-9pm. **Credit** MC, V.

Les Etages pulls in serious punters for an apéritif, a handful of sugary peanuts and an evening of inelegant slumming. If squalor is your thing and you don't mind picking bits of ceiling out of your caipirinha, snagging your Wolfords on a sofa spring and contorting yourself into yoga positions to sit down, then this is the place for you. Watch out for the weird caste system governing seating (apparently the top floors are the hippest places to squat) and don't forget to take a shih-tzu on a string for the authentic trustafarian traveller look. Go quickly before it's condemned.

Branch: 5 rue de Buci, 6th (01.46.34.26.26).

The Lizard Lounge ★

18 rue du Bourg-Tibourg, 4th (01.42.72.81.34/www.hip-bars.com). M° Hôtel-de-Ville. **Open** daily noon-2am. Food served Mon-Fri, Sun noon-2pm, 7-10.30pm; Sat noon-11pm (Sat, Sun brunch noon-4pm). Closed one week in Aug. **Beer** 25cl €2.70. **Cocktails** €6-7.80. **Happy hour** daily spirits 5-7pm; beer/cocktails 8-10pm. **Credit** MC, V.

Stone walls, modern art and a long, curved bar guarded by a lascivious-looking lizard provide the backdrop for an Anglophone/phile crowd to indulge in serious flirting over lethal cocktails. The mezzanine is perfect for talent spotting and houses the cleverly hidden copper loo. Trip hop and house music help everything along and from 8pm you can shake your stuff on the small dance floor in the cellar. Brunch is an institution at The Lizard Lounge; come early for the Sunday papers, cheap Bloody Marys and a mean eggs Benedict (€12.20-€18.30).

Le Pick-Clops

16 rue Vieille-du-Temple, 4th (01.40.29.02.18). M° Hôtel-de-Ville or St-Paul. **Open** Mon-Sat 8am-2am, Sun 9am-2am. Food served daily noon-midnight. **Beer** 25cl €2-€2.50. **Credit** MC, V.

Occupying a busy corner of the rue Vieille-du-Temple, this bar is shamelessly '70s. The leitmotif here is resolutely kitsch, with top-to-toe pink neon lights, furniture in clashing colours and a wonderfully awful clock with bauble-adorned hands. Seventies retro chicks vie with trendy Marais locals in geometric specs for space at the bar from which to survey passers-by. A place with as many shiny surfaces and mirrors as this is clearly designed for narcissists, and it does a roaring trade on a hot Parisian evening.

Stolly's

16 rue Cloche-Perce, 4th (01.42.76.06.76/ www.hip-bars.com). M° Hôtel-de-Ville or St-Paul. **Open** daily 4.30pm-2am. **Beer** 25cl €2.80. **Cocktails** €4-€8. **Happy hour** daily 4.30-8pm. **Credit** MC, V.

Proving that size really doesn't matter, Stolly's packs a large crowd into a small space. The hardcore cocktails, friendly staff and loud music create a welcoming atmosphere. Always full of expats getting steadily trolleyed, Stolly's is a great place to watch the football or the rugby, particularly if you have a scrum fetish. In summer the terrace provides welcome relief.

5th Arrondissement

Bombardier

2 pl du Panthéon, 5th (01.43.54.79.22/ www.bombardier.com). M° Maubert-Mutualité. **Open** daily 11am-2am. Food served Mon-Fri, Sun noon-3pm; Sat 1-4pm. **Beer** 50cl €4.70. **Cocktails** €4.20-€7. **Happy hour** 4-9pm. **Credit** AmEx, MC, V.

A real pork scratchings and pint pub, the Bombardier looks like the dodgy local you never went into at home. Despite the swirly glass, padded velour seats and olde worlde tapestry, it's a lot less hardcore Anglo than most English pubs, managing to pull in healthy measures of pretty young French things. A great place for a quiet Sunday drink or raucous rugby session.

Connolly's Corner

12 rue de Mirbel, 5th (01.43.31.94.22) M° Censier-Daubenton. **Open** daily 4pm-2am. **Beer** 25cl €3. **Happy hour** daily 4-8pm. **Credit** MC, V.

This cosy pub is unabashedly Irish. Revellers from the nearby rue Mouffetard join staunch regulars to knock back stout and generous measures of Paddy at beer-barrel tables. Beware of entering in a tie: it may end up joining the impressive wall collection, each with a dedication from its former owner. Live music on Tuesdays, Thursdays and Sundays at 7.30pm, though charming, takes up half the main bar.

Le Crocodile ★

6 rue Royer-Collard, 5th. (01.43.54.32.37). M° Maubert-Mutualité. **Open** Mon-Sat 10.30pm-6am (closing variable). Closed Aug. **Cocktails** €5.33 (before midnight).

It's worth ignoring appearances – boarded-up windows – for a cocktail at Le Crocodile. Young, friendly regulars line the sides of this small, narrow bar and try to decide on a drink – extremely difficult given the length and complexity of the cocktail list. We were assured that there are 267 choices, most of them marginally less potent than meths. Pen and paper are provided to note your decision; the pen came in handy for point-and-choose decisions when everything got hazy. We think we can recommend an accroche-coeur, a supremely '70s mix of Champagne and goldschläger, served with extra gold leaf. We can definitely recommend headache pills for the morning after.

Finnegan's Wake

9 rue des Boulangers, 5th (01.46.34.23.65/ www.irishfrance.com). M° Jussieu. **Open** Mon-Fri 11am-2am; Sat 6pm-2am. Snacks served all day. **Beer** 25cl €3-€3.50. **Happy hour** Mon-Sat 6-8pm. **No credit cards.**

The interior decoration of Finnegan's Wake is courtesy of Murphy's, Hennessy and Kilkenny and the constant Irish folk music provides an interesting soundtrack to the muted MTV in the corner. The cheery bar staff serve beer-food in the shape of piping-hot quiche Lorraine and ring a firebell every time they receive a tip. Although not the most happening bar in the area, it's a nice place for a quiet pint and boasts an indoor wishing well, beamed ceilings and Welsh lessons on Wednesday evenings.

La Gueuze

19 rue Soufflot, 5th (01.43.54.63.00). RER Luxembourg. **Open** Mon-Thur 11am-2am; Fri, Sat 11am-4am; Sun 11am-midnight. Food served Mon-Sat 11am-1am; Sun 11am-11pm. **Beer** 25cl €4. **Happy hour** daily 4-7pm. **Credit** AmEx, MC, V.

This roomy Alsatian café is a lively and fun establishment on an otherwise quiet street. It's a beer-drinker's paradise, with more than 120 brands on offer, including Vietnamese, Scottish and Russian brews. The decor is rather gloomy but the service is ultra-friendly and the atmosphere is relaxed – the waiters spend as much time chatting as they do taking orders. It's not cheap, but they do have a happy hour with two drinks for the price of one.

The Hideout

11 rue du Pot-de-Fer 5th (01.45.35.13.17/ www.irishfrance.com). M° Place Monge. **Open** daily 4pm-2am. **Beer** 25cl €2.60-€3.50. **Cocktails** €2.60. **Happy hour** Fri, Sat 4-10pm Sun-Thu 4pm-midnight. **Credit** AmEx, DC, MC, V.

The Hideout is everything an Irish pub in Paris should be – dark, smoky and down-to-earth. With its blasting Britpop and don't-care decor it attracts a young, international bunch who crowd in at weekends to down cheap pints at happy hour and do a little drunken flirting. After sipping *demis* on elegant terraces this place is the perfect antidote; their only minor concession to sophistication is the list of lethal cocktails. There's an excellent DJ on Thursdays.

Le Pantalon

7 rue Royer-Collard, 5th (01.40.51.85.85). RER Luxembourg. **Open** Mon-Sat 5.30pm-2am. Snacks served all day. **Beer** 25cl €1.70-€2.28. **Happy hour** Mon-Sat 5.30-7.30pm. **No credit cards.**

A bastion of anarchic kook in an otherwise respectable area, this place is like the café equivalent of a 'where's Wally' poster – the more you look, the more new and bizarre things you see. An ancient hoover attached to a dustbin lid hangs precariously from the ceiling but manages to seem run-of-the-mill next to the disembodied arm holding a sun umbrella and the beautifully patterned naked body-casts. A student crowd downs drinks to the sound of what can only be described as funked-up bagpipe music while a mangy stuffed sheep overlooks proceedings from a miniature balcony.

Le Piano Vache

8 rue Laplace, 5th (01.46.33.75.03). M° Maubert-Mutualite. **Open** daily noon-2am. Food served daily noon- 2.30pm. **Beer** 25cl €2-€3.50. **Credit** MC, V.

Perfect for '80s revivalists dying to get into goth, Le Piano Vache is the place to relive previous experiments with manic-depressive music and far too much cheap black lace. Posters dating back to the '70s are plastered all over the walls, lights are low and a dense cloud of smoke shrouds the bar and tardis-like back room. Indie nights here look like a Robert Smith tribute evening staged on the set of The Lost Boys. Steer clear on Wednesday nights (*soirée gothique*) and go in when it's in a better mood and people wearing colour are welcome.

Aux Trois Mailletz ★

56 rue Galande, 5th (01.43.54.00.79/ www.lestroismailletz.com). M° St-Michel. **Open** daily 6pm-5am (closing variable). Food served daily 7.30pm-3am. **Beer** bottle €3.75-€4.90. **Credit** AmEx, MC,V.

Life is a cabaret in the bowels of Aux Trois Mailletz on weekends from 11pm until the wee small hours. For a €15-€20 entry fee you'll be tunefully entertained with everything from Latin to rock n' roll and discover how sophisticated, image-conscious Parisians let their hair down. It's a small price to pay for such a privilege. Upstairs, a more civilised set line up numbers for a pianist and enjoy a good ol' singalong. Dine on typical French cuisine, or guzzle the odd cocktail including the house special, coco punch. Be warned, prices go up after 10pm (coco punch increases to €11) but that's when the fun begins.

Le Violon Dingue

46 rue de la Montagne-Ste-Geneviève, 5th (01.43.25.79.93). M° Maubert-Mutualité. **Open** Mon-Thur, Sun 6pm-5am; Fri-Sat 8pm-5am. **Beer** 50cl €5.34-€6.10. **Happy hour** daily 6pm-10pm. **Credit** MC, V.

Despite the Latin Quarter location and French name, this bar is full of expats downing pints and hoping that they might take advantage of the low-lit, alcohol-fuelled atmosphere to strike up a linguistically-challenged conversation with one of the French students who stray into the bar. The sticky floor and the third-world toilets complete the image of a reliably grotty boozer. The real attraction must therefore be the extended happy hour prices, but beware – there

Stay the night

Aesthetic satisfaction is guaranteed through rosé-coloured glasses of Perrier – Laurent Perrier, that is.

Hôtel Ritz

15 pl Vendôme, 1st (01.43.16.30.31/ www.ritzparis.com). Mº Madeleine or Concorde. **Open** daily 11am-1am. **Credit** AmEx, DC, MC, V. **Wheelchair access.**

The Hemingway Bar is pretty close to alcoholic Valhalla. Colin, possibly the best barman in the world, presides over his own pearly gates, dispensing nectar to all. The sybaritic *Cognac aux truffes* at €38.11 is sublime.

Hôtel Lutétia

45 bd Raspail, 6th (01.49.54.46.46/ www.lutetia-paris.com). Mº Sèvres-Babylone. **Open** daily 9am-1am. **Credit** AmEx, DC, MC, V.

You have a choice of three different settings in which to tipple at the Lutétia: a *fumoir* heavily populated by blowhard cigar smokers, the main hall, or the wonderfully louche, low-lit art deco bar with its cushy armchairs, friendly bartender Gilles, generously poured drinks and appealing assortment of international odd-bods letting their hair down. We watched a pack of young French banker types with their shirts untucked surf a wave of vodka tonics and ultimately figure out how four boys could go home with three girls; no one got left out.

Mathis

Hôtel Elysées-Matignon, 3 rue de Ponthieu, 8th (01.53.76.01.62). Mº Champs-Elysées-Clemenceau. **Open** 10pm-dawn. **Credit** AmEx, MC, V.

If you make it past the formidable hostess, expect to be pampered by the staff and exchange daring witticisms with your neighbours (if you can't be witty in at least four languages then you shouldn't be here). No-one arrives until at least midnight and things hot up after 2am, when the pretty boys and girls that make the bar look like a Prada shoot really start to party. Achingly hip.

Hôtel Plaza Athénée *

25 av Montaigne, 8th (01.53.67.66.65). Mº Franklin D. Roosevelt. **Open** 11.30am-2am. **Credit** AmEx, DC, MC, V. **Wheelchair access.**

An ice-cool phoenix has risen from the ashes (the previous bar caught fire) at the Plaza. Decked out by Patrick Jouin, it's all luminosity, glass, metal and a Louis XV stool or 30. The famed vodka jellies, favoured by the ladies who lunch then lurch, are back; so too the elegant rose royale – Champagne and raspberry coulis.

6th Arrondissement

Le Bar Dix ★
*10 rue de l'Odéon, 6th (01.43.26.66.83).
M° Odéon.* **Open** daily 5.30pm-2am.
Beer bottle €2.90-€3.70. **Happy hour** daily 6-9pm. **No credit cards**.

If you want to converse with the natives, this is the place to do it. Students and oldies merge into a convivial, laid-back *mêlée*. Faded posters, genre Toulouse-Lautrec, cover shabby walls in the deceptively small ground floor bar, but a precariously steep staircase, to be used only when stone cold sober, leads down to a much larger, but equally packed, cellar. Spot a space, make a beeline for it, wedge yourself in alongside the locals, order a pitcher of the set drink – home-brewed sangria – and settle in.

Café Mabillon
*164 bd St-Germain, 6th (01.43.26.62.93).
M° Mabillon or St-Germain-des-Prés.* **Open** daily 7.30am-6.30am. Food served daily from 9am. **Beer** 25cl €3-€5.30. **Cocktails** €9-€11.50. **Happy hour** daily 7-9pm. **Credit** MC, V.

Café Mabillon is a funky place, with a flashy modern interior, pumping soundtrack and a cast list of trendies, *poseurs, dragueurs* and out-of-place tourists trying to be part of the Parisian in-crowd. The place to be seen is the terrace, but unless you fancy a gulp of boulevard St-Germain's finest fumes then the side seats are better. The waiters have been through the Parisian school of charm so expect lots of attitude with little aptitude, and, annoyingly, your bill may bear little resemblance to listed prices – staff seem to work on the assumption that their is a price hike later on, at which stage you'll probably have had too many cocktails to care.

Le Comptoir des Canettes
*11 rue des Canettes, 6th (01.43.26.79.15).
M° Mabillon.* **Open** Tue-Sat noon-2am. Closed Aug, Christmas. **Beer** bottle €3.50-€3.80. **Credit** MC, V.

The heart of St-Germain still runs red as wine in this historic *bar à vins* (aka Chez Georges), despite the demise of old Georges himself. Street-level, run by Georges' son, is filled with local shop owners and residents sipping a beer or one of the many regional wines on offer. Downstairs, the domaine of Georges' grandsons, is host to a younger, rowdier student crowd that huddles at long tables in the dank basement, catching an occasional live band, and drinking lots of beer. On warm summer nights both young and old spill out of the front door, turning the narrow street into one big party.

Corcoran
*28 rue St-André-des-Arts, 6th
(01.40.46.97.46/www.corcoranirishpub.com).
M° St-Michel.* **Open** daily 11.30am-2am. Food served Mon-Sat noon-4pm.
Beer 25cl €3.40. **Happy hour** daily 5-8pm.
Credit AmEx, DC, MC, V.

A typical Irish pub, stuffed with homesick natives of the Emerald Isle in search of a well-poured pint of the black stuff, plus Kilkenny and Beamish. There's also Golden Wonder crisps, an excellent selection of Irish whiskey, and a live Irish band every Sunday night from 6-9pm. Take advantage of cheap 'student night' on Thursdays 9.30pm-2am. A prime venue for watching sport on the telly.

The Frog & Princess
*9 rue Princesse, 6th (01.40.51.77.38/
www.frogpubs.com). M° Mabillon.* **Open** Mon-Fri 5.30pm-2am; Sat, Sun noon-2am. Food served all day until 11.30pm. Brunch Sat, Sun.
Beer pint €4.20-€5.70. **Happy hour** 5.30-8pm. **Credit** MC, V.

This little bit of Leeds on the Left Bank boasts above-average pub grub, decent micro-brewery beer and extremely friendly staff. Weekends are popular with students pooling their centimes for a final round, 'laydeez' on ill-advised girls' nights outs and barely post-pubescent French teenagers trying out their school exchange chat-up lines. School nights (except for 'student night' Tuesdays, when shots are €1.50 with every pint) are more chilled out, attracting grown-ups keen for a pint-and-packet of crisps with pub pop.

Fu Bar
*5 rue St-Sulpice, 6th (01.40.51.82.00).
M° Odéon.* **Open** daily 4pm-2am. **Beer** 25cl €2.80-€3.20. **Cocktails** €6.20-€7.
Happy hour Mon, Wed-Sat 4-9pm; Tue 4pm-2am; Sun 4pm-midnight. **Credit** MC, V.

Proving that size doesn't matter, the tiny Fu Bar is a brilliant addition to any serious bar hopper's itinerary; it's full of up-for-it Anglos making friends and inroads into the cocktail list. The friendly staff make a superb cosmopolitan but beware Patsy's martinis which have led to some absolutely fabulous mistakes. Practically obscene measures and plenty of punter interaction make this a top choice for a huge night out.

De La Ville is so à la mode

Coolín
*Marché St-Germain, 15 rue Clément, 6th
(01.44.07.00.92/www.irishfrance.com).
M° Mabillon.* **Open** Mon-Sat 10.30am-2am, Sun noon-2am. Food served daily 6.30-10.30pm. **Beer** 25cl €2.90. **Happy hour** Mon-Sat 5-8pm. **Credit** MC, V.
Wheelchair access.

This rather chilled bar tucked into the Marché St-Germain steers clear of the fiddle-de-dee Oirishness peddled elsewhere. There are no leprechauns or shamrocks, and plenty of seats and floor space mean it's easy to mingle or go *tête-à-tête*. The clientele is well-behaved as Coolín is better suited to a quiet pint than to a

The Moose
*16 rue des Quatre-Vents, 6th (01.46.33.77.00/
www.mooseheadparis.com). M° Odéon.*
Open Mon-Fri 4pm-2am; Sat, Sun 11am-2am. Food served Mon-Fri 4-11pm; Sat, Sun 11am-11pm. Brunch 11am-3.30pm. **Beer** 25cl €2.75-€3.50. **Cocktails** €4-€9.20. **Happy hour** daily 4-9pm. **Credit** MC, V.

A giant plastic moosehead behind the bar, ice hockey regalia on the walls, Bryan Adams tunes, and national flags affirm the Canadian theme. Although there were no Mounties or lumberjacks at the bar, there were plenty of inebriated Canadians – including a bar-room sportsman in hockey jersey and shorts. The bar boasts that 'Canadian speciality' food is served, though this seems to mean that everything, including meat, is served with maple syrup. Themed nights feature regularly.

7th Arrondissement

Café Thoumieux
*4 rue de la Comète, 7th (01.45.51.50.40).
M° La Tour-Maubourg.* **Open** Mon-Fri noon-2am; Sat 5pm-2am. Food served Mon-Fri noon-3pm. Closed three weeks in Aug, 24 Dec-2 Jan. **Beer** 25cl €4. **Cocktails** €6-€9.
Happy hour Mon-Sat 5-6pm. **Credit** AmEx, MC, V.

It may be little brother to the vintage bistro Thoumieux around the corner, but the Café is a laid-back, sultry destination for cocktails, tapas or big-screen sport. Banquettes snake around the room and spiky Aztec-pattern lamps send light flickering up the walls. There's a good tapas platter (€13 for two) and vodkas include vanilla, caramel and banana. Don't blame the vodka for the image of a monstrous, pebble-dashed sink in the toilets – it's real.

8th Arrondissement

Barfly
*49 av George V, 8th (01.53.67.84.60).
M° George V.* **Open** Mon-Fri noon-3pm, 7.30pm-1am; Sat 7.30pm-2am; Sun noon-4pm; 7.30pm-1am. **Beer** 25cl €5. **Cocktails** €11-€12. **Credit** AmEx, MC, V.

The Liz Taylor of the bar world (still trading on its former glory), Barfly should have been put out of its misery a long time ago. Once home to B-list beautiful people it now plays raddled hostess to quiz show contestants and expense account Germans trying to reel in bottle-blondes with Bollinger and BMWs. If you must go then tango-tans, last season's Vuitton clutch and a gold card are indispensable and may help you get served by attitude-junkie staff who don't seem to realise they're serving drinks in the Paris equivalent of Stringfellows.

The Bowler
*13 rue d'Artois, 8th (01.45.61.16.60).
M° St-Philippe du Roule.* **Open** daily 11am-2am. Hot food served daily noon-2.30pm; curry Sun 7.30-10.30pm. **Happy hour** Mon-Fri 5-6.30pm, Sat, Sun 7-9pm.
Beer 25cl €3.50. **Credit** AmEx, MC, V.

The Bowler is the refuge of the love-France-loathe-the-French expat. It's full of rugger buggers, students and bankers shooting weak-chinned smiles at pashmina 'n' pearls girls. Aided and abetted by jugs of Courage and vats of flavoured vodka, things can get noisy. Sunday's pub quiz is legendary. Plan hen nights for Saturdays when drinks are cheaper for 'ladies'.

Freedom
*8 rue de Berri, 8th (01.53.75.25.50).
M° George V.* **Open** Mon-Fri noon-2am, Sat, Sun noon-5am. Food served Mon-Fri noon-4pm; Sat, Sun noon-3pm. **Beer** 25cl €3.
Happy hour Mon-Fri 5.30-7.30pm.
Credit AmEx, DC, MC, V.

The Freedom (no longer part of the Firkin chain) pulls in gangs of regulars for after-work frolics, lunchtime sessions and some serious sharking on weekends. There are pub games, decent grub, genuinely friendly staff and some fiercely patriotic decor. Weekends are packed till 5am with goodtime girls and boys, delighted that the supersonic volume levels render traditional courting rituals (names and 30 seconds of small talk) useless. Like a school disco for grown-ups, it's great fun.

Latina Café
114 av des Champs-Elysées, 8th (01.42.89.98.89). M° George V. **Open** daily noon-5am. Food served Mon-Sat noon-3pm, 7pm-2am. **Beer** 25cl €4-€4.50. **Cocktails** €4-€8.50. **Credit** MC, V.

The Latina Café is a deeply sexy place, from the funky stained glass, curvy wrought-iron, deep leather armchairs and ludicrously fat cigars to the hordes of pretty young things who come here to flirt. But the most important element is the music. And the dancing. Run in partnership with Radio Latina, the music – including live concerts on Tuesday and Thursdays – is streets away from the Ricky Martin/Enrique Iglesias combos peddled at ersatz 'Latino' joints across town. A great place to put last summer's salsa classes into practice, or to learn during the Sunday brunch lessons.

Polo Room
3 rue Lord-Byron, 8th (01.40.74.07.78/ www.poloroom.com). M° George V. **Open** Mon-Thur noon-3pm, 5pm-1am; Fri, Sat noon-3pm, 5pm-2am; Sun 7pm-1am. **Beer** 25cl €2-€4. **Cocktails** €5-€10. **Happy hour** daily 5-8pm. **Credit** AmEx, DC, MC, V. **Wheelchair access**.

Like a social climbing teenager undergoing an identity crisis, the Polo Room can't quite decide what it wants to be when it grows up. It likes to think that it's all martinis and chukkas, but it is sadly closer to alcopops and chucking. The 'posh' decor mixes ye olde colonial club pieces with the type of net curtains that haven't been seen in suburbia since the arrival of Ikea, migraine-inducing laser lights and low tables that make it look like a drinking den for leprechauns. Choose from a suave and sophisticated drinks list featuring gems such as the mandarintini, a sexy mix of vodka and fizzy orange served in a fancy triangular glass. Punters gingerly sipping their cocktails included plenty of predatory dirty old men and some divine young things who clearly didn't realise they were in the wrong place.

9th Arrondissement

Le Barramundi
3 rue Taitbout, 9th (01.47.70.21.21). M° Richelieu-Drouot. **Open** Mon-Fri noon-3pm, 7.30pm-2am; Sat 8pm-5am. Closed two weeks in Aug. Food served Mon-Fri noon-3pm, 7.30pm-midnight; Sat 8-11pm. **Beer** 25cl €6. **Cocktails** €7-€10. **Credit** AmEx, DC, MC, V. **Wheelchair access**.

Firmly on the bandwagon of all things world (think African art, Aboriginal sculpture, Oriental lighting and global food), Barramundi just about manages to pull it off. Relaxed, pretty young things disappear into vast squishy sofas while nursing potent cocktails and looking faintly bored. The menu isn't particularly inspiring so don't bother with dinner, but the Indian-inspired DJ box pumps out decent chill-out music on Friday nights (there is a 'dance party' on Saturdays) and the drinks list is reassuringly expensive.

The best After hours

Le Tambour (2nd)
Wacky Alpine chalet.

Harry's New York Bar
For serious cocktails.

Les Chimères (4th)
Hectic and hedonistic.

Café Mabillon (6th)
Funky and flashy.

Mathis (8th)
Achingly hip.

Le Barramundi (9th)
A world apart.

La Fabrique (11th)
For the beer necessities.

Ten out of ten for Le Bar Dix

10th Arrondissement

L'Atmosphère ★
49 rue Lucien-Sampaix, 10th (01.40.38.09.21). M° Gare de l'Est. **Open** Tue-Sat 10am-2am; Sun 5-9pm. Food served Tue-Sat 8-11pm. **Beer** 25cl €2-€3. **No credit cards**.

Despite having lost its evening live music permit after years of push and pull with neighbours and the mayor's office, L'Atmosphère remains at the centre of the Canal St-Martin renaissance. Parisians of all kinds chat, read and people-watch on the canal-side terrace, while within the simple, tasteful interior, animated conversation and cheapish drinks provide spectacle enough for locals. Drop in for world and experimental music Sundays from 5-7pm.

Chez Adel
10 rue de la Grange-aux-Belles, 10th (01.42.08.24.61). M° Jacques Bonsergent. **Open** Mon-Fri 11am-2am; Sat 5pm-2am; Sun noon-2am. Food served Mon-Fri noon-2.30pm, 8pm-2am; Sat, Sun 8pm-2am. Closed Aug. **Beer** 25cl €2-€2.50. **Credit** MC, V.

For 12 years Chez Adel has played host to musicians and performing artists nightly at 9pm. Locals and wannabe bohemians sip, sit, smirk and occasionally applaud talent from the quartier and 'as far away as Texas'. The decor is exceptional for its utter disregard for rhyme, reason or taste. Outsiders should expect to be treated as such by hardcore habitués.

De La Ville Café ★
34 bd Bonne Nouvelle, 10th (01.48.24.48.09). M° Bonne Nouvelle. **Open** Mon-Sat 11am-2am; Sun 3pm-2am. **Beer** €2.80-€3.40. **Credit** MC, V

De La Ville is a new addition to the art-squat-as-style-statement gang. The industrial-squalor entrance is terribly Berlin, the bio-food themed mural off-putting. Upstairs looks like a turn-of-the-century church hall and the apothecary-and-cobbler-sharing-office-space corner is a deeply weird design concept. But, bizarrely, it works. The comfy rattan sofas, brilliant service, perfectly chilled beer and punters make this a top place for apéro. The scene gets trendier and the music more serious later on as the clubbers take over.

La Patache
60 rue de Lancry, 10th (01.42.08.14.35). M° Jacques Bonsergent. **Open** daily 6pm-2am. **Beer** 25cl €2-€2.60. **No credit cards**. **Wheelchair access**.

Pleasantly seedy and small, this unlikely haunt of local lushes and slummers manages to keep its authentically alternative edge. The styling is humble with faded black-and-white photos and you can add to, or read, the rantings, poems and polemics of drinkers past on the scraps of paper provided in old biscuit tins at the tables. If your language skills are up to par, ask the softly-spoken owner and barman exactly what a 'patache' is anyway. On nights without live music or drama, the jukebox runs the gamut from Jacques Brel to MC Hammer.

Le Sainte Marthe
32 rue Ste-Marthe, 10th (01.44.84.36.96). M° Belleville. **Open** Mon-Sat 7pm-2am; Sun noon-2pm. Food served Mon-Fri 8.15-11.30pm; Sat noon-2pm, 8.15-11.30pm; Sun noon-2pm. **Beer** 25cl €2-€2.50. **Happy hour** daily 6-10pm. **No credit cards**.

Deep in the heart of this neglected, ethnic quartier, on a village square that's more reminiscent of rural France than of the throbbing metropolis, sits Sainte Marthe. Tables are lined up outside canteen-style, and it's up to you to squeeze in on sultry summer evenings when it heaves with chatty regulars. Otherwise, dark-red walls, swathes of crimson curtains and smooth soulful jazz entice you inside. Good for eats, too, with a straightforward menu of modern French or tapas if you just fancy a nibble.

11th Arrondissement

Les Abats Jour à Coudre
115 rue Oberkampf, 11th. No telephone/www.paris-zoom.com. M° Ménilmontant. **Open** Mon-Sat 5pm-2am. **Beer** 25cl €2.50-€3.50. **Cocktails** €6. **Credit** AmEx, MC, V.

A curious little bar which looks as if it's been furnished by a Clignancourt-obsessed kleptomaniac. Full of standard Oberkampf junk plus a few interesting lampshades, a package-holiday sombrero, pedal sewing machine tables (as tables) and lots of duff old records. Desperately friendly bar staff dole out uninspiring cocktails from an extensive list, while most of the rather subdued punters are stuck into the cheap beer.

L'Armagnac
104 rue de Charonne, 11th (01.43.71.49.43). M° Charonne. **Open** Mon-Fri 7am-2am; Sat 10.30am-2am; Sun 10.30am-midnight. **Beer** 25cl €1.85-€2.90. **Credit** MC, V.

A ceiling dotted with playing cards indicates you're missing a trick, which is in fact the weekly magic night on Wednesdays at 9pm. Locals prop up the bar, sipping an occasional margarita and putting the world to right with the amicable staff. There's a good selection of wines starting at €2.75 a glass.

L'Autre Cafe
62 rue Jean-Pierre Timbaud, 11th (01.40.21.03.07). M° Parmentier. **Open** daily 8pm-2am. **Beer** 25cl €2.50-€3.25. **Credit** MC, V. **Wheelchair access**.

An updated and expanded version of the traditional corner caff, L'Autre Café is more a pit stop than a drinking destination. The BCBG clientele looked as if they'd cabbed in from the 16th for a bit of rough and seemed vaguely disappointed at the lack of dust.

Bar des Ferailleurs
18 rue de Lappe, 11th (01.48.07.89.12). M° Bastille. **Open** Mon-Fri 5pm-2am; Sat, Sun 3pm-2am. **Beer** 25cl €2.43-€3.04. **Happy hour** daily 5-10pm. **Credit** MC, V.

Decorated with the old junk from a French grandad's garage (the name alludes to scrap metal merchants), this quirky little bar is one of the few places on the rue de Lappe where you're likely to find genuine Parisians hanging out with hard-drinking out-of-towners. The staff is attentive and the thirsty clientele is grateful for the excellent happy hour prices on everything from pints of beer to frozen daiquiris.

Boca Chica
58 rue de Charonne, 11th (01.43.57.93.13/ www.labocachica.com). M° Ledru-Rollin. **Open** Mon-Thur, Sun 10am-2am; Fri-Sat 10am-5am. Food served all day. **Beer** 25cl €3-€4. **Cocktails** €7.62-€9. **Happy hour** daily 4-7pm. **Credit** AmEx, MC, V. **Wheelchair access**.

Although it's another Bastille club/bar/café/ restaurant extravaganza, the Boca Chica's point of difference is its Spanish flavour. Inside is an airy space with ochre walls housing separate restaurant and bar areas as well as a small dance floor, where things hot up on the weekend. You might have to pay a cover charge of €15 after midnight on Friday and Saturday nights. Apart from serving breakfast, brunch, lunch and dinner and operating as a bar and nightclub, Boca Chica also markets its customised chairs and plates, as well as delicious olive oil and other Spanish specialities.

The Bottle Shop
5 rue Trousseau, 11th (01.43.14.28.04/ www.hip-bars.com). M° Ledru-Rollin. **Open** daily 11.30am-2am. Food served daily noon-3.30pm. **Beer** 25cl €2-€3. **Cocktails** €4.50-€6.80. **Happy hour** daily 5-8pm. **Credit** AmEx, MC, V. **Wheelchair access**.

A casual, young Franco/Anglo haunt with boppy vibes and trendy, understated decor, apart from the bizarre papier maché ducks, cunningly disguised as bumble bees, that dangle from the ceiling. Pints at €3.80 during

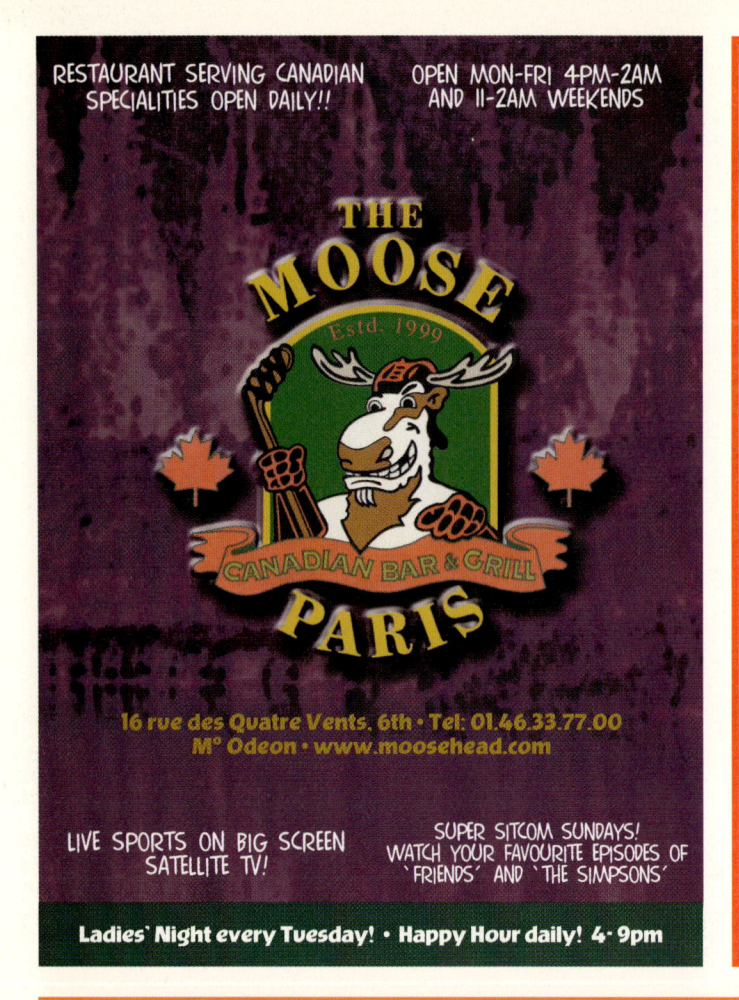

THE MOOSE — Canadian Bar & Grill — PARIS

Estd. 1999

RESTAURANT SERVING CANADIAN SPECIALITIES OPEN DAILY!!
OPEN MON-FRI 4PM-2AM AND 11-2AM WEEKENDS

16 rue des Quatre Vents, 6th • Tel: 01.46.33.77.00
M° Odeon • www.moosehead.com

LIVE SPORTS ON BIG SCREEN SATELLITE TV!

SUPER SITCOM SUNDAYS! WATCH YOUR FAVOURITE EPISODES OF 'FRIENDS' AND 'THE SIMPSONS'

Ladies' Night every Tuesday! • Happy Hour daily! 4-9pm

The Molly Malone Lounge Bar

Entertainement 7 nights a week
Tel: 01.47.42.07.77
21 rue Godot de Mauroy, 9th
M° Havre-caumartin or Madeleine
RER Auber

Au Caveau Montpensier

15 rue Montpensier, 1st
Open daily from 6pm till late
Tel: 01.47.03.33.78
M° Palais Royal

---

the DUTCH bars in Paris

We make you go up•side down !!!

LE PORT d'Amsterdam — The Dutch Party !!! Bar in Paris

20, rue du Croissant
75002 Paris
M° Bourse / Grand Boulevard
Tel: 01 40 39 02 63
Open from 5pm to 2am every day

Mondays international Students Party Night !!! Happy Hour ALL NIGHT
Hop by and Party along with the Dutch party crew and Dance on the Tables
Food served till 22.00

café KLEIN HOLLAND — The Dutch Place to be in the Marais

36 rue du Roi de Sicile
75004 Paris
M° Saint Paul - Hotel de Ville
Tel: 01 42 71 43 13
Open from 5pm to 2am every day

Come in, enjoy our food, have a drink and let's have a Party
Wide selection of Cocktails and Beers
International crowd

happy hour make this a good place to get in the mood for a big night out. Cocktails, including a house special bumble bee, start at €6.80 and you can also find a decent pint of Guinness. A menu heavy on comfort food favourites caters to the crowd.

Café Cannibale

93 rue Jean-Pierre Timbaud, 11th (01.49.29.95.59). M° Couronnes. **Open** daily 8am-2am. Food served daily noon-3pm, 8pm-midnight; Sun brunch noon-4pm. **Beer** 25cl €2-€2.60. **Credit** MC, V.

The Cannibale is the perfect antidote to the ersatz-bohemia that prevails on nearby rue Oberkampf. It pulls in a crowd of hipsters, struggling artist-types and bourgeois night-trippers alike. The food is rather good, particularly the Sunday brunch, and the long zinc bar is perfect for hanging around if a long night's drinking is on the agenda. Proof that there's still reason to head up the hill.

Café Charbon

109 rue Oberkampf, 11th (01.43.57.55.13/ www.nouveaucasino.net). M° Parmentier. **Open** Mon-Thur, Sun 9am-2am; Fri-Sat 9am-4am. Food served daily 11am-5pm, 7.30-11.30pm. **Beer** 25cl €2-€2.40. **Credit** MC, V. **Wheelchair access**.

With probably the loveliest interior in the area, this former turn-of-the-century dance hall boasts dazzling mirrors stretching to the ceiling, where antique light fixtures cast a warm glow over the bar. Unfortunately, as the granddaddy of Oberkampf nightlife, Charbon draws an ever-more-enthusiastic but uninspiring crowd. Wannabes and aspiring Casanovas pout and pose in time to the house-heavy DJ while over-worked and under-mannered bar staff fight the urge to throw your drink in your face. So if you can get their attention, be very polite. A recent expansion has added the moodily lit Nouveau Casino, a funky concert venue that contrasts sharply with the original bar.

Les Couleurs ★

117 rue St-Maur, 11th (01.43.57.95.61). M° Parmentier. **Open** daily 3pm-2am. Closed two weeks in Aug. **Beer** 25cl €2.10-€2.40. **Cocktails** €5-€8.40. **No credit cards.**

A deliberately dilapidated stop on the Ménilmontant haul, Les Couleurs pulls in the punters with its punch: stout, oversized shot glasses of eerie yellow/green *ti ponch* will test even the hardiest drinker's ability to keep up with the *habitués*. The decor is grungy and casual with old Christmas-tree lights and a serpentine bar lending an Alice-in-Wonderland hue. Street musicians wander in and out while boho locals tirelessly pursue their goal: to drink and have a good time.

Floating Assets

The *péniches* or river boats moored along the Seine really come alive in the summer months as many of them have chairs and tables on deck or on the quay side. Even in colder weather, however, these boats can be an original place to spend an evening, as each *péniche* has its own identity and attracts a loyal clientele who make the boat their own. As boats tend to move from one mooring point to another, here is a selection of the more permanent ones on both sides of the river. The largest gathering of *péniches* is now on the Left Bank just below the Bibliothèque Nationale in the 13th. The ample parking space on the quayside has turned this strip into a hive of activity with *péniches* of every shape and size competing for the crowds who come down on mild evenings or at the weekends.

Right Bank:

Port de La Gare, quai François Mauriac, 13th. M° Quai de la Gare.

Le Kiosque Flottant (01.45.86.41.60) looks like a floating bandstand with a 360° view of the outside world. It does particularly well in the winter months and on wet summer nights as there is no terrace and you can drink tea, watch the rain outside and imagine you're on a ship in a storm.

Péniche Makara (no telephone) is the boat version of Dr Who's Tardis; you could never image that anyone, let alone a band, could fit inside it. The Makara specialises in world music; to find it just listen to the call of the drum – there's always a gaggle of enthusiastic *djembe* players hanging out outside.

El Alamein (01.45.86.41.60) has an array of beautifully tended plants which create a deckside pub garden equipped with long wooden tables. Downstairs is a piano bar that could almost be a captain's cabin. The specialty is cocktails, most of which have a rum edge.

La Guingette Pirate (01.56.29.10.20), as the name suggests, looks like a mini-pirate ship but it's actually a Chinese junk. The Guingette has a very loyal clientele with a penchant for French *chanson*, alternative rock and French/world music. Characters from any Jean-Pierre Jeunet film would be quite at home here.

La Cantine (01.45.83.33.06) is the restaurant annexe of the electronic music venue Batofar; Although the mother-ship attracts a young, fashionable crowd, La Cantine has developed its own identity. Punters come for a cosy plate of foie gras or pasta. When the restaurant closes at 1am a DJ takes over and the barman pulls a beer a second. The music ranges from rock to hardcore techno.

Left Bank:

Le Café Barge (no telephone). BCBGs mingle with shirt and tie-clad tax workers out for a glass of Champagne; during summer, lie back on a sun lounge with a cocktail and pretend you're on the Riviera.

Péniche Déclic (7 quai Saint Bernard, 5th) further up river in the more touristy 5th and 6th specialises in Australian didgeridoo concerts on weekends.

Kiosque Flottant 2 (Quai Montebello, 5th) is a restaurant offering traditional French cuisine as well as Sunday brunch (€21.50). Later in the evening at the cocktail witching hour, below deck turns into a piano bar.

Metamorphosis (55 quai de la Tournelle, 5th) attracts many a tourist for a dinner show priced at €28. The acts range from plays to magic shows, all ending in a *bal* which runs into the wee small hours on weekends. *Lucia Scazzoccio*

L'Entre-potes

14 rue de Charonne, 11th (01.48. 06.57.04). M° Ledru-Rollin. **Open** daily 5pm-2am. **Beer** 25cl €3. **Cocktails** €8.40-€9.90. **Happy hour** daily 5-8pm. **Credit** AmEx, MC, V.

The name is a pun, playing on a standard French bar name 'entrepôt', meaning warehouse, and 'entre-potes', meaning between friends. We found it to be an apt description of what takes place here. Rather than nervous groups of boys and girls hoping to pull, as can be the case in some of the blockbuster Bastille bar/clubs, there were intimate groups of friends enjoying each other's company. Curiously, the front window of the bar proclaims 'American Bar', but the place felt utterly French. The familiar sight of nicotine-stained walls and candles on tables, combined with the reggae music, friendly staff and trendy twentysomething crowd, combine to produce an amicable and quietly groovy atmosphere.

La Fabrique

53 rue du Fbg-St-Antoine, 11th (01.43.07.67.07/www.fabrique.fr). M° Bastille. **Open** daily noon-5am. Food served daily noon-3pm, 8pm-midnight. **Beer** 25cl €2.90-€4.57. **Cocktails** €6.86. **Happy hour** Mon-Fri 5.30-9pm. **Credit** AmEx, MC, V. **Wheelchair access**.

La Fabrique brews its own beer, a point emphasised by the huge shiny copper vats lining the room as you enter, but it also offers a huge range of bottled beers from around the world. The place goes off on the weekend thanks to the surge of people who flood the Bastille to paaaarrrty!, but is a nicer spot mid-afternoon and mid-week. A spacious, simply designed restaurant at the back serves contemporary cuisine.

F.B.I. Paris (Freestyle Bar)

45 rue de la Folie-Méricourt, 11th (01.43.14.26.36/www.fbiparis.com). M° St-Ambroise. **Open** Mon-Sat 7pm-2am. **Cocktails** €6.50-€8.50. **Happy hour** Mon-Sat 7-10pm. **Credit** MC, V.

It's well worth wandering over to this cringingly named bar for a cocktail before heading up to Oberkampf. The bartender will serve you a beer, but he'd rather juggle his bottles and mix up a concoction worthy of a legendary American bar. Why not experiment with the Japanese slipper (Midori, Cointreau and lime juice cordial) or stick to the tried and true gimlet, gin with lime, served here in a bathtub-sized glass. With a well-mixed cocktail in your hand, it's easy to be cheerfully entertained by the bottle-flinging barman and the atmosphere.

Le Lèche-Vin

13 rue Daval, 11th (01.43.55.98.91). M° Bastille. **Open** Mon-Sat 6pm-2am; Sun 7pm-midnight. **Beer** 25cl €2.15. **Credit** MC, V.

The Lèche-Vin has raised idolatry to a new level with its bar-as-shrine-to-the-Virgin-Mary. Every available nook, cranny and wall offers up a kitsch, often irreverent tribute to the holiest of mothers. If the idea of knocking back pints under her tearful gaze doesn't make you fear for the safety of your soul, a trip to the toilets will surely be enough to make you abandon any hope of salvation. On the bright side, you will be richly rewarded on earth with some of the cheapest and best drinks in the *quartier*.

Le Mecano Bar

99 rue Oberkampf, 11th (01.40.21.35.28). M° Parmentier. **Open** daily 9am-2am. Food served daily 11am-2am. **Beer** 25cl €2.15-€3.60. **Cocktails** €6.01-€9.15. **Happy hour** daily 6-8pm. **Credit** MC, V. **Wheelchair access**.

Located in an old tool factory, this slightly scruffy bar contains relics from its industrial past: pipes and obscure bits of machinery poke out among the numerous paintings on the walls. It's a good reminder of eastern Paris' working-class roots; these days the area is inhabited by a young and increasingly prosperous population. The night we were there, the Mecano was host to an unpretentious and relaxed local crowd indulging in an apéritif or an early dinner. Our drinks came with a plate of sourdough bread topped with fresh goat's cheese and rosemary. With double doors opening onto the street, the Mecano is a great place to sit and watch the groovy young things go by.

La Mercerie

98 rue Oberkampf, 11th (01.43.38.81.30). M° Parmentier. **Open** Mon-Fri 5pm-2am; Sat, Sun 3pm-2am. **Beer** 25cl €2.20-€2.50. **Cocktails** €4.90-€6.80. **Credit** MC, V.

It's all too easy to miss the ivy-obscured entrance to La Mercerie. But, once inside there's room for large groups of boisterous, arty types, while comfy alcoves provide couples with an atmosphere more conducive to seduction. The distressed decor, exposed brick and mismatched furniture are pretty typical of the *quartier*, but carefully chosen accoutrements add a flavour that many other bars in the area lack.

Le Réservoir

16 rue de la Forge-Royal, 11th (01.43.56.39.60/www.reservoir-dogs.com). M° Ledru-Rollin. **Open** Mon-Thur 8pm-2am; Fri, Sat 8pm-4am; Sun noon-5pm (brunch). **Beer** €5.33-€8.38. **Credit** AmEx, DC, MC, V. **Wheelchair access**.

Part resaurant (with a menu ranging from foie gras to sushi), part club, part concert venue; there's always something happening here, even in the wee hours (call their friendly reception for a list of the current week's program). Past performers have included Tricky, Brian May, and, gasp, Toto. But day-to-day shows generally feature lesser-known acts. The Sunday jazz brunch remains popular with families, while students and late risers keep the place going until dawn.

Le Sanz Sans

49 rue du Fbg-St-Antoine, 11th (01.44.75.78.78). M° Bastille or Ledru-Rollin. **Open** Mon-Thur 9am-2am; Fri, Sat 9am-5am; Sun 11am-2am. Food served Mon-Sat noon-3pm, 8pm-midnight; Sun 8pm-midnight. **Beer** 25cl €2.50-€4. **Cocktails** €9. **Credit** DC, MC, V. **Wheelchair access**.

One of the rue du Fbg-St-Antoine triumvirate, the other two being the Fabrique and the Barrio Latino, the Sanz Sans draws in a huge, usually non-local crowd on the weekends. Prior to this visit, we'd only ever been there at 5am, when critical faculties were functioning at a minimum. The place is always packed at that hour, and invariably there are a couple of girls in hot pants gyrating on the bar to the DJ's beats. It has a number of faces, depending on the hour and your condition, although the crowd tends toward young and bouncy whatever the time.

Les Trois Têtards ★

46 rue Jean Pierre Timbaud, 11th (01.43.14.27.37). M° Oberkampf or Parmentier. **Open** Mon-Fri 8am-2am; Sat, Sun 5pm-2am. **Beer** 25cl €2-€3.30. **Happy hour** Thur-Sat 7-9pm. **Credit** MC, V.

This friendly neighbourhood drinking den has already achieved cult status among bobo *buveurs*. A familiar interior of rickety chairs and murals is presided over by genial staff and a raucous crowd. It's a bit like a chi-chi Cheers: everyone seems to know everyone else, or maybe they're just very good with strangers. The eponymous house speciality is an intoxicating (if weird) combination of vodka, grapefruit juice, mint and some 'secret' ingredient that we didn't dare pry into.

Le Zéro Zéro

89 rue Amelot, 11th (01.49.23.51.00/ www.zerozero.com). M° Bastille. **Open** daily 6pm-2am. **Beer** 25cl €2.59. **Happy hour** daily 6-8.30pm. **Credit** MC, V.

Part '70s kitsch, part teenage fantasy, the Zéro Zéro attracts a loyal – and lush – international and local crowd of the hip and the alcholic hardcore. Don't go here for an intimate assignation – when you're practically sitting on a stranger's lap, it's not suprising that you end up talking to him. Probably the best mojitos in town.

12th Arrondissement

Barrio Latino

46-48 rue du Fbg-St-Antoine, 12th (01.55.78.84.75). M° Bastille. **Open** daily 11.30am-2am. Food served daily noon-3pm, 7.30pm-midnight. **Beer** 25cl €4.50-€5. **Cocktails** €8-€9. **Credit** AmEx, DC, MC, V. **Wheelchair access**.

After getting past a serious security check, similar, we imagine, to what you might en-

McBrides Irish Pub

Follow the lead ... ...to McBride's

Happy Hour 5pm-8pm

Big Screen TV
SKY Digital / Canal Satellite
Chamipons League / Premiership Matches / Six Nations / World Cup

All Major Sports Events Shown

Live Music Tuesdays and Sundays
Food served from 10am till 10pm (Sunday 11am-7pm)
Sunday Roast / Traditional Irish Breakfast / Full Menu

54 rue St Denis, 1st. M° Chatelet/Chatelet les Halles
Tel: 01.40..26.46.70 - Fax: 01.40.26.56.31
Credit cards - Visa, mastrecard, diners Club, CB - Pool Table, Darts

Celtic Corner pub

- Live music
- Big screen
- Rugby spirit
- Sky

88 rue de la Croix Nivert, 15th
Metro Commerce or Cambronne
Tel/Fax: 01.42.50.74.11
celtic.corner.pub@wanadoo.fr

counter as a US citizen trying to enter Cuba, we arrived at a large central atrium flanked by three floors of ascending cast-iron balconies. The style is meant to be Latin but the decor is an odd hybrid – one suspects that the closest the interior decorator ever got to South America was a Taco Bell. Once settled into one of the large velvet couches, pisco sour in hand, we started to feel we'd inadvertently wandered into a singles club. There were lots of tables of 'ladies' drinking elaborate cocktails with maraschino cherries, counterbalanced by groups of lads, eyeing each other nervously. The place is very popular, and the owners know what they're doing, having already made big successes of the Buddha Bar and Barfly.

China Club
50 rue de Charenton, 12th (01.43.43.82.02/ www.chinaclub.cc). M° Ledru-Rollin or Bastille. **Open** Mon-Thur, Sun 7pm-2am; Fri, Sat 7pm-3am. Food served daily 7pm-midnight. Closed 20 Jul-20 Aug. **Beer** 25cl €3.81. **Cocktails** €7.46-€10.67. **Happy hour** daily 7-9pm. **Credit** AmEx, MC, V.

With huge Chesterfields, low lighting and a sexy long bar, it's impossible not to feel glamorous here. It's like an extremely relaxed gentleman's club with a distinctly colonial Cohibas and cocktails feel. They take their martinis seriously and you can't go wrong with a well-made Champagne cocktail. This is ideal seduction territory, but equally good for a gossip session, particularly during happy hour. The basement bar is divine – but for serious jazz lovers only.

La Distillerie
50 rue du Fbg-St-Antoine, 12th (01.40.01.99.00/www.la-distillerie.com). M° Bastille. **Open** Mon-Sat 7pm-5am. Food served Mon-Fri 7pm-3am; Sat 7pm-midnight. **Beer** 25cl €3.40. **Credit** MC, V.

The extensive selection of exotic punches lets drinkers choose from a rainbow of tropical poisons while bobbing and swaying to hip-hop, reggae and Latin beats. After other Bastille bars close down at 2am, the friendly but forceful staff keep a rollicking late-night crowd in check. It also serves up Caribbean dishes to the pre-club crowd, with most *plats* around €13.

OPA ★
9 rue Biscornet, 12th (01.49.28.97.16/ www.opabastille.com). M° Bastille. **Open** Tue-Thur noon-2am; Fri noon-4am; Sat 5pm-4am. Food served Tues-Sat noon-3.30pm, 8-11pm. **Beer** 25cl €3.50-€4. **Cocktails** €8-€10.50. **Happy hour** Tue-Sat 6-8pm. **Credit** MC, V.

OPA is the ultimate in warehouse chic with its exposed brick, overexposed bar staff and serious music conspiring to create the perfect playground for record producers and film industry bods on their night off from posing elsewhere. The first-floor restaurant churns out decent enough *m'as-tu-vu* food while providing a perfect vantage point for checking out the flirting young things on the dance floor. A chilled atmosphere helps reduce the air-kissing quota.

13th Arrondissement

La Folie en Tête
33 rue de la Butte-aux-Cailles, 13th (01.45.80.65.99). M° Corvisart or Place d'Italie. **Open** Mon-Sat 5pm-2am. Closed 25 Dec-2 Jan. **Beer** 25cl €2.40. **Happy hour** Mon-Sat 5-8pm. **Credit** MC, V.

On summer evenings this throbbing bar is reminiscent of a Mediterranean student hangout where youths stand around their Vespas chatting outside. The four Belgian beers on tap are good value and happy hour is unbeatable: *kir*, *pastis* and a small selection of wines cost €1.50 while €3 will buy a pint of Gothic beer. It's bar service only and last orders at 1.30am. Saturdays are now animated by DJs or live music.

Le Merle Moqueur
11 rue de la Butte-aux-Cailles, 13th (01.45.65.12.43). M° Corvisart or Place d'Italie. **Open** daily 5pm-2am. **Beer** 25cl €2.29-€2.74. **Happy hour** daily 5-9pm. **Credit** MC, V. **Wheelchair access.**

Come here for the atmosphere of a beach party but be prepared for the loud Europop and mad topless surfer types showing off to drunken girls in skimpy outfits. Large glass vats of rum are temptingly displayed behind the bar, each one containing a different fruit or spice. Take your pick of rum-based shots flavoured with vanilla, coconut, lime, banana, grapefruit, ginger, and more – at €15 for six it's a bargain. The drunken atmosphere is incredibly infectious and you'll soon find yourself singing along with the rest of them and joining in with the dancing, shots or no shots.

14th Arrondissement

La Jamaïque
2 pl Catalogne, 14th (01.43.35.50.50). M° Gaîté. **Open** daily noon-5am. **Beer** 25cl €3.81. **Cocktails** €10.57-€12.96. **Credit** MC, V.

Looking for a second-date bar or a cheesy cocktail lounge in the 14th? This is it. During the week couples sink into the orange bamboo couches sharing a giant punch, or smooch in dark corners. On weekends the Zouk music is cranked up and punters dance to Creole beats. Of the more than 60 cocktails we liked the king's creole, a concoction of rum, coconut cream, pineapple juice and grenadine. It didn't come in the coconut promised but the sweets on the swizzle stick were nice. At around €11 the cocktails are pricey, but the measures are generous. Fruit cocktails and ice creams also on offer.

Le Rosebud
11bis rue Delambre, 14th (01.43.20.44.13). M° Vavin or Edgar Quinet. **Open** daily 7pm-2am. Hot food served 7-11pm. Closed Aug. **Beer** bottle €5.50. **Cocktails** €10. **Credit** MC, V.

It's unclear whether or not the name of this bar is meant to invoke any cinematic references, but entering is akin to stepping on to a 1950s film set. The night we visited, the cast of characters included ageing Lotharios, wannabe starlets and an Indiana Jones knock-off who arrived in full safari gear complete with leather driving gloves and a weather-stained fedora. The white-jacketed waiting staff and martini-sipping *habitués* traded sugar-coated insults in good-natured competition for our attention.

17th Arrondissement

L'Endroit ★
67 pl du Dr-Félix-Lobligeois, 17th (01.42.29.50.00). M° Villiers. **Open** daily noon-2am. Food served daily noon-3pm, 7.30-11.30pm. Closed 1 Jan-15 Feb. **Beer** bottle €4.12-€4.73. **Cocktails** €7.62-€8.38. **Credit** MC, V.

A real find in this *quartier*, L'Endroit is a slick café on a charming square, where well-dressed, well-behaved thirtysomethings lounge. Movie-set lamps diffuse soft light over a art deco-style interior featuring spring-loaded barstools that keep the barflies bouncing while the barmen serve cocktails like chihuahua pearls and purple rains from a motorised carousel of bottles. At weekends, take advantage of the American-style brunch on the lovely terrace.

The James Joyce
71 bd Gouvion-St-Cyr, 17th (01.44.09.70.32). M° Porte-Maillot. **Open** daily 7am-2am. Food served daily noon-2.30pm, 7.30-10pm. **Beer** 25cl €3.81. **Credit** AmEx, DC, MC, V.

Conveniently situated near several large hotels catering to business travellers, the James Joyce is a friendly Irish corner pub where there's always a football game and a pint of Guinness to be had. Faded Joycean memorabilia covers the dark wood panelling and fills the display cases, and the stained-glass windows are colourful renderings of scenes from *Ulysses*. Upstairs the restaurant specialises in Irish cuisine, including excellent smoked salmon.

18th Arrondissement

Chào-Bà-Café
22 bd de Clichy, 18th (01.46.06.72.90). M° Pigalle. **Open** Mon-Wed, Sun 8.30am-2am; Thur 8.30am-4am; Fri, Sat 8.30am-5am. Food served daily noon-1am. **Beer** 25cl €2.50-€4.50. **Cocktails** €9.50-€11.50. **Credit** MC, V.

This French Indochina theme bar blends in seamlessly with the neon peep show parlours flanking it on the Pigalle strip. A bust of Ho Chi Minh looks on approvingly as the thirsty toast and the hungry dine in fine capitalist style on Franco-Vietnamese food such as spicy noodles. Dance and Latino music doesn't seem out of place among the pink lights and bamboo. Die-hard drinkers should expect a knowing wink from the staff when ordering a *double express serré* after hours.

La Jungle
32 rue Gabrielle, 18th (01.46.06.75.69). M° Abbesses. **Open** daily 6pm-2am. Food served daily 8pm-midnight. **Cocktails** €5. **Credit** MC, V.

Earthy tones, leopard skin table-tops, wooden sculptures and bright ambient lights give off a distinctive Afro vibe in this small but lively Senegalese bar and restaurant hidden in the quiet back streets of Montmartre. Live music is a regular part of the scene with a mix of upbeat Afro lilts and chilled-out reggae. Get up and dance if you're in the mood, or sit back with a cocktail or a pitcher of the ginger-infused house punch (€7 for 25cl, €13 for 50cl).

La Fourmi
74 rue des Martyrs, 18th (01.42.64.70.35). M° Pigalle. **Open** Mon-Thur 8am-2am; Fri-Sat 8am-4am; Sun 10am-2am. Food served daily noon-11pm. **Beer** 25cl €1.50-€2.30. **Credit** MC, V.

With a retro-industrial decor, long zinc bar and trademark Duchampian bottle-rack chandelier, this spacious bar in happening Pigalle buzzes all day and night with a young, arty crowd and even artier staff, joined by the odd tour-bus driver and postman. It makes a handy jumping-off point for the neighbourhood's music venues – the windows are plastered with flyers for upcoming gigs.

20th Arrondissement

La Flèche d'Or ★
102bis rue de Bagnolet, 20th (01.43.72.04.23/www.flechedor.com). M° Alexandre Dumas. **Open** Tue-Sun 10am-2am. Food served Tue-Sat 8.30pm-midnight; Sun noon-4pm. **Beer** 25cl €2-€3.30. **Credit** AmEx, DC, MC, V. **Wheelchair access.**

Music fans and a grungy young crowd flock to this funky venue on the eastern outskirts of the city, in a former station on the defunct Petite Ceinture railway line, to catch local groups performing live or dig the decidedly alternative scene that runs from Télébocal community TV and salsa *bals* to impassioned debates. In the daytime the enclosed terrace overlooking the abandoned tracks is a fantastic spot for brunch or an afternoon cocktail. At night, the place is packed to the point where getting a drink or getting to an exit is decidedly tricky.

Lou Pascalou
14 rue des Panoyaux, 20th (01.46.36.78.10). M° Ménilmontant. **Open** daily 9am-2am. Food served daily noon-2am. **Beer** 25cl €2-€2.30. **Cocktails** €4.75-€5. **Credit** MC, V.

Dress down for a visit to this Ménilmontant mainstay, where a bohemian crowd hangs out until the small hours, and spills onto the pavement on warm evenings. Chess matches roll on for hours as regulars settle scores over a *pression* or two. Satisfyingly chunky sets and a roll-out board are available from behind the bar for free, as well as a timer for the real pros. Guinness and Kilkenny (€5.80 pint) are not much cop, but the selection of cocktails is remarkable. Don't miss the chrome loos; you half expect to bump into Captain Kirk himself washing his hands.

Arty, antsy La Fourmi

Reasonable ? in Paris ?

Tea & Tattered Pages
English second hand Bookstore & Tea room

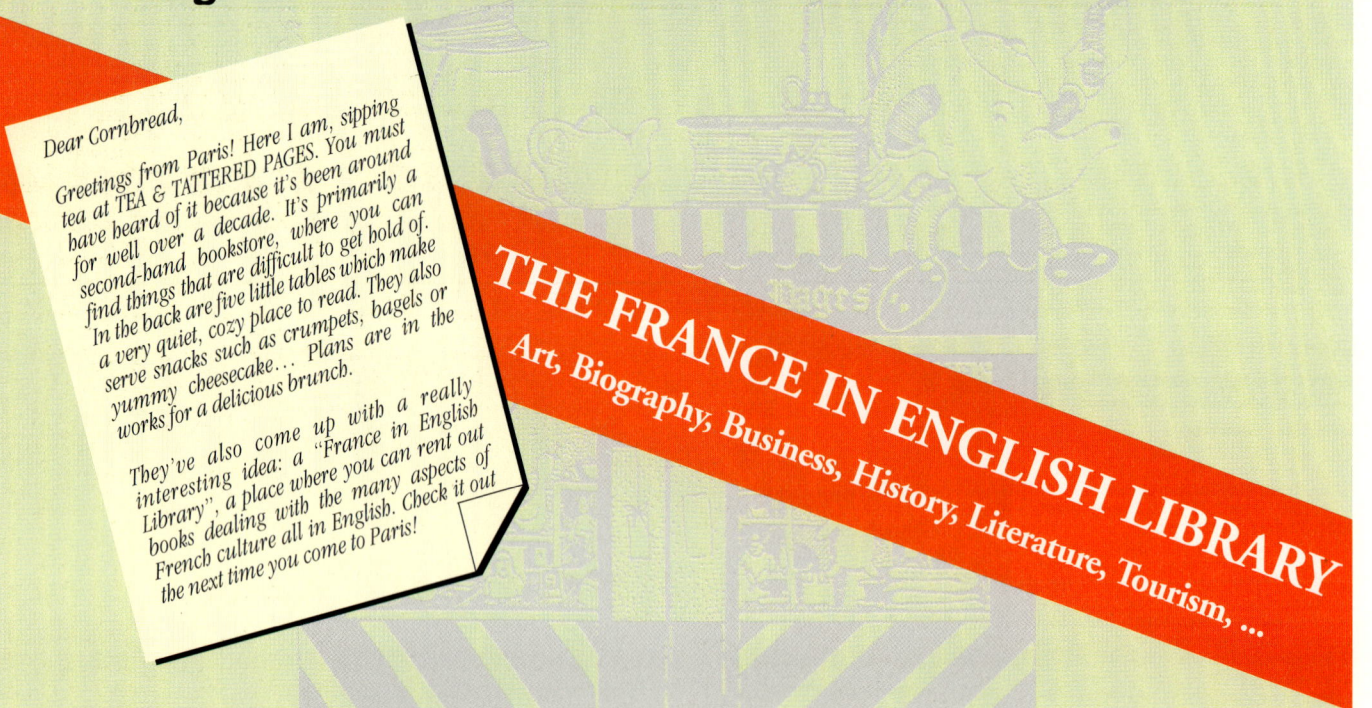

Dear Cornbread,

Greetings from Paris! Here I am, sipping tea at TEA & TATTERED PAGES. You must have heard of it because it's been around for well over a decade. It's primarily a second-hand bookstore, where you can find things that are difficult to get hold of. In the back are five little tables which make a very quiet, cozy place to read. They also serve snacks such as crumpets, bagels or yummy cheesecake… Plans are in the works for a delicious brunch.

They've also come up with a really interesting idea: a "France in English Library", a place where you can rent out books dealing with the many aspects of French culture all in English. Check it out the next time you come to Paris!

THE FRANCE IN ENGLISH LIBRARY
Art, Biography, Business, History, Literature, Tourism, …

Open Monday to Saturday from 11am-7pm and Sundays from noon-6pm

24 rue Mayet, 6th. M° Duroc/Falguière. Bus lines: 28, 39, 70, 82, 89, 92
Tel: 01.40.65.94.35 – Fax: 01.42.19.05.54 – e-mail: ttp@noos.fr

Tea Rooms & Ice Cream

Heavenly scented tea and seriously sticky cakes are the order of the day in Paris salons.

Once a very British ritual, tea appreciation today is taken almost as seriously as fine wine tasting by discerning Parisians. Tea suppliers and salons have sprung up across the city offering an extraordinary variety of brews.

Angelina's
226 rue de Rivoli, 1st (01.42.60.82.00). M° Tuileries. **Open** daily 9.45am-7pm. Wed-Mon in July and Aug. **Tea** €5.65-€6. **Pâtisseries** €4.55-€5.95. **Credit** AmEx, V.
Between the two world wars, the smart set needed only to say, 'meet you on the rue de Rivoli' when arranging a tea date, such was the fame of this neo-rococo tearoom. The salon was originally known as Rumpelmeyer's and the cakes still have an Austrian gooeyness; this also partly explains the excellence of the hot chocolate, made with African cocoa (€6). The speciality has always been the *mont blanc*: soft and chewy meringue with whipped cream and chestnut cream topping. Although as sublime as ever, the *mont* has diminished in size over the years. Still, Angelina's is currently in its element, with an excellent lunch menu. Seated in plump leather armchairs at solid green marble tables with flamboyant murals as a backdrop, the *haute bourgeoisie* and *hoi polloi* are equally content.
Branches: Galeries Lafayette (3rd floor), 40 bd Haussmann, 9th (01.42.32.30.32); Palais des Congrès, 2 pl de la Porte-Maillot, 17th (01.40.68.22.50).

Jean-Paul Hévin
231 rue St-Honoré, 1st (01.55.35.35.97). M° Tuileries. **Open** tea and shop Mon-Sat 10am-7.30pm. Closed one week in Aug. **Tea** €5.50. **Pâtisseries** €3.90-€5.80. **Credit** AmEx, DC, MC, V.
If black minimalist à la Gucci is your cup of tea, and you have a cocoa habit, then Jean-Paul Hévin is your man. His dark chocolate desserts gleam like edible accessories against the silver and dark-wood furnishings of his shop. Take the futuristic stairway to the first floor to the surprisingly warm tea room with bare teak floorboards, dark wood panels and wicker chairs. Surprisingly, given Hévin's fame, our *quito*, a dark chocolate sponge cake, tasted a bit artificial. The caramelised apples of his *tarte Tatin* melted in the mouth, though the pastry was suspiciously chewy. From the short but high-quality selection of teas we chose Imperial Lapsang Souchong and mango tea. The black-clad staff are friendly and courteous.

Toraya
10 rue St-Florentin, 1st (01.42.60.13.48). M° Concorde. **Open** Mon-Sat 10am-7pm. **Tea** €3.10-€6.90. **Pâtisseries** €3.90. **Credit** AmEx, DC, MC, V.
The high proportion of Japanese at this branch of the supplier of cakes to Tokyo's Imperial Palace attests to the authenticity of the teas and cakes on offer. The bold redecoration may not be to everyone's taste (pale wood panelling, beige-and-orange leather chairs), but the teas alleviate any doubts. Don't miss the soul-warming *gyokuro*, which, like the other teas, you can buy in packets to take away. Sweet delicacies include red bean cakes and *abekawa-mochi* – delicious rice cakes coated in soya flour – all served on exquisite Japanese tableware.

La Charlotte en l'Ile
24 rue St-Louis-en-Ile, 4th (01.43.54.25.83). M° Pont-Marie. **Open** Thur-Sun noon-8pm. Wed tea and puppet show by reservation only; Fri 6-8pm piano tea. **Closed** July and Aug. **Tea** €4. **Pâtisseries** €2.50-€4.50. **Credit** MC, V.
This tiny tea shop has all the stuff of fairy tales – pictures of witches on broomsticks, lanterns, carnival masks – the only thing lacking is gingerbread. Poetess and chocolatier par excellence Sylvie Langlet has been spinning her sweet fantasies here for more than 25 years. In the miniscule front room she sells her superb dark chocolate and candied fruit sticks, while at six tightly-packed round tables she offers 36 teas of a quality that would put some five-star hotels to shame. Our choice of violet and apricot were served in simple blue and yellow bowls from dinky cast-iron teapots; their aroma alone perked us up. The desserts are magic and beware the potent hot chocolate.

Les Enfants Gâtés
43 rue des Francs-Bourgeois, 4th (01.42.77.07.63). M° St-Paul. **Open** daily 11am-8pm. Closed Aug. **Tea** €4.12. **Pâtisseries** €5.49. **Credit** MC, V.
Despite being in the heart of the intensely posey Marais, this tearoom is refreshingly casual. The worn wicker chairs that curve around your shoulders offer solace after near-fatal run-ins with cars which, bent on avoiding traffic jams, take to the narrow pavements. The teas such as Marco Polo, a Parisian favourite, ylang ylang, jasmine, caramel and cinnamon are supplied by Mariage Frères so you can be certain of a good pick-me-up. Our *thé vert sur le Nil*, a green tea with a fruity aroma, was served in an oval white teapot, the leaves cleverly strained through the top. If you crave a sticky cake with your tea, don't hold your breath. Ice cream by the ubiquitous Berthillon is the speciality here. Down scoops of nougat and honey, vanilla and caramel, or intense sorbets and you'll leave ready to stop traffic.

Le Loir dans la Théière
3 rue des Rosiers, 4th (01.42.72.90.61). M° St-Paul. **Open** Mon-Fri 11am-7pm; Sat, Sun 10am-7pm. **Tea** €4. **Pâtisseries** €6. **Credit** MC, V.
Alice in Wonderland would love this place, and not least because it's named after her old friend 'the dormouse in the teapot'. There is a charming disorder about the setting: vast, wrinkled armchairs and battered poufs crowd around square, rectangular and round tables, while ancient prams and cartoon-like teapots line deep shelves. Besides darjeeling, Earl Grey, sencha and other staples, Le Loir has excellent perfumed teas, including the fabulously fragrant lotus. Desserts, including a sky-high lemon meringue pie, *clafoutis* packed with fat cherries plus a divine rhubarb and crème brûlée tart, all look equally scrumptious.

Mariage Frères
30-32 rue du Bourg-Tibourg, 4th (01.42.72.28.11/www.mariagefreres.com). M° Hôtel-de-Ville. **Open** tea room daily noon-7pm, shop and museum daily 10.30am-7.30pm. **Tea** €6. **Pâtisseries** €7. **Credit** AmEx, MC, V.
Established in 1854, Mariage Frères still has a colonial feel, thanks to its dark wood furnishings, staff in white linen suits and the slightly battered gold and black tea tins arranged in racks behind the counters. The tea room is surprisingly relaxed with staff only too happy to discuss the menu with its very refined-looking clientele. The names alone send you into a reverie – 'the tea of solitary poets', 'Himalaya mist', 'opium hill' – there are more than 500 varieties. We knocked back Jamaica, a black tea with a rum bouquet, with relish whereas the 'island vanillas' tasted more of a straight black Ceylon. 'Tea party', a selection of mini macaroons and sponges, was rather dry so try instead a slice of sumptuous cake.
Branches: 13 rue des Grands-Augustins, 6th (01.40.51.82.50); 260 rue du Fbg-St-Honoré, 8th (91.46.22.18.54).

Le Café Maure de la Mosquée de Paris
39 rue Geoffroy-St-Hilaire, 5th (01.43.31.38.20). M° Censier-Daubenton. **Open** daily 9am-11.30pm. **Tea** €2. **Pâtisseries** €2. **Credit** MC, V.
Inspired by the Alhambra, the Paris Mosque was built between 1922 and 1926. Most people make a beeline for the terrace with its landscaped garden and luminous, cobalt-blue

Moorish mint tea at Le Café Maure

A touch of *glace*

Simply the best

Myriad possibilities await those who crave a frozen feast – but beware, as many ice cream shops take the rather unusual (and unfair) decision to close in August.
The most famous Parisian *glacier*, **Berthillon** (31 rue St-Louis-en-l'Ile, 4th/01.43.54.31.61) dominates the tourist ice-cream scene on the Ile St-Louis. Although their ices are available in almost every cafe on the island, people still queue up at all hours at the original outlet on the rue St-Louis. Seventy flavours are on offer, ranging from sweet wild strawberry to wickedly strong whisky and the extra-zingy *cocktail exotique*.
Raimo (59-61 bd de Reuilly, 12th/01.43.43.70.17) has been in this frosty business since 1947. Though the white-shirted waiters are not overly attentive, the ice cream more than makes up for it. At €2.70 for a small serving, it's not cheap, but the *fleur de lait* is heavenly as is the woody Vermont maple. Cheaper scoops are available at **La Tropicale** (180 bd Vincent-Auriol, 13th/01.42.16.87.27), which offers jazz music, friendly service, and fabulous curaçao and mango, and strawberry with mint sorbets.
Paris' best value *boules* are at the **Gelati d'Alberto** (45 rue Mouffetard, 5th/01.43.37.88.07) where €3.05 buys you a selection of Italy's finest, shaped into a rose. Traditional flavours include passion fruit and *panna cotta*. A stone's throw away is **Octave** (138 rue Mouffetard, 5th/01.45.35.20.56) whose beautiful sorbets and ices include fresh pineapple and blood orange. A special treat is the Palais de Chaillot chestnut ice cream.
Another place for Italian gelati is **La Butte Glacée** (14 rue Norvins, 18th/01.42.23.91.58), an unpretentious ice cream parlour. After the long climb to Sacré Coeur reward yourself with *stracciatella* and banana yoghurt sorbet or a jaw-crunching *crocante*.
At **Glacier Calabrese** (15 rue d'Odessa, 15th/01.43.20.31.63), a 70s-style *glacier*, septuagenarian owner Luigi Calabrese serves up ginger, liquorice and a brilliant basil sorbet along with more pedestrian options.
Finally, for taste thrill-seekers, there's **Le Bac à Glaces** (109 rue du Bac, 7th/01.45.48.87.65) and its creamy roquefort, camembert, carrot and avocado concoctions; they also do great sundaes and more orthodox flavours. *Rob Orchard*

Tea ceremony

Hôtel de Crillon: the *dernier cri* in tea

What could be more alluring, on a scale of after-shopping pampering, than to clock in at a grand hotel?

Hôtel Meurice

228 rue de Rivoli, 1st (01.44.58.10.10/www.meuricehotel.com). Mº Tuileries. **Open** 3-7pm. **Tea** €8-€11. **Pâtisseries** €8-€11. **Credit** AmEx, DC, MC, V.

Since its recent refurbishment, the Meurice has become the favoured venue for a spot of tea, a cocktail, even lunch (for money-burning Parisians). The Jardin d'Hiver is a riot of colour and detail – Bergère chairs that fold round the shoulders like fine fur and curved velvet banquettes conspire to loosen your urban armour. The peaceful ambiance inspired us to try 'monk's tea'. Expecting a religious elixir we were surprised by the tea's blandness. Our misgivings were appeased, however, by the superb homemade madeleines and the dinky scones and muffins. If we had only opted for one of the tempting hot chocolates, then the Meurice may well have scored full marks.

Hôtel Ritz

15 pl Vendôme, 1st (01.43.16.30.30/www.ritzparis.com). Mº Concorde. **Open** daily 4-6pm. **Tea** €8.40. **Pâtisseries** €17.50. **Credit** AmEx, DC, MC, V.

The sombre Bar Vendôme may disappoint those used to the sumptuous interior of the London Ritz. Summertime is best when the bar opens onto a narrow terrace prettily decorated with geranium-filled urns. Mysteriously, tea bags (or *mousselines* as they put it) figure prominently in the hotel's understanding of this art. Our *mousseline Sultane* was admittedly well-structured with a refreshing bouquet, but the super-strong dosage considerably weakened the Ritz's claim of tea artistry. The wild strawberry tart with its perfect pastry and delicately spiced *crème anglaise* was, however, a masterpiece.

Le Bristol

112 rue du Fbg-St-Honoré, 8th (01.53.43.43.00). Mº Miromesnil. **Open** daily 3-6.30pm. **Tea** €8. **Pâtisseries** €10-€11. **Credit** AmEx, DC, MC, V.

Cross the apricot marble foyer and trip down the steps to the right to a vast lounge complete with marble columns, magnificent bouquets and a view to the lawns. The hotel's teas appear to have been picked by a connoisseur. Our choice of the excellent *grand foochow fumé pointes blanches* and *assam doomou* confirmed that Le Bristol takes teatime seriously. The accompanying little sandwiches of tuna, smoked salmon and cheese were delicously buttery, although the absence of cucumber was a tad disappointing.

Hôtel de Crillon

10 pl de la Concorde, 8th (01.44.71.15.00). Mº Concorde. **Open** daily 3.30-6pm. **Tea** €9-€12. **Pâtisseries** €9-€12. **Credit** AmEx, DC, MC, V.

There are few more grandiose settings for tea than the Crillon's Jardin d'Hiver, the gilt-edged chamber adjoining its renowned restaurant Les Ambassadeurs. Decor aside, the salon has an impersonal feel that's not much fun if you have come expressly to be pampered. The pretty terrace is the best idea in summer, especially as the tables are set wide apart. The cakes are delicious, especially the *crème brulée à la vanille Bourbon.* Teas are confined to a select number with an excellent pedigree. While the large silver teapots can't fail to impress,our lukewarm tea did – the tea seems to be in a perpetually tepid state here.

Hôtel Plaza Athénée ★

25 av Montaigne, 8th. Mº Alma Marceau (01.53.67.66.65). **Open** 8am-8pm daily. **Tea** €8. **Pâtisseries** €11-€15.**Credit** AmEx, DC, MC, V.

In the 18th century-style Galerie des Gobelins, you can watch the wealthy mingle. On our visit, the Iranian royal family had gathered for tea, next to them a famous opera singer and further down an eminent statesman. People-gazing, however, is a very minor pleasure compared to the Plaza's superb teas and dessert trolley. Try the *fraisier*, a strawberry and pistachio cream cake ... perfection. As for the teas, don't miss *mélange Plaza*, a masterly blend of fig, hazelnut, quince and grape. Listening to the harpist and pouring another cup from the armoury of silverware, we felt part of it all. Even the head waiter played the game, slipping us some juicy celebrity gossip.

Hotel Raphaël

17 av Kléber, 16th (01.53.64.32.00). Mº Kléber. **Open** daily 8am-10pm. **Tea** €6.10. **Pâtisseries** €10. **Credit** AmEx, DC, MC, V.

The seventh-floor Jardins Plein Ciel offers an extraordinary view of almost every Paris monument. Strategically placed lavender bushes and potted geraniums make it popular with privacy-conscious celebrities. The tea selection is tiny and uninspired; €9.15 for a Brooke Bond herb tea seemed outrageous. Our lemon meringue tart and chocolate mousse, though, would have been worthy accompaniments to the most rarefied Sauternes. And, on a crystal-clear day in June with all Paris at your feet, why count the cents?

pebbles. Overworked waiters have been known to short-change tourists marvelling at the cheapness (10F/€1.52 a glass) of the mint tea. The interior tearooms decorated in elaborate Moorish style are more comfortable, and air-conditioned, which improves everyone's humour no end. Indulge your ultra-sweet tooth with little mounds of almond paste encrusted with pine nuts and fat squares of Turkish delight while reclining on plump cushions.

La Fourmi Aillée

8 rue du Fouarre, 5th (01.43.29.40.99). Mº Maubert-Mutualité. **Open** tea daily noon-3pm, 7pm-midnight; shop daily noon-midnight. Evenings only in July and Aug. **Tea** €3.50-€4.50. **Pâtisseries** €5-€6. **Credit** MC, V.

Walking into this tea salon is like stepping into a Vanessa Bell painting. The intimate atmosphere is created by caramel-coloured hessian walls packed from floor to exceptionally high ceiling with books, a log pile by the chimney, a gilt-edged mirror, pretty lamps and a collection of homely-looking blue and white teapots. Try the Ceylon and China blend, perfumed with mango or hazelnut, or the mixed fruits and flowers. The lemon tart with a plum base is as perfectly composed as ever, while the apple strudel with cep mushrooms and custard sounds so unlikely it must be good. Not so good is the the background pop music.

La Maison des Trois Thés ★

33 rue Gracieuse, 5th (01.43.36.93.84). Mº Monge. **Open** Tue-Sun 11am-7.30pm. **Tea** €8.5-€687. **No pastries**. **Credit** MC, V.

There is probably no better place in France than here to indulge in *gongfu cha*, the ancient ritual of taking tea. The proprietor, Yu Hua Tseng, is one of the ten leading tea experts in the world. For years connoisseurs visited her tiny premises at rue du Pot au Fer to dip into her library of teas, harvested and aged at the house's plantations in Taiwan.This year, the company moved to larger premises. Madame Tseng, whose new address suits her to a tee, supplies the sommeliers of various grand hotels. The blue-green tea *dong ding wulong* is among the specialities. Grown in the Taiwanese mountains, it features a heady aroma of orchid, magnolia and blackcurrant. You might find yourself sitting next to a tea fiend savouring a rare oolong at €687 a tiny pot while you sample an exquisite *feng yan* jasmine tea at a mere €9.91. Tea is taken so seriously here that perfume-wearers are not admitted.

L'Artisan de Saveurs ★

72 rue du Cherche-Midi, 6th (01.42.22.46.64). Mº St-Placide. **Open** Tue-Sun noon-6.30pm (food served Tue-Fri noon-2.30pm; Sat, Sun noon-3pm). **Tea** €5.40-€6.40. **Pâtisseries** €6.40-€7.50. **Credit** MC, V.

Taking tea here is as good as curling up at a friend's house. There are even piles of interior design magazines to flick through should the conversation flag. The centrepiece of the dining area is a crockery-filled dresser topped with a huge still life of dried branches and silver-sprayed pine cones. From a deep red banquette we studied the concise and inviting menu, finally plumping for the black *thé des lettrés*, 'both spicy and malty with hints of honey and chocolate', and *Bourbon*, 'a South African Roibosch tannin-free tea flavoured with vanilla'. Deciding on a cake could have been equally tricky given the imaginative selection, but no true Brit could resist a scone or a muffin. The mini scones and apple and walnut muffins came with redcurrant jelly, butter and rather synthetic-tasting whipped cream.

Forêt Noire

9 rue de l'Eperon, 6th (01.44.41.00.09). Mº Odéon. **Open** tea Mon-Sat noon-7pm; Sun brunch noon-3pm, tea 3pm-7.30pm. **Tea** €4-€6. **Pâtisseries** €5-€7. **Credit** V.

Curiously, nothing in the eclectic decor conjures up the tea room's title, the Black Forest. Still, fans of this famed cake needn't lose heart; owner Denise Siegal hails from this part of Germany, and the cake heads the short list of desserts. Connoisseurs won't be disappointed with her version, oozing fresh cream and a moist, jammy interior. The *gâteau au fromage blanc*, a less sweet, creamy version of a cheesecake, was equally wicked. Naturally, from an intriguing tea list we chose the *Fôret Noire*, a black tea with a scintillating bouquet of blackberries, bilberries and blackcurrants.

La Maison de la Chine

76 rue Bonaparte, 6th (01.40.51.95.16). Mº St-Sulpice. **Open** Mon-Sat 10am-6.30pm. **Tea** €7.67-€13.72 (pâtisserie included). **Credit** MC, V.

Prepare yourself, this place conspires to make you fall for the East. First, there are the clocks giving the time in Rangoon, Hanoi, Peking and Hong Kong. Next, saleswomen sell package tours to places you sighed over in Bertolucci's 'The Last Emperor'. Then there's the interior design area filled with Chinese-lacquered furniture, lamps and exquisite celadon ceramics and, finally, the beautifully decorated tea room. The amiable staff offer four blends prepared following *gongfu cha,* the ancient ritual of taking tea; fine blue-green teas are brewed with infinite care in tiny vessels, then sipped like a liqueur. Their aromas can be so intense that too much tippling can result in a hangover.

Tch'a

6 rue du Pont-de-Lodi, 6th (01.43.29.61.31). Mº Odéon. **Open** Tue-Sun 11am-7.30pm (food served noon-3pm). *Gongfu cha* tea ceremony after 4pm. Closed Aug. **Tea** €3.50-€8.50. **Pâtisseries** €4.80. **Credit** MC, V.

This austere Chinese tearoom offers one of the most comprehensive tea lists in Paris. The parchment divides teas into white, yellow, green, blue-green, red and black varieties with a short description of each tea's history and qualities. Watch a ball of lychee white tea unfold as the hot water penetrates its complex mesh of threads, nibble on fresh ginger rock cakes, and let the soft Chinese chants unpick your knitted brow. For home, choose tea from large silver and red tins at the front. Sadly, the monastic atmosphere can't be wrapped up along with your tea.

Ladurée

16 rue Royale, 8th (01.42.60.21.79). Mº Madeleine or Concorde. **Open** Mon-Sat 8.30am-7pm; Sun 10am-7pm. **Tea** €4.85-€7. **Pâtisseries** €4-€5.60. **Credit** AmEx, DC, MC, V.

Avoiding someone's eye when they're desperately seeking yours is an art that French waiters have perfected, and Ladurée staff do it exceptionally well. Once you accept this, the effects on your temper will be neutralised and you can settle back and enjoy one of Paris' favourite institutions. The cake descriptions are Proustian, but it's the macaroons that regulars devour by the mound, whether coffee (arguably the best), coconut, chocolate, pistachio or mint. We chose mint and verbena, a large pot filled with dozens of fresh leaves steeped to perfection, and *yin hao* jasmine, whose aroma conjured up acres of the flowers in full bloom.

Branches: 75 av des Champs-Elysées, 8th (01.40.75.08.75); Printemps, 64 bd Haussmann, 9th (01.42.82.40.10); Franck et Fils, 80 rue de Passy, 16th (01.44.14.38.80).

Les Petits Plus ★

20 bd Beaumarchais, 11th (01.48.87.01.40/www.lespetitsplus.com). Mº Bastille. **Open** Mon-Sun 10am-7pm. **Tea** €3.81. **Pâtisseries** €5.34. **Credit** AmEx, DC, MC, V.

Once upon a time there was a funky tea room in the toy and gift shop Marais Plus on the rue des Francs-Bourgeois, then it vanished. Luckily, the owner Charlotte Bensoussan has resurfaced with Les Petits Plus. Her new venue has the same array of whimsical gifts to browse, then it's up the spiral staircase for tea. This is 'Goldilocks and the Three Bears' territory: scrubbed wood floor, tables and chairs, dressers and shelving set against pristine white walls. Our apricot tart tasted as if the fruit had been picked that morning, while the pecan pie, thick lemon and blackcurrant tarts and chocolate fudge cake were indecently inviting. The 21 teas, served in transparent, strainer teapots teapots so you can see the leaves but not chew them,, include the poetic *sonate d'automne, voyage d'hiver, secret tibétain* and Etna. Oh, and there's lemonade with fruit syrups, made to traditional recipes, and milkshakes for the kids.

Wine Bars

Where to go for rustic red by the glass or an exceptional bottle served with class.

The French may be drinking less wine (and more whisky, apparently), but Paris retains a fascinatingly diverse collection of wine bars, from the simple, working class *comptoirs* serving rough and ready *rouge* to places offering truly superb wines, painstakingly sourced by passionate owners. Although the importance of food means that there may be very little difference between many *bars à vins* and the city's bistros, bar opening hours tend to be more flexible, and it is often possible to get a glass of decent wine at the counter. With a few notable exceptions, such as L'Enoteca and Juvéniles, wines are uniformly French.

Aux Bons Crus
7 rue des Petits-Champs, 1st (01.42.60.06.45). M° *Palais Royal or Bourse.* **Open** daily 9am-2am. Food served Mon-Thur 9am-11.30pm; Fri-Sun 9am-midnight. **Glass** €3.05-€4.55. **Bottle** €15.25-€36.60. **Credit** DC, MC, V.
Opened in 1905, Aux Bons Crus is a solid, down-to-earth wine bar offering unpretentious hospitality along with wine and food menus that change weekly. Each *plat* is twinned with a suggested wine to make the ideal gastronomic combination, although no offence is taken if you choose something different. The day we visited, a chunky *entrecôte de boeuf* with *dauphinoise* potatoes went perfectly with the suggested '99 Côtes du Rhône, as did the *tartare de poisson* with a chilled glass of Brouilly.

Juvéniles
47 rue de Richelieu, 1st (01.42.97.46.49). M° *Palais Royal.* **Open** Mon-Sat noon-midnight. Food served Mon-Sat, noon-11pm. **Glass** €2.75-€7.62. **Bottle** €14.95-€60.98. **Credit** AmEx, MC, V.
Juveniles, run by the oenophile Tim Johnston, provides a constantly changing range of high-quality wines as well as some excellent Ports and sherries. This is one of the rare bars to offer a good selection of foreign wines; recent bottles have come from Italy, Spain, Portugal, Australia and even Iraq. Food is either *charcuterie* or a limited range of more substantial *plats chauds*. Its proximity to the Bourse means Juveniles is full of businessmen at lunch, but in the evenings half the clientele is Anglophone. If any of the wines take your fancy, you can buy a bottle or two to take home.

Le Père Fouettard
9 rue Pierre-Lescot, 1st (01.42.33.74.17). M° *Etienne-Marcel or RER Châtelet-Les Halles.* **Open** daily 8am-2am. Food served 11.30am-1am. **Glass** €2.60-€3.65. **Bottle** €13.35-€41.15. **Credit** MC, V. **Wheelchair access.**
As far as we could discern from the waiter's lively and involved description, a *père fouettard* is a sort of whip-wielding Father Christmas, a bogeyman *à la française* used for scaring children into behaving. Quite what this has to do with Parisian wining is unclear, but with good main courses, top-notch desserts and smiling waiters, one can afford to overlook this sort of Gallic eccentricity. The crowded, traditionally decorated bar serves a range of wine classics but fails to mention the producers and manages to misspell half the names. Still, with low prices and an outdoor terrace, it's one of the nicest spots in Les Halles.

Le Rubis
10 rue du Marché-St-Honoré, 1st (01.42.61.03.34). M° *Tuileries.* **Open** Mon-Fri 8am-10pm; Sat 9am-4pm. Hot food served 11.30am-3.30pm, cold food all day. Closed three weeks in Aug, two weeks at Christmas. **Glass** €1.20-€4.40. **Bottle** €12-€30. No credit cards.
Shoe-horned into the upstairs dining room, you have no choice but to make friends with your neighbours. Blackboards announce a selection of about 30 wines – there's no mention of producers – and bottles arrive on the table with generic labels. Our Brouilly tasted like vinegar, so we sent it back. The replacement was not a great deal better. The real draw is the generous, tasty, robust and astoundingly cheap lunchtime food – *saucisse aux lentilles, chou farci, tarte Tatin* – which will set you up nicely for the rest of the day. Le Rubis is also renowned for its Beaujolais Nouveau celebrations.

La Côte
77 rue de Richelieu, 2nd (01.42.97.40.68). M° *Bourse.* **Open** Mon-Fri 7.30am-8pm. Food served noon-3pm. **Glass** €3-€4.40. **Bottle** €14-€22. **Credit** MC, V. **Wheelchair access.**
An unsophisticated and friendly bar near the stock exchange, La Côte has been done up since last year, with wheelchair access and air conditioning, of which the owners are mightily proud. The main decoration remains a selection of trophies for wine and (more oddly) tray-carrying. Solid dishes such as lamb steak and *pavé de boeuf* with potatoes are washed down with an extensive range of wines which is regularly updated. The staff are more than happy to advise you on the best match for your meal.

La Belle Hortense
31 rue Vielle-du-Temple, 4th (01.48.04.71.60). M° *St-Paul or Hôtel-de-Ville.* **Open** daily 5pm-2am. **Glass** €3-€5.50. **Bottle** €14-€30. **Credit** MC, V.
Bookshop, literary salon, wine bar and off-licence, this highly original Marais spot certainly crams a lot into a tiny space. A good range of wines by the glass features a strong contingent of Rhônes from Guigal (most of the Guigal range is also available to take away at competitive prices), along with the likes of Vouvray, Cahors and Bordeaux. It's standing room only at the bar, but the non-smoking reading room in the back is guaranteed to enhance your intellectual credibility.

L'Enoteca ★
25 rue Charles V, 4th (01.42.78.91.44). M° *St-Paul.* **Open** Mon-Fri noon-2.30pm, 7.30-11.30pm. Closed one week in Aug. **Glass** €3-€7. **Bottle** €15-€35. **Credit** MC, V.
If you like Italian wine, then this classy Marais trattoria is a must. The list is astounding, with hard-to-find wines from all the best producers: Gaja, Aldo Conterno, Vajra, Felsina Berardenga and a stack of vintages. And what a pleasure to taste by the glass – we tried Moscato d'Asti and Barbera from Piedmont, and Sant'Agata dei Goti from Campania (the selection changes weekly). The food is delicious too, with antipasti like *porchetta alla Romana*, generous portions of *pappardelle al ragu di salsiccie* and a few meat and fish mains. It does get very busy though, so booking is recommended.

Le Felteu
15 rue Pecquay, 4th (01.42.72.14.51). M° *Rambuteau.* **Open** Mon-Sat 11am-2am. Food served noon-2.30pm, 8-10.30pm. **Glass** €2.60-€4. **Bottle** €14.50-€30. No credit cards.
The sign on the wall says, 'There's no wine in heaven. Let's have a drink now.' This seems to be the personal motto of the hugely jovial barman who doles out excellent drinks while haranguing his customers on the evils of modern-day life. Modernity certainly hasn't filtered through to the decor – the bulging walls are hung with filthy peeling wallpaper, stained mirrors and occasional patches of mock brick. However, the limited wine list is excellent – firm favourites join wines of the week (when we visited, a Gamay d'Anjou red and a St-Chinian rosé) all at a reasonable €2.60 a glass. A €13.72 *formule* of daily specials is mainly meaty (although we did have a lovely *duo de poissons* in creamy sauce) and comes with warm bread. You can sit at the small bar or in the restaurant where you can ogle the exceptionally ugly collection of souvenir plates.

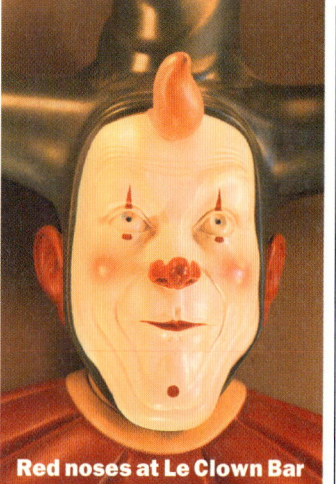

Le Rouge Gorge ★
8 rue St-Paul, 4th (01.48.04.75.89). M° *St-Paul.* **Open** Mon-Sat 10am-4pm, 6pm-1am, Sun 10am-4pm. Food served Mon-Sat noon-3pm, 7.30-11pm; Sun noon-3pm. Closed two weeks in Aug. **Glass** €2.30-€5.80. **Bottle** €14-€64. **Credit** MC, V.
This charming little wine bar, with its wooden beams, exposed stone and excellent cellar, has undergone a change of focus recently. Owner François Briclot and passionate young sommelier Guillaume Dupré have introduced a programme of changing themes, rotating roughly every two or three weeks. On our visit, it was the Loire and we were treated to a terrific selection of artisan-produced, unfiltered wines like Chinon Le Clos des Roches 1997 from Guy Lenoir, and the unclassified white, Les Bulles du Clos du Tue-Boeuf. On the food side, the savoury dishes – goat's cheese and hazelnut terrine, *paupiettes de veau, oignons farcis* – are tasty and well-executed, if pricey. Wines are also available to take away.

Le Soleil en Cave
21 rue Rambuteau, 4th (01.42.72.26.25). M° *Rambuteau.* **Open** Wed-Sun 10am-9pm. Food served Wed-Sun 12.30-9.30pm. **Glass** €3.05-€9.15. **Bottle** €12.20-€230. **Credit** MC, V.
The former Au Soleil en Coin has been replaced by the brightly polished Le Soleil en Cave, a wine bar-boutique, which, despite a modern, somewhat soulless interior of veneer shelving and yellow tiled tables, nonetheless feels inviting. *Tartines* are the speciality: little open-faced sandwiches combining sunny, top-notch ingredients. More rib-sticking *plats du jour* such as an exceptionally moist turkey with lemon sauce and tagliatelle are also available. The pleasure of Le Soleil en Cave is its knowledgeable and helpful owner who has picked a list of winning wines, such as a fruity Corbières Tentation 1998, many available by the glass.

Les Cépages
6 rue des Fossés-St-Marcel, 5th (01.47.07.91.25). M° *Gobelins.* **Open** Mon-Fri noon-3.30pm, 7.30-10.30pm; Sat noon-3.30pm. Hot food served 11.30am-3.30pm. Closed Aug. **Glass** €2.45-€4.15. **Bottle** €10.70-€27.45. **Credit** MC, V.
This is a neighbourhood bistro specialising in wine rather than a *bar à vins*; you can have just a glass at the bar if it's not too busy but eating is compulsory during the lunch service. The standard of food is commendable, with good, robust French regional dishes such as *saucisson chaud* with steamed potatoes, *rognons de veau à la moutarde* with braised endives and crème brûlée. Wash these down with excellent Morgon or Côtes du Rhône from Guigal, from a short but well-chosen list. Ambiance, however, can be a bit lacking; on our rainy Saturday lunchtime visit, *patron* Jacques Petit was exhibiting severe signs of world-weariness.

Le Mauzac
7 rue de l'Abbé de l'Epée, 5th (01.46.33.75.22). RER *Luxembourg.* **Open** Mon-Fri 7.30am-2am. Food served daily noon-2.30pm; Thur, Fri from 8pm with a reservation. Closed Aug. **Glass** €2-€3.05. **Bottle** €12.20-€42.70. **Credit** MC, V.
Named after a white grape from Gaillac, Le Mauzac sits on a quiet road lined with trees and antiquarian bookshops. The relaxed service reflects the sleepiness of the street, although it's a popular place, so booking is advised. Excellent glasses of Morgon and Beaujolais complement an ultra-tender ribsteak, and dessert wine is available to accompany the buttery fruit crumbles. If you're not peckish, you can also sip a glass at the counter.

Les Papilles
30 rue Gay-Lussac, 5th (01.43.25.20.79/ www.lespapilles.fr). RER *Luxembourg.* **Open** Mon-Sat 9am-8.30pm. Food served Mon-Sat noon-2.45pm; Tue, Thur noon-2.45pm, 8-10.30pm. **Glass** €2.74 and up. **Bottle** €13.72 and up. **Credit** MC, V. **Wheelchair access.**
Decorated in the style of a Provençal kitchen, Les Papilles ('tastebuds') is all about eating and drinking well. It's run by two couples dedicated to gastronomy – Brigitte and Julie look after the food while their husbands Gérard and Pierre trawl the countryside looking for new wines. The regularly changing menu – choose from a hot *plat du jour* or lighter plates – emphasises seasonal cooking. There's a good selection of *vins de la semaine* and the regulars were lapping up an excellent red from Corsica. Jams, vinegars, olive oils, pasta, whiskies and vintage Ports are all there to take home, and shelves of wine await, like a fine library, to be perused with pleasure.

Red noses at Le Clown Bar

Le Grand Colbert

... a first rate, typically French Brasserie, open until late and affordable for all budgets. Meals vary from simple dishes to the most exquisite cuisine. Whatever takes your fancy, you can savour a relaxing moment in a lovely Parisian atmosphere.

New lunch menu (Monday-Friday): €17.50
Menu: €25 (including coffee)
Open daily from noon-1am (with last orders taken up until 1am)

2 rue Vivienne, 2nd. Tel: 01.42.86.87.88. M° Bourse

Le Nez Rouge • The Red Nose
Great choice • Great quality • Great prices
e-mail: lenezrouge@wanadoo.fr

Yves is a winemaker (5th generation) working in the south of France and southern hemisphere. Benoit also comes from a wine producing family. He has worked in some of the most famous French wine shops before joining 'Le Nez Rouge'. All selected wines are regularly quoted by Hugh Johnson, Wine Enthusiast, Gamberro Rosso, R. Parker, Decanter, Wine Spectator, Wine...

Over 400 wines from France and from all around the World (short list of our selection):

<u>Argentina</u>: Bianchi Elsa's Malbec, Luz Cabernet Sauvignon Reserve. <u>Australia</u>: Wolf Blass Yellow Label, Bailey's Shiraz, Metal Langhorne Creek. <u>New-Zealand</u>: Mount Riley, Marlborough, Kim Crawford <u>USA</u>: Hogue Washington State, De Loach California <u>Chile</u>: Villard Wines, Dallas Conte, Andes Peak <u>Italy</u>: La Carraia-Umbria, Falesco-Lazio, Coppo-Piemonte, Livio Felluga-Friuli, Castello di Querceto-Chianti Classico, Vasco Sasetti-Brunello di Montalcino, La Morrmoraia - Toscana... <u>Spain</u>: Nekeas-Navarra, Marqués de Vitoria Rioja, Ribera del duero, Cava... <u>South Africa</u>: Altus - Paarl, Landskroon-Paarl, Kanonkop-Stellenbosch, Beyerskloof-Stellenbosch...

<u>Loire</u>: Domaine de Cray, Sancerre Vatan, Pouilly Fumé Landrat Guyollot <u>Rhône</u>: Domaine de la Soumade Rasteau, Gigondas, Châteauneuf du Pape... <u>Languedoc & South West</u>: Borie de Maurel, Domaine de Chiroulet and over 30 wine estates <u>Bordeaux-Burgundy</u>: a selection of the best estates of which some less known, interesting to discover

<u>WE CAN DELIVER ANYWHERE IN FRANCE</u>
Over 15% discount when you buy by the case!!!
On presentation of this add from Time Out, get a free bottle of our excellent Claret:
Château Pardaillan, Bordeaux Supérieur

<u>See you soon, "à bientôt"... Benoit & Yves</u>
11 rue Alexandre CABANEL, 15th. Tel/Fax: +33 (0)1.47.34.87.40
M° CAMBRONNE (off the square on the right as you come out)

Caves Miard
9 rue des Quatre-Vents, 6th (01.43.54.99.30). M° Odéon. **Open** Mon 2.30-8pm, Tue-Sat 10am-8pm. Food served noon-3pm. Closed two weeks in Aug. **Glass** €2.50-€9. **Bottle** €12-€316.
Credit AmEx, MC, V.
The marble shelves and cupboards of this tiny vintage *crèmerie* are now stacked with wine bottles. At lunch the staff get out the tables and chairs and serve an array of savoury tarts, salads and *charcuterie* and a selection of wines by the glass. But it's more than just a question of picturesque charm – our warm tart of *girolles*, duck gizzards and tangy reblochon cheese was crisp and appetising, the red from near Perpignan zingy and refreshing. A good place for a light lunch and interesting wines.

Fish
69 rue de Seine, 6th (01.43.54.34.69). M° Odéon or Mabillon. **Open** Tue-Sun noon-11pm. Food served noon-3pm, 7-11pm. **Glass** €2.70-€8.54. **Bottle** €13-€655.
Credit MC, V.
Set up by a New Zealander who runs the panini shop Cosi across the road and an American with a wine shop around the corner, this friendly, informal place attracts well-heeled young French and slightly worse-heeled young Anglos in roughly equal numbers. The wine list is strong on the sunny, big-hitter wines of Languedoc-Roussillon (we chose a bottle of smooth, ample St-Chinian) and there's an interesting selection from the Rhône Valley. The food is Mediterranean (polenta, rocket salad, salt cod, tomatoes-a-gogo) and not bad at all.

La Tour de Pierre ★
53 rue Dauphine, 6th (01.43.26.08.93/www.latouredepierre.com). M° Odéon. **Open** Mon-Sat 8am-9pm. Food served noon-8.30pm. Closed two weeks in Aug, one week at Christmas. **Glass** €1.98-€4.88. **Bottle** €13.72-€36.59. **Credit** MC, V. **Wheelchair access.**
Time stands still in this tiny, award-winning *tabac*/wine bar on the Left Bank. OK, so it might take an age to get served (particularly if you come in simply to buy a pack of cigarettes) but what atmosphere! Where else would you meet an Appeals Court judge dressed in tweeds and quoting Oscar Wilde, the elderly spouse of a newspaper war correspondent and a member of the jury for one of France's most notorious serial-killer trials? The wine is excellent – riesling late harvest, Médoc, Burgundy – and reasonably priced, and the food is decent.

Le Griffonier
8 rue des Saussies, 8th (01.42.65.17.17). M° Champs-Elysées-Clemenceau. **Open** Mon-Wed, Fri 7.30am-9pm; Thur 7.30am-11pm. Hot food served Mon-Fri noon-3.30pm; Thur until 10.30pm, cold food all day. **Glass** €3.51-€6.10. **Bottle** €19.06-€57.93.
Credit MC, V.
You might catch a bit of excitement as the sirens wail and a motorcade swoops by – this sophisticated bistro is a stone's throw from the Elysée Palace and directly opposite the Ministry of the Interior. At lunch, the upstairs room is thronging with suits discussing power politics or business over nicely cooked lamb chops, juicy *entrecôte*, rhubarb tart and profiteroles. There is a good choice of reasonably priced Beaujolais, Loire and Rhône wines along with some more unusual and expensive bottles, including our Alsace pinot noir '98.

Ma Bourgogne
133 bd Haussmann, 8th (01.45.63.50.61). M° Miromesnil. **Open** Mon-Fri 7am-10pm. Hot food served noon-2pm, 7-10pm. Closed Aug. **Glass** €1.40-€2.50. **Bottle** €15.24-€45.73. **Credit** AmEx, MC, V. **Wheelchair access.**
After 40 years behind the counter of this Parisian institution, Louis Prin has retired. Prin was at the centre of many wine associations. Sad to say, therefore, that on first impressions, the new regime fails to live up to its predecessor. Our experience was one of indifferent service, indifferent food (the bread at dinner was left over from lunch) and, shock-horror, indifferent wine (we sent our vinegary Chiroubles back and it was exchanged, but without any hint of an apology). Add to this the frankly old-fashioned and unwelcoming décor (lace curtains and dark-stained wood) and it becomes hard to find a reason to go.

La Cave Drouot
8 rue Drouot, 9th (01.47.70.83.38). M° Richelieu-Drouot. **Open** Mon-Sat 7am-9pm. Hot food served noon-3pm. **Glass** €1.20-€4.60. **Bottle** €14.60-€121.95.
Credit MC, V.
Three seating options await the visitor to La Cave Drouot – bar, brasserie and restaurant. Each has its advantages, but if you just want to drink take a seat at the bar for a proper sampling session. Beaujolais bottled on the premises is the speciality, and though not super-cheap, it is outstandingly good. At the bar you can fill up on cheese *tartines* and home-smoked salmon, while the brasserie and restaurant offer more filling dishes, accompanied by delicious crunchy *pommes allumettes*.

Le Verre Volé
67 rue de Lancry, 10th (01.48.03.17.34). M° République. **Open** Sun 11am-8pm; Tue-Sat 10.30am-midnight. Closed one week in Aug. Food served all day Tue-Sat. **Glass** €2.80-€3.90. **Bottle** €5-€40. **Credit** MC, V.
A popular favourite of this newly-cool quartier near Canal St-Martin, Le Verre Volé specialises in food and drink from the Ardèche region of France. Unsulphured, unfiltered wines join hearty black puddings, *andouillette* and pâté in a cheery atmosphere. Opened only in 2000, it is run by two friends who clearly love their job and make every effort to ensure their customers have a good time. It's tiny, little more than a few very basic tables in a shop, but it's always full to bursting in the evening.

Le Café du Passage
12 rue de Charonne, 11th (01.49.29.97.64). M° Bastille. **Open** Mon-Fri, Sun 6pm-2am, Sat noon-2am. Food served all day. **Glass** €3.81-€6.86. **Bottle** €15.24-€609.76.
Credit AmEx, DC, MC, V.
Visitors to this velvet-curtained café can look forward to a good selection of wine from all the major producing regions of France. Wonderful Côtes du Rhône, Burgundy and Bordeaux as well as wines from Provence and Jurançon are on offer, all at relatively high prices. The presentation is nice – sparkling decanters and tapered glasses for certain wines – and the food is standard well-executed French cuisine. In summer the bar opens onto an inner courtyard where you can bask in the sun on wicker chairs, clutching a cold glass of Sauvignon.

Le Clown Bar
114 rue Amelot, 11th (01.43.55.87.35). M° Filles du Calvaire. **Open** Mon-Sat noon-2.30pm, 7.00pm-midnight; Sun 7pm-midnight. Hot food served during opening hours. **Glass** €3-€4.50. **Bottle** €15-€52.
No credit cards.
Nestling next to the Cirque d'Hiver, a shortish walk from the Bastille or the Marais, the Clown Bar is decorated with the comic-yet-sinister circus memorabilia. Much of the listed interior dates from 1919, but owner Jo Vitte, a former antique dealer, has added period bistro tables and a beautiful sculpted zinc bar. Open on Sunday evenings, Le Clown Bar serves excellent food for locals who'd rather not cook – *petit salé aux lentilles* or *filet mignon de porc à l'ancienne*, with mustard, cream and fried potatoes and a wonderfully moist *pain d'épices* dessert. Good selection of wines from the Rhône, Languedoc-Roussillon and the Loire.

Jacques Mélac ★
42 rue Léon-Frot, 11th (01.43.70.59.27). M° Charonne. **Open** Tue-Sat 9am-midnight. Hot food served noon-3pm, 7-10.30pm, cold food all day. Closed Christmas and New Year, Aug. **Glass** €2.80-€3.66. **Bottle** €14.50-€44.30. **Credit** MC, V. **Wheelchair access.**
Jacques Mélac, the owner of this crowded locals' bar, used to own a vineyard and his love of wine shows in every aspect of the place. The walls are draped with creeping vines and shelves bursting with bottles. Hams and cantal cheeses loom behind the bar, and Jacques hacks off generous chunks to accompany the good-value glasses of hardy young wines. Unusually, there is a non-smoking section, reached by walking through the bare-bones kitchen. Every September there is a little festival in the street, where people with vines in Paris bring grapes to be pressed, having fun but producing mainly foul fermentations.

Le Baron Bouge
1 rue Théophile-Roussel, 12th (01.43.43.14.32). M° Ledru-Rollin. **Open** Mon 5-10pm; Tue-Thur 10am-2pm, 5-10pm; Fri, Sat 10am-10pm; Sun 10am-3.30pm. Cold food served all day. **Glass** €1.30-€4. **Bottle** €10.70-€25.
Credit MC, V. **Wheelchair access.**
Easter Sunday and the place was literally awash! Soapy water was gushing from a defective washing machine on the floor above and the owners were doing their best to keep us from going under. But punters – an eclectic crowd of artists, musicians and other locals – continued to smoke, drink and tuck into fresh oysters from the stand outside (October to April), oblivious to the rising tide. Le Baron Bouge may appear rather rough and ready, but the wines, including varied Loire selections, small châteaux from Bordeaux or Condrieu from the Rhône, are chosen with an eye for quality. There's a bit of bar food – *charcuterie* and some good goat's cheese – and they also sell honey and various other delights in jars.

Les Cailloux
58 rue des Cinq Diamants, 13th (01.45.80.15.08). M° Corvisart or Place d'Italie. **Open** Tue-Sat 12.30-2.30pm, 7.30-11pm. Closed Aug, 25 Dec-3 Jan. **Glass** €2-€3. **Bottle** €14-€59.50. **Credit** AmEx, MC, V.
Les Cailloux offers more than 40 wines, only six or so by the glass, and half the list is Italian, reflecting the first language of the staff and cooks. You can't really hang out by the bar, but expect a fine Italian meal with superb service and atmosphere. Mozzarella salad and grilled vegetables with gorgonzola, pastas such as linguine with crab or *girolle* mushrooms, and *panna cotta*, a wobbly baked cream, are some of the carefully prepared and satisfying dishes. With lights hanging over each table and plenty of distractions for the tastebuds, we could happily while away many a winter's evening here.

Le Rallye-Peret
6 rue Daguerre, 14th (01.43.22.57.05). M° Denfert-Rochereau. **Open** Tue-Sat 9am-11.30pm; Mon, Sun 9am-8pm. Food served all day. Closed at Christmas. **Glass** €3.35-€6.10. **Bottle** €16.80-€42. **Credit** MC, V.
The main attraction of this long-established café-style *bar à vins* on a busy pedestrianised street is the terrace, perfect for sipping chilled Sancerre on a summer evening. Otherwise, though, and particularly on a rainy winter's evening, it's a pretty charmless affair. There's a reasonable selection of wines on offer – we tried the Loupiac '98 and a Brouilly, and food, from *charcuterie* and salads, to snails and Berthillon ice cream, is served all day. Service is free of all pretension – when we asked what the stuffing was in the *chou farci*, we were told quite simply 'stuffing'.

Le Baratin
3 rue Jouye-Rouve, 20th (01.43.49.39.70). M° Pyrénées. **Open** Tue-Fri, Sat 6pm-midnight. Closed for two weeks in Aug and first week in Jan. Food served noon-3pm, 8pm-midnight. **Glass** €1.64-€2.90. **Bottle** €15-€80. **Credit** MC, V.
Way up in deepest Belleville, Philippe Pinoteau runs this great, buzzing bar with marble tables and black-and-white photos. Like his predecessor Olivier Camus, he prefers the hands-on artistry of young winemakers to the industrial perfection too often found with the big names. The food is well-presented and the menu is updated daily. As with many bars in Paris, the staff tend to be friendlier to the regulars – they can be a bit cool the first time you visit.

Having a grape old time at Jacques Mélac

Moulin Rouge BAL du

Féerie

New Show!

Dinner & Show at 7PM from €125 - Show at 9PM: €89 & at 11PM: €79
Montmartre - 82 BD de Clichy - 75018 Paris - **Reservations** : 01 53 09 82 82
www.moulin-rouge.com

Eating & Entertainment

If classic bistros leave you restless, swing for your supper or trip the night fantastic.

Beyond this timeless selection, an increasing number of bars (see p117) also offer entertainment in unexpected forms.

Bawdy Songs

Les Assassins
40 rue Jacob, 6th (no telephone). M° St-Germain-des-Prés. **Open** Mon-Sat 7pm-midnight. **Average** €17. **No credit cards**.
This relic of St-Germain's pre-chi-chi days, littered with naughty postcards, attracts students, hen parties and provincials for double entendres and trad fare such as *lapin à la moutarde*. Singer-guitarist Maurice Duluc swings on seaside humour: you need a smattering of gutter French to keep up.

Boats

La Balle au Bond
(01.40.51.87.06/www.laballeaubond.fr). Oct-Mar: facing 55 quai de la Tournelle, 5th. M° Maubert-Mutualité. Apr-Sept: quai Malaquais, 6th. M° Pont-Neuf. **Bar** Mon-Sat 11am-2am; Sun 6-10pm. **Concerts** 9pm. **Admission** €6. **Credit** AmEx, MC, V.
A café-bar with prime mooring positions, sunny deck terrace, live jazz and *chanson*.

Bateaux Parisiens
Port de La Bourdonnais, 7th (01.44.11.33.44/ meal reservations 01.44.11.33.55/ www.bateauxparisiens.com). M° Bir-Hakeim or RER Champ de Mars. **Departs** *lunch cruise* daily 12.15pm; *dinner cruise* daily 7.45pm. **Lunch** €49-€69. **Dinner** €89-€125. **Credit** DC, MC, V.
Whether the spiel is in French or English, the secrets don't seem much more confidential than those divulged by a standard guidebook. Lunch, too, is less than riveting: fairly imaginative, fairly fresh, fairly priced. The cruise lasts a leisurely two hours, enough time to digest both the meal and the major Parisian monuments.

Bateaux-Mouches
Pont de l'Alma, rive droite, 8th (01.42.25.96.10/recorded information 01.40.76.99.99/www.bateaux-mouches.fr). M° Alma-Marceau. **Departs** *lunch cruise* Tue-Sun 1pm; *dinner cruise* daily 8.30pm. **Lunch** €50. **Dinner** €85, €125. **Credit** AmEx, DC, MC, V.
Though blandly commentated, the Bateaux-Mouches offer a scenic ride through Paris by day or night (after dark, the boats switch on powerful lights). Two of the boats have high-priced restaurants.

Cabaret

Un Piano dans la Cuisine
20 rue de la Verrerie, 4th (01.42.72.23.81). M° Hôtel-de-Ville. **Dinner and show** daily 8.30pm. **Prix fixe** €36 (Mon-Fri, Sun), €46 (Sat). **No credit cards**.
Owner and ring-leader Serge Gilles greets guests at the door wearing sequins and his body weight in lipstick; later in the evening, he leads his troupe of middle-aged, tragicomic drag artists through a manic program of *chanson* and cheese – Juliette Greco, Dalida, Mireille Mathieu, Barbra Streisand. Expect anything and be warned – the closer you sit to the stage, the greater your chances are of becoming a last-minute addition to the show. Food is passable, but clearly not the attraction. Small, packed and good fun.

Le Lido
116bis av des Champs-Elysees, 8th (01.40.76.56.10/www.lido.fr). M° Georges V. **Dinner** daily 8pm. **Show** 10pm, midnight. **Admission** *with Champagne* €70.13, €85.37; *with dinner* €124.25, €154.74. **Credit** AmEx, DC, MC, V. **Wheelchair access**.
Operating since 1928, when it was known as La Plage de Paris, The Lido – renamed in 1946 after the Lido beach in Venice – still draws the tourists and the business revellers. Its galas have seen the likes of Elvis Presley, Sammy Davis Jr. and Richard Nixon. The current show is still (since 2000) *C'est magique*: a series of hyper-choreographed stage numbers featuring ice-skating and flying beauties. Beware of ordering extortionately priced *à la carte* extras with the already pricey – and still disappointing – dinner *menus* crafted by Paul Bocuse.

La Nouvelle Eve
25 rue Fontaine, 9th (01.48.78.37.96). M° Blanche. **Dinner** daily 6.30pm, 10pm. **Show** 8pm, 10.15pm. Closed Nov-Apr. **Admission** *with dinner* €111; *with Champagne* €73. **Credit** AmEx, MC, V.
Small fry compared to the big-name cabarets, La Nouvelle Eve offers a more intimate peek at Pigalle traditions. With its flashy disco interior, you expect Travolta to strut his stuff at any moment. The garish, high-kick-littered show has audiences bellowing for more but the same cannot be said of the food: a chateaubriand steak, followed by ice cream fancies, was a feeble fanfare to the delights of the show that followed.

Olé Bodega ★
Square Victor, rue Lucien Bossoutrot, 15th (01.53.02.90.85/www.olebodega.com). M° Balard. **Open** *restaurant bookings* Wed-Sat 8.30-9.30pm. *Bar/club* 10pm-2am. **Prix fixe** €29.37-€54. **Credit** AmEx, MC, V.
Having cautiously pulled back the curtain and ventured into the big top we were enveloped in a mellow, candle-lit atmosphere. At 11pm the arena comes alive with circus entertainers (jugglers, acrobats, trapeze artists or clowns depending on the night) who perform two acts and receive raucous praise from the animated audience. Somewhat confused waiters deliver a range of hot and cold tapas (more cold than hot by the time they reach you) and lamb chops in rosemary or beef ribs. The house red and rosé, at €15.24, help you get into the circus vibe. Once the entertainers disperse the arena becomes a dance floor and the eclectic crowd struts its stuff to French pop.

Chez Michou ★
80 rue des Martyrs, 18th (01.46.06.16.04/ www.michou.com). M° Pigalle. **Dinner** daily 8.30pm. **Show** 11pm. **Admission** *with dinner* €95; *show and one drink* €31. **Credit** MC, V.
With his blonde locks, blue glasses and Chelsea boots, the over-the-top master of ceremonies and owner, Michou, is a Paris icon (he has even shared his stage with Jacques Chirac) and he orchestrates the evening's entertainment: drag diva *chanson* (from Piaf to to Cher to Whoopi Goldberg).

Moulin Rouge
82 bd de Clichy, 18th (01.53.09.82.82/ www.moulin-rouge.com). M° Blanche. **Dinner** daily 7pm. **Show** 9pm, 11pm. **Admission** *with dinner* €125-€155; *show* €79, €89. **Credit** AmEx, DC, MC, V. **Wheelchair access**.
With new publicity courtesy of Nicole Kidman, you'll find more of her fans among the coachloads of tourists than people interested in Toulouse-Lautrec's inspiration or Edith Piaf's concerts. Every year the Moulin Rouge boasts about a 'new show', but it's usually the same basic idea – prancing flawless bods – with a little twist (they alter the 1000-plus costumes or chuck a few of the Doriss girls into a giant aquarium, etc.). It's the 'go once to say you've been' business they're after. With the dinner option you can expect to munch on posh nosh such as foie gras, veal and caviar.

Comedy & Lit Crit

Hôtel du Nord
102 quai de Jemmapes, 10th, (01.40.40.78.78 dinner concerts/01.53.19.98.88 comedy). M° République or Jacques Bonsergent. **Open** Mon 11am-3pm; Tue-Sat 11am-3pm, 6-11pm; Sun 11am-3pm. No comedy in Aug. **Admission** varies. **Credit** DC, MC, V. No credit cards for comedy.
The setting of Marcel Carné's film of the same name, this legendary hotel houses varied cultural events, often with set dinners. Regular English comedy nights have seen such stars as Al Murray and Johnny Vegas. Concerts run from Muscovite musicians to blues. The front bar looks on to the pretty Canal St-Martin.

La Maroquinerie
23 rue Boyer, 20th (01.40.33.30.60). M° Gambetta. **Open** Mon-Sat 11am-1am. **Average** €23. **Admission** free-€17. **Concerts** Mon-Sat 8.30pm; Sun 4pm. **Credit** MC, V. **Wheelchair access**.
Though this ancient warehouse is beautiful, the non-decor doesn't do it justice. The main attraction is the eclectic readings (poetry, theatre), debates (sociologists, philosophers) and concerts (blues to Celtic harp) – and there is now a concert venue downstairs. Dishes such as marinated salmon and duck *magret* are appetising, but are served only before and after concerts, so time your arrival carefully.

Guinguette & Dancing

Les Etoiles
61 rue du Château d'Eau, 10th (01.47.70.60.56). M° Château d'Eau. **Open** Thur 9pm-3.30am; Fri-Sat 9pm-4.30am. Closed Aug. **Admission** *with dinner* €18.29 (9pm); *with drink from 11pm* €9.15. **Drinks** €3-€6. **No credit cards**.
Up-for-it 30-somethings frequent this tatty music hall which holds friendly salsa nights with infectious Latino bands. Canteen-like tables encourage mingling, while a spicy Latin-American menu ensures that even those who aren't dancing get hot under the collar.

Chez Raymonde ★
119 av Parmentier, 11th (01.43.55.26.27). M° Parmentier or Goncourt. **Open** Tue-Fri 7pm-1am; Sat 8pm-1am. **Average** €22. **Prix fixe** €19 (Tue-Fri), €38 (Sat). **Credit** AmEx, DC, MC, V.
Beware, ladies: the chef may ask you to tango (though only on Saturdays). Halfway through the *diner-dansant* meal here – solidly French and scrumptious – the lights dim to rosy reds, the host sprinkles magic dust on the tiny dance floor, introduces a piano/accordion duo and invites the chef out of the kitchen and into his arms to inaugurate an evening of waltz, swing and other fancy steps. The meal is satisfying enough on its own; add in the dance, and the *soirée* delivers pure enchantment.

Chez Louisette
130 av Michelet, Marché Vernaison, 93400 St-Ouen (01.40.12.10.14). M° Porte de Clignancourt. **Open** Mon, Sat, Sun noon-6pm. **Average** €30. **No credit cards**.
This *guinguette* in the heart of the Clignancourt flea market is deliciously over-the-top. On a Saturday lunch it was in full swing: a heavy-metal junkie in a two-tone wig strummed on a pink electric guitar while Georges-Paul and Manuela crooned French oldies. Acts change regularly.

Chez Gégène
162bis quai de Polangis, allée des Guinguettes, 94345 Joinville-le-Pont (01.48.83.29.43/ www.chez-gegene.com). RER Joinville-le-Pont. **Open** Tue-Sun noon-2.30pm, 7-10.30pm. Closed Jan-Mar. **Average** €28. **Admission** *with dinner* €32.01 (Fri, Sat); *with drink* €13.72, €15.24 (Fri, Sat). **Credit** AmEx, MC, V. **Wheelchair access**.
Typically French and thoroughly un-Parisian, Chez Gégène attracts dance addicts, grannies and urban hipsters. The band (Friday, Saturday nights, Sunday afternoons) sprinkles tangos, foxtrots and *musette* with disco hits, so those less sure of foot don't feel left out. Between dances, feast on steaks, *moules-frites* and wine.

Le Guinguette de l'Ile du Martin-Pêcheur
41 quai Victor-Hugo, 94500 Champigny-sur-Marne (01.49.83.03.02). RER Champigny-sur-Marne. **Open** *May-Aug* Wed-Sat 7pm-2am; Sun noon-8pm (live band). Closed Wed in Sept. *Oct-Dec, Apr* Fri, Sat 8pm-2am; Sun noon-8pm. **Prix fixe** €21.34, €25.92. **Admission** €6.10-€10.67. **No credit cards**.
The Martin-Pêcheur (kingfisher), built on an island which is reached by raft, dates from the 1980s – but the bunting, gingham cloths, red plonk and gently lapping water are more real than real. Parisian trendies and local families laze on the lawns or jive and rumba.

Let the chef lead at Chez Raymonde

Gay & Lesbian

The lesbian scene is revving up while the boys show signs of coming of age.

It's frisky business as usual in gay bars and clubs in Paris, while in restaurants you'll find hot dishes posted on the menu and at the table. The gay heartland is in the Marais but there are loud and proud rainbow pockets throughout the city.

Gay bars & cafés

Banana Café ★
*13 rue de la Ferronnerie, 1st
(01.42.33.35.31/www.bananacafe.com).
Mº Châtelet.* **Open** daily 4pm-5am.
Credit AmEx, MC, V. **Wheelchair access**.
Pumping nightly with hedonistic 30-somethings, gay and straight, the Banana Café hosts legendary theme nights. Singers belt out showtunes in the cellar bar and upstairs you might find a beautiful buns contest.

Le Tropic Café
*66 rue des Lombards, 1st (01.40.13.92.62).
Mº Châtelet.* **Open** daily noon-dawn. **Credit** AmEx, MC, V. **Wheelchair access**.
This bright, upbeat bar is going through a renaissance with some groovy parties that draw a loyal band.

Le Duplex
*25 rue Michel-le-Comte, 3rd
(01.42.72.80.86). Mº Rambuteau.*
Open daily 8pm-2am. **Credit** MC, V.
Monthly exhibitions and eclectic music attract all sorts to this smoky bar, but don't be fooled: cruising is down to a fine art. Attracts those seeking Socratic master/pupil relationships.

Onix
*9 rue Nicolas-Flamel, 4th (01.42.72.37.72).
Mº Hôtel-de-Ville.* **Open** daily 3pm-5am.
Credit MC, V.
A glossy, orange and terracotta bar with arty fittings, plum centre on the pink route linking the Marais to Les Halles. Crowded with the smart set, it is also a jumping-off point for clubbers.

Amnesia
*42 rue Vieille-du-Temple, 4th
(01.42.72.16.94). Mº Hôtel-de-Ville.* **Open** daily 10am-2am. **Credit** MC, V.
A warm meeting place with comfy sofas and easy-going clientele, known to hold Nana Mouskouri soirées in the basement.

Le Bar du Palmier
*16 rue des Lombards, 4th (01.42.78.53.53).
Mº Hôtel-de-Ville.* **Open** daily 5pm-5am.
Credit AmEx, MC, V.
The bar gets busy late, but is also good during happy hour (6-8pm). It has a bizarre pseudo-tropical decor and a nice terrace. One of the few places where women are welcome.

Le Central
*33 rue Vieille-du-Temple, 4th
(01.48.87.99.33/www.hotelcentralmarais.com).
Mº Hôtel-de-Ville.* **Open** Mon-Fri 4pm-2am; Sat, Sun 2pm-2am. Closed 24 Dec.
Credit MC, V. **Wheelchair access**.
One of the oldest gay hangouts, Le Central still passes muster against its sprightly neighbours. No attitude, cute bar staff. Popular with tourists.

Coffee Shop
*3 rue Ste-Croix-de-la-Bretonnerie, 4th
(01.42.74.24.21/www.coffeeshop.fr).
Mº Hôtel-de-Ville.* **Open** daily 9am-2am.
No credit cards. **Wheelchair access**.
Popular rendezvous and pick-up joint. MTV plays in a corner and decent food is served until late. Great for gossip.

Baked beings galore at Sun Café

Le Cox
*15 rue des Archives, 4th (01.42.72.08.00).
Mº Hôtel-de-Ville.* **Open** daily 1pm-2am.
No credit cards.
One of the hottest and most militant Marais gay bars. Afternoons are calm, but evenings rev up with loud music and dishy barmen.

Okawa
*40 rue Vieille-du-Temple, 4th
(01.48.04.30.69/www.okawa.fr).
Mº Hôtel-de-Ville.* **Open** daily 11am-2am.
Credit AmEx, MC, V.
This French-Canadian bar/coffee shop excels in word play. Okawa is native-American for peace pipe; *pipe* is French slang for blow job.

Open Café ★
*17 rue des Archives, 4th (01.42.72.26.18).
Mº Hôtel-de-Ville.* **Open** daily 11am-2am.
Credit MC, V.
A Mecca for gay boys meeting up before heading into the night. A facelift has only increased its popularity. The management also runs the extended Open Bar Coffee Shop.

Quetzal
10 rue de la Verrerie, 4th (01.48.87.99.07/www.quetzal.com). Mº Hôtel-de-Ville.
Open daily 1pm-5am. **Credit** MC, V .
Quetzal, the cruisiest bar in the Marais with a strategically-placed terrace, attracts a beefy crowd. It's at the end of rue des Mauvais-Garçons (bad boys' street). Enough said! Midweek thrills to the sight of Lolo and the go-go boys.

Sun Café
*35 rue Ste-Croix-de-la-Bretonnerie, 4th
(01.40.29.44.40). Mº Hôtel-de-Ville.*
Open daily 8am-2am. **Credit** MC, V.
Upstairs has cosy nests of low stools and a food bar; downstairs has state-of-the-art sunbeds. Morning tanning comes with a free breakfast .

Gay restaurants

L'Amazonial
*3 rue Ste-Opportune, 1st (01.42.33.53.13).
Mº Châtelet.* **Open** Mon-Fri noon-3pm, 7pm-1am; Sat, Sun noon-5pm, 7pm-1am.
Average €26 **Prix fixe** €14, €25 (dinner only). **Lunch menu** €11, €15 (Mon-Fri). **Credit** AmEx, DC, MC, V.
Wheelchair access.
Paris' largest gay restaurant has expanded its terrace with a lot of fake stone and tack. Decent French cuisine and tight T-shirted waiters.

Au Rendezvous des Camionneurs
*72 quai des Orfèvres, 1st (01.43.54.88.74).
Mº Pont-Neuf.* **Open** Mon-Sat noon-11pm, Sun noon-5pm. **Average** €28.
Prix fixe €21.50. **Lunch menu** €15.
Credit AmEx, MC, V.
Classic French food and a charming location equals consistent success.

Aux Trois Petits Cochons
*31 rue Tiquetonne, 2nd (01.42.33.39.69/www.auxtroispetitscochons.com).
Mº Etienne-Marcel.* **Open** daily 8.30pm-1am.
Closed Aug, one week in Mar. **Average** €27 **Prix fixe** €23, €27. **Credit** AmEx, MC, V. **Wheelchair access**.
Three Little Pigs eschews the gimmickry of international boystown cuisine in favour of a tasty, daily-changing menu.

The Open Bar Coffee Shop
*23 rue du Temple, 4th (01.42.77.04.88).
Mº Hôtel-de-Ville.* **Open** daily noon-midnight. **Average** €13. **Credit** MC, V.
The management of the Open Café has taken over this spot and sensibly not departed much from its previous formula. It's a convivial place with mostly gay dinners and a reasonably priced, largely French menu .

L'Eclèche et Cie
*10 rue St-Merri, 4th (01.42.74.62.62).
Mº Hôtel-de-Ville.* **Open** daily 9am-1am.
Average €20. **Prix fixe** €16 (dinner).
Lunch menu €10. **Credit** AmEx, MC, V.
Popular gay restaurant offers bistro fare such as *gigot d'agneau* and steak tartare. Relaxed by day; a great hubbub prevails by mid-evening.

Gay clubs & discos

Check press and flyers for one-nighters. Not much gets going before 1am and admission prices often include one drink.

Club 18
*18 rue de Beaujolais, 1st (01.42.97.52.13).
Mº Palais Royal.* **Open** Thur-Sat 11pm-dawn; Sun 5pm-dawn. **Admission** Thur, Sun free; Fri, Sat €11. **Credit** AmEx, MC, V.
Time travel for real in this soopa-doopa camp club. Friendly, but the music isn't adventurous.

L'Insolite
*33 rue des Petits-Champs, 2nd
(01.40.20.98.59). Mº Pyramides.* **Open** daily 11pm-5am. **Admission** Mon-Thur, Sun free; Fri, Sat €8. **Credit** MC, V.
Bright and brassy with a 90s disco glitter ball, you can rely on this club blasting out floor-filling dance hits. No-nonsense and friendly.

Le Dépôt
10 rue aux Ours, 3rd (01.44.54.96.96/www.ledepot.com). Mº Rambuteau. **Open** daily 2pm-8am. **Admission** Mon-Thur €6-€7.50; Fri-Sun €7.50-€10 **Credit** MC, V.
The decor is blockhouse chic with jungle netting and exposed air ducts. Ladies Room every Wednesday; Gay Tea Dance on Sundays (2-11pm, €7.50-€10).

Le Tango
13 rue au Maire, 3rd (01.42.72.17.78/www.boite-a-frissons.fr). Mº Arts et Métiers.
Open Thur 8pm-2am;, Fri, Sat 10.30pm-5am; Sun 5-10pm. **Admission** Fri-Sat €6.50; Sun €5, **No credit cards**.
Le Tango returns to its dancehall roots for dancing *à deux*. Clientele is mixed.

Le Queen ★
*102 av des Champs-Elysées, 8th
(01.53.89.08.90/www.queen.fr).
Mº George V.* **Open** daily midnight-dawn.
Admission Mon-Thur, Sun €9; Fri, Sat and eve of holidays €18.
Credit AmEx, DC, MC, V (at the bar).
Still the pick of the crop, even if going to Le Queen takes courage – the door staff are rude and ruthless, especially with women. Top DJs, extravagant (un)dress, drag queens and go-gos galore. House music and hedonism, or don your gaudiest shirt for Monday's Disco Inferno.

Scorp
*25 bd Poissonnière, 9th (01.40.26.28.30).
Mº Grands Boulevards.* **Open** Wed-Sun midnight-7am. **Admission** Wed, Thur, Sun €9; Fri, Sat €12. **Credit** AmEx, MC, V.
Shortened in name and sharpened in style, the former Scorpion proves that long relationships are possible in *gai* Paris. House and dance hits.

Lesbian restaurant

Restaurant Le Sofa
21 rue St Sabin, 11th (01.43.14.07.46/www.lesofa.com). Mº Bréguet-Sabin.
Open Tue, Wed 6pm-midnight; Thur-Sat 6pm-2am; Sun 12.30-3.30pm. **Average** €27.
Prix fixe (Sun brunch) €15. **Credit** MC, V.
Expect a warm welcome at this laid-back spot. Menu items are beautifully presented by the photographer/chef, and complemented by a simple, well-selected wine list. Desserts are a highlight, including crème brulée flavored with orange flower and a decadent *moelleux au chocolat*. Reserve on weekends.

Lesbian bars

L'Alcântara
*30 rue de Roi-de-Sicile, 4th (01.42.74.45.00).
Mº St-Paul.* **Open** daily 6pm-2am.
Credit MC, V.
The newest women's bar in the Marais. From the outside, it doesn't look like much but inside, the lounge is sleek and stylish. There is a basement dance floor.

Unity Bar
*176/178 rue St. Martin, 3rd
(01.42.72.70.59).* Mº Rambuteau.
Open daily 4pm-2am. **No credit cards**.
Ex-New Yorker Jean and her Parisian lover Corinne own this bright, spacious gathering spot, where you're more likely to see gals in jeans and sweatshirts than in pretty much any other women's bar in Paris.

Lesbian clubs

Pulp ★
25 bd Poissonnière, 2nd. Mº Bonne Nouvelle (01.40.26.01.93). **Open** Thur-Sat 11pm-dawn. **Admission** Thur free; Fri-Sat €7.50 with drink. **Credit** AmEx, MC, V.
Pulp is women-only Saturday and lesbian-centric other nights. Thursday nights are the most mixed in terms of gender and sexual preference. The club regularly draws top DJs. The crowd is young, fashionable and frisky.

Le Rive Gauche
*1 rue du Sabot, 6th (01.42.22.51.70).
Mº St-Germain-des-Prés.* **Open** Fri-Sat 11pm-dawn. **Admission** €14 with drink.
Credit MC, V.
The women-only Rive Gauche attracts a mixed, in terms of ages and styles, crowd. It has a fun, party atmosphere as long as you don't sit at one of the tables marked 'reserved'. Those who do will be selectively requested to relocate as the 'A' list regulars arrive.

Clubs

Leave the trainers behind as you rock the boat, sway to Latin rhythms or just chill out.

Most Paris clubs rely on resident DJs who play anything from chart music to French pop oldies. Thankfully, a handful of clubs do experiment with new trends (**Batofar, Rex Club, Le Gibus**). Credit cards are usually accepted at the bar but not at the door. Fashionable restaurants, such as **Korova** and **Man Ray** (see p51, **Trendy**), also increasingly hold DJ nights.

Cool clubs

Rex Club
5 bd Poissonnière, 2nd (01.42.36.28.83). M° Bonne-Nouvelle. **Open** Wed-Sat 11pm-dawn. **Admission** Wed €10; Thur-Fri €11; Sat €12. **Drinks** €5-€8. **Credit** AmEx, MC, V.
The Rex prides itself on booking quality, up-to-date DJs. Entry is refused only when the club is too full, so arrive early when big name guests play. Friday's Automatik is one of Paris' few authentic techno nights. The bar is the unofficial hang out for DJs.

Les Bains
7 rue du Bourg-l'Abbé, 3rd (01.48.87.01.80). M° Etienne-Marcel. **Open** daily 11.30pm-5am. Restaurant 8.30pm-1am. **Admission** €20. **Drinks** €14. **Credit** AmEx, DC, MC, V. **Wheelchair access**.
The concentration of beautiful people here is quite an eye opener, and the door policy is draconian. Unfortunately, the music policy has become a bit dated: house and garage. Look for hip hop stars at 'Be-Fly' (Wed). Booking a table at the restaurant should ensure you get in.

Le Queen
102 av des Champs-Elysées, 8th (01.53.89.08.90). M° George V. **Open** daily midnight-dawn. **Admission** Sun-Thur €9 with drink; Fri-Sat €18 with drink. **Drinks** from €9. **Credit** AmEx, DC, MC, V.
This is the nearest Paris gets to London's super clubs, with its own merchandising and magazine. Wednesday night's Break is open to all, Saturday is especially gay and Friday is the night to look out for big names. Mondays, Sundays and Thursdays rely on kitsch disco to bring in the crowds.

Bus Palladium
6 rue Fontaine, 9th (01.53.21.07.33). M° Pigalle. **Open** Tue-Thur 11.30pm-dawn; Fri, Sat 7pm-dawn. **Admission** Tue €16, women free; Wed €8; Thur-Sat €16. **Drinks** €8-€13. **Credit** AmEx, MC, V.
New management at this venerable bourgeois haunt has adopted a house music policy. Wednesday night is run by the Respect team, recalling the glory days of French Touch.

Nouveau Casino
109 rue Oberkampf, 11th (01.43.57.57.40). M° Parmentier or St-Maur. **Open** daily 9pm-2am, sometimes till 5am. **Admission** €8-€14. **Drinks** €3.50-€7. **Credit** AmEx, MC, V.
This newcomer has started to make its mark. Offering an alternative to the Batofar, it has an eclectic music policy of live music and DJs. The decor is a little cold and the early closing is maybe a tad restrictive, but this is a space to watch out for.

Batofar ★
in front of 11 quai François-Mauriac, 13th (01.40.33.37.17/www.batofar.org). M° Bibliothèque or Quai de la Gare. **Open** Tue-Thur 9pm-3am; Fri, Sat 9pm-4am; two Sun per month 5am-noon. **Admission** €6.50-€9.50. **Drinks** €3-€8. **Credit** MC, V.
This boat has become the most interesting night-time venue in town. Alternative and often electronic music concerts are followed by quality DJs. Paris' fashion brigade turns up for the Sunday morning afters and on summer Sunday afternoons for a musical tanning session.

Le Divan du Monde
75 rue des Martyrs, 18th (01.44.92.77.66). M° Pigalle. **Open** concerts daily 7.30-10.30pm, club Thur-Sat 11.30pm-dawn. **Admission** €10-€15. **Drinks** €4-€8. **Credit** MC, V. **Wheelchair access**.
Le Divan sees an eclectic mix of alternative club nights at weekends. There are regular jungle, raï, ragga, R&B, Brazilian and trance events. There is no strict dress code.

Elysée Montmartre
72 bd Rochechouart, 18th (01.44.92.45.38). M° Anvers. **Open** varies. Closed Aug. **Admission** €13-€24. **Drinks** €2.50-€10. Credit MC, V. **Wheelchair access**.
This fine concert venue has a sprung dancefloor and a quality sound system. Regular nights include Scream, Club Europa and Panik. Every second and fourth Saturday in the month is the popular Le Bal.

Gilded youth

Club Castel
15 rue Princesse, 6th (01.40.51.52.80). M° Mabillon. **Open** Tue-Sat 9pm-dawn. **Admission** free (members and guests only). **Drinks** €16. **Credit** AmEx, DC, MC, V.
The nearest Paris gets to St-Tropez. The strict door policy – members and friends only – ensures an elite clientele. Pretend you've just arrived from Cannes.

Duplex
2bis av Foch, 16th (01.45.00.45.00). M° Charles de Gaulle-Etoile. **Open** Tue-Sun 11pm-dawn. **Admission** Tue-Thur, Sun €15 (girls free before midnight); Fri, Sat €19-€24 with drink. **Drinks** €11. **Credit** AmEx, MC, V. **Wheelchair access**.
The Duplex caters for young wannabes and privileged youths. Regulars look as though they have raided a parent's wardrobe. A sultry restaurant upstairs (8.30pm-1am) is transformed into a chill-out room later on.

Le Monkey Club
67 rue Pierre-Charron, 8th (01.58.56.20.50). M° George V. **Open** Mon-Sat 11.30pm-dawn. **Admission** Mon-Wed free; Thur-Sat €16. **Drinks** €15. **Credit** AmEx, DC, MC, V. **Wheelchair access**.
Resident DJ Marco plays house and disco on Wednesdays, house/funk/groove on Thursdays and house on Fridays. Weekends are more mainstream. A restaurant takes up one floor.

Latino, jazz & world

Caveau de la Huchette
5 rue de la Huchette, 5th (01.43.26.65.05). M° St-Michel. **Open** Mon-Thur, Sun 9.30pm-2.30am; Fri, Sat 9.30pm-3.30am. **Admission** Mon-Thur, Sun €9.50; €9 students; Fri, Sat €13. **Drinks** from €4.60. **Credit** MC, V.
This is enduringly popular with ageing divorcées and wannabe Stones during the week. At weekends it attracts a mixed bunch who boogie to soulful jazz or enjoy live rock 'n' roll or jazz.

Le Balajo
9 rue de Lappe, 11th (01.47.00.07.87). M° Bastille. **Open** Tue-Thur 10.30pm-4.30am; Fri, Sat 11.30pm-5am; Sun 3-7pm, 9pm-1am (tango). **Admission** Tue-Thur €16 with drink; Fri, Sat €17 with drink; Sun afternoon and evening €8 and €9. **Drinks** €8. **Credit** MC, V.
Bal-à-Jo (Jo's ball) has been going for more than 60 years. Wednesday's boogie and swing session attracts some colourful customers and the tango crowd is surprisingly young.

L'Atlantis
32 quai d'Austerlitz, 13th (01.44.23.24.00/www.atlantis-club.com). M° Quai de la Gare. **Open** Fri-Sun, public holidays 11pm-dawn. **Admission** Fri €17; Sat €19. **Drinks** €11. **Credit** MC, V. **Wheelchair access**.
A very popular French Caribbean club. Women wear painted-on dresses and men wear suits; the dancing is always close contact.

Les Etoiles ★
61 rue du Château d'Eau, 10th (01.47.70.60.56). M° Château d'Eau. **Open** Thur 9pm-3.30am; Fri-Sat 9pm-4.30am. Closed Aug. **Admission** €19 with meal; €10 with drink from 11pm. **Drinks** €3-€6. No credit cards.
Top-notch musicians electrify a soulful crowd here. There is not much space, but that doesn't slow down the night-owl crowd. Women are unlikely to be left standing still for more than a minute, and veterans dish out footwork advice.

La Java
105 rue du Fbg-du-Temple, 10th (01.42.02.20.52). M° Belleville. **Open** Thur-Sat 11pm-6am; Sun 2-7pm. **Admission** Thur €10; Fri, Sat €16; Sun €5 with drink. **Drinks** €5.50-€8. **Credit** AmEx, DC, MC, V. **Wheelchair access**.
Hidden away in a disused Belleville market, La Java is a Mecca for the salsa-loving community. DJs and live bands play anything tropical and Latino to a fun-loving crowd. A new Thursday soirée is venturing into house.

Bar clubs

Cithéa
112 rue Oberkampf, 11th (01.40.21.70.95/www.cithea.com). M° Parmentier. **Open** daily 10pm-5.30am. **Admission** Mon, Tue, Sun free; Wed, Thur €5; Fri, Sat €10. **Drinks** €6-€10. **Credit** MC, V. **Wheelchair access**.
The Cithéa has become a prime concert venue for world music and jazz. At weekends, however, disco and funk nights pull everyone in at closing time – the result is a sweaty nightmare.

Popin
105 rue Amelot, 11th (01.48.05.56.11). M° St-Sébastien-Froissart. **Open** Tue-Sun 6.30pm-1.30am. **Admission** free. **Drinks** €1.50-€6. **Credit** AmEx, MC, V.
Predominantly French, with more than a smattering of students, Popin also attracts savvy young internationals looking for a pint (€5.50 for Kilkenny or Guinness). On weekends the tiny downstairs dance floor heaves.

Wax
15 rue Daval, 11th (01.40.21.16.16). M° Bastille. **Open** Mon-Sat 8pm-2am. **Admission** free. **Drinks** €3.50-€9. **Credit** AmEx, DC, MC, V. **Wheelchair access**.
Wax is worth going to just for the orange swirly paintwork and plastic tables, but you have to spend to be allowed near the white leather sofas. The music is essentially house.

The glittering scene at Le Queen

BRÛLERIE DES GOBELINS

Our coffee is roasted daily on the premises. Choose coffee from 14 different pure origins or one of our wide range of delicious blends.

We aslo have a rotating selection of quality fresh teas. Many authentic jams from the Savoie and natural honeys as well as delicious treats to accompany your coffee.

2 avenue des Gobelins, 5th. M° Censier-Daubenton
Tel: 01.43.31.90.13 • Fax: 01.45.35.83.00

La Maison du Miel
founded in 1898

40 flavours of honey from different regions and plants, and a wide range of honey-related and hive produce on offer.

Taste before you buy...

Open Mon-Sat, from 9am-7pm.
24 RUE VIGNON, 9TH.
M° MADELEINE, HAVRE-CAUMARTIN, AUBER.
TEL,FAX: 01.47.42.26.70

THE REAL McCOY
U·S·FOOD

The American grocery store

Open 7 days a week

From 10 am to 8pm

Hundreds of US grocery items • Special events year round
Over-stuffed sandwiches and home-baked goods
Bilingual service with a smile

You can find it at The Real Mc Coy

194 rue de Grenelle, 7th. M° Ecole Militaire
Tel/Fax: 01.45.56.98.82

Shops & Markets

Velvety foie gras and snow-white goat's cheese still define the Parisian way of life.

Every Parisian neighbourhood has its market and speciality shops where the faithful wait patiently in slow-moving queues for rustic corn-fed chicken, farmhouse camembert or briny oysters fresh from Brittany. Supermarkets and suburban *hypermarchés* are indeed a force to be reckoned with but the latest food scares have produced a renewed attention to quality and a willingness to pay a little extra. Where else but in France can you buy a chicken identifying not only its region and diet but also its name, 'Henri'?

Bakeries

Au Levain du Marais ★
32 rue de Turenne, 3rd (01.42.78.07.31). Mº St-Paul. **Open** Mon-Sat 7am-8pm. Closed Aug. **No credit cards.**
Thierry Rabineau took over this gorgeous but formerly uninspired bakery in 1994 and made it the talk of the town with his organic baguettes and hefty country *miches*.
Branches: 142 av Parmentier, 11th (01.43.57.36.91); 28 bd Beaumarchais, 11th (01.48.05.17.14).

Au Noisetier
33 rue Rambuteau, 4th (01.48.87.68.12). Mº Rambuteau. **Open** Mon, Tue, Fri-Sun 8am-7.45pm. Closed July or Aug. **No credit cards.**
Jean-Pierre Malzis has seen the neighbourhood change in his 28 years here, but his speciality, the noisetier, remains the same: twisty or round, with a crunchy crust and nutty-coloured, naturally leavened crumb.

Maison Kayser
8, 14 rue Monge, 5th (01.44.07.01.42/31.61). Mº Cardinal Lemoine. **Open** Nº 8 Mon, Wed-Sun 7.30am-8pm; Nº 14 Tue-Sun 8am-8pm. **Credit** AmEx, MC, V.
In a few years this bakery has established itself as one of the best in town: it provides bread for Alain Ducasse's Spoon restaurant and the range of intensely flavoured and wonderfully textured breads is impressive. The moist baguette au froment is particularly delicious.
Branches: 79 rue du Commerce, 15th (01.44.19.88.54); 87 rue d'Alsace, 6th (01.43.54.92.31).

Poilâne
8 rue du Cherche-Midi, 6th (01.45.48.42.59/www.poilane.com). Mº Sèvres-Babylone or St-Sulpice. **Open** Mon-Sat 7.15am-8.15pm. **No credit cards.**
You can now buy the dark-crusted, chewy-centred Poilâne loaf in many supermarkets but if you want it fresh out of the oven this tiny, old-fashioned bakery is the place to go. The buttery apple tarts almost better the bread.
Branch: 49 bd de Grenelle, 15th (01.45.79.11.49).

Jean-Luc Poujauran ★
20 rue Jean-Nicot, 7th (01.47.05.80.88). Mº Invalides or Latour-Maubourg. **Open** Tue-Sat 8am-8.30pm. Closed Aug. **No credit cards.**
This little pink shop bursts with breads studded with nuts, apricots, figs, anchovies, raisins or olives. The baguette recipe changes with the seasons for perfect crunch every time.

René-Gérard St-Ouen
111 bd Haussmann, 8th (01.42.65.06.25). Mº Miromesnil. **Open** Mon-Sat 7.30am-7.30pm. Closed Aug. **No credit cards.**
Celebrated for his edible 'bread sculptures' shaped like cats, horses, bicycles and the Eiffel Tower, this baker also does more conventional breads, including highly prized baguettes.

L'Autre Boulange
43, rue de Montreuil, 11th (01.43.72.86.04). Mº Nation or Faidherbe-Chaligny. **Open** Mon-Fri 7.30am-1.30pm, 4-7.30pm; Sat 7.30am-12.30pm. Closed Aug. **No credit cards.**
Michel Cousin bakes 23 kinds of organic bread in his wood-fired oven including the *flutiot* (rye bread with raisins, walnuts and hazelnuts), the *sarment de Bourgogne* (sourdough and a little rye) and a spiced cornmeal bread ideal for foie gras. Great croissants and *chaussons*, too.

Max Poilâne
87 rue Brancion, 15th (01.48.28.45.90/www.max-poilane.fr). Mº Porte de Vanves. **Open** Mon-Sat 7.30am-8pm, Sun 10am-7pm. **No credit cards.**
Using the Poilâne family recipe, the lesser-known Max produces bread that rivals that of his more famous brother Lionel.
Branches: 29 rue de l'Ouest, 14th (01.43.27.29.91); 42 pl du Marché-St-Honoré, 1st (01.42.61.10.53).

Le Moulin de la Vierge
166 av de Suffren, 15th (01.47.83.45.55). Mº Sèvres-Lecourbe. **Open** Mon-Sat 7am-8pm. **No credit cards.**
Basile Kamir learned breadmaking after falling in love with an abandoned bakery. His naturally leavened country loaf is thick-crusted, dense and fragrant.
Branches include: 82 rue Daguerre, 14th (01.43.22.50.55); 105 rue Vercingétorix, 14th (01.45.43.09.84); 77 rue Cambronne, 15th (01.44.49.05.05).

Pâtisseries

Gérard Mulot ★
76 rue de Seine, 6th (01.43.26.85.77). Mº Odéon. **Open** Mon, Tue, Thur-Sun 6.45am-8pm. Closed Aug. **No credit cards.**
Picture-perfect cakes – bitter chocolate tart and the *mabillon*, caramel mousse with apricot marmalade – attract the local celebrities.

Maison Rollet Pradier
6 rue de Bourgogne, 7th (01.45.51.78.36). Mº Assemblée Nationale. **Open** Mon-Sat 8am-8pm, Sun 8am-7pm. Closed three weeks in Aug. **Credit** AmEx, DC, MC, V.
Enjoy sumptious gâteaux laden with chocolate curls or hazelnuts, or bread specialities *flûte rollet* and *boule de levain*. Upstairs, there is a sandwich counter and tea room.

Dalloyau
101 rue du Fbg-St-Honoré, 8th (01.42.99.90.00). Mº St-Philippe du Roule. **Open** daily 8am-9pm. **Credit** DC, MC, V.
This temple to pastry, opened in 1802, has gone modern with a three-level space including a vast boutique, plush tea room and snack bar.
Branches: 2 pl Edmond-Rostand, 6th (01.43.29.31.10); 63 rue de Grenelle, 7th (01.45.49.95.30); 69 rue de la Convention, 15th (01.45.77.84.27); 5 bd Beaumarchais, 4th (01.48.87.89.88).

Démoulin
6 bd Voltaire, 11th (01.47.00.58.20/www.chocolat-paris.com). Mº République. **Open** Tue-Sat 8.30am-7.30pm; Sun 8am-1.30pm, 3-7pm. Closed Aug. **Credit** MC, V.
Chocolate maker and pastry chef Philippe Démoulin's Ali Baba, filled with vanilla custard, rum and raisins, is not to be missed. Nor, his bitter chocolate and meringue Negresco, and chocolate tart with chocolate *sablé* pastry.

Cheese

The sign *maître fromager affineur* denotes master cheese merchants who buy young cheeses from farmers and age them on their premises. *Fromage fermier* and *fromage au lait cru* signify farm-produced and raw (unpasteurised) milk cheeses respectively.

Marie-Anne Cantin ★
12 rue du Champs-de-Mars, 7th (01.45.50.43.94/www.cantin.fr). Mº Ecole-Militaire. **Open** Mon-Sat 8.30am-7.30pm; Sun 9am-1pm. **Credit** MC, V.
Cantin, a vigorous defender of unpasteurised cheese, is justifiably proud of her creamy st-marcellins, aged chèvres and nutty beauforts. The cheeses are ripened in her cellars.

Fil o'Fromage
4 rue Poirier-de-Narçay, 14th (01.40.44.86.75). Mº Porte d'Orléans. **Open** Tue-Fri 9am-1pm, 4-7.45pm; Sat 9am-7.30pm. Closed Aug. **Credit** MC, V.
Husband and wife team Sylvie and Chérif Boubrit offer a top-class selection of authentic farmhouse cheeses such as fresh Corsican brocciu, the house cow's milk creation, figuette, and a rare, naturally fermented gorgonzola.

Laurent Dubois
2 rue de Lourmel, 15th (01.45.78.70.58). Mº Dupleix. **Open** Tue-Fri 9am-1pm, 4-7.45pm; Sat 8.30am-1pm, 3.30-7.45pm; Sun 9am-1pm. Closed Aug. **Credit** MC, V.
Nephew of the famous cheese specialist Alain Dubois, Laurent Dubois is a master in his own right. Especially impressive are his nutty two-year-old comté and crackly vieille mimolette.

Alain Dubois
80 rue de Tocqueville, 17th (01.42.27.11.38). Mº Malesherbes or Villiers. **Open** Tue-Fri 9am-1pm, 4-8pm; Sat 8.30am-8pm; Sun 9am-1pm. Closed first and two weeks in Aug. **Credit** MC, V.
Dubois, who stocks some 70 varieties of goat's cheese plus prized, aged st-marcellin and st-félicien, is the darling of the superchefs. Fortunately, he will ship orders.
Branch: 79 rue de Courcelles, 17th (01.43.80.36.42).

Alléosse
13 rue Poncelet, 17th (01.46.22.50.45). Mº Ternes. **Open** Tue-Fri 9am-1pm, 4-7pm; Sat 9am-1pm, 3.30-7pm; Sun 9am-1pm. **Credit** MC, V.
People cross town for the cheeses – wonderful farmhouse camemberts, delicate st-marcellins, a choice of *chèvres* and several rareties – ripened in the cellars here.

Chocolate

Cacao et Chocolat
29 rue de Buci, 6th (01.46.33.77.63). Mº Mabillon. **Open** Tue-Sat 10.30am-7.30pm. **Credit** AmEx, MC, V.
Opened in 1998, this shop in burnt-orange and ochre recalls chocolate's Aztec origins with

Loafing around at Le Moulin de la Vierge

Time Out Book of **Paris Walks**

23 walks around the French capital

The Time Out Book of **Paris** Short Stories

Edited by Nicholas Royle

23 walks and maps exploring and illuminating the French capital.

16 original, cutting-edge short stories by French, British and American authors.

A breath of French air...

Available from all good booksellers and at www.timeout.com/shop

Time Out
www.timeout.com

www.penguin.com

spicy fillings (honey and chilli, nutmeg, clove and citrus), chocolate masks and pyramids.
Branch: 63 rue St Louis en l'Ile, 4th (01.46.33.33.33).

Christian Constant
37 rue d'Assas, 6th (01.53.63.15.15). Mº St-Placide. **Open** Mon-Fri 8.30am-9pm; Sat, Sun 8am-8.30pm. **Credit** MC, V.
A master chocolate maker and *traiteur*, Constant is revered by *le tout Paris*. Trained in *pâtisserie* and chocolate, he scours the globe for new ideas. *Ganaches* are subtly flavoured with verbena, jasmine or cardamom.

Jean-Paul Hévin ★
3 rue Vavin, 6th (01.43.54.09.85). Mº Vavin. **Open** daily 10am-7.30pm. Closed 6-27 Aug. **Credit** MC, V.
A stylish window display tempts you to test florentines, and *ganaches* scented with smoked tea, or honey, and bitter chocolate-orange.
Branches: 231 rue St-Honoré, 1st (01.55.35.35.96); 16 av de La Motte-Picquet, 7th (01.45.51.77.48).

Debauve & Gallais
30 rue des Sts-Pères, 7th (01.45.48.54.67). Mº St-Germain-des-Prés. **Open** Mon-Sat 9am-7pm. Closed Aug. **Credit** MC, V.
This former pharmacy, with a facade dating from 1800, once sold chocolate for medicinal purposes. Its intense tea, honey or praline-flavoured chocolates do, indeed, heal the soul.
Branches: 33 rue Vivienne, 2nd (01.40.39.05.50); 107 rue Jouffroy d'Abbans, 17th (01.47.63.15.15).

Richart
258 bd St-Germain, 7th (01.45.55.66.00/ www.richart.com). Mº Solférino. **Open** Mon-Sat 10am-7pm. Closed one week in Aug. **Credit** MC, V.
Each chocolate *ganache* has an intricate design, packages look like jewel boxes and each purchase comes with a tract on how best to savour chocolate.

A la Petite Fabrique
12 rue St-Sabin, 11th (01.48.05.82.02). Mº Bastille. **Open** Tue-Sat 10.30am-7.30pm. Closed two weeks in Aug. **Credit** MC, V.
Colourfully-wrapped chocolate flavoured with orange, hazelnuts or almonds from this little 'laboratory' makes a perfect gift.

La Maison du Chocolat
89 av Raymond-Poincaré, 16th (01.40.67.77.83/www.lamaisonduchocolat. com). Mº Victor-Hugo. **Open** Mon-Sat 10am-7pm. **Credit** AmEx, MC, V.
Robert Linxe opened his first Paris shop in 1977 and has been inventing new chocolates ever since. Using Asian spices, fresh fruits and herbal infusions he has won over the most demanding chocolate-lovers.
Branches: 19 rue de Sèvres, 6th (01.45.44.20.40); 225 rue du Fbg-St-Honoré, 8th (01.42.27.39.44); 52 rue François 1er, 8th (01.47.23.38.25); 8 bd de la Madeleine, 9th (01.47.42.86.52).

L'Artisan Chocolatier
102 rue de Belleville, 20th (01.46.36.67.60). Mº Pyrénées. **Open** Tue-Sat 5.30am-1pm, 2.30pm-7.30pm; Sun 9.30am-1pm. Closed Aug. **Credit** MC, V.
Stuffed with handmade chocolates, old-style sweets, teas and toys, this shop is a childish delight. Dark *ganache* fillings come in adult flavours, though, such as Poire Williams, ginger and juniper berry.

Treats & traiteurs

Comptoir de la Gastronomie
34 rue Montmartre, 1st (01.42.33.31.32). Mº Etienne-Marcel. **Open** Tue-Sat 6am-1pm, 2.30-7pm. **Credit** AmEx, MC, V.
This old-fashioned grocery is laden with foie gras from south-west France, along with other regional specialities such as snails, whole hams, *confit de canard*, truffles and dried mushrooms.

L'Epicerie
51 rue St-Louis-en-l'Ile, 4th (01.43.25.20.14). Mº Pont-Marie. **Open** daily 10.30am-8pm. **Credit** MC, V.

Izraël: a pleasure trove

A perfect gift shop crammed with pretty bottles of blackcurrant vinegar, five-spice mustard, orange sauce, tiny pots of jam, honey with figs and boxes of chocolate snails.

Huilerie Artisanale Leblanc ★
6 rue Jacob, 6th (01.46.34.61.55). Mº St-Germain-des-Prés. **Open** Mon 2.30-7.30pm; Tue-Sat 11am-7.30pm. Closed three weeks in Aug. **No credit cards.**
The Leblanc family started out making walnut oil from its family tree in Burgundy and selling to its neighbours before branching out to press pure oils from hazelnuts, almonds, pine nuts, grilled peanuts, pistachios and olives.

Oliviers & Co
28 rue de Buci, 6th (01.44.07.15.43/ www.oliviers-co.com). Mº St-Germain-des-Prés. **Open** daily 10.30am-7pm. **Credit** AmEx, MC, V.
Oliviers & Co has quickly established itself as the leading purveyor of Mediterranean olive oil in Paris. Each oil is tested daily to be sure it is at its peak. The rue de Lévis and Mouffetard branches serve food.
Branches include: 34-36 rue Montorgueil, 2nd (01.42.33.89.95); 47 rue Vieille-du-Temple, 4th (01.42.74.38.40); 128 rue Mouffetard, 5th (01.55.43.83.42); 8 rue de Lévis, 17th (01.53.42.18.04).

Fauchon
26-30 pl de la Madeleine, 8th (01.47.42.60.11). Mº Madeleine. **Open** Mon-Sat 9.30am-7pm. **Credit** AmEx, DC, MC, V.
Paris' most famous food store is like every specialist deli rolled into one with windows as much for tourists as buyers. There's a museum-like prepared-food section, cheese, fish and exotic fruit counters, an Italian deli, wines in the cave, chocolates and a plush tea room.

Hédiard
21 pl de la Madeleine, 8th (01.43.12.88.88/ www.hediard.fr). Mº Madeleine. **Open** shop Mon-Sat 9.30am-10pm; *traiteur* Mon-Sat 9am-10pm. **Credit** AmEx, DC, MC, V.
The first shop to bring exotic foods to Parisians, Hédiard specialises in rare teas and coffees, unusual spices, imported produce, jams and candied fruits. The original shop, dating from 1880, has a posh tea room upstairs.
Branches include: 126 rue du Bac, 7th (01.45.44.01.98); 70 av Paul-Doumer, 16th (01.45.04.51.92); 106 bd des Courcelles, 17th (01.47.63.32.14).

La Maison de la Truffe
19 pl de la Madeleine, 8th (01.42.65.53.22/ www.maison-de-la-truffe.com). Mº Madeleine. **Open** Mon 9am-8pm; Tue-Sat 9am-9pm. **Credit** AmEx, DC, MC, V.
Come here for truffles worth more than gold – Piedmontese white truffles from Alba cost a cool €4573 a kilo – or for more affordable truffle oils, sauces and vinegars.

Les Cakes de Bertrand
7 rue Bourdaloue, 9th (01.40.16.16.28). Mº Notre Dame de Lorette. **Open** Tue-Sun 9am-7pm. Closed Aug. **Credit** MC, V.
Bertrand's tiny tea room at 21 rue St-Lazare has been re-invented as La Cantine de Bertrand, while the tea room and *traiteur* has moved to rue Bourdaloue. Hand-picked treasures include exceptional teas (Japanese *sencha* and Russian *baikal*), *marmielade* (marmelade made with honey), poppy and violet sweets and freshly made cakes, crumbles and soups.

Poissonerie du Dôme
4 rue Delambre, 14th (01.43.35.23.95). **Open** Tue-Sat 8am-1pm, 4-7pm; Sun 8am-1pm. **Credit** MC, V.
Jean-Pierre Lopez' tiny shop is probably the best fishmonger in Paris, for all his fish are individually selected, many coming straight from small boats off the Breton coast. Each and every one is bright of eye and sound of gill. Try the drool-inducing (but bank-breaking) turbot, the giant crabs or the scallops when in season.

Lenôtre
61 rue Lecourbe, 15th (01.42.73.20.97/ www.lenotre.com). Mº Sèvres-Lecourbe. **Open** daily 9am-9pm. Closed two weeks in Aug. **Credit** AmEx, DC, MC, V.
The Lenôtre shops are known for their prepared dishes, cakes and catering service but don't miss their intensely flavoured chocolate truffles and Roland Durant's unusual jams.
Branches include: 15 bd de Courcelles, 8th (01.45.63.87.63); 48 av Victor-Hugo, 16th (01.45.02.21.21); 121 av de Wagram, 17th (01.47.63.70.30).

La Maison de l'Escargot
79 rue Fondary, 15th (01.45.75.31.09). Mº Emile-Zola. **Open** Tue-Sat 9.30am-7.30pm; Sun 10am-1pm. Closed 14 July-31 Aug. **Credit** MC, V.
Two women sit stuffing garlic butter into *petits gris* and Burgundy snails, which you can taste on the premises or take away to heat up at home. Traditional duck foie gras direct from the south-west is also on sale.

Boucherie Lamartine Prosper et Cie
172 av Victor Hugo, 16th (01 47.27.82.29). Mº Victor Hugo. **Open** Tues-Sat 6am-1pm, 3.30-7.30pm. Closed Aug. **Credit** V
Jean-Christophe Prosper is a prince when it comes to meat; he supplies the Elysées Palace. His top quality lamb and beef, sourced from the very best suppliers, is always in heavy demand in the sophisticated 16th as is his expertise and willingness to prepare cuts of meat exactly the way the customer wants.

Regional specialities

La Cigogne
61 rue de l'Arcade, 8th (01.43.87.39.16). Mº St-Lazare. **Open** Mon-Fri 8.30am-7pm. Closed Aug. **Credit** MC, V.
Hearty Alsatian fare at La Cigogne includes scrumptious tarts, strüdel, *beravecka* fruit bread plus sausages laced with pistachios.

Charcuterie Lyonnaise
58 rue des Martyrs, 9th (01.48.78.96.45). Mº Notre-Dame de Lorette. **Open** Tue-Sat 8.30am-1.30pm, 4-7.30pm; Sun 9am-12.30pm. Closed 15 July-15 Aug. **Credit** MC, V.
Jean-Jacques Chrétienne prepares Lyonnais delicacies *quenelles de brochet*, *jambon persillé* and *hure* (pistachio-seasoned tongue).

Henri Ceccaldi
21 rue des Mathurins, 9th (01.47.42.66.52). Mº Havre-Caumartin/RER Auber. **Open** Mon-Fri 9am-7.30pm; (Sat 2-6pm Nov-Mar). Closed Aug. **Credit** MC, V.

Jewel-toned gifts at L'Epicerie

Ceccaldi sells freshly imported Corsican specialities: charcuterie, goat's and sheep's cheese, chestnut flour, cakes and wines.

La Campagne
111 bd de Grenelle, 15th (01.47.34.77.05). Mº La Motte-Picquet. **Open** Tue-Sat 8.30am-1pm, 3.30-8pm; Sun 8am-1pm. Closed Aug. **Credit** MC, V.
Bask in all things Basque: Pyrenean sheep's cheese, Bayonne ham, Espelette peppers and Irouléguy wines.

Le Comptoir Corrézien ★
8 rue des Volontaires, 15th (01.47.83.52.97). Mº Volontaires. **Open** Mon-Sat 9.30am-1.30pm, 3.30-8pm. Closed Aug. **Credit** AmEx, MC, V.
For foie gras, fresh and dried mushrooms and a tempting array of duck-based products.

Markets
Market streets open Tue-Sat 8am-1pm and 4-7pm; Sun 8am-1pm. The roving markets set up two or three times a week from 8am-1pm. For locally grown products, look for the sign '*producteur*' – and arrive early for the best selection, late for bulk bargains.

Market streets

Rue Mouffetard
5th. Mº Censier-Daubenton.
Wind your way up from medieval St-Médard to prod peaches, sample the flûte Gana at Steff le Boulanger (No 123) or take a pit stop off at the Bar des Papillons (No 129).

Marché d'Aligre
rue and pl d'Aligre, 12th. Mº Ledru-Rollin. **Open** mornings only.
One of the cheapest markets in Paris offers North African and Caribbean produce, herbs, unusual potatoes and onions and cheap fruit. The covered market next door, although more expensive, is open in the afternoon.

Rue Daguerre
14th. Mº Denfert-Rochereau.
A good local market with products from the Aveyron region, the Vacroux cheese stall and the Daguerre Marée fishmonger.

Rue Poncelet
rue Poncelet and rue Bayen, 17th. Mº Ternes.
Take in the coffee aromas at the Brûlerie des Ternes on this classy street which also boasts cheese shop Alléosse and a German deli.

Roving markets

Marché Biologique ★
bd Raspail, 6th. Mº Sèvres-Babylone. **Open** Sun.
Très chic organic market with produce direct from the farm at far from rustic prices. Other organic markets: boulevard des Batignolles, 17th (Sat) and rue St-Charles, 15th (Tue, Fri).

Saxe-Breteuil
av de Saxe, 7th. Mº Ségur. **Open** Thur, Sat.
Possibly the most scenic of Paris' markets, with the Eiffel Tower poking up between tree-lined rows of impeccable stalls.

Marché Bastille ★
bd Richard-Lenoir, 11th. Mº Bastille. **Open** Thur, Sun.
A big daddy which seems to go on for miles.

Look out for Provençal olives and oils, game, cheese, fish and wild mushrooms.

Cour de Vincennes
12th. Mº Nation. **Open** Wed, Sat.
A classy kilometre-long market reputed for fruit, veg and free-range poultry.

Boulevard Auguste-Blanqui
between pl d'Italie and rue Baurrault, 13th. Mº Place d'Italie or Corvisart. **Open** Tue, Fri, Sun.
A tree-shaded market with loads of veggies, roasting free-range chickens, Alpine cheeses, steaming *choucroute* and ham.

International

Le Mille-Pâtes
5 rue des Petits-Champs, 1st (01.42.96.03.04). Mº Palais-Royal. **Open** Mon 9am-3.15pm; Tue-Thur 9.30am-3.15pm; 4.40-7.30pm; Fri, Sat 9.30am-7.30pm. Closed Aug. **Credit** AmEx, DC, MC, V.
A treasure trove of Italian delicacies: amaretti biscuits, *charcuterie*, white truffles in season, and takeaway panini and hot pastas.

Kioko
46 rue des Petits-Champs, 2nd (01.42.61.33.65). Mº Pyramides. **Open** Tue-Sat 10am-8pm; Sun 11am-7pm. **Credit** MC, V.
Everything you need to make sushi (or good ready-made sushi for the lazy), plus sauces, snacks, sake, Japanese beer, tea and kitchen utensils. Ten per cent off on weekends.

Izraël
30 rue François-Miron, 4th (01.42.72.66.23). Mº Hôtel-de-Ville. **Open** Tue-Fri 9.30am-1pm, 2.30-7pm; Sat 9-7pm. **Closed** Aug. **Credit** MC, V.
Spices and other delights from as far afield as Mexico, Turkey and India – juicy dates, feta cheese, *tapenades* and lots of spirits.

Mexi & Co
10 rue Dante, 5th (01.46.34.14.12). Mº Maubert-Mutualité. **Open** daily noon-midnight. **No credit cards.**
Everything you need for a fiesta, including marinades for *fajitas*, dried chillies, South American beers, *cachaça* and tequilas.

Jabugo Iberico & Co.
11 rue Clément Marot, 8th (01.47.20.03.13). Mº Alma-Marceau, Franklin Roosevelt. **Open** Mon-Sat 10am-8pm. **Credit** AmEx, DC, MC, V.
This shop specialises in Spanish hams with the Bellota-Bellota label, meaning the pigs have feasted on acorns. Manager Philippe Poulachon compares the complexity of his cured hams (at nearly €91.46 a kilo) to truffles.

Sarl Velan Stores
87 passage Brady, 10th (01.42.46.06.06). Mº Château d'Eau. **Open** Mon-Sat 9.30am-8.30pm. **Credit** MC, V.
In an alley of Indian cafés and shops, discover spices and vegetables from Kenya and India.

Saveurs d'Irlande
5 cité du Vauxhall, 10th (01.42.00.36.20). Mº République or Jacques-Bonsergent. **Open** Mon-Fri 10am-7pm; Sat 11am-7pm. Closed Aug. **Credit** MC.
The place for real Irish soda bread, smoked and wild salmon, beers, whiskeys and Celtic CDs.
Branch: Saveurs d'Irlande et d'Ecosse, 139 rue Ordener, 18th (01.42.55.10.31).

Tang Frères
48 av d'Ivry, 13th (01.45.70.80.00). Mº Porte d'Ivry. **Open** Tue-Fri 9am-7.30pm; Sat, Sun 8.30am-7.30pm. **Credit** MC, V.
Chinatown's biggest Asian supermarket is great for flat, wind-dried duck and all sorts of unidentifiable fruit and veg.

Les Délices d'Orient
52 av Emile Zola, 15th (01.45.79.10.00). Mº Charles-Michels. **Open** Tue-Sun 8.30am-9pm. **Credit** MC, V.
Shelves here brim with houmous, stuffed aubergines, *halva*, fava beans, stuffed vine-leaves, Lebanese bread, felafel, olives and all manner of Middle Eastern delicacies.
Branch: 14 rue des Quatre-Frères Peignot, 15th.

Wines, Beers & Spirits
Most *cavistes* happily dispense advice, so ask if you have a specific wine or menu in mind. To buy direct from producers, visit the Salon des Caves Particulières at Espace Champerret in March and December.

Legrand Filles et Fils ★
1 rue de la Banque, 2nd (01.42.60.07.12). Mº Bourse. **Open** Mon, Wed-Fri 9am-7pm; Thur 9am-9pm; Sat 9am-7pm. **Credit** AmEx, MC, V.
This old-fashioned shop offers fine wines, brandies, tasting glasses and gadgets amid chocolates, teas, coffees and bonbons. Wine tastings take place on Thursday evenings.

Ryst Dupeyron
79 rue du Bac, 7th (01.45.48.80.93/ www.dupeyron.com). Mº Rue du Bac. **Open** Mon 12.30-7.30pm; Tue-Sat 10.30am-7.30pm. Closed one week in Aug. **Credit** AmEx, MC, V.
The Dupeyron family has sold Armagnac for four generations. You'll find bottles dating from 1868 (and nearly every year since) in this listed shop; labels can be personalised on the spot. Other treasures include some 200 fine Bordeaux, vintage Port and rare whiskeys.

Les Caves Augé
116 bd Haussmann, 8th (01.45.22.16.97). Mº St-Augustin. **Open** Mon 1-7.30pm; Tue-Sat 9am-7.30pm. Closed Mon in Aug. **Credit** AmEx, MC, V.
The oldest wine shop in Paris – Marcel Proust was a regular customer – is serious and professional, with sommelier Marc Sibard advising.

Les Caves Taillevent
199 rue du Fbg-St-Honoré, 8th (01.45.61.14.09/www.taillevent.com). Mº Charles-de-Gaulle-Etoile or Ternes. **Open** Mon 2-8pm; Tue-Fri 9am-8pm; Sat 9am-7.30pm. Closed first three weeks in Aug. **Credit** AmEx, DC, MC, V.
Half a million bottles make up the Taillevent cellar. Saturday tastings with the three head sommeliers. Wines start from €3.65 a bottle.

La Maison du Whisky
20 rue d'Anjou, 8th (01.42.65.03.16/ www.whisky.fr). Mº Madeleine. **Open** Mon 9.30am-7pm; Tue-Fri 9.15am-8pm; Sat 9.30am-7.30pm. **Credit** AmEx, MC, V.
Jean-Marc Bellier is fascinating as he explains which whisky matches with food or waxes lyrical about different flavours such as honey and tobacco. He also hosts a whisky club.

Bières Spéciales
77 rue St-Maur, 11th (01.48.07.18.71). Mº St-Maur. **Open** Mon 4-9pm; Tue-Sat 10:30am-1pm, 4-9pm. **Credit** AmEx, MC, V.
Single bottles and cans from 16 nations (at last count) neatly cover the walls. Belgium might dominate but you'll also find Polish, Scottish, Corsican, Portuguese and Chinese brews.

Les Domaines qui Montent
136 bd Voltaire, 11th (01.43.56.89.15). Mº Voltaire. **Open** Tue-Sat 10am-8pm. Lunch served noon-2.30pm. **Credit** MC, V.
This is not only a wine shop but a convivial place to have breakfast, lunch or tea. Wines cost the same as they would at the producer's, with no extra charge for drinking them on the premises (with food). Saturday tastings with up-and-coming producers featured in the shop.

Les Ultra-Vins
16 rue Lacuée, 12th (01.43.46.85.81). Mº Bastille. **Open** Mon-Sat 9am-8.15pm. Closed 10-20 Aug. **Credit** MC, V.
With 1800 different wines in its cellars, this is the place to come if you crave a 1921 Yquem or a 1989 Pétrus. Owner Alain Audry specialises in prestigious Bordeaux and Burgundies but he's also realistic enough to offer rather more accessible wines starting at €2.75. Among his favourites: Languedoc-Roussillon, 1998.

Look, but don't touch at Rue Mouffetard

Home Delivery

From Champagne breakfast in bed to a soothing couscous or curry, Paris delivers.

Until recently, the only option for at-home Parisian eating was *traiteur* take-aways. However, a wide range of delivery food is now on offer, from Russian caviar to couscous. There are a few limitations, though; few of the firms accept credit cards, and most won't deliver after 11pm. Try to have exact change ready, as delivery people usually carry less than €15 cash. A €2-€5 tip is polite.

Asian

Le Lotus Bleu
17 rue de la Pierre-Levée, 11th (01.43.55.57.75/fax 01.43.14.02.72/ www.lotus-bleu.fr). **Open** Mon-Fri 11.30am-2.30pm, 6.30-10.30pm; Sat, Sun 6.30-10.30pm. Closed Aug. **Minimum order** €12. **Delivery time** 30 mins. **No delivery charge. Area** 3rd, 10th, 11th (also 4th, 12th, 19th and 20th, but with a higher minimum order). **No credit cards.**
With generous *menus*, Le Lotus Bleu offers a quick and easy way to satisfy a Chinese food craving. Our marinated beef with black mushrooms was tender with a delicate sauce. The *nems*, under a pile of fresh mint, were fresh if tepid on arrival. A small selection of Thai dishes is also available; if you like it hot, be sure to let them know, as even the spicy beef was quite tame. Not the best Chinese cuisine has to offer, but still head and shoulders above the reheat masters that reign at the many street *traiteurs*. Online ordering now available.
Branches: 26 rue Lakanal, 15th (01.45.32.24.20) – area 15th; 66 rue Anatole France, Levallois (01.47.58.05.55) – area Levallois, 17th, Neuilly; 108 rue du Vieux Pont de Sèvres, Boulogne (01.58.17.04.04) – area Boulogne

French

Croissant Bon'Heur
83 rue de la Mare, 20th (tel/fax 01.43.58.43.43/www.croissantbonheur.com). **Open** daily 7-11am. Closed first three weeks in Aug. **Minimum order** €15. **Delivery time** 30 mins (best to call night before). **Delivery charge** included. **Area** Paris and suburbs (call for delivery prices to suburbs). **Credit** MC, V (by phone at time of order).
Looking to spoil yourself? The perfect start to any day is surely breakfast in bread; so why not have it brought straight to your door in a wrapped wicker basket by the friendly owner and operator of this essential service. The baskets come loaded with *pains suédois*, croissants, *pains aux raisins* and little glass jars of butter and homemade jams, and can be supplemented with a range of goodies such as fresh orange juice, fruit salad, and Champagne – for those difficult mornings. They will even bring along a morning paper. Orders can be placed online, by calling the evening before, or in the morning.

Indian

Allô Indes
Vijaya, 22 rue Daubenton, 5th (01.47.07.56.78/fax 01.43.36.60.27/ www.allo-indes.com). **Open** daily 7-11pm. **Minimum order** €12. **Delivery time** 1 hour. **Delivery charge** free in 4th-6th, 13th, 14th; €3.05-in 1st-3rd, 7th-12th, 15th-20th. **No credit cards.**
Formerly Allô Curi, Allô Indes is the delivery wing of the Vijay, a charming Indian restaurant with excellent service. We phoned an order through from the pub and it arrived as promised just after we got home, 45 minutes later. A huge bag of onion bhaji was fairly bland but perked up with dollops of hot pickle, while vegetable samosas were very tasty. A chicken tikka masala was fine and an *aaloo-palak* (potatoes and spinach) dish was a good vegetarian option. The lamb madras was heavily spiced with a devilishly hot sauce. Not a gourmet experience, but a good place if you need some comfort food for a lazy night.

Japanese

Sushi Company
22 rue des Pyramides, 1st (01.40.15.04.04/fax 01.42.46.19.36). **Open** Mon-Sat 11am-2.30pm, 6-10.30pm; Sun 6-10.30pm. **Minimum order** €15.24 (in Paris). **Delivery time** 40 mins. **Delivery charge** free-€3.81 in Paris, free-€5.34 in suburbs. **Credit** MC, V.
As well as having a slick but laid-back restaurant, all steel and glass, with high stools and swanky tableware, the Sushi Company provides a delivery service. The sushi and sashimi are of surprisingly good quality: well prepared, fresh and moist, with all the trimmings: thin-sliced pink ginger, *wasabi* and soy sauce. The choice goes well beyond the usual Westerner-friendly tuna and salmon.

Matsuri Sushi
26 rue Leopold Bellan, 2nd (01.40.26.11.13/fax 01.42.33.10.38/ www.matsuri-sushi.com) **Open** daily 11am-3pm, 5.30-11pm. **Minimum order** €20.87. **Delivery time** 45mins. **Delivery charge** €5.34. **Credit** MC, V.
Our pre-selected boxes of sashimi and various maki arrived in a 12°C refrigerated container in precisely the time quoted to us on the phone- to the minute. The salmon sashimi was, like the ginger, delicious while the rice of the *nigiri* sushi was expertly prepared with just the right amount of vinegar. Our only complaints were the slight over-saltiness of the seaweed of the rolled sushi and the exorbitant cost of ordering *à la carte* from their vast menu. Lunch orders are the best value, for food and delivery charges. Sake and Japanese beer are available as well as a sushi-making kit.

Lebanese

Radis Olive
27 rue de Marignan, 8th (01.42.56.55.55/ fax 01.42.56.22.37). **Open** daily noon-3pm, 7-11.30pm. **Minimum order** €23. **Delivery time** 45 mins. **Delivery charge** free in 8th, 15th-17th. Varies elsewhere. **Area** 8th, 15th-17th. Check for others. **No credit cards.**
Getting food delivered from the Radis Olive is a feel-good experience from start to finish. We ordered a *chawarma poulet* (€10.98) and a *plateau mezze* (€13.72) and they were delivered just half an hour later. The delivery man climbed the stairs with a huge bag of delicacies and was still smiling when he reached the fifth floor. The two dishes came in enormous portions, and contained pretty much the same stuff – slivers of chicken, tubs of creamy houmous topped with chickpeas, packs of fluffy pitta bread and Lebanese-style salad. It's essentially a delicious make-your-own-kebab kit, with high-quality, freshly-prepared ingredients. The *plateau mezze* came with two sweet little honey cakes.

North African

Allô Couscous
70 rue Alexandre-Dumas, 11th (01.43.70.82.83). **Open** Mon 6-10pm; Tue-Sun 11am-2pm, 6-10pm. Closed three weeks in Aug. **Minimum order** €21. **Delivery charge** €5 and up. **Delivery time** 60-90 mins. **Area** Paris, suburbs. **No credit cards.**
Pack of wolves to feed on a shoe-string at short notice? Allô Couscous, run by the Halimi family, remains the easiest way to make heaps of hot food appear in your living-room. Be sure to have some large containers ready to receive the chicken, mutton, beef and meatball stews; or request that they be delivered in disposable containers. Our *couscous Royal* – all of the above plus *merguez* – arrived promptly and piping hot. We could not come close to finishing it all, which is a shame (it doesn't keep). If there are four of you, order for three.

Pizza

Pizza Hut
(central phone 08.10.30.30.30/ www.pizzahut.fr). **Open** Mon-Fri noon-2.30pm, 6-11pm. **Minimum order** €10.91. **Delivery time** 30 mins. **No delivery charge. Area** Paris/suburbs. **No credit cards.**
From Manhattan to Moscow, Pizza Hut has seemingly global control over efficiently delivered American-style pizzas. Assorted toppings or create-your-own come with 'classic' thin-crust or doughier pan-crust. They can also bring you guacamole, addictive barbecued chicken wings, ice cream, fizzy drinks, Heineken beer and rosé wine (but only if you order a pizza).

Speed Rabbit Pizza
14 bd de Reuilly, 12th (01.43.44.80.80). **Open** daily 11am-2.30pm, 6-11pm. **Minimum order** €9.50. **Delivery time** 30 mins. **No delivery charge. Area** 12th and Charenton (see below for other branches). **No credit cards.**
Speed Rabbit describes itself as 'the true American pizza' and offers a range of toppings from basic Harlem to the Mega Rabbit or build-your-own. Our *'spicey lover'* (sic) came generously garnished with beef, *merguez*, cheese and tomatoes with a spicy sauce. Extras include mixed salad, onion rings and chicken wings.
Branches include: 47 bd du Montparnasse, 7th (01.45.44.28.81); 37 rue La Fayette, 9th (01.42.81.38.38); 167 av de Versailles, 16th (01.45.20.38.38); 205 rue Ordener, 18th (01.40.25.08.08).

Liquid Luxuries

Allô Apéro
9bis rue Labie, 17th (01.71.71.69.69). **Open** Mon-Thur 7pm-2am; Fri, Sat 7pm-4am; Sun 7pm-midnight. **Minimum order** €20. **Delivery time** 30 mins. **Delivery charge** €3-€9; free with minimum €30 order (7th, 8th, 16th, 17th). **Area** 1st-18th, Neuilly. **Credit** AmEx, MC, V.
Opened early in 1997, this service delivers spirits, plus the fruit juices and mixers necessary for cocktails. Margaritas for four cost €18.14. They can also bring you beer, tortilla chips, Chipsters and pistachios.

Intermagnum
(08.00.80.20.20/fax 01.41.73.55.79/ www.nicolas-wines.com). **Open** Mon-Sat 9am-7pm. **No minimum order. Delivery time** 24-72 hours. **Delivery charge** €9 standard, €14.50 express France; €9-€14 anywhere in Europe. **Credit** AmEx, MC, V.
Say it with a bottle rather than flowers – this offshoot of off-licence chain Nicolas will deliver gift-boxed bottles, with a message, all over France and even the world. The web site includes tasting notes and offers discounts.

Croissant Bon'Heur: say it with pastries

LE PARADIS DU FRUIT
le péché original

BAR A FRUITS

Exotic Ambiance
Candlelight Dinners
Specialties : Salads,
Vegetarian Dishes
& Fruits, lots
of Fruits!

Our large mezzanine
& Shaded tropical terrace
will welcome you, and offer
a wonderful view
of Saint Eustache
& the Jardins
des Halles

You'll even find trivial Pursuit
cards on each table!

Lunch offers :
7.50 € - main course & drink
11.50 € - main course,
drink & desert

Dinner Menus:
15 € - main course,
drink & desert

Formule Prestige:
18 € - aperitif, dish,
drink, desert & coffee

Our Dinner Menu
& Formule Prestige
are offered all week,
weekends included.

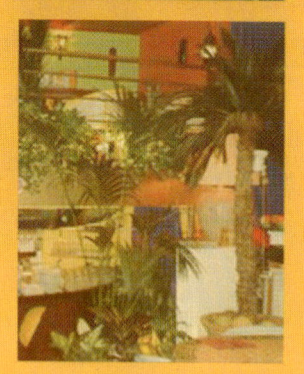

- LETCHEE
- PASSION
- POMME
- KIWI
- BANANE
- MELON
- ANANAS
- ABRICOT
- COCO
- PÊCHE
- POIRE
- CAROTTE
- FRAISE
- MANGUE
- FRAMBOISE
- AVOCAT

Le Paradis du Fruit - Les Halles

4, rue Saint Honoré (at the corner of rue du Pont Neuf) - Paris 1st
Telephone : 01 40 39 93 99 - Fax : 01 40 39 04 40
Metro : Châtelet or Châtelet - Les Halles
Open 7 days a week - SERVICE NON STOP from 11:30am to 1:30am
www.pagesrestos.com/paradis-du-fruit

Learning & Tasting

Soufflé dunces take heart: this is the city in which to become acquainted with a whisk.

Cookery Courses

Ritz Escoffier Ecole de Gastronomie Française
38 rue Cambon, 1st (01.43.16.30.50). Mº Opéra. **Courses** start each Mon; demonstrations Mon, Thur 3-5.30pm. **Fees** demonstration €45.75; half-day hands-on from €122; three-day (Aug only) €488; one-week from €885; diploma €5,336. **Enrolment** in advance. **Credit** AmEx, DC, MC, V.
Few cooking schools can boast an address as prestigious as the Hôtel Ritz. Students, unfortunately, don't fully enjoy this as they enter through the modest rear door/underground parking entrance. The school is deep in the bowels of the hotel, next to the famous hotel kitchen; designed by Auguste Escoffier, it was the first to run like an assembly line, the modern standard. This gives the school some warranted legitimacy, as many graduates of the 30-week professional course go on to internships at the hotel. Like the other big schools, the Ritz has many courses to choose from ranging from workshops for children to master classes for professionals; from half-day bread-baking classes to the 30-week 'Ritz Escoffier Superior Diploma'. The carefully prepared materials – recipes, lists of ingredients, etc – for any course you choose are available in English. Simultaneous translation of all the courses is also provided; the quality was a bit sub-standard on our visit. There are demonstrations every afternoon by the school's gifted and entertaining chefs, although the absence of desks makes it tricky to take notes.

Françoise Meunier
7 rue Paul-Lelong, 2nd (01.40.26.14.00/ www.intiweb.com/fmeunier). Mº Bourse. **Classes** Tue-Sat 10.30am-1.30pm; Wed 7.30-10.30pm. **Fees** €80 per class; five classes €320; classes and exam/diploma €1,200. **No credit cards**.
A graduate of the Ecole Hôtelière de Toulouse, Françoise presides over casual and informative classes for amateur cooks in her custom-built kitchen. During a three-hour class, an international mix of students (English, Spanish and Japanese translation is available with notice) prepares a three-course meal, dresses the dishes, sets the table and, finally, with a glass of wine in hand, comments on the results. A typical menu, usually created to cater to students' requests, might include such dishes as a duck *magret* salad with poached egg, chicken fricassée with mushrooms, and an apple and Calvados soufflé. Classes with simpler themes are also offered to children. All the best cooking classes have one thing in common – regulars – and Françoise's are no exception. Be sure to register in advance as places are snapped up quickly and numbers are limited to ten. Recipes and complete lists of ingredients are provided.

Promenades Gourmandes
187 rue du Temple, 3rd (01.48.04.56.84/ www.theinternationalkitchen.com/ promen.htm). Mº Temple. **Classes** Tue, Thur, Fri, Sat, Sun. Closed Aug. **Fees** half day €210, full day €300. **Enrolment** preferably at least one week in advance. **No credit cards**.
If the seriousness of the bigger schools' workshops puts you off, or if you're looking for something a little more interactive than a mass demonstration, this could be the answer. A class with Paule Caillat begins with a trip to buy the ingredients from the local market and then moves on to her large personal kitchen where aprons are donned, recipes are handed out, and the tasks for the preparation of a three-course meal are delegated: this might consist of cheese soufflé, chicken in white wine, tarragon and mushroom sauce, and chocolate tart. The classes cater to Americans, especially those new to or visiting Paris. Paule is bilingual, so all classes are available in English.

L'Ecole du Thé
Le Palais des Thés, 64 rue Vieille-du-Temple, 3rd (01.43.56.96.38/www.le-palais-des-thes.fr). Mº Hôtel-de-Ville. **Classes** daily. **Fees** *découvertes* €8; *connaissances* €16; *évasions* €32. **Credit** AmEx, MC, V.
Who would have thought that such a humble drink could inspire so much admiration? Three types of courses are offered. The 45-minute *découvertes* workshops for €8, and the 90-minute *connaissances* tastings for €16 have various themes that change each month. On our visit, we were introduced to the very serious business of formal tea tasting: isolating the essential flavours and fragrances; testing our new skills on a worldwide selection of brews, and even studying complex graphs of the effects of aftertaste over time. The third course option, the 90-minute, €32 *évasions*, offers in-depth sessions on a large variety of subjects, often held at other locations: study the Tea Ceremony with a Japanese master; discuss the health benefits of green tea with a researcher at the Faculté de Pharmacie de Paris Sud; or savour mint brews at La Mosquée de Paris – no leaf is left unturned. You can save some money by buying books of tickets which can be used for any of the sessions described above. All students go home with a sample pack of teas with exact instructions for steeping and serving.

Astuces et Tours de Main
29 rue Censier, 5th (03.44.54.37.21). Mº Censier-Daubenton. **Classes** Mon, Tue, Thur, Fri 1-4pm; Sat 10am-2pm; children's class (age 9 and up) Wed 3-4.30pm; Sat 10am-2pm. **Fees** €57.93 each; children €22.87; Sat €73.18. **Enrolment** in advance. **No credit cards**.
Laurence Guarneri's lovely little school is located in her custom-built kitchen in a renovated tannery with lots of natural light. Seated on comfortable stools at the counter, students can take notes on Laurence's tips while having a good view of the day's creation. Classes vary from broad themes to specific workshops depending on the students' interests, and most courses are booked up well in advance. The atmosphere is both professional and convivial as most of the students are regulars – an opportunity to meet people with similar interests and pick up valuable skills. Excellent, if your French is up to it or if you can convince a bilingual friend to come along.

La Cuisine de Marie-Blanche
18 av de la Motte-Picquet, 7th (01.45.51.36.34). Mº Ecole-Militaire. **Classes** Mon-Fri 10.30am-1.30pm, 2.30-4.30pm. Closed Aug. **Fees** one class €145; 5-20 classes €550-€1,850; one week intensive €1000. **Enrolment** two weeks in advance. **No credit cards**.
Marie-Blanche de Broglie founded her school almost 25 years ago. Working from an elegant apartment, she helps aspiring hosts launch themselves into the world of sophisticated dinner parties. Courses include classic cookery using seasonal recipes, pastry and desserts and 'Art de Vivre', in which table presentation, flower arranging, table manners, the history of French gastronomy, and the role of the host are all covered. Classes, limited to six students, are given in French, English or Spanish, with a Japanese interpreter on request. For youngsters keen to try pastry-making, classes can be organised on demand.

Ecoles Grégoire Ferrandi
28 rue de l'Abbé-Grégoire, 6th (01.49.54.28.03). Mº St-Placide or Montparnasse-Bienvenüe. **Classes** cooking and pâtisserie courses Wed 6.30-10.30pm. **Fee** €53.36. **No credit cards**.
This state-run cooking school offers a choice of cooking or pâtisserie classes, each consisting of an evening session with a maximum of 12 students. Each evening of the cooking course is organised around a different theme according to the season: for example, in autumn, single-dish meals such as *cassoulet*, autumn dishes and 'Les Plats de Fêtes'. Among the desserts you can learn to make are classics such as crêpes and *fondant au chocolat*.

Le Cordon Bleu
8 rue Léon-Delhomme, 15th (01.53.68.22.50). Mº Vaugirard. **Classes** Mon-Fri 8.30am-8.30pm; Sat 9am-3.30pm. **Fees** demonstrations €38; one-day workshop from €125; four-day course €820; three-month certificate €4,950 (cooking), €6,750 (pastry); nine-month diploma from €13,500 (pastry), €18,950 (cooking), €29,550 (both). **Enrolment** three months ahead for long courses, two weeks for one-day courses. **Credit** MC, V.
Although it's the oldest cooking school in Paris – teaching the culinary arts since 1895 – the Cordon Bleu still has greater recognition internationally than domestically (branches now exist in ten countries, including Peru). Thus, most of the students are Japanese or American, and the only French people you're likely to encounter are the chefs (simultaneous translation into English is available for demonstrations and is excellent). Many types of classes are offered: half-day demonstrations; one-time workshops for keen amateurs; week-long themed courses; and, of course, the full nine-month diploma programme. With mirrors on the ceilings and video monitors on the walls, the classrooms allow you to follow the chef's every move. Despite these visual aids, it's worth arriving early as the demonstrations are often packed and excitable students of the diploma programmes quickly snap up the best seats. Also, be sure to go on a full stomach. The demonstrations are long and, although the sample tastings are often divine, they're by no means a meal. A selection of cookbooks, gourmet products and kitchen equipment is also available.

Ecole Lenôtre
48 av Victor-Hugo, 16th (01.45.02.21.19). Mº Victor-Hugo. **Classes** Mon, Tue, Thur-Sat 9am-1pm, 2-6pm; Wed 2-3.30pm, 4-5.30pm (children's classes). Closed 21 July-28 Aug, 8 Dec-4 Jan, two weeks in Feb, one week at Easter. **Fees** half-day €77-€107; one-day €214; children €27.50. **Enrolment** three weeks in advance. **Credit** AmEx, DC, MC, V.
With branches of its *traiteurs* and *chocolatiers* all over Paris, Lenôtre has become a temple for foodies as well as a few sheepish professionals (some private cooking school instructors admit to coming here occasionally to hone their skills). From old-hat topics such as the elusive perfect soufflé to nouvelle cuisine concoctions to simple bread-baking, there are workshops here on just about every topic under the sun (although most classes deal with classic French desserts). All the menus are planned well in

Experience grape passion at Le Jardin des Vignes

Time Out Reader Survey

Paris Eating & Drinking Guide — 5th Edition

We would like to find out more about you and what you think about this guide. Please find time to fill in this questionnaire and return it (or a photocopy) by 31 December 2002. This information will be treated in the strictest confidence. If your reply is among the first ten picked out, we will send you your choice of *Time Out* Guide (worth up to £12.99), so don't forget to fill in your name and address. Thank you for your help.

1. How did you get this copy of the *Time Out Paris Eating & Drinking Guide*?
- ❏ Newsagent
- ❏ Bookshop
- ❏ Online

Please specify outlet, city & country:
_____

2. How did you first hear of this guide?
- ❏ Advertising in a *Time Out* publication
- ❏ Advertising in *Pariscope*
- ❏ A poster or sticker
- ❏ Personal recommendation
- ❏ Bookshop or newsagent
- ❏ www.timeout.com
- ❏ Other _____

3. How do you rate the quality and usefulness of this guide?
- ❏ Excellent
- ❏ Very good
- ❏ Good
- ❏ Fair
- ❏ Poor

4. How many times do you estimate you have or will consult this Guide?
- ❏ Once
- ❏ 2-9 times
- ❏ 10-19 times
- ❏ 20 times or more

5. Have you (or will you) use this Guide to choose (tick as many as apply)?
- ❏ Restaurants
- ❏ Cafés, Bars or Pubs
- ❏ Clubs or Cabarets
- ❏ Shops or Markets
- ❏ Cooking or Wine Classes

6. Would you purchase future editions of this Paris Eating & Drinking Guide?
- ❏ Yes, even at a higher cover price
- ❏ Yes, but only at the same cover price
- ❏ Yes, but only at a lower cover price
- ❏ No

7. What format would you prefer for future editions of this Guide?
- ❏ Perfect-bound magazine (current size)
- ❏ Paperback book

8. Do you speak French?
- ❏ Not at all
- ❏ A little
- ❏ Proficiently
- ❏ Fluently
- ❏ Mother tongue

9. How much time do you spend in Paris?
- ❏ Long-term resident
- ❏ Short-term resident
- ❏ Visit more than 3 times a year
- ❏ Visit 2-3 times a year
- ❏ Visit once a year
- ❏ Visit less than once a year

10. How often do you go out to lunch when in Paris?
- ❏ Every day
- ❏ 2-6 times a week
- ❏ Once a week
- ❏ Less than once a week

11. How often do you go out to dinner when in Paris?
- ❏ Every night
- ❏ 2-6 times a week
- ❏ Once a week
- ❏ Less than once a week

12. What is the average price per person you pay when eating out in Paris, including wine?
- ❏ Less than €20 (less than £12)
- ❏ €20 - €40 (£12-£25)
- ❏ €40 - €80 (£25-£50)
- ❏ over €80 (over £50)

13. Do you pay for meals by credit card?
- ❏ Yes   ❏ No

14. Do you purchase or use these products or services (tick all that apply)?

	In France	Outside
Mineral water	❏	❏
Wine	❏	❏
Beer	❏	❏
Champagne	❏	❏
Fortified wine/Apéritifs	❏	❏
Cognac/Digestifs	❏	❏
Other spirits	❏	❏
Soft drinks	❏	❏
Food products	❏	❏

15. What is the total annual income of your household?
- ❏ €25,000 or less (£15,000 or less)
- ❏ €25-50,000 (£15-30,000)
- ❏ over €50,000 (over £30,000)

16. Your sex:
- ❏ Male
- ❏ Female

17. What is your nationality?
- ❏ British
- ❏ American
- ❏ French
- ❏ Other _____

18. What is your occupation?
- ❏ Senior manager or Professional
- ❏ Middle manager or Technician
- ❏ Self-employed/Small business owner
- ❏ Employee
- ❏ Manual worker
- ❏ Housewife
- ❏ Student
- ❏ Unemployed
- ❏ Retired
- ❏ Specify _____

19. What is your level of education?
- ❏ Postgraduate qualification
- ❏ University degree or equivalent
- ❏ Some university study
- ❏ Technical or other further education
- ❏ Secondary school

20. Are you:
- ❏ Single
- ❏ Married or living with a partner

21. What is your year of birth? _____

22. Have you bought or read: (tick all that apply)
- ❏ Previous editions of this guide
- ❏ Penguin *Time Out* Paris City Guide
- ❏ Other Penguin *Time Out* City Guides
- ❏ *Time Out Paris* inside *Pariscope*
- ❏ *Time Out Paris Free Guide*
- ❏ *Time Out Paris Visitors' Guide*
- ❏ *Time Out London*
- ❏ Other *Time Out* London Guides
- ❏ *Time Out New York*
- ❏ www.timeout.com

23. Which section of this guide have you found most useful / interesting? _____

24. Which sections have you found least useful / interesting? _____

25. Do you have any comments on the Guide, or suggestions for inclusion in future editions? _____

Title: _____ **First Name:** _____ **Surname:** _____
Address: _____ **City:** _____ **Postcode:** _____
Country: _____ **Phone:** _____ **E-mail:** _____

Please indicate here your choice of free Penguin *Time Out* Guide:
- ❏ Amsterdam ❏ Barcelona ❏ Berlin ❏ Boston ❏ Brussels ❏ Budapest ❏ Buenos Aires ❏ Chicago ❏ Copenhagen ❏ Dublin ❏ Edinburgh ❏ Florence ❏ Havana ❏ Hong Kong ❏ Istanbul ❏ Las Vegas ❏ Lisbon ❏ London ❏ Los Angeles ❏ Madrid ❏ Miami ❏ Moscow ❏ Naples ❏ New Orleans ❏ New York ❏ Paris ❏ Prague ❏ Rome ❏ San Francisco ❏ South of France ❏ Sydney ❏ Tokyo ❏ Venice ❏ Vienna ❏ Washington DC

❏ Tick here if you do not wish to receive mailings from third parties.   ❏ Tick here if you do not wish to receive information from Time Out

Please complete this questionnaire (or a photocopy) and post or fax it to:

Time Out Paris - Libre Réponse Nº 2423/75 - 75566 Paris Cedex 12 (Postage free in France) • **Fax: +33 (0)1.44.73.90.60**
Time Out Magazine - Freepost 20 (WC 3187) - London W1E 0DQ (Postage free in U.K.) • **Fax: +44 (0)20 7813 6001**

Learning & Tasting

advance for the year and are printed in a programme available at the school. Class size is limited to seven (eight for children) so there are plenty of opportunities to have your questions answered by the professional instructor, provided, of course, that you speak French (no translation is offered). Lenôtre also runs a professional school in Versailles.

Wine Courses

Le Jardin des Vignes
91 rue de Turenne, 3rd (01.42.77.05.00). Mº St-Sébastien-Froissart. **Courses** on request, usually Tue, Wed or Thur 8-10pm. **Fees** tasting session €46-€61, four-session introductory course €145. **Credit** MC, V.
Caviste Jean Radford is passionate about helping people understand the art of *dégustation*. His four starter classes cover the history of winemaking, different grapes and regions and the basics of tasting.

Grains Nobles
5 rue Laplace, 5th (01.43.54.93.54). Mº Cardinal-Lemoine. **Fees** classes from €69; courses from €130. **Enrolment** by post with cheque. **No credit cards**.
Set up in 1991, Grains Nobles offers a range of different wine-tasting events. There are the *dégustations*, for a maximum of 24 people, at which a different wine is considered and dissected every few days. There are the pricier *études de terroirs*, in which the wines of a certain area are considered, followed by a meal. For more dedicated oenophiles, *sessions initiation/perfectionnement* comprise three classes of three hours each, covering 18 quality wines. If this seems a bit much, a one-off three hour class (which can be taken in English) is available at a price of €69. The school's founder André Bessou will take you down to his cellar, where you can swirl, sniff, sip and spit some of France's finest wines. Some advance knowledge of wine, and of French, helps.

Centre de Dégustation Jacques Vivet
48 rue de Vaugirard, 6th (01.43.25.96.30). RER Luxembourg. **Classes** Mon, Tue, Thur evening, times vary. **Fees** four introductory classes €180; four advanced classes €160. **Enrolment** in advance. **No credit cards**.
Jacques Vivet created his tasting centre 20 years ago. At the time, the majority of his clients were foreigners, French people apparently believing innate knowledge of wine to be a national birthright. However, the French have now wised up and flock to his introductory and *perfectionnement* courses. Based around a desire to bring the appreciation of wine to as many people as possible and to avoid wine snobbery, he keeps his prices relatively low. The introductory course covers the theoretical side of wine – the elements that make up its flavour – as well as lots of dedicated tasting practice. The *perfectionnement* course brings in more developed vocabulary and some very special wines. After his courses, Vivet hopes that 'you'll no longer just drink wine, as you did before, instead you'll taste it'.

Sugar, spice and cooking advice with Françoise Meunier

Gadget fantastic

Paris, home to people who think of lobster soufflé as a TV snack and can rustle up a *bourguignon* with their eyes closed, is awash with impressive cook-shops. If you're ready to throw out your knackered non-stick and join the dinner-party people, there's a store out there with your name on it.

The kitchen section of **BHV** (52 rue de Rivoli, 4th/01.42.74.90.00) is a glittery Aladdin's den of saucepans bordered by soft furnishings and men's fashion. As well as its own range of sturdy copper pans, it stocks Cuisinox, Hackman, Cristel and Le Creuset. The best place to pick up the basics, it has a wide range of knives and frying pans and no fewer than 24 types of whisk. Fondue sets, foie gras containers and unfeasibly large garlic presses are available for authentic French cooking.

For those who love kitchen gadgets, there are *moules à boules* (melon ballers), oyster openers and hand-operated food mills.

With a pitiful total of only nine different whisks, **Kitchen Bazaar** (11 av du Maine, 15th/01.42.22.91.17) is a smaller store but a classier one. It's a festival of chrome gadgetry and modish accessories, perfect for buying a few luxury items after sorting out the essentials. Fifties-throwback KitchenAid blenders join space-age kettles, graphite cutlery, and (insofar as pepper grinders can be sexy) sexy pepper grinders. Top gadget awards go to the €43.45 automatic chip cutter and the zip-up wine-coolers, although the double-headed herb cutters come a close second.

At the other end of the fashion scale is **E. Dehillerin** (8 rue Coquillière, 1st/01.42.36.53.13), a no-nonsense store patronised by professional chefs since 1820 and now a favourite with Japanese and US tourists. A great warehouse of a shop on two floors, its walls and ceilings are hung with cauldron-like saucepans and chunky baking trays. Though it's more geared to the catering trade than to individual customers, it's excellent for knives, selling several dozen different sizes from hatchet to fruit-slicer. It's the best and cheapest shop in Paris for copper pots, as well as one of the very few places in the world you can buy a specially-made razor blade for slitting baguettes.

Culinarion (75 rue du Commerce, 15th/01.42.50.37.50) straddles the hazy border between cute and tacky. Big colourful aprons, kettles painted as strawberries and novelty egg timers are among the delights on offer in this small boutique in the 15th. The service is friendly and there is a limited range of useful equipment, including Cristel pots and pans, baking trays and nice serving dishes. It's a good place to go if you live nearby or have an urgent need for ladybird fridge magnets, but it's not in the premier league of Paris cookshops.

A. Simon (48, 52 rue Montmartre, 2nd/01.42.33.71.65) caters to the restaurant trade as well as individuals, supplying both quality goods and cheery tat. Chefs' briefcases of knives sit next to Tefal woks and beautiful glassware shares a shelf with cheekily phallic salt cellars. Sabatier, Au Nain and Culineer knives are reasonably priced and there is an excellent selection of cake-making equipment, from mixing bowls to miniature dolls for wedding cakes. *Rob Orchard*

E. Dehillerin: a pot-aholic's fantasy

Ecoles Grégoire Ferrandi
28 rue de l'Abbé-Grégoire, 6th (01.49.54.28.03). Mº St-Placide or Montparnasse-Bienvenüe. **Classes** four Wed or Thur evenings, 6.30-9pm. **Fee** €229. **No credit cards**.
The 'initiation' course at the *Ecoles Grégoire Ferrandi* covers all aspects of wine tasting – the influence of the soil and climate, tasting techniques, wine vocabulary, and the significance of the *grandes appellations*. A whole session is dedicated to the discovery of Champagne, and the last session is held over dinner, at which various wines are tasted with the dishes to which they are best suited.

Les Vins du Terroir
34 av Duquesne, 7th (01.40.61.91.87). Mº St François-Xavier. **Classes** Tue, Thur 8.30-10pm. **Fees** €30-€45 per class. **Enrolment** in advance. **Credit** MC, V.
At the wine shop that he opened in 1998, owner Alexandre Gerbe runs an evening class once a month or so, each time tasting ten wines from a different region. Classes run throughout the year except during the summer holidays, and accept a maximum of 12 people.

L'Ecole du Vin Ylan Schwartz
17 passage Foubert, 13th (01.45.89.77.39). Mº Tolbiac. **Fees** €300-€500. **Enrolment** two months in advance. **No credit cards**.
Oenologist Ylan Schwarz brings an original approach to learning about wine. An advocate of 'the harmony between wine and music', Schwarz works with a Baroque ensemble and musicians from the Orchestre Philharmonique de Radio France in evenings (prices vary) that combine dinner, wine tasting and the music to suit it, matching a specific château to a particular piece or even movement of music. Other classes deal with matching wine and cheese, regional tastings, *grands crus* to go with grand food, and vineyard tours. Some classes are available in English or Spanish.

CIDD Découverte du Vin
30 rue de la Sablière, 14th (01.45.45.44.20). Mº Pernéty. **Open** Mon-Fri 10am-8pm. **Classes** days and times vary. **Fees** three-hour class €70; cycles of 3-14 classes €182-€738. **Enrolment** at least two weeks in advance. **No credit cards**.
The CIDD (Centre d'Information, de Documentation et de Dégustation) was founded in 1982 by Alain Ségelle, winner of the best Paris wine steward of the year award in 1978. Entirely devoted to every aspect of wine, the centre offers high-level training for professionals, conferences, themed weekends, organised trips around vineyards and much more. Most classes are taught by Ségelle himself and '*Découverte de vin*' classes are available in French, English and Japanese. Some focus on regions, while others have themes such as 'how to stock your cellar'. Other activities include day trips to regional vineyards.

Institut du Vin du Savour Club
11-13 rue Gros, 16th (01.42.30.94.18). RER Kennedy-Radio France. **Classes** Tue or Thur 8-10pm. **Fees** three classes (or two including a *soirée gastronomique*) €140. **Enrolment** book early. **Credit** AmEx, DC, MC, V.
Georges Lepré, former Ritz and Grand Véfour sommelier, heads these courses, taught in French, which focus on how to match wine to dishes. Two *cycles* are on offer, entitled 'an approach to wine' and 'the passion of wine'. The first involves three sessions, each covering six wines. People attending the courses are taught the basics of tasting, how best to build up their own wine cellar and how to pick the best wine for a meal. The second cycle concerns special wines, for example *vins moelleux, vendanges tardives* and *vin jaune* and includes a section on the '*mystère des cépages*', looking at Château Poujeaux wines. Horizontal and vertical tastings and special wine-making processes are part of a second set of three classes, while a third includes an evening at a local restaurant.

Le Musée du Vin
5 sq Charles-Dickens, 16th (01.45.25.63.26). Mº Passy. For information about courses, contact Monique Josse on 01.64.09.44.80. **Open** museum Tue-Sun 10-6pm; courses Sept-June Sat 10am-noon, 2-4pm. **Fees** €38.11 per session; students €33.54. **Enrolment** one week in advance. **Credit** AmEx, MC, V.
This small museum is housed in 14th-century vaulted cellars that were once part of the Abbaye de Passy, which produced a wine enjoyed by Louis XIII himself. Discover the history and processes of wine-making (labels in French only) through displays of vats, corkscrews and cutouts of medieval peasants, followed by a short *dégustation*. Classes cover many different regions of France, grape varieties and sensory analysis.

Time Out Paris Eating & Drinking 145

Lexicon

Tongue-tied *à table*? This guide will help take the stress out of French menu-speak.

Food

Abats offal.
Accra salt-cod fritter.
Agneau lamb.
Aiglefin haddock.
Aiguillettes thin slices.
Ail garlic.
Aile wing.
Aïoli ground garlic sauce.
Airelle cranberry.
Algues seaweed.
Aligot mashed potatoes with cheese and garlic.
Aloyau beef loin.
Amande almond; **– de mer** small clam.
Amer/amère bitter.
Ananas pineapple.
Anchoïade anchovy paste.
Anchois anchovy.
Andouille pig's offal sausage, served cold.
Andouillette grilled chitterling (offal) sausage.
Aneth dill.
Anguille eel.
Anis aniseed.
Araignée de mer spider crab.
Artichaut artichoke.
Asperge asparagus.
Assiette plate.
Aubergine aubergine (GB), eggplant (US).
Avocat avocado.

Baies roses pink peppercorns.
Ballotine stuffed, rolled-up piece of boned fish or meat.
Bar sea bass.
Barbue brill.
Basilic basil.
Bavarois moulded cream dessert.
Bavette beef flank steak.
Béarnaise *hollandaise* sauce with tarragon and shallots.
Belon flat, round oyster.
Betterave beetroot.
Beurre butter; **– blanc** butter sauce with white wine and shallots; **– rouge** butter sauce with red wine.
Beignet fritter or doughnut.
Biche deer, venison.
Bifteck steak.
Bigorneau periwinkle.
Biologique organic.
Blanc white; **– de poulet** chicken breast.
Blanquette a 'white' stew (with eggs and cream).
Blette Swiss chard.
Boeuf beef; **– bourguignon** beef stew with red wine; **– de charolais** charolais beef (a breed); **– gros sel** boiled beef with vegetables; **– miroton** sliced boiled beef in onion sauce; **– de salers** salers beef (a breed).
Bordelaise sauce with red wine, shallots and marrow.
Boudin blanc white veal, chicken or pork sausage.
Boudin noir black (blood) pudding.
Bouillabaisse Mediterranean fish and shellfish soup.
Bouillon stock.
Bourride fish stew.
Brandade de morue salt cod puréed with potatoes.
Brebis sheep's milk cheese.
Brik North African filo pastry package.
Brochet pike.
Brochette kebab.
Brouillé scrambled.
Brûle(é) literally, burned, usually caramelised.
Bulot whelk.

Cabillaud fresh cod.
Cabri young goat.
Caille quail.
Calamar squid.
Campagne/campagnard country-style.
Canard duck.
Canette duckling.
Cannelle cinnamon.
Carbonnade beef stew with onions and beer.
Carré d'agneau rack or loin of lamb.
Carrelet plaice.
Carvi caraway seeds.
Cassis blackcurrants, also blackcurrant liqueur in *kir*.
Cassoulet stew of haricot beans, sausage and preserved duck.
Céleri celery.
Céleri rave celeriac.
Céleri rémoulade grated celariac in mustard mayonnaise.
Cèpe fleshy, dark-brown mushroom.
Cerfeuil chervil.
Cerise cherry.
Cervelas garlicky Alsatian pork sausage.
Cervelle brains.
Champignon mushroom; **– de Paris** cultivated button mushroom.
Chantilly whipped cream.
Chapon capon.
Charcuterie cured meat, such as *saucisson* or pâté.
Charlotte moulded cream dessert with a biscuit edge.
Chasseur sauce with white wine, mushrooms, shallots and tomato.
Châtaigne chestnut.
Chateaubriand fillet steak.
Chaud hot.
Chaud-froid glazing sauce with gelatine or aspic.
Chausson pastry turnover.
Cheval horse.
A cheval with egg on top.
Chèvre goat's cheese.
Chevreuil young roe deer.
Chicorée *frisée*, or curly endive (GB), chicory (US).
Chiffonade shredded herbs and vegetables.
Chipiron squid.
Choron *Béarnaise* sauce with tomato purée.
Chou cabbage; **– de Bruxelles** Brussels sprout; **– frisé** kale; **– rouge** red cabbage; **–fleur** cauliflower.
Choucroute sauerkraut (*garnie* if topped with cured ham and sausages).
Ciboulette chive.
Citron lemon.
Citron vert lime.
Citronelle lemongrass.
Citrouille pumpkin.
Civet game stew in blood-thickened sauce.
Clafoutis thick batter baked with fruit.
Cochon pig; **– Cochon de lait** suckling pig.
Cochonnailles cured pig parts (ears, snout, cheeks...).
Coeur heart.
Coing quince.
Colin hake.
Concombre cucumber.
Confit preserved.
Confiture jam.
Congre conger eel.
Contre-filet sirloin.
Coq rooster.
à la Coque in its shell.
Coquelet baby rooster.
Coquillages shellfish.
Coquille shell; **– St-Jacques** scallop.
Cornichon pickled gherkin.
Côte de boeuf rib beef.
Cotriade Breton fish stew.
Coulis thick sauce or purée.
Courge vegetable marrow (GB), squash (US).
Courgette courgette (GB), zucchini (US).
Crème anglaise custard.
Crème brûlée caramelised custard dessert.
Crème fraîche thick, slightly soured cream.
Crêpe pancake.
Crépinette small, flattish sausage, often grilled.
Cresson watercress.
Creuse oyster with long, crinkly shell.
Crevette prawn (GB), shrimp (US); **– grise** grey shrimp.
Croque-madame *croque monsieur* topped with an egg.
Croque-monsieur toasted cheese and ham sandwich.
Crottin small, round goat cheese (literally, turd).
Croustade bread or pastry case, deep-fried.
en Croûte in a pastry case.
Crudités raw vegetables.
Crustacé shellfish.
Cuisse leg (poultry).
Curcuma turmeric.

Darne fish steak.
Datte date.
Daube meat braised slowly in red wine.
Daurade/dorade sea bream.
Demi-glace brown stock with meat jelly or veal.
Désossé(e) boned.
Diable *demi-glace* with cayenne and white wine.
Dinde turkey.
Duxelles chopped, sautéed mushrooms with shallots.

Echalote shallot.
Ecrémé skimmed (milk).
Ecrevisse crayfish.
Emincé fine slice.
Encornet squid.
Endive chicory (GB), Belgian endive (US).
Entrecôte beef rib steak.
Entremets cream or milk-based dessert.
Eperlan smelt; whitebait.
Epicé(e) spicy.
Epices spices.
Epinards spinach.
Escabèche fish fried, marinated and served cold.
Escalope cutlet.
Escarole slightly bitter, slightly curly salad leaves.
Espadon swordfish.
Espelette small, hot Basque pepper.
Estouffade meat stew.
Estragon tarragon.
Etrille small crab.

Faisan pheasant.
Farci(e) stuffed.
Faux-filet sirloin steak.
Fenouil fennel.
Feuille de chêne oak leaf lettuce.
Feuilleté puff pastry.
Fève broad bean.
Figue fig.
Filet mignon tenderloin.
Financier small rectangular cake.
Fines de claire crinkle-shelled oysters.
Fines herbes mixed herbs.
Flambé(e) sprinkled with alcohol, then set alight.
Flet flounder.
Flétan halibut.
Florentine with spinach.
Foie liver.
Foie gras fattened liver of goose or duck; **– cru** raw foie gras; **– entier** whole foie gras; **– mi-cuit** barely cooked (alsocalled *frais* or *nature*); **pâté de –** liver pâté with a foie gras base.
Fondant chocolate dessert.
Fondu(e) melted.
Fondue savoyarde bread dipped into melted cheese.
Fondue bourguignonne beef dipped in heated oil.
Forestière with mushrooms.
au four oven-baked.
Fourré(e) filled or stuffed.
Frais/fraîche fresh.
Fraise strawberry; **– des bois** wild strawberry; **– de veau** part of the calf's intestine.
Framboise raspberry.
Frappé(e) iced or chilled.
Fricadelle meatball.
Frisée curly endive (GB), chicory (US).
Frit(e) fried.
Frites chips (UK), French fries (US).
Friture tiny fried fish.
Froid cold.
Fromage cheese; **– blanc** smooth cream cheese.
Froment wheat flour.
Fruits de mer seafood, especially shellfish.
Fumé(e) smoked.
Fumet strong stock.

Galantine pressed meat or fish, usually stuffed.
Galette flat cake of savoury pastry, potato pancake or buckwheat *crêpe*.
Garbure thick vegetable and meat soup.
Garni(e) garnished.
Gelée jelly or aspic.
Genièvre juniper berry.
Gésiers gizzards.
Gibier game.
Gigot d'agneau leg of lamb.
Gigue haunch of game, usually venison or boar.
Gingembre ginger.
Girofle clove.
Girolle wild mushroom.
Gîte shin of beef.
Gîte à la noix topside or silverside of beef.
Glace ice, also ice cream.
Glacé(e) frozen; ice-cold; iced (as in cake).
Glaçon ice cube.
Gombo okra.
Gougère *choux* pastry and cheese mixture in a ring.
Goujon breaded, fried strip of fish; also a small catfish.
Goût taste.
Goûter to taste, or snack.
Graisse fat, grease.
Granité water-ice.
Gras(se) fatty.
Gratin dauphinois sliced potatoes baked with milk, cheese and garlic.
Gratiné(e) browned with breadcrumbs or cheese.
Grattons pork crackling.
à la Grecque served cold in olive oil and lemon juice.
Grenade pomegranate.
Grenadier delicate, white-fleshed sea fish.
Grenoblois sauce with cream, capers and lemon.
Grenouille frog.
Gribiche sauce of vinegar, capers, gherkins and egg.
Grillade grilled food, often mixed grill.
Grillé(e) grilled.
Griotte morello cherry.
Gros(se) large.
Groseille redcurrant.
Groseille à maquereau gooseberry.
Gros sel rock salt.

Haché(e) chopped, minced (GB), ground (US).
Hachis minced meat (hash); **– parmentier** beef mince with mashed potato topping.
Hareng herring.
Haricot bean.
Herbe herb; grass.
Hollandaise sauce of egg, butter, vinegar, and lemon.
Homard lobster.
Huile oil.
Huître oyster.
Hure cold sausage made from boar's or pig's head.

Ile flottante poached, whipped-egg white 'island' in vanilla custard.

Jambon ham; **– de Paris** cooked ham; **– cru** raw, cured ham; **– fumé** smoked ham; **– de pays** cured country ham.
Jambonneau hamhock; **– de canard** stuffed duck drumstick.
Jardinière with vegetables.
Jarret shin or knuckle.
Joue cheek or jowl.
Julienne finely cut vegetables; also ling (fish).
Jus juice.

Lait milk. **(agneau/cochon) de lait** milk-fed lamb/suckling pig.
Laitier made with milk.
Laitue lettuce.
Lamproie lamprey eel.
Landaise in goose fat with garlic, onion and ham.
Langue tongue.
Langouste spiny lobster or crawfish.
Langoustine Dublin Bay prawns or scampi.
Lapereau young rabbit.
Lapin rabbit.
Lard bacon.
Lardon cubed bacon bit.
Légume vegetable.
Lentille lentil.
Levraut young hare.
Lièvre hare.
Liégoise coffee or chocolate ice-cream sundae.
Lieu pollock.
Limande lemon sole.
Lisette small mackerel.
Litchi lychee.
Lotte monkfish.
Loup sea bass.
Lyonnais served with onions or sautéed potatoes.

Lexicon

Mâche lamb's lettuce.
Madère Madeira.
Magret de canard duck breast.
Maïs maize, corn.
Maison homemade, or house special.
Mangue mango.
Maquereau mackerel.
Marcassin young wild boar.
Mariné(e) marinated.
Marjolaine marjoram.
Marmite small cooking pot, or a stew served in one; – **dieppoise** Normandy fish stew.
Marquise mousse-like cake.
Marron chestnut.
Matelote freshwater fish stew cooked in wine.
Mélange mixture.
Ménagère home-style.
Menthe mint.
Merguez spicy lamb or lamb and beef sausage.
Merlan whiting.
Mesclun mixed young salad leaves.
Meunière fish seasoned, floured and fried in butter.
Meurette red wine and stock used for poaching.
Mi-cuit(e) half/semi-cooked.
Miel honey.
Mignon small meat fillet.
Millefeuille puff pastry with many layers.
Minute fried quickly.
Mirabelle tiny yellow plum.
Mirepoix chopped carrots, onion and celery.
Moelle bone marrow.
Morille morel mushroom.
Mornay béchamel sauce with cheese.
Morue cod, usually salt cod.
Mou lights (lungs).
Moules mussels; – **marinières** cooked in white wine with shallots.
Moulu(e) ground, milled.
Mousseline hollandaise sauce with whipped cream.
Mousseron type of wild mushroom.
Moutarde mustard.
Mouton mutton.
Mulet grey mullet.
Mûre blackberry.
Muscade nutmeg.
Myrtille bilberry/blueberry.

Nage poaching liquid.
Nantua crayfish sauce.
Nature plain, ungarnished.
Navarin lamb stew.
Navet turnip.
Nid nest.
Noisette hazelnut, or small, round piece of meat, or coffee with a little milk.
Noix walnut.
Nouilles noodles.

Oeuf egg; – **à la coque** soft-boiled; – **cocotte** baked with cream; – **dur** hard-boiled; – **en meurette** poached in red wine; – **à la neige** île flottante.
Oie goose.
Oignon onion.
Onglet similar to bavette.
Oreille ear, usually pig's.
Orge barley.
Ortie nettle, used in soup.
Os bone.
Oseille sorrel.
Oursin sea urchin.

Pain bread (see also p107); – **d'épices** honey gingerbread; – **grillé** toast; – **perdu** French toast.
Palombe wood pigeon.
Palourde a type of clam.
Pamplemousse grapefruit.
en Papillote steamed in foil or paper packet.
Panaché mixture.
Panais parsnip.
Pané(e) breaded.
Parfait sweet or savoury mousse-like mixture.
Parmentier with potato.
Pastèque watermelon.
Pâte pastry.
Pâtes pasta or noodles.
Pâté meat or fish pâté; – **en croûte** in a pastry case (similar to pork pie).
Paupiette meat or fish rolled up and tied, usually stuffed.
Pavé thick, square steak.
Pêcheur based on fish.
Perdreau young partridge.
Perdrix partridge.
Persil parsley.
Petit gris small snail.
Petit pois pea.
Petit salé salt pork.
Pétoncle queen scallop.
Pets de nonne ('nuns farts') light puffy fritters.
Pied foot (or trotter).
Pigeonneau young pigeon.
Pignon pine kernel.
Piment pepper or chilli.
Pimenté(e) spicy.
Pince claw.
Pintade/pintadeau guinea fowl.
Pipérade Basque egg, pepper, tomato, onion and ham mixture.
Pissaladière anchovy, tomato and onion tart.
Pistache pistachio nut.
Pistou basil and garlic paste, similar to pesto.
Plat dish; main course.
Plate flat-shelled oyster.
Pleurote oyster mushroom.
Poché(e) poached.
Pochetot skate.
Poêlé(e) pan-fried.
Poire pear.
Poireau leek.
Poisson fish.
Poitrine breast cut.
Poivrade peppery brown sauce served with meat.
Poivre pepper.
Poivron red or green pepper.
Pomme apple.
Pomme de terre potato (often referred to as pomme); – **à l'huile** cold, boiled potatoes in oil; – **au four** baked potato; – **dauphines** deep-fried croquettes of puréed potato; – **lyonnaises** sliced potatoes fried with onions; – **parisiennes** potatoes fried and tossed in a meat glaze; – **soufflées** puffed up, deep-fried potato skins; – **voisin** grated potato cake with cheese.
Porc pork.
Porcelet suckling pig.
Potage thick soup.
Pot-au-feu boiled beef with vegetables.
Potée meat and vegetable stew.
Potiron pumpkin.
Poudre powder or granules.
Poularde chicken or hen.
Poule hen; –**au-pot** stewed with vegetables and broth.
Poulet chicken
Poulpe octopus.
Poussin small chicken.
Praire small clam.
Pressé(e) squeezed.
Primeur early or young, of fruit, vegetables or wine.
Printanière springtime; served with vegetables.
Profiterole ice-cream filled pastry puff, served with melted chocolate.
Provençal(e) with garlic and tomatoes, and often onions, anchovies or olives.
Prune plum.
Pruneau prune.

Quenelle poached dumplings, usually pike.
Quetsch damson plum.
Queue tail.
Queue de boeuf oxtail.

Râble saddle.
Racine root.
Raclette melted cheese served with boiled potatoes.
Radis radish.
Ragoût meat stew.
Raie skate.
Raifort horseradish.
Raisin grape.
Râpé(e) grated.
Rascasse scorpion fish.
Ratte small, firm potato.
Ravigote thick vinaigrette.
Ravioles de Royans tiny cheese ravioli.
Recette recipe.
Récolte harvest.
Régime diet.
Réglisse liquorice.
à la Reine with chicken.
Reine-claude greengage (plum).
Reinette dessert apple.
Rémoulade mayonnaise with mustard, chopped herbs, capers and gherkins.
Rillettes potted meat, usually pork and/or goose.
Rillons crispy chunks of pork belly.
Ris sweetbreads.
Riz rice; – **sauvage** wild rice.
Rognon kidney.
Romarin rosemary.
Roquette rocket.
Rosbif roast beef.
Rosette dry, salami-like pork sausage from Lyon.
Rôti roast.
Rouget red mullet.
Roulade rolled-up portion.
Rouille red, cayenne-seasoned mayonnaise.
Roussette rock salmon (dogfish).
Roux flour- and butter-based sauce.
Rumsteack rump steak.

Sabayon frothy sauce made with wine and egg yolks, sometimes a dessert.
Sablé shortbread biscuit.
Safran saffron.
St Pierre John Dory.
Saisonnier seasonal.
Salé(e) salted.
Salmis game or poultry stew.
Sandre pike-perch.
Sang blood.
Sanglier wild boar.
Sarrasin buckwheat.
Sarriette savory (herb).
Saucisse fresh sausage.
Saucisson small sausage.
Saucisson sec dried sausage, eaten cold.
Sauge sage.
Saumon salmon.
Saumonette sea eel, or dog fish.
Sauvage wild.
gratin Savoyard potatoes baked in stock with cheese.
Scarole see escarole.
Sec/sèche dry.
Seiche squid.
Sel salt.
Selle saddle or back.
Sirop syrup.
Soisson white bean.
Soja soya.
Soubise béchamel sauce with rice and cream.
Souper supper.
Souris d'agneau lamb knuckle.
Sucre sugar.
Sucré(e) sweet.
Suppion small cuttlefish.
Suprême breast; – **de volaille** fowl in a white roux with cream and meat juice.
crêpe Suzette pancake flambéed in orange liqueur.

Tapenade Provençal black olive and caper paste, usually with anchovies.
Tartare raw minced steak (also tuna or salmon).
Tarte Tatin caramelised upside-down apple tart.
Tartine buttered baguette or open sandwich.
Tendron de veau veal rib.
Tête head.
Thon tuna.
Thym thyme.
Tian Provençal gratin cooked in an earthenware dish.
Tiède tepid or warm.
Timbale rounded mould, or food cooked in one.
Tisane herbal tea.
Tomate tomato; – **de mer** sea anemone.
Topinambour Jerusalem artichoke.
Toulouse large sausage.
Tournedos thick slices taken from a fillet of beef.
Tournesol sunflower.
Tourte covered tart or pie, usually savoury.
Tourteau large crab.
Tranche slice.
Travers de porc spare ribs.
Trénels lamb's tripe.
Tripes tripe.
Tripoux Auvergnat dish of sheep's tripe and feet.
Trompette-de-la-mort horn of plenty mushroom.
Truffade fried potato cake or mashed potato with cheese.
Truffe truffles, the ultimate fungus, blanche (white) or noire (black).
Truffé(e) stuffed or garnished with truffles.
Truite trout; – **de mer/– saumonée** salmon trout.

Vacherin a meringue, fruit and ice cream cake; or soft, cow's milk cheese.
Vapeur steam.
Veau veal; – **élevé sous la mère** milk-fed veal.
Velouté sauce made with white roux and bouillon; creamy soup.
Ventre belly, breast or stomach.
Vénus American clam.
Verdurette vinaigrette with herbs and egg.
Véronique with grapes.
Viande meat.
Vichyssoise cold leek and potato soup.
Volaille poultry.

Yaourt yoghurt.

Zeste zest or peel.

Drinks

Appellation d'Origine Contrôlée (AOC) wine (or food) conforming to specific strict quality rules.
Bière beer.
Bock 12cl of beer.
Boire to drink.
Boisson a drink.
Blanche pale wheat beer.
Blonde lager (GB), beer (US).
Brune dark beer.
Café small espresso coffee; – **allongé** 'lengthened' (twice the water); – **au lait** milky coffee; – **crème** coffee with steamed milk; – **serré** strong espresso, (half the water); **grand –** double espresso.
Calvados apple brandy.
Cardinal kir with red wine.
Chope tankard.
Citron pressé freshly squeezed lemon juice.
Chocolat (chaud) (hot) chocolate.
Décaféiné/déca decaffeinated coffee.
Demie (demie-pression) 25cl of draught beer; – **ordinaire** 25cl of the least-expensive lager.
Demi-litre half a litre (50cl).
Express espresso; **double –** double espresso.
Gazeuse fizzy/carbonated.
Grand cru top-quality wine.
Infusion herbal or fruit tea.
Jus de fruits fruit juice.
Kir crème de cassis and dry white wine – **royale** crème de cassis and Champagne.
Lait milk.
Marc clear brandy made from grape residues.
Mauresque pastis with almond syrup.
Mirabelle plum brandy.
Noisette espresso with a drop of milk.
Orange pressée freshly squeezed orange juice.
Panaché beer and lemonade shandy.
Pastis anise apéritif.
Perroquet pastis with mint syrup.
Pichet jug or carafe.
Plat(e) still, non-carbonated.
Poire Williams pear brandy.
Porto port.
Pot lyonnais 46cl carafe.
Pression draught lager.
Quart quarter litre (25cl).
Rousse red, bitter-like beer.
Thé tea.
Tilleul linden flower tea.
Tisane herbal tea.
Tomate pastis with grenadine syrup.
Verveine verbena tea.
Vieille Prune plum brandy.
Xérès sherry.

Savoir-faire

Addition bill.
Amuse-gueule (or amuse-bouche) appetiser or hors d'oeuvre.
Assiette plate.
A la carte ordered separately (i.e. not on the fixed-price menu or formule).
Carte des vins wine list.
Cendrier ashtray.
Commande order.
Commander to order.
Compris included.
Comptoir counter.
Couvert cutlery, also used to express number of diners.
Couteau knife.
Cuillère spoon.
Dégustation tasting.
Eau du robinet tap water.
Entrée starter.
Espace non-fumeur non-smoking area.
Formule set-price menu.
Fourchette fork.
Majoration price increase.
Menu set-price selection, also called a formule or prix fixe.
Menu dégustation tasting menu, sampling several different dishes.
Monnaie change.
Plat main course.
Pourboire tip.
Serveur/serveuse waiter/waitress.
Rince-doigts finger bowl.
Verre glass.
Zinc bar counter.

Alphabetical Index

Les 100 Kilos p70
2 rue de la Folie Méricourt, 11th (01.43.55.12.74). Budget
Au 35 p20
35 rue Jacob, 6th (01.42.60.23.24). Bistros
404 p99
69 rue des Gravilliers, 3rd (01.42.74.57.81). North African
59 Poincaré p60
Hôtel Le Parc, 59 av Raymond-Poincaré, 16th (01.47.27.59.59). Contemporary

A

Les Abats-Jour à Coudre p121
115 rue Oberkampf, 11th. Bars & Pubs
L'Absinthe p13
24 pl du Marché-St-Honoré, 1st (01.49.26.90.04). Bistros
L'Affriolé p23
17 rue Malar, 7th (01.44.18.31.33). Bistros
L'Afghani p101
16 rue Paul-Albert, 18th (01.42.51.08.72). Other International
L'Aimant du Sud p31
40 bd Arago, 13th (01.47.07.33.57). Bistros
Aki p96
2 bis rue Daunou, 2nd (01.42.61.48.38). Japanese
Alain Dubois p137
80 rue de Tocqueville, 17th (01.42.27.11.38). Shops & Markets
Alain Ducasse au Plaza Athénée p41
Hôtel Plaza Athénée, 25 av Montaigne, 8th (01.53.67.65.00/ www.alain-ducasse.com). Haute Cuisine
Alcazar p45
62 rue Mazarine, 6th (01.53.10.19.99/ www.conran.com). Brasseries
Allard p20
41 rue St-André-des-Arts, 6th (01.43.26.48.23). Bistros
Alléosse p137
13 rue Poncelet, 17th (01.46.22.50.45). Shops & Markets
Allô Apéro p133
9bis rue Labie, 17th (01.71.71.69.69). Home Delivery
Allô Couscous p133
70 rue Alexandre-Dumas, 11th (01.43.70.82.83). Home Delivery
Allô Indes p133
Vijaya, 22 rue Daubenton, 5th (01.47.07.56.78/fax 01.43.36.60.27/ www.allo-indes.com). Home Delivery
Altitude 95 p23
First level, Eiffel Tower, Champ de Mars, 7th (01.45.55.00.21). Bistros
Les Ambassadeurs p41
Hôtel de Crillon, 10 pl de la Concorde, 8th (01.44.71.16.16/ www.crillon.com). Haute Cuisine
L'Ambroisie p40
9 pl des Vosges, 4th (01.42.78.51.45). Haute Cuisine
L'Ami Louis p14
32 rue du Vertbois, 3rd (01.48.87.77.48). Bistros
Les Amognes p28
243 rue du Fbg-St-Antoine 11th (01.43.72.73.05). Bistros
Anacréon p31
53 bd St-Marcel, 13th (01.43.31.71.18). Bistros
Anahi p82
49 rue Volta, 3rd (01.48.87.88.24). The Americas
Angelina's p127
226 rue de Rivoli, 1st (01.42.60.82.00). Tea Rooms & Ice Cream
L'Angle du Faubourg p59
195 rue du Fbg St-Honoré, 8th (01.40.74.20.20). Contemporary
Anahuacalli p82
30 rue des Bernardins, 5th (01.43.26.10.20). The Americas
L'Apparemment Café p105
18 rue des Coutures-St-Gervais, 3rd (01.48.87.12.22). Cafés
Aquarius p75
40 rue de Gergovie, 14th (01.45.41.36.88). Vegetarian
L'Ardoise p13
28 rue du Mont-Thabor, 1st (01.42.96.28.18). Bistros
L'Armagnac p121
104 rue de Charonne, 11th (01.43.71.49.43). Bars & Pubs
L'Arpège p41
84 rue de Varenne, 7th (01.45.51.47.33/ www.alain-passard.com). Haute Cuisine
Arriba Mexico p82
32 av de la République, 11th (01.49.29.95.40). The Americas
L'Art Brut p117
78 rue Quincampoix, 3rd (01.42.72.17.36). Bars & Pubs
L'Artisan Chocolatier p139
102 rue de Belleville, 20th (01.46.36.67.60). Shops & Markets
L'Artisan de Saveurs p128
72 rue du Cherche-Midi, 6th (01.42.22.46.64). Tea Rooms & Ice Cream
L'Assiette p32
181 rue du Château, 14th (01.43.22.64.86). Bistros
Astier p28
44 rue Jean-Pierre-Timbaud 11th (01.43.57.16.35). Bistros
L'Astor p59
Sofitel Demeure Hôtel Astor, 11 rue d'Astorg, 8th (01.53.05.05.20/ www.hotel-astor.net). Contemporary
L'Astrance p60
4 rue Beethoven, 16th (01.40.50.84.40). Contemporary
Astuces et Tours de Main p143
29 rue Censier, 5th (03.44.54.37.21). Learning & Tasting
L'Atelier Berger p58
49 rue Berger, 1st (01.40.28.00.00/ www.atelierberger.com). Contemporary
Atelier Renault p111
53 av des Champs-Elysées, 8th (01.49.53.70.00). Cafés
L'Atlas p99
12 bd St-Germain, 5th (01.44.07.23.66). North African
L'Atmosphère p121
49 rue Lucien-Sampaix, 10th (01.40.38.09.21). Bars & Pubs
L'Auberge du Champ de Mars p70
18 rue de l'Exposition, 7th (01.45.51.78.08). Budget
L'Auberge Nicolas Flamel p14
51 rue de Montmorency, 3rd (01.42.71.77.78/ www.nicolasflamel.forez.com). Bistros
L'Auberge le Quincy p29
28 av Ledru-Rollin, 12th (01.46.28.46.76). Bistros
The Auld Alliance p117
80 rue François-Miron, 4th (01.48.04.30.40). Bars & Pubs
L'Autre Boulange p137
43 rue de Montreuil, 11th (01.43.72.86.04). Shops & Markets
L'Autre Café p121
62 rue Jean-Pierre Timbaud, 11th (01.40.21.03.07). Bars & Pubs
L'Avant-Goût p31
26 rue Bobillot, 13th (01.53.80.24.00). Bistros
L'Avenue p46
41 av Montaigne, 8th (01.40.70.14.91). Brasseries

B

Baan-Boran p89
43 rue Montpensier, 1st (01.40.15.90.45). Far East
Au Babylone p70
13 rue de Babylone, 7th (01.45.48.72.13). Budget
Bali Bar p89
9 rue St-Sabin, 11th (01.47.00.25.47). Far East
Le Balzar p45
49 rue des Ecoles, 5th (01.43.54.13.67). Brasseries
Bar Basile p109
34 rue de Grenelle, 7th (01.42.22.59.46). Cafés
Bar de la Croix-Rouge p107
2 carrefour de la Croix-Rouge, 6th (01.45.48.06.45). Cafés
Le Bar Dix p120
10 rue de l'Odéon, 6th (01.43.26.66.83). Bars & Pubs
Bar de l'Entr'acte p104
47 rue Montpensier, 1st (01.42.97.57.76). Cafés
Bar des Ferailleurs p121
18 rue de Lappe, 11th (01.48.07.89.12). Bars & Pubs
Le Bar à Huîtres p66
112 bd du Montparnasse, 14th (01.43.20.71.01/ www.lebarahuitres.fr). Fish & Seafood
Bar du Marché p109
75 rue de Seine, 6th (01.43.26.55.15). Cafés
Bar à Coupes p69
33 rue de Charonne, 11th (01.43.57.53.79). Budget
Bar des Théâtres p111
6 av Montaigne, 8th (01.47.23.34.63). Cafés
Baracane p17
38 rue des Tournelles, 4th (01.42.71.43.33). Bistros
Le Baratin p131
3 rue Jouye-Rouve, 20th (01.43.49.39.70). Wine Bars
Barfly p120
49 av George V, 8th (01.53.67.84.60). Bars & Pubs
Le Baromètre p105
17 rue Charlot, 3rd (01.48.87.04.54). Cafés
Le Baron Rouge p131
1 rue Théophile-Roussel, 12th (01.43.43.14.32). Wine Bars
Le Barramundi p121
3 rue Taitbout, 9th (01.47.70.21.21). Bars & Pubs
Barrio Latino p123
46-48 rue du Fbg-St-Antoine, 12th (01.55.78.84.75). Bars & Pubs
Ba'ta'clan Café p111
50 bd Voltaire, 11th (01.49.23.96.33). Cafés
Baz'Art Café p105
36, bd Henri IV, 4th. (01.42.78.62.23). Cafés
La Belle Hortense p129
31 rue Vielle-du-Temple, 4th (01.48.04.71.60). Wine Bars
Bennelong p101
31 bd Henri IV, 4th, (01.42.71.07.71). Other International
Benoît p17
20 rue St Martin, 4th (01.42.72.25.76). Bistros
La Biche au Bois p29
45 av Ledru Rollin, 12th (01.43.43.34.38). Bistros
Bières Spéciales p140
77 rue St-Maur, 11th (01.48.07.18.71). Shops & Markets
Bio.It p69
15 rue des Halles, 1st (01.42.21.10.21). Budget
Le Bistro du 19 p39
45 rue des Alouettes, 19th (01.42.00.84.85). Bistros
Bistro Beaubourg p67
25 rue Quincampoix, 4th (01.42.77.48.02). Budget
Le Bistro de Gala p25
45 rue du Fbg-Montmartre, 9th (01.40.22.90.50). Bistros
Bistro Jef p19
9 rue Cujas, 5th (01.43.29.20.20). Bistros
Le Bistro des Soupirs (Chez Raymonde) p39
49 rue de la Chine, 20th (01.44.62.93.31). Bistros
Le Bistroquet p70
52 rue du Colisée, 8th (01.45.61.01.82). Budget
Le Bistrot d'Anglas p24
29 rue Boissy d'Anglas, 8th (01.42.65.63.73). Bistros
Le Bistrot des Capucins p39
27 av Gambetta, 20th (01.46.36.74.75/ www.le-bistrot-des-capucins.com). Bistros
Bistrot Côté Mer p65
16 bd St-Germain, 5th (01.43.54.59.10/ www.michelrostang.com). Fish & Seafood
Le Bistrot d'à Côté Flaubert p36
10 rue Gustave-Flaubert, 17th (01.42.67.05.81/ www.michelrostang.com). Bistros
Le Bistrot du Dôme Bastille p65
2 rue de la Bastille, 4th (01.48.04.88.44). Fish & Seafood
Le Bistrot d'Hubert p33
41 bd Pasteur, 15th (01.47.34.15.50). Bistros
Le Bistrot du Peintre p111
116 av Ledru-Rollin, 11th (01.47.00.34.39). Cafés
Le Bistrot des Vignes p35
1 rue Jean-Bologne, 16th (01.45.27.76.64). Bistros
Blue Bayou p81
111-113 rue St-Maur, 11th (01.43.55.87.21). The Americas
Blue Elephant p89
43 rue de la Roquette, 11th, (01.47.00.42.00). Far East
Board Café Restaurant p81
8 rue Coquillère, 1st (01.40.28.97.98). The Americas
Boca Chica p121
58 rue de Charonne, 11th (01.43.57.93.13/ www.labocachica.com). Bars & Pubs
Au Boeuf Couronné p48
188 av Jean-Jaurès, 19th (01.42.39.54.54/ www.au-boeuf-couronne.com). Brasseries
Le Boeuf sur le Toit p46
34 rue du Colisée, 8th (01.53.93.65.55). Brasseries
Bofinger p45
5-7 rue de la Bastille, 4th (01.42.72.87.82). Brasseries
Bombardier p119
2 pl du Panthéon, 5th (01.43.54.79.22/ www.bombardier.com). Bars & Pubs
Les Bombis Bistrot p31
22 rue de Chaligny, 12th (01.43.45.36.32). Bistros
Bon p53
25 rue de la Pompe, 16th (01.40.72.70.00). Trendy
Au Bon Accueil p23
14 rue Monttessuy 7th (01.47.05.46.11). Bistros
Au Bon Saint-Pourçain p20
10bis rue Servandoni, 6th (01.43.54.93.63). Bistros
Aux Bons Crus p129
7 rue des Petits-Champs, 1st (01.42.60.06.45). Wine Bars
Les Bookinistes p21
53 quai des Grands-Augustins, 6th (01.43.25.45.94). Bistros
Botequim p82
1 rue Berthollet, 5th (01.43.37.98.46). The Americas
The Bottle Shop p121
5 rue Trousseau, 11th (01.43.14.28.04/ www.hip-bars.com). Bars & Pubs
Boucherie Lamartine Prosper et Cie p139
172 av Victor Hugo, 16th (01 47.27.82.29). Shops & Markets
Le Bouclard p37
1 rue Cavalotti, 18th (01.45.22.60.01). Bistros
La Boulangerie p73
15 rue des Panoyaux, 20th (01.43.58.45.45). Budget
Boulevard Auguste-Blanqui p140
between pl d'Italie and rue Baurrault, 13th. Shops & Markets
The Bowler p120
13 rue d'Artois, 8th (01.45.61.16.60). Bars & Pubs
Brasserie Fernand p21
13 rue Guisarde, 6th (01.43.54.61.47). Bistros
Brasserie Flo p47
7 cour des Petites-Ecuries, 10th (01.47.70.13.59). Brasseries
Brasserie de l'Isle St-Louis p45
55 quai de Bourbon, 4th (01.43.54.02.59). Brasseries
Brasserie Lipp p45
151 bd St-Germain, 6th (01.45.48.53.91/ www.brasserie-lipp.fr). Brasseries
Brasserie Lorraine p46
2-4 place des Ternes, 8th (01.56.21.22.00). Brasseries
Brasserie de la Poste p48
54 rue de Longchamp, 16th (01.47.55.01.31/ www.brasserie-de-la-poste.com). Brasseries
Bricolo Café p105
Basement of BHV department store, 52 rue de Rivoli, 4th (01.42.74.90.00/ www.cyberbricoleur.com). Cafés
Le Bristol p41; p128
112 rue du Fbg-St-Honoré, 8th (01.53.43.43.00/ www.hotel-bristol.com). Haute Cuisine; Tea Rooms & Ice Cream
Le Buddha Bar p51
8 rue Boissy d'Anglas, 8th (01.53.05.90.00). Trendy
Buffalo Grill p81
1 bd St-Germain, 5th (01.56.24.34.49/ www.buffalo-grill.com). The Americas
Le Buisson Ardent p19
25 rue Jussieu, 5th (01.43.54.93.02). Bistros
La Butte Chaillot p36
110bis av Kléber, 16th (01.47.27.88.88). Bistros

C

C'Amelot p28
50 rue Amelot, 11th (01.43.55.54.04). Bistros
Cabaret p51
2 pl du Palais-Royal, 1st (01.58.62.56.25). Trendy
Cacao et Chocolat p137
29 rue de Buci, 6th (01.46.33.77.63). Shops & Markets
Le Cadran p113
38 rue Raymond-Losserand, 14th (01.43.21.69.45). Cafés
Le Café p104
62 rue Tiquetonne, 2nd (01.40.39.08.00). Cafés
Café Antoine p115
17 rue La Fontaine, 16th (01.40.50.14.30). Cafés
Café Beaubourg p105
43 rue St-Merri, 4th (01.48.87.63.96). Cafés
Café Cannibale p123
93 rue Jean-Pierre-Timbaud, 11th (01.49.29.95.59). Bars & Pubs
Café Charbon p123
109 rue Oberkampf, 11th (01.43.57.55.13/ www.nouveaucasino.net). Bars & Pubs
Café du Commerce p72
51 rue du Commerce, 15th (01.45.75.03.27). Budget
Le Café des Délices p58
87 rue d'Assas, 6th (01.43.54.70.00). Contemporary
Café Delmas p107
2-4 pl de la Contrescarpe, 5th (01.43.26.51.26). Cafés
Café Le Dôme p109
149 rue St-Dominique, 7th (01.45.51.45.41). Cafés
Café de Flore p109
172 bd St-Germain, 6th (01.45.48.55.26). Cafés
Café de l'Industrie p111
16 rue St-Sabin, 11th (01.47.00.13.53). Cafés
Café de la Jatte p53
60 bd Vital Bouhot, Ile de la Jatte, 92200 Neuilly-sur-Seine (01.47.45.04.20). Trendy
Café des Lettres p109
53 rue de Verneuil, 7th (01.42.22.52.17/www. cafedeslettres.com). Cafés
Café Mabillon p120
164 bd St-Germain, 6th (01.43.26.62.93). Bars & Pubs
Café de la Mairie p109
8 pl St-Sulpice, 6th (01.43.26.67.82). Cafés
Café du Marché p109
38 rue Cler, 7th (01.47.05.51.27). Cafés
Café Marly p104
93 rue de Rivoli, cour Napoléon du Louvre, 1st (01.49.26.06.60). Cafés
Le Café Maure de la Mosquée de Paris p127
39 rue Geoffroy-St-Hilaire, 5th (01.43.31.38.20). Tea Rooms & Ice Cream
Café Le Nemours p104
2 pl Colette, 1st (01.42.61.34.14). Cafés
Café Noir p39
15 rue St-Blaise, 20th (01.40.09.75.80). Bistros
Café Noir p117
65 rue Montmartre, 2nd (01.40.39.07.36). Bars & Pubs
Café de la Nouvelle Mairie p107
19-21 rue des Fossés St-Jacques, 5th (01.44.07.04.41). Cafés
Café Oz p117
18 rue St-Denis, 1st (01.40.39.00.18/ www.cafe-oz.com). Bars & Pubs
Le Café du Passage p131
12 rue de Charonne, 11th (01.49.29.97.64). Wine Bars
Café des Phares p105
7 pl de la Bastille, 4th (01.42.72.04.70). Cafés
Café de la Place p113
23 rue d'Odessa, 14th (01.42.18.01.55). Cafés
Café de la Poste p68
13 rue Castex, 4th (01.42.72.95.35). Budget
Café de la Poste p107
7 rue l'Epée-de-Bois, 5th (01.43.37.05.58). Cafés
Café Ruc p104
159 rue St-Honoré, 1st (01.42.60.97.54). Cafés
Café Thoumieux p120
4 rue de la Comète, 7th (01.45.51.50.40). Bars & Pubs
Café du Trésor p105
7-9 rue du Trésor, 4th (01.42.71.78.34). Cafés
La Cagouille p66
10-12 pl Constantin-Brancusi, 14th(01.43.22.09.01/www.la-cagouille.fr). Fish & Seafood
Les Cailloux p131
58 rue des Cinq Diamants, 13th (01.45.80.15.08). Wine Bars
Les Cakes de Bertrand p139
7 rue Bourdaloue, 9th (01.40.16.16.28). Shops & Markets
Le Cambodge p87
10 av Richerand, 10th (01.44.84.37.70). Far East
Camille p14
24 rue des Francs-Bourgeois, 3rd (01.42.72.20.50). Bistros
La Campagne p140
111 bd de Grenelle, 15th (01.47.34.77.05). Shops & Markets
La Canaille p68
4 rue Crillon, 4th (01.42.78.09.71). Budget
Le Carré des Feuillants p40
14 rue de Castiglione, 1st (01.42.86.82.82). Haute Cuisine
La Casa del Habano p82

Alphabetical Index

169 bd St-Germain, 6th (01.45.44.33.56). The Americas

Casa Olympe p25
48 rue St-Georges, 9th (01.42.85.26.01). Bistros

La Cave Drouot p131
8 rue Drouot, 9th (01.47.70.83.38). Wine Bars

La Cave Gourmande p39
10 rue du Général Brunet, 19th (01.40.40.03.30). Bistros

Les Caves Augé p140
116 bd Haussmann, 8th (01.45.22.16.97). Shops & Markets

Caves Miard p131
9 rue des Quatre-Vents, 6th (01.43.54.99.30). Wine Bars

Caves Saint Gilles p100
4 rue St-Gilles, 3rd (01.48.87.22.62). Spanish

Les Caves Taillevent p140
199 rue du Fbg-St-Honoré, 8th (01.45.61.14.09/ www.taillevent.com). Shops & Markets

Centre de Dégustation Jacques Vivet p145
48 rue de Vaugirard, 6th (01.43.25.96.30). Learning & Tasting

Les Cépages p129
6 rue des Fossés-St-Marcel, 5th (01.47.07.91.25). Wine Bars

Chào-Bà-Café p125
22 bd de Clichy, 18th (01.46.06.72.90). Bars & Pubs

Charcuterie Lyonnaise p139
58 rue des Martyrs, 9th (01.48.78.96.45). Shops & Markets

Chardenoux p28
1 rue Jules-Vallès, 11th (01.43.71.49.52). Bistros

Charlot, Roi des Coquillages p47
81 bd de Clichy, 9th (01.53.20.48.00). Brasseries

La Charlotte en l'Ile p127
24 rue St-Louis-en-l'Ile, 4th (01.43.54.25.83). Tea Rooms & Ice Cream

Aux Charpentiers p21
10 rue Mabillon, 6th (01.43.26.30.05). Bistros

Chartier p70
7 rue du Fbg-Montmartre, 9th. (01.47.70.86.29). Budget

Le Chateaubriand p28
129 av Parmentier, 11th (01.43.57.45.95). Bistros

La Cheminée p70
7 rue Jean-Pierre Timbaud, 11th (01.49.23.06.76). Budget

Chen p88
15 rue du Théâtre, 15th (01.45.79.34.34). Far East

Chez Adel p121
10 rue de la Grange-aux-Belles, 10th (01.42.08.24.61). Bars & Pubs

Chez Arthur p27
25 rue du Fbg St-Martin, 10th (01.42.08.34.33). Bistros

Chez Camille p115
8 rue Ravignan, 18th (01.46.06.05.78). Cafés

Chez Casimir p27
6 rue de Belzunce, 10th (01.48.78.28.80). Bistros

Chez Catherine p25
65 rue de Provence, 9th (01.45.26.72.88). Bistros

Chez Foong p89
32 rue de Frémicourt, 15th (01.45.67.36.99). Far East

Chez Les Frères Gaudet p33
19 rue Duranton, 15th (01.45.58.43.17).

Chez Georges p14
1 rue du Mail, 2nd, (01.42.60.07.11). Bistros

Chez Germaine p70
30 rue Pierre-Leroux, 7th (01.42.73.28.34). Budget

Chez Gladines p72
30 rue des Cinq-Diamants, 13th (01.45.80.70.10). Budget

Chez Gudule p113
58 bd de Picpus, 12th (01.43.40.08.28). Cafés

Chez Janou p14
2 rue Roger-Verlomme, 3rd (01.42.72.28.41). Bistros

Chez Jean p73
38 rue Boyer, 20th (01.47.97.44.58). Budget

Chez Jean p25
8 rue St-Lazare, 9th (01.48.78.62.73). Bistros

Chez Marcel p21
7 rue Stanislas, 6th (01.45.48.29.94). Bistros

Chez Michel p27
10 rue de Belzunce, 10th (01.44.53.06.20). Bistros

Chez Omar p99
47 rue de Bretagne, 3rd (01.42.72.36.26). North African

Chez Papa p70
206 rue Lafayette, 10th (01.42.09.53.87). Budget

Chez Paul p32
22 rue de la Butte-aux-Cailles, 13th (01.45.89.22.11). Bistros

Chez Paul p28
13 rue de Charonne, 11th (01.47.00.34.57). Bistros

Chez Prune p111
71 quai de Valmy, 10th (01.42.41.30.47). Cafés

Chez Ramulaud p28
269 rue du Fbg-St-Antoine, 11th (01.43.72.23.29). Bistros

Chez René p19
14 bd St-Germain, 5th (01.43.54.30.23). Bistros

Chez Richard p119
37 rue Vieille-du-Temple, 4th (01.42.74.31.65). Bars & Pubs

Chez Toinette p73
20 rue Germain-Pilon, 18th (01.42.54.44.36). Budget

Chez Toutoune p19
5 rue de Pointoise, 5th (01.43.26.56.81). Bistros

Chez La Vieille p13
1 rue Bailleul/37 rue de l'Arbre Sec, 1st (01.42.60.15.78). Bistros

Chez Vong p87
10 rue de la Grande Truanderie, 1st (01.40.26.09.36). Far East

Chiberta p60
3 rue Arsène-Houssaye, 8th (01.53.53.42.00). Contemporary

The Chicago Pizza Pie Factory p81
5 rue Berri, 8th (01.45.62.50.23). The Americas

Les Chimères p119
133 rue St-Antoine, 4th (01.42.72.71.97). Bars & Pubs

China Club p125
50 rue de Charenton, 12th (01.43.43.82.02/ www.chinaclub.cc). Bars & Pubs

La Chine Masséna p87
Centre Commercial Masséna, 13 pl de Vénétie, 13th (01.45.83.98.88). Far East

Le Chinois p87
3 rue Monsieur le Prince, 6th (01.43.25.36.88). Far East

Le Chinon p115
49 rue des Abbesses, 18th (01.42.62.07.17). Cafés

La Chope Daguerre p113
17 rue Daguerre, 14th (01.43.22.76.59). Cafés

Christian Constant p139
37 rue d'Assas, 6th (01.53.63.15.15). Shops & Markets

CIDD Découverte du Vin p145
30 rue de la Sablière, 14th (01.45.45.44.20). Learning & Tasting

La Cigale p23
11bis rue Chomel, 7th (01.45.48.87.87). Bistros

La Cigogne p139
61 rue de l'Arcade, 8th (01.43.87.39.16). Shops & Markets

Le Cinq p42
Hôtel Four Seasons George V, 31 av George V, 8th (01.49.52.70.00/ www.fourseasons.com). Haute Cuisine

A la Cloche d'Or p25
3 rue Mansart, 9th (01.48.74.48.88). Bistros

Le Clos des Gourmets p23
16 av Rapp, 7th (01.45.51.75.61). Bistros

Le Clou p36
132 rue Cardinet, 17th (01.42.27.36.78). Bistros

Le Clown Bar p131
114 rue Amelot, 11th (01.43.55.87.35). Wine Bars

Le Cochon à l'Oreille p13
15 rue Montmartre, 1st (01.42.36.07.56). Bistros

Coffee India p91
33-35 rue de Lappe, 11th (01.48.06.18.57/ www.coffee-india.com). Indian

Au Coin des Gourmets p88
5, rue Dante, 5th (01.43.26.12.92). Far East

Le Colimaçon p17
44 rue Vieille-du-Temple, 4th (01.48.87.12.01/ www.lecolimacon.com). Bistros

Columbus Café p105
25 rue Vieille-du-Temple, 3rd (01.42.72.20.25/ www.columbuscafe.com). Cafés

Les Comédiens p27
1 rue de la Trinité, 9th (01.40.82.95.95). Bistros

... Comme Cochons p71
135 rue de Charenton, 12th (01.43.42.43.36). Budget

Le Comptoir p104
37 rue Berger, 1st (01.40.26.26.66). Cafés

Le Comptoir des Canettes p120
11 rue des Canettes, 6th (01.43.26.79.15). Bars & Pubs

Le Comptoir Corrézien p140
8 rue des Volontaires, 15th (01.47.83.52.97). Shops & Markets

Comptoir de la Gastronomie p139
34 rue Montmartre, 1st (01.42.33.31.32). Shops & Markets

Le Comptoir du Panthéon p107
5 rue Soufflot, 5th (01.43.54.75.36). Cafés

La Connivence p71
1 rue de Cotte, 12th (01.46.28.46.17). Budget

Connolly's Corner p119
12 rue de Mirbel, 5th (01.43.31.94.22). Bars & Pubs

Contre-Allée p32
83 av Denfert-Rochereau, 14th (01.43.54.99.86). Bistros

Coolín p120
Marché St-Germain, 15 rue Clément, 6th (01.44.07.00.92/ www.irishfrance.com). Bars & Pubs

La Coquille p104
30 rue Coquillière, 1st (01.40.26.55.36). Cafés

Corcoran p120
28 rue St-André-des-Arts, 6th (01.40.46.97.46/ www.corcoranirishpub.com). Bars & Pubs

Le Cordon Bleu p143
8 rue Léon-Delhomme, 15th (01.53.68.22.50). Learning & Tasting

Cosi p69
54 rue de Seine, 6th (01.46.33.35.36). Budget

La Côte p129
77 rue de Richelieu, 2nd (01.42.97.40.68). Wine Bars

Les Couleurs p123
117 rue St-Maur, 11th (01.43.57.95.61). Bars & Pubs

Le Coupe-Chou p19
11 rue de Lanneau, 5th (01.46.33.68.69/ www.lecoupechou.com). Bistros

Le Coupe Gorge p68
2 rue de la Coutellerie, 4th (01.48.04.79.24). Budget

La Coupole p48
102 bd du Montparnasse, 14th (01.43.20.14.20). Brasseries

Cour de Vincennes p140
12th. Mº Nation. Shops & Markets

Le Crocodile p119
6 rue Royer-Collard, 5th. (01.43.54.32.37). Bars & Pubs

Croissant Bon'Heur p133
83 rue de la Mare, 20th (tel/fax 01.43.58.43.43/ www.croissantbonheur.com). Home Delivery

Aux Crus de Bourgogne p14
3 rue Bachaumont, 2nd (01.42.33.48.24). Bistros

La Cuisine de Marie-Blanche p143
18 av de la Motte-Picquet, 7th (01.45.51.36.34). Learning & Tasting

D

Dalloyau p137
101 rue du Fbg-St-Honoré, 8th (01.42.99.90.00). Shops & Markets

Dame Jeanne p28
60 rue de Charonne, 11th (01.47.00.37.40/ www.damejeanne.fr). Bistros

Le Dauphin p13
167 rue St-Honoré, 1st (01.42.60.40.11). Bistros

De La Ville Café p121
34 bd Bonne Nouvelle, 10th (01.48.24.48.09). Bars & Pubs

Debauve & Gallais p139
30 rue des Sts-Pères, 7th (01.45.48.54.67). Shops & Markets

Les Degrés de Notre-Dame p19
10 rue des Grands-Degrés, 5th (01.55.42.88.88). Bistros

Les Délices d'Aphrodite p85
4 rue de Candolle, 5th (01.43.31.40.39). Eastern Mediterranean

Les Délices d'Orient p140
52 av Emile Zola, 15th (01.45.79.10.00). Shops & Markets

Démoulin p137
6 bd Voltaire, 11th (01.47.00.58.20/ www.chocolat-paris.com). Shops & Markets

Le Dénicheur p104
4 rue Tiquetonne, 2nd (01.42.21.31.01). Cafés

Au Dernier Métro p115
70 bd de Grenelle, 15th (01.45.75.01.23/www.auderniermetro.com). Cafés

Aux Deux Canards p27
8 rue du Fbg-Poissonnière, 10th (01.47.70.03.23). Bistros

Les Deux Magots p109
6 pl St-Germain-des-Prés, 6th (01.45.48.55.25/ www.lesdeuxmagots.com). Cafés

La Dînée p33
85 rue Leblanc, 15th (01.45.54.20.49). Bistros

La Distillerie p125
50 rue du Fbg-St-Antoine, 12th (01.40.01.99.00/ www.la-distillerie.com). Bars & Pubs

Le Divellec p65
107 rue de l'Universite, 7th (01.45.51.91.96). Fish & Seafood

Les Dix Vins p72
57 rue Falguière, 15th (01.43.20.91.77). Budget

Djakarta Bali p88
9 rue Vauvilliers, 1st (01.45.08.83.11). Far East

Doïna p101
149 rue St-Dominique, 7th (01.45.50.49.57). Other International

Les Domaines qui Montent p140
136 bd Voltaire, 11th (01.43.56.89.15). Shops & Markets

Le Dôme p66
108 bd du Montparnasse, 14th (01.43.35.25.81). Fish & Seafood

Le Dôme du Marais p17
53bis rue des Francs-Bourgeois, 4th (01.42.74.54.17). Bistros

Dominique p101
19 rue Bréa, 6th (01.43.27.08.80). Other International

Dong Huong p90
14 rue Louis-Bonnet, 11th (01.43.57.18.88). Far East

Le Duc p66
243 bd Raspail, 14th (01.43.20.96.30/ 01.43.22.59.59). Fish & Seafood

E

L'Ebauchoir p31
45 rue de Cîteaux, 12th (01.43.42.49.31). Bistros

Ecole Lenôtre p143
48 av Victor-Hugo, 16th (01.45.02.21.19). Learning & Tasting

L'Ecole du Thé p143
Le Palais des Thés, 64 rue Vieille-du-Temple, 3rd (01.43.56.96.38/www.le-palais-des-thes.fr). Learning & Tasting

L'Ecole du Vin Ylan Schwartz p145
17 passage Foubert, 13th (01.45.89.77.39). Learning & Tasting

Ecoles Grégoire Ferrandi p143; p145
28 rue de l'Abbé-Grégoire, 6th (01.49.54.28.03). Learning & Tasting

L'Ecurie p68
2 rue Laplace, 5th (01.46.33.68.49). Budget

Les Editeurs p109
4 carrefour de l'Odéon, 6th (01.43.26.67.76/ www.lesediteurs.fr). Cafés

El Bacha p85
74, rue de la Croix-Nivert, 15th (01.45.32.15.42). Eastern Mediterranean

El Bodegon de Pancho p83
8 rue Guy-Môquet, 17th (01.53.31.00.73). The Americas

El Paladar p83
26bis rue de la Fontaine au Roi, 11th. (01.43.57.42.70). The Americas

El Palenque p82
5 rue de la Montagne-Ste-Geneviève, 5th (01.43.54.08.99). The Americas

Les Elysées p60
Hôtel Vernet, 25 rue Vernet, 8th (01.44.31.98.98/www.hotelvernet.com). Contemporary

L'Encrier p71
55 rue Traversière, 12th (01.44.68.08.16). Budget

L'Endroit p125
67 pl du Dr-Félix-Lobligeois, 17th (01.42.29.50.00). Bars & Pubs

Les Enfants Gâtés p127
43 rue des Francs-Bourgeois, 4th (01.42.77.07.63). Tea Rooms & Ice Cream

L'Enoteca p129
25 rue Charles V, 4th (01.42.78.91.44). Wine Bars

L'Entracte p37
44 rue d'Orsel, 18th (01.46.06.93.41). Bistros

Entre Ciel et Terre p74
5 rue Hérold, 1st (01.45.08.49.84/www.entrecieletterre.com). Vegetarian

L'Entre-potes p123
14 rue de Charonne, 11th (01.48. 06.57.04). Bars & Pubs

L'Entrepôt p115
7-9 rue Francis-de-Pressensé, 14th (01.45.40.60.70). Cafés

L'Epi Dupin p21
11 rue Dupin, 6th (01.42.22.64.56). Bistros

L'Epicerie p139
51 rue St-Louis-en-l'Ile, 4th (01.43.25.20.14). Shops & Markets

L'Equitable p19
1 rue des Fossés-St-Marcel, 5th (01.43.31.69.20). Bistros

L'Escale p107
1 rue des Deux-Ponts, 4th (01.43.54.94.23). Cafés

L'Escapade p69
10 rue de la Montagne-Ste-Geneviève, 5th (01.46.33.23.85). Budget

L'Espadon p40
Hôtel Ritz, 15 pl Vendôme, 1st (01.43.16.30.80/ www.ritzparis.com). Haute Cuisine

L'Esplanade p51
52 rue Fabert, 7th (01.47.05.38.80). Trendy

Les Etages p119
35 rue Vielle-du-Temple, 4th (01.42.78.72.00). Bars & Pubs

L'Été en Pente Douce p115
23 rue Muller, 18th (01.42.64.02.67). Cafés

L'Etoile Manquante p107
34 rue Vieille-du-Temple, 4th (01.42.72.48.34/ www.cafeine.com). Cafés

L'Etrier Bistrot p37
154 rue Lamarck, 18th (01.42.29.14.01). Bistros

Extra Old Café p111
307 rue du Fbg-St-Antoine, 11th (01.43.71.73.45). Cafés

F

F.B.I. Paris (Freestyle Bar) p123
45 rue de la Folie-Méricourt, 11th (01.43.14.26.36/ www.fbiparis.com). Bars & Pubs

La Fabrique p123
53 rue du Fbg-St-Antoine, 11th (01.43.07.67.07/ www.fabrique.fr). Bars & Pubs

Fajitas p82
15 rue Dauphine, 6th (01.46.34.44.69). The Americas

Fakhr el Dine p85
3 rue Quentin-Bauchart, 8th. (01.47.23.44.42). Eastern Mediterranean

Fauchon p139
26-30 pl de la Madeleine, 8th (01.47.42.60.11). Shops & Markets

Favela Chic p83
18 rue du Fbg-du-Temple, 11th (01.40.21.38.14/ www.favelachic.com). The Americas

Le Felteu p129
15 rue Pecquay, 4th (01.42.72.14.51). Wine Bars

La Ferme Opéra p69
55-57 rue St-Roch, 1st (01.40.20.12.12). Budget

La Fermette Marbeuf 1900 p46
5 rue Marbeuf, 8th (01.53.23.08.00/ www.blanc.net). Brasseries

Fil o'Fromage p137
4 rue Poirier-de-Narçay, 14th (01.40.44.86.75). Shops & Markets

Finnegan's Wake p119
9 rue des Boulangers, 5th (01.46.34.23.65/ www.irishfrance.com). Bars & Pubs

Fish p131
69 rue de Seine, 6th (01.43.54.34.69). Wine Bars

Flann O'Brien's p117
6 rue Bailleul, 1st (01.42.60.13.58/ www.irishfrance.com/ flannobrien). Bars & Pubs

La Flèche d'Or p125
102bis rue de Bagnolet, 20th (01.43.72.04.23/ www.flechedor.com). Bars & Pubs

Le Flore en l'Isle p107
42 quai d'Orléans, 4th (01.43.29.88.27). Cafés

Fogon Saint-Julien p100
10 rue St-Julien-le-Pauvre, 5th (01.43.54.31.33). Spanish

La Folie en Tête p125
33 rue de la Butte-aux-Cailles, 13th (01.45.80.65.99). Bars & Pubs

La Folletterie p33
34 rue Letellier, 15th (01.45.75.55.95). Bistros

La Fontaine de Mars p23
129 rue St-Dominique, 7th (01.47.05.46.44). Bistros

La Fontaine Gourmande p14
11 rue Charlot, 3rd (01.42.78.72.40). Bistros

Les Fontaines p19
9 rue Soufflot, 5th (01.43.26.42.80). Bistros

Fontaines d'Elysabeth p67
1 rue Ste-Elysabeth, 3rd (01.42.74.36.41). Budget

Foody's Brunch Café p74
26 rue Montorgueil, 1st (01.40.13.02.53). Vegetarian

Forêt Noire p128
9 rue de l'Eperon, 6th (01.44.41.00.09). Tea Rooms & Ice Cream

Le Fouquet's p46

99 av des des Champs-Elysées, 8th (01.47.23.70.60/ www.lucienbarriere.com). Brasseries

La Fourchette des Anges p73
17 rue Biot, 17th (01.44.69.07.69). Budget

La Fourmi p125
74 rue des Martyrs, 18th (01.42.64.70.35). Bars & Pubs

La Fourmi Aillée p128
8 rue du Fouarre, 5th (01.43.29.40.99). Tea Rooms & Ice Cream

Françoise Meunier p143
7 rue Paul-Lelong, 2nd (01.40.26.14.00/ www.intiweb.com/fmeunier). Learning & Tasting

Freedom p120
8 rue de Berri, 8th (01.53.75.25.50). Bars & Pubs

La Frégate p109
1 rue du Bac, 7th (01.42.61.23.77/ www.la-fregate.com). Cafés

La Fresque p67
100 rue Rambuteau, 1st (01.42.33.17.56). Budget

The Frog & Princess p120
9 rue Princesse, 6th (01.40.51.77.38/ www.frogpubs.com). Bars & Pubs

The Frog & Rosbif p117
116 rue St-Denis, 2nd (01.42.36.34.73/ www.frogpubs.com). Bars & Pubs

Fu Bar p120
5 rue St-Sulpice, 6th (01.40.51.82.00). Bars & Pubs

Le Fumoir p117
6 rue de l'Amiral-de-Coligny, 1st (01.42.92.00.24/ www.lefumoir.com). Bars & Pubs

G

La Galère des Rois p37
8 rue Cavallotti 18th (01.42.93.34.58). Bistros

Galerie 88 p71
88 quai de l'Hôtel de Ville, 4th (01.42.72.17.58). Vegetarian

Gallopin p45
40 rue Notre-Dame-des-Victoires, 2nd (01.42.36.45.38.). Brasseries

Gandhi-Opéra p91
66 rue Ste-Anne, 2nd (01.47.03.41.00/ www.restaurant-gandhi.com). Indian

Ganesha Corner p91
16 rue Perdonnet, 10th (01.46.07.35.32). Indian

La Gare p48
19 chaussée de la Muette, 16th (01.42.15.15.31). Brasseries

Garnier p46
111 rue St-Lazare, 8th (01.43.87.50.40). Brasseries

Le Gavroche p14
19 rue St-Marc, 2nd (01.42.96.89.70). Bistros

Georges p51
Centre Pompidou, 6th floor, rue Rambuteau, 4th. (01.44.78.47.99). Trendy

Georget p15
64 rue Vieille-du-Temple, 3rd (01.42.78.55.89). Bistros

Gérard Mulot p137
76 rue de Seine, 6th (01.43.26.85.77). Shops & Markets

Ghislaine Arabian p43
16 av Bugeaud, 16th (01.56.28.16.16). Haute Cuisine

Gin Go Gae p88
28 rue Lamartine, 9th (01.48.78.24.64). Far East

La Girondine p32
48 bd Arago, 13th (01.43.31.64.17). Bistros

Les Glénan p65
54 rue de Bourgogne, 7th (01.45.51.61.09). Fish & Seafood

Goumard p65
7-9 rue Duphot, 1st (01.42.60.36.07/ www.goumard.fr). Fish & Seafood

Au Grain de Folie p75
24 rue de La-Vieuville, 18th (01.42.58.15.57). Vegetarian

Grains Nobles p145
5 rue Laplace, 5th (01.43.54.93.54). Learning & Tasting

Gr& Appétit p74
9 rue de la Cerisaie, 4th (01.40.27.04.95). Vegetarian

Le Grand Colbert p45
2-4 rue Vivienne, 2nd (01.42.86.87.88). Brasseries

Le Grand Véfour p40
17 rue de Beaujolais, 1st (01.42.96.56.27). Haute Cuisine

La Grande Armée p48
3 av de la Grande-Armée, 16th (01.45.00.24.77). Brasseries

Les Grandes Marches p48
6 pl de la Bastille, 12th (01.43.42.90.32/ www.lesgrandesmarches.com). Brasseries

A la Grange Batelière p27
16 rue de la Grange-Batelière, 9th (01.47.70.85.15). Bistros

Granterroirs p111
30 rue de Miromesnil, 8th (01.47.42.18.18). Cafés

Le Grenier de Notre Dame p75
18 rue de la Bûcherie, 5th (01.43.29.98.29/ www.legrenierdenotredame.com). Vegetarian

Le Grenier Voyageur p111
3 rue Yves-Toudic, 10th (01.42.02.25.50). Cafés

Le Griffonier p131
8 rue des Saussaies, 8th (01.42.65.17.17). Wine Bars

Grizzli Café p17
7 rue St-Martin, 4th (01.48.87.77.56). Bistros

Guen Maï p75
2bis rue de l'Abbaye, 6th. (01.43.26.03.24). Vegetarian

La Gueuze p119
19 rue Soufflot, 5th (01.43.54.63.00). Bars & Pubs

Le Guilvinec p66
34 Cour St-Emilion, 12th (01.44.68.01.35). Fish & Seafood

Gustavia p101
26-28 rue des Grands-Augustins, 6th (01.40.46.86.70). Other International

Guy Savoy p43
18 rue Troyon, 17th (01.43.80.40.61/ www.guysavoy.com). Haute Cuisine

H

Han Lim p88
6 rue Blainville, 5th (01.43.54.62.74). Far East

Handmade p111
19 rue Jean-Mermoz, 8th (01.45.62.50.05). Cafés

Le Hangar p15
12 impasse Berthaud, 3rd (01.42.74.55.44). Bistros

Hard Rock Café p81
14 bd Montmartre, 9th (01.53.24.60.00/ www.hardrockcafe.com). The Americas

Harry's New York Bar p117
5 rue Daunou, 2nd (01.42.61.71.14/ www.harrys-bar.fr). Bars & Pubs

Hédiard p139
21 pl de la Madeleine, 8th (01.43.12.88.88/ www.hediard.fr). Shops & Markets

Hélices et Délices p101
8 rue Thénard, 5th (01.43.54.59.47). Other International

Henri Ceccaldi p139
21 rue des Mathurins, 9th (01.47.42.66.52). Shops & Markets

L'Hermitage p27
5 bd de Denain, 10th (01.48.78.77.09). Bistros

The Hideout p119
11 rue du Pot-de-Fer, 5th (01.45.35.13.17/ www.irishfrance.com). Bars & Pubs

Hiramatsu p40
7 quai de Bourbon, 4th (01.56.81.08.80). Haute Cuisine

L'Homme Bleu p99
55bis rue Jean-Pierre Timbaud, 11th (01.48.07.05.63). North African

Hôtel Costes p51
239 rue St-Honoré, 1st (01.42.44.50.25). Trendy

Hôtel de Crillon p128
10 pl de la Concorde, 8th (01.44.71.15.00). Tea Rooms & Ice Cream

Hôtel Lutétia p119
45 bd Raspail, 6th (01.49.54.46.46/ www.lutetia-paris.com). Bars & Pubs

Hôtel Meurice p128
228 rue de Rivoli, 1st (01.44.58.10.10/www.meuricehotel.com). Tea Rooms & Ice Cream

Hôtel Plaza Athenée p119; p128
25 av Montaigne, 8th (01.53.67.66.65). Bars & Pubs; Tea Rooms & Ice Cream

Hôtel Raphaël p128
17 av Kléber, 16th (01.53.64.32.00). Tea Rooms & Ice Cream

Hôtel Ritz p119; p128
15 pl Vendôme, 1st (01.43.16.30.31/ www.ritzparis.com). Bars & Pubs; Tea Rooms & Ice Cream

Huilerie Artisanale Leblanc p139
6 rue Jacob, 6th (01.46.34.61.55). Shops & Markets

L'Huître et Demie p65
80 rue Mouffetard, 5th (01.43.37.98.21). Fish & Seafood

L'Huîtrier p66
16 rue Saussier-Leroy, 17th (01.40.54.83.44). Fish & Seafood

I

L'Imprévu Café p107
7-9 rue Quincampoix, 4th (01.42.78.23.50). Cafés

Indiana Café p81
1 pl de la République, 3rd (01.48.87.82.35/ www.indiana-cafe.com). The Americas

Institut du Vin du Savour Club p145
11-13 rue Gros, 16th (01.42.30.94.18). Learning & Tasting

L'Intermède p19
4 bd du Port-Royal, 5th (01.47.07.08.99). Bistros

Iode p65
48 rue d'Argout, 2nd (01.42.36.46.45). Fish & Seafood

Isami p97
4 quai d'Orléans, 4th (01.40.46.06.97). Japanese

Isse p97
56 rue Ste-Anne, 2nd (01.42.96.67.76). Japanese

Izraël p140
30 rue François-Miron, 4th (01.42.72.66.23). Shops & Markets

J

Jabugo Iberico & Co. p140
11 rue Clément Marot, 8th (01.47.20.03.13). Shops & Markets

Jacques Mélac p131
42 rue Léon-Frot, 11th (01.43.70.59.27). Wine Bars

La Jamaïque p125
2 pl Catalogne, 14th (01.43.35.50.50). Bars & Pubs

The James Joyce p125
71 bd Gouvion-St-Cyr, 17th (01.44.09.70.32). Bars & Pubs

Jamin p43
32 rue de Longchamp, 16th (01.45.53.00.07). Haute Cuisine

Japotori p97
41 rue Monsieur-le-Prince, 6th (01.43.29.00.54). Japanese

Le Jardin des Pâtes p69
4 rue Lacépède, 5th (01.43.31.50.71). Budget

Le Jardin des Vignes p145
91 rue de Turenne, 3rd (01.42.77.05.00). Learning & Tasting

Jean-Luc Poujauran p137
20 rue Jean-Nicot, 7th (01.47.05.80.88). Shops & Markets

Jean-Paul Hévin p127
231 rue St-Honoré, 1st (01.55.35.35.97). Tea Rooms & Ice Cream

Jean-Paul Hévin p139
3 rue Vavin, 6th (01.43.54.09.85). Shops & Markets

Jemmapes p111
82 quai de Jemmapes, 10th (01.40.40.02.35). Cafés

Jipangue p97
96 rue La Boétie, 8th (01.45.63.77.00). Japanese

Joe Allen Restaurant p81
30 rue Pierre Lescot, 1st (01.42.36.70.13). The Americas

Josephine 'Chez Dumonet' p21
117 rue du Cherche-Midi, 6th (01.45.48.52.40). Bistros

Le Jules Verne p41
Second Level, Eiffel Tower, Champ de Mars, 7th (01.45.55.61.44). Haute Cuisine

Julien p47
16 rue du Fbg-St-Denis, 10th (01.47.70.12.06). Brasseries

Les Jumeaux p28
73 rue Amelot, 11th (01.43.14.27.00). Bistros

La Jungle p125
32 rue Gabrielle, 18th (01.46.06.75.69). Bars & Pubs

La Jungle p117
56 rue d'Argout, 2nd (01.40.41.03.45). Bars & Pubs

Juveniles p129
47 rue de Richelieu, 1st (01.42.97.46.49). Wine Bars

K

Kambodgia p87
15 rue de Bassano, 16th (01.47.23.08.19). Far East

La Kaskad' p115
2 pl Armand-Carrel, 19th (01.40.40.08.10). Cafés

Kastoori p91
4 pl Gustave Toudouze, 9th (01.44.53.06.10). Indian

Le Keryado p66
32 rue Regnault, 13th (01.45.83.87.58). Fish & Seafood

Khun Akorn p89
8 av de Taillebourg, 11th (01.43.56.20.03). Far East

Kibele p85
12 rue de l'Echiquier, 10th (01.48.24.57.74). Eastern Mediterranean

Kifuné p97
44 rue St-Ferdinand, 17th (01.45.72.11.19). Japanese

Kim Ahn p90
49 av. Emile Zola, 15th (01.45.79.40.96). Far East

Kinugawa p96
9 rue du Mont-Thabor, 1st (01.42.60.65.07). Japanese

Kioko p140
46 rue des Petits-Champs, 2nd (01.42.61.33.65). Shops & Markets

Kirane's p91
85 av des Ternes, 17th (01.45.74.40.21). Indian

Le Kitch p113
10 rue Oberkampf, 11th (01.40.21.94.14). Cafés

Kok p90
129bis av de Choisy, 13th (01.45.84.10.48). Far East

Korean Barbecue p88
22, rue Delambre, 14th (01.43.35.44.32). Far East

Korova p51
33 rue Marbeuf, 8th (01.53.89.93.93). Trendy

Krung Thep p89
93 rue Julien-Lacroix, 20th (01.43.66.83.74). Far East

L

Ladurée p128
16 rue Royale, 8th (01.42.60.21.79). Tea Rooms & Ice Cream

Laï Laï Ken p96
7 rue Ste-Anne, 1st (01.40.15.96.90). Japanese

Lao Siam p89
49 rue de Belleville, 19th (01.40.40.09.68). Far East

Las Ramblas p100
14 rue Miollis, 15th (01 47 83 32 98). Spanish

Latina Café p121
114 av des Champs-Elysées, 8th (01.42.89.98.89). Bars & Pubs

Laurent p42
41 av Gabriel, 8th (01.42.25.00.39/ www.le-laurent.com). Haute Cuisine

Laurent Dubois p137
2 rue de Lourmel, 15th (01.45.78.70.58). Shops & Markets

Le Lèche-Vin p123
13 rue Daval, 11th (01.43.55.98.91). Bars & Pubs

Ledoyen p42
1 av Dutuit, 8th (01.53.05.10.01). Haute Cuisine

Legrand Filles et Fils p140
1 rue de la Banque, 2nd (01.42.60.07.12). Shops & Markets

Lenôtre p139
61 rue Lecourbe, 15th (01.42.73.20.97/ www.lenotre.com). Shops & Markets

Au Levain du Marais p137
32 rue de Turenne, 3rd (01.42.78.07.31). Shops & Markets

Lézard Café p104
32 rue Etienne Marcel, 2nd (01.42.33.22.73). Cafés

The Lizard Lounge p119
18 rue du Bourg-Tibourg, 4th (01.42.72.81.34/ www.hip-bars.com). Bars & Pubs

Le Loir dans la Théière p127
3 rue des Rosiers, 4th (01.42.72.90.61). Tea Rooms & Ice Cream

Le Lotus Bleu p133
17 rue de la Pierre-Levée, 11th (01.43.55.57.75/ fax 01.43.14.02.72/ www.lotus-bleu.fr). Home Delivery

Lou Pascalou p125
14 rue des Panoyaux, 20th (01.46.36.78.10). Bars & Pubs

Lucas Carton p42
9 pl de la Madeleine, 8th (01.42.65.22.90/ www.lucascarton.com). Haute Cuisine

M

M's Coffee Room p109
71 rue du Cherche-Midi, 6th (01.45.44.20.57). Cafés

Ma Bourgogne p131
133 bd Haussmann, 8th (01.45.63.50.61). Wine Bars

Ma Bourgogne p17
19 pl des Vosges, 4th (01.42.78.44.64). Bistros

Ma Pomme p73
107 rue de Ménilmontant, 20th (01.40.33.10.40). Budget

Macéo p58
15 rue des Petits-Champs, 1st (01.42.97.53.85). Contemporary

Le Mâchon d'Henri p21
8 rue Guisarde, 6th (01.43.29.08.70). Bistros

Macis & Muscade p36
110 rue Legendre, 17th (01.42.26.62.26). Bistros

La Maison de l'Aubrac p46
37 rue Marbeuf, 8th (01.43.59.05.14). Brasseries

Maison Blanche p60
15 av Montaigne, 8th (01.47.23.55.99). Contemporary

La Maison de la Chine p128
76 rue Bonaparte, 6th (01.40.51.95.16). Tea Rooms & Ice Cream

La Maison du Chocolat p139
89 av Raymond-Poincaré, 16th (01.40.67.77.83/www.lamaisonduchocolat.com). Shops & Markets

La Maison de l'Escargot p139
79 rue Fondary, 15th (01.45.75.31.09). Shops & Markets

Maison Kayser p137
8, 14 rue Monge, 5th (01.44.07.01.42/ 31.61). Shops & Markets

Maison Prunier p66
16 av Victor Hugo, 16th (01.44.17.35.85/www.maisonprunier.com). Fish & Seafood

Maison Rollet Pradier p137
6 rue de Bourgogne, 7th (01.45.51.78.36). Shops & Markets

La Maison des Trois Thés p128
33 rue Gracieuse, 5th (01.43.36.93.84). Tea Rooms & Ice Cream

La Maison de la Truffe p139
19 pl de la Madeleine, 8th (01.42.65.53.22/ www.maison-de-la-truffe.com). Shops & Markets

La Maline p24
40 rue de Ponthieu, 8th (01.45.63.14.14). Bistros

Man Ray p52
34 rue Marbeuf, 8th (01.56.88.36.36/ www.manray.fr). Trendy

Le Mansouria p100
11 rue Faidherbe, 11th (01.43.71.00.16). North African

Marché Bastille p140
bd Richard-Lenoir, 11th. Shops & Markets

Marché Biologique p140
bd Raspail, 6th. Shops & Markets

Marché d'Aligre p140
rue and pl d'Aligre, 12th. Shops & Markets

Mariage Frères p127
30-32 rue du Bourg-Tibourg, 4th (01.42.72.28.11/www.mariagefreres.com). Tea Rooms & Ice Cream

Marie-Anne Cantin p137
12 rue du Champ-de-Mars, 7th (01.45.50.43.94/ www.cantin.fr). Shops & Markets

Market p60
15 av Matignon, 8th (01.56.43.40.90). Contemporary

Marmite et Cassolette p69
157 bd du Montparnasse, 6th (01.43.26.26.53). Budget

Mathis p119
3 rue de Ponthieu, 8th (01.53.76.01.62). Bars & Pubs

Matsuri Sushi p133
26 rue Leopold Bellan, 2nd (01.40.26.11.13/ fax 01.42.33.10.38/ www.matsuri-sushi.com). Home Delivery

Le Mauzac p129
7 rue de l'Abbé de l'Epée, 5th (01.46.33.75.22). Wine Bars

Mavrommatis p85
5 rue du Marché des Patriarches, 5th (01.43.31.17.17). Eastern Mediterranean

Max Poilâne p137
87 rue Brancion, 15th (01.48.28.45.90/ www.max-poilane.fr). Shops & Markets

Le Maxence p58
9bis bd du Montparnasse, 6th (01.45.67.24.88). Contemporary

Mazeh p85
65 rue des Entrepreneurs, 15th (01.45.75.33.89). Eastern Mediterranean

Mazurka p101
3 rue André-del-Sarte, 18th (01.42.23.36.45). Other International

Le Mecano Bar p123
99 rue Oberkampf, 11th (01.40.21.35.28). Bars & Pubs

La Méditerranée p65
2 pl de l'Odéon, 6th (01.43.26.02.30/www.la-mediterranee.com). Fish & Seafood

La Mercerie p123

Alphabetical Index

98 rue Oberkampf, 11th (01.43.38.81.30). Bars & Pubs

Le Merle Moqueur p125 11 rue de la Butte-aux-Cailles, 13th (01.45.65.12.43). Bars & Pubs

Le Meurice p40 Hôtel Meurice, 228 rue de Rivoli, 1st (01.44.58.10.10). Haute Cuisine

Mexi & Co p82; p140 10 rue Dante, 5th (01.46.34.14.12). The Americas; Shops & Markets

A la Mexicaine p81 68 rue Quincampoix, 3rd (01.48.87.99.34). The Americas

Michel Rostang p43 20 rue Rennequin, 17th (01.47.63.40.77/ www.michelrostang.com). Haute Cuisine

Le Mille-Pâtes p140 5 rue des Petits-Champs, 1st (01.42.96.03.04). Shops & Markets

Mimosa p67 44 rue d'Argout, 2nd (01.40.28.15.75). Budget

Mirama p87 17 rue Saint-Jacques, 5th (01.43.54.71.77). Far East

The Moose p120 16 rue des Quatre-Vents, 6th (01.46.33.77.00/ www.mooseheadparis. com). Bars & Pubs

Le Morosophe p37 83 rue Legendre, 17th (01.53.06.82.82). Bistros

Morry's p113 1 rue de Charonne, 11th (01.48.07.03.03). Cafés

Le Moulin à Vent - Chez Henri p20 20 rue des Fossés-St-Bernard, 5th (01.43.54.99.37). Bistros

Le Moulin à Vins p37 6 rue Burq, 18th (01.42.52.81.27). Bistros

Moulin de la Vierge p137 166 av de Suffren, 15th (01.47.83.45.55). Shops & Markets

La Mousson p87 9 rue Thérèse, 1st (01.42.60.59.46). Far East

Le Musée du Vin p145 5 sq Charles-Dickens, 16th (01.45.25.63.26). Learning & Tasting

N

Nabuchodonosor p23 6 av Bosquet, 7th (01.45.56.97.26). Bistros

Natacha p32 17bis rue Campagne-Première, 14th (01.43.20.79.27). Bistros

Aux Négociants p37 27 rue Lambert, 18th (01.46.06.15.11). Bistros

Le Nemrod p21 51 rue du Cherche-Midi, 6th (01.45.48.17.05). Bistros

New Nioullaville p87 32 rue de l'Orillon, 11th. (01.40.21.96.18). Far East

New Pondichery p91 189 rue du Fbg-St-Denis, 10th (01.40.34.30.70). Indian

Nils p69 36 rue Montorgueil, 1st (01.55.34.39.49). Budget

No Stress Café p115 27 rue Balard, 15th (01.45.58.45.68). Cafés

Nobu p52 15 rue Marbeuf, 8th (01.56.89.53.53). Trendy

Au Noiseiter p137 33 rue Rambuteau, 4th (01.48.87.68.12). Shops & Markets

O

L'O à la Bouche p32 124 bd du Montparanasse, 14th (01.56.54.01.55). Bistros

L'Oeillade p24 10 rue St-Simon, 7th (01.42.22.01.60). Bistros

Oliviers & Co p139 28 rue de Buci, 6th (01.44.07.15.43/ www.oliviers-co.com). Shops & Markets

OPA p125 9 rue Biscornet, 12th (01.49.28.97.16/ www.opabastille.com). Bars & Pubs

Les Ormes p36 8 rue Chapu, 16th (01.46.47.83.98). Bistros

L'Os à Moëlle p35 3 rue Vasco-de-Gama, 15th (01.45.57.27.27). Bistros

P

La Palette p109 43 rue de Seine, 6th (01.43.26.68.15). Cafés

Le Pamphlet p15 38 rue Debellyme, 3rd (01.42.72.39.24). Bistros

Le Pantalon p119 7 rue Royer-Collard, 5th (01.40.51.85.85). Bars & Pubs

Les Papilles p129 30 rue Gay-Lussac, 5th (01.43.25.20.79/ www.lespapilles.fr). Wine Bars

Papou Lounge p104 74 rue Jean-Jacques Rousseau, 1st (01.44.76.00.03). Cafés

Le Paprika p101 28 av Trudaine, 9th (01.44.63.02.91/ www.le-paprika.com). Other International

Le Parc aux Cerfs p21 50 rue Vavin, 6th (01.43.54.87.83). Bistros

Le Parmentier p28 12 rue Arthur Groussier, 10th. (01.42.40.74.75). Bistros

Le Passage p28 18 passage de la Bonne-Graine, 11th (01.47.00.73.30). Bistros

La Patache p121 60 rue de Lancry, 10th (01.42.08.14.35). Bars & Pubs

Pause Café p113 41 rue de Charonne, 11th (01.48.06.80.33). Cafés

Le Pavé p68 7 rue des Lombards, 4th (01.44.54.07.20). Budget

Le Pays de Vannes p72 34bis rue Wattignies, 12th (01.43.07.87.42). Budget

Pema Thang p90 13 rue de la Montagne Ste-Geneviève, 5th (01.43.54.34.34). Far East

Le Père Claude p35 51 av de la Motte-Picquet, 15th (01.47.34.03.05). Bistros

Le Père Fouettard p129 9 rue Pierre-Lescot, 1st (01.42.33.74.17). Wine Bars

Perraudin p69 157 rue St-Jacques, 5th (01.46.33.15.75). Budget

Le Petit Bergson p111 10 pl Henri-Bergson, 8th (01.45.22.63.25). Cafés

Le Petit Caboulot p37 6 pl Jacques-Froment, 18th (01.46.27.19.00). Bistros

Au P'tit Cahoua p100 39 bd St-Marcel, 13th (01.47.07.24.42). North African

Le Petit Château d'Eau p111 34 rue du Chateau d'Eau, 10th (01.42.08.72.81). Cafés

P'tit Creux du Faubourg p111 66 rue du Fbg-Montmartre, 9th (01.48.78.20.57). Cafés

Au Petit Fer à Cheval p107 30 rue Vieille-du-Temple, 4th (01.42.72.47.47/ www.cafeine.com). Cafés

Le Petit Flore p67 6 rue Croix des Petits Champs, 1st (01.42.60.25.53). Budget

Le P'tit Gavroche p68 15 rue Ste-Croix de la Bretonnerie, 4th (01.48.87.74.26). Budget

Le Petit Keller p70 13bis rue Keller, 11th (01.47.00.12.97). Budget

Le Petit Marcel p107 65 rue Rambuteau, 4th (01.48.87.10.20). Cafés

Au Petit Marguery p32 9 bd du Port-Royal, 13th (01.43.31.58.59). Bistros

Le Petit Marseillais p15 72 rue Vieille-du-Temple, 3rd (01.42.78.91.59). Bistros

Le Petit Rétro p36 5 rue Mesnil, 16th (01.44.05.06.05). Bistros

Au Petit Riche p47 25 rue Le Peletier, 9th (01.47.70.68.68/ www.aupetitriche.com). Brasseries

Le Petit Robert p39 10 rue Cauchois, 18th (01.46.06.04.46). Bistros

Le Petit Saint-Benoît p69 4 rue Saint-Benoît, 6th (01.42.60.27.92). Budget

Au Petit Suisse p109 16 rue de Vaugirard, 6th (01.43.26.03.81). Cafés

Le Petit Troquet p24 28 rue de l'Exposition, 7th (01.47.05.80.39). Bistros

La Petite Chaise p24 36 rue de Grenelle, 7th (01.42.22.13.35). Bistros

A la Petite Fabrique p139 12 rue St-Sabin, 11th (01.48.05.82.02). Shops & Markets

La Petite France p67 14 rue de la Banque, 2nd (01.42.96.17.19). Budget

Les Petites Sorcières p32 12 rue Liancourt, 14th (01.43.21.95.68). Bistros

Les P'tits Bouchons de François Clerc p35 32 bd du Montparnasse, 15th (01.45.48.52.03/ www.lesbouchonsdefrancoisclerc.com). Bistros

Les Petits Plus p128 20 bd Beaumarchais, 11th (01.48.87.01.40/ www.lespetitsplus.com). Tea Rooms & Ice Cream

Les Philosophes p17 28 rue Vieille-du-Temple, 4th (01.48.87.49.64/ www.cafeine.com). Bistros

Le Piano Vache p119 8 rue Laplace, 5th (01.46.33.75.03). Bars & Pubs

Piccolo Teatro p75 6, rue des Ecouffes, 4th (01.42.72.17.79/ www.piccoloteatro.com). Vegetarian

Le Pick-Clops p119 16 rue Vieille-du-Temple, 4th (01.40.29.02.18). Bars & Pubs

Au Pied de Cochon p45 6 rue Coquillière, 1st (01.40.13.77.00/ www.pieddecochon.com). Brasseries

Pierre Gagnaire p42 6 rue Balzac, 8th (0158.36.12.50/ www.pierre-gagnaire.com). Haute Cuisine

Pizza Hut p133 (central phone 08.10.30.30.30/ www.pizzahut.fr). Home Delivery

La Plancha p100 34 rue Keller, 11th (01.48.05.20.30). Spanish

Planet Hollywood p81 76-78 av des Champs-Elysées, 8th (01.53.83.78.27/www.planethollywood.com). The Americas

Poilâne p137 8 rue du Cherche-Midi, 6th (01.45.48.42.59/ www.poilane.com). Shops & Markets

Poissonerie du Dôme p139 4 rue Delambre, 14th (01.43.35.23.95). Shops & Markets

Le Polidor p69 41 rue Monsieur-le-Prince, 6th (01.43.26.95.34). Budget

Polo Room p121 3 rue Lord-Byron, 8th (01.40.74.07.78/ www.poloroom.com). Bars & Pubs

Le Potager du Marais p74 22 rue Rambuteau, 3rd (01.44.54.00.31). Vegetarian

La Potée des Halles p67 3 rue Etienne-Marcel, 1st (01.40.41.98.15). Budget

Le Pré Catelan p43 route de Suresnes, Bois de Boulogne, 16th (01.44.14.41.14/www.lenotre.fr). Haute Cuisine

Le Président p87 120-124 rue du Fbg-du-Temple, 11th (01.47.00.17.18). Far East

Promenades Gourmandes p143 187 rue du Temple, 3rd (01.48.04.56.84/ www.theinternationalkitchen.com/promen.htm). Learning & Tasting

Q

Quai Ouest p53 1200 quai Marcel Dassault, 92210 St-Cloud (01.46.02.35.54). Trendy

Les Quatre et Une Saveurs p75 72 rue du Cardinal-Lemoine, 5th. (01.43.26.88.80). Vegetarian

R

Radis Olive p133 27 rue de Marignan, 8th (01.42.56.55.55/ fax 01.42.56.22.37). Home Delivery

Le Rallye p107 11 quai de la Tournelle, 5th (01.43.54.29.65). Cafés

Le Rallye-Peret p131 6 rue Daguerre, 14th (01.43.22.57.05). Wine Bars

Le Récamier p24 4 rue Récamier, 7th (01.45.48.86.58). Bistros

Le Réconfort p15 37 rue de Poitou, 3rd (01.49.96.09.60). Bistros

Le Reflet p107 6 rue Champollion, 5th (01.43.29.97.27). Cafés

La Régalade p33 49 av Jean-Moulin, 14th (01.45.45.68.58). Bistros

Le Relais Gascon p73 6 rue des Abbesses, 18th (01.42.58.58.22). Budget

Le Reminet p20 3 rue des Grands-Degrés, 5th (01.44.07.04.24). Bistros

Au Rendez-Vous des Camionneurs p72 34 rue des Plantes, 14th (01.45.42.20.94). Budget

Le Rendez-Vous des Chauffeurs p73 11 rue des Portes Blanches, 18th (01.42.64.04.17). Budget

Le Rendez-vous des Quais p115 MK2 sur Seine, 10-14 quai de la Seine, 19th (01.40.37.02.81). Cafés

René-Gérard St-Ouen p137 111 bd Haussmann, 8th (01.42.65.06.25). Shops & Markets

Renoma Café Gallery p60 32 av George V/45 rue Pierre-Charron, 8th (01.56.89.05.89). Contemporary

Le Repaire de Cartouche p28 8 bd des Filles-du-Calvaire/99 rue Amelot, 11th (01.47.00.25.86). Bistros

Le Réservoir p123 16 rue de la Forge-Royal, 11th (01.43.56.39.60/ www.reservoir-dogs.com). Bars & Pubs

Restaurant des 4 Frères p100 127 bd de Ménilmontant, 11th (01.43.55.40.91). North African

Restaurant Al Wady p85 153-155 rue de Lourmel, 15th (01.45.58.57.18). Eastern Mediterranean

Restaurant Cap Vernet p46 82 av Marceau, 8th (01.47.20.20.40). Brasseries

Restaurant E Marty p45 20 av des Gobelins, 5th (01.43.31.39.51/ www.marty-restaurant.com). Brasseries

Restaurant GR5 p72 19 rue Gustave Courbet, 16th (01.47.27.09.84). Budget

Restaurant Haiku p75 63 rue Jean-Pierre Timbaud, 11th. (01.56.98.11.67). Vegetarian

Restaurant Hélène Darroze p58 4 rue d'Assas, 6th (01.42.22.00.11). Contemporary

Restaurant L'Hermès p39 23 rue Mélingue, 19th (01.42.39.94.70). Bistros

Restaurant du Palais-Royal p58 110 galerie Valois, 1st (01.40.20.00.27). Contemporary

Restaurant Petrossian p59 18 bd de La Tour-Maubourg, 7th (01.44.11.32.32). Contemporary

Restaurant Pho p90 3 rue Volta, 3rd (01.42.78.31.70). Far East

Richart p139 258 bd St-Germain, 7th (01.45.55.66.00/ www.richart.com). Shops & Markets

Ritz Escoffier Ecole de Gastronomie Française p143 38 rue Cambon, 1st (01.43.16.30.50). Learning & Tasting

Le Rocher Gourmand p25 89 rue du Rocher, 8th (01.40.08.00.36). Bistros

Le Roi du Café p115 59 rue Lecourbe, 15th (01.47.34.48.50). Cafés

Roller Café p113 50 bd de la Bastille, 12th (01.43.46.55.22). Cafés

Le Rosebud p125 11bis rue Delambre, 14th (01.43.20.44.13). Bars & Pubs

Le Rostand p109 6 pl Edmond-Rostand, 6th (01.43.54.61.58). Cafés

La Rôtisserie de Beaujolais p20 19 quai de la Tournelle, 5th (01.43.54.17.47). Bistros

Rôtisserie Ste-Marthe p70 4 rue Ste-Marthe, 10th (01.40.03.08.30). Budget

Le Rouge Gorge p129 8 rue St-Paul, 4th (01.48.04.75.89). Wine Bars

La Route du Cacao p113 Quai de la Gare, 13th (01.53.82.10.35/www.larouteducacao.com). Cafés

Le Rubis p129 10 rue du Marché-St-Honoré, 1st (01.42.61.03.34). Wine Bars

Rue Balzac p52 3-5 rue Balzac, 8th (01.53.89.90.91). Trendy

Rue Daguerre p140 14th. Shops & Markets

Rue Mouffetard p140 5th. Shops & Markets

Rue Poncelet p140 rue Poncelet and rue Bayen, 17th. Shops & Markets

Ryst Dupeyron p140 79 rue du Bac, 7th (01.45.48.80.93/ www.dupeyron.com). Shops & Markets

S

Le Sabot Saint-Germain p21 6 rue du Sabot, 6th (01.42.22.21.56). Bistros

Le Safran p13 29 rue d'Argenteuil, 1st (01.42.61.25.30). Bistros

Le Saint Amarante p31 4 rue Biscornet, 12th (01.43.43.00.08). Bistros

Le Sainte Marthe p121 32 rue Ste-Marthe, 10th (01.44.84.36.96). Bars & Pubs

Le Salon d'Hélène p58 4 rue d'Assas, 6th (01.42.22.00.11). Contemporary

Salon de Thé Wenzhou p88 24 rue de Belleville, 20th (01.46.36.56.33). Far East

Le Sancerre p115 35 rue des Abbesses, 18th (01.42.58.47.05). Cafés

Le Sanz Sans p123 49 rue du Fbg-St-Antoine, 11th (01.44.75.78.78). Bars & Pubs

Sarl Velan Stores p140 87 passage Brady, 10th (01.42.46.06.06). Shops & Markets

Saveurs d'Irlande p140 5 cité du Vauxhall, 10th (01.42.00.36.20). Shops & Markets

Savy p25 23 rue Bayard, 8th (01.47.23.46.98). Bistros

Sawadee p89 53 av Emile Zola, 15th (01.45.77.68.90). Far East

Saxe-Breteuil p140 av de Saxe, 7th. Shops & Markets

Le Scheffer p36 22 rue Scheffer, 16th (01.47.27.81.11). Bistros

Sèbillon p25 66 rue Pierre-Charron, 8th (01.43.59.28.15). Bistros

Le Select p109 99 bd du Montparnasse, 6th (01.42.22.65.27). Cafés

Le Sept/Quinze p35 29 av de Lowendal, 15th (01.43.06.23.06). Bistros

Shah Jahan p91 4 rue Gauthey, 17th (01.42.63.44.06). Indian

Shalimar p91 59 Passage Brady, 10th (01.45.23.31.61). Indian

Shozan p60 11 rue de la Trémoïlle, 8th (01.47.23.37.32). Contemporary

Sinostar p88 27-29 av de Fontainebleau, 94270 Le Kremlin-Bicêtre (01.49.60.88.88). Far East

Le Soleil p39 109 av Michelet, 93400 St-Ouen (01.40.10.08.08). Bistros

Le Soleil p115 136 bd de Ménilmontant, 20th (01.46.36.47.44). Cafés

Au Soleil d'Austerlitz p113 18 bd de l'Hôpital, 13th (01.43.31.22.38.). Cafés

Le Soleil en Cave p129 21 rue Rambuteau, 4th (01.42.72.26.25). Wine Bars

Au Soleil de Minuit p101 15 rue Desnouettes, 15th (01.48.28.15.15). Other International

Le Souk p100 1 rue Keller, 11th (01.49.29.05.08). North African

A Sousceyrac p29 35 rue Faidherbe, 11th (01.43.71.65.30). Bistros

Speed Rabbit Pizza p133 14 bd de Reuilly, 12th (01.43.44.80.80). Home Delivery

Spoon, Food & Wine p52 14 rue de Marignan, 8th (01.40.76.34.44). Trendy

Le Square Trousseau p31 1 rue Antoine-Vollon, 12th (01.43.43.06.00). Bistros

Stella Maris p60 4 rue Arsène-Houssaye, 8th (01.42.89.16.22). Contemporary

Stolly's p119 16 rue Cloche-Perce, 4th (01.42.76.06.76/ www.hip-bars.com). Bars & Pubs

The Studio p81 41 rue du Temple, 4th (01.42.74.10.38). The Americas

Le Suffren p48 84 av de Suffren, 15th (01.45.66.97.86). Brasseries

Sushi Company p133 22 rue des Pyramides, 1st (01.40.15.04.04/ fax 01.42.46.19.36). Home Delivery

T

T pour 2 Café p113 23 cour St-Emilion, 12th (01.40.19.02.09/ www.tpour2cafe.com). Cafés

Tabac de la Sorbonne p107 7 pl de la Sorbonne, 5th (01.43.54.52.04). Cafés

La Table de la Fontaine p27 5 rue Henri-Monnier, 9th (01.45.26.26.30). Bistros

Time Out Paris Eating & Drinking 151

La Table de Lucullus
129 rue Legendre, 17th (01.40.25.02.68). Bistros
La Table de Michel p20
13 quai de la Tournelle, 5th (01.44.07.17.57). Bistros
La Table du Marquis p31
3 rue Beccaria, 12th (01.43.41.56.77). Bistros
Taco Loco p83
116 rue Amelot, 11th (01.43.57.90.24). The Americas
Taillevent p43
15 rue Lamennais, 8th (01.44.95.15.01/ www.taillevent.com). Haute Cuisine
Takara p96
14 rue Molière, 1st (01.42.96.08.38). Japanese
Le Tambour p117
41 rue Montmartre, 2nd (01.42.33.06.90). Bars & Pubs
Tang Frères p140
48 av d'Ivry, 13th (01.45.70.80.00). Shops & Markets
Taninna p100
14 rue Abel, 12th (01.40.19.99.04). North African
Tanjia p52
23 rue de Ponthieu, 8th (01.42.25.95.00). Trendy
Tante Jeanne p37
116, bd Péreire, 17th (01.43.80.88.68/ www.bearnard-loiseau.com). Bistros
La Taverne p47
24 bd des Italiens, 9th (01.55.33.10.00/ www.taverne.fr). Brasseries
Taxi Jaune p17
13 rue Chapon, 3rd (01.42.76.00.40). Bistros
Tch'a p128
6 rue du Pont-de-Lodi, 6th (01.43.29.61.31). Tea Rooms & Ice Cream
Le Temps des Cerises p72
18 rue de la Butte-aux-Cailles, 13th (01.45.89.69.48). Budget
Le Temps des Cerises p68
31 rue de la Cerisaie, 4th (01.42.72.08.63). Budget
Le Temps au Temps p70
13 rue Paul Bert, 11th (01.43.79.63.40/ www.ifrance.com/ restaurant75). Budget
Terminus Nord p47
23 rue de Dunkerque, 10th (01.42.85.05.15). Brasseries
Le Terroir p32
11 bd Arago, 13th (01.47.07.36.99). Bistros
Tête de Goinfre/ Cave du Cochon p37
16/18, rue Jacquemont, 17th (01.42.29.89.80). Bistros
Thiou p51
49 quai d'Orsay, 7th (01.45.51.58.58). Trendy
Thoumieux p24
79 rue St-Dominique, 7th (01.47.05.49.75). Bistros
Thu Thu p90
51bis rue Hermel, 18th (01.42.54.70.30). Far East
Thuy Long p90
111 rue de Vaugirard, 6th (01.45.49.26.01). Far East
Au Tibourg p17
29 rue du Bourg-Tibourg, 4th (01.42.74.45.25/ www.autibourg.com). Bistros
Timgad p100
21 rue Brunel, 17th (01.45.74.23.70). North African
Le Tir-Bouchon p14
22 rue Tiquetonne, 2nd (01.42.21.95.51). Bistros
Toraya p127
10 rue St-Florentin, 1st (01.42.60.13.48). Tea Rooms & Ice Cream
Le Totem p115
Musée de l'Homme, 17 pl du Trocadéro, 16th (01.47.27.28.29). Cafés
La Tour d'Argent p40
15-17 quai de la Tournelle, 5th (01.43.54.23.31/ www.tourdargent.com). Haute Cuisine
La Tour de Montlhéry (Chez Denise) p14
5 rue des Prouvaires, 1st (01.42.36.21.82). Bistros
La Tour de Pierre p131
53 rue Dauphine, 6th (01.43.26.08.93/www.latouredepierre.com). Wine Bars
Le Train Bleu p48
Gare de Lyon, Place Louis-Armand, 12th (01.43.43.09.06). Brasseries
Tricotin p87
15 av de Choisy, 13th (01.45.84.74.44). Far East
Aux Trois Mailletz p119
56 rue Galande, 5th (01.43.54.00.79/www.lestroismaillezt.com). Bars & Pubs
Les Trois Têtards p123
46 rue Jean Pierre Timbaud, 11th (01.43.14.27.37). Bars & Pubs
Le Troquet p35
21 rue François-Bonvin, 15th (01.45.66.89.00). Bistros
Le Troyon p37
4 rue Troyon, 17th (01.40.68.99.40). Bistros
Le Trumilou p68
84 quai de l'Hôtel-de-Ville, 4th (01.42.77.63.98). Budget
Tsukizi p97
2bis rue des Ciseaux, 6th (01.43.54.65.19). Japanese

U

U Sampiero Corsu p72
12 rue de l'Amiral Roussin, 15th. No telephone. Budget
Les Ultra-Vins p140
16 rue Lacuée, 12th (01.43.46.85.81). Shops and Markets

V

Vagenende p46
142 bd St-Germain, 6th (01.43.26.68.18). Brasseries
Vasco da Gama p101
39 rue Vasco de Gama, 15th (01.45.57.20.01). Other International
Le Vaudeville p45
29 rue Vivienne, 2nd (01.40.20.04.62). Brasseries
Velly p27
52 rue Lamartine, 9th (01.48.78.60.05). Bistros
Verdibus p75
48 rue du Cherche Midi, 6th (01.40.49.06.17). Vegetarian
Le Verre à Pied p107
118bis rue Mouffetard, 5th (01.43.31.15.72). Cafés
Le Verre Volé p131
67 rue de Lancry, 10th (01.48.03.17.34). Wine Bars
La Verte Tige p74
13 rue Ste-Anastase, 3rd (01.42.77.22.15). Vegetarian
Le Viaduc Café p113
43 av Daumesnil, 12th (01.44.74.70.70). Cafés
La Victoire Suprême du Coeur p74
41 rue des Bourdonnais, 1st (01.40.41.93.95). Vegetarian
Au Vide Gousset p105
1 rue Vide-Gousset, 2nd (01.42.60.02.78). Cafés
Le Vieux Bistro p19
14 rue du Cloître-Notre-Dame, 4th (01.43.54.18.95). Bistros
Au Vieux Chêne p70
7 rue Dahomey, 11th (01.43.71.67.69). Budget
Au Vieux Colombier p109
65 rue de Rennes, 6th (01.45.48.53.81). Cafés
Le Vin des Rues p33
21 rue Boulard, 14th (01.43.22.19.78). Bistros
Vin et Marée p66
183, bd Murat, 16th (01.46.47.91.39). Fish & Seafood
Les Vins du Terroir p145
34 av Duquesne, 7th (01.40.61.91.87). Learning & Tasting
Le Violon Dingue p119
46 rue de la Montagne-Ste-Geneviève, 5th (01.43.25.79.93). Bars & Pubs
Au Virage Lepic p73
61 rue Lepic, 18th (01.42.52.46.79). Budget
La Voie Lactée p85
34 rue du Cardinal-Lemoine, 5th (01.46.34.02.35). Eastern Mediterranean

W

Wadja p21
10 rue de la Grande-Chaumière, 6th (01.46.33.02.02). Bistros
Wally le Saharien p99
36 rue Rodier, 9th (01.42.85.51.90). North African
Web Bar p105
32 rue de Picardie, 3rd (01.42.72.66.55/ www.webbar.fr). Cafés
Le Wepler p48
14 pl de Clichy, 18th (01.45.22.53.24/ www.wepler.com). Brasseries
Willi's Wine Bar p14
13 rue des Petits-Champs, 1st (01.42.61.05.09/ www.williswinebar.com). Bistros
Wok p87
23 rue des Taillandiers, 11th (01.55.28.88.77). Far East

Y

Yen p97
22 rue St-Benoît, 6th (01.45.44.11.18). Japanese
Yogi's p52
13 rue du Commandant-Mouchotte, 14th (01.45.38.92.93). Trendy
Yugaraj p91
14 rue Dauphine, 6th (01.43.26.44.91). Indian

Z

Zagros p85
21 rue de la Folie-Méricourt, 11th (01.48.07.09.56). Eastern Mediterranean
Ze Kitchen Galerie p58
4 rue des Grands-Augustins, 6th (01.44.32.00.32). Contemporary
Zebra Square p48
3 pl Clément-Ader, 16th (01.44.14.91.91/ www.zebrasquare.com). Brasseries
Zen p96
18 rue du Louvre, 1st (01.42.86.95.05). Japanese
Le Zéphyr p39
1 rue du Jourdain, 20th (01.46.36.65.81). Bistros
Le Zéro Zéro p123
89 rue Amelot, 11th (01.49.23.51.00/ www.zerozero.com). Bars & Pubs
Le Zimmer p104
1 pl du Châtelet, 1st (01.42.36.74.03). Cafés
Ziryab p99
Institut du Monde Arabe, 1 rue des Fossés-St-Bernard, 5th (01.53.10.10.20). North African
Les Zygomates p31
7 rue de Capri, 12th (01.40.19.93.04). Bistros
La Zygotissoire p71
101 rue de Charonne, 11th (01.40.09.93.05). Budget

Arrondissement Index

1st

The Americas

Board Café Restaurant p81
8 rue Coquillière, 1st (01.40.28.97.98)
Joe Allen Restaurant p81
30 rue Pierre Lescot, 1st (01.42.36.70.13)

Bars & Pubs

Café Oz p117
18 rue St-Denis, 1st (01.40.39.00.18/ www.cafe-oz.com)
Le Comptoir p117
37 rue Berger, 1st (01.40.26.26.66)
Flann O'Brien's p117
6 rue Bailleul, 1st (01.42.60.13.58/ www.irishfrance.com/ flannobrien)
Le Fumoir p117
6 rue de l'Amiral-de-Coligny, 1st (01.42.92.00.24/ www.lefumoir.com)
Hôtel Ritz p119
15 pl Vendôme, 1st (01.43.16.30.31/ www.ritzparis.com)

Bistros

L'Absinthe p13
24 pl du Marché-St-Honoré, 1st (01.49.26.90.04)
L'Ardoise p13
28 rue du Mont-Thabor, 1st (01.42.96.28.18)
Chez La Vieille p13
1 rue Bailleul/37 rue de l'Arbre Sec, 1st (01.42.60.15.78)
Le Cochon à l'Oreille p13
15 rue Montmartre, 1st (01.42.36.07.56)
Le Dauphin p13
167 rue St-Honoré, 1st (01.42.60.40.11)
Le Safran p13
29 rue d'Argenteuil, 1st (01.42.61.25.30)
La Tour de Montlhéry (Chez Denise) p14
5 rue des Prouvaires, 1st (01.42.36.21.82)
Willi's Wine Bar p14
13 rue des Petits-Champs, 1st (01.42.61.05.09/ www.williswinebar.com)

Brasseries

Au Pied de Cochon p45
6 rue Coquillière, 1st (01.40.13.77.00/ www.pieddecochon.com)

Budget

Bio.lt p69
15 rue des Halles, 1st (01.42.21.10.21)
La Ferme Opéra p69
55-57 rue St-Roch, 1st (01.40.20.12.12)
La Fresque p67
100 rue Rambuteau, 1st (01.42.33.17.56)
Nils p69
36 rue Montorgueil, 1st (01.55.34.39.49)
Le Petit Flore p67
6 rue Croix des Petits Champs, 1st (01.42.60.25.53)
La Potée des Halles p67
3 rue Etienne-Marcel, 1st (01.40.41.98.15)

Cafés

Bar de l'Entr'acte p104
47 rue Montpensier, 1st (01.42.97.57.76)
Café Le Nemours p104
2 pl Colette, 1st (01.42.61.34.14)
Café Marly p104
93 rue de Rivoli, cour Napoléon du Louvre, 1st (01.49.26.06.60)
Café Ruc p104
159 rue St-Honoré, 1st (01.42.60.97.54)
Le Comptoir p104
37 rue Berger, 1st (01.40.26.26.66)
La Coquille p104
30 rue Coquillière, 1st (01.40.26.55.36)
Papou Lounge p104
74 rue Jean-Jacques Rousseau, 1st (01.44.76.00.03)
Le Zimmer p104
1 pl du Châtelet, 1st (01.42.36.74.03)

Contemporary

L'Atelier Berger p58
49 rue Berger, 1st (01.40.28.00.00/ www.atelierberger.com)
Macéo p58
15 rue des Petits-Champs, 1st (01.42.97.53.85)
Restaurant du Palais-Royal p58
110 galerie Valois, 1st (01.40.20.00.27)

Far East

Baan-Boran p89
43 rue Montpensier, 1st (01.40.15.90.45)
Chez Vong p87
10 rue de la Grande Truanderie, 1st (01.40.26.09.36)
Djakarta Bali p88
9 rue Vauvilliers, 1st (01.45.08.83.11)
La Mousson p87
9 rue Thérèse, 1st (01.42.60.59.46)

Fish & Seafood

Goumard p65
7-9 rue Duphot, 1st (01.42.60.36.07/ www.goumard.fr)

Haute Cuisine

Le Carré des Feuillants p40
14 rue de Castiglione, 1st (01.42.86.82.82)
L'Espadon p40
Hôtel Ritz, 15 pl Vendôme, 1st (01.43.16.30.80/ www.ritzparis.com)
Le Grand Véfour p40
17 rue de Beaujolais, 1st (01.42.96.56.27)
Le Meurice p40
Hôtel Meurice, 228 rue de Rivoli, 1st (01.44.58.10.10)

Home Delivery

Sushi Company p133
22 rue des Pyramides, 1st (01.40.15.04.04/fax 01.42.46.19.36)

Japanese

Kinugawa p96
9 rue du Mont-Thabor, 1st (01.42.60.65.07)
Lai Laï Ken p96
7 rue Ste-Anne, 1st (01.40.15.96.90)
Takara p96
14 rue Molière, 1st (01.42.96.08.38)
Zen p96
18 rue du Louvre, 1st (01.42.86.95.05)

Learning & Tasting

Ritz Escoffier Ecole de Gastronomie Française p143
38 rue Cambon, 1st (01.43.16.30.50)

Shops and Markets

Comptoir de la Gastronomie p139
34 rue Montmartre, 1st (01.42.33.31.32)
Le Mille-Pâtes p140
5 rue des Petits-Champs, 1st (01.42.96.03.04)

Tea Rooms & Ice Cream

Angelina's p127
226 rue de Rivoli, 1st (01.42.60.82.00)
Hôtel Meurice p128
228 rue de Rivoli, 1st (01.44.58.10.10/ www.meuricehotel.com)
Hôtel Ritz p128
15 pl Vendôme, 1st (01.43.16.30.30/ www.ritzparis.com)
Jean-Paul Hévin p127
231 rue St-Honoré, 1st (01.55.35.35.97)
Toraya p127
10 rue St-Florentin, 1st (01.42.60.13.48)

Trendy

Cabaret p51
2 pl du Palais-Royal, 1st (01.58.62.56.25)
Hôtel Costes p51
239 rue St-Honoré, 1st (01.42.44.50.25)

Vegetarian

Entre Ciel et Terre p74
5 rue Hérold, 1st (01.45.08.49.84/ www.entrecieletterre.com)
Foody's Brunch Café p74
26 rue Montorgueil, 1st (01.40.13.02.53)
La Victoire Suprême du Coeur p74
41 rue des Bourdonnais, 1st (01.40.41.93.95)

Wine Bars

Aux Bons Crus p129
7 rue des Petits-Champs, 1st (01.42.60.06.45)
Juvéniles p129
47 rue de Richelieu, 1st (01.42.97.46.49)

Arrondissement Index

Le Père Fouettard p129
9 rue Pierre-Lescot, 1st
(01.42.33.74.17)

Le Rubis p129
10 rue du Marché-St-Honoré,
1st (01.42.61.03.34)

2nd

Bars & Pubs

Café Noir p117
65 rue Montmartre, 2nd
(01.40.39.07.36)

The Frog & Rosbif p117
116 rue St-Denis, 2nd
(01.42.36.34.73/
www.frogpubs.com)

Harry's New York Bar p117
5 rue Daunou, 2nd
(01.42.61.71.14/
www.harrys-bar.fr)

La Jungle p117
56 rue d'Argout, 2nd
(01.40.41.03.45)

Le Tambour p117
41 rue Montmartre, 2nd
(01.42.33.06.90)

Bistros

Chez Georges p14
1 rue du Mail, 2nd,
(01.42.60.07.11)

Aux Crus de Bourgogne p14
3 rue Bachaumont, 2nd
(01.42.33.48.24)

Le Gavroche p14
19 rue St-Marc, 2nd
(01.42.96.89.70)

Mellifère p14
8 rue Monsigny, 2nd
(01.42.61.21.71)

Brasseries

Gallopin p45
40 rue Notre-Dame-des-Victoires, 2nd
(01.42.36.45.38.)

Le Grand Colbert p45
2-4 rue Vivienne, 2nd
(01.42.86.87.88)

Le Vaudeville p45
29 rue Vivienne, 2nd
(01.40.20.04.62)

Budget

Mimosa p67
44 rue d'Argout, 2nd
(01.40.28.15.75)

La Petite France p67
14 rue de la Banque,
2nd (01.42.96.17.19)

Cafés

Le Café p104
62 rue Tiquetonne, 2nd
(01.40.39.08.00)

Le Dénicheur p104
4 rue Tiquetonne, 2nd
(01.42.21.31.01)

Lézard Café p104
32 rue Etienne Marcel,
2nd (01.42.33.22.73)

Au Vide Gousset p105
1 rue Vide-Gousset, 2nd
(01.42.60.02.78)

Fish & Seafood

Iode p65
48 rue d'Argout, 2nd
(01.42.36.46.45)

Home Delivery

Matsuri Sushi p133
26 rue Leopold Bellan,
2nd (01.40.26.11.13/
fax 01.40.33.10.38/
www.matsuri-sushi.com)

Indian

Gandhi-Opéra p91
66 rue Ste-Anne, 2nd
(01.47.03.41.00/
www.restaurant-gandhi.com)

Japanese

Aki p96
2 bis, rue Daunou, 2nd
(01.42.61.48.38)

Isse p97
56 rue Ste-Anne, 2nd
(01.42.96.67.76)

Learning & Tasting

Françoise Meunier p143
7 rue Paul-Lelong, 2nd
(01.40.26.14.00/
www.intiweb.com/fmeunier)

Shops and Markets

Kioko p140
46 rue des Petits-Champs,
2nd (01.42.61.33.65)

Legrand Filles et Fils p140
1 rue de la Banque, 2nd
(01.42.60.07.12)

Wine Bars

La Côte p129
77 rue de Richelieu, 2nd
(01.42.97.40.68)

3rd

The Americas

Anahi p82
49 rue Volta, 3rd
(01.48.87.88.24)

Indiana Café p81
1 pl de la République, 3rd
(01.48.87.82.35/
www.indiana-café.com)

A la Mexicaine p81
68 rue Quincampoix, 3rd
(01.48.87.99.34)

Bars & Pubs

L'Art Brut p117
78 rue Quincampoix, 3rd
(01.42.72.17.36)

Bistros

L'Ami Louis p14
32 rue du Vertbois, 3rd
(01.48.87.77.48)

L'Auberge Nicolas Flamel p14
51 rue de Montmorency,
3rd (01.42.71.77.78/www.
nicolasflamel.forez.com)

Camille p14
24 rue des Francs-Bourgeois, 3rd
(01.42.72.20.50)

Chez Janou p14
2, rue Roger-Verlomme,
3rd (01.42.72.28.41)

La Fontaine Gourmande p14
11 rue Charlot, 3rd
(01.42.78.72.40)

Georget p15
64 rue Vieille-du-Temple,
3rd (01.42.78.55.89)

Le Hangar p15
12 impasse Berthaud,
3rd (01.42.74.55.44)

Le Pamphlet p15
38 rue Debellyme, 3rd
(01.42.72.39.24)

Le Petit Marseillais p15
72 rue Vieille-du-Temple,
3rd (01.42.78.91.59)

Le Réconfort p15
37 rue de Poitou, 3rd
(01.49.96.09.60)

Taxi Jaune p17
13 rue Chapon, 3rd
(01.42.76.00.40)

Budget

Fontaines d'Elysabeth p67
1 rue Ste-Elysabeth, 3rd
(01.42.74.36.41)

Cafés

L'Apparement Café p105
18 rue des Coutures-St-Gervais, 3rd
(01.48.87.12.22)

Le Baromètre p105
17 rue Charlot, 3rd
(01.48.87.04.54)

Columbus Café p105
25 rue Vieille-du-Temple,
3rd (01.42.72.20.25/
www.columbuscafe.com)

Web Bar p105
32 rue de Picardie, 3rd
(01.42.72.66.55/
www.webbar.fr)

Far East

Restaurant Pho p90
3 rue Volta, 3rd
(01.42.78.31.70)

Learning & Tasting

L'Ecole du Thé p143
Le Palais des Thés, 64 rue
Vieille-du-Temple, 3rd
(01.43.56.96.38/
www.le-palais-des-thes.fr)

Le Jardin des Vignes p145
91 rue de Turenne, 3rd
(01.42.77.05.00)

Promenades Gourmandes p143
187 rue du Temple, 3rd
(01.48.04.56.84/
www.theinternationalkitchen.com/promen.htm)

North African

404 p99
69 rue des Gravilliers, 3rd
(01.42.74.57.81)

Chez Omar p99
47 rue de Bretagne, 3rd
(01.42.72.36.26)

Shops and Markets

Au Levain du Marais p137
32 rue de Turenne, 3rd
(01.42.78.07.31)

Spanish

Caves Saint Gilles p100
4 rue St-Gilles, 3rd
(01.48.87.22.62)

Vegetarian

Le Potager du Marais p74
22 rue Rambuteau, 3rd
(01.44.54.00.31)

La Verte Tige p74
13 rue Ste-Anastase, 3rd
(01.42.77.22.15)

4th

The Americas

The Studio p81
41 rue du Temple, 4th
(01.42.74.10.38)

Bars & Pubs

The Auld Alliance p117
80 rue François-Miron, 4th
(01.48.04.30.40)

Chez Richard p119
37 rue Vieille-du-Temple,
4th (01.42.74.31.65)

Les Chimères p119
133 rue St-Antoine, 4th
(01.42.72.71.97)

Les Etages p119
35 rue Vieille-du-Temple,
4th (01.42.78.72.00)

The Lizard Lounge p119
18 rue du Bourg-Tibourg,
4th (01.42.72.81.34/
www.hip-bars.com)

Le Pick-Clops p119
16 rue Vieille-du-Temple,
4th (01.40.29.02.18)

Stolly's p119
16 rue Cloche-Perce, 4th
(01.42.76.06.76/
www.hip-bars.com)

Bistros

Baracane p17
38 rue des Tournelles, 4th
(01.42.71.43.33)

Benoît p17
20 rue St Martin, 4th
(01.42.72.25.76)

Le Colimaçon p17
44 rue Vieille-du-Temple,
4th (01.42.71.12.01/
www.lecolimacon.com)

Le Dôme du Marais p17
53bis rue des Francs-Bourgeois, 4th
(01.42.74.54.17)

Grizzli Café p17
7 rue St-Martin, 4th
(01.48.87.77.56)

Ma Bourgogne p17
19 pl des Vosges, 4th
(01.42.78.44.64)

Les Philosophes p17
28 rue Vieille-du-Temple,
4th (01.48.87.49.64/
www.cafeine.com)

Au Tibourg p17
29 rue du Bourg-Tibourg, 4th
(01.42.74.45.25/
www.autibourg.com)

Le Vieux Bistro p19
14 rue du Cloître-Notre-Dame, 4th (01.43.54.18.95)

Brasseries

Bofinger p45
5-7 rue de la Bastille, 4th
(01.42.72.87.82)

Brasserie de l'Isle St-Louis p45
55 quai de Bourbon, 4th
(01.43.54.02.59)

Budget

Bistro Beaubourg p67
25 rue Quincampoix, 4th
(01.42.77.48.02)

Café de la Poste p68
13 rue Castex, 4th
(01.42.72.95.35)

La Canaille p68
4 rue Crillon, 4th
(01.42.78.09.71)

Le Coupe Gorge p68
2 rue de la Coutellerie,
4th (01.48.04.79.24)

Le Pavé p68
7 rue des Lombards, 4th
(01.44.54.07.20)

Le P'tit Gavroche p68
15 rue Ste-Croix de la
Bretonnerie, 4th
(01.48.87.74.26)

Le Temps des Cerises p68
31 rue de la Cerisaie, 4th
(01.42.72.08.63)

Le Trumilou p68
84 quai de l'Hôtel-de-Ville,
4th (01.42.77.63.98)

Cafés

Baz'Art Café p105
36, bd Henri IV, 4th.
(01.42.78.62.23)

Bricolo Café p105
Basement of BHV
department store,
52 rue de Rivoli, 4th
(01.42.74.90.00/
www.cyberbricoleur.com)

Café Beaubourg p105
43 rue St-Merri, 4th
(01.48.87.63.96)

Café des Phares p105
7 pl de la Bastille, 4th
(01.42.72.04.70)

Café du Trésor p105
7-9 rue du Trésor, 4th
(01.42.71.78.34)

L'Escale p107
1 rue des Deux-Ponts,
4th (01.43.54.94.23)

L'Etoile Manquante p107
34 rue Vieille-du-Temple,
4th (01.42.72.48.34/
www.cafeine.com)

Le Flore en l'Isle p107
42 quai d'Orléans, 4th
(01.43.29.88.27)

L'Imprévu Café p107
7-9 rue Quincampoix, 4th
(01.42.78.23.50)

Au Petit Fer à Cheval p107
30 rue Vieille-du-Temple, 4th
(01.42.72.47.47/
www.cafeine.com)

Le Petit Marcel p107
65 rue Rambuteau, 4th
(01.48.87.10.20)

Fish & Seafood

Le Bistrot du Dôme Bastille p65
2 rue de la Bastille, 4th
(01.48.04.88.44)

Haute Cuisine

L'Ambroisie p40
9 pl des Vosges, 4th
(01.42.78.51.45)

Hiramatsu p40
7 quai de Bourbon, 4th
(01.56.81.08.80)

Japanese

Isami p97
4 quai d'Orléans, 4th
(01.40.46.06.97)

Other International

Bennelong p101
31 bd Henri IV, 4th,
(01.42.71.07.71)

Shops and Markets

L'Epicerie p139
51 rue St-Louis-en-l'Ile,
4th (01.43.25.20.14)

Izraël p140
30 rue François-Miron, 4th
(01.42.72.66.23)

Au Noisetier p137
33 rue Rambuteau, 4th
(01.48.87.68.12)

Tea Rooms & Ice Cream

La Charlotte en l'Ile p127
24 rue St-Louis-en-Ile, 4th
(01.43.54.25.83)

Les Enfants Gâtés p127
43 rue des Francs-Bourgeois, 4th
(01.42.77.07.63)

Le Loir dans la Théière p127
3 rue des Rosiers, 4th
(01.42.72.90.61)

Mariage Frères p127
30-32 rue du Bourg-Tibourg,
4th (01.42.72.28.11/
www.mariagefreres.com)

Trendy

Georges p51
Centre Pompidou, 6th floor,
rue Rambuteau, 4th.
(01.44.78.47.99)

Vegetarian

Galerie 88 p74
88 quai de l'Hôtel de Ville,
4th (01.42.72.17.58)

Grand Appétit p74
9 rue de la Cerisaie, 4th
(01.40.27.04.95)

Piccolo Teatro p75
6, rue des Ecouffes, 4th
(01.42.72.17.79/
www.piccoloteatro.com)

Wine Bars

La Belle Hortense p129
31 rue Vieille-du-Temple,
4th (01.48.04.71.60)

L'Enoteca p129
25 rue Charles V, 4th
(01.42.78.91.44)

Le Felteu p129
15 rue Pecquay, 4th
(01.42.72.14.51)

Le Rouge Gorge p129
8 rue St-Paul, 4th
(01.48.04.75.89)

Le Soleil en Cave p129
21 rue Rambuteau, 4th
(01.42.72.26.25)

5th

The Americas

Anuhuacalli p82
30 rue des Bernardins,
5th (01.43.26.10.20)

Botequim p82
1 rue Berthollet, 5th
(01.43.37.98.46)

Buffalo Grill p81
1 bd St-Germain, 5th
(01.56.24.34.49/
www.buffalo-grill.com)

El Palenque p82
5 rue de la Montagne-Ste-Geneviève, 5th
(01.43.54.08.99)

Mexi & Co p82
10 rue Dante, 5th
(01.46.34.14.12)

Bars & Pubs

Bombardier p119
2 pl du Panthéon, 5th
(01.43.54.79.22/
www.bombardier.com)

Connolly's Corner p119
12 rue de Mirbel, 5th
(01.43.31.94.22)

Le Crocodile p119
6 rue Royer-Collard, 5th
(01.43.54.32.37)

Finnegan's Wake p119
9 rue des Boulangers, 5th
(01.46.34.23.65/
www.irishfrance.com)

La Gueuze p119
19 rue Soufflot, 5th
(01.43.54.63.00)

The Hideout p119
11 rue du Pot-de-Fer 5th
(01.45.35.13.17/
www.irishfrance.com)

Le Pantalon p119
7 rue Royer-Collard, 5th
(01.40.51.85.85)

Le Piano Vache p119
8 rue Laplace, 5th
(01.46.33.75.03)

Le Violon Dingue p119
46 rue de la Montagne-Ste-Geneviève, 5th
(01.43.25.79.93)

Aux Trois Mailletz p119
56 rue Galande, 5th
(01.43.54.00.79/
www.lestroismailletz.com)

Bistros

Bistro Jef p19
9 rue Cujas, 5th
(01.43.29.20.20)

Le Buisson Ardent p19
25 rue Jussieu, 5th
(01.43.54.93.02)

Chez René p19
14 bd St-Germain, 5th
(01.43.54.30.23)

Chez Toutoune p19
5 rue de Pointoise, 5th
(01.43.26.56.81)

Le Coupe-Chou p19
11 rue de Lanneau, 5th
(01.46.33.68.69/
www.lecoupechou.com)

Les Degrés de Notre-Dame p19
10 rue des Grands-Degrés,
5th (01.55.42.88.88)

L'Equitable p19
1 rue des Fossés-St-Marcel,
5th (01.43.31.69.20)

Les Fontaines p19
9 rue Soufflot, 5th
(01.43.26.42.80)

L'Intermède p19
4 bd du Port-Royal, 5th
(01.47.07.08.99)

Le Moulin à Vent p20
20 rue des Fossés-St-Bernard, 5th
(01.43.54.99.37)

Le Reminet p20
3 rue des Grands-Degrés,
5th (01.44.07.04.24)

Time Out Paris Eating & Drinking 153

La Rôtisserie de
Beaujolais
19 quai de la Tournelle,
5th (01.43.54.17.47)

La Table de Michel p20
13 quai de la Tournelle,
5th (01.44.07.17.57)

Brasseries

Le Balzar p45
49 rue des Ecoles, 5th
(01.43.54.13.67)

Restaurant E Marty p45
20 av des Gobelins, 5th
(01.43.31.39.51/
www.marty-restaurant.com)

Budget

L'Ecurie p68
2 rue Laplace, 5th
(01.46.33.68.49)

L'Escapade p69
10 rue de la Montagne-Ste-
Geneviève, 5th
(01.46.33.23.85)

Le Jardin des Pâtes p69
4 rue Lacépède, 5th
(01.43.31.50.71)

Perraudin p69
157 rue St-Jacques, 5th
(01.46.33.15.75)

Cafés

Café Delmas p107
2-4 pl de la Contrescarpe,
5th (01.43.26.51.26)

Café de la Nouvelle
Mairie p107
19-21 rue des Fossés St-
Jacques, 5th
(01.44.07.04.41)

Café de la Poste p107
7 rue l'Epée-de-Bois, 5th
(01.43.37.05.58)

Le Comptoir du
Panthéon p107
5 rue Soufflot, 5th
(01.43.54.75.36)

Le Rallye p107
11 quai de la Tournelle, 5th
(01.43.54.29.65)

Le Reflet p107
6 rue Champollion, 5th
(01.43.29.97.27)

Tabac de la
Sorbonne p107
7 pl de la Sorbonne, 5th
(01.43.54.52.04)

Le Verre à Pied p107
118bis rue Mouffetard, 5th
(01.43.31.15.72)

Eastern Mediterranean

Les Délices
d'Aphrodite p85
4 rue de Candolle, 5th
(01.43.31.40.39)

Mavrommatis p85
5 rue du Marché des
Patriarches, 5th
(01.43.31.17.17)

La Voie Lactée p85
34 rue du Cardinal-Lemoine,
5th (01.46.34.02.35)

Far East

Au Coin des
Gourmets p88
5, rue Dante, 5th
(01.43.26.12.92)

Han Lim p88
6 rue Blainville, 5th
(01.43.54.62.74)

Mirama p87
17 rue Saint-Jacques, 5th
(01.43.54.71.77)

Pema Thang p90
13 rue de la Montagne
Ste-Geneviève, 5th
(01.43.54.34.34)

Fish & Seafood

Bistrot Côté Mer p65
16 bd St-Germain, 5th
(01.43.54.59.10/
www.michelrostang.com)

L'Huître et Demie p65
80 rue Mouffetard, 5th
(01.43.37.98.21)

Haute Cuisine

La Tour d'Argent p40
15-17 quai de la Tournelle,
5th (01.43.54.23.31/
www.tourdargent.com)

Home Delivery

Allô Indes p133
Vijaya, 22 rue Daubenton,
5th (01.47.07.56.78/fax
01.43.36.60.27/
www.allo-indes.com)

Learning & Tasting

Astuces et Tours
de Main p143
29 rue Censier, 5th
(03.44.54.37.21)

Grains Nobles p145
5 rue Laplace, 5th
(01.43.54.93.54)

North African

L'Atlas p99
12 bd St-Germain, 5th
(01.44.07.23.66)

Ziryab p99
Institut du Monde Arabe,
1 rue des Fossés-St-Bernard,
5th (01.53.10.10.20)

Other International

Hélices et Délices p101
8 rue Thénard, 5th
(01.43.54.59.47)

Shops and Markets

Maison Kayser p137
8, 14 rue Monge, 5th
(01.44.07.01.42/ 31.61)

Mexi & Co p140
10 rue Dante, 5th
(01.46.34.14.12)

Rue Mouffetard p140
5th. Mº Censier-Daubenton.

Spanish

Fogon Saint-Julien p100
10 rue St-Julien-le-Pauvre,
5th (01.43.54.31.33)

Tea Rooms & Ice Cream

Le Café Maure de la
Mosquée de Paris p127
39 rue Geoffroy-St-Hilaire,
5th (01.43.31.38.20)

La Fourmi Aillée p128
8 rue du Fouarre, 5th
(01.43.29.40.99)

La Maison des Trois
Thés p128
33 rue Gracieuse, 5th
(01.43.36.93.84)

Vegetarian

Le Grenier de Notre
Dame p75
18 rue de la Bûcherie,
5th (01.43.29.98.29/
www.legrenierdenotredame.com)

Les Quatre et Une
Saveurs p75
72 rue du Cardinal-Lemoine,
5th. (01.43.26.88.80)

Wine Bars

Les Cépages p129
6 rue des Fossés-St-Marcel,
5th (01.47.07.91.25)

Le Mauzac p129
7 rue de l'Abbé de l'Epée,
5th (01.46.33.75.22)

Les Papilles p129
30 rue Gay-Lussac, 5th
(01.43.25.20.79/
www.lespapilles.fr)

6th

The Americas

La Casa del Habano p82
169 bd Saint Germain, 6th
(01.45.44.33.56)

Fajitas p82
15 rue Dauphine, 6th
(01.46.34.44.69)

Bars & Pubs

Le Bar Dix p120
10 rue de l'Odéon, 6th
(01.43.26.66.83)

Café Mabillon p120
164 bd St-Germain, 6th
(01.43.26.62.93)

Le Comptoir des
Canettes p120
11 rue des Canettes,
6th (01.43.26.79.15)

Coolín p120
Marché St-Germain,
15 rue Clément, 6th
(01.44.07.00.92/
www.irishfrance.com)

Corcoran p120
28 rue St-André-des-Arts,
6th (01.40.46.97.46/
www.corcoranirishpub.com)

The Frog &
Princess p120
9 rue Princesse, 6th
(01.40.51.77.38/
www.frogpubs.com)

Fu Bar p120
5 rue St-Sulpice, 6th
(01.40.51.82.00)

Hôtel Lutétia p119
45 bd Raspail, 6th
(01.49.54.46.46/
www.lutetia-paris.com)

The Moose p120
16 rue des Quatre-Vents,
6th (01.46.33.77.00/
www.mooseheadparis.com)

Bistros

Au 35 p20
35 rue Jacob, 6th
(01.42.60.23.24)

Allard p20
41 rue St-André-des-Arts,
6th (01.43.26.48.23)

Aux Charpentiers p21
10 rue Mabillon, 6th
(01.43.26.30.05)

Au Bon Saint-
Pourçain p20
10bis rue Servandoni, 6th
(01.43.54.93.63)

Les Bookinistes p21
53 quai des Grands-
Augustins, 6th
(01.43.25.45.94)

Brasserie Fernand p21
13 rue Guisarde, 6th
(01.43.54.61.47)

Chez Marcel p21
7 rue Stanislas, 6th
(01.45.48.29.94)

L'Epi Dupin p21
11 rue Dupin, 6th
(01.42.22.64.56)

Josephine 'Chez
Dumonet' p21
117 rue du Cherche-Midi,
6th (01.45.48.52.40)

Le Mâchon d'Henri p21
8 rue Guisarde, 6th
(01.43.29.08.70)

Le Nemrod p21
51 rue du Cherche-Midi,6th
(01.45.48.17.05)

Le Parc Aux Cerfs p21
50 rue Vavin, 6th
(01.43.54.87.83)

Le Sabot Saint-
Germain p21
6 rue du Sabot, 6th
(01.42.22.21.56)

Wadja p21
10 rue de la Grande-
Chaumière, 6th
(01.46.33.02.02)

Brasseries

Alcazar p45
62 rue Mazarine, 6th
(01.53.10.19.99/
www.conran.com)

Brasserie Lipp p45
151 bd St-Germain, 6th
(01.45.48.53.91/
www.brasserie-lipp.fr)

Vagenende p46
142 bd St-Germain, 6th
(01.43.26.68.18)

Budget

Così p69
54 rue de Seine, 6th
(01.46.33.35.36)

Marmite et
Cassolette p69
157 bd du Montparnasse,
6th (01.43.26.26.53)

Le Petit Saint-Benoît p69
4 rue St-Benoît, 6th
(01.42.60.27.92)

Le Polidor p69
41 rue Monsieur-le-Prince,
6th (01.43.26.95.34)

Cafés

Bar de la Croix-
Rouge p107
2 carrefour de la Croix-
Rouge, 6th
(01.45.48.06.45)

Bar du Marché p109
75 rue de Seine, 6th
(01.43.26.55.15)

Café de Flore p109
172 bd St-Germain, 6th
(01.45.48.55.26)

Café de la Mairie p109
8 pl St-Sulpice, 6th
(01.43.26.67.82)

Les Deux Magots p109
6 pl St-Germain-des-Prés,
6th (01.45.48.55.25/
www.lesdeuxmagots.com)

Les Editeurs p109
4 carrefour de l'Odéon,
6th (01.43.26.67.76/
www.lesediteurs.fr)

M's Coffee Room p109
71 rue du Cherche-Midi,
6th (01.45.44.20.57)

La Palette p109
43 rue de Seine, 6th
(01.43.26.68.15)

Au Petit Suisse p109
16 rue de Vaugirard, 6th
(01.43.26.03.81)

Le Rostand p109
6 pl Edmond-Rostand, 6th
(01.43.54.61.58)

Le Select p109
99 bd du Montparnasse,
6th (01.42.22.65.27)

Au Vieux Colombier p109
65 rue de Rennes, 6th
(01.45.48.53.81)

Contemporary

Le Café des Délices p58
87 rue d'Assas, 6th
(01.43.54.70.00)

Le Maxence p58
9bis bd du Montparnasse,
6th (01.45.67.24.88)

Restaurant Hélène
Darroze p58
4 rue d'Assas, 6th
(01.42.22.00.11)

Le Salon d'Hélène p58
4 rue d'Assas, 6th
(01.42.22.00.11)

Ze Kitchen Galerie p58
4 rue des Grands-Augustins,
6th (01.44.32.00.32)

Far East

Le Chinois p87
3 rue Monsieur le Prince,
6th (01.43.25.36.88)

Thuy Long p90
111 rue de Vaugirard, 6th
(01.45.49.26.01)

Fish & Seafood

La Méditerranée p65
2 pl de l'Odéon, 6th
(01.43.26.02.30/
www.la-mediterranee.com)

Indian

Yugaraj p91
14 rue Dauphine, 6th
(01.43.26.44.91)

Japanese

Japotori p97
41 rue Monsieur-le-Prince,
6th (01.43.29.00.54)

Tsukizi p97
2bis rue des Ciseaux, 6th
(01.43.54.65.19)

Yen p97
22 rue St-Benoît, 6th
(01.45.44.11.18)

Learning & Tasting

Centre de Dégustation
Jacques Vivet p145
48 rue de Vaugirard, 6th
(01.43.25.96.30)

Ecoles Grégoire Ferrandi
p145
28 rue de l'Abbé-Grégoire,
6th (01.49.54.28.03)

Other International

Dominique p101
19 rue Bréa, 6th
(01.43.27.08.80)

Gustavia p101
26-28 rue des Grands-
Augustins, 6th
(01.40.46.86.70)

Shops and Markets

Cacao et Chocolat p137
29 rue de Buci, 6th
(01.46.33.77.63)

Christian Constant p139
37 rue d'Assas, 6th
(01.53.63.15.15)

Gérard Mulot p137
76 rue de Seine, 6th
(01.43.26.85.77)

Huilerie Artisanale
Leblanc p139
6 rue Jacob, 6th
(01.46.34.61.55)

Jean-Paul Hévin p139
3 rue Vavin, 6th
(01.43.54.09.85)

Marché Biologique p140
bd Raspail, 6th.

Oliviers & Co p139
28 rue de Buci, 6th
(01.44.07.15.43/
www.oliviers-co.com)

Poilâne p137
8 rue du Cherche-Midi, 6th
(01.45.48.42.59/
www.poilane.com)

Tea Rooms & Ice Cream

L'Artisan de Saveurs
p128
72 rue du Cherche-Midi, 6th
(01.42.22.46.64)

Forêt Noire p128
9 rue de l'Eperon, 6th
(01.44.41.00.09)

La Maison de la Chine
p128
76 rue Bonaparte, 6th
(01.40.51.95.16)

Tch'a p128
6 rue du Pont-de-Lodi, 6th
(01.43.29.61.31)

Vegetarian

Guen Maï p75
2bis rue de l'Abbaye, 6th.
(01.43.26.03.24)

Verdibus p75
48 rue du Cherche Midi, 6th
(01.40.49.06.17)

Wine Bars

Caves Miard p131
9 rue des Quatre-Vents, 6th
(01.43.54.99.30)

Fish p131
69 rue de Seine, 6th
(01.43.54.34.69)

La Tour de Pierre p131
53 rue Dauphine, 6th
(01.43.26.08.93/
www.latourdepierre.com)

7th

Bars & Pubs

Café Thoumieux p120
4 rue de la Comète, 7th
(01.45.51.50.40)

Bistros

L'Affriolé p23
17 rue Malar, 7th
(01.44.18.31.33)

Altitude 95 p23
First level, Eiffel Tower,
Champ de Mars,
7th (01.45.55.00.21)

Au Bon Accueil p23
14 rue Monttessuy 7th
(01.47.05.46.11)

La Cigale p23
11bis rue Chomel, 7th
(01.45.48.87.87)

Le Clos des
Gourmets p23
16 av Rapp, 7th
(01.45.51.75.61)

La Fontaine de Mars p23
129 rue St-Dominique,
7th (01.47.05.46.44)

Nabuchodonosor p23
6 av Bosquet, 7th
(01.45.56.97.26)

L'Oeillade p24
10 rue St-Simon, 7th
(01.42.22.01.60)

Le Petit Troquet p24
28 rue de l'Exposition, 7th
(01.47.05.80.39)

La Petite Chaise p24
36 rue de Grenelle, 7th
(01.42.22.13.35)

Le Récamier p24
4 rue Recamier, 7th
(01.45.48.86.58)

Thoumieux p24
79 rue St-Dominique, 7th
(01.47.05.49.75)

Budget

L'Auberge du Champ
de Mars p70
18 rue de l'Exposition,
7th (01.45.51.78.08)

Au Babylone p70
13 rue de Babylone, 7th
(01.45.48.72.13)

Chez Germaine p70
30 rue Pierre-Leroux, 7th
(01.42.73.28.34)

Cafés

Bar Basile p109
34 rue de Grenelle, 7th
(01.42.22.59.46)

Café Le Dôme p109
149 rue St-Dominique, 7th
(01.45.51.45.41)

Café des Lettres p109
53 rue de Verneuil, 7th
(01.42.22.52.17/
www.cafedeslettres.com)

Café du Marché p109
38 rue Cler, 7th
(01.47.05.51.27)

La Frégate p109
1 rue du Bac, 7th
(01.42.61.23.77/
www.la-fregate.com)

Contemporary

Restaurant
Petrossian p59
18 bd de La Tour-Maubourg,
7th (01.44.11.32.32)

Fish & Seafood

Le Divellec p65
107 rue de l'Universite, 7th
(01.45.51.91.96)

Les Glénan p65
54 rue de Bourgogne, 7th
(01.45.51.61.09)

Haute Cuisine

L'Arpège p41
84 rue de Varenne, 7th
(01.45.51.47.33/
www.alain-passard.com)

Le Jules Verne p41
Second Level, Eiffel
Tower, Champ de Mars,
7th (01.45.55.61.44)

Arrondissement Index

Learning & Tasting

La Cuisine de Marie-Blanche p143
18 av de la Motte-Picquet, 7th (01.45.51.36.34)

Les Vins du Terroir p145
34 av Duquesne, 7th (01.40.61.91.87)

Other International

Doïna p101
149 rue Saint-Dominique, 7th (01.45.50.49.57)

Shops and Markets

Debauve & Gallais p139
30 rue des Sts-Pères, 7th (01.45.48.54.67)

Jean-Luc Poujauran p137
20 rue Jean-Nicot, 7th (01.47.05.80.88)

Maison Rollet Pradier p137
6 rue de Bourgogne, 7th (01.45.51.78.36)

Marie-Anne Cantin p137
12 rue du Champs-de-Mars, 7th (01.45.50.43.94/www.cantin.fr)

Richart p139
258 bd St-Germain, 7th (01.45.55.66.00/www.richart.com)

Ryst Dupeyron p140
79 rue du Bac, 7th (01.45.48.80.93/www.dupeyron.com)

Saxe-Breteuil p140
av de Saxe, 7th. M° Ségur.

Trendy

L'Esplanade p51
52 rue Fabert, 7th (01.47.05.38.80)

Thiou p51
49 quai d'Orsay, 7th (01.45.51.58.58)

8th

The Americas

The Chicago Pizza Pie Factory p81
5 rue Berri, 8th (01.45.62.50.23)

Planet Hollywood p81
76-78 av des Champs-Elysées, 8th (01.53.83.78.27/www.planethollywood.com)

Bars & Pubs

Barfly p120
49 av George V, 8th (01.53.67.84.60)

The Bowler p120
13 rue d'Artois, 8th (01.45.61.16.60)

Freedom p120
8 rue de Berri, 8th (01.53.75.25.50)

Hôtel Plaza Athénée p119
25 av Montaigne, 8th (01.53.67.66.65)

Latina Café p121
114 av des Champs-Elysées, 8th (01.42.89.98.89)

Mathis p119
3 rue de Ponthieu, 8th (01.53.76.01.62)

Polo Room p121
3 rue Lord-Byron, 8th (01.40.74.07.78/www.poloroom.com)

Bistros

Le Bistro de Gala p25
45 rue du Fbg-Montmartre, 9th (01.40.22.90.50)

Le Bistrot d'Anglas p24
29 rue Boissy d'Anglas, 8th (01.42.65.63.73)

La Maline p24
40 rue de Ponthieu, 8th (01.45.63.14.14)

Le Rocher Gourmand p25
89 rue du Rocher, 8th (01.40.08.00.36)

Savy p25
23 rue Bayard, 8th (01.47.23.46.98)

Sébillon p25
66 rue Pierre-Charron, 8th (01.43.59.28.15)

Brasseries

L'Avenue p46
41 av Montaigne, 8th (01.40.70.14.91)

Le Boeuf sur le Toit p46
34 rue du Colisée, 8th (01.53.93.65.55)

Brasserie Lorraine p46
2-4 place des Ternes, 8th (01.56.21.22.00)

La Fermette Marbeuf 1900 p46
5 rue Marbeuf, 8th (01.53.23.08.00/www.blanc.net)

Le Fouquet's p46
99 av des Champs-Elysées, 8th (01.47.23.70.60/www.lucienbarriere.com)

Garnier p46
111 rue St-Lazare, 8th (01.43.87.50.40)

La Maison de l'Aubrac p46
37 rue Marbeuf, 8th (01.43.59.05.14)

Restaurant Cap Vernet p46
82 av Marceau, 8th (01.47.20.20.40)

Budget

Le Bistroquet p70
52 rue du Colisée, 8th (01.45.61.01.82)

Cafés

Atelier Renault p111
53 av des Champs-Elysées, 8th (01.49.53.70.00)

Bar des Théâtres p111
6 av Montaigne, 8th (01.47.23.34.63)

Granterroirs p111
30 rue de Miromesnil, 8th (01.47.42.18.18)

Handmade p111
19 rue Jean-Mermoz, 8th (01.45.62.50.05)

Le Petit Bergson p111
10 pl Henri-Bergson, 8th (01.45.22.63.25)

Contemporary

L'Angle du Faubourg p59
195 rue du Fbg St-Honoré, 8th (01.40.74.20.20)

L'Astor p59
Sofitel Demeure Hôtel Astor, 11 rue d'Astorg, 8th (01.53.05.05.20/www.hotel-astor.net)

Chiberta p60
3 rue Arsène-Houssaye, 8th (01.53.53.42.00)

Les Elysées p60
Hôtel Vernet, 25 rue Vernet, 8th (01.44.31.98.98/www.hotelvernet.com)

Maison Blanche p60
15 av Montaigne, 8th (01.47.23.55.99)

Market p60
15 av Matignon, 8th (01.56.43.40.90)

Renoma Café Gallery p60
32 av George V/45 rue Pierre-Charron, 8th (01.56.89.05.89)

Shozan p60
11 rue de la Trémoïlle, 8th (01.47.23.37.32)

Stella Maris p60
4 rue Arsène-Houssaye, 8th (01.42.89.16.22)

Eastern Mediterranean

Fakhr el Dine p85
3 rue Quentin-Bauchart, 8th (01.47.23.44.42)

Haute Cuisine

Alain Ducasse au Plaza Athénée p41
Hôtel Plaza Athénée, 25 av Montaigne, 8th (01.53.67.65.00/www.alain-ducasse.com)

Les Ambassadeurs p41
Hôtel de Crillon, 10 pl de la Concorde, 8th (01.44.71.16.16/www.crillon.com)

Le Bristol p41
Hôtel Bristol, 112 rue du Fbg-St-Honoré, 8th (01.53.43.43.00/www.hotel-bristol.com)

Le Cinq p42
Hôtel Four Seasons George V, 31 av George V, 8th (01.49.52.70.00/www.fourseasons.com)

Laurent p42
41 av Gabriel, 8th (01.42.25.00.39/www.le-laurent.com)

Ledoyen p42
1 av Dutuit, 8th (01.53.05.10.01)

Lucas Carton p42
9 pl de la Madeleine, 8th (01.42.65.22.90/www.lucascarton.com)

Pierre Gagnaire p42
6 rue Balzac, 8th (0158.36.12.50/www.pierre-gagnaire.com)

Taillevent p43
15 rue Lamennais, 8th (01.44.95.15.01/www.taillevent.com)

Home Delivery

Radis Olive p133
27 rue de Marignan, 8th (01.42.56.55.55/fax 01.42.56.22.37)

Japanese

Jipangue p97
96 rue La Boétie, 8th (01.45.63.77.00)

Shops and Markets

Les Caves Augé p140
116 bd Haussmann, 8th (01.45.22.16.97)

Les Caves Taillevent p140
199 rue du Fbg-St-Honoré, 8th (01.45.61.14.09/www.taillevent.com)

La Cigogne p139
61 rue de l'Arcade, 8th (01.43.87.39.16)

Dalloyau p137
101 rue du Fbg-St-Honoré, 8th (01.42.99.90.00)

Fauchon p139
26-30 pl de la Madeleine, 8th (01.47.42.60.11)

Hédiard p139
21 pl de la Madeleine, 8th (01.43.12.88.88/www.hediard.fr)

Jabugo Iberico & Co. p140
11 rue Clément Marot, 8th (01.47.20.03.13)

La Maison de la Truffe p139
19 pl de la Madeleine, 8th (01.42.65.53.22/www.maison-de-la-truffe.com)

René-Gérard St-Ouen p137
111 bd Haussmann, 8th (01.42.65.06.25)

Tea Rooms & Ice Cream

Le Bristol p128
112 rue du Fbg-St-Honoré, 8th (01.53.43.43.00)

Hôtel de Crillon p128
10 pl de la Concorde, 8th (01.44.71.15.00)

Hôtel Plaza Athénée p128
25 av Montaigne, 8th. M° Alma Marceau (01.53.67.66.65)

Ladurée p128
16 rue Royale, 8th (01.42.60.21.79)

Trendy

Le Buddha Bar p51
8 rue Boissy d'Anglas, 8th (01.53.05.90.00)

Korova p51
33 rue Marbeuf, 8th (01.53.89.93.93)

Man Ray p52
34 rue Marbeuf, 8th (01.56.88.36.36/www.manray.fr)

Nobu p52
15 rue Marbeuf, 8th (01.56.89.53.53)

Rue Balzac p52
3-5 rue Balzac, 8th (01.53.89.90.91)

Spoon, Food & Wine p52
14 rue de Marignan, 8th (01.40.76.34.44)

Tanjia p52
23 rue de Ponthieu, 8th (01.42.25.95.00)

Wine Bars

Le Griffonier p131
8 rue des Saussaies, 8th (01.42.65.17.17)

Ma Bourgogne p131
133 bd Haussmann, 8th (01.45.63.50.61)

9th

The Americas

Hard Rock Café p81
14 bd Montmartre, 9th (01.53.24.60.00/www.hardrockcafe.com)

Bars & Pubs

Le Barramundi p121
3 rue Taitbout, 9th (01.47.70.21.21)

Bistros

A la Cloche d'Or p25
3 rue Mansart, 9th (01.48.74.48.88)

Casa Olympe p25
48 rue St-Georges, 9th (01.42.85.26.01)

Chez Catherine p25
65 rue de Provence, 9th (01.45.26.72.88)

Chez Jean p25
8 rue St-Lazare, 9th (01.48.78.62.73)

Les Comédiens p27
1 rue de la Trinité, 9th (01.40.82.95.95)

A la Grange Batelière p27
16 rue de la Grange-Batelière, 9th (01.47.70.85.15)

La Table de la Fontaine p27
5 rue Henri-Monnier, 9th (01.45.26.26.30)

Velly p27
52 rue Lamartine, 9th (01.48.78.60.05)

Brasseries

Charlot, Roi des Coquillages p47
81 bd de Clichy, 9th (01.53.20.48.00)

Au Petit Riche p47
25 rue Le Peletier, 9th (01.47.70.68.68/www.aupetitriche.com)

La Taverne p47
24 bd des Italiens, 9th (01.55.33.10.00/www.taverne.fr)

Budget

Chartier p70
7 rue du Fbg-Montmartre, 9th. (01.47.70.86.29)

Cafés

P'tit Creux du Faubourg p111
66 rue du Fbg-Montmartre, 9th (01.48.78.20.57)

Far East

Gin Go Gae p88
28 rue Lamartine, 9th (01.48.78.24.64)

Indian

Kastoori p91
4 pl Gustave Toudouze, 9th (01.44.53.06.10)

North African

Wally le Saharien p99
36 rue Rodier, 9th (01.42.85.51.90)

Other International

Le Paprika p101
28 av Trudaine, 9th (01.44.63.02.91/www.le-paprika.com)

Shops and Markets

Les Cakes de Bertrand p139
7 rue Bourdaloue, 9th (01.40.16.16.28)

Charcuterie Lyonnaise p139
58 rue des Martyrs, 9th (01.48.78.96.45)

Henri Ceccaldi p139
21 rue des Mathurins, 9th (01.47.42.66.52)

Wine Bars

La Cave Drouot p131
8 rue Drouot, 9th (01.47.70.83.38)

10th

Bars & Pubs

L'Atmosphère p121
49 rue Lucien-Sampaix, 10th (01.40.38.09.21)

Chez Adel p121
10 rue de la Grange-aux-Belles, 10th (01.42.08.24.61)

De La Ville Café p121
34 bd Bonne Nouvelle, 10th (01.48.24.48.09)

La Patache p121
60 rue de Lancry, 10th (01.42.08.14.35)

Le Sainte Marthe p121
32 rue Ste-Marthe, 10th (01.44.84.36.96)

Bistros

Chez Arthur p27
25 rue du Fbg St-Martin, 10th (01.42.08.34.33)

Chez Casimir p27
6 rue de Belzunce, 10th (01.48.78.28.80)

Chez Michel p27
10 rue de Belzunce, 10th (01.44.53.06.20)

Aux Deux Canards p27
8 rue du Fbg-Poissonnière, 10th (01.47.70.03.23)

L'Hermitage p27
5 bd de Denain, 10th (01.48.78.77.09)

Le Parmentier p28
12 rue Arthur Groussier, 10th (01.42.40.74.75)

Brasseries

Brasserie Flo p47
7 cour des Petites-Ecuries, 10th (01.47.70.13.59)

Julien p47
16 rue du Fbg-St-Denis, 10th (01.47.70.12.06)

Terminus Nord p47
23 rue de Dunkerque, 10th (01.42.85.05.15)

Budget

Chez Papa p70
206 rue Lafayette, 10th (01.42.09.53.87)

Rôtisserie Ste-Marthe p70
4 rue Ste-Marthe, 10th (01.40.03.08.30)

Cafés

Chez Prune p111
71 quai de Valmy, 10th (01.42.41.30.47)

Le Grenier Voyageur p111
3 rue Yves-Toudic, 10th (01.42.02.25.50)

Jemmapes p111
82 quai de Jemmapes, 10th (01.40.40.02.35)

Le Petit Château d'Eau p111
34 rue du Chateau d'Eau, 10th (01.42.08.72.81)

Eastern Mediterranean

Kibele p85
12 rue de l'Echiquier, 10th (01.48.24.57.74)

Far East

Le Cambodge p87
10 av Richerand, 10th (01.44.84.37.70)

Indian

Ganesha Corner p91
16 rue Perdonnet, 10th (01.46.07.35.32)

New Pondichery p91
189 rue du Fbg-St-Denis, 10th (01.40.34.30.70)

Shalimar p91
59 Passage Brady, 10th (01.45.23.31.61)

Shops and Markets

Sarl Velan Stores p140
87 passage Brady, 10th (01.42.46.06.06)

Saveurs d'Irlande p140
5 cité de Vauxhall, 10th (01.42.00.36.20)

Wine Bars

Le Verre Volé p131
67 rue de Lancry, 10th (01.48.03.17.34)

11th

The Americas

Arriba Mexico p82
32 av de la République, 11th (01.49.29.95.40)

Blue Bayou p81
111-113 rue St-Maur, 11th (01.43.55.87.21)

El Paladar p83
26bis rue de la Fontaine au Roi, 11th. (01.43.57.42.70)

Favela Chic p83
18 rue du Fbg-du-Temple, 11th (01.40.21.38.14/www.favelachic.com)

Taco Loco p83
116, rue Amelot, 11th (01.43.57.90.24)

Bars & Pubs

Les Abats-Jour à Coudre p121
115 rue Oberkampf, 11th.

L'Armagnac p121
104 rue de Charonne, 11th (01.43.71.49.43)

L'Autre Cafe p121
62 rue Jean-Pierre Timbaud, 11th (01.40.21.03.07)

Bar des Ferailleurs p121
18 rue de Lappe, 11th (01.48.07.89.12)

Boca Chica p121
58 rue de Charonne, 11th (01.43.57.93.13/www.labocachica.com)

The Bottle Shop p121
5 rue Trousseau, 11th (01.43.14.28.04/www.hip-bars.com)

Time Out Paris Eating & Drinking 155

Café Cannibale p123
93 rue Jean-Pierre-Timbaud, 11th (01.49.29.95.59)

Café Charbon p123
109 rue Oberkampf, 11th (01.43.57.55.13/ www.nouveaucasino.net)

Les Couleurs p123
117 rue St-Maur, 11th (01.43.57.95.61)

L'Entre-potes p123
14 rue de Charonne, 11th (01.48.06.57.04)

La Fabrique p123
53 rue du Fbg-St-Antoine, 11th (01.43.07.67.07/ www.fabrique.fr)

Le Lèche-Vin p123
13 rue Daval, 11th (01.43.55.98.91)

Le Mecano Bar p123
99 rue Oberkampf, 11th (01.40.21.35.28)

La Mercerie p123
98 rue Oberkampf, 11th (01.43.38.81.30)

F.B.I. Paris (Freestyle Bar) p123
45 rue de la Folie-Méricourt, 11th (01.43.14.26.36/ www.fbiparis.com)

Le Réservoir p123
16 rue de la Forge-Royal, 11th (01.43.56.39.60/ www.reservoir-dogs.com)

Le Sanz Sans p123
49 rue du Fbg-St-Antoine, 11th (01.44.75.78.78)

Les Trois Têtards p123
46 rue Jean Pierre Timbaud, 11th (01.43.14.27.37)

Le Zéro Zéro p123
89 rue Amelot, 11th (01.49.23.51.00/ www.zerozero.com)

Bistros

Les Amognes p28
243 rue du Fbg-St-Antoine, 11th (01.43.72.73.05)

Astier p28
44 rue Jean-Pierre-Timbaud, 11th (01.43.57.16.35)

C'Amelot p28
50 rue Amelot, 11th (01.43.55.54.04)

Chardenoux p28
1 rue Jules-Vallès, 11th (01.43.71.49.52)

Le Chateaubriand p28
129 av Parmentier, 11th (01.43.57.45.95)

Chez Paul p28
13 rue de Charonne, 11th (01.47.00.34.57)

Chez Ramulaud p28
269 rue du Fbg-St-Antoine, 11th (01.43.72.23.29)

Dame Jeanne p28
60 rue de Charonne, 11th (01.47.00.37.40/ www.damejeanne.fr)

Les Jumeaux p28
73 rue Amelot, 11th (01.43.14.27.00)

Le Passage p28
18 passage de la Bonne-Graine, 11th (01.47.00.73.30)

Le Repaire de Cartouche p28
8 bd des Filles-du-Calvaire/99 rue Amelot, 11th (01.47.00.25.86)

A Sousceyrac p29
35 rue Faidherbe, 11th (01.43.71.65.30)

Budget

Les 100 Kilos p70
2 rue de la Folie Méricourt, 11th (01.43.55.12.74)

Bar à Soupes p69
33 rue de Charonne, 11th (01.43.57.53.79)

La Cheminée p70
7 rue Jean-Pierre Timbaud, 11th (01.49.23.06.76)

Le Petit Keller p70
13bis rue Keller, 11th (01.47.00.12.97)

Le Temps au Temps p70
13 rue Paul Bert, 11th (01.43.79.63.40/ www.ifrance.com/ restaurant75)

Au Vieux Chêne p70
7 rue Dahomey, 11th (01.43.71.67.69)

La Zygotissoire p71
101 rue de Charonne, 11th (01.40.09.93.05)

Cafés

Ba'ta'clan Café p111
50 bd Voltaire, 11th (01.49.23.96.33)

Le Bistrot du Peintre p111
116 av Ledru-Rollin, 11th (01.47.00.34.39)

Café de l'Industrie p111
16 rue St-Sabin, 11th (01.47.00.13.53)

Extra Old Café p111
307 rue du Fbg-St-Antoine, 11th (01.43.71.73.45)

Le Kitch p113
10 rue Oberkampf, 11th (01.40.21.94.14)

Morry's p113
1 rue de Charonne, 11th (01.48.07.03.03)

Pause Café p113
41 rue de Charonne, 11th (01.48.06.80.33)

Eastern Mediterranean

Zagros p85
21 rue de la Folie-Méricourt, 11th (01.48.07.09.56)

Far East

Bali Bar p89
9 rue St-Sabin, 11th (01.47.00.25.47)

Blue Elephant p89
43 rue de la Roquette, 11th (01.47.00.42.00)

Dong Huong p90
14 rue Louis-Bonnet, 11th (01.43.57.18.88)

Khun Akorn p89
8 av de Taillebourg, 11th (01.43.56.20.03)

New Nioullaville p87
32 rue de l'Orillon, 11th (01.40.21.96.18)

Le Président p87
120-124 rue du Fbg-du-Temple, 11th (01.47.00.17.18)

Wok p87
23 rue des Taillandiers, 11th (01.55.28.88.77)

Home Delivery

Allô Couscous p133
70 rue Alexandre-Dumas, 11th (01.43.70.82.83)

Le Lotus Bleu p133
17 rue de la Pierre-Levée, 11th (01.43.55.57.75/ fax 01.43.14.02.72/ www.lotus-bleu.fr)

Indian

Coffee India p91
33-35 rue de Lappe, 11th (01.48.06.18.57/ www.coffee-india.com)

North African

L'Homme Bleu p99
55bis rue Jean-Pierre Timbaud, 11th (01.48.07.05.63)

La Mansouria p100
11 rue Faidherbe, 11th (01.43.71.00.16)

Restaurant des 4 Frères p100
127 bd de Ménilmontant, 11th (01.43.55.40.91)

Le Souk p100
1 rue Keller, 11th (01.49.29.05.08)

Shops and Markets

L'Autre Boulange p137
43, rue de Montreuil, 11th (01.43.72.86.04)

Bières Spéciales p140
77 rue St-Maur, 11th (01.48.07.18.71)

Les Domaines qui Montent p140
136 bd Voltaire, 11th (01.43.56.89.15)

A la Petite Fabrique p139
12 rue St-Sabin, 11th (01.48.05.82.02)

Marché Bastille p140
bd Richard-Lenoir, 11th.

Démoulin p137
6 bd Voltaire, 11th (01.47.00.58.20/ www.chocolat-paris.com)

Spanish

La Plancha p100
34 rue Keller, 11th (01.48.05.20.30)

Tea Rooms & Ice Cream

Les Petits Plus p128
20 bd Beaumarchais, 11th (01.48.87.01.40/ www.lespetitsplus.com)

Vegetarian

Restaurant Haiku p75
63 rue Jean-Pierre Timbaud, 11th. (01.56.98.11.67)

Wine Bars

Le Café du Passage p131
12 rue de Charonne, 11th (01.49.29.97.64)

Le Clown Bar p131
114 rue Amelot, 11th (01.43.55.87.35)

Jacques Mélac p131
42 rue Léon-Frot, 11th (01.43.70.59.27)

12th

Bars & Pubs

Barrio Latino p123
46-48 rue du Fbg-St-Antoine, 12th (01.55.78.84.75)

China Club p125
50 rue de Charenton, 12th (01.43.43.82.02/ www.chinaclub.cc)

La Distillerie p125
50 rue du Fbg-St-Antoine, 12th (01.40.01.99.00/ www.la-distillerie.com)

OPA p125
9 rue Biscornet, 12th (01.49.28.97.16/ www.opabastille.com)

Bistros

L'Auberge le Quincy p29
28 av Ledru-Rollin, 12th (01.46.28.46.76)

Les Bombis Bistrot p31
22 rue de Chaligny, 12th (01.43.45.36.32)

L'Ebauchoir p31
45 rue de Cîteaux, 12th (01.43.42.49.31)

A La Biche du Bois p29
45 av Ledru Rollin, 12th (01.43.43.34.38)

Le Saint Amarante p31
4 rue Biscornet, 12th (01.43.43.00.08)

Le Square Trousseau p31
1 rue Antoine-Vollon, 12th (01.43.43.06.00)

La Table du Marquis p31
3 rue Beccaria, 12th (01.43.41.56.71)

Les Zygomates p31
7 rue de Capri, 12th (01.40.19.93.04)

Brasseries

Les Grandes Marches p48
6 pl de la Bastille, 12th (01.43.42.90.32/ www.lesgrandesmarches.com)

Le Train Bleu p48
Gare de Lyon, Place Louis-Armand, 12th (01.43.43.09.06)

Budget

... Comme Cochons p71
135 rue de Charenton, 12th (01.43.42.43.36)

La Connivence p71
1 rue de Cotte, 12th (01.46.28.46.17)

L'Encrier p71
55 rue Traversière, 12th (01.44.68.08.16)

Le Pays de Vannes p72
34bis rue Wattignies, 12th (01.43.07.87.42)

Cafés

Chez Gudule p113
58 bd de Picpus, 12th (01.43.40.08.28)

Roller Café p113
50 bd de la Bastille, 12th (01.43.46.55.22)

T pour 2 Café p113
23 cour St-Emilion, 12th (01.40.19.02.09/ www.tpour2cafe.com)

Le Viaduc Café p113
43 av Daumesnil, 12th (01.44.74.70.70)

Fish & Seafood

Le Guilvinec p66
34 Cour St-Emilion, 12th (01.44.68.01.35)

Home Delivery

Speed Rabbit Pizza p133
14 bd de Reuilly, 12th (01.43.44.80.80)

North African

Taninna p100
14 rue Abel, 12th (01.40.19.99.04)

Shops and Markets

Cour de Vincennes p140
12th.

Marché d'Aligre p140
rue and pl d'Aligre, 12th.

Les Ultra-Vins p140
16 rue Lacuée, 12th (01.43.46.85.81)

Wine Bars

Le Baron Bouge p131
1 rue Théophile-Roussel, 12th (01.43.43.14.32)

13th

Bars & Pubs

La Folie en Tête p125
33 rue de la Butte-aux-Cailles, 13th (01.45.80.65.99)

Le Merle Moqueur p125
11 rue de la Butte-aux-Cailles, 13th (01.45.65.12.43)

Bistros

L'Aimant du Sud p31
40 bd Arago, 13th (01.47.07.33.57)

Anacréon p31
53 bd St-Marcel, 13th (01.43.31.71.18)

L'Avant-Goût p31
26 rue Bobillot, 13th (01.53.80.24.00)

Chez Paul p32
22 rue de la Butte-aux-Cailles, 13th (01.45.89.22.11)

La Girondine p32
48 bd Arago, 13th (01.43.31.64.17)

Au Petit Marguery p32
9 bd du Port-Royal, 13th (01.43.31.58.59)

Le Terroir p32
11 bd Arago, 13th (01.47.07.36.99)

Budget

Chez Gladines p72
30 rue des Cinq-Diamants, 13th (01.45.80.70.10)

Le Temps des Cerises p72
18 rue de la Butte-aux-Cailles, 13th (01.45.89.69.48)

Cafés

La Route du Cacao p113
Quai de la Gare, 13th (01.53.82.10.35/ www.larouteducacao.com)

Au Soleil d'Austerlitz p113
18 bd de l'Hôpital, 13th (01.43.31.22.38.)

Far East

La Chine Masséna p87
Centre Commercial Masséna, 13 pl de Vénétie, 13th (01.45.83.98.88)

Kok p90
129bis av de Choisy, 13th (01.45.84.10.48)

Tricotin p87
15 av de Choisy, 13th (01.45.84.74.44)

Fish & Seafood

Le Keryado p66
32 rue Regnault, 13th (01.45.83.87.58)

Learning & Tasting

L'Ecole du Vin Ylan Schwartz p145
17 passage Foubert, 13th (01.45.89.77.39)

North African

Au P'tit Cahoua p100
39 bd St-Marcel, 13th (01.47.07.24.42)

Shops and Markets

Boulevard Auguste-Blanqui p140
between pl d'Italie and rue Baurrault, 13th.

Tang Frères p140
48 av d'Ivry, 13th (01.45.70.80.00)

Wine Bars

Les Cailloux p131
58 rue des Cinq Diamants, 13th (01.45.80.15.08)

14th

Bars & Pubs

La Jamaïque p125
2 pl Catalogne, 14th (01.43.35.50.50)

Le Rosebud p125
11bis rue Delambre, 14th (01.43.20.44.13)

Bistros

L'Assiette p32
181 rue du Château, 14th (01.43.22.64.86)

Contre-Allée p32
83 av Denfert-Rochereau, 14th (01.43.54.99.86)

Natacha p32
17bis rue Campagne-Première, 14th (01.43.20.79.27)

L'O à la Bouche p32
124 bd du Montparanasse, 14th (01.56.54.01.55)

Les Petites Sorcières p32
12 rue Liancourt, 14th (01.43.21.95.68)

La Régalade p33
49 av Jean-Moulin, 14th (01.45.45.68.58)

Le Vin des Rues p33
21 rue Boulard, 14th (01.43.22.19.78)

Brasseries

La Coupole p48
102 bd du Montparnasse, 14th (01.43.20.14.20)

Budget

Au Rendez-Vous des Camionneurs p72
34 rue des Plantes, 14th (01.45.42.20.94)

Cafés

Le Cadran p113
38 rue Raymond-Losserand, 14th (01.43.21.69.45)

Café de la Place p113
23 rue de l'Odessa, 14th (01.42.18.01.55)

La Chope Daguerre p113
17 rue Daguerre, 14th (01.43.22.76.59)

L'Entrepôt p115
7-9 rue Francis-de-Pressensé, 14th (01.45.40.60.70)

Far East

Korean Barbecue p88
22, rue Delambre, 14th (01.43.35.44.32)

Fish & Seafood

Le Bar à Huîtres p66
112 bd du Montparnasse, 14th (01.43.20.71.01/ www.lebarahuitres.fr)

La Cagouille p66
10-12 pl Constantin-Brancusi, 14th (01.43.22.09.01/ www.la-cagouille.fr)

Le Dôme p66
108 bd du Montparnasse, 14th (01.43.35.25.81)

Le Duc p66
243 bd Raspail, 14th (01.43.20.96.30/ 01.43.22.59.59)

Learning & Tasting

CIDD Découverte du Vin p145
30 rue de la Sablière, 14th (01.45.45.44.20)

Shops and Markets

Fil o'Fromage p137
4 rue Poirier-de-Narçay, 14th (01.40.44.86.75)

Poissonerie du Dôme p139
4 rue Delambre, 14th (01.43.35.23.95)

Rue Daguerre p140
14th.

Trendy

Yogi's p52
13 rue du Commandant-Mouchotte, 14th (01.45.38.92.93)

Vegetarian

Aquarius p75
40 rue de Gergovie, 14th (01.45.41.36.88)

Wine Bars

Le Rallye-Peret p131
6 Daguerre, 14th (01.43.22.57.05)

15th

Bistros

Le Bistrot d'Hubert p33
41 bd Pasteur, 15th (01.47.34.15.50)

Chez Les Frères Gaudet p33
19 rue Duranton, 15th (01.45.58.43.17)

Arrondissement Index

La Dînée p33
85 rue Leblanc, 15th
(01.45.54.20.49)

La Folletterie p33
34 rue Letellier, 15th
(01.45.75.55.95)

L'Os à Moëlle p35
3 rue Vasco-de-Gama, 15th (01.45.57.27.27)

Les P'tits Bouchons de François Clerc p35
32 bd du Montparnasse, 15th (01.45.48.52.03/ www.lesbouchonsdefrancoisclerc.com)

Le Père Claude p35
51 av de la Motte-Picquet, 15th (01.47.34.03.05)

Le Sept/Quinze p35
29 av de Lowendal, 15th (01.43.06.23.06)

Le Troquet p35
21 rue François-Bonvin, 15th (01.45.66.89.00)

Brasseries

Le Suffren p48
84 av de Suffren, 15th
(01.45.66.97.86)

Budget

Café du Commerce p72
51 rue du Commerce, 15th
(01.45.75.03.27)

Les Dix Vins p72
57 rue Falguière, 15th
(01.43.20.91.77)

U Sampiero Corsu p72
12 rue de l'Amiral Roussin, 15th.

Cafés

Au Dernier Métro p115
70 bd de Grenelle, 15th
(01.45.75.01.23/
www.auderniermetro.com)

No Stress Café p115
27 rue Balard, 15th
(01.45.58.45.68)

Le Roi du Café p115
59 rue Lecourbe, 15th
(01.47.34.48.50)

Eastern Mediterranean

El Bacha p85
74, rue de la Croix-Nivert, 15th (01.45.32.15.42)

Mazeh p85
65, rue des Entrepreneurs, 15th (01.45.75.33.89)

Restaurant Al Wady p85
153-155 rue de Lourmel, 15th (01.45.58.57.18)

Far East

Chen p88
15 rue du Théâtre, 15th
(01.45.79.34.34)

Chez Foong p89
32 rue de Frémicourt, 15th
(01.45.67.36.99)

Kim Anh p90
49 av. Emile Zola, 15th
(01.45.79.40.96)

Sawadee p89
53 av Emile Zola, 15th
(01.45.77.68.90)

Learning & Tasting

Le Cordon Bleu p143
8 rue Léon-Delhomme, 15th
(01.53.68.22.50)

Other International

Au Soleil de Minuit p101
15 rue Desnouettes, 15th
(01.48.28.15.15)

Vasco da Gama p101
39 rue Vasco de Gama, 15th
(01.45.57.20.01)

Shops and Markets

La Campagne p140
111 bd de Grenelle, 15th
(01.47.34.77.05)

Le Comptoir Corrézien p140
8 rue des Volontaires, 15th
(01.47.83.52.97)

Les Délices d'Orient p140
52 av Emile Zola, 15th
(01.45.79.10.00)

Laurent Dubois p137
2 rue de Lourmel, 15th
(01.45.78.70.58)

Lenôtre p139
61 rue Lecourbe, 15th
(01.42.73.20.97/
www.lenotre.fr)

La Maison de l'Escargot p139
79 rue Fondary, 15th
(01.45.75.31.09)

Max Poilâne p137
87 rue Brancion, 15th
(01.48.28.45.90/
www.max-poilane.fr)

Moulin de la Vierge p137
166 av de Suffren, 15th
(01.47.83.45.55)

Spanish

Las Ramblas p100
14 rue Miollis, 15th (01 47 83 32 98)

16th

Bistros

Le Bistrot des Vignes p35
1 rue Jean-Bologne, 16th
(01.45.27.76.64)

La Butte Chaillot p36
110bis av Kléber, 16th
(01.47.27.88.88)

Les Ormes p36
8 rue Chapu, 16th
(01.46.47.83.98)

Le Petit Rétro p36
5 rue Mesnil, 16th
(01.44.05.06.05)

Le Scheffer p36
22 rue Scheffer, 16th
(01.47.27.81.11)

Brasseries

Brasserie de la Poste p48
54 rue de Longchamp, 16th (01.47.55.01.31/ www.brasserie-de-la-poste.com)

La Gare p48
19 chaussée de la Muette, 16th (01.42.15.15.31)

La Grande Armée p48
3 av de la Grande-Armée, 16th (01.45.00.24.77)

Zebra Square p48
3 pl Clément-Ader, 16th
(01.44.14.91.91/
www.zebra-square.com)

Budget

Restaurant GR5 p72
19 rue Gustave Courbet, 16th (01.47.27.09.84)

Cafés

Café Antoine p115
17 rue La Fontaine, 16th
(01.40.50.14.30)

Le Totem p115
Musée de l'Homme,
17 pl du Trocadéro, 16th
(01.47.27.28.29)

Contemporary

59 Poincaré p60
Hôtel Le Parc, 59 av Raymond-Poincaré, 16th
(01.47.27.59.59)

L'Astrance p60
4 rue Beethoven, 16th
(01.40.50.84.40)

Far East

Kambodgia p87
15 rue de Bassano, 16th
(01.47.23.08.19)

Fish & Seafood

Maison Prunier p66
16 av Victor Hugo, 16th
(01.44.17.35.85/
www.maisonprunier.com)

Vin et Marée p66
183, bd Murat, 16th
(01.46.47.91.39)

Haute Cuisine

Ghislaine Arabian p43
16 av Bugeaud, 16th
(01.56.28.16.16)

Jamin p43
32 rue de Longchamp, 16th (01.45.53.00.07)

Le Pré Catelan p43
route de Suresnes,
Bois de Boulogne, 16th
(01.44.14.41.14/
www.lenotre.fr)

Learning & Tasting

Ecole Lenôtre p143
48 av Victor-Hugo, 16th
(01.45.02.21.19)

Institut du Vin du Savour Club p145
11-13 rue Gros, 16th
(01.42.30.94.18)

Le Musée du Vin p145
5 sq Charles-Dickens, 16th (01.45.25.63.26)

Shops and Markets

Boucherie Lamartine Prosper et Cie p139
172 av Victor Hugo, 16th
(01.47.27.82.29)

La Maison du Chocolat p139
89 av Raymond-Poincaré, 16th (01.40.67.77.83/ www.lamaisonduchocolat.com)

Tea Rooms & Ice Cream

Hôtel Raphaël p128
17 av Kléber, 16th
(01.53.64.32.00)

Trendy

Bon p53
25 rue de la Pompe, 16th
(01.40.72.70.00)

17th

The Americas

El Bodegon de Pancho p83
8 rue Guy-Môquet, 17th
(01.53.31.00.73)

Bars & Pubs

L'Endroit p125
67 pl du Dr-Félix-Lobligeois, 17th (01.42.29.50.00)

The James Joyce p125
71 bd Gouvion-St-Cyr, 17th
(01.44.09.70.32)

Bistros

Le Bistrot d'à Côté Flaubert p36
10 rue Gustave-Flaubert, 17th (01.42.67.05.81/
www.michelrostang.com)

Le Clou p36
132 rue Cardinet, 17th
(01.42.27.36.78)

Macis & Muscade p36
110 rue Legendre, 17th
(01.42.26.62.26)

Le Morosophe p37
83 rue Legendre, 17th
(01.53.06.82.82)

La Table de Lucullus p37
129 rue Legendre, 17th
(01.40.25.02.68)

Tante Jeanne p37
116, bd Péreire, 17th
(01.43.80.88.68/
www.bearnard-loiseau.com)

Tête de Goinfre/ Cave du Cochon p37
16/18, rue Jacquemont, 17th (01.42.29.89.80)

Le Troyon p37
4 rue Troyon, 17th
(01.40.68.99.40)

Vin et Marée p66
183, bd Murat, 16th
(01.46.47.91.39)

Budget

La Fourchette des Anges p73
17 rue Biot, 17th
(01.44.69.07.69)

Fish & Seafood

L'Huîtrier p66
16 rue Saussier-Leroy, 17th (01.40.54.83.44)

Haute Cuisine

Guy Savoy p43
18 rue Troyon, 17th
(01.43.80.40.61/
www.guysavoy.com)

Michel Rostang p43
20 rue Rennequin, 17th
(01.47.63.40.77/
www.michelrostang.com)

Home Delivery

Allô Apéro p133
9bis rue Labie, 17th
(01.71.71.69.69)

Indian

Kirane's p91
85 av des Ternes, 17th
(01.45.74.40.21)

Shah Jahan p91
4 rue Gauthey, 17th
(01.42.63.44.06)

Japanese

Kifuné p97
44 rue St-Ferdinand, 17th
(01.45.72.11.19)

North African

Timgad p100
21 rue Brunel, 17th
(01.45.74.23.70)

Shops and Markets

Alain Dubois p137
80 rue de Tocqueville, 17th (01.42.27.11.38)

Alléosse p137
13 rue Poncelet, 17th
(01.46.22.50.45)

Rue Poncelet p140
rue Poncelet and rue Bayen, 17th.

18th

Bars & Pubs

Chào-Bà-Café p125
22 bd de Clichy, 18th
(01.46.06.72.90)

La Fourmi p125
74 rue des Martyrs, 18th
(01.42.64.70.35)

La Jungle p125
32 rue Gabrielle, 18th
(01.46.06.75.69)

Bistros

Le Bouclard p37
1 rue Cavalotti, 18th
(01.45.22.60.01)

L'Entracte p37
44 rue d'Orsel, 18th
(01.46.06.93.41)

L'Etrier Bistrot p37
154 rue Lamarck, 18th
(01.42.29.14.01)

La Galère des Rois p37
8 rue Cavallotti 18th
(01.42.93.34.58)

Le Moulin à Vins p37
6 rue Burq, 18th
(01.42.52.81.27)

Aux Négociants p37
27 rue Lambert, 18th
(01.46.06.15.11)

Le Petit Caboulot p37
6 pl Jacques-Froment, 18th (01.46.27.19.00)

Le Petit Robert p39
10 rue Cauchois, 18th
(01.46.06.04.46)

Brasseries

Le Wepler p48
14 pl de Clichy, 18th
(01.45.22.53.24/
www.wepler.com)

Budget

Chez Toinette p73
20 rue Germain-Pilon, 18th
(01.42.54.44.36)

Le Relais Gascon p73
6 rue des Abbesses, 18th
(01.42.58.58.22)

Le Rendez-Vous des Chauffeurs p73
11 rue des Portes Blanches, 18th (01.42.64.04.17)

Au Virage Lepic p73
61 rue Lepic, 18th
(01.42.52.46.79)

Cafés

Chez Camille p115
8 rue Ravignan, 18th
(01.46.06.05.78)

Le Chinon p115
49 rue des Abbesses, 18th
(01.42.62.07.17)

L'Été en Pente Douce p115
23 rue Muller, 18th
(01.42.64.02.67)

Le Sancerre p115
35 rue des Abbesses, 18th
(01.42.58.47.05)

Far East

Thu Thu p90
51bis rue Hermel, 18th
(01.42.54.70.30)

Other International

L'Afghani p101
16 rue Paul-Albert, 18th
(01.42.51.08.72)

Mazurka p101
3 rue André-del-Sarte, 18th (01.42.23.36.45)

Vegetarian

Au Grain de Folie p75
24 rue de La-Vieuville, 18th
(01.42.58.15.57)

19th

Bistros

Le Bistro du 19 p39
45 rue des Alouettes, 19th (01.42.00.84.85)

La Cave Gourmande p39
10 rue du Général Brunet, 19th (01.40.40.03.30)

Restaurant L'Hermès p39
23 rue Mélingue, 19th
(01.42.39.94.70)

Brasseries

Au Boeuf Couronné p48
188 av Jean-Jaurès, 19th (01.42.39.54.54/
www.au-boeuf-couronne.com)

Cafés

La Kaskad' p115
2 pl Armand-Carrel, 19th
(01.40.40.08.10)

Le Rendez-vous des Quais p115
MK2 sur Seine, 10-14 quai de la Seine, 19th
(01.40.37.02.81)

Far East

Lao Siam p89
49 rue de Belleville, 19th
(01.40.40.09.68)

20th

Bars & Pubs

La Flèche d'Or p125
102bis rue de Bagnolet, 20th (01.43.72.04.23/
www.flechedor.com)

Lou Pascalou p125
14 rue des Panoyaux, 20th (01.46.36.78.10)

Bistros

Le Bistro des Soupirs (Chez Raymonde) p39
49 rue de la Chine, 20th
(01.44.62.93.31)

Le Bistrot des Capucins p39
27 av Gambetta, 20th
(01.46.36.74.75/
www.le-bistrot-des-capucins.com)

Café Noir p39
15 rue St-Blaise, 20th
(01.40.09.75.80)

Le Zéphyr p39
1 rue du Jourdain, 20th
(01.46.36.65.81)

Budget

La Boulangerie p73
15 rue des Panoyaux,
20th (01.43.58.45.45)

Chez Jean p73
38 rue Boyer, 20th
(01.47.97.44.58)

Ma Pomme p73
107 rue de Ménilmontant, 20th (01.40.33.10.40)

Cafés

Le Soleil p115
136 bd de Ménilmontant,
20th (01.46.36.47.44)

Far East

Krung Thep p89
93 rue Julien-Lacroix,
20th (01.43.66.83.74)

Salon de Thé Wenzhou p88
24 rue de Belleville, 20th
(01.46.36.56.33)

Home Delivery

Croissant Bon'Heur p133
83 rue de la Mare, 20th
(tel/fax 01.43.58.43.43/
www.croissantbonheur.com)

Shops and Markets

L'Artisan Chocolatier p139
102 rue de Belleville, 20th
(01.46.36.67.60)

Wine Bars

Le Baratin p131
3 rue Jouye-Rouve, 20th
(01.43.49.39.70)

Outside Paris

Bistros

Le Soleil p39
109 av Michelet, 93400 St-Ouen (01.40.10.08.08)

Far East

Sinostar p88
27-29 av de Fontainebleau, 94270 Le Kremlin-Bicêtre
(01.49.60.88.88)

Home Delivery

Pizza Hut p133
(central phone
08.10.30.30.30/
www.pizzahut.fr)

Trendy

Café de la Jatte p53
60 bd Vital Bouhot, Ile de la Jatte, 92200
Neuilly-sur-Seine
(01.47.45.04.20)

Quai Ouest p53
1200 quai Marcel Dassault, 92210 St-Cloud
(01.46.02.35.54)

London's best-selling Eating & Drinking Guide

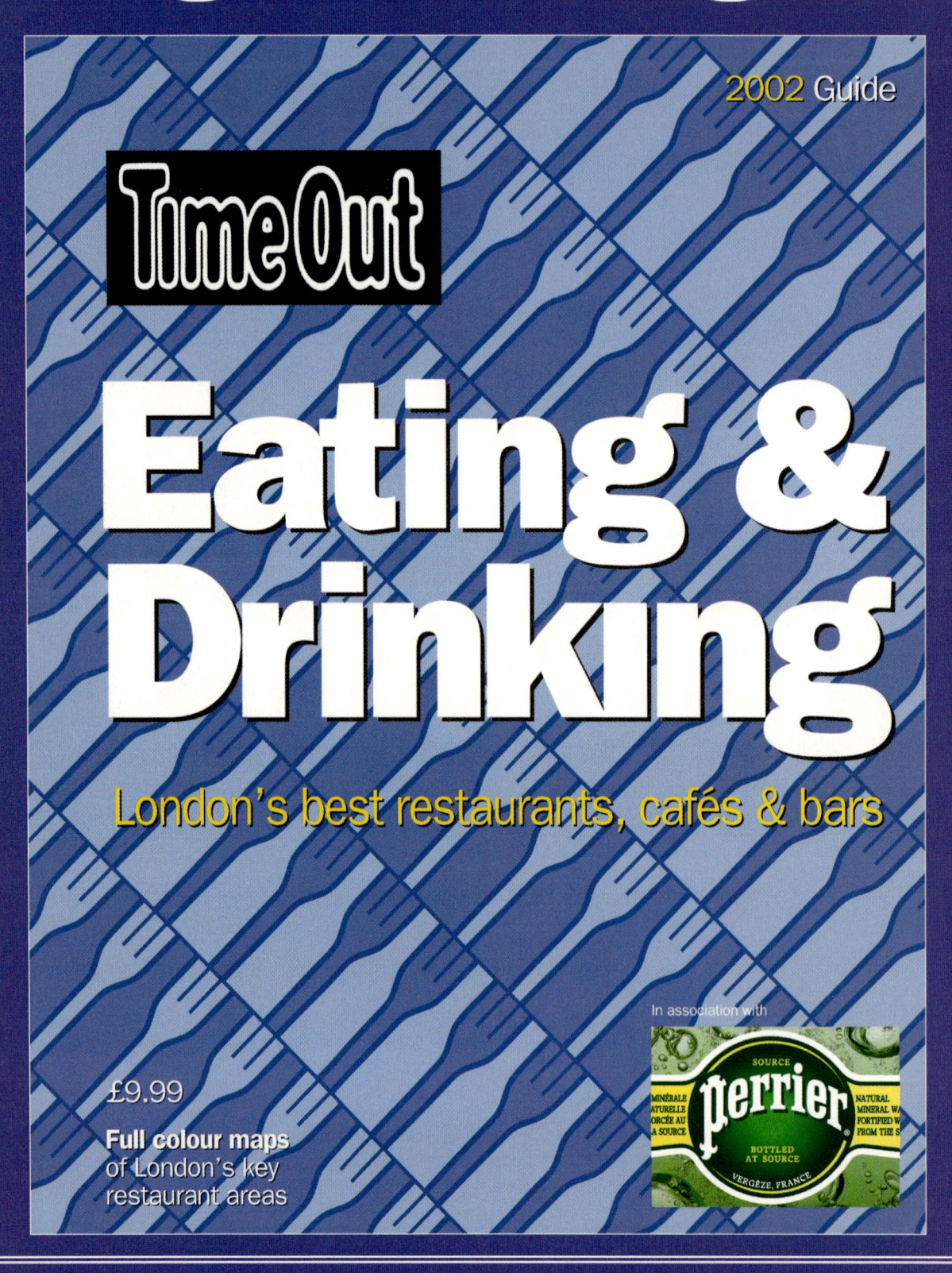

Time Out

2002 Guide

Eating & Drinking

London's best restaurants, cafés & bars

£9.99

Full colour maps of London's key restaurant areas

In association with **Perrier**

Available from all good bookshops, newsagents and online at timeout.com/shop

Time Out

Paris Maps

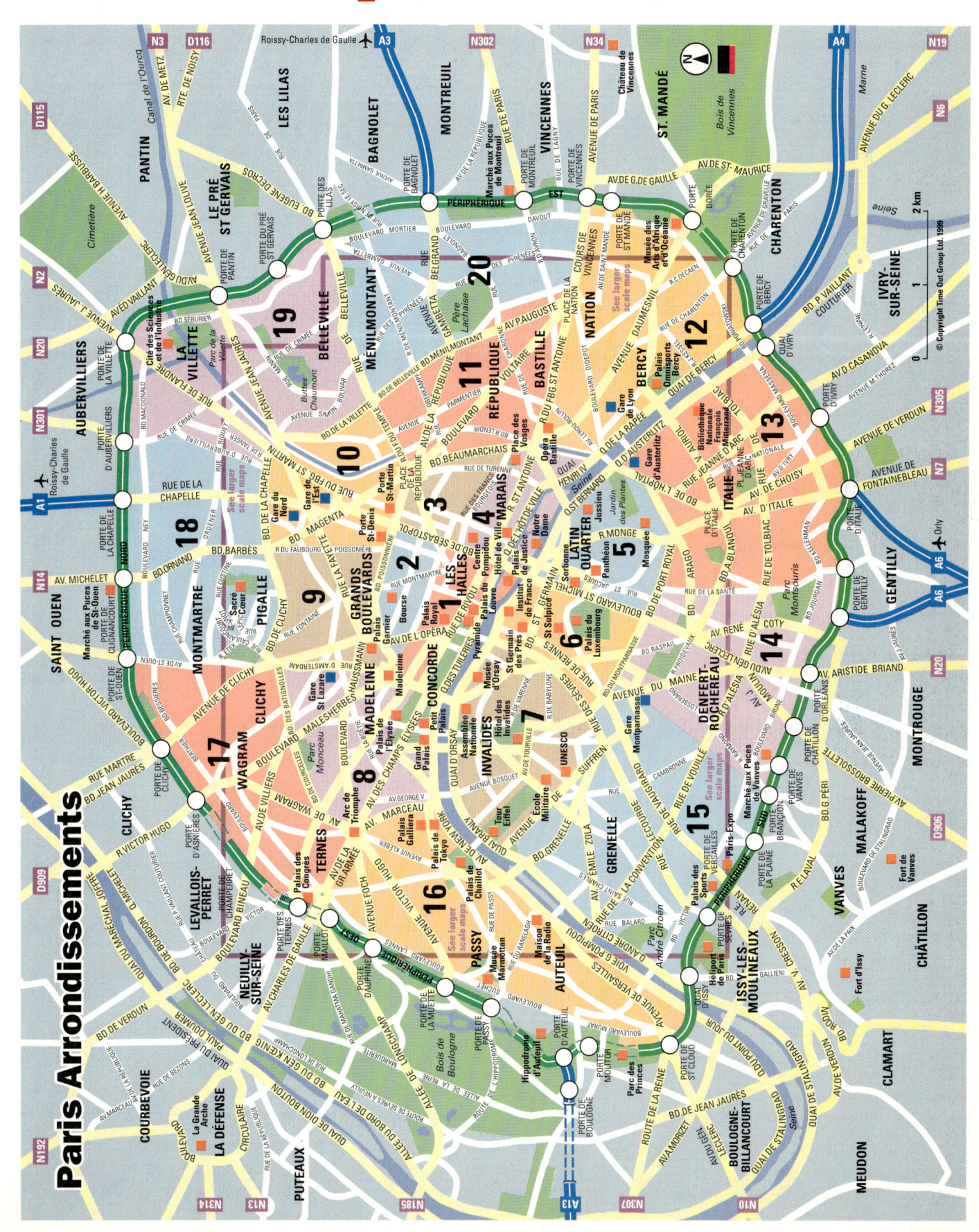

Central Paris

- Place of Interest and/or Entertainment
- Hospital or College
- Arrondissement Boundary & Number —16
- Paris Métro & RER station
- Railway line & station
- Pedestrians only

0 — 500 m

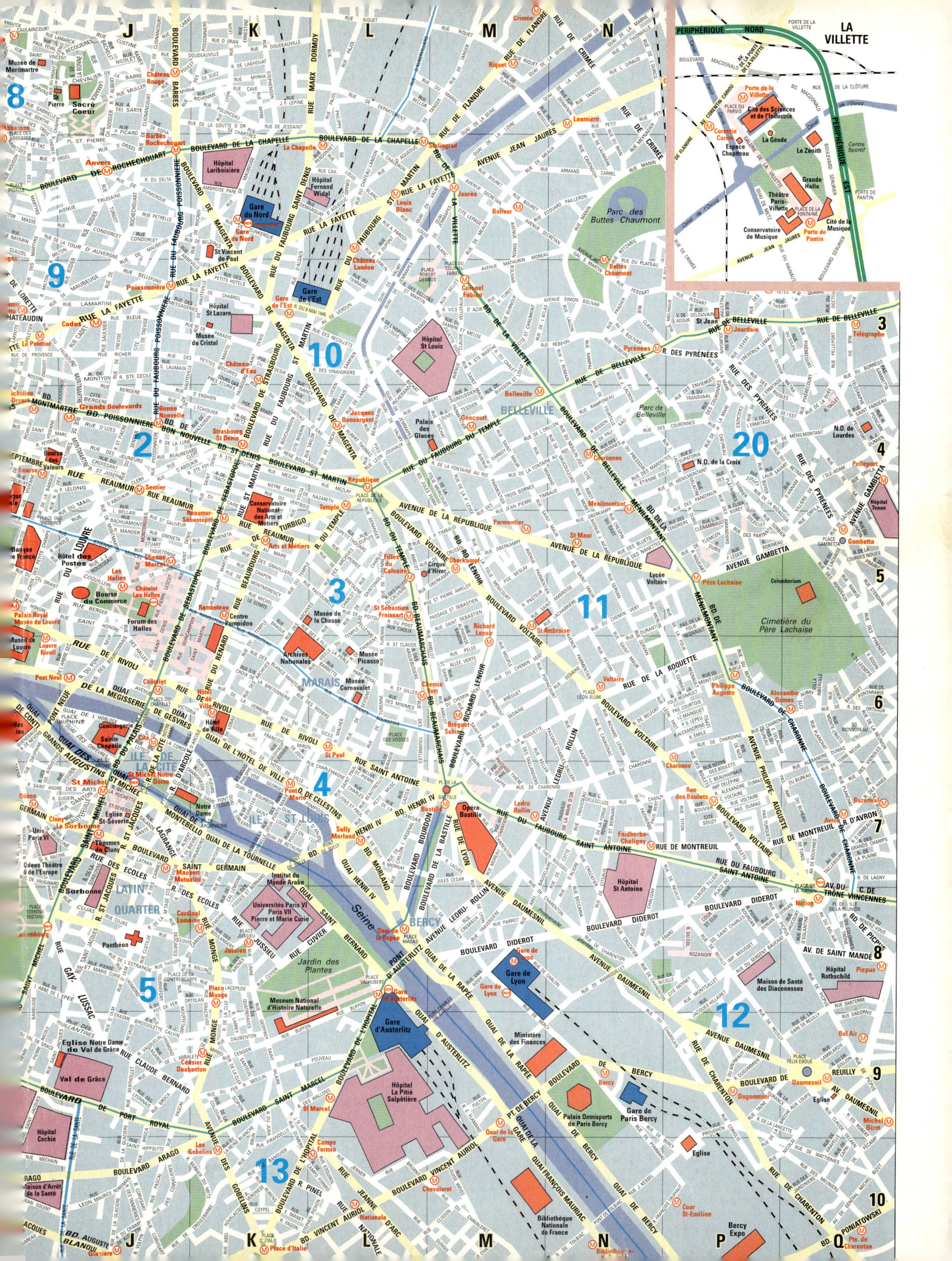

LA VILLETTE
PERIPHÉRIQUE NORD
Cité des Sciences et de l'Industrie
La Géode
Le Zénith
Grande Halle
Théâtre Paris Villette
Conservatoire de Musique
Cité de la Musique
Porte de Pantin
Porte de la Villette
Corentin Cariou
Espace Chapiteau
Centre Sportif
Musée de Montmartre
Sacré Coeur
Anvers
Barbès Rochechouart
Château Rouge
La Chapelle
BOULEVARD DE ROCHECHOUART
BOULEVARD DE LA CHAPELLE
Hôpital Lariboisière
Gare du Nord
Gare de l'Est
Hôpital Fernand Widal
Stalingrad
Jaurès
Louis Blanc
Château Landon
Colonel Fabien
Riquet
Crimée
Laumière
Bolivar
Parc des Buttes Chaumont
Buttes Chaumont
AVENUE JEAN JAURÈS
RUE LA FAYETTE
Poissonnière
Cadet
Le Peletier
Hôpital St Lazare
Musée du Cristal
Château d'Eau
Hôpital St Louis
Jacques Bonsergent
Goncourt
Belleville
BELLEVILLE
Parc de Belleville
Pyrénées
Jourdain
Télégraphe
St Jean
RUE DE BELLEVILLE
Bonne Nouvelle
Grands Boulevards
Strasbourg St Denis
BD. POISSONNIÈRE
BD. MONTMARTRE
BOULEVARD ST MARTIN
République
Bourse des Valeurs
Sentier
Réaumur Sébastopol
Conservatoire National des Arts et Métiers
Arts et Métiers
Temple
AVENUE DE LA RÉPUBLIQUE
Parmentier
Ménilmontant
St Maur
Couronnes
N.D. de la Croix
N.D. de Lourdes
Pelleport
Hôpital Tenon
Gambetta
Père Lachaise
Cimetière du Père Lachaise
Lycée Voltaire
Banque de France
Hôtel des Postes
Etienne Marcel
Les Halles
Bourse du Commerce
Châtelet Les Halles
Forum des Halles
Centre Pompidou
Rambuteau
Musée de la Chasse
Archives Nationales
Musée Picasso
MARAIS
Musée Carnavalet
Filles du Calvaire
Oberkampf
Cirque d'Hiver
St Sébastien Froissart
Richard Lenoir
St Ambroise
Voltaire
Philippe Auguste
Alexandre Dumas
Palais Royal Musée du Louvre
Musée du Louvre
Louvre Rivoli
RUE DE RIVOLI
Pont Neuf
Châtelet
Hôtel de Ville
Chemin Vert
Bréguet Sabin
Charonne
Conciergerie
Sainte Chapelle
Cité
ILE DE LA CITÉ
St Michel
Notre Dame
ILE ST LOUIS
St Paul
Pont Marie
Sully Morland
Bastille
Opéra Bastille
RUE SAINT ANTOINE
Ledru Rollin
Faidherbe-Chaligny
Rue des Boulets
Avron
Hôpital St Antoine
Nation
Buzenval
Odéon
Cluny La Sorbonne
Eglise St-Séverin
Thermes de Cluny
Maubert Mutualité
Sorbonne
LATIN QUARTER
Institut du Monde Arabe
Universités Paris VI Paris VII Pierre et Marie Curie
Cardinal Lemoine
Jussieu
Panthéon
Luxembourg
Jardin des Plantes
Museum National d'Histoire Naturelle
Place Monge
Censier Daubenton
Quai de la Rapée
Gare d'Austerlitz
Gare de Lyon
BERCY
Ministère des Finances
Palais Omnisports de Paris Bercy
Gare de Paris Bercy
Bercy
Dugommier
Daumesnil
Maison de Santé des Diaconesses
Hôpital Rothschild
Picpus
Bel Air
Michel Bizot
Eglise Notre Dame de Val de Grâce
Val de Grâce
Hôpital Cochin
Les Gobelins
St Marcel
Hôpital La Pitié Salpêtrière
Campo Formio
Quai de la Gare
Chevaleret
Bibliothèque Nationale de France
Nationale
Place d'Italie
Glacière
Cour St-Emilion
Bercy Expo
Pte. de Charenton
Seine

www.citefutee.com
M RER T
Paris
RATP
RER C Pontoise Argenteuil
RER B D Aéroport Ch. de Gaulle CDG
Mitry – Claye
Orry-la-Ville
Coye
T 1 Gare de Saint-Denis
7 La Courneuve 8 Mai 1945
T 1 Tramway tarification bus
5 Bobigny Pablo Picasso
RER E Chelles – Gournay
Villiers-sur-Marne
Le Plessis-Trévise
7bis Pré-St-Gervais
11 Mairie des Lilas
3bis Porte des Lilas
3 Galliéni
Mairie de Montreuil 9
RER A Boissy-St-Léger
Marne-la-Vallée
Parc Disneyland
1 Château de Vincennes
Créteil Préfecture 8
RER D Melun
Malesherbes
RER C Massy – Palaiseau
Versailles - Chantiers
Dourdan
Saint-Martin-d'Etampes
7 Villejuif Louis Aragon
Mairie d'Ivry 7
14 Bibliothèque Fr. Mitterrand
Orly Tatification spéciale
Orly Ouest
Orly Sud
St-Rémy-lès-Chevreuse
RER B
Châtillon Montrouge 13
Porte d'Orléans 4
Mairie d'Issy 12
RER C Versailles – Rive Gauche
Château de Versailles
St-Quentin-en-Yvelines
T 2 Tramway tarification bus
Issy – Val de Seine
Balard 8
Pont de Sèvres 9
10 Boulogne Pont de St-Cloud
Porte Dauphine 2
T 2 Tramway tarification bus
1 Pont de Neuilly
La Défense Grande Arche
RER A St-Germain en-Laye
Cergy
Poissy
3 Pont de Levallois Bécon
Gabriel Péri Asnières – Gennevilliers 13
13 St-Denis Université
4 Porte de Clignancourt
12 Porte de la Chapelle
Ch. de Gaulle Étoile
Haussmann – St-Lazare
Madeleine
Châtelet
Châtelet Les Halles
Gare du Nord
Gare de l'Est
Gare de Lyon
Gare d'Austerlitz
Nation
République
Place d'Italie
Montparnasse Bienvenüe
Louis Blanc
Gambetta
♦ Liège et Rennes : fermées après 20 h et dimanches et fêtes.
Trajets en Ile-de-France
Horaires et tarifs
Métro, Bus, RER, Tram
24 h sur 24
www.citefutee.com
08 92 68 77 14
0,34 € la minute ou 2,21 F
36 15 RATP
RATP - CML - Agence Cartographique
PPM 12.01 - Reproduction interdite